Why You Need This New Edition

The field of public relations is always changing. New forms of media and technology have revolutionized public relations practice in the last few years, causing organizations to reach multiple audiences in ways that were not even conceived when the last edition of this book was published.

Our goal with this new edition, therefore, is to discuss the most current issues and developments in the field. This revision includes many new examples of today's public relations campaigns, real-life ethical situations, and other popular examples to illustrate public relations issues and practice in a familiar and stimulating way.

Substantial changes were made to this edition to ensure that the text remains a current, engaging, and practical resource for today's public relations students. Pages xix–xxiv of this preface present detailed information on what is new to the tenth edition. A brief overview of some of the most important changes follows:

- The Internet and Social Media, Chapter 13, is a completely new chapter and shows how today's public relations professionals are using social media as a major tactic in various programs and campaigns. In addition, Internet and social media campaigns are frequently the topic of many casebooks and real-world examples throughout the entire book.

- Meetings and Events, Chapter 16, is another new addition to the book. This chapter, not found in other introductory textbooks, reflects the suggestion of several reviewers that such a chapter would have high interest among their students who want to know how to organize meetings and plan everything from a reception to a trade show.

- Entertainment, Sports, and Tourism, Chapter 18, is another chapter found only in this textbook. Students have always expressed interest in the entertainment and tourism fields, and this revised chapter satisfies their desire for more information about working in these fields.

- This edition incorporates the most current statistical and demographic data to accurately reflect current practice. There are charts and tables showing salary levels, job categories, effectiveness of various media, and the use of various social media; organizational charts; and other easy-to-understand checklists.

- Over 75 percent of the PR Casebooks are new to this edition and reflect yesterday's headlines. Students read about the public relations aspects of Obama's presidential election, the battle over health care reform, BP's oil spill in the Gulf of Mexico, the fall of Tiger Woods, Toyota's auto recall, the Wall Street meltdown of Goldman Sachs, Google's problems with Chinese censorship, and even the World Cup of soccer in South Africa. PR Casebooks engage students and help them apply basic public relations concepts to actual situations.

- Two other features, also updated, help students develop critical thinking skills. One is an ethics box in each chapter that asks students to decide what is morally and professionally correct in a particular situation. Another key component of each chapter is a new case activity that poses a real-world situation and asks students to apply what they have learned to formulate a strategy or program.

- New quotations from experienced professionals appear in each chapter. These concise, pointed statements provide the essence of professional insight and wisdom, not only highlighting important themes from the text, but also piquing student interest in the material.

- This edition also has an expanded interactive element on the Web, giving students access to MyCommunicationLab (MCL) for videos and other materials applicable to each chapter. This is further discussed in the supplements section.

Public Relations
Strategies and Tactics

Public Relations
Strategies and Tactics

Tenth Edition

Dennis L. Wilcox

School of Journalism & Mass Communications
San Jose State University

Glen T. Cameron

School of Journalism
University of Missouri

Allyn & Bacon

Boston   Columbus   Indianapolis   New York   San Francisco   Upper Saddle River
Amsterdam   Cape Town   Dubai   London   Madrid   Milan   Munich   Paris   Montréal   Toronto
Delhi   Mexico City   São Paulo   Sydney   Hong Kong   Seoul   Singapore   Taipei   Tokyo

Editor-in-Chief, Communication: Karon Bowers
Senior Acquisitions Editor: Jeanne Zalesky
Senior Development Editor: Carol Alper
Executive Marketing Manager: Wendy Gordon
Editorial Assistant: Stephanie Chaisson
Senior Managing Editor: Linda Mihatov Behrens
Associate Managing Editor: Bayani Mendoza de Leon
Media Producer: Megan Higginbotham
Manufacturing Buyer: Mary Ann Gloriande
Art Director: Leslie Osher
Project Coordination, Interior Design, and Electronic Page Makeup: Integra Software
   Services, Inc.
Cover Designer: Ximena Tamvakopoulos
Cover Image: Jeff Malet Photography/Newscom; HO/Reuters/Newscom

Library of Congress Cataloging-in-Publication Data
Public relations : strategies and tactics/Dennis L. Wilcox, Glen T. Cameron.—10th ed.
    p. cm.
Includes bibliographical references and index.
ISBN 978-0-205-77088-5
1. Public relations.   I. Wilcox, Dennis L.   II. Cameron, Glen T.
HM1221.P8 2012
659.2—dc22   2010033355

Allyn & Bacon
is an imprint of

www.pearsonhighered.com

4 5 6 7 8 9 10—RDH—14 13

ISBN-13: 978-0-205-77088-5
ISBN-10:   0-205-77088-6

Brief Contents

Contents

CHAPTER 3
Ethics and
Professionalism   65

CHAPTER 4
Public Relations Departments
and Firms   92

PART 2   Process   119

CHAPTER 5
Research   119

CHAPTER 6
Program Planning   144

CHAPTER 7
Communication   163

CHAPTER 8
Evaluation   189

PART 3   Strategy   211

CHAPTER 9

Public Opinion and Persuasion   211

CHAPTER 10

Conflict Management: Dealing with Issues, Risks, and Crises   242

CHAPTER **11**
Reaching Diverse
Audiences **271**

CHAPTER **12**
Public Relations and the
Law **292**

PART 4　**Tactics**　**326**

CHAPTER 13
**The Internet and Social
Media**　**326**

CHAPTER 14
Preparing Materials for Mass
Media   353

CHAPTER 15
Radio and Television   383

PART 5 Application 440

CHAPTER 18

Entertainment, Sports, and
Tourism   470

CHAPTER 19

Politics and Government   495

Preface

A textbook should be more than packaged information. It should also be written and designed to (1) provide learning objectives, (2) offer relevant examples of today's practice, and (3) actively engage students in critical thinking, analysis, and problem solving.

That's why the tenth edition of *Public Relations: Strategies and Tactics* continues its widely acclaimed reputation for being the most comprehensive, up-to-date introductory public relations text on the market. This edition, like others before it, also continues to successfully blend theory, concepts, and actual practice into a highly attractive format that is clear and easy for students to understand without being superficial or shallow.

Students will find interesting examples, case studies, and applications throughout that will encourage them to actively engage in critical thinking, analysis, and problem solving. The authors' narrative writing style and the sleek new design will capture the interest of students; in every chapter they will find interesting tidbits that will give them a preview of what a career in public relations might be like. At the same time, the book will appeal to instructors who want their students to have an in-depth understanding of public relations as a problem-solving process involving ethical responsibility and the application of key principles. Indeed, the continuing popularity of this book among both students and faculty relates to the consistent inclusion of new issues and case studies that students recognize from yesterday's headlines. This new edition is no exception. Every chapter has examples of award-winning campaigns and current issues that students will find relevant, informative, and interesting.

New in the Tenth Edition

We have revised and updated major portions of the book to reflect today's diverse public relations practice on the local, national, and global levels. The suggestions of adopters and reviewers regarding the ninth edition have been given serious consideration, and the result is a strong new edition that retains the best of past editions but also captures the essence of today's current practice and concerns in a more streamlined style. New content includes:

A new chapter on meeting and event management

An important component of daily public relations practice is conducting successful meetings and planning special events. Chapter 16, "Meetings and Events," gives students practical advice and checklists for organizing everything from a local club meeting to a cocktail reception and a banquet. It also discusses the mechanics of regional and national conventions and participating in trade shows. Corporate-sponsored events, as well as promotional events for new products, are also discussed.

A new chapter on the Internet and social media

The use of the Internet and social media is now commonplace in almost all public relations programs and campaigns. Chapter 13, "The Internet and Social Media," is a primer that outlines the use of such tactics as blogs, websites, webcasts, YouTube,

Facebook, and Twitter in various public relations campaigns. It gives new statistics about Internet usage on a global basis, tips for designing an effective website, and even the future of mobile-enabled content.

Examples of social media used in public relations campaigns are found in the text and highlighted in boxes throughout the book. Some examples include:

- Ethical guidelines for the Web and social media (Chapter 3)
- SanDisk using social media to promote a new memory chip (Chapter 4)
- The Department of Defense using a creative website to control binge drinking in the military (Chapter 5)
- Nestlé's false start in using social media (Chapter 7)
- Discussion of whether women are better at social media than men (Chapter 7)
- YouTube videos promoting World Water Day (Chapter 8)
- How the millennial generation is using social media (Chapter 11)
- New FTC rules for bloggers accepting gifts and getting paid for endorsements (Chapter 12)
- Employee rights regarding e-mail and use of social media in the workplace (Chapter 12)
- The characteristics of an online newsroom (Chapter 14)
- Working with bloggers (Chapter 14)
- Making reservations on the Web (Chapter 16)
- Ford's social media program (Chapter 17)
- Coke's success at the 2010 World Cup (Chapter 18)
- Social media in the 2008 election (Chapter 19)
- Nonprofit health educators using text messages to answer students' sex education questions (Chapter 21)

A revised chapter on preparing materials for mass media

Chapter 14, "Preparing Materials for Mass Media," has been revised and reorganized to place more emphasis on digital preparation of basic news releases, multimedia news releases, and media kits. There is more discussion about the components of an organization's online newsroom and the pervasive use of electronic news services to distribute media materials. How to pitch stories to the media, conduct media interviews, and organize news conferences have also been incorporated into the chapter.

A continuing focus on diverse and multicultural audiences

A completely revised Chapter 11, "Reaching Diverse Audiences," explores the characteristics of many special publics and how to effectively include them in various public relations programs. The fastest-growing ethnic group in the United States, Hispanics, is thoroughly covered, as are such publics as millennials, baby boomers, seniors, women, the gay community, the African American community, and the physically disabled. Charts show the demographic makeup of today's American society, and what it will be like in 2050.

A more graphic explanation of competition, conflict, and crisis

This book is unique among introductory texts in that it reflects groundbreaking research on the role of public relations in managing competition, conflict, and crisis. The complexity of Chapter 10, "Conflict Management: Dealing with Issues, Risks, and Crises," has been simplified with the addition of colorful graphics that help students understand how organizations assess risks and threats, and decide on a course of action that ranges from advocacy (defense) to accommodation (apology for misdeeds). In this chapter, some new situations are explored such as Toyota's crisis communications during a widely publicized recall of defective autos. Another case involves conflict between an Australian winery's charitable contribution to an animal charity that was widely criticized by farmers and ranchers. Other chapters that include case studies on conflict and crisis include the following:

- Use of front groups in issue and political campaigns (Chapter 3)
- Conflict between environmentalists and pro-growth advocates (Chapter 6)
- Google opposing censorship by the Chinese government (Chapter 9)
- The bottled water industry under attack (Chapter 9)
- Chevron dealing with a filmmaker's exposé about oil drilling in Ecuador (Chapter 12)
- BP's oil spill crisis in the Gulf of Mexico (Chapter 17)
- Goldman Sachs struggling to improve its image after Wall Street bailout (Chapter 17)
- Tiger Woods' reputation crisis (Chapter 18)
- President Obama dealing with the BP oil spill (Chapter 19)
- Israel taking the offensive in a war of words (Chapter 20)
- Apple splitting with the U.S. Chamber of Commerce over climate change (Chapter 21).

Updated statistics about the public relations industry

The most current statistical and demographic data have been incorporated into this edition. Students and professors will find new data throughout the book that accurately reflect current practice. Some examples include:

- Salaries for entry-level jobs and for experienced practitioners in various areas of public relations, including breakouts showing salaries for men and women (Chapter 1)
- The size and revenues of the U.S. public relations industry (Chapter 1)
- The number of female professionals in the field and their progress toward management titles (Chapter 2)

- The current breakdown of employment categories for members of PRSA and IABC (Chapter 3)
- Current staffing profiles and expenditures of public relations departments from the USC Strategic Public Relations Center (Chapter 4)
- Revenue breakdown of global communication conglomerates (Chapter 4)
- Key functions of a corporate communications department in order of importance (Chapter 4)
- The relative effectiveness of various measurement tools (Chapter 8)
- Census information about ethnic groups in the United States (Chapter 11)
- Current court rulings about employers' monitoring of employee e-mails (Chapter 12)
- Amount of time individuals spend using various media (Chapter 13)
- Internet users by world region (Chapter 13)
- The demographics of Facebook (Chapter 13)
- Updated charts about philanthropy from Giving USA (Chapter 21).

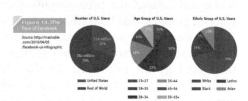

New "On the Job" boxed features in every chapter

On the Job: A Multicultural World   Each chapter highlights recent programs and campaigns that have reached diverse audiences in the United States and around the world. New examples in this edition include:

- The beginnings of public relations in other nations (Chapter 2)
- Ford promoting its pickup trucks in Argentina through sponsorship of plays about local legends (Chapter 4)
- Australia promoting the four-minute shower to conserve water during a drought (Chapter 6)
- Google grappling with the Chinese government over censorship (Chapter 9)
- Terrorist groups using the Web for recruitment (Chapter 12)
- Coca-Cola sponsoring three young people as they blog their way around the world (Chapter 13)
- Global news releases requiring language and cultural sensitivity (Chapter 14)
- A beer fest putting Belgrade on the map (Chapter 16)
- Environmentalism and sustainability being the new mantra of global corporations (Chapter 17)
- Mexican tourism responding to the H1N1 virus (Chapter 18)
- Debating whether aid to African nations is a waste of time and money (Chapter 21).

On the Job: Ethics   A major strength of this book is its exploration of ethical issues relevant to the subject matter of each chapter. Particular attention is given to current situations and issues familiar to students. Because the objective is to encourage robust class discussion, each Ethics box ends with several questions to help students understand the crux of moral dilemmas faced by practitioners in daily practice. New examples of moral dilemmas and questionably ethical situations that are presented in this edition include:

- Canada using fake photos in a tourism campaign (Chapter 1)
- A hospital being criticized for accepting Abercrombie & Fitch's gift for a children's wing (Chapter 3)
- The CEO of Burson-Marsteller being accused of "conflict of interest" (Chapter 4)
- Word-of-mouth (WOM) campaigns raising ethical issues (Chapter 7)
- The ethics of a new generation in the workplace using social media (Chapter 11)
- Ann Taylor Loft offering gift cards to bloggers (Chapter 12)
- The rules of etiquette for cell phones, texting, and tweeting (Chapter 13)
- Cruise ship passengers visiting Haiti for fun in the sun after an earthquake (Chapter 18)
- Student loan industry launching lobbying campaign (Chapter 19)
- Uproar in India concerning a $23,000 pen honoring Gandhi (Chapter 20).

New PR Casebooks to generate interest and discussion

Each chapter, as in past editions, has a PR Casebook that describes the "nuts and bolts" of a public relations program or campaign. This edition features many new PR Casebooks that will engage students and heighten their knowledge of, as well as enthusiasm for, the field of public relations. Some new examples include:

- Go Red for Women cancer campaign (Chapter 1)
- The dilemma of being a spokesperson for Steve Jobs, CEO of Apple, or former Gov. Mark Sanford of South Carolina (Chapter 3)
- SanDisk using the Internet and social media to promote its Extreme Pro memory chip (Chapter 4)
- Green being the new color of UPS (Chapter 6)
- Apple iPad exploiting early adoption buzz (Chapter 7)
- Health care reform at the crossroads (Chapter 9)
- Corporate culture hindering Toyota's car recall (Chapter 10)
- Google preparing for possible litigation (Chapter 12)
- Domino's being ambushed by a YouTube video (Chapter 13)
- A nonprofit scoring a front page story in *USA Today* (Chapter 14)
- B-roll driving Shell's Eco-Mileage Competition (Chapter 15)

- Charmin's restroom promotion in Times Square (Chapter 16)
- BP's oil spill causing gusher of problems (Chapter 17)
- Tiger Woods teeing off fans and sponsors (Chapter 18)
- NGO campaign going after fishing subsidies (Chapter 20).

Quotations from leading professionals

Selected quotations from experienced professionals are highlighted in each chapter. These short, pithy statements give the essence of a professional's insights and wisdom. We feel this approach provides practitioners' viewpoints for students with brevity instead of long interviews.

Organization of the Book

The text is divided into five parts in order to give a comprehensive overview of the public relations field: Part 1: Role; Part 2: Process; Part 3: Strategy; Part 4: Tactics; and Part 5: Application.

Part 1: Role

This section of the book gives students a thorough grounding in public relations as a pervasive, fully developed field of activity in today's society and global economy. It properly defines the broad scope of public relations, its societal value, and the workplace settings in which public relations is practiced. **Chapter 1** explains what public relations is, and students learn to understand public relations as a systematic, problem-solving process. **Chapter 2** discusses the evolution of public relations in terms of major eras of development and the individuals that made a significant contribution to the field. Emphasis is placed on the last half of the 20th century, and how the role and function of public relations have evolved over the years. **Chapter 3** exposes students to the ethical and professional standards of today's practice and discusses the codes of conduct of several professional organizations. **Chapter 4** covers the structure of public relations departments and their role in various organizational structures.

Part 2: Process

The four chapters in this part form a unified whole, taking students in sequence through the basic steps involved in a public relations program—research, planning, communication, and evaluation. In this way, students gain a deeper understanding and appreciation of public relations as a multiple-step process. To explain the process, the chapters follow the public relations programs of several organizations from conception to evaluation. **Chapter 5** discusses the essential first step: research. Students are exposed to different levels of qualitative and quantitative research and are taught how to construct a basic questionnaire and how to reach respondents. **Chapter 6** discusses program planning and the importance of setting goals and objectives for a public relations program. It also covers the eight essential parts of a public relations plan, including information on how to identify target audiences, create budgets, develop timelines, and evaluate the effort. **Chapter 7** is an overview of major communication theories as they apply to various techniques for accomplishing everything from making individuals aware of a message to actually changing their behavior in terms of opinions or product purchases. **Chapter 8** discusses the pros and cons of various measurement methods and defines techniques for measuring message exposure, audience awareness, audience attitudes, and audience action.

Part 3: Strategy

This part discusses the fundamental concepts of strategy from the standpoint of acquainting students with broad-based concepts such as persuasion, audience characteristics, law, and new technologies. **Chapter 9** covers the influence of opinion leaders and explains source credibility, timing and context, and appeal to self-interest. **Chapter 10** provides students with an easy-to-understand theoretical framework so that they can systematically respond to risks and crises. **Chapter 11** teaches students that the "general public" is really a group of "publics" with specific characteristics. The demographics of various publics are outlined by ethnic group, age, gender, and lifestyle, with tips on how to effectively reach each group. **Chapter 12** explains libel, privacy, copyright, plagiarism, and trademarks. Rules and regulations of regulatory agencies—such as the FTC, SEC, FCC, and FDA—that affect the content of public relations materials are also outlined.

Part 4: Tactics

This section focuses on the "how-to" skills that students will need to actually produce and write public relations materials. With the rapid rise of the Internet and social media, **Chapter 13** covers blogs, podcasts, webcasts, online newsrooms, and other online phenomena such as YouTube, Facebook, and Twitter. Its focus is on how public relations professionals are using the Internet and social media in practically every program and campaign. **Chapter 14** teaches students how to prepare materials for the mass media, which are now referred to as "traditional media." The focus is on how to write news releases, media alerts, pitch letters, and media kits. There are numerous "how-to" checklists, samples from various public relations campaigns, and even a section on what makes a good publicity photo. In **Chapter 15,** students are exposed to broadcast news writing, how to arrange guest appearances on talk shows, satellite media tours, and the components of a video news release. **Chapter 16** concerns the mechanics of organizing meetings and various other kinds of events. Information about club meetings, receptions, banquets, conventions, promotional events, and trade shows gives students a "how-to" guide that they will find useful in their careers.

Part 5: Application

This section teaches students about the practical ways in which process, strategies, and tactics are applied in major areas of practice. These chapters, which make the text comprehensive, build upon the basics that students have learned in the first sixteen chapters. **Chapter 17** outlines the public relations challenges facing today's modern, global corporation. Such topics as media relations, consumer boycotts, multicultural marketing, investor relations, cause-related marketing, environmental activism, philanthropy, and corporate sponsorship of events are covered. Because a major part of the American economy deals with entertainment, sports, and tourism, **Chapter 18** focuses on the cult of celebrity and how public relations is conducted for individuals in politics, entertainment, and sports. Tourism is another major industry, so the chapter also includes detailed information about working in that field. **Chapter 19** discusses lobbying and the problems of influence peddling, as well as the nature of governmental public relations work at the federal, state, and city levels. In **Chapter 20,** students gain an appreciation of global public relations and the challenges of cross-cultural communications. **Chapter 21** discusses the nature of public relations work in trade groups, labor unions, professional associations, charities, social agencies, and universities. Resource development and how to conduct a fund-raising campaign are also explored.

Student Learning Tools

Each chapter of *Public Relations: Strategies and Tactics* includes several learning tools to help students better understand and remember the principles of public relations, and to give them the practice they need to apply those principles to real-life situations. This edition continues the tradition of providing key student learning aids at the beginning and end of every chapter. In each chapter, you will find:

- **Chapter-opening preview.** Learning objectives for students are succinctly stated at the beginning of every chapter.
- **End-of-chapter summary.** The major themes are summarized at the end of each chapter.
- **End-of-chapter Case Activity.** A public relations situation or dilemma based on actual cases is posed, and students are asked to apply what they have just read to the real-life situation. These activities have been updated for the tenth edition. Some examples of activities for students to complete individually or in small groups include:
  - Organize a public relations program to celebrate Bubble Wrap's 50th anniversary (Chapter 1)
  - Discuss the impact of so many women (about 70 percent) in the field (Chapter 2)
  - Plan an employee communication program (Chapter 5)
  - Promote a coffee house near a college campus (Chapter 6)
  - Draft a program to persuade individuals to make a donation to a nonprofit (Chapter 9)
  - Conduct a campaign for new sunscreen use among Hispanic women (Chapter 11)
  - Design a social media program for a yogurt company (Chapter 13)
  - Plan the grand opening of a new city university library (Chapter 14)
  - Get media and Internet coverage for a peanut butter sandwich contest (Chapter 15)
  - Plan a banquet for the college of business at your local university (Chapter 16)
  - Plan a public relations and promotion campaign to increase tourism in the Azores (Chapter 18).
- **Questions for Review and Discussion.** A list of questions at the end of each chapter helps students prepare for tests and also stimulates class discussion.
- **Media Resources.** These updated end-of-chapter lists of readings and websites give students additional references for exploring topics brought up in the chapter.
- **Useful websites and bibliography.** This updated collection of selected books, periodicals, and directories at the end of the book provides a more complete list of references for students wishing to conduct further research.

See also the next section on supplements, for new online materials that are now available to students.

Resources in Print and Online

Name of Supplement	Instructor or Student Supplement	Description
Available in Print and Online		
Instructor's Manual and Test Bank ISBN: 0205799701	Instructor Supplement	This comprehensive instructor resource provides learning objectives, chapter outlines, sample syllabi, class activities, and discussion questions. The fully-reviewed Test Bank offers more than 700 test questions in multiple-choice, true/false, and essay format. Each question is referenced by page. Available for download at www.pearsonhighered.com/irc (access code required).
Available Online		
MyTest ISBN: 0205799728	Instructor Supplement	This flexible online test-generating software includes all questions found in the Test Bank, allowing instructors to create their own personalized exams, edit any or all of the existing test questions, and even add new questions. Other special features of this program include random generation of test questions, creation of alternate versions of the same test, scrambling of question sequence, and test preview before printing. Available at www.pearsonmytest.com (access code required).
PowerPoint™ Presentation Package ISBN: 020579968X	Instructor Supplement	This text-specific package provides lecture slides based on key concepts in the text. Available for download at www.pearsonhighered.com/irc (access code required).
Pearson Allyn & Bacon Public Relations Study Site	Student Supplement	This open-access student website features public relations study materials. There is a complete set of practice tests (multiple choice, true/false, and essay questions) for all major topics as well as weblinks to valuable sites for further exploration. The site can be accessed at http://www.pearsonpublicrel.com.
MyCommunicationLab	Student and Instructor Supplement	MyCommunicationLab is a state-of-the-art, interactive, and instructive solution for communication courses. Designed to be used as a supplement to a traditional lecture course or to completely administer an online course, MyCommunicationLab combines Pearson's eText, MySearchLab™, MediaShare, multimedia, video clips, activities, research support, tests, and quizzes to completely engage students. See next page for more details.

Save Time and Improve Results with

mycommunicationlab

Designed to amplify a traditional course in numerous ways or to administer a course on-line, **MyCommunicationLab** for Public Relations courses combines pedagogy and assessment with an array of multimedia activities—videos, assessments, research support, a portfolio tool, multiple newsfeeds, and more—to make learning more effective for all types of students. Now featuring more resources, including a video-upload tool, this new release of **MyCommunicationLab** is visually richer and even more interactive than the previous version—a leap forward in design with more tools and features to enrich learning and aid students in classroom success.

Teaching and Learning Tools

Pearson eText: Identical in content and design to the printed text, a Pearson eText provides students access to their text whenever and wherever they need it. In addition to contextually placed multimedia features in every chapter, the Pearson eText allows students to take notes and highlight, just like in a traditional book.

Videos and Video Quizzes: Interactive videos provide students with the opportunity to watch video clips that discuss various well-known public relations cases and interviews with public relations professionals. Many videos include short, assignable quizzes that report to the instructor's gradebook.

Assessments: Pre- and post-tests for every chapter help students assess their level of understanding of the material in the chapter. The tests generate a customized study plan that focuses students on content areas they need to study. Instructors can also use these tools to demonstrate student improvement and learning outcomes over the duration of the course.

ABC news RSS feed: MyCommunicationLab provides an online feed from ABC news, updated hourly, to keep class and assignments current. Through this feed, students can read about the PR aspects of situations, events, and challenges as they unfold, providing them with additional opportunities to apply text concepts to actual situations.

MySearchLab: Pearson's MySearchLab™ is the easiest way for students to start a research assignment or paper. Complete with extensive help on the research process and four databases of credible and reliable source material, MySearchLab™ helps students quickly and efficiently make the most of their research time.

Cutting-Edge Technology

Portfolio Builder: The easy-to-use Portfolio Builder guides students step-by-step as they develop each part of their portfolio. This tool allows students to practice writing various types of press releases and other public relations documents. With only a few clicks, students can create portfolios of their work that they can e-mail, print, and download.

MediaShare: With this video-upload tool, students are able to upload public relations role plays and video news releases for their instructor and classmates to watch (whether face-to-face or online) and provide online feedback and comments. MediaShare assignments can be graded via an exportable gradebook that can be imported into most learning management systems. Structured much like a social networking site, MediaShare can help promote a sense of community among students.

Audio Chapter Summaries: Every chapter includes an audio summary that can be streamed online, perfect for students reviewing material before a test or instructors reviewing material before class.

Online Administration

No matter what course management system you use—or if you do not use one at all, but still wish to easily capture your students' grades and track their performance—Pearson has a **MyCommunicationLab** option to suit your needs. Contact one of Pearson's Technology Specialists for more information and assistance.

A **MyCommunicationLab** access code is available at no additional cost when packaged with selected Pearson Communication texts. To get started, contact your local Pearson Publisher's Representative at www.pearsonhighered.com/replocator.

Acknowledgments

We would like to thank the following reviewers for their expertise and their helpful and insightful suggestions for the development of this text:

Josh Boyd, Purdue University

Karyn Brown, Mississippi State University

Christopher Caldiero, Farleigh Dickinson University

Robert A. Carroll, York College of Pennsylvania

Jennifer Chin, University of North Carolina, Wilmington

Janine W. Dunlap, Freed-Hardeman University

Gregg Feistman, Temple University

W. Gerry Gilmer, Florida State University

Randy Hines, Susquehanna University

Steve G. Mandel, Pennsylvania State University

Teresa Mastin, Michigan State University

Ronda L. Menke, Drake University

Maureen Taylor, Rutgers University

Kelly Kinner Tryba, University of Colorado at Boulder

Beth Wood, Indiana University

Brenda J. Wrigley, Syracuse University

About the Authors

Dennis L. Wilcox, Ph.D., is professor emeritus of public relations and past director of the School of Journalism & Mass Communications at San Jose State University, California. He is a Fellow and accredited (APR) member of the Public Relations Society of America, former chair of the PRSA Educator's Academy, and past chair of the public relations division of AEJMC. Among his six books, Dr. Wilcox is the lead author of *Public Relations: Strategies and Tactics* and *Think: Public Relations.* He is also the author of *Public Relations Writing and Media Techniques.* His honors include PRSA's "Outstanding Educator," the Xifra Award from the University of Girona (Spain), and an honorary doctorate from the University of Bucharest. He is active in the International Public Relations Association (IPRA) and a member of the Arthur W. Page Society, a group of senior communication executives. Dr. Wilcox currently consults and gives lectures/workshops to students and professionals in such diverse nations as Thailand, India, Latvia, Serbia, and Argentina. His philosophy, to quote St. Augustine, is "The world is a book, and those who do not travel read only a page." Dr. Wilcox welcomes your feedback via email: Dennis.Wilcox@sjsu.edu

Glen T. Cameron, Ph.D., is Gregory Chair in Journalism Research and founder of the Health Communication Research Center at the University of Missouri. Dr. Cameron has authored more than 300 articles, chapters, and award-winning conference papers on public relations topics. In addition to being coauthor of *Public Relations: Strategies and Tactics*, he is also coauthor of *Think: Public Relations.* A popular lecturer internationally, Dr. Cameron has received the **Baskett-Mosse** and **Pathfinder** awards for career achievement. The University of Missouri honored him in 2006 with the 21st Century Corps of Discovery Lectureship, given once each year to a globally recognized campus scholar. Dr. Cameron gains ongoing public relations experience by managing over $42 million in external funding of health public relations projects for sources such as NIH, NCI, Missouri Foundation for Health, USDA, CDC, the U.S. Department of Defense, and Monsanto. Whenever he can, Dr. Cameron enjoys the rivers and mountains of his native Montana as well as wild spots around the world. Dr. Cameron welcomes your feedback via email: camerong@missouri.edu

What Is Public Relations?

After reading this chapter, you will be able to:

Be familiar with the global scope of the public relations industry

Have a good definition of public relations

Understand that public relations is a process, not an event

Know the difference between public relations, journalism, advertising, and marketing

Assess the skills needed for a public relations career and what salary to expect

The Challenge of Public Relations

It is 9 A.M. and Anne-Marie, a senior account executive in a San Francisco public relations firm, is at her desk getting ready for a full day of busy activity. She takes a few minutes to answer some text messages, scan her e-mails, and Tweet a printing firm about the status of a brochure. She also quickly flips through the local daily and checks RSS feeds from client companies and various trade groups.

She downloads a *Wall Street Journal* article about the increasing risk of tainted food from foreign suppliers and makes a note to have her student intern do some more research about this issue. One of Anne-Marie's clients is a restaurant chain, and she senses an opportunity for the client to capitalize on the media interest by informing the press and the public about what the restaurant chain is doing to ensure the quality and safety of their meals.

She then finishes a draft of a news release about a client's new tablet computer and e-mails it to the client for approval. She also attaches a note that an electronic news service can deliver it to newspapers across the country later in the day. Anne-Marie's next activity is a brainstorming session with other staff members in the conference room to generate creative ideas about creating a Facebook page for a yogurt company.

When she gets back to her office, she finds more text messages, Tweets, and voice-mails. A reporter for a trade publication needs background information on a story he is writing; a graphic designer has finished a rough draft of a client's new logo; a catering manager has called about final arrangements for a VIP reception at an art gallery; and a video producer asks whether Anne-Marie can preview a video news release (VNR) that will be uploaded to YouTube and distributed by satellite to television stations throughout the nation.

Lunch is with a client who wants her counsel on how to position the company as environmentally conscious and dedicated to sustainable development. After lunch, Anne-Marie walks back to the office while talking on her phone to a colleague in the New York office about an upcoming news conference to announce a new celebrity clothing line. She also calls an editor to "pitch" a story about a client's new product. He's interested, so she follows up by sending some background material via her BlackBerry. Back in the office, Anne-Marie touches base with other members of her team, who are working on a 12-city media tour by an Olympic champion representing Nike.

Then it's back to the computer. She checks several online databases to gather information about the industry of a new client. She also reviews online news updates and postings on popular blogs to find out if anything is being said about her clients. At 5 P.M., as she winds down from the day's hectic activities, she reviews news stories from an electronic monitoring service about another client, an association of strawberry producers. She is pleased to find that her feature story, which included recipes and color photos, appeared in 150 dailies.

But the day isn't quite done. Anne-Marie is on her way to attend a chapter meeting of the Public Relations Society of America (PRSA), where the speaker will discuss trends in reputation management. It's her way of continuing her education since her graduation from college four years ago with a public relations major and a minor in marketing. After the meeting, she networks with several other members over a glass of wine and a quick dinner. It's a nice respite from the bulging briefcase, text messages, and e-mails that must be dealt with before she calls it a day.

As this scenario illustrates, the profession of public relations is multifaceted and quite challenging. A public relations professional must have skills in written and interpersonal communication, media relations and social media, research, negotiation, creativity, logistics, facilitation, and problem solving.

Indeed, those who want a challenging career with plenty of variety often choose the field of public relations. The U.S. Bureau of Labor Statistics estimates that the field already employs almost 300,000 people nationwide, and its 2010–2011 *Occupational Outlook Handbook* (OOH) projects a 24 percent growth rate through 2018. The handbook also gives an excellent description of a public relations specialist, which is highlighted in the Insights box below.

More good news: Public relations is somewhat recession-proof. The Bureau of Labor Statistics reported a national unemployment rate of 9.5 percent in June 2009, but an analysis by the professional recruiting firm Robert Half International found that the unemployment rate among public relations managers was less than half of 1 percent. Jim Rutherford, executive vice president (EVP) of private equity firm Veronis Suhler Stevenson (VSS), quipped to *PRWeek*, "The economy may have been in a downturn, but even companies in bankruptcy protection had to communicate to their stakeholders."

on the job

INSIGHTS

The Nature of Public Relations Work

The *Occupational Outlook Handbook 2010–11*, published by the U.S Bureau of Labor Statistics (www.bls.gov/oco), describes various jobs. The following is the description for public relations specialists:

An organization's reputation, profitability, and its continued existence can depend on the degree to which its targeted public supports its goals and policies. Public relations specialists—also referred to as *communication specialists* and *media specialists*, among other titles—serve as advocates for clients seeking to build and maintain positive relationships with the public. Their clients include businesses, nonprofit associations, universities, hospitals, and other organizations, and build and maintain positive relationships with the public. As managers recognize the link between good public relations and the success of their organizations, they increasingly rely on public relations specialists for advice on the strategy and policy of their communications.

Public relations specialists handle organizational functions, such as media, community, consumer, industry, and governmental relations; political campaigns, interest-group representation; conflict mediation; and employee and investor relations. Public relations specialists must understand the attitudes and concerns of community, consumer, employee, and public interest groups to establish and maintain cooperative

The need for good public relations in an increasingly competitive business environment should spur demand for PR specialists in organizations of all types and sizes.

—*U.S. Bureau of Labor Statistics*

(continued)

relationships between them and representatives from print and broadcast journalism.

Public relations specialists draft press releases and contact people in the media who might print or broadcast their material. Many radio or television special reports, newspaper stories, and magazine articles start at the desks of public relations specialists. Sometimes, the subject of a press release is an organization and its policies toward employees or its role in the community. For example, a press release might describe a public issue, such as health, energy, or the environment, and what an organization does to advance that issue.

Public relations specialists also arrange and conduct programs to maintain contact between organization representatives and the public. For example, public relations specialists set up speaking engagements and prepare speeches for officials. These media specialists represent employers at community projects; make film, slide, and other visual presentations for meetings and school assemblies; and plan conventions.

In government, public relations specialists may be called *press secretaries*. They keep the public informed about the activities of agencies and officials. For example, *public affairs specialists* in the U.S. Department of State alert the public of travel advisories and of U.S. positions on foreign issues. A press secretary for a member of Congress informs constituents of the representative's accomplishments.

In large organizations, the key public relations executive, who often is a vice president, may develop overall plans and policies with other executives. In addition, public relations departments employ public relations specialists to write, research, prepare materials, maintain contacts, and respond to inquiries.

People who handle publicity for an individual or who direct public relations for a small organization may deal with all aspects of the job. These public relations specialists contact people, plan and research, and prepare material for distribution. They also may handle advertising or sales promotion work to support marketing efforts.

In addition to the ability to communicate thoughts clearly and simply, public relations specialists must show creativity, initiative, and good judgment. Decision-making, problem-solving, and research skills also are important. People who choose public relations as a career should have an outgoing personality, self-confidence, an understanding of human psychology, and an enthusiasm for motivating people. They should be assertive but able to participate as part of a team and be open to new ideas.

A Global Industry

Public relations, however, is not just an American activity. It is also a worldwide industry. The global dimensions of public relations can be illustrated in several ways. The following gives some background on (1) the global market, (2) the number of practitioners, (3) regions of major growth, and (4) the growth of public relations as an academic discipline.

Global Expenditures on Public Relations   In terms of economics, the public relations field is most extensively developed in the United States. Private equity firm Veronis Suhler Stevenson (VSS), which has been tracking the communications industry for the past 15 years, reported that spending on public relations in the U.S. grew more than 4 percent in 2008 and nearly 3 percent in 2009 to $3.7 billion. In addition, VSS also predicts that spending on public relations will top $8 billion by 2013.

The projected spending, according to *PRWeek* reporter Chris Daniels, includes "...$3 billion that will be spent on word-of-mouth marketing, which includes social media outreach as well as offline brand ambassador programs." The *Economist* adds,

"The rise of the Internet and social media has given PR a big boost. Many big firms have a presence on social networking sites, such a Facebook and Twitter, overseen by PR staff. PR firms are increasingly called on to track what consumers are saying about their clients online and to respond directly to any negative commentary."

The amount spent on public relations for the rest of the world is somewhat sketchy and not well documented. One major reason is that public relations can include a number of activities that overlap into such areas as marketing, promotion, direct mail, and even advertising. The 2008 president of the Public Relations Society of America (PRSA), Michael Cherenson, estimated that the industry was a $6 billion global business. It's also been estimated that European spending on public relations is currently about $3 billion annually, but continues to increase due to the expansion of the European Union (EU) and the developing market economies of Russia and the other nations of the former Soviet Union. There is also considerable growth in other regions of the world, particularly China, which will be discussed shortly.

Despite the billions spent on public relations around the world, it should be noted that it's still a cottage industry compared to advertising. The *Financial Times* reports that global spending on advertising was more than $450 billion in 2009.

An Estimated Three Million Practitioners The Global Alliance (www.global alliancepr.org), with about 60 national and regional public relations associations representing 160,000 members, estimates that some 3 million people worldwide practice public relations as their main professional activity. This includes the estimated 300,000 practitioners in the U.S., and also the estimated 50,000 located in the United Kingdom (UK). It's also estimated that there are between 7,000 and 10,000 public relations firms in the United States, and the directory *Hollis Europe 2009* lists almost 3,000 public relations firms (consultancies) in 40 European nations. Many of these firms are one-person operations, but also included are firms with several hundred employees. There are, of course, literally thousands of companies, governmental organizations, and nonprofits around the world that also have in-house public relations departments and staffs.

There are also an estimated 200 national and regional public relations organizations around the world. A partial list that shows the geographic diversity includes the following: Public Relations Institute of Southern Africa (PRISA), the Spanish Association of Communicators (DIRCOM), the Public Relations Institute of Australia (PRIA), the Public Relations Society of Serbia, the Canadian Public Relations Society (CPRS), the Public Relations Society of Kenya (PRSK), the Institute of Public Relations (United Kingdom), the Romania Public Relations Association (RPRA), the Public Relations Agencies Association of Mexico (PRAA), Relaciones Publigas America Latina (ALARP), the Consejo Professional de Relaciones Publicas of Argentina, the Public Relations Society of India (PRSI), and the Middle East Public Relations Association (MEPRA).

An Explosion of Growth in China, Other Nations Major growth is also occurring in Asia for several reasons. China is literally the "new frontier." Since opening its economy to market capitalism 30 years ago, China today is the world's second largest economy after the United States. And the public relations industry is thriving. The China International Public Relations Association (CIPRA) reports that there are

> The rise of the Internet and social media has given PR a big boost.
>
> *The* Economist

more than 20,000 practitioners in the country and that every major global public relations firm has offices in the country. According to the *Economist*, an estimated $1.8 billion was spent on public relations in China in 2010, second only to Japan in the region.

China's membership in the World Trade Organization (WTO) opened the floodgate for more public relations activity by international companies engaged in a fierce competition for the bonanza of reaching more than a billion potential customers. The biggest trend, according to the *Economist*, is now a soaring demand for public relations among Chinese companies as they actively seek local consumers, foreign investments, and international outlets for their goods. The 2008 Beijing Olympics and the 2010 Shanghai World Expo further fueled the dynamic growth of public relations in China.

Other nations, such as Malaysia, Korea, Thailand, Singapore, Indonesia, and India, are also rapidly expanding their domestic and international markets, which creates a fertile environment for increased public relations activity. India has great economic and public relations potential because, like China, it has over 1 billion people and is also moving toward a more robust market economy. Africa and Latin America also present growth opportunities, stimulated in part by hosting international events. South Africa hosted the World Cup soccer championship in 2010 and Brazil will host the Summer Olympics in 2016. A more detailed discussion of international public relations is found in Chapter 20.

A Proliferation of University Courses   Large numbers of students around the world are studying public relations as a career field. One study by Professor Elizabeth Toth and her colleagues at the University of Maryland surveyed English-only websites and found 218 degree, certificate, and diploma programs offered in 39 countries. In another study by Chunhui He and Jing Xie at Zheijiang University's Communications Studies Institute, they report that more than 300 universities in China have now added public relations to their course offerings.

An estimated 600 American universities and colleges also offer a curriculum in public relations. There are also courses in departments of communication and schools of business, but most students are enrolled in departments or schools of journalism. In these units, the Association for Education in Journalism and Mass Communications' (AEJMC) annual enrollment survey for 2007–2008 reported there were more than 30,000 students majoring in public relations

In Europe, an estimated 100 universities also offer studies in the subject. Unlike the United States, however, many courses are taught in a faculty of economics or business. Public relations study is popular in such nations as the Netherlands, Germany, Serbia, Romania, Latvia, Estonia, and Finland. Many Asian universities, particularly those in Thailand, Korea, Indonesia, India, and the Philippines, also offer major programs. Australia and New Zealand have a long history of public relations education.

In South America, particularly in Argentina, Chile, and Brazil, public relations is taught at many universities. South African universities have the most developed public relations curriculum on the African continent, but programs of study can also be found in Nigeria, Ghana, and Kenya. The Middle East, particularly the United Arab Emirates, introduced public relations into university curriculums during the mid-1990s. In sum, public relations is a well-established academic subject that is taught and practiced on a global scale.

A Definition of Public Relations

Public relations has been defined in many ways. Rex Harlow, a Stanford professor and founder of the organization that became the Public Relations Society of America, once compiled more than 500 definitions from almost as many sources. The definitions ranged from the simple, "Doing good and getting credit for it," to more verbose definitions. Harlow's collective definition, for example, is almost 100 words.

One early definition that gained wide acceptance was formulated by the newsletter *PR News*: "Public relations is the management function which evaluates public attitudes, identifies the policies and procedures of an individual or an organization with the public interest, and plans and executes a program of action to earn public understanding and patience."

Other definitions are provided by theorists and textbook authors. One of the first textbooks in the field, *Effective Public Relations* by Scott Cutlip and Allen Center, stated, "Public relations is the management function that identifies, establishes, and maintains mutually beneficial relationships between an organization and the various publics on whom its success or failure depends." The management function was also emphasized more than 25 years ago in *Managing Public Relations* by James E. Grunig and Todd Hunt. They said, "Public relations is the management of communication between an organization and its publics."

> Public relations is the management of communication between an organization and its publics.
>
> *James E. Grunig and Todd Hunt,*
> *Managing Public Relations*

National and international public relations organizations, including the PRSA, also have formulated definitions. Here are two examples:

- "Public relations is influencing behaviour to achieve objectives through the effective management of relationships and communications." (British Institute of Public Relations, whose definition has also been adopted in a number of Commonwealth nations)
- "Public relations practice is the art and social science of analyzing trends, predicting their consequences, counseling organization leaders, and implementing planned programs of action which serve both the organization's and the public's interest." (1978 World Assembly of Public Relations in Mexico City and endorsed by 34 national public relations organizations)

A good definition for today's modern practice is offered by Professors Lawrence W. Long and Vincent Hazelton, who describe public relations as "a communication function of management through which organizations adapt to, alter, or maintain their environment for the purpose of achieving organizational goals." Their approach promotes the idea that public relations should also foster open, two-way communication and mutual understanding, with the idea that an organization—not just the target audience—changes its attitudes and behaviors in the process.

Although current definitions of public relations have long emphasized the building of mutually beneficial relationships between the organization and its various publics, a more assertive approach has emerged over the past decade. Professor Glen Cameron, at the University of Missouri School of Journalism, defines public relations as the "strategic management of competition and conflict for the benefit of one's own organization—and when possible—also for the mutual benefit of the organization and its various stakeholders or publics."

It isn't necessary, however, to memorize any particular definition of public relations. It's more important to remember the key words that are used in most definitions that frame today's modern public relations. The key words are:

- **Deliberate.** Public relations activity is intentional. It is designed to influence, gain understanding, provide information, and obtain feedback from those affected by the activity.
- **Planned.** Public relations activity is organized. Solutions to problems are discovered and logistics are thought out, with the activity taking place over a period of time. It is systematic, requiring research and analysis.
- **Performance.** Effective public relations is based on actual policies and performance. No amount of public relations will generate goodwill and support if the organization has poor policies and is unresponsive to public concerns.
- **Public interest.** Public relations activity should be mutually beneficial to the organization and the public; it is the alignment of the organization's self-interests with the public's concerns and interests.
- **Two-way communication.** Public relations is not just disseminating information but also the art of listening and engaging in a conversation with various publics.
- **Management function.** Public relations is most effective when it is a strategic and integral part of decision making by top management. Public relations involves counseling, problem solving, and the management of competition and conflict.

To summarize, you can grasp the essential elements of effective public relations by remembering the following words and phrases: deliberate . . . planned . . . performance . . . public interest . . . two-way communication . . . strategic management function. The elements of public relations just described are part of the process that defines today's public relations.

Other Popular Names

Public relations is used as an umbrella term on a worldwide basis. Most national membership associations, from the Azerbaijan Public Relations Association to the Zimbabwe Institute of Public Relations, identify themselves with that term.

Individual companies and other groups, however, often use other terms to describe the public relations function. The most popular term among *Fortune* 500 companies is *corporate communications*. This description is used by such companies as McDonald's, BMW of North America, Toyota, Walt Disney, and Walgreens. Other companies, such as GM and United Technologies, just use the term *communications*.

A number of corporations also use combination titles to describe the public relations function within the organization. IBM, for example, has a senior vice president (SVP) of marketing and communications. At Facebook, the public relations executive is in charge of *communications and public policy*. Johnson & Johnson goes with *public affairs and corporate communications*, while L'Oreal USA uses *corporate communications and external affairs*. Other companies think in more global terms. The public relations executive at Coca-Cola, for example, is in charge of *worldwide public affairs and communications*, and FedEx uses *worldwide communications and investor relations*.

The use of *corporate communications* is based, in part, on the belief that the term is broader than *public relations*, which is often incorrectly perceived as only *media relations*. Corporate communications, many argue, encompasses all communications of the company, including advertising, marketing communications, public affairs, community relations, and employee communications. Others believe that such terms as *corporate communications* sound more impressive and get away from some of the negative stereotypes about "public relations," which will be discussed shortly.

Public information and *public affairs* are the most widely used terms by nonprofits, universities, and government agencies. The implication is that only information is being disseminated, in contrast to persuasive communication, generally perceived as the purpose of public relations. Social services agencies often use the term *community relations*, and the military is fond of *public affairs*. Increasingly, many nonprofits are also using the term *marketing communications*, as they reorient to the idea that they must sell their services and generate donations in a highly competitive environment.

Other organizations use a term that better describes the primary activity of the department. It is clear, for example, that a department of investor relations deals primarily with stockholders, institutional investors, and the financial press. Likewise, a department of environmental affairs, community relations, or employee communications is self-explanatory. A department of marketing communications primarily emphasizes product publicity and promotion. The organization and functions of communications departments are discussed in Chapter 4.

Like departments, individuals specialize in subcategories of public relations. A person who deals exclusively with placement of stories in the media is, to be precise, a *publicist*. A *press agent* is also a specialist, operating within the subcategory of public relations that concentrates on finding unusual news angles and planning events or "happenings" that attract media attention—a stunt by an aspiring Hollywood actress, for example, or an attempt to be listed in the *Guinness Book of Records* by baking the world's largest apple pie. *Publicist* is an honorable term in the entertainment and celebrity business, but is somewhat frowned on by the mainstream public relations industry. Chapter 18 discusses the work of New York and Hollywood publicists.

Stereotypes and Less Flattering Terms

Unfortunately, the public often has a much different image of public relations. A common stereotype is that public relations is a glamorous field because public relations practitioners meet exciting and interesting people, go to parties, and generally spend the day doing a lot of schmoozing. On the more sinister side, many people think public relations is a synonym for propaganda, manipulation, and even lying on behalf of special interests such as corporations and politicians.

Many people gain their perceptions from television programs such as *Sex and the City*, which is now in reruns and even became two movies. Ellen Tashie Frisna, a professor at Hofstra University, writes in *Tactics*, "Samantha Jones (Kim Cattrall), the sexiest of the show's characters, owns a PR agency. And she is—shall we say—experienced. She talks about her career as a way to meet men. (Her conquests include clients and temps.) Sorry, kids—the real world of public relations isn't like that."

Of course, other television programs and movies also give somewhat negative stereotypes about public relations. ABC's *Spin City*, for example, featured Michael J. Fox as the deputy mayor of New York, who protected his bumbling boss from the media and public. More recently, Bravo launched a reality show, *Kell on Earth*, that the *New York Times* described as "a reality show that follows a publicist, Kelly Cutrone, as she bullies and cajoles her

Public Relations Hollywood Style

Samantha Jones (Kim Cattrall) leads a glamorous life as the owner of a public relations firm in the television series *Sex and the City*. In the second movie sequel, she even goes to Abu Dhabi to plan a public relations campaign for a luxury hotel. Public relations work, however, requires more than wearing designer clothes and going to dinner parties.

way through the underbelly of the New York fashion world." *Mad Men*, a series about an advertising firm in the 1960s, has also portrayed public relations as a somewhat dubious activity.

The movies *Phone Booth*, *The Sweet Smell of Success*, and even *The Devil Wears Prada* also add to the portrayals of sleazy publicists who have virtually no personal or professional moral compass. Some films are satires, but still project a negative image of public relations. *Thank You for Smoking*, a movie adapted from the book by Christopher Buckley, is a particularly good satire about a public relations person defending the tobacco industry. *Wag the Dog*, starring Dustin Hoffman and Robert DeNiro, is also a satire focusing on how an embattled president creates a fake war with the help of public relations pros to improve his image. A more recent film, *Bruno*, with leading actor Sacha Baron Cohen, played up the "dumb blonde" syndrome. At one point in the film, Sacha's fictional character asks two sisters who run a public relations firm in Los Angeles, "What charities are hot now?" They replied, "Darfur." He then asked them where Darfur is, and they didn't have a clue.

Other negative stereotypes are perpetuated by journalists who use terms such as "PR gimmick" or "PR fluff." One journalist once described public relations as "the art of saying nothing." Frank Rich, an influential columnist for the *New York Times*, has used a number of adjectives over the years to describe public relations. They include "marketing," "sales," "sloganeering," "propaganda," and "lacking in principles and substance." Gene Weingarten, a columnist for the *Washington Post*, seems to agree, once calling public relations people "pathetic, desperate dillweeds." Joe Norcera, a business columnist for the *New York Times*, used less colorful language to describe his frustration

Public Relations as "Image Building"

The image of an organization is made up of many factors, and public relations is only one of them. (Copyright © The New Yorker Collection 2004. Mick Stevens from cartoonbank.com. All rights reserved.)

with Apple public relations reps. He wrote, "This is another Apple innovation: the robotic spokesman who says only what he's programmed to say."

Journalists often express frustration when they feel that public relations personnel are stonewalling, providing misleading information, or not being readily accessible to fully answer questions. This is traditionally a problem of effective media relations and, quite frankly, incompetence occurs in all fields, including public relations. Chapters 14 and 15 discuss the responsibilities of public relations personnel to provide assistance to media personnel.

Public relations is also referred to as *spin*. This term first appeared in a 1984 *New York Times* editorial about the activities of President Ronald Reagan's reelection campaign. In the beginning, the meaning of *spin* was restricted to what often were considered the unethical and misleading activities and tactics of political campaign consultants. Today, however, the media widely use the term to describe any effort by an individual or organization to interpret an event or issue according to a particular viewpoint. On occasion, however, spin can lead to a question of ethics, which is highlighted in the Ethics box below. A more academic term for spin is the concept of *framing*. Multiple research studies show how journalists, as well as public relations personnel, "frame" issues. See Chapter 9 for more on the theory of framing.

Another term with a long history is *flak* or *flack*. These words are derisive slang terms that journalists often use for a press agent or anyone else working in public relations. It's like calling a journalist a "hack." Although in recent years most publications, including the *Wall Street Journal*, have refrained from using the "F" word in news stories, columnists still occasionally use the word.

on the job

ETHICS

Canada Outed for Scenery Theft

The Canadian province of Alberta launched an image campaign to somewhat offset the controversy over oil extraction in Alberta's wetlands. The campaign artwork included a photo of two children playing on a seaside beach with the slogan, "Alberta: Freedom to Create. Spirit to Achieve."

The only problem was that Alberta has no coastline and is 800 kilometers from the nearest body of water, the Pacific Ocean. A sailing enthusiast tracked down the actual site of the photo, which was Beadnell Bay on the north coast of England, 8,000 kilometers away from landlocked Alberta.

Martin Wainwright, a reporter for the *Guardian Weekly*, asked Canadian officials about using the photo. The head of media relations for the Canadian prime minister told him that the photograph merely symbolized the fact that "Albertans are a worldly people. There's no attempt to mislead here. The picture used just fitted the mood and tone of what we were trying to do." And the Alberta public relations bureau, who was managing the public relations campaign, issued the statement, "This represents Albertans' concern for the future of the world. There's no attempt to make people think that the place pictured is Alberta." The PR firm Calder Bateman, which devised the campaign, issued a "no comment."

What do you think of the rationale given for using the photo? Do you think the use of such a picture was misleading, unethical, or OK?

The term has a mixed history. According to Wes Pedersen, a former director of communications for the Public Affairs Council, the term *flack* originated in 1939 in *Variety*, the show business publication. It began using *flack* as a synonym for *press agent*, he says, "in tribute to the skills of Gene Flack in publicizing motion pictures." Others say the word *flak* was used during World War I to describe heavy ground fire aimed at aircraft. At times, journalists consider the barrage of daily news releases they receive a form of flak that interferes with their mission of informing the public.

Within the public relations community, feeling also exists that *PR* is a slang term that carries a somewhat denigrating connotation. The late Sam Black, a public relations consultant in the United Kingdom and author of several books on public relations, said, "The use of 'PR' probably originated as a nickname for 'press relations,'" the primary activity of public relations in its early years (see Chapter 2).

Although PR is now more than press relations, the nickname is commonly used in daily conversation and is widely recognized around the world. A good compromise, which this book uses, is to adopt the style of spelling out "public relations" in the body of a text or article but to use the shorter term, "PR," if it is used in a direct quote.

Public Relations as a Process

Public relations is a process—that is, a series of actions, changes, or functions that bring about a result. One popular way to describe the process, and to remember its components, is to use the RACE acronym, first articulated by John Marston in his book *The Nature of Public Relations*. Essentially, RACE means that public relations activity consists of four key elements:

- **Research.** What is the problem or situation?
- **Action** (program planning). What is going to be done about it?
- **Communication** (execution). How will the public be told?
- **Evaluation.** Was the audience reached and what was the effect?

Part Two of this text (Chapters 5–8) discusses this key four-step process.

Another approach is to think of the process as a never-ending cycle in which six components are links in a chain. Figure 1.1 shows the process.

1. **Step 1: *Research and Analysis.*** This consists of inputs that determine the nature and extent of the public relations problem or opportunity. These may include feedback from the public, media reporting and editorial comment, analysis of trend data, other forms of research, personal experience, and government pressures and regulations.

2. **Step 2: *Policy Formulation.*** Public relations personnel, as advisors to top management, make recommendations on policy and what actions should be taken by the organization.

3. **Step 3: *Programming.*** Once a policy or action is agreed on, public relations staff begin to plan a communications program that will further the organization's objectives. They will set objectives, define audiences, and decide on what strategies will be used on a specific timeline. Budget and staffing are also major considerations.

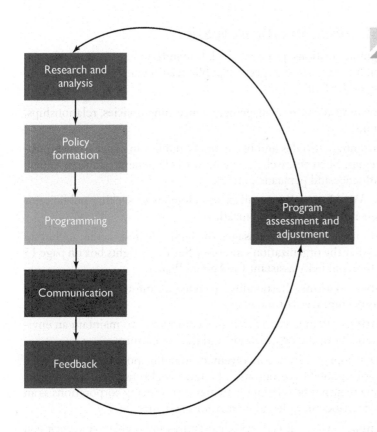

Figure 1.1 The Public Relations Process

The conceptualization of public relations as a cyclical process, feedback, or audience response leads to assessment of the program, which becomes an essential element in the development of another public relations project.

4. **Step 4: *Communication.*** Public relations personnel execute the program through such vehicles as news releases, media advisories, newsletters, Internet and Web postings, special events, speeches, and community relations programs.

5. **Step 5: *Feedback.*** The effect of these efforts is measured by feedback from the same components that made up the first step. Did the media mention the key messages? Did people change their attitudes or opinions? Did sales go up? Did the organization preserve or enhance its reputation?

6. **Step 6: *Assessment.*** The cycle is then repeated. The success or failure of the policy or program is assessed as a way of determining whether additional efforts are needed, or whether new issues or opportunities must be addressed. Thus, it is a continuing loop process.

Note that public relations plays two distinct roles in this process, thus serving as a "middle ground" or "linking agent." On one level, public relations interacts directly with external sources of information, including the public, media, and government, and relays these inputs to management along with recommendations. On a second level, public relations becomes the vehicle through which management reaches the public with assorted messages.

We provide a voice in the marketplace of ideas, facts, and viewpoints to aid informed public debate.

Public Relations Society of America, defining the role of public relations in today's society

The Diversity of Public Relations Work

The basic process of public relations, just described, is manifested in a variety of ways. The PRSA Foundation lists the various aspects of public relations activity that are done by individuals working in the field.

- **Counseling.** Providing advice to management concerning policies, relationships, and communications.

- **Research.** Determining attitudes and behaviors of publics in order to plan public relations strategies. Such research can be used to (1) generate mutual understanding or (2) influence and persuade publics.

- **Media relations.** Working with journalists and bloggers in seeking publicity or responding to their interests in the organization.

- **Publicity.** Disseminating planned messages through selected media, including social media, to further the organization's interests. See the Insights box on page 15 for a job posting for a publicity assistant for Animal Planet.

- **Employee/member relations.** Responding to concerns, informing, and motivating an organization's employees or members.

- **Community relations.** Planned activity with a community to maintain an environment that benefits both the organization and the community.

- **Public affairs.** Developing effective involvement in public policy and helping an organization adapt to public expectations. The term is also used by government agencies to describe their public relations activities and by many corporations as an umbrella term to describe multiple public relations activities.

- **Government affairs.** Relating directly with legislatures and regulatory agencies on behalf of the organization. Lobbying can be part of a government affairs program.

- **Issues management.** Identifying and addressing issues of public concern that affect the organization.

- **Financial relations.** Creating and maintaining investor confidence and building good relationships with the financial community. Also known as investor relations or shareholder relations.

- **Industry relations.** Relating with other firms in the industry of an organization and with trade associations.

- **Development/fund-raising.** Demonstrating the need for and encouraging the public to support an organization, primarily through financial contributions.

- **Multicultural relations/workplace diversity.** Relating with individuals and groups in various cultural groups. A good example is the Bank of America's outreach to the Hispanic community on page 16.

- **Special events.** Stimulating an interest in a person, product, or organization by means of a well-planned event; also, activities designed to interact with publics and listen to them.

- **Marketing communications.** Combination of activities designed to sell a product, service, or idea, including advertising, collateral materials, publicity, promotion, direct mail, trade shows, and special events.

These components, and how they function, constitute the substance of this textbook. The next sections, however, will help you more fully understand the differences between public relations and the related fields of journalism, advertising, and marketing.

on the job

INSIGHTS

Wanted: A Publicity Assistant for Animal Planet

Entry-level jobs in public relations often focus on media relations and logistics. A good example is a job posting for a publicity assistant by Discovery Communications, a media company that owns multiple cable channels such as the Discovery Channel and Animal Planet.

The following job description was posted on *prnewsonline.com*:

Position Summary

Support communications activities for *Animal Planet*. The Publicity Assistant position reports to the manager of publicity or director, communications (pending location) and supports team managers on various projects. Discovery Communications is the number-one nonfiction media company reaching more than 1.5 billion subscribers in over 170 countries.

Responsibilities

- Provide administrative support and project support on projects in a timely and efficient manner.
- Press lists and database development and maintenance.
- Distribution and formatting of news releases and press materials

(via e-mail lists, PR Newswire, PressWeb, and new online distribution methods.

- Tracking of press coverage and preparation of press research reports and analyses.
- Managing publicity stills on PressWeb and Virtual Library.
- Compiling, writing, editing, and distributing monthly program highlights.
- Submitting event photos/captions to the press.
- Drafting of executive personnel announcements and bios.
- Other press release writing, editing, and pitching.
- Special events support.
- Talent management and staffing.
- Manage upkeep of press website and materials including boilerplates and fast facts, network overview, and executive bios and photos.
- Maintain long lead and seasonal programming documents.
- Maintain editorial and PR calendars, which include upcoming special reports in key trade and business publications.

- Execute multiple press campaigns.
- Perform other duties as required.

Job Requirements

- One-year of hands-on communications and media relations work experience and appropriate number of internships in the field.
- Demonstrated ability to work under pressure, meet tight deadlines, and work on multiple projects simultaneously.
- Superb written, verbal, and interpersonal skills.
- Ability to juggle a myriad of tasks simultaneously.
- Must be independent, strategic thinker who is a strong team player (no job is too small or too large) and willing to take on additional responsibilities if necessary.
- Ability to cultivate and sustain strong relationships with members of the media and with coworkers.
- Strong computer skills, including proficiency in social networking skills.

on the job

A MULTICULTURAL WORLD

Bank of America Reaches Out to the Hispanic Community

More than half of the Hispanics living in the United States regularly send money to loved ones in their home countries. At the same time, 70 percent of them use wire transfer services that charge relatively high fees.

The Bank of America (BofA), realizing the potential market of the 25 million Latin Americans living in the United States, had a better idea. The bank launched a program called SafeSend, which allowed Hispanics to send remittances free if they opened a BofA checking account.

Fleishman-Hillard public relations was engaged to generate awareness among the Hispanic community about the SafeSend program. The kickoff focused on Mexican Mother's Day because that traditionally was the time of year when remittances were the highest. A national news release, a radio news release, and a video news release (VNR) were distributed to major Spanish-language media outlets, as well as the general press.

In addition, the bank began hosting Fiesta Fridays in its various facilities and provided materials in Spanish so

A Better Way to Send Money
A 10-foot-high Mexican piggy bank symbolized the Bank of America's SafeSend program at an event in Los Angeles.

that potential customers could become better acquainted with its products and services. Other events also were used. At a Los Angeles event, for example, a 10-foot-high Mexican piggy bank was used to symbolize the savings that SafeSend could offer. Piggy banks were also used at regional Cinco de Mayo festivals in California and Texas.

As a result, the SafeSend program received considerable coverage in the Hispanic press. More important, BofA opened 3,295 new direct-deposit accounts with SafeSend in the initial weeks. Before this campaign, the bank had already been the first one to introduce Spanish-language ATMs, bilingual customer service, and a Spanish-language website.

Public Relations vs. Journalism

Writing is a common activity of both public relations professionals and journalists. Both also do their jobs in the same way. They interview people, gather and synthesize large amounts of information, write in a journalistic style, and are trained to produce good copy on deadline. In fact, many reporters eventually change careers and become public relations practitioners.

This has led many people, including journalists, to the incorrect conclusion that little difference exists between public relations and journalism. For these people, public relations is simply being a "journalist-in-residence" for a nonmedia organization. However, despite the sharing of many techniques, the two fields are fundamentally different in scope, objectives, audiences, and channels.

Scope   Public relations, as stated earlier, has many components, ranging from counseling to issues management and special events. Journalistic writing and media relations, although important, are only two of these elements. In addition, effective practice of public relations requires strategic thinking, problem-solving capability, and other management skills.

Objectives   Journalists gather and select information for the primary purpose of providing the public with news and information. Public relations personnel also gather facts and information for the purpose of informing the public, but the objective is not only to inform but also to change people's attitudes and behaviors in order to further an organization's goals and objectives. Harold Burson, chairman of Burson-Marsteller, makes the point: "To be effective and credible, public relations messages must be based on facts. Nevertheless, we are advocates, and we need to remember that. We are advocates of a particular point of view—our client's or our employer's point of view. And while we recognize that serving the public interest best serves our client's interest, we are not journalists. That's not our job."

Audiences   Journalists write primarily for a mass audience—readers, listeners, or viewers of the medium for which they work. By definition, mass audiences are not well defined, and a journalist on a daily newspaper, for example, writes for the general public. A public relations professional, in contrast, carefully segments audiences into various demographic and psychological characteristics. Such research allows messages to be tailored to audience needs, concerns, and interests for maximum effect.

Channels   Most journalists, by nature of their employment, reach audiences through one channel—the medium that publishes or broadcasts their work. On the other hand, public relations professionals use a variety of channels to reach the audiences previously described. The channels employed may be a combination of mass media outlets— newspapers, magazines, radio, and television. Or they may include direct mail, brochures, posters, newsletters, trade journals, special events, podcasts, blogs, websites, and even video postings on YouTube.

Public Relations vs. Advertising

Just as many people mistakenly equate publicity with public relations, there is also some confusion about the distinction between publicity (one area of public relations) and advertising.

Although publicity and advertising both utilize mass media for dissemination of messages, the format and context each uses are different. Publicity—information about an event, an individual or group, or a product—appears as a news item or feature story in the mass media or online. Material is prepared by public relations personnel and submitted to the news department for consideration. Editors, known as gatekeepers, determine whether the material will be used or simply thrown away.

We're beginning to see research that supports the superiority of PR over advertising to launch a brand.

Al and Laura Ries, authors of The Fall of Advertising and The Rise of Public Relations

Advertising, in contrast, is paid space and broadcast time. Organizations and individuals typically contract with the advertising department of a mass media outlet for a full-page ad or a one-minute commercial. An organization writes the advertisement, decides the type and graphics, and controls where and when the advertisement will be run. In other words, advertising is simply renting space in a mass medium. The lion's share of revenue for traditional media and even Google comes from the selling of advertising space.

Other differences between public relations activities and advertising include:

- Advertising works almost exclusively through mass media outlets; public relations relies on a number of communication tools—brochures, slide presentations, special events, speeches, news releases, feature stories, and so forth.

- Advertising is primarily directed to consumers of goods and services; public relations presents its message to specialized external audiences (stockholders, vendors, community leaders, environmental groups, and so on) and internal publics (employees).

- Advertising is readily identified as a specialized communication function; public relations is broader in scope, dealing with the policies and performance of the entire organization, from the morale of employees to the amount of money given to local community organizations.

- Advertising is often used as a communication tool in public relations, and public relations activity often supports advertising campaigns. Advertising's primary function is to sell goods and services; public relations' function is to create an environment in which the organization can thrive. The latter calls for dealing with economic, social, and political factors that can affect the organization.

The major disadvantage of advertising, of course, is the cost. A full-page ad in the national edition of the *Wall Street Journal*, for example, costs $164,000 for black and white and $220,000 for full color. Advertising campaigns on network television, of course, can run into the millions of dollars. For example, advertisers paid $2.5 to $3 million for a 30-second Super Bowl ad in 2010. Consequently, companies often use a tool of public relations—product publicity—that is more cost effective and often more credible because the message appears in a news context. One poll by Opinion Research Corporation, for example, found that online articles about a product or service were more persuasive than banner ads, pop-up ads, e-mail offers, and sponsored links.

Public Relations vs. Marketing

Public relations is distinct from marketing in several ways, although their boundaries often overlap. Both disciplines deal with an organization's external relationships and employ similar communication tools to reach the public. Both also have the ultimate purpose of ensuring an organization's success and economic survival. Public relations and marketing, however, approach this task from somewhat different perspectives or worldviews.

Objectives   The purpose of marketing is to sell goods and services through attractive packaging, competitive pricing, retail and online promotions, and efficient distribution systems. The purpose of public relations is to build relationships with a variety of publics that can enhance the organization's reputation and establish trust in its policies, products, and services.

Audiences   The primary audiences for marketing are consumers and customers. Public relations deals with a much broader array of audiences, or publics. They may include investors, community leaders, environmental groups, vendors, government officials, and even employees, who can affect the organization's success and profitability through boycotts, legislation, and the generation of unfavorable publicity.

Competition vs. Opposition   Marketing professionals tend to rely exclusively on competitive solutions, whereas public relations professionals often perceive the problem as effectively dealing with opposition. When meeting opposition to a product, marketing often thinks the solution is lower pricing or better packaging. However, public relations professionals realize that pricing doesn't make any difference if a consumer group is opposed to the product because they think it is unsafe. See the PR Casebook in Chapter 4 about the Toyota product recall.

Role in Management   Marketing is a distinct function primarily dealing with product positioning and sales. Public relations, however, deals with all departments of the organization to advance overall business goals and objectives. An organization, to be successful in the marketplace, must pay constant attention to its reputation and have policies that enhance trust and credibility among its multiple publics. Public relations, in its ideal form, directly deals with upper management to shape and promote the organization's core values.

> Marketing is transaction oriented. While public relations can be part of a marketing strategy, it has a much larger responsibility within the organization.
>
> *Dave Imre, an executive at Imre Communications, Baltimore*

How Public Relations Supports Marketing

Philip Kotler, professor of marketing at Northwestern University and author of a leading marketing textbook, says public relations is the fifth "P" of marketing strategy, which includes four other Ps—Product, Price, Place, and Promotion. As he wrote in the *Harvard Business Review*, "Public relations takes longer to cultivate, but when energized, it can help pull the company into the market."

When public relations is used to support directly an organization's marketing objectives, it is called *marketing communications*. Thomas Harris, author of *The Marketer's Guide to Public Relations*, prefers the term *marketing public relations*. This, he says, distinguishes the function from *corporate public relations* that define the corporation's relationships with its non-customer publics.

Dennis L. Wilcox, in his text *Public Relations Writing and Media Techniques*, lists eight ways in which public relations activities contribute to fulfilling marketing objectives:

1. Developing new prospects for new markets, such as people who inquire after seeing or hearing a product release in the news media

2. Providing third-party endorsements—via newspapers, magazines, radio, and television—through news releases about a company's products or services, community involvement, inventions, and new plans

3. Generating sales leads, usually through articles in the trade press about new products and services

4. Paving the way for sales calls

5. Stretching the organization's advertising and promotional dollars through timely and supportive releases about it and its products

6. Providing inexpensive sales literature, because articles about the company and its products can be reprinted as informative pieces for prospective customers

7. Establishing the corporation as an authoritative source of information on a given product

8. Helping to sell minor products that don't have large advertising budgets

Toward an Integrated Perspective

Although well-defined differences exist among the fields of advertising, marketing, and public relations, there is an increasing realization that an organization's objectives can be best accomplished through an integrated approach.

This understanding has given rise to such terms as *integrated marketing communications (IMC)*, *convergent communications*, and *integrated communications*. Don Schulz, Stanley Tannenbaum, and Robert Lauterborn, authors of *Integrated Marketing Communications*, explain the title of their book as follows:

> A concept of marketing communication planning that recognizes the added value of a comprehensive plan that evaluates the strategic roles of a variety of communication disciplines—e.g., General Advertising, Direct Response, Sales Promotion, and Public Relations—and combines these disciplines to provide clarity, consistency, and maximum communication impact.

Several factors have fueled the trend toward IMC. (See the IMC model in Figure 1.2.) First is the downsizing of organizations. Many of them have consolidated departments and have also reduced staff dedicated to various communication disciplines. As a result, one department, with fewer employees, is expected to do a greater variety of communication tasks.

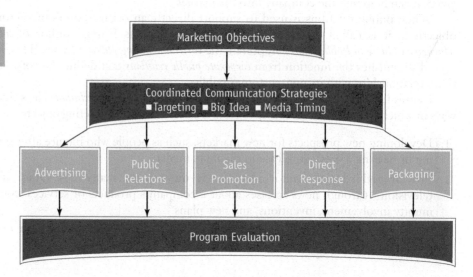

Figure 1.2   The IMC Model

This illustration shows the components of an integrated marketing communications model.

Second, organizational marketing and communication departments are making do with tighter budgets. Many organizations, to avoid the high cost of advertising, look for alternative ways to deliver messages. These may include (1) building buzz via word of mouth, (2) targeting influentials, (3) Web marketing, (4) grassroots marketing, (5) media relations and product publicity, and (6) event sponsorship.

Third is the increasing realization that advertising, with its high costs, isn't the silver bullet that it used to be. The problem is the increasing clutter of advertising, the fragmentation of audiences among multiple media, and a general lack of credibility among consumers.

Al and Laura Ries, authors of the popular book (at least among public relations people) *The Fall of Advertising and the Rise of PR*, write, "We're beginning to see research that supports the superiority of PR over advertising to launch a brand. A recent study of 91 new product launches shows highly successful products are more likely to use PR-related activities than less successful ones." They continue, ". . . PR creates the brand. Advertising defends the brand."

> It comes down to economics. If you're coming up with one idea that can be used across five different marketing disciplines, it just makes the idea much stronger, that much more cohesive when you are communicating it to your audience, and it makes your dollar work that much harder.
>
> *Andrea Morgan,*
> *EVP of consumer brands for Euro RSCG*

Fourth, it is now widely recognized that the marketing of products and services can be affected by public and social policy issues. Environmental legislation influences packaging and the content of products, a proposed luxury tax on expensive autos affects sales of those cars, and a company's support of Planned Parenthood or health benefits for same-sex partners may spur a product boycott.

The impact of such factors, not traditionally considered by marketing managers, has led many professionals to believe that organizations should do a better job of integrating public relations and public affairs into their overall marketing considerations. In fact, David Corona, writing in the *Public Relations Journal* some years ago, was the first one to advance the idea that marketing's sixth "P" should be public policy.

The concept of integration, therefore, is the ability of organizations to use a variety of strategies and tactics to convey a consistent message in a variety of forms. The metaphor might be the golfer with a variety of clubs in her bag. She may use one club (public relations) to launch a product, another club (advertising) to reinforce the message, and yet another club (Web marketing) to actually sell the product or service to a well-defined audience.

The golf metaphor also reflects a realization on the part of management and marketing executives that public relations is an effective strategy in several important areas. A *PRWeek* survey of marketing executives, for example, found that public relations ranked higher in effectiveness than advertising or marketing in nine areas: (1) brand reputation, (2) corporate reputation, (3) cultivating thought leaders, (4) strategy development, (5) launching a new product, (6) building awareness, (7) generating word of mouth, (8) message development, and (9) overcoming a crisis.

A good example of an integrated marketing campaign is a back-to-school program by Sears. The campaign featured *High School Musical* star Vanessa Hudgens, who was used across different channels, primarily social networks where many of her fans are located. Hudgens took part in another Sears campaign that also used celebrities LL Cool J and Ty Pennington in advertising, in-store promotions, and online Web videos. A public relations component had the celebrities participate in satellite media tours (SMTs) and radio media tours (RMTs), which are discussed in Chapter 15.

A Career in Public Relations

The growth of public relations as a career field has spawned any number of public relations courses, sequences, and majors.

The Commission on Public Relations Education, which includes public relations educators and representatives from all of the major professional organizations, has set the standard by specifying a minimum of five courses that should be required in a public relations major. They are:

- Introduction to public relations (including theory, origin, and principles)
- Public relations research, measurement, and evaluation
- Public relations writing and production
- Supervised work experience in public relations (internship)
- An additional public relations course in law and ethics, planning and management, and case studies or campaigns

In addition, the Commission highly recommends that students take courses in such areas as marketing, management, economics, social psychology, and multicultural communication. Other experienced professionals agree that coursework is important, but also feel networking skills should not be overlooked. See the Insights box about a first-person account.

Public relations, at least in the United States, has traditionally been taught in departments and schools of journalism. Consequently, a number of journalism graduates also consider employment in public relations, as job opportunities on newspapers and other traditional media continue to decline. Lindsey Miller, in a *Ragan.com* article, writes, "As curricula

> PR people are the story tellers. It's our job to help find the authenticity at the core of our companies and clients, and tell those stories to the world in real words that will really be heard.
>
> *Fred Cook, president of Golin Harris public relations*

on the job

INSIGHTS

Networking: The Key to Career Success
By Robin Carr

We all take different paths to reach our professional and personal goals. Whatever you do, be sure to network, network and network some more. Every job I have ever had has been the direct result of networking and I cannot stress this enough.

Even while you're still in school, take the time to go to various mixers and events and meet people. IABC (International Association of Business Communicators) and PRSA (Public Relations Society of America) have open events and

you don't have to be a member. While in school, get actively involved and with your PRSSA (Public Relations Student Society of America) chapter. Often times, your area PRSA chapter will host PRSSA students and create professional

Robin Carr

partner programs. This is an excellent way to not only network, but find a mentor or two.

And while social media sites such as LinkedIn and Twitter are great tools to network and learn, there's nothing like getting out and meeting people face to face. Go to monthly luncheons, mixers and attend business conferences with interesting speakers and panels.

The terrific thing about public relations as a discipline is that you can apply it to practically anything.

Collect business cards, follow up with an email or LinkedIn invitation, and your network will grow.

After graduation, I worked at a PR agency for one year to get general experience in the work world. Agencies are very good places for PR graduates to start. There are a variety of clients and you can learn and discover what your interests are and, of course, network. There are many agencies that have different specialties: technology, hospitality, consumer products and youth "buzz" marketing, to name a few.

I stayed at the agency for more than a year, but my first love was sports, so I was able to land an informational interview with the Publicity Director for the San Francisco Giants. There are very limited PR openings in sports, however, and while I felt discouraged at the time, I was told to be patient and wait for an available opportunity. Sure enough, about six months later, I attended a Giants game and I ran into the gentleman I had interviewed with. He said "call me tomorrow—my assistant quit today!" So I got the job as an administrative assistant in the publicity department. It was very entry level, but it was a foot in the door. And the Giants had always promised me that I would move up and I was promoted several times. I worked there ten years,

before moving on to Nike and EA Sports.

The terrific thing about public relations as a discipline is that you can apply it to practically anything. I worked in sports public relations for 18 years, however, my career path has included video gaming, retail and health care. There are also networking events besides PR groups that you can join that is catered to your field of PR. For instance, I'm a member of the Association for Women in Sports Media, WISE (Women in Sports/Entertainment) and the National Sports Marketing Association.

Finally, if possible, do more than one internship. Take advantage of opportunities when they come up and get in on the ground floor if you have to. Be patient—if you really want to move up to the next level, work hard and prove yourself. It will pay off.

Robin Carr has worked almost 20 years in the sports industry, including stints at the San Francisco Giants, Nike, and EA Sports. She also has experience at the Gap as manager of its Product Red program and at Kaiser Permanente as director of national public relations. She is a graduate of the public relations degree program at San Jose State University and lives in San Francisco with her husband, Thomas Bonk, a Los Angeles Times *sports columnist.*

diversify and career options widen, many J-school grads are seeing the more stable and better-paying corporate communications field as fertile ground for their skills. They're armed not only with the ability to write a good article, but they can also tell a good story on a range of platforms, using a variety of media."

Such skills, of course, are important in public relations work, but there's some debate whether journalism majors have the training and temperament that lead to successful careers in public relations. Richard Mintz, managing director of the Harbour Group in Washington, D.C., told an *Atlantic* magazine blogger, "Journalists, by their nature, don't make great advocates or public relations people, because they're trained to be objective rather than take sides. They also tend to work alone, and they have no business experience." Michele Horaney, a former journalist and now a communications director for a nonprofit organization, disagrees. She told *Ragan.com*, "PR people with news coverage background have a leg up over folks … who have never written a news story. Being able to write and do research from 'in the news' and 'in the public's interest' perspective is invaluable."

In sum, there are many paths to a career in public relations. Majoring in public relations, or at least taking some basic courses in the subject, is considered the best preparation, but majors from other fields such as journalism, communication studies, and marketing also have skills that are valued by many employers. Former TV news producer Bev Carlson, a board member of Nebraska's chapter of the Public Relations Society of America (PRSA), told *Ragan.com*, "It all depends on the person and their willingness to be flexible and learn."

There's also some thought that public relations courses should be in a school of business instead of a journalism department or school. The argument is that today's public relations is no longer exclusively a journalistic-type activity that involves working with the media. James Lukaszewski, a well-known consultant and speaker in the public relations field, is quite blunt. He wrote in *The Strategist*, "At minimum, PR programs belong in marketing sequences rather than journalism sequences. The sooner we can reflect a more managementlike perspective, the more quickly we'll find ourselves called in for our advice and counsel."

Indeed, many European universities offer a public relations curriculum in other academic areas. At the University of Belgrade in Serbia, for example, public relations is located in the Faculty of Economics. And in Latvia, the strongest public relations program in the country is taught at the Turiba School of Business Administration. Management schools in India also offer the most courses in public relations and corporate communications. In the United States, however, the vast majority of public relations programs continue to be part of J-schools.

Essential Career Skills

A student's choice of a major in college is important, but equally important is participating in campus clubs, taking internships, and even working part-time at jobs that develop essential skills for a successful career in public relations. These are (1) writing skill, (2) research ability, (3) planning expertise, (4) problem-solving ability, (5) business/economics competence, and (6) expertise in social media.

1. **Writing skill.** The ability to put information and ideas onto paper clearly and concisely is essential. Good grammar and good spelling are vital. Misspelled words and sloppy sentence structure are unacceptable. The importance of writing skill is emphasized in a career advice column in *Working Woman*: "I changed careers, choosing public relations as having the best potential, but found it difficult to persuade employers that my writing and interpersonal skills were sufficient for an entry-level job in the profession."

2. **Research ability.** Arguments for causes must have factual support instead of generalities. A person must have the persistence and ability to gather information from a variety of sources, as well as to conduct original research by designing and implementing opinion polls or audits. Too many public relations programs fail because the organization does not assess audience needs and perceptions. Skillful use of the Internet and computer databases is an important element of research work. Reading current newspapers and magazines also is important.

on the job

INSIGHTS

Personality Quiz: Do You Have the "Right Stuff"?

This checklist, based on careful evaluation, can measure the effectiveness of your personality in terms of the public relations profession.

Rate each item "yes" or "no." Each "yes" counts for 4 points. A "no" does not count. Anything below 60 is a poor score. A score between 60 and 80 suggests you should analyze your weak areas and take steps to correct them. Scores above 80 indicate an effective public relations personality.

_____ Good sense of humor

_____ Positive and optimistic

_____ Friendly, meet people easily

_____ Can keep a conversation going with anybody

_____ Take frustration and rejection in stride

_____ Able to persuade others easily

_____ Well-groomed, businesslike appearance

_____ Flair for showmanship

_____ Strong creative urge

_____ Considerate and tactful

_____ Adept in use of words

_____ Able to gain management's confidence

_____ Enjoy being with people

_____ Enjoy listening

_____ Enjoy helping other people resolve problems

_____ Curious about many things

_____ Enjoy reading in diverse areas

_____ Determined to complete projects

_____ High energy level

_____ Can cope with sudden emergencies

_____ See mistakes as learning experiences

_____ Factual and objective

_____ Respect other people's viewpoints

_____ Perceptive and sensitive

_____ Quickly absorb and retain information

Source: PRSSA Forum.

3. **Planning expertise.** A public relations program involves a number of communication tools and activities that must be carefully planned and coordinated. A person needs to be a good planner to make certain that materials are distributed in a timely manner, events occur without problems, and budgets are not exceeded. Public relations people must be highly organized, detail-oriented, and able to see the big picture. Caryn Alagno, vice president of Edelman Worldwide, adds, "Pay attention to details ... and when it comes to the 'small stuff', make sure you treat all tasks like a big deal."

4. **Problem-solving ability.** Innovative ideas and fresh approaches are needed to solve complex problems or to make a public relations program unique and memorable. Increased salaries and promotions go to people who show top management how to solve problems creatively. Two examples of creative public relations campaigns are given in the PR Casebook on page 26.

5. **Business/economics competence.** The increasing emphasis on public relations as a management function calls for public relations students to learn the "nuts and bolts" of business and economics. According to Joel Curren, senior vice president of CKPR in Chicago, "The greatest need PR people have is understanding how a business and, more importantly, how a public company operates." Rachel Beanland, a professional

PRCasebook

The Wonderful World of Public Relations

Public relations is an exciting field that offers variety, creativity, and opportunity to work on any number of projects. The following are two programs that received "campaign of the year" awards by judges in *PRWeek*'s 2009 competition:

Go Red for Women

Heart disease claims one woman's life per minute, but only one in five women view it as a significant health threat. The American Heart Association and its public relations firm, Edelman Worldwide, decided to do something about this by creating a website, *GoRedForWomen.org*, that would use testimonials from "women like me" who had been affected by heart disease.

Edelman also created forums, both online and offline, where women could share their stories of heart disease to motivate others to donate funds and get a heart checkup. Research had shown that women are most likely to believe and act on information that is delivered by peers. Media coverage for Go Red for Women was generated by having Sigourney Weaver serve as the host of "Rhapsody in Red," Go Red's signature event to honor its supporters and draw attention to the lifestyle implications of women's heart disease.

The result was an increase of 75,000 visitors per month to the website, and more than 220,000 new women signed up to support *GoRedForWomen.org* and its fund-raising efforts. Almost $125 million was raised for education, scientific outreach, and medical research. Another measurement of the campaign's success was a survey that showed 65 percent of women were now aware that heart disease is the major killer of women, as opposed to only 57 percent before the campaign.

Papa John's Pizza Only a Text Away

Papa John's led the industry in 2007 by introducing text message ordering, but it raised the question of whether texting was quicker and more effective than phone ordering. The pizza chain, working with its public relations firm Fleishman-Hillard (F-H), decided to raise public awareness about its texting capability by having a contest staged at the Mall of America in Minneapolis. It pitted the *Guinness Book of World Records'* fastest talker and fastest texter against each other in a pizza-ordering challenge.

The pizza challenge was a device for generating media coverage, but the more important objective was to generate more business by encouraging pizza lovers to register on www.papajohns.com and save their favorite orders, payment information, and delivery instructions. Fleishman-Hillard got an exclusive story in the *Wall Street Journal*, but was also able to get stories distributed by the Associated Press (AP) and many other print outlets. In addition, F-H reached out to influential bloggers, offering a flash video on the pizza chain's website and giving a tutorial on how to text-message an order.

The campaign result was more than 600 media placements in print publications and broadcast outlets. A YouTube video of the contest at the Mall of America was also viewed by 75,000 people. The most important result, however, was that almost 120,000 people registered their mobile numbers with Papa John's.

Sigourney Weaver

PEARSON
mycommunicationlab

interviewed by *Public Relations Tactics*, noted that almost all of the recent public relations grads she talked to wished they had taken a marketing course. In sum, students preparing for careers in public relations should obtain a solid grounding by taking courses in economics, management, and marketing.

6. **Expertise in social media.** Employers still value expertise in mainstream media relations, but it's now just as important to have social media savvy. A survey of employers by online MarketingVOX found 80 percent of the respondents agreed that knowledge of social networks is either important or very important. The three most important skills for job applicants are social networking, blogging, and tweeting. Employers also prefer job applicants who know about podcasting, search engine optimization (SEO), e-mail outreach, Web content management, and social bookmarking. According to MarketingVox, "These social media skills will likely increase in importance as PR professionals continue to take the lead in managing most organizations' social media communications channels."

> The future belongs to those who not only know public relations, but also know business—and who can think strategically and write.
>
> *Jeff Conley, partner in Stratacomm, Washington, D.C, quoted in* PR Tactics

on the job

INSIGHTS

How to Succeed in Public Relations

The following is a list of skills you need to succeed in public relations, which has been distilled from a variety of sources:

- Be a media junkie. Absorb large quantities of information and track trend lines, issues that will impact your industry, employer, or clients.

- Stand up for transparency. Make transparency a core value for you and your organization.

- Join the social media bandwagon. Today's public relations requires expert knowledge of social media and the art of engaging in a conversation with multiple audiences.

- Avoid a technician mentality. Hone your ability to be a

strategic thinker and do creative problem solving.

- Get on management's wavelength. Be knowledgeable about business, economics, and the triple bottom line: profits, the environment, and sustainability.

- Never forget the basics. Excellent writing and presentation skills are still fundamental.

- Develop global cultural literacy. Remember that there are no kangaroos in Austria.

- Learn for life. Make continuing education through reading, seminars, and short courses a prerequisite for being a professional.

- Give something back. Mentor young professionals; be a vocal advocate for advancing public relations ethics and professionalism.

- Master the media universe. Be aware of the symbiotic relationship between traditional media and the "new" media and how they reinforce each other.

- Do your homework. Have an in-depth knowledge of research and evaluation strategies as an integral part of campaign planning.

- Cut the B.S. Be authentic, real, and ethical in all your communications.

It should be noted, of course, that all jobs in public relations don't require all these essential skills in equal proportion. It often depends on your specific job responsibilities and assignments. Other skills required for today's practitioner are in the Insights box on page 27. You may also want to take the personality quiz on page 25.

> Internship programs can be much more than a means to get young, inexpensive talent. Designed properly, they can offer a significant return on investment for agencies.
>
> *Mark Hand, reporter for* PRWeek

The Value of Internships

Internships are extremely popular in the communications industry, and a student whose résumé includes practical work experience along with a good academic record has an important advantage. The Commission on Public Relations Education believes the internship is so important that it is one of the five basic courses it recommends for any quality college or university public relations curriculum.

An internship is a win-win situation for both the student and the organization. The student, in most cases, not only receives academic credit, but also gets firsthand knowledge of work in the professional world. This gives the student an advantage in getting that all-important first job after graduation. In many cases, recent graduates are hired by their former internship employers because they have already proved themselves.

Indeed, *PRWeek* reporter Sara Calabro says:

> Agencies and corporate communications departments are beginning to see interns as the future of their companies, not merely as gophers that they can pass the grunt work off to. While a few years ago, it was typical for an intern to work for nothing, it is almost unheard of for an internship to be unpaid these days. Examples of the essential work now entrusted to interns include tasks such as media monitoring, writing press releases, financial estimating, and compiling status reports. In many cases, interns are being included in all team and client meetings, as well as brainstorming sessions.

Many major public relations firms have formal internship programs. At Edelman Worldwide, for example, students enroll in "Edel-U," an internal training program that exposes them to all aspects of agency work. The summer internship program at Weber Shandick in Boston is called "Weber University." Calabro cites Jane Dolan, a senior account executive, who says that upper management is always incredibly impressed with the work that interns do for their final projects. "It is amazing to see them go from zero to 100 in a matter of months," says Dolan.

Hill & Knowlton also has an extensive internship training program in its New York office, taking about 40 interns a year. In its view, the internship program is "the cheapest and most effective recruiting tool available." Ketchum also gets about 800 résumés each year for 12 to 14 summer positions, which pay a weekly stipend. According to Scott Proper, SVP at Ketchum, "You can walk the halls any day and find former interns in pretty senior positions."

It's not always possible, of course, for a student to do an internship in Chicago or New York. However, many opportunities are available at local public relations firms, businesses, and nonprofit agencies. It is important, however, that the organization have at least one experienced public relations professional who can mentor a student and ensure that he or she gets an opportunity to do a variety of tasks to maximize the learning experience.

Most national and international firms pay interns. This often is not the case at the local level. Many smaller companies and nonprofits claim that they cannot afford to pay,

on the job

INSIGHTS

Want an Internship?: Can You Do This Assignment?

Employers use a variety of techniques to select students for internships. In addition to personal interviews, they also test students on their knowledge of basic public relations concepts and ask for samples of their writing ability. Another approach is to have an applicant write a case study.

The following is a case study assignment used by Deveney Communication (www.deveney.com) for college students applying for its summer program. Applicants were judged on their creativity, research, writing, critical thinking, and knowledge of basic public relations tactics for an internship with the firm in its New Orleans headquarters.

Louisiana Office of Tourism (LOT)

Overview

The Louisiana Office of Tourism is a state agency responsible for supporting tourism, one of the state's largest industries. The public relations objective is to promote the state as a travel destination to specific audiences, including families, African Americans, young adults 18–24, and the gay and lesbian (GLBT) market.

Assignment

Research Component

Review media coverage of Louisiana and answer the following questions: (I) what key messages regarding travel to the state are already in the media?; (2) what challenges do you think LOT faces today in attracting visitors?; and (3) what messages should LOT use to address issues that detract visitors?

Strategy

Based on your review of the media coverage, develop a public relations plan to attract visitors *to the state.

Intended Audiences: Who are your primary and secondary audience? What demographics and characteristics do they represent?

Goals and Objectives: What broad goal should this plan accomplish for the client? What measurable objectives should this plan accomplish for LOT?

Tactics: What will you do and how will you do it? What is your rationale? How does the plan showcase a creative solution? What are the key messages? What is the proposed budget?

Measurement of Success: How would you measure your results, and how do these measurements relate back to your goals and objectives?

Creativity: Choose one tactic from your plan (news release, public service announcement, webpage, etc.) and write or produce it to show your writing ability.

or that the opportunity to gain training and experience should be more than adequate compensation. Dave DeVries, a senior public relations manager for the PCS Division of Sprint, disagrees. He wrote in PRSA's *Tactics*, "Unpaid internships severely limit the field of potential candidates" because, as he points out, the best and brightest students will always gravitate to employers who pay.

Paid internships, however, are very competitive and a student has to demonstrate his or her abilities in order to be selected. Deveney Communications in New Orleans, for example, requires submission of a case study (see the Insights box above). Many employers also use writing and current event tests to screen internship applicants.

Salaries in the Field

Public relations work pays relatively well compared to other communications professions. Many practitioners say they like the income and opportunities for steady advancement. They also enjoy the variety and fast pace that the field provides. Blogger Todd Defren of *pr.squared.com* writes, "PR is hard work, strategic work, under promoted and infinitely interesting work—hard to describe or appreciate until you're in the trenches."

Several surveys have attempted to pinpoint the national median annual salary for recent graduates in their first full-time jobs in the public relations field. Probably the most definitive survey is the one conducted by Lee Becker and his associates at the University of Georgia. They work with journalism and mass communications programs throughout the nation to compile a list of recent graduates, who are then surveyed (www.grady.uga.edu/annualsurveys/).

on the job

INSIGHTS

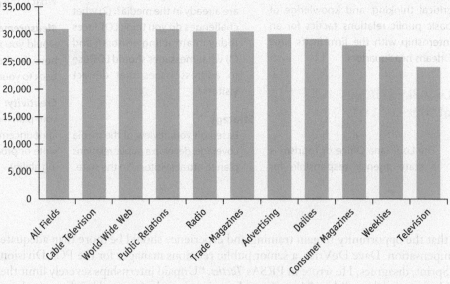

A national survey of 2008 graduates from 86 departments and schools of journalism and mass communications found that recent public relations graduates earned a median annual salary of $31,000.

The survey, conducted by Professor Lee Becker and his associates at the University of Georgia, also found that public relations graduates differed in a key way from other majors in journalism and mass communications. They didn't necessarily seek and find jobs in traditional areas such as public relations departments and firms.

Professor Becker concludes, "The evidence is that public relations students are more entrepreneurial, less tied to traditional definitions of what is communications work, and more flexible about what kinds of work they actually do. They did better in the job market in 2008, and that may say a lot about the future of employment for graduates of the nation's journalism and mass communications programs."

Source: L. B. Becker, T., Vlad, & D. Olin. (2009, November). Annual survey of journalism & mass communication graduates. AEJMC News, 1, 4–8.

The latest data available, published in 2009, show that the median entry-level salary for all recent graduates working in the communications field was $31,000. Public relations graduates, as the chart on page 30 indicates, also made this amount. It, however, was considerably more than the salaries of graduates working in television ($24,000) and those working for weekly newspapers ($26,000), which is probably one reason why journalism grads begin to think about public relations as a career option. On the other hand, recent graduates working in cable television or at sites on the Web make slightly more than public relations graduates.

Another survey, conducted by *PRWeek*, places a more optimistic figure on starting salaries in public relations. Its 2010 survey of salaries, for example, found that median salaries for professionals with less than two years' experience was $37,000.

Key findings of *PRWeek*'s 2010 salary survey are listed in the Insights box below, which shows the progression of income with years of experience. Practitioners with 3–4 years of experience have median incomes of $52,000 and those with 5 to 6 years of

> Although employment is projected to grow much faster than average, keen competition is expected for entry-level jobs.
>
> *U.S. Bureau of Labor Statistics,* Occupational Outlook Handbook 2010–11 edition

on the job
INSIGHTS

An Overview of Salaries in the Public Relations Field

*P*RWeek conducts an annual survey of salaries. The following charts are excerpted from the 2010 survey, which polled 1,000 practitioners in the field.

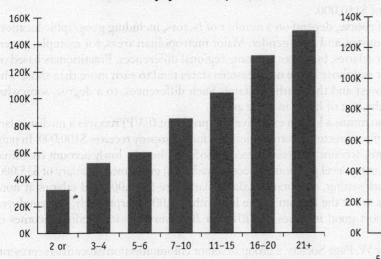

Median Salary by Years of Experience

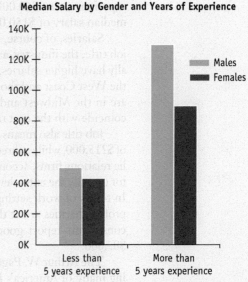

Median Salary by Gender and Years of Experience

(continued)

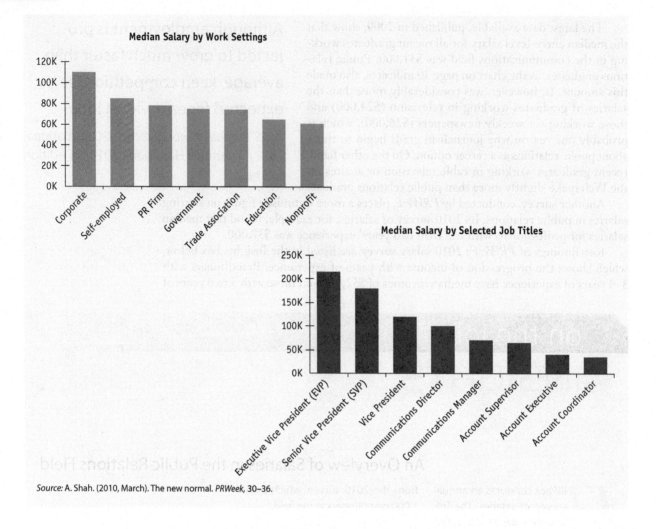

Median Salary by Work Settings

Median Salary by Selected Job Titles

Source: A. Shah. (2010, March). The new normal. *PRWeek*, 30–36.

experience earn $60,000. The most experienced individuals (21 years or more) have a median salary of $150,000.

Salaries, of course, depend on a number of factors, including geographic location, job title, the industry, and even gender. Major metropolitan areas, for example, generally have higher salaries, but there are some regional differences. Practitioners based on the West Coast and those in the northeastern states tend to earn more than those who are in the Midwest and the southern states. Such differences, to a degree, somewhat coincide with the cost of living in these areas.

Job title also means a lot. An executive vice president (EVP) receives a median salary of $215,000, while a director of communications for a company receives $100,000. In public relations firms, account supervisors receive $65,000, but the lowly account coordinator (usually the entry-level position for recent graduates) gets a median salary of $35,000. In terms of work setting, corporate median salaries are $110,000 and salaries at nonprofits/charities are at the bottom of the list, with $61,000. Surprisingly, self-employed consultants report good incomes in *PRWeek*'s 2010 survey, with median incomes of $85,000.

The Arthur W. Page Society, a group of senior communication executives representing many of America's *Fortune* 500 corporations, also conducts an annual survey of its members regarding budgets and executive compensation. In general, compensation for the top communications officer in a large corporation ranges from $269,000 to $500,000+. There are, of course, other forms of compensation. Former Edelman Worldwide vice chairman Leslie Dach is reported to have received $3 million in Wal-Mart shares for taking the EVP post at the retail giant, according to Jack O'Dwyer's newsletter.

Gender also makes a difference. National statistics show that females earn only 80 percent of what men earn for full-time work, and this disparity is also reflected in the public relations field. *PRWeek*'s survey, for example, found that men with less than five years' experience earn $50,000, compared to women's median salary of $43,000. The gap becomes even greater with five-plus years of experience, $130,000 versus $90,000. Despite the salary differences, there continues to be an influx of women into the field, which is discussed in Chapter 2.

A good source for checking current salaries for public relations in major cities throughout the United States and around the world is www.workinpr.com, which posts current openings and also provides the salary ranges for various job classifications.

The Value of Public Relations

This chapter has outlined the size and global scope of public relations, provided some definitions, discussed the various activities of public relations, and explored how it differs from and is similar to journalism, advertising, and marketing. The case for an organization integrating all of its communications for maximum effectiveness has also been made. Careers in public relations, the qualities needed in public relations professionals, and the salaries that can be earned in the field of public relations have also been discussed.

Today more than ever, the world needs not more information but sensitive communicators and facilitators who can explain the goals and aspirations of individuals, organizations, and governments to others in a socially responsive manner. Experts in communication and public opinion must provide their employers and clients with knowledge of what others are thinking to guide them in setting their policies for the common good.

Indeed, in this era of heightened environmental concern, accountability, and transparency, no organization exists solely for its own purposes; it must also serve society as a whole. Another way of expressing this point is the idea that no organization can exist without the express permission of the government and society at large.

Tom Glover, writing in *Profile*, the magazine of the Institute of Public Relations in the United Kingdom, believes "clear and consistent communication helps organizations achieve their goals, employees to work to their potential, customers to make informed choices, investors to make an accurate assessment of an organization, and society to form fair judgments of industries, organizations, and issues."

Public relations provides businesses and society with a vital service. On a practical level, Laurence Moskowitz, chairman and CEO of Medialink, says that public relations is "...informative. It's part of the news, the program, the article, the stuff readers and viewers want..." Indeed, the Harris Interactive/PRSA survey previously mentioned also found that 71 percent of its respondents agreed with the statement that public relations professionals can "help raise awareness about important issues that the public might not know about."

The late Patrick Jackson, a former president of the PRSA and publisher of *PR Reporter*, said it best:

> As soon as there was Eve with Adam, there were relationships, and in every society, no matter how small or primitive, public communication needs and problems inevitably emerge and must be resolved. Public relations is devoted to the essential function of building and improving human relationships.

Summary

The Challenge of Public Relations

- Public relations is well established in the United States and throughout the world. Growth is strong in Europe and Asia, particularly China.

- Common terms in most definitions of public relations are *deliberate*, *planned*, *performance*, *public interest*, *two-way communication*, and *strategic management function*.

- Organizations use a variety of terms to describe the public relations function, calling it *corporate communications*, *public affairs*, *communication*, and even *external affairs*. Less flattering terms used in the media include *flack* and *spin doctor*.

Public Relations as a Process

- The public relations process can be described with the RACE acronym: **R**esearch, **A**ction, **C**ommunication, and **E**valuation. The process is a constant cycle; feedback and program adjustment are integral components of the overall process.

- Public relations work includes the following specializations: counseling, media relations, publicity, community relations, governmental affairs, employee relations, investor relations, development/fund-raising, special events, and marketing communications.

- Public relations is a distinct discipline separate from journalism, advertising, and marketing. Although the disciplines share some basic concepts of effective communication, public relations is much broader in scope and works to build relationships with multiple publics.

- An organization's goals and objectives are best achieved by integrating the activities of advertising, marketing, and public relations to create a consistent message. Integration requires teamwork and the recognition that each field has strengths that complement and reinforce one another.

A Career in Public Relations

- The recommended path to a career in public relations is to major or take courses in the subject. Journalism majors and communication majors, however, are also attracted to the field. Students, in addition to having excellent writing skills, should also take courses in management, marketing, and economics.

- Those who plan careers in public relations should be competent in the following areas: writing, research, planning, problem solving, business/economics, and social media.

- Students should participate in internships throughout college as part of their preprofessional training in public relations. Paid internships are the most desirable.

- Entry-level salaries are higher in public relations than in many other communications fields. An entry-level person can earn a salary in the $30,000 to $40,000 range. A more experienced professional can earn a salary in the six figures.

Case Activity   Bubble Wrap Celebrates Its 50th Anniversary

People have walked to the altar dressed in it, artists have made exhibits using it, and companies around the world have used it to ship their products. The product is Bubble Wrap, which has been manufactured by Sealed Air Corporation for the past 50 years.

The product has become somewhat of a pop icon loved by many who, for whatever reason, like the feel and sound when they destroy it, piece by piece, popping all the little bubbles. In fact, enthusiasts have even created more than 250 Facebook pages devoted to Bubble Wrap.

The company would like to celebrate its 50th anniversary by organizing various activities and events that will generate publicity in the mainstream media and on the Web. Your public relations firm has been retained to do some creative brainstorming about how the Sealed Air Corporation can generate more public awareness about a product that's been on the market for a half-century. Attracting media coverage, however, will be a challenge; Bubble Wrap is a fairly mundane product and there's nothing new or "sexy" about it. What would you recommend?

Questions   For Review and Discussion

1. How many people are estimated to work in public relations around the world?
2. Is public relations growing as a field in terms of employees and revenues?
3. What key words and phrases are found in most definitions of public relations?
4. What does the acronym RACE stand for?
5. Public relations is described as a loop process. What makes it a loop rather than a linear process?
6. Review the description for a public relations specialist on page 3. Did it change your initial perception of public relations as a field?
7. What are the components of basic public relations practice? Which one sounds the most interesting to you as a possible career specialty?
8. What other terms are used by organizations to describe the public relations function? Do you have preference for any of them? Explain.
9. Do you think portrayals of public relations people in films and on television are negative or positive?
10. How does public relations differ from the fields of journalism, advertising, and marketing?
11. Some experts say that public relations can launch a new product or service better than advertising can. Do you agree or disagree?
12. Public relations people work for a variety of organizations. What type of organization would you prefer if you want to work in public relations?
13. The text mentions six essential qualities for working in public relations. On a scale of 1 to 10, how would you rate yourself on each ability?
14. Discuss entry-level salaries in public relations. Are they about what you expected? What about the salaries for experienced professionals?
15. After reading this chapter, do you think you would enjoy a career in public relations? Why or why not?

Media Resources

Becker, L. B., Vlad, T., & Olin, D. (2009). Job market turns much worse. Retrieved from http://aejmc.org/topics/2009

Bowen, S. A. (2009). All glamour, no substance? How public relations majors and potential majors in an exemplar program view the industry and function. *Public Relations Review, 35*(1), 402–410.

Bureau of Labor Statistics. (2010). *Occupational outlook handbook 2010–11: Public relations specialists*. Retrieved from www.bls.gov/ocos086.htm

Council of Public Relations Firms. (2009) Careers in public relations: A guide to opportunities in a dynamic industry, pp. 1–18. Retrieved from www.prfirms.org/career_guide.pdf

Council of Public Relations Firms, PRSA Counselor's Academy. (2010) Free Web-based program offering three modules for individuals new to the public relations industry: What is public relations? The agency life, and Media relations. Retrieved from www.prquickstart.com

Good news: Other firms' suffering has bolstered the public relations business. (2010, January 14). *Economist*, 61–62.

Jacques, A. (2009, May). Graduating into a recession: The hopes, fears—and job prospects—of PR students. *Public Relations Tactics, 1*, 14–15.

Levco, J. (2009, June). Veteran communicators share advice with newbies. *The Ragan Report*, 27–28.

Lukaszewski, J. E. (2007, Winter). What's next? The relationship of public relations to management, journalism, and society. *The Strategist*, 21–23.

Maul, K. (2009, July). Creative collaboration: Integrated marketing. *PRWeek*, 36–38.

Miller, L. (2009, April 23). As newspapers dwindle, J-school students eye a communications path. Retrieved from www.ragan.com

Shah, A. (2010, March). 2010 salary survey: The new normal. *PRWeek*, 30–36.

Study: New hires must blog, Tweet, use social media. (2009, August 17). Retrieved from www.marketingvox.com

Toth, E. L. (2009, October). Global graduates: Examining PR education around the world. *Public Relations Tactics*, 21.

The Evolution of Public Relations

P. T. Barnum

After reading this chapter, you will be able to:

Understand the evolution of public relations from ancient empires to today's practice

Know how public relations tactics have contributed to American independence, the settlement of the West, and social causes such as voting rights for women

Appreciate the contributions of visionaries such as Ivy Lee and Edward Bernays, who laid the foundation of today's practice

Have insight into the reasons for the massive influx of women into the field

Be knowledgeable about current developments and trends in the field

Early Beginnings

The concept of public relations is probably as old as human communication itself. In many ancient civilizations, people were persuaded to accept the authority of government and religion through common public relations techniques such as interpersonal communication, speeches, art, literature, staged events, and publicity. None of these endeavors were called public relations, of course, but their purpose and effect were often the same as those of today's modern practice.

Herodotus, writing about the Persian Wars, noted that the Greeks carved messages on stones near watering holes to demoralize the Ionian fleet. And Alexander the Great publicized his battlefield victories by sending glowing reports back to the Macedonian Court. In India, Emperor Asoka (273–326 B.C.) was communicating with his subjects through messages on large stone pillars erected at major crossroads. The Rosetta Stone, dating back to 196 B.C., was basically a publicity release touting an Egyptian pharaoh's accomplishments. Similarly, the ancient Olympic Games were promoted to enhance the aura of athletes as heroes in much the same way as the 2010 Vancouver Winter Games.

Julius Caesar was probably the first politician to publish a book, *Commentaries*, which he used to further his ambitions to become emperor of the Roman Empire. He also organized elaborate parades whenever he returned from a successful battle to burnish his image as an outstanding commander and leader. After Caesar became a consul of Rome in 59 B.C., he had public proceedings posted on walls throughout the city. These *Acta Diurna*, or "Daily Doings," were probably one of the world's first newspapers.

Saint Paul, the New Testament's most prolific author, also qualifies for the public relations hall of fame. According to James Grunig and Todd Hunt, authors of *Managing Public Relations*:

> It's not stretching history too much to claim the success of the apostles in spreading Christianity through the known world in the first century A.D. as one of the great public relations accomplishments of history. The apostles Paul and Peter used speeches, letters, staged events, and similar public relations activities to attract attention, gain followers, and establish new churches. Similarly, the four gospels in the New Testament, which were written at least 40 years after the death of Jesus, were public relations documents, written more to propagate the faith than to provide a historical account of Jesus' life.

Emperor Asoka

Emperor Asoka of India used stone pillars as early as 300 B.C. to publicize his accomplishments and policies.

The Middle Ages

The Roman Catholic Church was a major practitioner of public relations throughout the Middle Ages. Pope Urban II used symbolism, staged events, and propaganda to persuade thousands of followers to join the Crusades. Six centuries later, the Church was among the first to use the word *propaganda*, with the establishment by Pope Gregory XV of the College of Propaganda to supervise foreign missions and train priests to propagate the faith.

Meanwhile, in Venice, bankers in the 15th and 16th centuries practiced the fine art of investor relations and were probably the first, along with local Catholic bishops, to adopt the concept of corporate philanthropy by sponsoring such artists as Michelangelo.

It was also during the Middle Ages that Gutenberg developed the printing press (1450), which profoundly influenced the gathering and distribution of information for the next 500 years. The printing press essentially made it possible for individuals and organizations to communicate directly with the public and to publicize any number of endeavors.

Colonial America

The United States was first settled by immigrants, primarily those from England. Various land companies with a license from the Crown actively promoted colonization to generate revenues from what the colonists were able to manufacture or grow. In other words, colonization was strictly a commercial proposition. As early as 1584, for example, Sir Walter Raleigh was sending back glowing accounts to England of what was actually a swamp-filled Roanoke Island. The Virginia Company, in 1620, distributed flyers and brochures throughout Europe, offering 50 acres of free land to anyone willing to migrate.

After the American colonies were well established, publicity and public relations techniques were used to promote various institutions. In 1641, Harvard College published a fund-raising brochure and sent representatives to England to raise funds. In addition, 10 other colleges founded between 1745 and 1775 also raised funds through promotional brochures, special events, lotteries, and cultivating wealthy donors. King's College (now Columbia University) issued its first news release in 1758, which announced its commencement exercises.

Public relations also played an active role in American independence. A major promoter of independence was Sam Adams, whom one historian once called "The father of press agentry." Adams was the founder of the Sons of Liberty and organized rallies and demonstrations in the 1760s to protest the Stamp Act. By the early 1770s, Adams had polished his organizing and publicity skills. For example, he is credited with organizing the Boston Tea Party—which *PRWeek* has called "... the greatest and best-known publicity stunt of all time ..."—in which a group of colonists dressed as Indians threw crates of tea from a British trade ship into Boston Harbor as a symbolic protest of British taxation, which received widespread publicity throughout the colonies. Another major success of Adams was to label the killing of five colonists by British troops at a demonstration as the "Boston Massacre," which further inflamed public opinion against Great Britain. Adams had a refined sense of how symbolism could sway public opinion.

Also instrumental in bringing lukewarm citizens around to the cause of American independence was Tom Paine's *Common Sense*. More than 120,000 copies of the pamphlet were sold in three months, an early example of political communication to a national audience. After independence, Alexander Hamilton, John Jay, and James Madison wrote the *Federalist Papers* to rally public support for the ratification of the U.S. Constitution. The effort laid the foundation for distributing syndicated opinion pieces via the mass media, a concept that is still being used today in public relations.

The 1800s: The Golden Age of Press Agentry

The 1800s was a period of growth and expansion in the United States. It also was the golden age of the press agent, which Webster's *New World Dictionary* defines as "a person whose work is to get publicity for an individual, organization, etc." The period was also the age of hype, which is the shrewd use of the media and other devices to promote an individual, a cause, or even a product or service, such as a circus.

Press agents were able to glorify Davy Crockett as a frontier hero to draw political support away from Andrew Jackson, attract thousands to the touring shows of Buffalo Bill and sharpshooter Annie Oakley, make a legend of frontiersman Daniel Boone, and promote hundreds of other personalities.

These old-time press agents played on the credulity of the public in its longing to be entertained. Advertisements and press releases were exaggerated to the point of being outright lies. Doing advance work for an attraction, the press agent dropped tickets on the desk of a newspaper editor, along with the announcements. Voluminous publicity generally followed, and the journalists and their families flocked to their free entertainment, with scant regard for the ethical constraints that largely prohibit such practices today.

The Legacy of P. T. Barnum

The individual who best represents the hype and press agentry of the 19th century is Phineas T. Barnum, the great American showman. He was the master of what historian Daniel Boorstin calls the pseudoevent, which is a planned happening that occurs primarily for the purpose of being reported. Barnum used flowery language, exaggeration, controversy, massive advertising, and publicity to promote his various attractions in an age when the public was hungry for any form of entertainment.

Barnum first gained fame in 1835 as the exhibitor of Joice Heth. She was an African American who was billed as George Washington's nursemaid, which would have made her 161 years old. Barnum and his advance man, Levi Lyman, encouraged public debate about her background and age because it generated not only media coverage but the sale of tickets as the public came to see for themselves. In the 1840s, another Barnum exhibit that generated controversy (and much media coverage) was the Fejee Mermaid, a stuffed creature that was half-monkey and half-fish. Barnum quoted some clerics who said it might be possible to merge species, but that the public should come to his American Museum in New York and judge for themselves—which they did in great numbers.

> He [Barnum] is a direct ancestor of everything from Bat Boy in the *Weekly World News* to all those pseudoscience shows on the History Channel like 'MonsterQuest' to ... the creators of reality television.
>
> *James Hynes, reviewing a book by Candace Fleming,*
> The Tremendous, Stupendous Life of
> Showman P. T. Barnum

Thanks to Barnum, Tom Thumb became one of America's first media celebrities. He was a midget, standing just over 2 feet and weighing 15 pounds, but he was exceptional at singing, dancing, and performing comedy monologues. Barnum made a public relations event of the marriage of "General" Tom Thumb to another midget. He even got extensive European bookings for Thumb by introducing him to society leaders in London, who were enchanted by him. An invitation to the palace followed, and from then on Thumb played to packed houses every night. Barnum, even in his day, knew the value of third-party endorsement.

Another Barnum success was the promotion of Jenny Lind, the "Swedish Nightingale." Lind was famous in Europe, but no one in America knew about her beautiful voice until Barnum took her on a national tour and made her one of America's first pop icons. He obtained full houses on opening nights in each community by donating part of the proceeds to charity. As a civic activity, the event attracted many of the town's opinion leaders, whereupon the general public flocked to attend succeeding performances—a device still employed today by entertainment publicists.

on the job

A MULTICULTURAL WORLD

The Beginnings of Public Relations in Other Nations

The British scholar J. A. R. Pimlott once wrote, "Public relations is not a peculiarly American phenomenon, but it has nowhere flourished as in the United States. Nowhere else is it so widely practiced, so lucrative, so pretentious, so respectable and disreputable, so widely suspected, and so extravagantly extolled."

It's important to realize, however, that other nations have their own histories. The following is a representative sample.

Germany

Railroads and other large business enterprises began publicity efforts as far back as the mid-19th century. Alfred Krupp, who founded the Krupp Company, the premier industrial firm in Germany and eventually the base of the Nazi war power, wrote in 1866, "We think . . . it is time that authoritative reports concerning factory matters, in

accordance with the facts should be propagated on a regular basis through newspaper reports which serve an enlightened public." In the 1870s, German Chancellor Otto von Bismarck set up a press office in the Foreign Ministry to do media relations, arrange interviews, and organize news conferences.

Great Britain

The Marconi Company, a world leader in wireless telegraphy, established a department in 1910 to distribute news releases about its achievements and operations. In 1911, the first government public relations campaign was launched by the Insurance Commission to explain the benefits of the National Insurance Act.

The Air Ministry appointed the first government press officer in 1919, and a year later the Ministry of Health selected Basil Clarke, a former Reuters correspondent, as director of

information. By 1922, the government launched the British Broadcasting Service (BBC) as a way to communicate British values and viewpoints to its colonies and other nations.

Professional public relations counseling for business was introduced in the country in 1924, when Basil Clarke started a firm in London. His first client was a dairy group that wanted to promote milk pasteurization, an innovation that had met with some resistance from the public.

Australia

Public relations in Australia largely consisted of publicity efforts until after World War II. When U.S. General Douglas MacArthur arrived after his escape from Corregidor in 1942, he introduced the term *public relations* and, with a highly skilled staff, demonstrated numerous ways of promoting his image and the war effort.

The industry grew steadily and, in 1960, the Public Relations Institute of Australia (PRIA) was formed. Notable practitioners included Eric White, who, according to one source, "virtually created the public relations industry" in Australia. As early as the 1960s, White oversaw extensions of his firm to six Pacific Rim countries.

India

Although India has a long history of kings and emperors who used various methods of communication and propaganda, modern public relations probably began during World War I, when the government set up publicity boards throughout the country to mobilize support for the war. According to C. V. Narasimha Reddi, editor of the *Public Relations Voice*, "Public relations or public communication played an active role in Indian independence." Gandhi, for example, used musicians, roadside meetings, rallies, speeches, and media interviews to reach both the urban and the rural populations to create awareness of the freedom struggle. Indeed, several Indian scholars have called Gandhi the "father of Indian public relations." TATA, now one of India's largest corporations, began programs in community relations and employee communications as early as 1912.

The Philippines

The public relations industry in the Philippines was transplanted from the West in the 1940s. In fact, the country is considered the "Pacific birthplace of public relations." U.S. Army public information officers regularly issued news releases to the Philippine press during World War II. After the war, the concept spread to local businesses, and the Business Writers Association of the Philippines was organized to promote the idea of corporate social responsibility.

Notable of the early Filipino pioneers is Pete Teodoro. He was public relations director of Elizalde & Company, a paint manufacturer, and is credited with undertaking the first organized public relations campaign to generate goodwill and business from local contractors and architects. In 1966, the San Miguel Corporation, one of the country's largest companies and known worldwide for its San Miguel beer, established the first public relations department.

Spain

The growth of public relations in Spain started in the 1950s and paralleled political, economic, and media developments in Spain. An advertising agency, Danis Advertising of Barcelona, launched a public relations campaign in 1955 to build community goodwill for a corporate client and its product. One of the directors of that campaign, Joaquin Maestre, started his own public relations firm in 1960. According to one historian, the advent of public relations consultancies "marked the beginning of a 'dynamic consumer market' for public relations services, which led to setting up the first public relations agencies as a direct response to the 'market demand for services.'"

The Russian Federation

The collapse of the Soviet Union in 1991 ushered in a free-market economy and democratic reforms that caused the rapid growth of the public relations field in government and private business. With the new openness, global companies began selling products and services in the new Russia, with the assistance of Western-style advertising, public relations, and promotion.

In addition, Russian companies began to understand the importance of publicizing their products and services. Before that time, most "public relations" was conducted by the government. In the mid-1990s, a Russian association of public relations professionals was organized to promote standards and provide continuing education.

Thailand

Public relations in Thailand, as in many nations, dates back to the 1950s. Esko Pajasalmi from Finland is credited with starting the first public relations firm in Thailand. He started his firm, Presko, after serving more than a decade as a Christian missionary in northern Thailand. Presko eventually became that nation's largest public relations firm and set the standard for other firms that followed.

One early Presko campaign was for Colgate-Palmolive, after its toothpaste was falsely accused of containing pork fat. The Muslim community was horrified, and Colgate immediately lost 100 percent of the market in southern Thailand. Pajasalmi contacted Muslim leaders, took them to inspect the factories, and convinced them that the rumors were unfounded. Business boomed again.

United Arab Emirates

Rapid business and economic development in the past two decades, particularly in Dubai, has encouraged the growth of public relations. By the mid-1980s, the majority of government departments and other major institutions had created a public relations department. In addition, a number of international public relations firms arrived in the mid-1980s to service the operations of multinational companies with operations in the Middle East.

Promoting the Westward Movement

Throughout the 19th century, publicity and promotion helped to populate the western United States. Land speculators distributed pamphlets and other publicity that described almost every community as "the garden spot of the West," which one critic of the time called "downright puffery, full of exaggerated statements, and high-wrought and false-colored descriptions." One brochure about Nebraska, for example, described the territory as the "Gulf stream of migration ... bounded on the north by the 'Aurora Borealis' and on the south by the Day of Judgment." Other brochures were more down-to-earth, describing the fertile land, the abundant water, and the opportunity to build a fortune.

American railroads, in particular, used extensive public relations and press agentry to attract settlers and expand operations. As Andy Piasecki, lecturer at Queen Margaret University College in Edinburgh, Scotland, describes it:

> The expansion of the railroads was dependent on publicity and promotion. This is hardly surprising that any investment in western expansion was dependent on finding a population. Many railroad companies were colonization agencies as much as they were transport companies. Without people, no railroads could be sustained and because there were, at this time, few people out West, they had to be brought in....

Consequently, such companies as the Burlington and Missouri Railroad promoted Western settlement from England and other European nations. The company set up an information office in Liverpool that distributed fact sheets and maps and placed stories in the local press. In addition, the railroad promoted lectures about migrating to the American West. According to Piasecki, "The pièce de resistance for the Burlington was a kind of early road show ... an elaborately illustrated lecture with 85 painted views, each covering 250 square feet."

The publicity and promotion paid off. Piasecki notes, "During the 1870s and the 1880s, the railroads attracted an estimated 5 million people to the Midwestern states, and they were responsible for the establishment there of almost 2 million farms. None of this could have been achieved without complex communication strategies closely linked to business objectives...."

Near the end of the 19th century, the Santa Fe Railway launched a campaign to lure tourists to the Southwest. It commissioned dozens of painters and photographers to depict the dramatic landscape and show romanticized American Indians weaving, grinding corn, and dancing.

Politics and Social Movements Take the Stage

The early 1800s also saw the development of public relations tactics on the political and activist front. Amos Kendall, a former Kentucky newspaper editor, became an intimate member of President Andrew Jackson's "kitchen cabinet" and probably was the first presidential press secretary.

Kendall sampled public opinion on issues, advised Jackson, and skillfully interpreted Jackson's rough ideas, putting them into presentable form as speeches and news releases. He also served as Jackson's advance agent on trips, wrote glowing articles that he sent to supportive newspapers, and probably was the first to use newspaper reprints in public relations; almost every complimentary story or editorial about Jackson was reprinted and widely circulated. Article reprints are still a standard tactic in today's modern practice.

on the job

INSIGHTS

Major Historical Themes Over the Centuries

The evolution of public relations can be placed on a timeline from ancient beginnings to today's practice, but there are also basic themes that transcend time and place. Margot Opdycke Lamme, at the University of Alabama, and Karen Miller Russell, at the University of Georgia, contend "...that the public relations function has remained remarkably consistent over time..." and there are five major historical themes.

Profit

In the historical literature, profit is consistently a motivation for the public relations function. In the 1500s, Pope Clement VIII used public relations tactics to raise money. Fifty years later, Harvard College was the first college in America to begin a development campaign. American railroads, in the 1800s, used media relations, exhibits, and press junkets to increase ticket sales.

Recruitment

Lamme and Russell write, "By the Middle Ages, Irish Monks, the Crusades, and the Catholic Church in Spain all employed public relations methods to recruit armies of the faithful." The Sons of Liberty, in the mid-1700s, used pamphlets, demonstrations, and staged events to recruit members opposed to British colonial rule.

Legitimacy

Third-party endorsements have been used throughout history to give legitimacy to causes and institutions. Glastonbury Abbey appropriated the King Arthur legends to legitimize England's rule over the Celts. P. T. Barnum and the railroads often engaged opinion leaders such as scholars and clerics to give their activities credibility.

Agitation

The temperance and woman's suffrage movements used agitation to rally the public against drunkenness and gender discrimination. Lamme and Russell also note, "The 1890s battle between Westinghouse and Edison for current included exploitative pathos and logos, while Standard Oil engaged in public relations to battle antitrust proponents."

Advocacy

Public relations tactics were used in the abolition movement to ban slavery, and were also used by Standard Oil to advocate its position against antitrust legislation. At the end of the 19th century, the Sierra Club's John Muir was advocating for conservation and the establishment of national parks.

Lamme and Russell note, "Collectively, these five motivations drove an enormous variety of tactics, such as brochures, pamphlets, and books, and other print materials, plays, music, art, third-party endorsements, slogans and symbols, media coverage, and showmanship and publicity stunts." Thus, they conclude, "The concept of public relations development over time is therefore relevant primarily to the scale at which tactics were employed and to the gradual development of the rules of engagement."

Source: M. O. Lamme & K. M. Russell. (2010, Winter). Removing the spin: Toward a new theory of public relations history. *Journalism Communication Monographs, 11*(4).

Supporters and leaders of such causes as abolition, suffrage, and prohibition employed publicity to maximum effect throughout the century. In 1848, for example, the organizers of the first women's rights convention in Seneca Falls, New York, used a variety of public relations tactics to promote the meeting and their cause. This included news releases, brochures, legislative petitions, special events, speaking tours, and even early concepts of issues management. One of the most influential publicity ventures for the abolition movement was the 1852 publication of Harriet Beecher Stowe's *Uncle Tom's Cabin.*

Ida B. Wells

Her writings and use of public relations tactics were instrumental in bringing antisegregation ideas to the forefront of American thinking.

The Women's Christian Temperance Union (WCTU), during the 1870s and beyond, also used a variety of public relations strategies to ban alcohol and promote the suffrage movement. Some of its techniques were (1) distributing information kits and fact sheets to the press, (2) establishing coffee houses, (3) holding demonstrations in front of liquor stores, and (4) going door to door to persuade voters. Another activist group, the Anti-Saloon League of America, used pamphlets, posters, lectures, and lobbying, which ultimately led to the enactment in 1920 of the Eighteenth Amendment, banning the selling and consumption of alcoholic products in the United States.

Other activists in the latter half of the 19th century focused on racial discrimination. Ida B. Wells was born a slave in 1862, and was just 22 when she refused to move when a railroad conductor ordered her to give up her seat. (This was more than 70 years before Rosa Parks, who became the symbol of the 1960s civil rights movement.) Ida went on to own and edit an anti-segregationist newspaper (which was later burned down by a white mob) and also be an advocate for anti-lynching laws, after three of her friends were lynched by a mob in Memphis. She wrote articles and books, gave hundreds of speeches, and skillfully crafted arguments to change public opinion in America and Europe. She was also a founder of the National Association of Colored People (NAACP) and became one of the most influential black leaders of her time.

There was also an environmental movement during the last half of the 19th century. In the 1860s, naturalist John Muir began a lifelong quest to protect wilderness areas and to establish national parks. He wrote several books and dozens of magazine articles, sent thousands of telegrams, and lectured throughout the country. In 1889 he worked with the influential *Century Magazine* to promote a campaign requesting congressional support to create Yosemite National Park. The activist public relations campaign succeeded, and today's citizens continue to enjoy the benefits of a protected Yosemite.

Early Corporate Initiatives

The wave of industrialization and urbanization that swept the nation after the Civil War created many new businesses that competed in the marketplace.

One department store owner, John Wannamaker of Philadelphia, was one of the first major retailers to use the tactics of public relations to attract customers. In the 1870s, he published a magazine that was given free to customers. Wannamaker also placed image ads about the quality of merchandise and service in his stores and even organized a lecture bureau to bring in noted speakers.

Another department store, Macy's, introduced its first Christmas window in 1870 that attracted the public to the store. Its greatest public relations coup, however, was the creation of the Macy's Thanksgiving Day Parade, which was started in 1924. By 1933, more than a million people lined the parade route in New York City. Today, the annual parade still draws large crowds and a national television audience.

Westinghouse Corporation established what is believed to be the first in-house publicity department, to promote the concept of alternating current (AC) versus

Thomas Edison's direct current (DC) system. George Westinghouse eventually won a bruising public relations battle with Edison, and AC became the standard in the United States. In 1897, the term *public relations* was first used, in a company listing, by the Association of American Railroads.

1900 to 1950: The Age of Pioneers

By the start of the 20th century, public relations had begun to reinvent itself along journalistic lines, as the emphasis shifted from the hype and press agentry of the Barnum era to the idea that facts and information were more effective strategies. Two factors were involved in this shift. First, the press agent model didn't really fit the operations and objectives of large corporations. Second, the new field of public relations attracted journalists, who are more comfortable with objectivity and the dissemination of information.

Ivy Lee: The First Public Relations Counsel

The leading pioneer in this new approach to public relations was Ivy Ledbetter Lee, a former business journalist for the *New York Times*, the *New York World*, and the *New York American*. He began as a publicist, but shortly expanded that role to be regarded as the first public relations counsel.

When Lee opened his public relations firm, Parker and Lee, in 1905, he issued a declaration of principles that signaled a new model of public relations practice: public information. Lee's emphasis was on the dissemination of truthful, accurate information rather than distortions, hype, and exaggerations.

One of Lee's first clients was the Pennsylvania Railroad, where he was retained as a "publicity counselor" to handle media relations. His first task was to convince management that the policy of operating in secret and refusing to talk with the press, typical of many large corporations at the time, was a poor strategy for fostering goodwill and public understanding. When the next rail accident occurred, Lee provided press facilities, issued what is claimed to be the first news release of the modern age, and took reporters to the accident site. Although such action appeared, to the conservative railroad directors, to be reckless indiscretion, they were pleasantly surprised that the company received fairer press comment than on any previous occasion.

It wasn't long before other railroads also adopted a more open information policy. By 1912, Lee had become the executive assistant to the president of the Pennsylvania Railroad, which Scott Cutlip, in his comprehensive history of public relations, calls "the first known instance of a public relations person being placed at the management level."

One of Lee's major accomplishments was the 1913–1914 railroad freight hike campaign. The Pennsylvania Railroad, after years of rising expenses, needed a 5 percent railroad freight rate hike to remain in business, but there was considerable public opposition and also a skeptical Interstate Commerce Commission (ICC). Lee believed the public and the ICC could be persuaded to accept higher rates if they were given the facts and made aware of the situation.

Burton St. John III, in a *Public Relations Review* article, recounts how Lee conducted his campaign. He not only widely distributed the railroad industry's case to the press, but he also broke with past publicity practices by clearly identifying the source of the information. After each ICC hearing, he distributed the railroad's testimony to the

Through his 20th century principles and practices, Ivy Lee, more than any other communicator in history, heralded the commencement of the 21st century practice of PR.

Fraser P. Seitel, author of
The Practice of Public Relations

press, railroad employees, railway riders, congressmen, state legislators, college presidents, and other opinion leaders such as the clergy. Other techniques were leaflets and bulletins for railway riders and community opinion leaders, a speaker's bureau, and reprints of speeches.

All these efforts paid off. Public opposition declined, and chambers of commerce around the country bombarded the ICC with resolutions supporting the railroad. The ICC approved the 5 percent rate hike. St. John concludes, "Lee's propaganda campaign for the Pennsylvania Railroad is a landmark in the history of public relations."

Lee counseled a number of companies and charitable organizations during his lifetime, but he is best known for his work with the Rockefeller family. In 1914, John D. Rockefeller Jr. hired Lee in the wake of the vicious strike-breaking activities, known as the Ludlow Massacre, at the Rockefeller family's Colorado Fuel and Iron Company (CF&I) plant. Lee went to Colorado to do some fact-finding (research) and talked to both sides. He found that labor leaders were effectively getting their views out by talking freely to the media, but that the company's executives were tight-lipped and inaccessible. The result, of course, was a barrage of negative publicity and public criticism directed at CF&I and the Rockefeller family.

Lee, drawing on his rate hike experience, proposed a series of informational bulletins by management that would be distributed to opinion leaders in Colorado and around the nation. The leaflets were designed to be thought pieces about various issues concerning mining, manufacturing, and labor. In all, 19 bulletins were produced over a period of several months and sent to a mailing list of 19,000. Even at this early time, Lee recognized the value of directly reaching opinion leaders, who, in turn, were highly influential in shaping public discussion and opinion.

Lee organized a number of other public relations activities on behalf of CF&I during 1914 and 1915, including convincing the governor of Colorado to write an article supporting the position taken by the company. Lee also convinced Rockefeller to visit the plant and talk with miners and their families. Lee made sure the press was there to record Rockefeller eating in the workers' hall, swinging a pickax in the mine, and having a beer with the workers after hours. The press loved it. Rockefeller was portrayed as being seriously concerned about the plight of the workers, and the visit led to policy changes and more worker benefits. As a result, the United Mine Workers failed to gain a foothold.

Lee continued as a counselor to the Rockefeller family and its various companies, but he also counseled a number of other clients. For example, he advised the American Tobacco Company to initiate a profit-sharing plan, the Pennsylvania Railroad to beautify its stations, the movie industry to stop inflated advertising, and the New York Subway to promote various stops along its route, such as the Museum of Natural History, as a way to increase ridership

He is remembered today for his four important contributions to public relations: (1) advancing the concept that business and industry should align themselves with the public interest, (2) dealing with top executives and carrying out no program without the active support of management, (3) maintaining open communication with the news media, and (4) emphasizing the necessity of humanizing business and bringing its public relations down to the community level of employees, customers, and neighbors.

Edward L. Bernays: Father of Modern Public Relations

Lee's public information model is still used today, but a new approach to the practice of public relations, introduced in the 1920s, emphasized the concept of "scientific persuasion." A leading proponent of this new approach was Edward L. Bernays, who, through brilliant campaigns and extensive self-promotion, became known as the "Father of Modern Public Relations" by the time of his death in 1995 at the age of 103.

Bernays, who was the nephew of Sigmund Freud, believed public relations should emphasize the application of social science research and behavioral psychology to formulate campaigns and messages that could change people's perceptions and encourage certain behaviors. Unlike Lee's public information model, which emphasized the accurate distribution of news, Bernays's model was essentially one of advocacy and scientific persuasion. It included listening to the audience, but the purpose of feedback was to formulate a more persuasive message. Professor emeritus James Grunig of the University of Maryland, a major theorist in public relations, has labeled this the two-way asymmetric model, one of four classic models that are outlined on page 52.

Bernays became a major spokesperson for the "new" public relations through his 1923 book *Crystallizing Public Opinion*, which outlined the scope, function, methods, techniques, and social responsibilities of a public relations counsel—a term that was to become the core of public relations practice.

The book, published a year after Walter Lippmann's insightful treatise on public opinion, attracted much attention, and Bernays was even invited by New York University to offer the first public relations course in the nation. Bernays, over the course of his long career, had many successful campaigns that have become classics. Here is a sampling:

Edward L. Bernays

This legendary figure in public relations had a career spanning about three-quarters of a century; he died at the age of 103 in 1995. He became known as the "father of modern public relations."

■ **Ivory Soap.** Procter & Gamble sold its Ivory Soap by the millions after Bernays came up with the idea of sponsoring soap sculpture contests for school-aged children. In the first year alone, 22 million schoolchildren participated in the contest, which eventually ran for 35 years. Bernays's brochure with soap sculpture tips, which millions of children received in their schools, advised them to "use discarded models for face, hands, and bath."

■ **"Torches of Liberty."** During the Roaring 20s, Bernays was hired by the American Tobacco Company to tap the women's market by countering the social taboo of women smoking in public. His solution was to have beautiful fashion models march in New York's popular Easter Parade, each waving a lit cigarette and wearing a banner proclaiming it a "torch of liberty." By making smoking a symbol of liberation, the sale of cigarettes to women skyrocketed. Later in his life, Bernays said he would have refused the account if he had known the dangers of tobacco.

■ **Light's Golden Jubilee.** To celebrate the 50th anniversary of Thomas Edison's invention of the electric light bulb, Bernays arranged the worldwide attention-getting

He [Bernays] was the first to demonstrate for future generations of PR people how powerful their profession could be in shaping America's economic, political, and cultural life.

Larry Tye, author of Father of Spin: Edward L. Bernays & the Birth of Public Relations

Light's Golden Jubilee in 1929. It was his idea, for example, that the world's utilities would shut off their power all at one time, for one minute, to honor Edison. President Herbert Hoover and many dignitaries were on hand, and the U.S. Post Office issued a commemorative two-cent postage stamp. Bill Moyers, in an interview with Bernays in 1984, asked, "You got the whole world to turn off its lights at the same time. That's not influence, that's power." Bernays responded, "But you see, I never thought of it as power. I never treated it as power. People want to go where they want to be led."

Journalist Larry Tye has outlined a number of campaigns conducted by Bernays in his book *The Father of Spin: Edward L. Bernays & the Birth of Public Relations*. Tye credits Bernays with having a unique approach to solving problems. Instead of thinking first about tactics, Bernays would always think about the "big idea" of how to motivate people. The bacon industry, for example, wanted to promote its product, so Bernays came up with the idea of doctors across the land endorsing a hearty breakfast. No mention was made of bacon, but sales soared anyway, as people took the advice and started eating the traditional breakfast of bacon and eggs.

Bernays, during his long, 20th-century-spanning life, constantly wrote about the profession of public relations and its ethical responsibilities—even to the point of advocating the licensing of public relations counselors. One historian described him as "the first and doubtless the leading ideologist of public relations."

Although he was named by *Life* magazine in 1990 as one of the 100 most important Americans of the 20th century, it should be noted that Bernays had a powerful partner in his wife, Doris E. Fleischman, who was a talented writer, ardent feminist, and former Sunday editor of the *New York Tribune*. Fleischman was an equal partner in the work of Bernays's firm, interviewing clients, writing news releases, editing the company's newsletter, and writing and editing books and magazine articles.

Other Pioneers in the Field

Ivy Lee and Edward Bernays were the most prominent pioneers in the public relations profession from 1900 to 1950, but the field is populated with a number of other brilliant practitioners and colorful personalities. The following gives a brief sketch of other leading historical figures:

■ **George Creel.** The public information model that Lee enunciated in his counseling was also used by George Creel, who was also a former newspaper reporter. He was asked by President Woodrow Wilson to organize a massive public relations effort to unite the nation and to influence world opinion during World War I.

In their book *Words That Won the War*, James O. Mock and Cedric Larson write: "Mr. Creel assembled a brilliant and talented group of journalists, scholars, press agents, editors, artists, and other manipulators of the symbols of public opinion as America had ever seen united for a single purpose." Among its numerous activities, the Creel Committee persuaded newspapers and magazines to contribute volumes of news and advertising space to encourage Americans to save food and to invest heavily in Liberty Bonds, which were purchased by more than 10 million people.

Such a massive publicity effort had a profound effect on the development of public relations by demonstrating the success of these techniques. It also awakened a public awareness of the power of mediated information in shaping public opinion and behavior.

■ **Arthur W. Page.** Page became vice president of the American Telephone & Telegraph (AT&T) Company in 1927 and is credited with establishing the concept that public relations should have an active voice in higher management. Page also expressed the belief that a company's performance, not press agentry, comprises its basis for public approval. More than any other individual, Page is credited with laying the foundation for the field of corporate public relations. He served on the boards of numerous corporations, charitable groups, and universities.

> . . . all business in a democratic country begins with public permission and exists by public approval.
>
> *Arthur W. Page*

After his death in 1960, a group of AT&T associates established a society of senior communication executives in his name. The Arthur W. Page Society, comprising about 350 senior-level public relations executives, has several meetings a year and publishes various monographs on communications management. The society posts on its website (www.awpagesociety.com) the six principles of public relations management developed by the society's namesake. In summary, Page's principles are: (1) tell the truth, (2) action speaks louder than words, (3) always listen to the consumer, (4) anticipate public reaction and eliminate practices that cause conflict, (5) public relations is a management and policy-making function that impacts the entire company, and (6) keep a sense of humor, exercise judgment, and keep a cool head in times of crisis.

■ **Benjamin Sonnenberg.** It was Sonnenberg who suggested that Texaco sponsor performances of the Metropolitan Opera on national radio. Sponsorship of the Saturday-afternoon series, which began in 1940, continued for a half-century and enhanced Texaco's reputation as a patron of the arts. Biographer Isadore Barmash described Sonnenberg as "the most influential publicist of the mid-twentieth century." He had an opulent townhouse in New York and entertained many of America's most powerful men and women. Asked what the secret of his success was, he quipped, "I build large pedestals for small people."

■ **Rex Harlow.** Considered by many to be the "father of public relations research," Harlow was probably the first full-time public relations educator. As a professor at Stanford University's School of Education, he taught public relations courses and also conducted multiple continuing education workshops around the nation for working practitioners. Harlow founded the American Council on Public Relations, which later became the Public Relations Society of America (PRSA). In 1952, he founded *Social Science Reporter*, one of the first newsletters in the field.

■ **Leone Baxter.** Baxter and her partner, Clem Whitaker, are credited with founding the first political campaign management firm in the United States. The firm handled several California governor and U.S. Senate campaigns, advised General Dwight Eisenhower when he ran for president in 1952, and counseled Richard Nixon on the famous "Checkers" speech that saved his career as vice president.

■ **Warren Cowan.** *Portfolio* magazine called Cowan the "consummate Hollywood PR man" because his firm, Rogers and Cowan, was one of the first firms to serve the movie industry in the 1930s. Cowan represented such celebrities as Judy Garland, Cary Grant, Frank Sinatra, Gary Cooper, and Paul Newman during his lifetime and is credited with mentoring today's leading Hollywood publicists. In 1944, Cowan invented the modern Oscar campaign by leaking a story about an actor's Academy Award chances. He once said, "If we don't have anything to publicize, let's create it." When Cowan died at age 87 in 2008, he was buried with his cell phone in his hand. As a footnote, his long-term partner, Henry Rogers, was once quoted as saying, "Dog food and movie stars are much alike because they are both products in need of exposure."

■ **Eleanor Lambert.** The "grande dame" of fashion public relations, Lambert is credited with putting American designers such as Bill Blass and Calvin Klein on the map when Europeans dominated the industry. She also compiled the "Best-Dressed" list for 62 years, which always received extensive media publicity.

■ **Elmer Davis.** President Franklin D. Roosevelt appointed Davis head of the Office of War Information (OWI) during World War II. Using the Creel Committee as a model, Davis mounted an even larger public relations effort to promote the sale of war bonds, obtain press support for wartime rationing, encourage the planting of "victory gardens," and spur higher productivity among American workers to win the war. The Voice of America (VOA) was established to carry news of the war to all parts of the world, and the movie industry made a number of feature films in support of the war. The OWI was the forerunner of the U.S. Information Agency (USIA), which was established in 1953. Its operations are now part of the U.S. State Department's public diplomacy efforts.

■ **Moss Kendrix.** "What the public thinks counts!" was the mantra of Kendrix, who founded his own public relations firm in 1944. He is credited with being the first African American to acquire a major corporate account, the Coca-Cola Company. During his lifetime, he designed countless public relations and advertising campaigns for major corporations. The Museum of Public Relations (www.prmuseum.com) notes: "He educated his corporate clients about the buying power of the African American consumer, and helped to make America realize that African Americans were more complex than the derogatory images depicted in the advertising of the past."

Major Contributions by Industrialists, Presidents

Major contributions to the development of public relations have also been made by nonpractitioners who had the vision to successfully harness many of its basic concepts. Some leading examples are Henry Ford, Samuel Insull, and Teddy Roosevelt.

Henry Ford   Henry Ford was America's first major industrialist, and he was among the first to use two basic public relations concepts. The first was the notion of positioning, the idea that credit and publicity always go to those who do something first. Second was the idea of being accessible to the press. Joseph Epstein, author of *Ambition*, says, "He may have been an even greater publicist than mechanic."

In 1900, Ford obtained coverage of the prototype Model T by demonstrating it to a reporter from the *Detroit Tribune*. By 1903, Ford achieved widespread publicity by racing his cars—a practice still used by today's automakers. He garnered further publicity and became the hero of working men and women by being the first automaker to double his worker's wages to $5 per day. A populist by nature, he once said, "Business is a service, not a bonanza," an idea reiterated by many of today's top corporate executives, who believe in what is now called corporate social responsibility (CSR).

Samuel Insull   At the corporate level, the Chicago Edison Company broke new ground in public relations techniques under the skillful leadership of its president, Samuel Insull. Well aware of the special need for a public utility to maintain a sound relationship with its customers, Insull created a monthly customer magazine, issued a constant stream of news releases, and even used films for public relations purposes. In 1912, he started the "bill stuffer" by inserting company information into customers' bills—a technique used by many utilities today. He did much to expand the market for electricity by promoting electrical appliances, with the theme that they liberate women from household drudgery.

Teddy Roosevelt   President Theodore Roosevelt (1901–1909) was a master at promoting and publicizing his pet projects. He was the first president to make extensive use of news conferences and press interviews to drum up public support when Congress was resistant. He was an ardent conservationist and knew the publicity value of the presidential tour. For example, he took a large group of reporters and photographers to see the wonders of Yosemite National Park, as a way of generating favorable press coverage and public support for the creation of additional national forests and national parks. While president, Roosevelt set

Teddy Roosevelt

Theodore Roosevelt gained public support for national parks by traveling with a corps of journalists and prominent business leaders to such places as Yosemite National Park.

aside 150 million acres for public recreational use and essentially became the "father" of the American conservation movement. Even his nickname, "Teddy," comes from the publicity that was generated after he spared a small bear on a hunting trip and a toy maker began to market "Teddy" bears in recognition of the president's humane gesture. He's probably the only U.S. president to have a stuffed animal named after him, a name that survives to this day.

President Franklin D. Roosevelt apparently took notes from his cousin Teddy. His supporters organized nationwide birthday balls in 1934 to celebrate his birthday and raise funds for infantile paralysis research. This led to the creation of the March of Dimes. The campaign by Carl Byoir & Associates, a leading public relations firm at the time, orchestrated 6,000 events in 3,600 communities and raised more than $1 million.

1950 to 2000: Public Relations Comes of Age

During the second half of the 20th century, the practice of public relations became firmly established as an indispensable part of America's economic, political, and social development.

The booming economy after World War II produced rapid growth in all areas of public relations. Companies opened public relations departments or expanded existing ones. Government staffs increased in size, as did those of nonprofits, such as educational institutions and health and welfare agencies. Television emerged in the early 1950s as a national medium and as a new challenge for public relations expertise. New counseling firms sprang up nationwide.

on the job

INSIGHTS

Four Classic Models of Public Relations

A four-model typology of public relations practice was formulated by Professors James Grunig of the University of Maryland and Todd Hunt of Rutgers University in their 1984 book *Managing Public Relations*. The models, which have been used widely in public relations theory, help to explain how public relations has evolved over the years.

Press Agentry/Publicity

This is one-way communication, primarily through the mass media, to distribute information that may be exaggerated, distorted, or even incomplete in order to "hype" a cause, product, or service. Its purpose is advocacy, and little or no research is required. P. T. Barnum was the leading historical figure of this model during the 19th century. Sports, theater, music, film, and the classic Hollywood publicist are the main fields of practice today.

Public Information

One-way distribution of information, not necessarily with a persuasive intent, is the purpose of public information. It is based on the journalistic ideal of accuracy and completeness, and the mass media are the primary channel. There is fact-finding for content, but little audience research regarding attitudes and dispositions. Ivy Lee, a former journalist, was the leading historical figure during this model's development from about 1910 into the 1920s. Government, nonprofit groups, and other public institutions are primary fields of practice today.

Two-Way Asymmetric

In this model, scientific persuasion is the purpose, and communication is two-way, with imbalanced effects. The model has a feedback loop, but the primary purpose of the model is to help the communicator better understand the audience and how to persuade it. Research is used to plan the activity and establish objectives as well as to learn whether an objective has been met. Edward Bernays was the leading historical figure during the model's beginning in the 1920s. Marketing and advertising departments in competitive businesses and public relations firms are the primary places of practice today.

Two-Way Symmetric

Gaining mutual understanding is the purpose of this model, and communication is two-way with balanced effects. Formative research is used mainly to learn how the public perceives the organization and to determine what consequences organizational actions/policy might have on the public. The result may counsel management to take certain actions or change policies. The idea, also expressed as "relationship building" and "engagement," is to have policies and actions that are mutually beneficial to both parties. Arthur W. Page is considered a leading advocate of this approach. Educators and professional leaders are the main proponents of this model, which has been around since the 1980s. The fields of practice today include organizations that engage in issue identification, crisis and risk management, corporate social responsibility, and long-range strategic planning.

The growth of the economy was one reason for the expansion of public relations, but there were other factors, too:

- major increases in urban and suburban populations
- the growth of a more impersonalized society, represented by big business, big labor, and big government

- scientific and technological advances, including automation and computerization
- the communications revolution in terms of mass media
- bottom-line financial considerations often replacing the more personalized decision making of a previous, more genteel society

Many citizens felt alienated and bewildered by such rapid changes, cut off from the sense of community that had characterized the lives of previous generations. They sought power through innumerable pressure groups, focusing on causes such as environmentalism, working conditions, and civil rights. Public opinion, registered through new, more sophisticated methods of polling, became increasingly powerful in opposing or effecting change.

Both physically and psychologically separated from their publics, American business and industry turned increasingly to public relations specialists for audience analysis, strategic planning, issues management, and even the creation of supportive environments for the selling of products and services. Mass media also became more complex and sophisticated, so specialists in media relations who understood how the media worked were also in demand.

Typical of the public relations programs of large corporations at midcentury was that of the Aluminum Company of America (ALCOA). Heading the operation was a vice president for public relations and advertising, who was aided by an assistant public relations director and advertising manager. Departments included community relations, product publicity, motion pictures and exhibits, employee publications, the news bureau, and speech writing. The *Alcoa News* magazine was published for all employees, and separate publications were published for each of the 20 plants throughout the United States.

The 1960s saw Vietnam War protests, the civil rights movement, the environmental movement, interest in women's rights, and a host of other issues. Antibusiness sentiment was high, and corporations adjusted their policies to generate public goodwill and understanding. Thus, the idea of issues management was added to the job description of the public relations manager. This was the first expression of the idea that public relations should be more than simply persuading people that corporate policy was correct. During this period, the idea emerged that perhaps it would be beneficial to have a dialogue with various publics and adapt corporate policy to their particular concerns. Grunig labeled this approach *two-way symmetrical communication* because there's balance between the organization and its various publics. In other words, the organization and the public can influence each other.

The 1970s was an era of reform in the stock market and investor relations. The Texas Gulf Sulfur case changed investor relations forever by establishing the idea that a company must immediately disclose any information that may affect the value of its stock. The field of investor relations boomed.

By the 1980s, the concept that public relations is a management function was in full bloom. The term *strategic* became a buzzword, and the concept of management by objective (MBO) was heavily endorsed by public relations practitioners as they sought to prove to higher management that public relations does indeed contribute to the bottom line. Many definitions from this time emphasized public relations as a management function. As Derina Holtzhausen of the University of Florida notes, "Public relations management highlights organizational effectiveness, the strategic management of the function through strategic identification of publics, and issues management to prevent crisis."

PRCasebook

Classic Campaigns Show the Power of Public Relations

During the last half of the 20th century, a number of organizations and causes have used effective public relations to accomplish highly visible results. *PRWeek* convened a panel of public relations experts and came up with some of the "greatest campaigns ever" during this time period.

- **The Civil Rights Campaign.** Martin Luther King Jr. was an outstanding civil rights advocate and a great communicator. He organized the 1963 civil rights campaign and used such techniques as well-written, well-delivered speeches; letter writing; lobbying; and staged events (nonviolent protests) to turn a powerful idea into reality.

- **NASA.** From the very beginning NASA fostered media accessibility at Houston's Johnson Space Center. For example, NASA director Chris Kraft insisted that television cameras be placed on the lunar lander in 1969, and in later years reporters were invited inside mission control during the Apollo 13 mission. According to *PRWeek*, "Those historic moments have helped the public overlook the huge taxpayer expense and numerous technical debacles that could otherwise have jeopardized the future of the organization."

- **Cabbage Patch Kids.** Public relations launched the craze for the adoptable dolls and created a "must-have" toy. The campaign set the standard for the introduction of a new product and showed what a strong media relations program can do for a product.

- **Seat Belt Campaign.** In the 1980s, the U.S. automotive industry got the nation to "buckle up" through a public relations campaign. Tactics included winning the support of news media across the country, interactive displays, celebrity endorsements, letter-writing campaigns, and several publicity events, such as buckling a 600-foot-wide safety belt around the Hollywood sign. Notes *PRWeek*, "The results of one of the biggest public relations campaigns of all time were phenomenal, with the number of people 'buckling up' rising from 12 to 50 percent—it is now even higher."

- **Hands Across America.** The largest human gathering in history was a public relations stunt in 1986 that saw 7 million people across 16 states join hands to form a human chain to raise money for the hungry and the homeless. Even President Ronald Reagan participated.

- **StarKist Tuna.** When negative media coverage threatened the tuna industry because dolphins were getting caught in fishermen's nets, StarKist led the industry in changing its fishing practices. The company publicized its efforts through conferences, print and broadcast news stories, and working with a coalition of environmental groups. About 90 percent of the public heard about the company's efforts, and StarKist was praised as an environmental leader.

- **Tylenol Crisis.** This has become the classic model for a product recall. When Johnson & Johnson found out that several people had died from cyanide-laced Tylenol capsules, a national panic erupted. Many thought the company would never recover from the damage caused by the tampering. However, the company issued a complete recall, redesigned the packaging so that it is tamper-proof, and launched a media campaign to keep the public fully informed. The result was that Tylenol survived the crisis and again became a best-seller.

- **Windows 95 Launch.** This campaign is easily in the product launch hall of fame. Microsoft, through media relations and publicity, achieved an unprecedented 99 percent awareness level among consumers before the product even hit the shelves.

- **Understanding AIDS.** This successful health education campaign changed the way that AIDS was perceived by Americans. In addition to a national mailing of a brochure titled "Understanding AIDS," there were grassroots activities that specifically targeted African Americans and Hispanics.

Source: The greatest campaigns ever. (2002, July 15). *PRWeek*, 14–15.

PEARSON
mycommunicationlab

Reputation, or *perception*, management was the buzzword of the 1990s. Burson-Marsteller, one of the largest public relations firms, decided that its business was not public relations but, rather, "perception management." Other firms also declared that their business was "reputation management." However, there was some debate as to whether reputations can be managed, because reputation is the cumulative effect of numerous actions and activities.

The basic idea, however, was that public relations people work to maintain credibility, to build solid internal and external relationships, and to manage issues. Inherent in this was the idea that public relations personnel should use research to do (1) environmental monitoring, (2) public relations audits, (3) communication audits, and (4) social audits. By doing these things, it would be possible to enhance corporate social responsibility (CSR).

The Influx of Women into the Field

In terms of personnel, the most dramatic change between 1950 and 2000 was the transformation of public relations from a male-dominated field to one in which women now constitute about 70 percent of practitioners.

The shift occurred over several decades. In 1979, women made up 41 percent of the public relations field. By 1983, they had become the majority (50.1 percent) of the public relations workforce. A decade later, the figure stood at 66.3 percent. By 2000, the percentage had leveled off at about 70 percent, where it remains today. National organizations also reflect the trend. About 75 percent of the membership in the International Association of Business Communicators (IABC) are now women, and the Public Relations Society of America (PRSA) estimates that more than 60 percent of its members are now women.

Such numbers also reflect the influx of women into the American workforce at all levels. Today, women make up 51 percent of the professional workers in the United States and also in many European nations. This can be somewhat explained by the massive influx of women into the nation's colleges and universities that has also taken place in the past several decades. Women have represented almost 60 percent of enrollments since at least 2000, according to a report by the American Council on Education. In terms of degrees, the U.S. Department of Education reports that women earn about 165 associate degrees and 135 bachelor's degrees for every 100 earned by males. And the *Economist* reports that by 2011, there will be 2.6 million more females than male university students in the United States.

Women traditionally earned degrees in such subjects as education, social work, and library science, but that has also changed.

on the job

ETHICS

Making a Hiring Decision

There's a shortage of men and minorities in the public relations field, and your public relations firm is no exception. About 80 percent of the professional staff are women, including one woman who is Hispanic. As the owner of the firm, you believe in diversity and have a job opening for an assistant account executive. Seven of the applicants are white women, and two applicants are men, including an African American. One of the female applicants has excellent credentials , but the white male and the African American male also have good qualifications for the job. What should you do? Given the high percentage of women already in your firm and the need for some gender balance in the workplace, would you hire one of the two men instead? And, if so, which one? Or would you go with the top candidate, who is female?

Blair Christie, SVP,
Global Corporate
Communications of Cisco

Genevieve Haldeman, VP,
Corporate Communications,
Symantec

Julie Hamp, SVP of
PepsiCo Communications

Betty Hudson, EVP of
Communications,
National Geographic Society

Anne McCarthy, EVP,
Corporate Communications and
Public Affairs, Western Union

Necole Merritt, VP of
Public Affairs,
Cox Communications

Zenia Mucha, EVP of Corporate
Communications,
The Walt Disney Company

Mary Stutts, SVP of
Corporate Relations,
Elan Pharmaceuticals

C. Perry Yeatman, SVP of
Corporate Affairs,
Kraft Foods

Women in Public Relations

This group of senior executives exemplifies the rise of women to major positions in large corporations and public relations firms.

Today, women earn more college degrees than men in all fields except the physical sciences, math, engineering, and business. This is particularly true in the communications field, according to the annual survey of journalism and mass communications departments at 480 colleges and universities conducted by Lee Becker and his associates at the University of Georgia. In 2008, for example, women made up 64 percent of the undergraduate enrollments and 67.5 percent of the master's degree programs.

Becker's survey also found that about 15 percent of the 201,000 students in departments and schools of journalism, or about 30,000 students, specialize in public relations. Of that number, it's estimated that females comprise about 70 to 75 percent of the majors, a percentage that hasn't changed much since 2000.

A number of reasons are given for the major influx of women into the field of public relations. Some of these reasons include the following:

- Women find public relations work a more flexible environment for juggling family responsibilities.
- Women earn higher salaries in public relations than in comparable fields such as newspapers, radio, and television.
- A woman can start a public relations firm without a lot of capital, or even work out of her home as an independent consultant.
- Women tend to have better listening and communication skills than men.
- Women are often considered more sensitive than men in facilitating two-way communication.

At the same time, a number of studies show that the majority of women in public relations earn less money than their male counterparts (see the salary survey information in Chapter 1). This, however, also reflects American society, where statistics show that full-time female workers in all fields earn only about 80 percent as much as the typical male.

A number of research studies have investigated the role and status of women in public relations. Some studies have explored the female/male salary gap and have come to various conclusions. Some scholars say that the gap is the result of women having less work experience in the field than typical males, so they are more likely to perform lower-level tactical functions instead of management duties. Other researchers have found that women have fewer mentors and role models than men, which limits their career aspirations. Still others have concluded that male-dominated corporate structures still impose a "glass ceiling" on the advancement of women into higher-level management.

> This industry doesn't look at gender, but rather attracts, nurtures, and promotes those who can provide business insights to their clients, understand influence and the power of storytelling, and drive business results.
>
> *Melissa Waggener Zorkin, CEO and founder of Waggener Edstrom public relations*

Although the executive ranks in the public relations field are still predominantly male, female representation has dramatically increased in recent years. One indication of this is the membership of the Arthur W. Page Society, which is composed of senior-level communication executives. It's now about 50 percent female. A representative grouping of female executives who are members of the Page Society is on page 56.

Today's Practice and Trends

By 2000, a number of scholars and practitioners began to conceptualize the practice of public relations as "relationship management," the basic idea being that public relations practitioners are in the business of building and fostering relationships with an organization's various publics. The idea has also caught on in marketing; *relationship marketing* is an effort to form a solid, ongoing relationship with the purchaser of a product or service.

Relationship management builds on Grunig's idea of two-way symmetrical communication, but goes beyond this by recognizing that an organization's publics are, as Stephen Bruning of Capital University notes, "active, interactive, and equal participants of an ongoing communication process." Bruning continues, "Typically, organizations are fairly effective at fulfilling content communication needs (communicating to key public members what is happening), but often fall short of fulfilling key public member relational communication needs (making the key public member feel they are valued in the relationship)."

An extension of relationship management is the *dialogic* (dialogue) model of public relations that has emerged since 2000. Michael Kent of Montclair University and Maureen Taylor of Rutgers University wrote in a *Public Relations Review* article that "A theoretical shift, from public relations reflecting an emphasis on managing communication, to an emphasis on communication as a tool of negotiating relationships, has been taking place for some time." Kent and Taylor say that good dialogic communication requires skills such as the following:

> . . . listening, empathy, being able to contextualize issues within local, national and international frameworks, being able to identify common ground between parties, thinking about long-term rather than short-term objectives, seeking out groups and individuals with opposing viewpoints, and soliciting a variety of internal and external opinions on policy issues.

The concept of dialogue places less emphasis on mass media distribution of messages and more on interpersonal channels. Kent and Taylor, for example, say that the Internet and World Wide Web are excellent vehicles for dialogue if the sites are interactive. They write, "The Web can be used to communicate directly with publics by offering real-time discussions, feedback loops, places to post comments, sources for organizational information, and postings of organizational member biographies and contact information."

The latest development, of course, is the advent of social media. The new buzzword is "engagement," which is another way of expressing Kent and Taylor's concept of dialogue between an organization and its various publics. Indeed, social media have revolutionized public relations practice in terms of how organizations now communicate with their customers, vendors, and employees on such sites as Facebook, YouTube, and even Twitter. This revolution in public relations is further explored in Chapter 13.

Although there has been a somewhat linear progression in public relations practice and philosophy as the field has expanded, today's practice represents a mixture of public relations models. The Hollywood publicist/press agent and the public information officer for the government agency are still with us. We also still have marketing communications, which almost exclusively uses the concept of scientific persuasion and two-way asymmetric communication. However, when it comes to issue management and relationship building, the two-way symmetric and dialogue models seem to be the most appropriate.

Another model that is gaining acceptance goes back to the idea that public relations should do more than build relationships. Professor Glen Cameron of the University of Missouri, and coauthor of this book, says public relations should be more assertive and is best defined as the strategic management of competition and conflict in the best interests of the organization and, when possible, also in the interest of key publics. This concept is discussed further in Chapter 10.

Current Developments

Throughout history, the practice of public relations has been a reflection of social, cultural, and economic forces that have shaped and influenced society through the centuries. The field of public relations is constantly evolving, and a number of ongoing developments will shape the practice of public relations in the coming years. The following are some current trend lines:

A Multicultural World   We now live in a multicultural world that requires sensitivity and knowledge of multiple audiences. Minorities, for example, will comprise more than one-third of the U.S. population by 2016. In terms of global economic growth projected to 2020, China and India will account for about 40 percent of this growth, as compared to the United States at 15 percent and Europe at less than 10 percent. For example, Dow Chemical already has 80 percent of its employees located at 156 manufacturing plants outside the United States; and Starbucks plans 30,000 stores worldwide in the coming years.

At the same time, by 2020, there will be an estimated 700 million individuals in the world over 65 years of age. By 2050, 42 percent of Japan's population will be over 60. There is also great potential for increased cultural clashes; 25 percent of France's population, for example, will be Muslim by 2030. The world is getting connected; 2 billion people are now on the Internet and 4 billion have cell phones, with the fastest growth in the developing nations. Fred Cook, president of Golin Harris, says, "The seismic shift to globalization and multiculturalism will transform communication. It will not be enough to address emerging cultures by simply creating separate practices to focus on individual ethnic groups. In the coming decades, the current ethnocentric approach to public relations will be replaced by a more holistic perspective." See Chapter 11, "Reaching Diverse Audiences."

Recruitment of Minorities   A continuing challenge is recruitment of a diversified workforce in public relations, one that more accurately reflects the demographics of the U.S. population.

According to the U.S. Census Bureau, the fastest-growing, and now largest, group is comprised of Hispanics. They are now 14 percent of the population, compared with 12.8 percent for African Americans. Asian/Pacific Islanders make up 4 percent, and Native Americans comprise 1 percent of the population. Unfortunately, despite the increase of minorities in the general population, not much has changed in the public relations industry. Whites still comprise nearly 90 percent of public relations specialists in the United States, according to the U.S. Bureau of Labor Statistics.

> The public relations industry, long an enclave of well-paid, college-educated, white professionals, is finally waking up to the reality that it needs to do better PR to attract people of color.
>
> *Tannette Johnson-Elie, columnist,*
> *Milwaukee Journal-Sentinel*

Many public relations employers express the desire to hire more minority candidates, but one obstacle is a shortage of qualified candidates. Racial or ethnic minority groups make up only about 30 percent of the students enrolled in journalism and mass communications programs. A diversity survey by *PRWeek* in 2009 also found that 62 percent of the black respondents working in public relations said "not enough role models" was the greatest barrier to generating more diversity in the industry.

Various national organizations, such as the Public Relations Society of America (PRSA), the National Black Public Relations Society (BPRS), the Hispanic Public Relations Association (HPRA), and the Asian American Advertising and Public Relations Association (AAAPRA), have ongoing programs to increase minorities in the field.

The Public Demand for Transparency   Instant global communications, corporate finance scandals, government regulation, and the increased public demand for accountability have made it necessary for all of society's institutions, including business and industry, to be more transparent in their operations.

A position paper by Vocus, a communications software firm, says it best: "An organization's every action is subject to public scrutiny. Everything—from the compensation provided to a departing CEO to the country from which a manufacturing plant orders its materials—is considered open to public discourse." Sir Martin Sorrell, CEO of communications conglomerate WPP, adds, "It is, like it or not, a more transparent world. Everything a company does and says will be dissected and discussed."

The Institute of Public Relations (IPR) in the United Kingdom says that the role of public relations has changed considerably over the last decade: "Instead of being used primarily as a way to influence and secure media coverage, organizations are using public relations to communicate with their stakeholders as society demands more transparency."

Expanded Role for Public Relations   Professionals have already repositioned public relations as being more than media relations and publicity, but those hard-fought gains will need to be reinforced in the coming years, as marketing and management consultants enter the field to also build relationships with various publics. Tom Gable, a public relations counselor in San Diego, says, "Our challenge and opportunity will be to own the areas of positioning, branding, reputation management, and building relationships for the long term with multiple constituencies." Increasingly, public relations personnel will play an even greater role in planning and executing integrated communications campaigns.

> The PR industry must continue to evolve beyond traditional media relations or it will end like buggy whip manufacturers—experts at placing stories with media that no longer exist.
>
> *Fred Cook, president and CEO,*
> *Golin Harris public relations*

Corporate Social Responsibility (CSR)   Global warming, environmental integrity, sustainable development, fair treatment of employees on a global basis, product quality and safety, and ethical supply chains are now on the agenda of all organizations. All elements of the organization are involved in the creation of the socially responsible corporation, but public relations will play a central role. James Murphy, global managing director of communications for Accenture, expresses it well: "PR staffs are in the forefront of building trust and credibility—and coordinating corporate social responsibility efforts. These are the people who deal with trust issues all the time; therefore, we're in a good position to address them." CSR is further discussed in Chapter 17 "Corporations."

Increased Emphasis on Measurement   Public relations professionals will continue to improve measurement techniques for showing management how their activities actually contribute to the bottom line. Helping them do this are increasingly sophisticated software programs that can measure all aspects of a public relations program.

One dimension is the return on investment (ROI). According to Kathy Cripps, chair of the Council of Public Relations Firms, two other important dimensions of measurement are: (1) measuring outcomes—the long-term effectiveness of a public relations program; and (2) measuring outputs—how well a program was executed and how effective its tactics were.

Management increasingly demands better measurement, and Ed Nicholson, director of media relations at Tyson Foods, says, "We're compelled to create measurable objectives and evaluation that goes beyond clip counts and impressions and demonstrate delivered value to the organization." Measurement and evaluation are further discussed in Chapter 8 "Evaluation."

Managing the 24/7 News Cycle   The flow of news and information is now a virtual cyclone that occurs every minute of the day. This means that public relations personnel must constantly monitor what is being reported or discussed in everything from traditional media outlets to blogs, chat groups, and social media such as Facebook or even YouTube. In addition, the demand for instant response and the distribution of even more information often leave little or no time for reasoned response or even ensure accuracy. A major challenge to today's practitioners is how to cope with the cascade of information and how to give it shape and purpose so that it's relevant to multiple audiences.

Continued Growth of Digital Media   Traditional media such as newspapers, magazines, radio, television, and even cable will continue to decline or remain static. Such media will also continue to be increasingly fragmented. "Mass media," according to Fred Cook of Golin Harris, "is rapidly being atomized—moving from mainstream to multistream."

In other words, public relations personnel will continue to expand their communication tools to account for the fact that no single mass medium, or combination of them, will be a good vehicle for reaching key publics. The greatest area of growth today and in the coming years will be the use of the Internet and various forms of social media.

Today, public relations professionals reach and interact with audiences via RSS feeds, blogs, vlogs, podcasts, webcasts, Facebook, YouTube, and Twitter. In 2010, about 24 hours of video were being uploaded every minute on YouTube, and Facebook users passed the half-billion mark. Twitter, within a year, had 110 million users. All these technologies are collectively called "social media" and offer public relations practitioners unparalleled opportunities for communicating, listening, and interacting with large numbers of individuals on a global basis. See Chapter 13, "The Internet and Social Media."

> By 2013, mobile phones will replace PCs as the most common device for Web access.
>
> *Center for Media Research, quoting predictions from Gartner Research*

Outsourcing to Public Relations Firms   The outsourcing trend developed some years ago, but now it's almost universal. A survey by Ian Mitroff, Gerald Swerling, and Jennifer Floto published in *The Strategist* notes, "The use of agencies is now the norm in American business across all revenue categories and industries in this study: 85 percent of respondents (corporate executives) work with outside PR firms." This is not to say that corporate public relations departments are disappearing, but, increasingly, that such tactics as media relations, annual reports, and sponsored events are being outsourced to public relations firms. In addition, it's entirely possible that basic tactics such as preparation of digital news releases and other collateral materials will be outsourced to places such as India. In fact, Indian companies already make about $280 million annually from outsourced advertising production. See Chapter 4, "Public Relations Departments and Firms."

The Need for Lifelong Professional Development   Public relations personnel, given the rapid additions to knowledge in today's society, will need to continually update their knowledge base just to stay current with new developments and even hundreds of new Internet-based applications. Deirdre Breakenridge, coauthor of *Putting the Public Back in Public Relations*, wrote on a PRSA blog (*comprehension.prsa.org*), "Social media is forcing a reform of the public relations industry and now requires public relations and communication professionals to act as research librarians, sociologists, cultural anthropologists, and content managers, among other responsibilities."

Summary

Early Beginnings

- Although public relations is a 20th-century term, the roots of the practice go back to the ancient empires of Egypt, Greece, Rome, and India.

- The Catholic Church in the Middle Ages extensively used public relations and propaganda techniques to promote the faith and rally followers to join the Crusades.

- Private companies attracted immigrants to the New World through promotion and glowing accounts of fertile land. The American Revolution, in part, was the result of such staged events as the Boston Tea Party and the writing of the *Federalist Papers*.

The 1800s: The Golden Age of Press Agentry

- P. T. Barnum, the master showman of the 19th century, pioneered many techniques that are still used today in the entertainment industry.

- The settlement of the West was due in large part to promotions by land developers and American railroads.

- The first presidential press secretary dates back to the administration of Andrew Jackson in the 1820s.

- Social movements for women's rights, racial equality, prohibition, and preservation of wilderness used multiple tools of publicity to influence public opinion.

- The Wannamaker department store in Philadelphia and Macy's in New York were the first to use public relations techniques to attract customers in the 1870s.

- The United States adopted alternating current (AC) in the 1890s, partly as a result of a successful public relations campaign by George Westinghouse who competed with Thomas Edison's advocacy of direct current (DC).

1900 to 1950: The Age of Pioneers

- Ivy Lee and Edward Bernays are considered the two outstanding pioneers who did much to establish the foundation for today's public relations practice.

- Other visionaries that dominated the field were Arthur W. Page, probably the first practitioner to establish public relations as an integral part of high-level corporate management.

- The pioneers also included a number of colorful personalities, including Hollywood publicist Warren Cowan and fashion publicist Eleanor Lambert.

1950 to 2000: Public Relations Comes of Age

- The field of public relations greatly expanded after World War II as a result of changes in American society. These changes included urbanization, the development of mass media including television, and the overall expansion of business.

- The concept of public relations as just media relations and publicity began to shift; the concepts of "reputation management" and "relationship building" became more prominent in the literature and in practice.

- Public relations matures as a management function at the highest levels of the organization.

- Public relations, traditionally a male domain, experienced the massive influx of women into the field, to the point that an estimated 70 percent of today's public relations practitioners are female.

Today's Practice and Trends

- Public relations, in the era of the Internet and social media, places increased emphasis on listening, engagement, and dialogue with respective publics.

- Current, ongoing trends in public relations include the effort to have a more diverse workforce, practice on a global scale, and the revolutionary shift from traditional mass media to digital media, including the Internet and social media.

- The concept of corporate social responsibility (CSR) and the necessity for transparency become mainstream in terms of widespread acceptance by all organizations.

Case Activity Women in Public Relations Today

A major trend in public relations has been the feminization of the field, with current estimates placing the percentage of women professionals at 70 percent. Working in class in groups of 2 to 5 students, discuss what you think the implications of this trend are for the profession. Select a spokesperson for your group and work together to prepare a five-minute briefing for the class on the role of women in public relations.

Some starting points might be:

- salary differentials
- the supposedly unique skills and strengths that women and men bring to public relations
- the historical role of women in public relations
- go in your own direction as a group!

Questions For Review and Discussion

1. The roots of public relations extend deep into history. What were some of the early antecedents to today's public relations practice?

2. The Boston Tea Party has been described as the "greatest and best-known publicity stunt of all time." Would you agree? Do you feel that staged events are a legitimate way to publicize a cause and motivate people?

3. Which concepts of publicity and public relations practiced by P. T. Barnum should modern practitioners use? Which should they reject?

4. What are the four important contributions Ivy Lee made to public relations?

5. Arthur W. Page enunciated six principles of public relations management. Do you think these "principles" are as relevant today as they were in the 1930s?

6. What's your assessment of Ivy Lee's work for the Rockefeller family in the Colorado Fuel & Iron Company labor strife? Do you think his approach was sound? What would you have done differently?

7. Summarize the major developments in the philosophy and practice of public relations from the 1920s to 2000.

8. James Grunig outlined four models of public relations practice. Name and describe each one. Do the models help explain the evolution of public relations theory?

9. Public relations is now described as "relationship management." How would you describe this concept to a friend?

10. Females now constitute the majority of public relations personnel. How do you personally feel about this? Does it make the field of public relations more attractive or less attractive to you?

11. Describe several recent developments and trends in the public relations field.

Media Resources

Aldoory, L., Reber, B. H., Berger, B. K., & Toth, E. L. (2008, Winter). Provocations in public relations: A study of gendered ideologies of power influence in practice. *Journalism & Mass Communications Quarterly, 85*(4), 735–750.

Brown, R. E. (2003). St. Paul as a public relations practitioner: A theoretical speculation on messianic communication and symmetry. *Public Relations Review, 29,* 229–240.

Cook, F. (2007, Winter). It's a small world after all: Multiculturalism, authenticity, connectedness among trends to watch in next 50 years. *The Strategist,* 30–33.

Cutlip, S. M. (1994). *The unseen power: A history of public relations.* Mahwah, NJ: Lawrence Erlbaum.

Frohlich, R., & Peters, S. B. (2007). PR bunnies caught in the agency ghetto? Gender stereotypes, organizational factors, and women's careers in PR agencies. *Journal of Public Relations Research, 19*(3), 229–254.

Grunig, L., Toth, E. & Hon, L. C. (2001). *Women in public relations: How gender influences practice.* New York, NY: Guilford Press.

Harrison, S., & Moloney, K. (2004). Comparing two public relations pioneers: American Ivy Lee and British John Elliott. *Public Relations Review, 30*(2), 205–214.

Lamme, M. O. (2009). The brewers of public relations history, 1909–1919. *Journal of Public Relations Research, 21*(4), 455–477.

Lamme, M. O., & Russell, K. M. (2010, Winter). Removing the spin: Toward a new theory of public relations history. *Journalism & Communication Monographs, 11*(4).

Martinelli, D. K., & Mucciarone, J. (2007, March). New Deal public relations: A glimpse into FDR Press Secretary Stephen Early's work." *Public Relations Review, 33*(1), 49–57.

Maul, K. (2009, December). Diversity survey 2009. *PRWeek,* 30–36.

Sorrell, M. (2009, Winter). The renaissance of public relations. *The Strategist,* 36, 38.

St. John, B. (2006). The case for ethical propaganda within a democracy? Ivy Lee's successful 1913–1914 railroad rate campaign. *Public Relations Review, 32,* 221–228.

Toth, E. L. *Diversity and Public Relations Practice* (pp. 1–15). Retrieved from Institute for Public Relations, Essential Knowledge Project website: www.instituteforpr.org

PEARSON
my**communication**lab

The Pearson Public Relations Podcasts: "The History of PR: The Beginning," "The History of PR: The Depression Years," "The History of PR: The 1960s"

Multimedia Library Case Studies: Merck: Giving Its Product Away, Harry Potter and the Magical Marketing Campaign, The Glamorous Life

Ethics Case Scenario: A Bad Apple?

chapter 3

Ethics and Professionalism

Bernie Madoff epitomized the worst in ethical standards.

After reading this chapter, you will be able to:

Understand the role of the ethical advocate

Appreciate the role that professional groups play in setting standards

Be familiar with the progress being made toward professionalism

Define the characteristics of being a public relations professional

Be ethical when working with the media.

Understanding Ethics and Values

There is some confusion about the difference between ethics and values, but public relations professionals should know the difference, as a framework for their daily work. The Markula Center for Applied Ethics at the University of Santa Clara in California says, "Ethics refers to the standards of conduct which indicates how one *should behave* based upon moral duties and virtues rising from principles of right and wrong." Values, however, are "central beliefs which determine how we *will behave* in certain situations."

"An ethical public relations professional," says University of Maryland Professor Shannon Bowen, "should have such values as honesty, openness, loyalty, fair-mindedness, respect, integrity, and forthright communication." These values are usually incorporated into codes of ethics, which will be discussed shortly. The reality, however, is that individuals interpret basic values in different ways as they struggle to assess what is "right" or "wrong" in a particular situation.

Public relations professionals also have the burden of making ethical decisions that take into consideration (1) the public interest, (2) the employer's self-interests, (3) the standards of the public relations profession, and (4) their personal values. In an ideal world, these four spheres would not conflict, and clear-cut guidelines would make ethical decisions easy. In reality, however, making the right ethical decision is often a complex process involving many considerations.

One consideration is your "discomfort" level. Google cofounder Sergey Brin, being interviewed by the *Wall Street Journal* about the company's exit from China because of censorship restrictions, said, "Ultimately, I guess it is where your threshold of discomfort is, so we obviously as a company crossed that threshold of discomfort." In other words, how comfortable would you feel if you were asked to (1) exaggerate the qualities of a product, (2) defend a company's poor environmental record, (3) speak on behalf of the tobacco or liquor industry, or (4) organize a "citizens' group" funded by the oil industry? See the Insights box below.

on the job

INSIGHTS

Use of "Front Groups" Poses Ethical Concerns

The proliferation of so-called front groups waging purported grassroots campaigns to achieve public relations goals has created much debate in the field in recent years.

The establishment of dozens of such groups evoked a strongly worded statement from the board of directors of the PRSA.

PRSA specifically condemns the efforts of those organizations, sometimes known as "front groups," that seek to influence the public policy process by disguising or obscuring the true identity of their members or by implying representation of a much more broadly based group than exists.

Almost every "save the environment" organization has spawned a countergroup. For example, the Forest

Citizens' Protest

Special interest groups such as political parties, labor unions, and industry trade groups often organize and fund a rally by a "citizens" group.

Alliance of British Columbia, composed of 25 "green" groups, posed as a grassroots movement opposing the International Coalition to Save British Columbia's Rainforests. It was later revealed that the Canadian timber industry paid Burson-Marsteller $1 million to create the alliance, whose aim was to convince the public that environmental destruction has been exaggerated and to persuade lawmakers to abolish unprofitable environmental regulations.

Names given to many of the organizations are confusing, if not downright deceptive. Northwesterners for More Fish was the name chosen for a "grassroots" coalition of utilities and other companies in the Northwest who were under attack from environmental groups for depleting the fish population. In California's Riverside County, a public relations firm organized Friends of Eagle Mountain on behalf of a mining company that wanted to create the world's largest landfill in an abandoned iron ore pit. A pro-hunting group known as the Abundant Wildlife Society of North America works to convince people that wildlife is so plentiful that there is no reason not to kill some of it.

A Gallup Poll once showed that the majority of Americans consider themselves environmentalists. In the face of such findings, "People sometimes create groups that try to fudge a little bit about what their goals are," said Hal Dash, president of Cerrell Associates, a Los Angeles public relations firm that has represented clients with environmental problems.

Questioned about the tactics used in so-called grassroots campaigns, more than half of professionals surveyed by *PRNews* said that it is unethical for parties to fail to mention that their impetus for contacting a government official or other organization is due to a vested interest or membership in another organization sponsoring the campaign.

Your answers to these questions reflect your values. If your orientation is Kant's *absolutist* philosophy, that something is either completely "right" or "wrong," you would refuse to do some of these activities. Or you might take Aristotle's *existential* approach, which calls for a balance between two extremes, and undertake the assignment but execute it in such a way that it doesn't cross your threshold of "discomfort." You could, for example, organize the "citizens' group" but also disclose its sponsor.

"Hold everything! The P.R. department just sent over this chart."

Public Relations Ethics

This *New Yorker* cartoon, although humorous, gives the impression that the purpose of public relations is to twist the facts. In reality, the moral imperative for public relations professionals is to tell the truth.

A third philosophical path is the *utilitarian* approach advocated by John Stewart Mill. He believed that the end could justify the means as long as the result caused the least harm or the most good. The most good, for example, is that you have a job. The extreme of the *utilitarian* approach is Hill & Knowlton's highly questionable campaign for the Citizens for a Free Kuwait in the 1990s. An H&K executive told his staff, "We'd represent Satan, if he paid."

The Ethical Advocate

Another consideration of students, as well as public relations critics, is whether a public relations practitioner can ethically communicate at the same time he or she is serving as an advocate for a particular client or organization. To some, traditional ethics prohibits a person from taking an advocacy role because that person is then "biased" and trying to "manipulate" people.

David L. Martinson of Florida International University makes the point, however, that the concept of role differentiation is important. This means that society, in general, expects public relations people to be advocates, just as society expects advertising copywriters to make a product sound attractive, journalists to be objective, and attorneys to defend someone in court. Because of this concept, Martinson believes that "Public relations practitioners are justified in disseminating persuasive information so long as objective and reasonable persons would view those persuasive efforts as truthful." He continues, in a monograph published by the public relations division of the Association for Education in Journalism and Mass Communications:

> We are advocates of what we believe to be the truth and not merely blind advocates for our organizations. We need to take all of this very seriously and on a very personal level.
>
> *W. D. (Bill) Nielsen, former VP of public affairs for Johnson & Johnson, speaking at the 44th annual lecture of the Institute for Public Relations*

Reasonable persons recognize that public relations practitioners can serve important societal goals in an advocacy (role defined) capacity. What reasonable persons require, however, is that such advocacy efforts be directed toward genuinely informing impacted publics. Communication efforts . . . will not attempt, for example, to present false/deceptive/misleading information under the guise of literal truth no matter how strongly the practitioner wants to convince others of the merits of a particular client/organization's position/cause. . . . Role differentiation is not a license to "lie, cheat, and/or steal" on behalf of clients whether one is an attorney, physician, or public relations practitioner.

The Role of Professional Organizations

Professional organizations have done much to develop the standards of ethical, professional public relations practice and to help society understand the role of public relations. A primary objective has been the development of professionals through continuing education in terms of publications, conferences, short courses, seminars, and speakers at local, regional, and national meetings. Although such organizations represent only a small percentage of the total number of individuals working in public relations, they set the ethical standards for, and foster professionalism among, public relations practitioners. The following sections give a thumbnail sketch of the largest professional groups serving the public relations profession.

The Public Relations Society of America (PRSA)

The largest national public relations organization in the world is the Public Relations Society of America (PRSA); the group's website can be found at www.prsa.org. PRSA is headquartered in New York City. It has almost 22,000 members organized into 110 chapters nationwide. It also has 20 professional interest sections that represent such areas as employee communications, counseling firms, entertainment and sports, food and beverages, multicultural communications, public affairs and government, nonprofit organizations, travel and tourism, and even public relations educators.

A fourth of PRSA members work in a corporate environment. Another 20 percent work for a public relations firm, and 17 percent work for nonprofits and associations. See Figure 3.1 on page 71. The top four responsibilities in rank order for PRSA members are (1) media relations, (2) writer/editor, (3) marketing communications, and (4) corporate communications. In terms of gender, 70 percent of PRSA's membership is now female.

PRSA has an extensive professional development program that offers short courses, seminars, teleconferences, and webcasts throughout the year. Some typical topics from a recent listing of online seminars available to members included social media strategies, reaching audiences via mobile devices, tapping the online video boom, search engine optimization tactics, crisis management, and starting word-of-mouth movements.

In addition to workshops and seminars, PRSA holds an annual meeting and publishes two major periodicals. *Public Relations Tactics* is a monthly tabloid of current news and professional tips. *The Strategist* is a quarterly magazine that contains in-depth articles about the profession and issues touching on contemporary public relations practice. The organization also sponsors the Silver Anvil and Bronze Anvil awards, which recognize outstanding public relations campaigns. The Silver Anvil awards, started 60-plus years ago, have honored more than 1,000 organizations for excellence in planning and implementation. In 2010, for example, there were more than 800 entries vying for top honors in 60 categories. The Bronze Anvils recognize outstanding examples of tactical communication vehicles such as media kits, newsletters, video news releases, and satellite media tours. A number of these award-winning campaigns and materials are included in this book.

PRSSA. PRSA is also the parent organization of the Public Relations Student Society of America (PRSSA),

PRSA's Publication

The Strategist and *Tactics* magazines are published by the Public Relations Society of America (PRSA) as one way of providing professional development for its members.

whose website can be found at www.prssa.org. This group celebrated its 40th anniversary in 2007 and is the world's largest preprofessional public relations organization, having 300 campus chapters (including one in Argentina) with almost 10,000 student members.

The student group, which has its own national officers, serves its members at the local chapter level through a variety of campus programs and maintains a close working relationship with the local sponsoring PRSA chapter. It has a national publication, *Forum*, and sponsors a national case study competition so that students have the opportunity to exercise the analytical skills and mature judgment required for public relations problem solving. The organization awards a number of scholarships, holds regional and national conventions, and actively promotes mentoring between students and professionals in the field. PRSSA members, after graduation, are eligible to become associate members of PRSA.

The International Association of Business Communicators (IABC)

The second largest organization is the International Association of Business Communicators (IABC). The group's website can be accessed at www.iabc.com. It has almost 16,000 members in 80 nations and about 100 chapters around the world, but about 90 percent of the membership is from the United States and Canada. The Toronto chapter is the largest, with more than 1,600 members; the three largest chapters outside North America are in Australia, the United Kingdom (UK), and South Africa. According to an IABC profile of members, 40 percent of the membership work in a corporate environment, 16 percent work for a public relations firm, and another 11 percent work in the nonprofit sector. The top four responsibilities for IABC members in rank order are (1) corporate communications, (2) employee communications, (3) marketing communications, and (4) media relations. In terms of gender, 75 percent of IABC's membership is now female.

IABC, headquartered in San Francisco, has similar objectives as the PRSA. Its mission is to "provide lifelong learning opportunities that give IABC members the tools and information to be the best in their chosen disciplines." It does this through sponsoring year-round workshops, publishing books and reports, and holding an annual meeting. The organization also has an awards program, the Gold Quill, that honors excellence in business communication. More than 1,000 entries are received every year from several dozen nations, and about 100 are selected to receive top awards for excellence. The IABC publication is *Communication World*; it features professional tips and in-depth articles on current issues. IABC also has the monthly *CW Bulletin*, which is e-mailed to members. IABC also sponsors 35 chapters on various campuses, with a combined membership of about 900 students.

The International Public Relations Association (IPRA)

A third organization, one that's thoroughly global in scope, is the International Public Relations Association (IPRA), which is based in London. The group's website is at www.ipra.org. IPRA has about 1,000 members in about 80 nations. Its membership is primarily senior-level public relations executives, and its mission is "to provide intellectual leadership in the practice of international public relations by making available to our members the services and information that will help them to meet their professional responsibilities and to succeed in their careers."

The international orientation of IPRA makes it somewhat different from national groups. It bases its code of ethics on the charter of the United Nations. The first point of its 13-point code states that members shall endeavor "to contribute to the achievement of the moral and cultural conditions enabling human beings to reach their full stature and enjoy the rights to each they are entitled under the 'Universal Declaration of Human Rights.'" In terms of dealing with misinformation, IPRA states that members shall refrain from "Circulating information which is not based on established and ascertainable facts."

IPRA organizes regional and international conferences to discuss issues in global public relations, but it also reaches its widespread membership through its website and *Frontline*, its major online publication. In addition, it issues Gold Papers on public relations practice and conducts an annual Golden World Awards competition to honor outstanding public relations programs and campaigns around the world. In 2009, IPRA received almost 350 entries from 42 nations. The organization continues its media transparency campaign to encourage media in various nations not to accept bribes in exchange for news coverage. See the Multicultural box on page 87.

Communications World
IABC's flagship publication

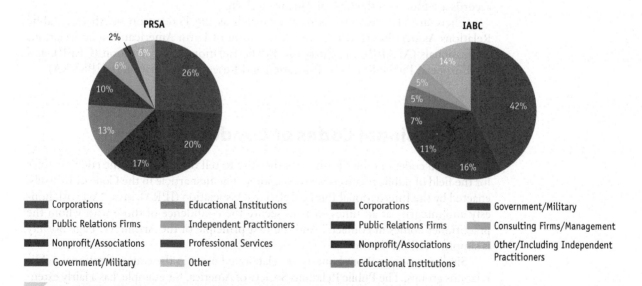

Figure 3.1 Employment Categories of PRSA and IABC Members

Other Groups

The PRSA, IABC, and IPRA are the largest broad-based membership organizations for communicators and public relations professionals. In addition, there are more specialized organizations in the United States. They include:

- Council for the Advancement and Support of Education (CASE), www.case.org (3,200 colleges and universities)
- National Investor Relations Institute (NIRI), www.niri.org (4,000 members in the financial industry)
- National School Public Relations Association (NSPRA), www.nspra.org (school communicators, K–12)
- National Black Public Relations Society (NBPRS), www.nbprs.org (about 1,000 members)
- Hispanic Public Relations Society (HPRA), www.hpra.org (network of Hispanic communicators)
- The Arthur W. Page Society, www.awpagesociety.com (senior-level communication executives in major corporations and public relations firms)
- Council of Public Relations Firms, www.prfirms.org (association of 100 public relations firms)

On an international level, there is the Global Alliance for Public Relations and Communication Management (www.globalalliancepr.org), which is an umbrella group of more than 70 national organizations representing more than 160,000 professionals around the world. The group's mission is to (1) unify the profession on a global basis, (2) raise professional standards, and (3) "to work in the public interest for the benefit of the profession." In June 2010, for example, alliance representatives approved *The Stockholm Accords* that further outlined the responsibilities of public relations professionals in such areas as environmental sustainability, organizational governance, management, internal communications, and external communications. The full text of the accords are found on the Global Alliance website.

There are also regional associations such as the Federation of African Public Relations Association (FAPRA), the Association of Latin American Public Relations Professionals (ALARP), the European Public Relations Confederation (CEPR), and the European Public Relations Education and Research Association (EUPRERA).

Professional Codes of Conduct

Virtually all codes of ethics begin with the duty to tell the truth, and the code of ethics for the field of public relations is no exception. The first article in the Code of Brussels, enacted by the International Public Relations Association (IPRA), says, "Act with honesty and integrity at all times so as to secure the confidence of those with whom the practitioner comes in contact." And the first principle of the Arthur W. Page Society is simply, "Tell the Truth."

Similar concepts about honesty are elaborated upon in the codes of national public relations groups. The Public Relations Society of America, for example, has a fairly extensive code of conduct that is summarized on page 73. In addition, the organization issues interpretations of its code when new situations arise. The PRSA code, for example, was

on the job
INSIGHTS

PRSA's Code of Ethics: Guidelines for Professional Practice

The Public Relations Society of America (PRSA) has a fairly comprehensive code of ethics for its members. The group believes that "professional values are vital to the integrity of the profession as a whole." Its six core values are as follows:

- Advocacy. Serving the public interest by acting as responsible advocates for clients or employers.

- Honesty. Adhering to the highest standards of accuracy and truth in advancing the interests of clients and employers.

- Expertise. Advancing the profession through continued professional development, research, and education.

- Independence. Providing objective counsel and being accountable for individual actions.

- Loyalty. Being faithful to clients and employers, but also honoring an obligation to serve the public interest.

- Fairness. Respecting all opinions and supporting the right of free expression.

The following is a summary of the major provisions and the kinds of activities that would constitute improper conduct.

Free Flow of Information

The free flow of accurate and truthful information is essential to serving the public interest in a democratic society. You should not bribe a journalist with an expensive gift so that he or she will write favorable stories about the organization or its products/services. Lavish entertainment and travel junkets for government officials, beyond the limits set by law, also are improper.

Competition

Healthy and fair competition among professionals should take place within an ethical framework. An employee of an organization should not share information with a public relations firm that is in competition with other firms for the organization's business. You should not disparage your competition or spread malicious rumors about them to recruit business or hire away their employees.

Disclosure of Information

Open communication is essential to informed decision making in a democratic society. You should not conduct grassroots and letter-writing campaigns on behalf of undisclosed interest groups. In addition, you should not deceive the public by employing people to pose as "volunteers" at a public meeting. This also applies to booking "spokespersons" on talk shows without disclosing that an organization or special interest is paying them to appear. Intentionally leaving out essential information or giving a false impression of a company's financial performance is considered "lying by omission." If you discover that inaccurate information has been given out, you have a responsibility to correct it immediately.

Safeguarding Confidences

Earning a client's trust results from appropriate protection of confidential information. You should not leak proprietary information that could adversely affect some other party. If you change jobs, you should not use confidential information from your previous employer to benefit the competitive advantage of your new employer.

Conflicts of Interest

Avoid real, potential, or perceived conflicts of interest among clients, employers, and the public. A public relations firm should inform a prospective client that it already represents a competitor or has a conflicting interest. For example, a firm should not handle public relations for two competing fast-food restaurant chains.

Enhancing the Profession

Public relations professionals should work constantly to strengthen the public's trust in the profession. You should not say a product is safe when it isn't. If it's unsafe under certain usages or conditions, you have an obligation to disclose this information.

For the complete code, please consult PRSA's website at www.prsa.org.

written before the age of the Internet, so it issued a statement condemning deceptive online practices, saying, "Any attempts to mislead or deceive an uninformed audience are considered malpractice." See the Insights box on page 76.

Most national organizations place heavy emphasis on educating their members about professional standards rather than having a highly structured grievance process in place. They do reserve the right, however, to censure or expel members who violate the organization's code or who are convicted of a crime in a court of law. PRSA, at one time, did have an elaborate judicial process, but in 33 years, only about 10 members were disciplined by the organization.

The IABC's code is based on the principle that professional communication is not only legal and ethical, but also in good taste and sensitive to cultural values and beliefs. Members are encouraged to be truthful, accurate, and fair in all of their communications.

According to IABC, the organization "fosters compliance with its code by engaging in global communication campaigns rather than through negative sanctions." The code is published in several languages, and IABC bylaws require that articles on ethics and professional conduct be published in the organization's monthly publication, *Communication World*. In addition, the organization includes sessions on ethics at its annual meeting, conducts workshops on ethics, and encourages chapters to include discussions of ethics in their local programs. PRSA and other organizations have similar programs.

A more aggressive form of enforcement, however, is conducted by the German Council for Public Relations, which is the umbrella organization for three German public relations associations. It actively investigates complaints about unethical behavior and publicly issues warnings and rebukes to organizations that violate professional standards. The Council, however, evaluates the behavior of organizations only, not the behavior of individuals.

Consequently, critics often complain that codes of ethics "have no teeth" because there's really no punishment for an individual who is unethical and unprofessional. About the only penalty that an organization can impose is to expel a person from the organization; that person can continue to work in public relations.

Problems with code enforcement, however, are not unique to public relations groups. Professional organizations, including the Society for Professional Journalists, are voluntary organizations, and they don't have the legal authority to ban members from the field, because no licensing is required. Such organizations run a high risk of being sued for defamation or restricting the First Amendment guarantee of free speech if they try to publicly censure a member or restrict his or her occupation.

Consequently, most professional groups believe that the primary purpose of establishing codes of ethics is not enforcement, but rather education and information. The Global Alliance strongly endorses professional development and states that members should "actively pursue personal professional development." Thus, all groups seek to enunciate standards of conduct that will guide members in their professional lives. It seems to work. Several studies have shown that the members of PRSA and other organizations have a much higher awareness of ethics and professional standards than do nonmembers.

Codes for Specific Situations

Various organizations, as noted, have established codes for the general practice of public relations, but various groups have also endorsed codes of conduct for specific situations and issues, such as the distribution of financial information, video news releases, Internet transparency, and even corporate practice.

Financial Information. The National Investors Relations Institute (NIRI), for example, has adopted a 12-point code of ethics in the wake of corporate financial scandals such as Enron, WorldCom, and Tyco. NIRI (www.niri.org) requires all its members to affirm the code in writing. The code holds members responsible for such things as (1) exercising independent professional judgment, (2) keeping track of financial laws and regulations, and (3) ensuring full and fair disclosure. Members who violate the law or SEC regulations are expelled from the organization.

Video News Releases Controversy about the use of video news releases (VNRs) by television stations and whether the viewing public has been informed about the source of information also has prompted greater attention to ethical behavior by the stations and the public relations industry that produces VNRs for any number of clients. On one hand, television stations are faulted for not telling viewers the source of video footage that is often used in newscasts. In fact, the Center for Media and Democracy found that 77 stations had aired VNRs without disclosing their sources. An earlier survey by *TV Guide* found that almost half of television station news directors failed to identify the source of VNRs on their news programs. *TV Guide*, as well as activist groups, has labeled VNRs "fake news."

On the other hand, producers of VNRs have been criticized for not properly identifying the sponsor (or client) of the material. One technique, for example, has been to have an actor pose as a newsperson on the VNR and simply say, "This is Jane Doe, reporting from Washington." VNR producers, however, say VNRs are clearly identified in the packaging and in advisories to television news editors.

The VNR controversy got the attention of the Federal Communications Commission (FCC), which began to investigate whether TV stations had violated its guidelines about disclosure of third-party information and sponsorship of material used in newscasts. This, in turn, prompted VNR producers to organize a National Association of Broadcast Communicators (NABC) (www.broadcastcommunicators.org) to promote ethical standards. The guidelines endorsed by the NABC include:

- Information contained in a VNR must be accurate and reliable. Intentionally false and misleading information must be avoided.

- A video news release must be identified as such, both on the video's opening slate and on any advisory material and scripts.

- The sponsor of the release must be clearly identified on the tape. The name and phone number of the sponsor must be provided on the video for journalists to contact for further information.

- Persons interviewed on the VNR must be accurately identified by name, title, and affiliation in the video.

Internet Transparency Should public relations personnel covertly build a buzz for their client's or employer's products in online postings without revealing that they are being paid to praise the product?

This question was raised by Richard Edelman, president and CEO of Edelman Worldwide, when he found out some of his staff was doing just that. "They were going in on an unattributed basis and saying, 'Well, the Game Cube—or whatever—is the world's greatest thing,' and, meanwhile, not revealing that 'Hi, I work for Nintendo,'" Edelman told *PRWeek*. He concluded, "No, we can't do that. It's wrong, and it ruins our credibility."

Because of such practices, the Arthur W. Page Society, an organization of senior-level communication executives, and 10 other major public relations organizations called for truth and accuracy in all Web content. See the Insights box below for Web and social media guidelines.

Corporate Practice   Many public relations firms and companies also have established codes of conduct and regularly schedule training sessions for their employees. CarryOn Communications in Los Angeles, for example, uses case studies that ask staff to evaluate ethically compromising situations and practice resolving the situation.

Ketchum tells its employees, as do many other firms, "We will deal with clients in a fair and businesslike fashion, providing unbiased, professional recommendations to move their business ahead." Ketchum's code deals with (1) truth and accuracy in communications, (2) how to handle confidential information, (3) what gifts and entertainment are acceptable and not acceptable, (4) fair dealings with suppliers and vendors, (5) safeguarding of client proprietary information, and (6) abuse of "inside" information.

on the job
INSIGHTS

Ethical Guidelines for the Web and Social Media

Public relations personnel are constantly using the Web and social networks to communicate information about their employers and clients, but they should do so within an ethical framework. The Public Relations Society of America (PRSA), for example, categorically states " . . . that misrepresenting the nature of editorial content or intentionally failing to clearly reveal the source of message contents is unethical." The following, compiled from other professional groups, elaborates on PRSA's key point about disclosure and honesty:

- The source of any material must be clearly identified. Any attempt to mislead or deceive the blogger or the intended audience is considered unethical.

- You must identify yourself and your connection to any employer or client in any postings in which you are promoting and publicizing a product or service.

- You must disclose your affiliation with a client or employer in any chat room postings, particularly if the affiliation is relevant to the topic or the conversation. If you want to make a personal comment about your client or employer's products or policies, you need to say something such as, "This is my personal opinion and doesn't necessarily reflect the policies or positions of my employer."

- It's considered unethical to offer cash or "gifts" to bloggers in return for posting favorable reviews concerning a product or service. Under new FTC guidelines, both you and the blogger are liable if any payments, free

products, or gifts are not disclosed in the posting.

- The owners of blogs, Facebook pages, and Twitter accounts must be clearly identified and disclosed. In other words, you can't use your name to establish a fake blog to promote a product or cause when the actual source/owner is the client or employer.

- Respect copyrights, trademarks, and fair use guidelines if you post material from other sources.

- Respect your audience. Don't use ethnic slurs, personal insults, or obscenity, or engage in any conduct that is not acceptable in the workplace.

- Try to add value. Provide worthwhile information and perspectives.

Of course, it is one thing to have a code of conduct in the employee handbook and another to actually practice what is being preached. Public relations executives have the responsibility to ensure that ethics becomes an integral part of the "corporate culture" and also that ethical considerations are part of senior management's policy decisions and how the organization responds to various situations. See the Insights box below.

On the job

INSIGHTS

Your Job: Ethics Counselor to Senior Management

The traditional role of a public relations manager is to build relationships and trust in an organization, but an equally important role is to counsel management about incorporating ethics and the organization's core values into every decision. Professor Shannon Bowen of the University of Maryland, in a monograph published by the Institute for Public Relations Research (IPR), gives some guidelines on how to become an ethics counselor to management:

Learn about Ethics

- Take courses in ethics while in college to build a framework for decision making.
- Once on the job, learn about the value systems of the organization.
- Incorporate those values into planning public relations activities for the organization.

Know Your Own Values

- Assess your own values and what is most important to you.

- Determine if your values match the values espoused by your client or employer.
- If they match, you have a solid foundation on which to build a professional career.
- If they don't match, you should find an organization more supportive of your values.

Spot Ethical Issues

- Be an early warning system in terms of identifying issues that pose ethical dilemmas for the organization.
- Early identification allows the organization to avoid loss of reputation and to take a proactive stance in managing an issue.

Identify and Shape the Organization's Core Values

- Identify what values are expressed in the organization's mission statement,

code of ethics, and other policies.
- Actively educate all employees about the organization's values.
- Encourage an atmosphere of open discussion about ethical issues.

Educate Management

- A public relations manager should provide ethical advisement to management using the concepts of issues management, research, and conflict resolution.

. . . the public relations function is ideally informed to counsel top management about ethical issues.

Shannon Bowen, University of Maryland

(continued)

- Management often doesn't realize the many ways that public relations can contribute to solving and preventing ethical problems, so public relations managers must continually educate management about such capabilities.

- Being accepted as an ethics counselor will give the public relations function more power and status in the organization.

Bowen concludes:

Although it is true that no single person or function can be the entire "conscience" of an organization, the public relations function is ideally informed to counsel top management about ethical issues. Public relations professionals know the values of key publics involved with ethical dilemmas, and can conduct rigorous ethical analysis to guide the policies of their organizations, as well as in

communications with publics and the news media. Careful and consistent ethical analyses facilitate trust, which enhances the building and maintenance of relationships—after all, that is the ultimate purpose of the public relations function.

Source: S. A. Bowen. (2010) Ethics and public relations. Retrieved from Institute for Public Relations website: www.instituteforpr.org

Other Steps Toward Professionalism

So what is a profession? C. V. Narasimha Reddi, an elder statesman of public relations in India and editor/publisher of *Public Relations Voice*, says there are five prerequisites for a profession like public relations. They are:

- **Education.** A body of knowledge for learning skills
- **Training.** Instruction, continuing education to improve and update skills
- **Literature.** Textbooks, case studies, reference books, and academic journals
- **Research.** Evaluation and measurement of programs and campaigns
- **Code of Ethics.** Standards that generate trust and credibility

Professor Reddi's prerequisites, for the most part, have been achieved in the public relations field, and some of his concepts have already been discussed, such as organizations having codes of conduct. The making of a profession, however, is an evolutionary process that includes a number of steps. They include (1) changing the mindset of many practitioners in the field who have no formal training in public relations, (2) establishing public relations as an academic discipline, (3) expanding the body of knowledge, (4) promoting certification and accreditation of practitioners, and (5) even moving toward required continuing education for members of professional organizations. The following sections outline what progress has been made.

Changing Practitioner Mindsets

Among public relations practitioners, there remains differences of opinion about whether public relations is a craft, a skill, or a developing profession. Certainly, at its present level, public relations does not qualify as a profession in the same sense that medicine and law do. Public relations does not have prescribed standards of educational preparation, a mandatory period of apprenticeship, or even state laws that govern admission to the profession.

Adding to the confusion about professionalism is the difficulty of ascertaining what constitutes public relations practice. John F. Budd Jr., a veteran counselor, wrote in *Public Relations Quarterly*: "We act as publicists, yet we talk of counseling. We perform as technologists in communication, but we aspire to be decision-makers dealing in policy." The debate whether public relations is a profession no doubt will continue for some time. But, for many who aspire to be true professionals, the most important principle is for the individual to act like a professional. This means that a practitioner should have:

> Staffers who feel their ethics aren't compromised by clients or colleagues will more likely succeed and do their best work.
>
> *Ted McKenna, reporter for* PRWeek

- A sense of independence.
- A sense of responsibility to society and the public interest.
- Manifest concern for the competence and honor of the profession as a whole.
- A higher loyalty to the standards of the profession and fellow professionals than to the employer of the moment.

Unfortunately, a major barrier to professionalism is the mindset that many practitioners themselves have toward their work. As James Grunig and Todd Hunt state in their text *Managing Public Relations*, many practitioners tend to hold more "careerist" values than professional values. In other words, they place higher importance on job security, prestige in the organization, salary level, and recognition from superiors than on the four values just listed.

On another level, many practitioners are limited in their professionalism by what might be termed a "technician mentality." These people narrowly define professionalism as the ability to do a competent job of executing the mechanics of communicating (preparing news releases, brochures, newsletters, etc.), even if the information provided by management or a client is in bad taste, is misleading, lacks documentation, or is just plain wrong.

Another aspect of the technician mentality is the willingness to represent issues or products that go against one's own beliefs and moral code. One survey on ethical awareness, conducted by Professors Lee Wilkins at the University of Missouri and Renita Coleman at the University of Texas, asked advertising personnel whether they would take a multimillion-dollar beer account even though they were against alcohol consumption. Most of respondents answered yes to this and similar questions, causing advertising to be ranked somewhat near the bottom of the list of occupations in terms of ethical awareness. Public relations personnel, given the same questions, did somewhat better; they ranked sixth on the list of occupations for ethical awareness.

Some practitioners defend the technician mentality, however, arguing that public relations people are like lawyers in the court of public opinion. In their view, everyone is entitled to his or her viewpoint, and whether the public relations person agrees or not, the client or employer has a right to be heard. Thus, a public relations representative is a paid advocate, just as a lawyer is. The only flaw in this argument is that public relations people are not lawyers, nor are they in a court of law where judicial concepts determine the roles of defendant and plaintiff. In addition, lawyers have been known to turn down clients or resign from a case because they doubted the client's story.

In sum, ethics in public relations boils down to deeply troubling questions for the individual practitioner: Will I lie for my employer? Will I deceive to gain information

ETHICS

Hospital Criticized for Taking Abercrombie & Fitch Gift

Hospitals build new facilities by soliciting corporate donations, and Children's Hospital in Columbus, Ohio, is no exception. For example, it renamed the facility Nationwide Children's Hospital after a $50 million donation from Nationwide Insurance.

What caused even more controversy, however, was the hospital's decision to name its new emergency department and trauma center after Abercrombie & Fitch, a local retailer, in exchange for a $10 million donation. A coalition of 15 organizations asked the hospital to reconsider its decision because they believed the naming sent the wrong message.

In a letter to the hospital, the coalition said, "It is troubling that a children's hospital would name its emergency room after a company that routinely relies on highly sexualized marketing to target teens and preteens." The letter continued, "The Abercrombie & Fitch Emergency Center and Trauma Center marries the Abercrombie brand to your reputation. A company with a long history of undermining children's well-being is now linked with healing."

Other critics also weighed in on the decision. Susan Linn, who is associate director at the media center at Judge Baker Children's Center and active in the Campaign for a Commercial-Free Childhood, told the *New York Times* that naming a facility for Abercrombie & Fitch "is more egregious" because of the retailer's reputation as "among the worst corporate predators for 'sexualizing and objectifying children.'" She

continued, "Selling corporate naming rights is a slippery slope, and this is way down the slope."

The president of the hospital foundation didn't answer the critics' concerns, simply telling the *New York Times*, "I like to focus on the philanthropy of it."

The hospital's decision to name one of its facilities after Abercrombie & Fitch raises some ethical questions. First, do you think the hospital violated any ethics in terms of its core values and mission by accepting the gift? Second, do you think the hospital should have considered, before naming the facility, how the retailer markets its products to teenagers? Third, what counsel would you have given to senior management about the ethics of the situation if you were the director of public relations for the hospital?

about another agency's clients? Will I cover up a hazardous condition? Will I issue a news release presenting only half the truth? Will I use the Internet to post anonymous messages promoting a client's product? Will I quit my job rather than cooperate in a questionable activity? In other words, to what extent, if any, will I compromise my personal beliefs?

These and similar questions plague the lives of public relations personnel, although surveys do show that a high number hold such strong personal beliefs and/or work for such highly principled employers that they seldom need to compromise their personal values. If employers make a suggestion that involves questionable ethics, the public relations person often can talk them out of the idea by citing the possible consequences of such an action—adverse media publicity, for example.

"To thine own self be true," advised New York public relations executive Chester Burger at an IABC conference. A fellow panelist, Canadian politician and radio commentator Stephen Lewis, observed: "There is a tremendous jaundice on the part of the public about the way things are communicated. People have elevated superficiality to an art form. Look at the substance of what you have to convey, and the honesty used in conveying it." Richard Levick, a crisis communications consultant in Washington, D.C., has a simple axiom: "If you can't justify it to your mother, don't do it."

Adherence to professional standards of conduct—being truly independent—is the chief measure of a public relations person. Faced with such personal problems as a mortgage to pay and children to educate, practitioners may be strongly tempted to become yes-men (or yes-women) and decline to express their views forcefully to an employer, or to resign. See the PR Casebook on page 82 about the dilemma of being a spokesperson. Yet, Norman Mineta, former Secretary of Transportation and now vice chairman of Hill & Knowlton, is quite blunt: "Yes-people need not apply. As professionals, we must encourage a culture of honesty, integrity, and intellectual curiosity among our peers and employees."

Thus, it can be readily seen that professionalism in public relations really begins with the self-image of the individual as a professional who adheres to a high standard of honesty and integrity in his or her daily work. Although it is important to show loyalty to an employer, practitioners must never allow a client or an employer to rob them of their self-esteem or undermine their reputation.

> You are your reputation. Never go against your beliefs, ethics, or morals. Trust is something that is easy to lose and almost impossible to gain back.
>
> *Jon Harris, SVP of global communications, Sara Lee*

A Standardized Curriculum

Public relations as an academic discipline is an important step toward professionalism. PRSA, IABC, and other organizations such as the National Communication Association (NCA) and the Association for Education in Journalism and Mass Communications (AEJMC) have worked toward professionalism by standardizing the curricula of public relations at the undergraduate and master's degree levels.

One result of this cooperation is the Commission on Public Relations Education (www.commpred.org), which consists of leading educators and practitioners representing a number of professional communication groups. The commission, also mentioned in Chapter 1, has called for more involvement by practitioners in the educational process. It noted, "While the record of broad support for public relations education by professional groups is growing, there is a critical need for similar action by individual practitioners and the firms, companies and organizations. ... "

The commission has also set the standard for coursework in public relations, saying it should comprise 25 to 40 percent of all undergraduate credit hours. Of that coursework, at least half should be clearly identified as public relations courses covering such topics as (1) principles, (2) case studies, (3) research and evaluation, (4) writing and production, (5) planning and management, (6) campaigns, and (7) supervised internships. One measure of success in establishing a standard curriculum is PRSSA's rule that a chapter cannot be established on a university campus unless the institution offers a minimum of five courses in public relations—and there are now more than 300 campuses with chapters.

PRCasebook

The Ethical Dilemma of Being a Spokesperson

One duty of a public relations practitioner is to serve as an organization's official spokesperson. What the practitioner tells the media is not considered his or her personal opinion, but management's response or stance on an issue or situation. Lauren Fernandez, a public relations professional who also blogs about the field, says, "As PR professionals, we represent a client, brand, and organization."

An ethical challenge arises however, when spokespersons are asked to say things on behalf of management that are misleading and even untrue. In such a situation, many practitioners take the approach that they are only the messengers and are not responsible for the accuracy of the message. Other practitioners, however, say that their own values and credibility are on the line as spokespeople and that it's unethical to intentionally distribute false or misleading information.

Steve Jobs: Is a Liver Transplant a "Hormonal Imbalance"?

Apple Computer is an example of the messenger approach. A spokesperson told the media that CEO Steve Jobs was taking a six-month leave of absence to correct a "hormonal imbalance." This was only partially true; Jobs actually took the leave to get a liver transplant in Memphis. In another situation, the spokesperson for large insurance firm AIG was criticized *for trying to justify* the company's decision to spend $300,000 for an executive retreat at a luxury resort barely one week after receiving $85 billion in bail-out funds from the government. One blogger called the spokesperson, "The world's worst PR guy."

Credibility Lapse

At a news conference, Governor Mark Sanford of South Carolina admits to having an affair.

Governor Sanford: A Hike on the Appalachian Trail—to Argentina?

Sometimes, however, media spokespeople do resign when they feel that they have been misled by their client or employer. Joel Sawyer, communications director for South Carolina Governor Mark Sanford, resigned after he lost considerable credibility by telling the media that the governor was hiking on the Appalachian Trail, when, in fact, Sanford was in Argentina having an affair. When reporters asked about reports that the governor was seen boarding a plane at the Atlanta airport, Sawyer flatly denied it. Upon returning after five days, Sanford admitted the affair and apologized to the citizens of South Carolina. The State Ethics Commission, in charging him with ethics violations, noted that Sanford "directed members of his staff in a manner that caused them to deceive and mislead the public."

Governor Paterson of New York: An Inept Cover-Up?

The communications director and the press secretary of New York's Governor David Paterson also resigned after the governor was involved in a scandal in which he used his influence to suppress charges of domestic violence against one of his closest aides. Peter E. Kauffmann, the communications director, announced that he could no longer "in good conscience" continue to serve because he had come to doubt the truthfulness of what Gov. Paterson wanted him to say about the allegations. Several weeks later, press secretary Marissa Shorenstein walked away from her $154,000 job, telling the New York *Daily News*, "Throughout

> Lying makes a problem part of the future; truth makes it part of the past.
>
> *Rick Pitino, college and professional basketball coach, quoted in* Feeding Frenzy: Crisis Management in the Spotlight *by Jon F. Harmon*

my career, I have performed my duties professionally and with integrity basing my actions on what I believe to be true at the time." Her friends told the *Daily News* that she resigned because the governor "duped her into playing a role in covering up the explosive domestic case against another top aide."

The role of spokesperson raises some ethical questions for you to think about. What would you do as a spokesperson if a client or employer gave you information that was false or misleading? Would you justify your actions by saying that you were only the "mouthpiece," or would you quit? Is there anything else between these two extremes you would do?

Expanding Body of Knowledge

Every profession is based on an accumulation of knowledge in the field. Various groups have added to the body of knowledge of public relations through the years by commissioning research studies, monographs, books, and reports. IPRA, for example, has issued a number of "gold papers" over the years on such topics as environmental communications and sustainability, consumerism, and corporate social responsibility. IABC has published a number of books and monographs on such topics as intranets, communication management, and employee communications. These organizations also publish magazines and newsletters, as has been mentioned earlier.

The two major academic journals in public relations are the *Public Relations Review* and the *Journal of Public Relations Research*. Both publications publish a variety of scholarly articles about public relations and communications theory, in-depth analyses of public relations issues and campaigns, and survey research. In addition, the body of knowledge is constantly expanding through trade publications such as *PRWeek*, *Ragan.com*, and *O'Dwyer's PR Report*, *Adweek*, and various newsletters. There are also about 3,000 blogs devoted to public relations, according to Technorati (www.technorati .com), which maintains a virtual catalog of blogs.

Major Centers of Research   The best-known think tank for public relations research is the Institute for Public Relations (IPR), which celebrated its 50th anniversary in 2006. Headquartered at the University of Florida, IPR is an independent, nonprofit organization of educators and practitioners "that builds and documents research-based knowledge in public relations, and makes this knowledge available and useful to practitioners, educators, and their clients." Research papers and other information are available for free on its website (www.instituteforpr. org). In recent years, it has commissioned a number of studies regarding measurement and evaluation in public relations practice. The IPR motto says a lot: "Dedicated to the science beneath the art."

Another research center is the Strategic Public Relations Center at the University of Southern California (USC) Annenberg School for Communication. It conducts an annual survey, among other research, that primarily documents public relations as a management function. Statistics on public relations evaluation methods, departmental budgets, level of staffing, and management reporting relationships are compiled. The center has an online database, PR Management Database (PRMD), that is available free of charge at www.annenberg.usc.edu/sprc.

FOUNDED 1956

Public relations and public affairs are becoming more scientific and professional. It's less a case of who you know. And more a case of what you know.

Sir Martin Sorrell, CEO of WPP communications conglomerate, London

Three other centers of public relations research are worth noting. One is the Arthur W. Page Center (www.pagecenter.comm.psu.edu) at Pennsylvania State University. Its goal is research and study for the advancement of ethics in the field. Since its founding in 2004, the center has awarded almost $300,000 in grants to researchers to examine integrity in communications and to identify best practices in corporate communications. The second center is the Plank Center for Leadership in Public Relations (www.plankcenter.ua.edu) at the University of Alabama. Its primary mission is "to help develop and recognize outstanding leaders and role models in public relations" through research and professional education efforts. For students and practitioners who want to increase their knowledge of international public relations, there is the Center for Global Public Relations (www.egpr.nccc.edu) at the University of North Carolina, Charlotte.

Professional Accreditation

One major step to improve standards and professionalism in public relations around the world has been the establishment of accreditation programs. This means that practitioners voluntarily go through a process in which they are "certified," by a national organization, to be competent, qualified professionals.

PRSA, for example, began its accreditation program a half-century ago. Other national groups, including the IABC, the Canadian Public Relations Society (CPRS), the British Institute of Public Relations (BIPR), the Public Relations Institute of Australia (PRIA), and the Public Relations Institute of Southern Africa (PRISA), to name just a few, also have established accreditation programs.

The IABC Model   The approach used by most national groups is to have written and oral exams and to have candidates submit a portfolio of work samples to a committee of professional peers. IABC, for example, places a major emphasis on the individual's portfolio as part of its ABC (Accredited Business Communicator) certification. The candidate must also have a minimum of five years' experience and pass a four-hour written and oral exam. Only about 6 percent of IABC's members, however, have earned ABC designation.

The PRSA Model   PRSA was the first public relations group in the world to establish an accreditation program, and so it's worth examining in some detail how it works. First, candidates are required to take a preview course (available online), complete a "readiness" questionnaire, and show a portfolio of work to a panel of professional peers before taking the written exam, which is available at test centers throughout the United States.

The 2.5-hour exam tests knowledge of the field and gives proportional weight to various core topics: research, planning, execution, and evaluation of programs (30 percent); ethics and law (15 percent); communication models and theories (15 percent); business literacy (10 percent); management skills (10 percent); crisis communication management (10 percent); media relations (5 percent); information technology (2 percent); history and current issues in public relations (2 percent); and advanced communication skills (1 percent). See Figure 3.2.

Candidates who pass earn the credential "APR" (Accredited in Public Relations). To date, about 20 percent of PRSA's membership have earned APR status. Administration of the APR exam falls under the auspices of the Universal Accreditation Board (UAB), which was created by PRSA in 1998 (www.praccreditation.org). It allows non-PRSA members from other professional groups that have affiliated with UAB to take the accreditation exam.

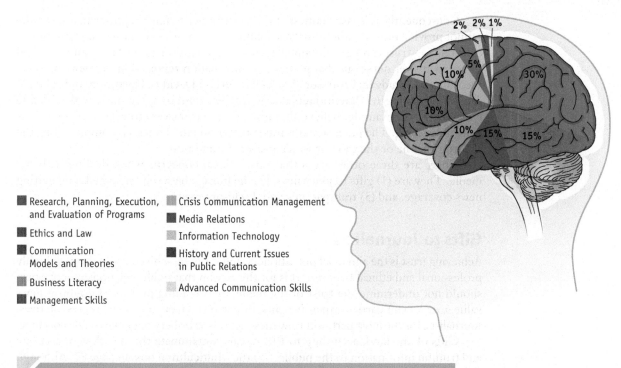

- ■ Research, Planning, Execution, and Evaluation of Programs
- ■ Ethics and Law
- ■ Communication Models and Theories
- ■ Business Literacy
- ■ Management Skills
- ▨ Crisis Communication Management
- ■ Media Relations
- ▨ Information Technology
- ■ History and Current Issues in Public Relations
- ▨ Advanced Communication Skills

Figure 3.2 The Core Areas of Knowledge in PRSA's Accreditation Exam

Required Continuing Education Some groups are beginning to require continuing education as a prerequisite for professional certification. Australia's PRIA, for example, requires its members to maintain Certified Practitioner (CP) status by completing 40 hours of continuing education each year. This, however, is the exception. The vast majority of national groups—including IABC and PRSA—have no continuing education requirements for their accredited members, let alone the rank and file. The failure to establish minimum continuing education requirements for members, quite frankly, gives public relations less status as a profession than other groups that require continuing education, such as dietitians and teachers.

Ethical Dealings with the News Media

The most practical consideration facing a public relations specialist is his or her dealings with the news media. The standard rubric is that he or she must be totally honest to maintain credibility and gain the trust of journalists and editors.

But the axiom "The devil is in the details" also applies. Honesty, for example, doesn't automatically mean that public relations professionals must answer every question that a reporter might ask. They often have to use discretion because of their obligation to represent the best interests of their clients or employers. There may be proprietary information or detailed information about organizational plans that cannot be released for public consumption. There also may be personal information about executives or employees that are protected by privacy laws.

> Our messages are credible only if the media that carry them are credible. If we hurt media credibility, we hurt our own.
>
> *Tim Yost, communications director for ASC, a Detroit automotive manufacturer, in* Public Relations Tactics

Consequently, it is also "honest" for a practitioner to tell a reporter that he or she cannot provide information or make a comment on an issue because of mitigating circumstances. Trust can be maintained even when practitioners say "no comment" and refuse to answer questions that go beyond information reported in the news releases, according to a study by Professors Michael Ryan and David L. Hartinson, published in *Journalism Quarterly*. Practitioners and journalists tend to agree on how they define lying. Both, for example, believe that giving evasive answers to reporters' questions constitutes lying. The practitioner is much better off (and honest) by simply telling the reporter that he or she can't or won't answer the question.

There are three other areas that raise ethical concerns when dealing with the media. They are (1) gifts to journalists, (2) the linkage between buying ads and getting news coverage, and (3) transparency and disclosure issues.

Gifts to Journalists

Achieving trust is the aim of all practitioners, and it can be achieved only through highly professional and ethical behavior. It is for this reason that public relations practitioners should not undermine the trust of the media by providing junkets of doubtful news value, extravagant parties, expensive gifts, or personal favors for media representatives. Journalists, for the most part, will view these actions as bribery to get favorable coverage.

Gifts of any kind, according to PRSA, can contaminate the free flow of accurate and truthful information to the public. See the Multicultural box on page 87. Although the exact words "corrupting the channels of communication" are no longer used in the PRSA code, there are still the same strictures about gifts of products, travel, and services to reporters. There is some blurring of lines, however, when it comes to such items as coffee mugs, T-shirts, or even a bottle of ketchup that is enclosed in media kits as a promotional gimmick. In most cases, such items are of little value and not considered a "gift." Some dailies, however, have a policy of not accepting even such minor items.

More expensive product samples, however, generate more scrutiny. A good example is Microsoft and its public relations firm, Edelman Worldwide, during the launch of the Vista operating system. Edelman chose 90 influential bloggers and asked them whether they wanted to receive an Acer Ferrari laptop loaded with the new Vista software to review. The bloggers were also told that they could return the laptop, donate it, or keep it.

Controversy arose when some bloggers mentioned their new laptops without disclosing that they were gifts from Microsoft. Other bloggers, who didn't get a computer, criticized Microsoft and Edelman for trying to buy favorable reviews of Vista with such an expensive gift. As far as Edelman was concerned, there was no attempt to bribe the recipients; it simply provided a product for review. What raised eyebrows, however, was that the product in question (the Vista software) came encased in an expensive laptop.

In most cases, publicists know it's not "cool" to offer reporters and bloggers gifts in return for coverage, and thus engage in a more indirect approach. DeVries public relations and its client Pantene, for example, were heavily criticized for sending out a survey to journalists, asking them which types of gifts they would prefer to receive, among other questions. Reporters could choose from a gift certificate at an upscale retailer, a certificate for a car service or cleaning service, fashion supplies, and electronics such as an iPod. Stephanie Smirnov, managing director of the beauty practice at DeVries, defended the survey. She told *Jack O'Dwyer's Newsletter*, "We would never put together a program that would ask any of our editor colleagues to compromise their own ethics."

A publicist for the television series *The Good Wife* also earned the ridicule of entertainment bloggers when she sent them a news release with the note "As a thank you for considering the story, I would love to send you a $20 Amazon gift certificate." A fashion retailer also generated considerable criticism when it offered bloggers a chance to be in a lottery for up to $500 in cash if they posted a favorable review. This raises an interesting question for public relations staffers. Is it ethical to offer a gift and then leave it to the journalist to either accept or reject it?

Although gift giving is considered unethical in the United States, other nations have different standards. A survey conducted by Insight and MediaSource, for example, found that two out of five Arabic-language journalists in the Middle East might be more inclined to use a news release if it came with a gift. Another area of ethical concern is paying a reporter's expenses for covering an event or news conference. Although the practice is not done in the United States, it's not uncommon in other nations. In one survey, almost a third of European journalists said they expect public relations people to pay their expenses. The percentage rises to almost 60 percent in Asian nations. The issue of "pay for play" is discussed in the Multicultural box below.

on the job

A MULTICULTURAL WORLD

"Pay for Play" Raises Ethical Concerns

In Russia and Eastern Europe, it's not uncommon for companies and public relations practitioners to pay journalists to get a news release or a product photo published in the news columns of a newspaper or mentioned on a television news program. The Russians call this practice "zakazukha." In the Ukraine, they call it "black propaganda."

A survey by the IPRA also found that "pay for play" is practiced extensively in Africa, the Middle East, and southern Europe. To a much lesser extent, it occurs in Asia, Western Europe, Australia, and the United States.

IPRA and five other global organizations—the International Press Institute, the International Federation of Journalists, Transparency International, the Global Alliance for Public Relations and Communications

Management, and the Institute for Public Relations Research and Education—have joined forces to support a set of principles designed to foster greater transparency between public relations professionals and the media, in an attempt to end bribery for media coverage throughout the world.

The guidelines call for the following:

- News material should appear as a result of the news judgment of journalists and editors, not as a result of any payment in cash or in kind or any other inducements.

- Material involving payment should be clearly identified as advertising, sponsorship, or promotion.

- No journalist or media representative should ever suggest that

news coverage will appear for any reason other than its merit.

- When samples or loans of products or services are necessary for a journalist to render an objective opinion, the length of time should be agreed on in advance and loaned products should be returned.

- The media should institute written policies regarding the receipt of gifts or discounted products and services, and journalists should be required to sign the policy.

PEARSON
mycommunicationlab

Some people might assume that public relations representatives would benefit from being able to influence journalists with gifts, but this is not the case. A major selling point of public relations work is the third-party credibility of reporters and editors. The public trusts journalists to be objective and somewhat impartial in their dissemination of information. If the public loses that trust because they feel the media can be "bought," the information provided by public relations sources also becomes less credible.

Linking Ads with News Coverage

"I don't think it's as blatant as putting cash in an editor's hand," says Mark Hass, chief executive of Manning, Selvage, and Lee, in a *New York Times* interview. He says it's often an implied agreement that the organization will buy advertising in the publication as long as an article or a product review will be part of the package. Indeed, a survey of marketing communication managers by *PRWeek* found that almost 20 percent of the respondents had purchased advertising in return for a news story.

Magazines serving a particular industry, such as home decorating or bridal fashions, often blur the line between news features and advertisements. Tony Silber, who writes about the magazine industry, told *PRWeek*, "If you look at shelter magazines, they are going to have advertisers' products in their decorated spreads of homes." Editors, however, defend the practice, arguing that organizations who receive coverage should also help the publication survive by buying advertising. That may be true, but the question still remains an ethical one for public relations practitioners. At what point does the transaction become "pay for play"?

Publications covering the auto industry can also be an ethical challenge. Some editors and journalists are paid consultants to the auto companies. As a *Wall Street Journal* article commented, "Welcome to the world of automotive enthusiast journalism where the barriers that separate advertisers from journalists are porous enough for paychecks to pass through." There's also considerable suspicion that the Car of the Year on the cover of an auto magazine is the result of an automaker's extensive purchase of advertising space in that magazine. Is this just coincidence, or part of an "understanding"?

Transparency and Disclosure Issues

Is it ethical for a public relations firm, for example, to hire a freelance writer to write favorable stories about its client? The Lewis Group, according to *PRWeek*, paid more than $10,000 to a freelancer to write flattering stories in the local newspaper about its client, Health South's Richard Scrushy, who was on trial for fraud. Again, there is some blurring of lines here. Whose responsibility was it to inform the public that the freelancer was being paid by Health South? Was this the obligation of the public relations firm, or the responsibility of the writer to inform the newspaper's editors or acknowledge payment in her article?

In another situation, Peter Ferrara wrote op-ed articles for various newspapers advocating Social Security privatization without disclosing that he was being paid by a major Washington lobbyist. According to the *AARP Bulletin*, Ferrara didn't think there was anything wrong with taking money from third parties for writing the articles under his own name. The *Manchester (NH) Union-Leader*, however, disagreed. The paper announced it would no longer run Ferrara's columns, commenting, "When a columnist is a paid shill—a trust is broken. A journalist's stock in trade is trust, and our op-ed pages are no place for columnists who have proven untrustworthy."

Transparency and disclosure also are issues in the broadcast industry. Should a spokesperson on a television talk show reveal his or her employer? This question came to the forefront when it was revealed in the press that the Toy Guy (Christopher Byrne), who appears on scores of local and national television shows with his selections of the best and hottest toys for the Christmas season, is actually paid hundreds of thousands of dollars by various toy companies to promote their products.

Paul Holmes, a columnist for *PRWeek*, wrote, "It's hard to read this kind of thing and not conclude that the entire toy industry is corrupt, united in its shared contempt for consumers and by its denial that this kind of sleazy practice is acceptable."

Celebrities appearing on talk shows such as NBC's *Today* show also raise the issue of transparency. Actress Kathleen Turner, for example, told Diane Sawyer on ABC's *Good Morning America* about her battle with rheumatoid arthritis and mentioned that a drug, Enbrel, helped ease the pain. What Turner didn't reveal, and Sawyer didn't tell the audience, was that Turner was being paid to appear by the company that manufactures the drug. After the *New York Times* broke the story, the networks said they would initiate a policy that viewers would be told about a celebrity's ties to a corporation or particular cause.

The blurring of lines in today's media continues to be a major concern for both public relations professionals and journalists. Indeed, a PRSA/Bacon's Inc. survey found that the greatest single challenge facing practitioners is "upholding credibility within an environment where the lines between PR, advertising, and journalism are growing increasingly vague."

> If something as basic as honesty does not appear to be instilled in the fabric of the PR department, I begin to question the entire PR program on down to its products and services.
>
> *Rose Gordon, news editor of* PRWeek

Summary

Understanding Ethics and Values

- Ethics is the study of how we should behave. Values drive our actual behavior in a given situation.

- It is possible to be an advocate and conduct yourself in a manner that is honest, open, and fair.

- Society understands that the advocate is operating within an assigned role, much like a defense lawyer has an assigned role in court.

The Role of Professional Organizations

- Groups such as PRSA, IABC, and IPRA play an important role in setting the standards and ethical behavior of the profession.

- A major mission of professional groups is to provide continuing education to its members and to raise standards in the industry.

Professional Codes of Conduct

- Virtually all professional organizations have published codes of conduct that set standards for professional behavior.

- There also are specialized codes of conduct for such areas as financial relations, production of video news releases, and working with bloggers and social media networks.

Other Steps Toward Professionalism

- An occupation becomes a profession through an evolutionary process that involves many steps including the acceptance of professional standards by practitioners with no formal training in the field.

- Public relations can be considered a profession in several ways. It has a body of knowledge, is now widely accepted as a discipline in colleges and universities, and has academic centers for research.

- Major groups such as IABC and PRSA have certification and accreditation programs in which members take prescribed coursework, submit work portfolios, and pass oral and written exams.

- True public relations professionals have a loyalty to the standards of the profession and the public interest.

Ethical Dealings with the News Media

- Both public relations and journalism groups condemn gift giving to journalists because the practice undermines the media's credibility and the public's trust.

- Other ethical issues that may come up when dealing with the media include gift giving, advertising influencing news coverage, and the lack of disclosure about the affiliation of celebrities on television talk shows.

Case Activity   Ethical Dilemmas in the Workplace

A number of situations can raise ethical questions in the public relations business. Resolving these situations often involve sifting through a number of factors including your philosophical orientation, your personal belief system, and your understanding of professional standards. The following are some situations that may arise in your work.

- Your employer wants you to write a news release about a new energy drink that is being launched. He asks you to mention that the U.S. Olympic Committee likes the product so much that it is planning to provide the drink to all U.S. Olympic athletes. In reality, there has been some contact with U.S. Olympic officials, but there has been no formal endorsement of the product.

- You make a pitch to a trade editor that your company would make a good feature in her magazine because

the company leads the industry in adopting "green" technology in its plants. The editor agrees that this is a good story, but then mentions that this feature would have a better chance of being published if your company also bought a full-page ad.

- Your public relations firm has a luxury resort hotel in Hawaii as a client. Your boss thinks a story about the property would be more appealing and credible to travel editors if you called them and said you are a freelance travel writer offering them an article that you wrote after visiting the hotel and the area.

What ethical concerns are raised by these situations? What would you do in each situation? You might review the PRSA code and review the ethical and professional concepts discussed in this chapter.

Questions   For Review and Discussion

1. Can a public relations person be an advocate for a cause and still be ethical? What is the concept of role differentiation?

2. What role do professional organizations play in setting the standards of public relations practice?

3. Describe, in general, the activities of PRSA, IABC, and IPRA.

4. A number of professional groups have codes of ethics. What are some common characteristics of these codes?

5. What is the controversy about television stations using video news releases (VNRs) provided by public relations sources?

6. What ethical rules apply to Internet public relations and participation in social networking sites?

7. Is public relations a profession? Why or why not?

8. In what ways do the concepts of "careerism" and "technician mentality" undermine the concept of public relations as a profession?

9. What is the accreditation process in public relations? Would you aspire to be accredited? Why or why not?

10. What is a "front" group? Why are they considered unethical?

11. Should public relations personnel give gifts to journalists? Why or why not?

12. What is the concept of "pay for play"? Who's more unethical: the public relations person who offers the cash, or the journalist who accepts it?

13. Should celebrities who appear on television talk shows disclose what company or organization is paying them to appear?

Media Resources

Are current economic conditions affecting the ethical practice of public relations? (2009, September). *Public Relations Tactics,* 15–17.

Bowen, S. A. (2007). Ethics and public relations. Retrieved from Institute for Public Relations website: www.instituteforpr.org

Bustillo, M., & Zimmerman, A. (2009, April 23). Paid to pitch: Product reviews by bloggers draw scrutiny. *Wall Street Journal,* pp. B9, B16.

Coleman, R., & Wilkins, L. (2009). The moral development of public relations practitioners: A comparison with other professions and influences on higher quality ethical reasoning. *Journal of Public Relations Research, 21*(3), 318–340.

DeSouza, A. (2009, April 30). Gifts to reporters? Don't bother. Retrieved from *Ragan PR Daily* website: www.ragan.com

Does social media affect the PR profession and ethics negatively? (2009, September). *Public Relations Tactics,* 18–19.

Gingerich, J. (2009, September). Study finds most PR professionals ethical. *O'Dwyer's PR Report,* 17.

Gower, K. K. (2003). *Legal and ethical restraints on public relations.* Prospect, IL: Waveland Press.

Guiniven, J. (2009, June). If your client is unethical, are you? *Public Relations Tactics,* 6.

Honick, J. J. (2008, June). Ethics, PR and the real world. *O'Dwyer's PR Report,* 33.

Jacobson, L. L. (2009, September). Understanding organizational ethics: How PR professionals can steer a safe course. *Public Relations Tactics,* 21.

O'Brien, T. (2009, Spring). Social networking media present new ethical challenges for public relations. *The Strategist,* 27–29.

Schmelzer, R. (2007, May 28). Accreditation receives high marks from most firms. *PRWeek,* 7.

Weiner, M. (2007, Spring). A trio of tests: Proving value, credibility, and maintaining ethical standards. *The Strategist,* 36–37.

PEARSON mycommunicationlab

The Pearson Public Relations Podcast. "Ethics in PR: Ethical Considerations in PR."

4

Public Relations
Departments
and Firms

After reading this chapter, you will be able to:

Understand the role and functions of a
public relations department

Be more knowledgeable about the
staff function of public relations

Understand the structure of a public
relations firm and its various activities

Know the difference between working
in a department and working in a firm

Public Relations Departments

A department of public relations, now usually called corporate communications or a similar term, has been an integral part of American business and industry for almost 150 years.

In the beginning, the primary objectives of a public relations department were promotion and publicity. American railroads in the 1870s, as explained in Chapter 2, had public relations departments that promoted settlement of the West. Also in the 1870s, department stores such as Wannamaker's in Philadelphia and Macy's in New York used public relations to attract customers. Of course, there is also George Westinghouse, who started a public relations department in 1889 to promote alternating current (AC) and his new company. Henry Ford also recognized the value of a public relations staff in promoting his cars in the early 1900s.

Today, public relations has expanded from its traditional functions and now exercises its influence on the highest levels of management. In a changing environment, and faced with the variety of pressures previously described, executives increasingly see public relations not as publicity and one-way communication, but as a complex and dynamic process of negotiation and compromise with a number of key audiences, which are often called "publics." James Grunig, now professor emeritus of public relations at the University of Maryland, calls the new approach "building good relationships with strategic publics," which requires public relations executives to be "strategic communication managers rather than communication technicians."

Grunig, head of a six-year IABC Foundation research study on *Excellence in Public Relations and Communications Management*, continues:

> When public relations helps that organization build relationships, it saves the organization money by reducing the costs of litigation, regulation, legislation, pressure campaign boycotts, or lost revenue that result from bad relationships with publics—publics that become activist groups when relationships are bad. It also helps the organization make money by cultivating relationships with donors, customers, shareholders and legislators.

The results of an IABC study seem to indicate that chief executive officers (CEOs) consider public relations to be a good investment. Another survey of 200 organizations shows that CEOs give public relations operations a 184 percent return on investment (ROI), a figure just below that of customer service and sales/marketing.

Ideally, professional public relations people assist top management in developing policy and communicating with various groups. Indeed, the IABC study emphasizes that CEOs want communication that is strategic, is based on research, and involves two-way communication with key publics. See the Insights box on page 94 about the attributes that a CEO wants in a chief communications officer.

Corporate Structure Shapes the Public Relations Role

Research indicates, however, that the role of public relations in an organization often depends on the type of organization, the perceptions of top management, and even the capabilities of the public relations executive.

Large and complex organizations, for example, have a greater tendency to include public relations in the policy-making process. Companies such as IBM and Cola-Cola, which operate in a highly competitive environment, are more sensitive to policy issues, public attitudes, and corporate reputation. Consequently, their public relations

on the job

INSIGHTS

So You Want to Make a Six-Figure Salary?

CEOs of major corporations have high expectations for their chief communications officers, who are commonly called vice president (VP) or even senior vice president (SVP) of corporate communications. The Arthur W. Page Society, an elite group of senior communications executives, surveyed CEOs to find out what key attributes they look for in a senior-level communications executive.

Detailed knowledge of the business. Be an expert in communications, but you should also have knowledge of business in general and the details of the company in particular.

Extensive communications background. Experience and extensive relationships are assumed, but you need expertise in what the company needs. A company in a highly regulated industry, for example, puts a premium on government and political experience.

A crystal ball. You need to anticipate how different audiences will react to different events, messages, and channels.

C-Suite credibility. It's crucial to be accepted in what is called the "C-Suite." Experience in actually running a business or a division is one form of earning one's "credentials."

Extensive internal relationships. You need to have your finger on the pulse of the company and know employees at every level of the operation.

Team player. Decisions are made on a collaborative basis. You thus need to have strong relationships with colleagues and the respect of the CEO's inner circle.

Educator. CEOs want you to educate them and the rest of the company on communications skills in general, and how to develop strategies for communicating the company's values.

departments place more emphasis on news conferences, formal contact with the media, writing executive speeches, and counseling management about issues that could potentially affect the bottom line.

In such organizations, which are classified as *mixed organic/mechanical* by management theorists, the authority and power of the public relations department are quite high; public relations is part of what is called the "dominant coalition" and has a great deal of autonomy.

In contrast, a small-scale organization of low complexity that offers a standardized product or service feels few public pressures and little governmental regulatory interest. It thus has scant public relations activity, and staff members perform basic duties such as producing the company newsletter and issuing routine news releases. Public relations in a traditional organization has virtually no input into management decisions and policy formation.

Research also indicates that the type of organization involved may be less significant in predicting the role of its public relations department than are the perceptions and expectations of its top management. In many organizations, top-level management perceives public relations as primarily a journalistic and technical function—media relations and publicity. In large-scale mechanical organizations of low complexity, there is also a tendency to think of public relations as only a support function of the marketing department.

Such perceptions by top management severely limit the role of the public relations department as well as its power to take part in management decision making. In such instances, public relations is relegated to being a tactical function, one of simply preparing messages without input on what should be communicated in those messages. In many cases, however, public relations personnel self-select technician roles because they lack a knowledge base in research, environmental scanning, problem solving, and managing total communications strategies. Research by Professors Elizabeth Toth, Linda Hon, Linda Aldoory, and Larissa Grunig also suggests that many practitioners prefer and choose the technician roles because they are more personally fulfilled by working with tactics than with strategy.

The most admired *Fortune* 500 corporations, in terms of reputation, tend to think of public relations as more of a strategic management tool. A study by the University of Southern California (USC) Annenberg Strategic Public Relations Center (www.annenberg.usc.edu/sprc) and the Council of Public Relations Firms found that these companies, compared to others, dedicate a larger percentage of their gross revenues to public relations activities, extensively use outside public relations firms to supplement their own large staffs, and don't have public relations personnel report to the marketing department.

PRWeek, summarizing the survey, said, "PR Departments that closely align their own goals with their companies' strategic business goals receive greater executive support, have larger budgets, and have a higher perceived contribution to their organizations' success." See the Multicultural World box on page 96 for a case study of a successful program that helped Ford increase its sales in Argentina.

The primary indicator of a department's influence and power, however, is whether the top communications officer has a seat at the management table. To gain and maintain a seat at the management table should be an ongoing goal of public relations practitioners. Experts indicate that it is increasingly common for the top public relations practitioner in an organization to report to the CEO. One survey of 500 senior-level practitioners, conducted by the Annenberg Strategic Public Relations Center, found that 64 percent of all respondents and 77 percent of *Fortune* 500 respondents report to the "C-Suite" (CEO, COO, or chairman). The report adds, "They were much more likely to indicate that their CEOs believe PR contributes to market share, financial success, and sales, than those reporting to other parts of the organization."

Julie O'Neil of Texas Christian University researched the sources influencing corporate public relations practitioners. She reported in a *Public Relations Review* article that having influence in the company is based on four factors: (1) perception of value by top management, (2) practitioners taking on the managerial role, (3) reporting to the CEO, and (4) years of professional experience. In another study, Bruce Berger of the University of Alabama and Bryan Reber of the University of Georgia interviewed public relations professionals and found that the top sources of influence among those practitioners are (1) relationships with others, (2) professional experience, (3) performance record, (4) persuasive skills with top executives, and (5) professional expertise.

Organization of Departments

The executive in charge of a corporate communications department usually has one of three titles: manager, director, or vice president. A vice president of corporate communications may have direct responsibility for the additional activities of advertising

on the job

A MULTICULTURAL WORLD

Ford Brings Theater to Argentina's Countryside

Ford had a problem. Its Ford Ranger had lost market share in Argentina's pickup truck market, and the only thing really "new" in the new model was the front bumpers. The company needed some magic to reverse the sales slump, and that's exactly what it found with the help of JWT, a joint advertising/public relations firm in Buenos Aires.

The creative idea was to tap into Argentina's traditional storytelling culture, which often involves legends and the supernatural. "Amor Galactico," for example, is based on a local legend about the *luz mala* ("bad light"), which appears at night and kills anyone who approaches it. The superstition probably got started from the reflection of animals' bleached bones in the moonlight amid the darkness of Argentina's sweeping plains.

Ford created a website where people could post stories that had been passed down in the oral tradition of the countryside. The idea was that a Ford Ranger is also handed down from one family member to another. More than 1,000 tales were submitted, and a final three were chosen to be transformed into 25-minute plays. The next step was to have a cast perform the plays in various towns around the countryside. Local Ford dealers helped promote the plays, and an average audience of 500 to 800 people watched all three plays in a single performance.

Ford, however, somewhat modernized the legend of "Amor Galactico." In the Ford version, Marcos and Laura are driving their Ford Ranger through the countryside when they spot a *luz mala* on the horizon. They discover that the light is really coming from a UFO, and they see another young couple just like them descend from the spaceship. The four quickly become friends and decide to switch places, with Marcos and Laura returning in the spaceship to an unknown universe. And, of course, Marcos insists that the Ford Ranger go with Laura and him.

The plays were so popular that many local mayors requested that they also be shown in their towns. Ford, sensing a great opportunity to expand its corporate social responsibility (CSR) visibility in Argentina, decided to produce even more plays and expand the number of performances. Ford spokesperson Ricardo Flaminni told *Advertising Age*, "It's a very expensive way of reaching people, more expensive than a TV spot, but it's a high-quality contact we needed to have. And we performed very well, both in top-of-mind and sales."

and marketing communications. Another title, which is promoted by the Arthur W. Page Society, is *chief communications officer* (CCO), to match the common management rubric of CMO (chief marketing officer), CFO (chief financial officer), or even CEO (chief executive officer). The various job levels in public relations are outlined in the Insights box on page 99.

A public relations department usually is divided into specialized sections, each of which has a coordinator or manager. Common sections found in a large corporation are media relations, investor relations, consumer affairs, governmental relations, community relations, marketing communications, and employee communications.

Large, global corporations such as IBM and General Motors have several hundred employees in various areas of corporate and marketing communications, and the IBM organizational chart (Figure 4.1) is a good example of how a large operation is structured.

> They need to be able to anticipate the reactions of governments, private interest groups, shareholders, factions, and so forth, in real time.
>
> *CEO of a large corporation on what he expects in a chief communications officer, in a survey by the Arthur W. Page Society*

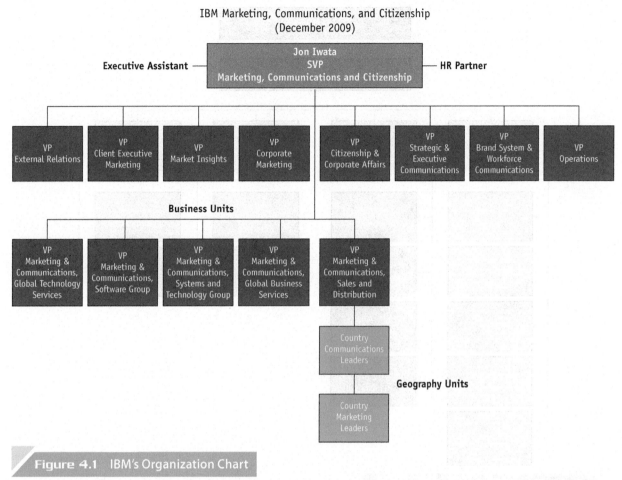

IBM's organization chart shows the integration of global marketing and communications under a senior vice president, Jon Iwata, who is a graduate of the public relations degree program at San Jose State University. There are 13 divisions headed by a vice president.

Corporate communications, under a senior vice president (SVP) of marketing, communications, and citizenship, has 13 vice presidents overseeing such areas as (1) marketing, (2) corporate affairs, (3) executive communications, (4) employee communications, and (5) communications for various business units. See the Insights box on page 100 for a job description for a director of corporate communications.

This example, however, should not mislead you about the size and budget of public relations departments. The USC Annenberg study found that *Fortune* 500 companies typically have 24 professionals in the corporate communications/public relations department. An example is the organization chart shown in Figure 4.2 on page 98 for Advance Micro Devices (AMD), which has 25 employees.

The majority of companies are much smaller in size and have fewer staff in the public relations area. One study of medium-sized U.S. corporations by the Conference Board found that the typical public relations department has nine professionals. Another survey, by PRSA and Bacon's Information, Inc., found that only 13 percent of the respondents work for an organization that has more than 10 employees in public relations. Another 45

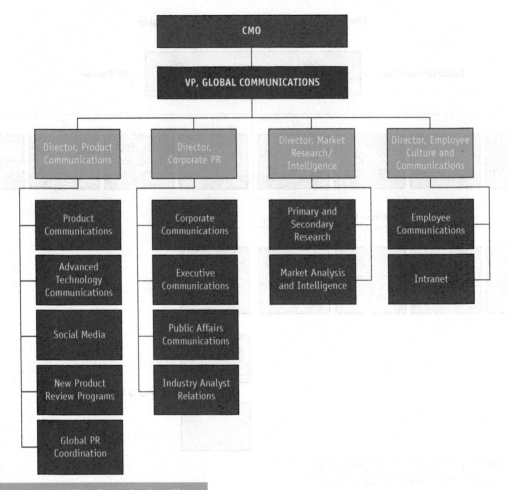

Figure 4.2   AMD's Organization Chart

Advanced Micro Devices (AMD) has a typical organization chart, showing the division of work among about 25 employees. In this chart, the vice president of global communications reports to the organization's chief marketing officer (CMO), which is the case in many high-technology companies.

percent work in a department with two to five employees. Almost a third of the respondents reported that they are the only public relations employee in their organization.

Public relations personnel may also be dispersed throughout an organization in such a manner that an observer has difficulty ascertaining the extent of public relations activity. For example, some personnel may be found in the marketing department working exclusively on product publicity, while others may be assigned to human resources as communication specialists who produce newsletters and announcements posted on the organization's intranet. Decentralization of the public relations function, and the frictions it causes, will be discussed later in this chapter.

Public Relations as a Staff Function

Traditional management theory divides an organization into *line* and *staff* functions. A line manager, such as a vice president of manufacturing, can delegate authority, set

on the job

INSIGHTS

Job Levels in Public Relations

- **Entry-Level Technician.** Uses technical "craft" skills to disseminate information, persuade, gather data, or solicit feedback

- **Supervisor.** Supervises projects, including planning, scheduling, budgeting, organizing, leading, controlling, and problem solving

- **Manager.** Constituency and issue-trend analysis; departmental management, including organizing, budgeting, leading, controlling, evaluating, and problem solving

- **Director.** Constituency and issue-trend analysis; communicating and operational planning at departmental level, including planning, organizing, leading, controlling, evaluating, and problem solving

- **Executive.** Organizational leadership and management skills, including developing the organizational vision, the corporate mission, strategic objectives, annual goals, businesses, broad strategies, policies, and systems

Source: Adapted from Public Relations Society of America. *Public Relations Professional Career Guide.*

---

production goals, hire employees, and make policy. Staff people, in contrast, have little or no direct authority. Instead, they indirectly influence the work of others through suggestions, recommendations, and advice.

According to accepted management theory, public relations is a staff function. Public relations people are experts in communication; line managers, including the chief executive officer, rely on them to use their skills in preparing and processing data, making recommendations, and executing communication programs to meet organizational objectives. Figure 4.3 on page 101 shows the primary functions of a communications department.

For example, public relations staff members may find through a community survey that people have only a vague understanding of what the company manufactures. To improve community comprehension and create greater rapport, the public relations department may recommend to top management that a community open house be held at which product demonstrations, tours, and entertainment would be featured.

Notice that the department can only recommend this action. It would have no direct authority to decide on its own to hold an open house or to order various departments within the company to cooperate. If top management approves the proposal, the department may take responsibility for organizing the event. The CEO, as a line manager, has the authority to direct all departments to cooperate in the activity. Although public relations departments can function only with the approval of top management, there are varying levels of influence that these departments may exert. These levels will be discussed shortly.

on the job
INSIGHTS

Wanted: A Director of Corporate Communications

Public relations managers often have a variety of responsibilities. A good example is this job posting on prnewsonline.com for a director of corporate communications at Wyndham Worldwide Corporation, an international hotel and resort company.

Job Description

The Director of Corporate Communications supports the goals and objectives of the Wyndham Worldwide Communications department as well as the goals and objectives of the organization overall. The individual is responsible for daily external communications operations with the goal of elevating public awareness of the brand, development and execution of a comprehensive media relations strategy, directing and managing messaging strategies. The individual will coordinate external messages with employee messages to ensure a cohesive internal and external messaging strategy. The position reports to the vice president of corporate communications.

Responsibilities Include

Public Relations
- Media outreach for company and programs including Women on Their Way, Wyndham Green, Wishes by Wyndham, and the Wyndham Championship.
- Pitching to consumer media and trades.
- Writing and distribution of press releases.
- Work closely with VP of Communications on crisis communications.
- Script writing for company executives.
- Award nominations and submissions for Fortune, Pink Magazine, Working Mother, etc.
- Work with Investor Relations when appropriate on media outreach and press inquiries.
- Tracking.
- Media tracking and reports on monthly basis.
- Year-end reports including key coverage by month.
- Website tracking and conversions.

Marketing
- Assist with creating and implementing campaigns for WOTW, Green and Wishes by Wyndham.
- Social media outreach and management of company sites where appropriate.
- Policing of branding and logo use.
- Social media task force lead.

- Assist with WOTW Foundation marketing—create and implement strategic plan.

Electronic Communications
- Oversee the company website.
- Manage content of website, recommend enhancements.
- SEO and other techniques to drive traffic to the site.

Job Requirements
- 7–10 years experience in corporate media relations or public relations agency.
- Travel or hospitality experience.
- B.A. degree in public relations, communications, English, journalism or related field.
- Experience in developing and executing strategic media relations plans.
- Excellent verbal and written communication skills.
- Experience with electronic press lists and database programs.
- Excellent computer skills.
- Excellent interpersonal skills.
- Ability to work as part of a team.
- Ability to be a self-starter and resourceful.
- Ability to multi-task and adapt quickly to change.
- Experience managing crisis communications.

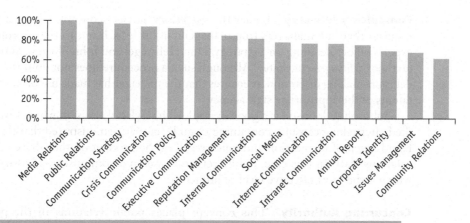

Figure 4.3 The Functions of a Corporate PR/Communications Department

A number of functions are performed by corporate communications departments. The number-one function, according to a 2009 survey by Corporate Communication International, is media relations, with 100 percent of the departments reporting that they perform this function. This chart lists the top 15 functions.

Source: Corporate Communication International. (2009). *2009 Corporate Communication Practices and Trends Survey.* Retrieved from www.corporatecomm.org

Access to Management The power and influence of a public relations department usually result from access to top management, which uses advice and recommendations to formulate policy. That is why public relations, as well as other staff functions, is located high in the organizational chart and is called on by top management to make reports and recommendations on issues affecting the entire company. In today's environment, public acceptance or nonacceptance of a proposed policy is an important factor in decision making—as important as costing and technological ability. This is why the former president of RJR Nabisco, F. Ross Johnson, told the *Wall Street Journal* in an interview that his senior public relations aide was "Numero Uno" and quipped, "He is the only one who has an unlimited budget and exceeds it every year." Being part of executive suite also has its rewards. Citigroup's EVP of global public affairs, according to the *Wall Street Journal*, was hired at an annual salary of $1 million.

> A significant part of our function has to do with strategic communications— altogether too much crisis communications.
>
> *John Buckley, EVP of corporate communications for AOL*

Levels of Influence

Management experts state that staff functions in an organization operate at three levels of influence and authority: advisory, compulsory-advisory, and concurring authority.

Advisory On the lowest level, the staff function may be only *advisory*: Line management has no obligation to take recommendations or even request them. When public relations is purely advisory, it is often ineffective. A good example is the Toyota recall. The auto company generated a great deal of public, legislative, and media criticism because its public relations department was relegated to a low level and was, for all practical purposes, nonexistent in the early stages of the crisis that caused Toyota's reputation for quality to fall off the charts.

Compulsory-Advisory   Under the *compulsory-advisory* concept, organization policy requires that line managers (top management) at least listen to the appropriate staff experts before deciding on a strategy. Don Hellriegel and John Slocum, authors of the textbook *Management*, state: "Although such a procedure does not limit the manager's decision-making discretion, it ensures that the manager has made use of the specialized talents of the appropriate staff agency."

Johnson & Johnson is a good example. The Tylenol crisis, in which seven persons died after taking capsules containing cyanide, clearly demonstrated that the company based much of its reaction and quick recall of the product on the advice of its public relations staff. In this case, public relations was in a compulsory-advisory position, which is the most effective level of influence.

Concurring Authority   This concept places public relations in the position of reviewing and approving all materials and communications with external audiences. For instance, an operating division wishing to publish a brochure or newsletter cannot do so unless the public relations department approves the key messages and design. If differences arise, the parties must agree before work can proceed.

Many firms use this mode to prevent departments and divisions from disseminating materials that do not conform to company graphic standards. In addition, the company must ascertain that its trademarks are used correctly to ensure continued protection. *Concurring authority*, however, may also limit the freedom of the public relations department. Some companies have a policy that all employee magazine articles and external news releases must be reviewed by the legal staff before publication. The material thus cannot be disseminated until legal and public relations personnel have agreed on what will be said.

Cooperation with Other Staff Functions

Ideally, public relations is part of the managerial subsystem and contributes to organizational strategy. Public relations is, say professors James and Larissa Grunig, "the management of communication between an organization and its publics." However, other staff functions also are involved in the communication process with internal and external publics. The four areas that require cooperation to avoid possible friction and turf battles are (1) legal, (2) human resources, (3) advertising, and (4) marketing.

Legal   The legal staff is concerned about the possible effect of any public statement on current or potential litigation. Consequently, lawyers often frustrate public relations personnel by taking the attitude that any public statement can potentially be used against the organization in a lawsuit. Conflicts over what to release, and when, often have a paralyzing effect on decision making, causing the organization to seem unresponsive to public concerns. This is particularly true in a crisis, when the public demands information immediately.

Human Resources   The traditional personnel department has now evolved into the expanded role of "human resources," and there is often confusion over who is responsible for employee communications. Human resources personnel believe they should control the flow of information. Public relations counters that satisfactory external communications cannot be achieved unless effective employee relations are conducted simultaneously. Layoffs, for example, affect not only employees, but also the community and investors.

Advertising   Advertising and public relations departments often collide because they compete for funds to communicate with external audiences. Philosophical differences also arise. Advertising's approach to communications is, "Will it increase sales?" Public relations asks, "Will it make friends?" These differing orientations frequently cause breakdowns in coordination of overall strategy.

Marketing   Marketing, like advertising, tends to think only of customers or potential buyers as key publics, whereas public relations defines publics in a broader way—any group that can have an impact on the operations of the organization. These publics include governmental agencies, environmental groups, neighborhood groups, and a host of other publics that marketing would not consider to be customers.

Logic dictates, however, that an organization needs a coordinated and integrated approach to its communications strategy. The following suggestions may help achieve this goal:

- Representatives of departments should serve together on key committees to exchange information on how various programs can complement each other to achieve overall organizational objectives. If representatives from human resources, public relations, legal, and investor relations present a united front to senior managers, their influence would likely be increased exponentially.

- Collaboration or coalition building among departments with shared interests in communication issues can also help achieve organization-wide business goals.

- Heads of departments should be equals in job title. In this way, the autonomy of one department is not subverted by that of another.

- All department heads should report to the same superior, so that all viewpoints can be considered before an appropriate strategy is formulated.

- Informal, regular contacts with representatives of other departments help dispel mindsets and create understanding and respect for each other's viewpoint.

- Written policies should be established to spell out the responsibilities of each department. Such policies are helpful in settling disputes over which department has authority to communicate with employees or alter a news release.

The Trend Toward Outsourcing

A major trend in business today has been the outsourcing of services, whether they be telecommunications, accounting, customer service, software engineering, or even legal. The trend line is also for more organizations to outsource their communication activities to public relations firms and outside contractors. Indeed, the USC and Council of Public Relations Firms study found that *Fortune* 500 companies now spend 25 percent of their public relations budgets on outside firms. In addition, almost 90 percent of those companies use outside public relations counsel to varying degrees. See the PR Casebook on page 104 about a campaign by SanDisk and its public relations firm.

> We're no longer in silos where marketing does its own thing, and PR does its own thing.
>
> *Kim Plaskett, director of corporate communications for Greyhound*

> We use agencies almost as extensions of our internal staff. We work as partners.
>
> *Paul James, communications manager of Harley-Davidson*

PRCasebook

SanDisk Focuses on Social Media for "Picture Perfect" Campaign

What's the best strategy for introducing a professional-grade flash memory card for cameras? That was the question facing SanDisk as it prepared to launch its Extreme Pro product. The standard news release, accompanied by a photo of the memory card, would be pretty dull.

Instead, SanDisk and its public relations firm, Cohn & Wolfe, decided that the ideal strategy would be to have professional photographers use the Extreme Pro to show its speed and reliability. Seven photographers specializing in fashion, sports, nature, and even weddings were selected to help engage audiences and illustrate the product's use. The strategy was then to post these photos on SanDisk microsites, in traditional media, on blogs, and in various social media channels.

Wendy Sept, director of worldwide retail public relations for SanDisk, told Tanya Lewis of *PRWeek*, "We wanted professional photographers' opinions . . . in their own words about what's important in the card. It puts it in a context and provides a halo for consumers." The following tactics were used:

- An Extreme Pro microsite contained the photographers' profiles and photos. Video profiles were also posted on the company's branded channels, including YouTube, MetaCafe, and Vimeo.

- Six months prior to the product's launch, SanDisk began using Facebook, Flickr, MySpace, Twitter, and Delicious to reach professional and camera enthusiasts with information, including the videos, photos, and tips.

- Bloggers specializing in photography, tech, and new gadget topics were sent information about SanDisk product innovations, such as Extreme Pro.

- Major consumer media, such as leading newspapers and magazines, were given briefings and shown photos taken by the professional photographers. The "show and tell" approach provided good visuals and brought the story to life.

- Chase Jarvis, a prominent outdoor photographer, was engaged to do a series of photos showing the ski jumpers of New Zealand. He wrote about his assignment daily on his blog and revealed on launch day that he had used SanDisk's new product to capture the action.

Outstanding Results

The campaign accomplished the objectives of (1) raising awareness among creative professionals, (2) distinguishing the product from the competition's, and (3) increasing sales. The following were some of the metrics used:

- Almost 50 Extreme Pro cards were sold in the first three weeks after its launch.

- There was a 60 percent increase in home page traffic on launch day.

- The blog of Chase Jarvis drew more than 40,000 views daily while he was in New Zealand.

Promoting a Product

The fast speed of SanDisk's Extreme Pro even allows photographers to get a photo of a boy in mid-air.

- The number of Facebook fans jumped from 370 to 2,270 in a nine-month period.

- Twitter audiences increased from 341 to 1,503 in the same period.

- Print and online audiences exceeded 112 million, with more than 740 stories appearing in such media as the *New York Times*, *Wired*, *Gizmodo*, and *CNET*.

The editors of *PRWeek* praised the campaign, saying, "Connecting with influencers such as respected photographer and blogger Jarvis was wise, as was letting all the photographers speak directly with the audiences. This team did an outstanding job of not only producing quality video and copy, but in circulating it." The editors also noted that the campaign was a good long-term investment for SanDisk in terms of continued visibility and reputation for quality products.

PEARSON
mycommunicationlab

A national survey by *PRWeek* found that companies of all sizes spend more than 40 percent of their public relations budget on the services of outside firms. In high technology, the percentage was even higher—a whopping 66 percent of the corporate budget. In contrast, nonprofits allocate an average of 38 percent of their budget for external public relations services.

The most frequent reason given for outsourcing is to bring expertise and resources to the organization that can't be found internally. A second reason is the need to supplement internal staffs during peak periods of activity. The most frequently outsourced activities, according to a study by Bisbee & Co. and Leone Marketing Research, are, in descending order, (1) writing and communications, (2) media relations, (3) publicity, (4) strategy and planning, and (5) event planning.

Public relations firms, and the services they offer, are discussed next.

Public Relations Firms

American public relations firms have proliferated in proportion to the trend toward outsourcing, which has just been mentioned. The growth of the global economy has also helped. As American companies expanded after World War II into booming domestic and worldwide markets, many corporations felt a need for public relations firms that could provide them with professional expertise in communications at the national and international level.

Executives of public relations firms predict even more growth, as more countries adopt free-market economies and as Internet applications continue to expand.

She votes with her thumbs, and her social network follows her lead. Where does she stand on your issues?

We can get you there.

be there.

www.fleishman.com

FLEISHMAN HILLARD

Public Relations Firm Services
This ad from Fleishman-Hillard focuses on its digital media capabilities.

Services Provided by Firms

Today, public relations firms provide a variety of services:

- **Marketing communications.** This involves promoting products and services through such tools as news releases, feature stories, special events, brochures, and media tours. See the Insights box below about a firm working with Olympic athletes.

- **Executive speech training.** Top executives are coached on public affairs activities, including personal appearances.

- **Research and evaluation.** Scientific surveys are conducted to measure public attitudes and perceptions.

- **Crisis communication.** Management is counseled on what to say and do in an emergency such as an oil spill or a recall of an unsafe product.

on the job

INSIGHTS

Public Relations Firm Steps Up to the Olympic Challenge

What do Winter Olympic medalists Lindsay Vonn, Bode Miller, Evan Lysacek, Julia Mancuso, and Apolo Anton Ohno have in common besides the medals hanging around their necks?

The answer is a Boston-based public relations firm, Fire It Up PR, which represented the athletes on behalf of NBC in terms of engaging viewers and fans of the Vancouver Olympics through telling lifestyle stories and facilitating media interviews. Those video clips, which presented the backgrounds of the athletes in terms of their childhoods, their challenges in life, and even their overcoming personal heartache in terms of a mother's death or serious accidents, were all organized and coordinated by Fire It Up PR.

"What we wanted to do is mine a bit deeper and tell their day-to-day stories, from fashion to their favorite movies, to personal stories, and how they came to be world class athletes," said Fire It Up President Diane McNamara in an interview with *PRNewser*. The public relations firm focused on long-lead media more than a year before the Vancouver Olympics.

During the Winter Olympics, the firm was flooded with media requests for interviews with the athletes. According to McNamara, "It's amazing people are actually calling me [on the night of the opening ceremonies] expecting actually to speak with [U.S. skier] Lindsay Vonn."

According to McNamara, a small firm such as hers succeeded because of determination and being able to craft a good story. She told *PRNewser*, "Large agencies are very top heavy and they have a good rolodex, but most of the good work is done by interns and recent college grads." In

Bode Miller

any case, the effort seemed to have worked. The Winter Games viewership on NBC set a new record.

"Young people today need heroes—that's why I hired a P.R. firm."

- **Media analysis.** Appropriate media, including digital media, are examined for their ability to target specific messages to key audiences.
- **Community relations.** Management is counseled on ways to achieve official and public support for such projects as building or expanding a factory.
- **Events management.** News conferences, anniversary celebrations, rallies, symposiums, and national conferences are planned and conducted.
- **Public affairs.** Materials and testimony are prepared for government hearings and regulatory bodies, and background briefings are prepared.
- **Branding and corporate reputation.** Advice is given on programs to establish a company brand and its reputation for quality.
- **Financial relations.** Management is counseled on ways to avoid takeover by another firm and effectively communicate with stockholders, security analysts, and institutional investors.

Public relations firms also offer specialty areas of service as trend lines are identified. Burson-Marsteller now has a practice specialty in labor to help corporations deal with unions. Earlier, the firm set up a specialty area in environmental communications. Other firms offer specialty services in such areas as litigation public relations, crisis management, technology, and health care. Fleishman-Hillard has even formed an animal care practice group to serve the growing interest in the health of the country's pets. More recently, many public relations firms have added digital and social media as a specialty area of practice.

Increasingly, public relations firms emphasize the counseling aspect of their services, although most of their revenues still come from implementing tactical aspects such as writing news releases and organizing special events or media tours. The transition to counseling is best expressed by Harold Burson, chairman of Burson-Marsteller, who once told an audience, "In the beginning, top management used to say to us, 'Here's the message, deliver it.' Then it became, 'What should we say?' Now, in smart organizations, it's 'What should we do?'"

Because of the counseling function, we use the phrase *public relations firm* instead of *agency* throughout this book. Advertising firms, in contrast, are properly called *agencies* because they serve as agents, buying time or space on behalf of a client.

A good source of information about public relations counseling is the Council of Public Relations Firms, which has about 100 member firms. The group provides information on its website (www.prfirms.org) about trends in the industry and how to select a public relations firm, as well as a variety of other materials. The Council also offers the popular publication *Careers in Public Relations: Opportunities in a Dynamic Industry.*

Global Reach

Public relations firms, large and small, usually are found in metropolitan areas. On an international level, firms and their offices or affiliates are situated in the world's major cities and capitals. Edelman Worldwide, the world's largest independently owned firm, has about 3,200 employees in 51 offices worldwide. Ogilvy PR Worldwide has 1,700 employees in 70 offices around the world. Ketchum, another major international firm, has more than 100 offices and affiliates in 66 nations. Some examples of campaigns conducted in other nations are highlighted in the Insights box below.

on the job

INSIGHTS

American PR Firms Have Clients Around the World

The following are some international campaigns conducted by U.S. firms for various clients:

Ketchum. Worked with the Russian government on a $3.5 million contract to provide services for a variety of activities. This included (1) publicizing Russia's viewpoint regarding its 2008 war with Georgia, (2) strategic counsel for positioning oil giant Gazprom's outreach to Western Europe, (3) organizing the Russian president's trip to the G20 summit in Pittsburgh, and (4) arranging the trip of the Russian ambassador to visit Fort Ross in California, a Russian outpost in the 1800s.

Weber Shandwick. Worked on behalf of client GlaxoSmithKline in Hong Kong to conduct an educational campaign among Asian women about the pharmaceutical company's cervical cancer vaccine, Cervarix. The campaign, which focused on the need to save lives through vaccination, successfully bridged the gap between Asian women's attitudes about cervical health and their awareness of how to prevent cervical cancer. The result was increased vaccination rates, more product sales, and—most important—saved lives.

Edelman Worldwide. Worked with client Microsoft to inform Italian teenagers about how to surf the Web safely to avoid such risks as online pedophilia. The campaign, "SicuramenteWeb" (Safety in the Web), was a multimedia corporate social responsibility (CSR) campaign aimed at promoting Web safety through media relations, school programs, Web campaigns, media partnerships, and viral activities. The campaign reached teenagers, parents, teachers, and law enforcement agencies to successfully raise awareness. At the school level, web-safety training reached 60,000 children and 4,000 teachers in 150 schools. The campaign also positioned Microsoft in Italy as a leader in Internet safety.

Fleishman-Hillard. Coordinated a global program with the World Hepatitis Alliance to raise public

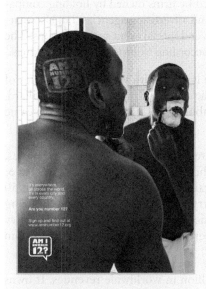
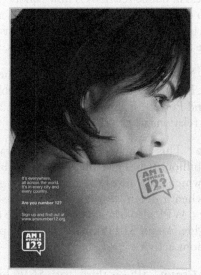

awareness about Hepatitis B and C, which affect 500 million people around the world. The theme of World Hepatitis Day was "Am I Number 12," which referred to the fact that 1 in 12 people worldwide is living with the disease. F-H

helped organize 200 patient groups in 50 nations, conducted 160 events (including rock concerts) around the world, hosted telephone support lines, prepared multiple public service announcements for broadcast outlets, and

set up multiple websites where people could get more information. There were thousands of "hits" from 135 nations, independent YouTube videos posted, and also social media engagement.

International operations are important because most major public relations firms generate substantial revenues from international clients. Edelman, for example, earned $450 million in 2008, but U.S. revenue accounted for only $287 million of the total. Although other large firms such as Burson-Marsteller, Ketchum, and Ogilvy PR Worldwide provide only broad estimates of total revenues, it is estimated that about 50 percent of their revenues come from global operations.

International work isn't only for large firms. Small- and medium-sized firms around the world have also formed working partnerships with each other to serve international client needs. The largest such group is Worldcom, with nearly 100 firms in 42 nations. Other major groups include Iprex, with nearly 60 firms in 25 nations; PROI, with 50 firms in 28 nations; and Pinnacle, with 40 firms in 16 nations.

Essentially, firms in an affiliation cooperate with each other to service clients with international needs. A firm in India, for example, may call its affiliate in Los Angeles to handle the details of news coverage for a visiting trade delegation from India. Bob Oltmanns, when he was head of Iprex, told *PRWeek*, "One of the reasons we started in the first place was to provide clients with a need for reach beyond their own markets with a viable alternative to the large multinational agencies." More information about global public relations is found in Chapter 20.

The Rise of Communication Conglomerates

Today, both public relations firms and advertising agencies have become part of large, diversified holding companies with global reach. In fact, an estimated 60 percent of the global business in public relations is now conducted by firms owned by holding companies that also own not only public relations firms and advertising agencies, but also marketing firms, billboard companies, direct mail firms, and special event specialty shops. The following are the three major holding companies, according to *PRWeek*'s 2009 rankings.

Omnicom   New York–based Omnicom was the largest, with worldwide revenues of $13.4 billion. It owns, for example, three major public relations firms—Fleishman-Hillard, Ketchum, and Porter Novelli. Of that amount, about $1.3 billion (9.5 percent) came from public relations work.

WPP Group   This London-based conglomerate is second in worldwide revenues, with $10.6 billion. It has a stable of major public relations firms, including Hill & Knowlton, which was one of the first firms to gain national visibility, more than 50 years ago, when it defended the tobacco industry against allegations that smoking causes cancer. WPP also owns two giants in the field—Burson-Marsteller and Ogilvy PR Worldwide. About $1 billion, or about 10 percent of global income, came from public relations activity.

Interpublic Group   IPG is third, with $6.96 billion in worldwide revenues. It owns Foote, Cone & Belding (now called DraftFCB) and other advertising agencies, but also six major public relations firms: Weber-Shandwick, Golin/Harris International, Carmichael Lynch Spong, DeVries PR, MWW Group, and Tierney Communications. Public relations work represented about 16 percent of the revenue, or about $1 billion.

Large conglomerates acquire public relations firms for several reasons. One is the natural evolutionary step of integrating various communication disciplines into "total communication networks." Supporters of integration say that no single-function agency or firm is equipped with the personnel or resources to handle complex, often global, integrated marketing functions efficiently for a client. In addition, joint efforts by public relations and advertising professionals can offer prospective clients greater communications impact, help them generate more business, and help them expand the number of their geographical locations around the world. London-based WPP, for example, now employs 69,000 people in more than 100 nations.

Sir Martin Sorrell, chairman of WPP (London), told a *Wall Street Journal* interviewer:

> If you want to upset me, call me an advertising agency. The strategic objective is for two-thirds of our revenue to come from nontraditional advertising in 5 to 10 years. Because of fragmentation, TiVo, and Sky Plus, clients and ourselves have to look at everything. Instead of focusing on network television, we have to look at public relations and radio and outdoor and mobile messaging and satellite. Media planning becomes more important.

Sir Martin also makes the point that one size doesn't fit all when it comes to global communications strategies and campaigns. Campaigns still have to be tailored to local customs, ethnic groups, and religious preferences. Muslims now constitute 26 percent of the world's population and, by 2014, they will be 30 percent. By that same year, two-thirds of the world's population will be Asian.

Structure of a Counseling Firm

A small public relations firm may consist only of the owner (president) and an assistant (vice president), who are supported by an administrative assistant. Larger firms have a more extended hierarchy.

The organization of Ketchum in San Francisco is fairly typical. The president is based in Ketchum's New York office, so the executive vice president is the on-site director in San Francisco. A senior vice president is associate director of operations. Next in line are several vice presidents, who primarily do account supervision or special projects.

An account supervisor is in charge of one major account or several smaller ones. An account executive, who reports to the supervisor, is in direct contact with the client and handles most of the day-to-day activity. At the bottom of the list is the assistant account executive, who does routine maintenance work compiling media lists, gathering information, and writing rough drafts of news releases.

Recent college graduates usually start as assistant account executives. Once they learn the firm's procedures and show ability, promotion to account executive may occur within 6 to 18 months. After two or three years, it is not uncommon for an account executive to become an account supervisor.

Executives at or above the vice presidential level usually are heavily involved in selling their firm's services. In order to prosper, a firm must continually seek new business and sell additional services to current clients. Consequently, the upper management of the firm calls on prospective clients, prepares proposals, and makes new business presentations. In this very competitive field, a firm not adept at selling itself frequently fails. See the Insights box below for a job description for a vice president of a public relations firm.

on the job

INSIGHTS

Wanted: A VP for a Public Relations Firm

A vice president of a public relations firm is similar to that of a director of corporate communications for a company, but the managerial duties are different. A good example is the following job posting for a vice president for health care clients, which was posted by Ketchum, an international public relations firm, on prnewsonline.com:

Job Description

Provide senior-level account planning and supervision for several accounts and/or provide specialized expertise in one or more ser-vice areas. Help set and achieve corporate goals through participation in decision-making and problem-solving processes. Serve as the strategic liaison among client, account team, and agency management.

Responsibilities

- Serve as senior contact for clients, demonstrating in-depth knowledge of clients' business; develop strategy for implementing successful client programs.

- Provide strategic guidance to clients on an ongoing basis; anticipate and address client needs.

- Troubleshoot clients' problems as they arise; seek senior management input whenever appropriate.

- Motivate team members by promptly reviewing work and providing constructive feedback; encourage teams to take advantage of

(continued)

training and development opportunities.

- Help account teams work effectively and in the best interests of clients; maximize agency's network of resources to enhance client services.

- Demonstrate proficiency in writing and editing materials including client media materials, byline articles, client correspondence and reports.

- Exhibit strong communication and presentation skills to effectively articulate ideas to clients, colleagues, and others.

- Take a leadership role in new business proposal development

and presentations; work with account teams to build incremental business.

- Manage account financials including budget allocation and control, time sheets, client billing, supplier invoicing and purchase orders; ensure team billability and account profitability.

- Participate in external company promotion through articles, speeches, presentations, professional memberships, etc.

- Begin to build a leadership role in outside organizations to increase Ketchum's visibility in the marketplace and to create new business opportunities.

Job Requirements

- Bachelor's degree in public relations, communications, journalism, marketing, or a related field. Master's degree in a communications field desirable.

- At least seven years of agency and/or corporate public relations experience.

- Experience in consumer healthcare, ophthalmology, optometric products, or diabetes a plus; experience in launching a new drug/medical device a definite plus.

- Experience in integrated marketing campaigns a definite plus.

- Experience in social media and digital strategy a must.

Firms frequently organize account teams, especially to serve a client whose program is multifaceted. One member of the team, for example, may set up a nationwide media tour in which an organization representative is booked on television talk shows. Another may supervise all materials going to the print media, including news stories, feature articles, background kits, and artwork. A third may concentrate on placements on social networking sites and on contacting influential bloggers.

How Public Relations Firms Get Business

Organizations, even if they have internal public relations staff, often use the services of public relations firms because they need supplemental staffing, help with a special project, or specific expertise in a particular situation. In fact, the Strategic Public Relations Center at the University of Southern California (USC) reports that public and private companies spend about 25 percent of their total public relations budget on the services of public relations firms.

A common approach to engaging the services of a public relations firm is to issue what is called a "Request for Proposal," known as an RFP. Firms are invited to make a presentation regarding their capabilities and express their ideas about what program they would create to address the potential client's particular needs. This is a highly competitive situation, and firms use their most skilled presenters to "sell" their services and ideas.

RFPs can be several pages or, in the case of governmental agencies, 50 to 100 pages. Public relations firms, after analyzing what is requested and the budget allocated, then decide whether to make a presentation or to pass up the opportunity. See the Insights box on page 113 about an RFP issued by the Jamaica Tourist Board.

Pros and Cons of Using a Public Relations Firm

Because public relations is a service industry, a firm's major asset is the quality of its people. Potential clients thinking about hiring a public relations firm usually base their decisions on that fact, according to a survey of *Fortune* 500 corporate vice presidents.

Basic attributes that an organization wants from a firm, according to another survey of 600 clients, are (1) understanding your business and the industry, (2) responding to all your needs and requests in a timely manner, and (3) working within your budget. Clients also give high priority to (1) accurate work, (2) high-quality staff, (3) consistent delivery of key messages to target audiences, (4) outstanding client service, (5) a measurable return on investment, and (6) creative programs that meet business objectives. Both firms and potential clients also consider possible conflicts of interest. A firm, for example, cannot ethically represent two clients that are directly competing with each other. Other concerns can also come up. See the Ethics box on page 114.

Advantages Public relations firms offer several advantages:

- **Objectivity.** The firm can analyze a client's needs or problems from a new perspective and offer fresh insights.
- **A variety of skills and expertise.** The firm has specialists, whether in speech writing, trade magazine placement, investor relations, or identifying influential bloggers.
- **Extensive resources.** The firm has abundant media contacts and works regularly with numerous suppliers of products and services. It has research materials, including data information banks, and experience in similar fields.

on the job

INSIGHTS

Jamaica Looks for a Public Relations Firm

Organizations seeking the services of a public relations firm often screen possible candidates by first requesting a "capabilities" profile. The Jamaica Tourist Board (JTB) began looking for qualified firms by asking for the following information:

- Agency background, size, geographic coverage, billing, agency principals and key personnel, client list.
- Record of experience in tourism and related industries. Prior experience in tourism and destination marketing and

promotion a prerequisite for consideration.

- Brief case histories of successful previous or current work in the tourism category.
- Experience and proven skills in creating, planning and executing promotions and events at the national, regional, and local level.
- Experience with crisis management, whether as a consequence of natural disaster, war, or sociopolitical problems.
- Experience with corporate reputation management.

- Any other specialized skills, resources, or services that differentiate the firm.
- A brief list of clients and media references, including names, titles, and contact information.

JTB, after screening various firms, then issued a Request for Proposal (RFP), in which a firm would propose a specific program to promote Jamaica as a tourist destination.

The process is usually very competitive and firms often spend considerable time and energy to give a presentation that will win the account.

ETHICS

Conflict of Interest Snags CEO of Major PR Firm

The code of conduct for PRSA, as well as other organizations, makes it very clear that public relations counselors should not represent clients who have competing interests. That apparently didn't register with the CEO of Burson-Marsteller, Mark Penn, who lost both of his clients over a conflict-of-interest controversy.

The conflict-of-interest charges came to light in April 2008 when Burson-Marsteller (B-M) had a lucrative, $300,000 annual contract with the government of Colombia to help convince the U.S. Congress to approve a controversial trade agreement between the two nations. Labor unions and human rights groups, however, opposed the agreement.

At the same time, Penn was serving as a major policy advisor in the campaign of Hillary Clinton, who was seeking the democratic presidential nomination. Clinton was campaigning against the trade agreement in the crucial Pennsylvania primary, where many blue-collar workers were concerned that the trade agreement would cost jobs. While this was going on, Penn attended a meeting with Colombia government officials to prepare more strategies for forcing a debate in Congress.

The *Wall Street Journal* broke the story about Penn's apparent conflict of interest, which embarrassed both Clinton and the Colombian government. Penn then issued the statement that meeting with the Colombian ambassador was "an error in judgment," but that only added fuel to the fire. The Colombian government issued a news release saying it was "insulted" by Penn's statement and that it was immediately terminating its contact with B-M. Within 24 hours, Clinton also sacked Penn.

Public relations professionals were surprised that the CEO of a major public relations firm would even try to represent two clients who were in direct opposition of one another. Public relations blogger Michael Tangeman wrote, " . . . for the CEO of Burson-Marsteller to have been engaged in such ethically challenged behavior is a disservice not only to the two clients involved, but to all the public relations professionals who work for the agency with their ethics intact."

Penn, however, remained the head of B-M. What do you think? Did he do a disservice to the employees of the firm? What about to the reputation of public relations?

- **Offices throughout the country.** A national public relations program requires coordination in major cities. Large firms have on-site staffs or affiliate firms in many cities around the world.

- **Special problem-solving skills.** A firm may have extensive experience and a solid reputation in desired areas. For example, Burson-Marsteller is well known for its expertise in crisis communications, health and medical issues, and international coordination of special projects. Hill & Knowlton is known for its expertise in public affairs, and Ketchum is the expert in consumer marketing.

- **Credibility.** A successful public relations firm has a solid reputation for professional, ethical work. If represented by such a firm, a client is likely to get more attention among opinion leaders in mass media, government, and the financial community.

Disadvantages   There are also drawbacks to using public relations firms:

- **Superficial grasp of a client's unique problems.** Although objectivity is gained from an outsider's perspective, there is often a disadvantage if the public relations firm does not thoroughly understand the client's business or needs.

- **Lack of full-time commitment.** A public relations firm has many clients. Therefore, no single client can monopolize its personnel and other resources.

- **Need for prolonged briefing period.** Some companies become frustrated because time and money are needed for a public relations firm to research the organization and make recommendations. Consequently, the actual start of a public relations program may take weeks or months.

- **Resentment by internal staff.** The public relations staff members of a client organization may resent the use of outside counsel, seeing it as an implication that they lack the ability to do the job.

- **Need for strong direction by top management.** High-level executives must take the time to brief outside counsel on the specific objectives sought.

- **Need for full information and confidence.** A client must be willing to share its information, including the skeletons in the closet, with outside counsel.

- **Costs.** Outside counsel is expensive. In many situations, routine public relations work can be handled at lower cost by internal staff.

on the job

INSIGHTS

Your Choice: A Corporation or a PR Firm?

Recent college graduates often ponder the pros and cons of joining a corporate department or going to work for a public relations firm. The following summarizes some of the pluses and minuses:

PR FIRM: BREADTH OF EXPERIENCE	CORPORATE PR: DEPTH OF EXPERIENCE
Jobs as administrative assistant or assistant account executive often considered entry-level for college grads.	Jobs more difficult to find without experience; duties more narrowly focused.
Variety. Usually work with several clients and projects at same time.	Sometimes little variety at entry level.
Possibility of rapid advancement.	Growth sometimes limited unless you are willing to switch employers.
Fast-paced, exciting.	Can be slower-paced.
Seldom see the impact of your work for a client; removed from "action."	Heavy involvement with executive staff; see impact almost instantly. You are an important component in the "big picture."

(continued)

Abilities get honed and polished. (This is where a mentor really helps). High emphasis on tactical skills, production of materials.	Same "client" all the time. Advantage: Get to know organization really well. Disadvantage: Can become boring.
Networking with other professionals leads to better job opportunities.	Sometimes so involved in your work, you don't have time for networking.
Learn other skills, such as how to do presentations and budgets and establish deadlines.	Strength in all areas expected. Not a lot of time for coaching by peers.
Intense daily pressure on billable hours, high productivity. Some firms are real "sweatshops."	Less intense daily pressure; more emphasis on accomplishing longer-term results.
Somewhat high employment turnover.	Less turnover.
Budgets and resources can be limited.	More resources usually available.
Salary traditionally low at entry level.	Salaries tend to be higher.
Insurance, medical benefits can be minimal.	Benefits usually good, sometimes excellent.
Little opportunity for profit sharing, stock options.	More opportunities available.

Fees and Charges

A public relations firm charges for its services in several ways. The three most common methods are:

- **Basic hourly fee, plus out-of-pocket expenses.** This method is commonly used by attorneys, accounting firms, and management consultants. The number of hours spent on a client's account is tabulated each month and billed to the client. Work by personnel is billed at various hourly rates. Out-of-pocket expenses, such as cab fares, car rentals, airline tickets, and meals, are also billed to the client. In a typical $100,000 public relations campaign, about 70 percent of the budget is spent on staff salaries.

- **Retainer fee.** A basic monthly charge billed to the client covers ordinary administrative and overhead expenses for maintaining the account and being "on call" for advice and strategic counseling. Many clients have in-house capabilities for executing communication campaigns but often need the advice of experts during the planning phase. Many retainer fees also specify the number of hours the firm will spend on an account each month. Any additional work is billed at normal hourly rates. Out-of-pocket expenses are usually billed separately.

- **Fixed project fee.** The public relations firm agrees to do a specific project, such as an annual report, a newsletter, or a special event, for a fixed fee. For example, a counseling firm may write and produce a quarterly newsletter for $30,000 annually. The fixed fee is the least popular among public relations firms because it is difficult to predict all work and expenses in advance. Many clients, however, like fixed fees for a specific project because it is easier to budget and there are no "surprises."

The primary basis of the most common methods—the basic hourly fee, the retainer fee, and the fixed project fee—is to estimate the number of hours that a particular project will take to plan, execute, and evaluate. The first method—the basic hourly fee—is the most flexible and most widely used among large firms. It is preferred by public relations people because they are paid for the exact number of hours spent on a project and because it is the only sound way that a fee can be determined intelligently. The retainer fee and the fixed project fee are based on an estimate of how many hours it will take to service a client.

A number of variables are considered when a public relations firm estimates the cost of a program. These may include the size and duration of the project, the geographical locations involved, the number of personnel assigned to the project, and the type of client. A major variable, of course, is billing the use of the firm's personnel to a client at the proper hourly rate.

A senior account executive, for example, may earn $60,000 annually and receive benefits (health insurance, pension plan, etc.) that cost the firm an additional $15,000, for a total of $75,000 in salary and benefits. Using 1,600 billable hours in a year (after deducting vacation time and holidays), the account executive makes about $47 per hour.

The standard industry practice, however, is to bill clients three to five times a person's salary. This multiple allows the firm to pay for such overhead expenses as office space, equipment, insurance, supplies, utilities, and even some potted plants. Of course, the object is to also make a net profit of 10 to 20 percent before taxes. Thus, the billing rate of a senior account executive could easily reach $200+ per hour, which one study by an executive search firm found was about the national average. An SVP of a public relations firm, according to a study by management consulting firm StevensGouldPincus (SGP), has an average billing rate of $287 per hour; a CEO of a public relations firm with over $25 million in revenues charges about $500 per hour.

The primary income of a public relations firm comes from the selling of staff time, but some additional income results from markups on photocopying, travel expenses, and materials provided by vendors such as graphic designers. The standard markup in the trade is between 15 and 20 percent.

▶ Summary

Public Relations Departments

- Most organizations have a public relations department, which is often called *corporate communications*.

- Organizations, depending on their culture and management, structure the public relations function in various ways.

- Public relations professionals often serve at the tactical level, but others are counselors to the top executive and have a major role in policy-making.

- In management theory, public relations is a staff function rather than a line function.

Public Relations Firms

- Public relations firms come in all sizes, are found worldwide, and provide a variety of services.

- Many large, international firms are part of giant communication conglomerates.

- The advantages of using outside firms include versatility and extensive resources.

- Revenues primarily come from charging a basic hourly fee, plus out-of-pocket expenses.

Case Activity   Planning a Career in Public Relations

You will graduate from college in several months and plan on pursuing a career in public relations. After several interviews, you receive two job offers.

One is with a high-technology company that makes inkjet printers and scanners for the consumer market. The corporate communications department has about 20 professionals, and it is customary for beginners to start in employee publications or product publicity. Later, with more experience, you might be assigned to do marketing communications for a product group or work in a specialized area such as investor relations, governmental affairs, or even community relations.

The second job offer is from a local office of a large, national public relations firm. You would begin as an assistant account executive and work on several accounts, including a chain of fast-food restaurants and an insurance company. The jobs pay about the same, but the high-tech company offers a better medical plan. Taking into consideration the pros and cons of working for public relations firms versus corporations, what job would best fit your abilities and preferences? Explain your reasons.

Questions   For Review and Discussion

1. How have the role and function of public relations departments changed in recent years?
2. In what ways do the structure and culture of an organization affect the role and influence of the public relations department?
3. What are the top five activities of a public relations department, according to a survey by CCI?
4. Name and describe the four job levels in public relations.
5. What is the difference between a line function and a staff function? To which function does public relations belong, and why?
6. Why is a compulsory-advisory role within an organization a good role for a public relations department to have?
7. Read the job description for a director of public relations for a corporation (page 100) and the job description for a vice president of a public relations firm (page 111). In what ways are they similar in terms of qualifications and skills required? How are they different?
8. What four areas in an organization have the potential for friction with the public relations department?
9. In your opinion, should public relations or human resources be responsible for employee communications? Why?
10. Name at least seven services that a public relations firm offers clients.
11. What are the three largest communications conglomerates in the world?
12. How important is international business to American public relations firms?
13. What are the pros and cons of using a public relations firm?
14. What are the standard methods used by a public relations firm to charge for its services?

Media Resources

Agency business report 2009. (2009, April 27). *PRWeek,* 1–50.

Are fixed monthly retainers the best billing option for PR agencies? (2009, June). *PRWeek,* 26.

Auletta, K. (2007, February 12). Annals of communications. The fixer: Why New Yorkers call Howard Rubenstein when they've got a problem. Profile of legendary public relations practitioner. *New Yorker.*

Gingerich, J. (2009, June). Global PR networks grow despite worldwide economic challenges. *O'Dwyer's PR Report,* 1, 26–27.

Miller, C. C. (2009, July 5). Spinning the Web: PR in Silicon Valley. *New York Times,* pp. B1, B6.

Moss, D., Newman, A., & DeSanto, B. (2005). What do communication managers do? Defining and refining the core elements of management in a public relations/corporate communications context. *Journalism and Mass Communications Quarterly, 82*(4), 873–890.

Skapinker, M. (2008, April 15). Perils of multi-client public relations agencies. *Financial Times,* 11.

Research

After reading this chapter, you will be able to:

Understand the importance of research in public relations planning

Conduct online and database research

Organize a focus group

Design a scientific survey

Write a survey questionnaire

Determine the best method of reaching respondents

The Importance of Research

Effective public relations is a process, and the essential first step in that process is research. Today, research is widely accepted by public relations professionals as an integral part of the planning, program development, and evaluation process. Beginning with the research phase, effective public relations is a process with four essential steps: (1) research, (2) planning, (3) communication, and (4) measurement.

Research provides the information required to understand the needs of publics and to develop powerful messages. Planning, the process of setting goals and objectives and determining ways to meet them, is referred to as the central function of management. Communication is related to message strategy—making a message more appealing and persuasive to the public. Measurement (or evaluation) is becoming increasingly important in the public relations profession. Executives justifiably demand accountability from public relations practitioners. Measurement techniques provide a means for demonstrating to management that public relations is achieving objectives and contributing in a meaningful way to the organization. This chapter describes the first of these steps—research.

Defining the Research Role

In basic terms, research is a form of careful listening. Broom and Dozier, in their book *Using Research in Public Relations*, say, "Research is the controlled, objective, and systematic gathering of information for the purpose of describing and understanding." Two standards are commonly considered for this listening process: validity and reliability.

Put simply, validity is achieved when research measures what it purports to measure. Reliability is achieved when very similar results are obtained when a study is repeated. For example, we cannot use a thermometer to gauge wind speed because it measures temperature, not wind speed. Similarly, a popularity poll for President Obama should not be used to gauge support for American foreign policy. An expensive thermometer will give consistent and stable measurements of temperature no matter how many times the temperature is read, making it highly reliable. But it is still not a valid measure of wind speed. In the same way, if the popularity poll were to be repeated, the study would be reliable if the results are consistent and stable. But those reliable results do not measure what people think of foreign policy.

> Measure what you claim to measure and do it so well that others can repeat your work.
>
> *A public relations research aphorism*

Determining the Research Role and Scope

Before any public relations program can be undertaken, information must be gathered and data must be collected and interpreted. Only by performing this first step can an organization begin to make policy decisions and map out strategies for effective communication programs. This research often becomes the basis for evaluating the program once it has been completed. The results of an evaluation can lead to greater accountability and credibility with upper management. (See Chapter 8 for details.)

Various types of research can be used to accomplish an organization's objectives and meet its need for information. What type of research to use really depends on the particular subject and situation. As always, time and budget are major considerations, as is the perceived importance of the situation. Consequently, many questions should be asked and answered before formulating a research project:

- What is the problem?
- What kind of information is needed?
- How will the results of the research be used?
- What specific public (or publics) should be researched?
- Should the organization do the research in-house or hire an outside consultant?
- How will the research data be analyzed, reported, or applied?
- How soon will the results be needed?
- How much will the research cost?

The answers to these questions will help the public relations person determine the extent and nature of the research needed. In some cases, informal research may be appropriate because of its low cost or the need for immediate information. In other cases, a random scientific survey may be used, despite its costs and time requirement, because a large retailer such as Wal-Mart or Home Depot wants to know how a community might vote on a referendum to approve the construction of a "big-box" store. The pros and cons of each research method will be discussed later in the chapter.

> Research gives a context in which to talk about the product.
>
> *Lisa Eggerton, SVP and head of consumer practice, RSCG Magnet*

Using Research

Research is a multipronged tool that is involved in virtually every phase of a communications program. In general, studies show that public relations departments spend about 3 to 5 percent of their budget on research. Some experts contend that it should be 10 percent. Public relations professionals use research in the following ways:

- **To achieve credibility with management.** Executives want facts, not guesses and hunches. The inclusion of public relations personnel in an organization's policy- and decision making, according to the findings of IABC's research on excellence in communication management, is strongly correlated with their ability to do research and relate their findings to the organization's objectives.

- **To define audiences and segment publics.** Detailed information about the demographics, lifestyles, characteristics, and consumption patterns of audiences helps to ensure that messages reach the proper audiences. A successful children's immunization information campaign in California was based on State Health Department statistics that showed that past immunization programs had not reached rural children and that Hispanic and Vietnamese children were not being immunized in the same proportion as other ethnic groups.

- **To formulate strategy.** Much money can be spent pursuing the wrong strategies. Officials of the New Hampshire paper industry, given the bad press about logging and waterway pollution, thought a campaign was needed to tell the public what it was doing to reduce pollution. An opinion survey of 800 state residents by a public relations firm, however, indicated that the public was already generally satisfied with the industry's efforts. Consequently, the new strategy focused on reinforcing positive themes such as worker safety, employment, and environmental responsibility.

■ **To test messages.** Research is often used to determine what particular message is most salient with the target audience. According to one focus group study for a campaign to encourage carpooling, the message that resonated the most with commuters was saving time and money, not air quality or environmental concerns. Consequently, the campaign emphasized how many minutes could be cut from an average commute by using carpool lanes and the annual savings in gasoline, insurance, and car maintenance.

■ **To help management keep in touch.** In a mass society, top management is increasingly isolated from the concerns of employees, customers, and other important publics. Research helps bridge the gap by periodically surveying key publics about problems and concerns. This feedback is a "reality check" for top executives and often leads to better policies and communication strategies.

■ **To prevent crises.** An estimated 90 percent of organizational crises are caused by internal operational problems rather than by unexpected natural disasters. Research can often uncover trouble spots and public concerns before they become page-one news. (See the section on issues management in Chapter 10.) Analyzing complaints made to a toll-free number or monitoring Internet chat rooms and blogs can often tip off an organization that it should act before a problem attracts widespread media attention.

We recommend that between 5 and 10% of your budget should be spent on measurement. Doesn't it make sense to spend that much to find out if the other 90–95% isn't doing anything for you?

Katie Paine, CEO of KD Paine and Partners

■ **To monitor the competition.** Savvy organizations keep track of what the competition is doing. Competition monitoring can be done using surveys that ask consumers to comment on competing products, content analysis of the competition's media coverage, and reviews of industry reports in trade journals. Monitoring can be made much easier by setting up alerts that are fed directly to an e-mail inbox. Google Alerts, for example, allows a user to choose a list of search terms; once it is set up, news information that mentions the selected terms is delivered via e-mail.

Google Alerts is promoted as being useful in "monitoring a developing news story" or "keeping current on a competitor or industry." Similarly, RSS (Real Simple Syndication) feeds provide timely updates from favored websites such as online news sites or aggregate feeds from many sites into one place on the professional's home page. For more sophisticated and targeted monitoring, commercial Internet-monitoring services are also available. Such research helps an organization shape its marketing and communication strategies to counter a competitor's strengths and capitalize on its weaknesses.

■ **To sway public opinion.** Facts and figures, compiled from a variety of primary and secondary sources, can change public opinion. Shortly before an election in Ohio, 90 percent of the voters supported a state ballot measure that would require cancer warnings on thousands of products from plywood to peanut butter. A coalition called Ohioans for Responsible Health Information, which opposed the bill, commissioned universities and other credible outside sources to research the economic impact of such legislation on consumers and major industries. The research, which was used as the basis of the grassroots campaign, caused the defeat of the ballot measure, with 78 percent of the voters voting "no."

■ **To generate publicity.** Polls and surveys can generate publicity for an organization. Indeed, many surveys seem to be designed with publicity in mind. Simmons Mattress once polled people to find out how many sleep in the nude. Norelco Phillips, which introduced a new shaver for men called BodyGroom, got publicity for the new product by citing a telephone survey that found that more than half of the male respondents prefer a hairless back to any other body part. Another 72 percent said they use a razor blade to remove hair in even the most sensitive places. See the news release regarding the survey on this page.

There are, however, some general rules about how to write news releases reporting the results of polls and surveys. (See the Insights box on page 125.)

■ **To measure success.** The bottom line of any public relations program is whether the time and money spent accomplished the stated objective. As one of its many programs to boost brand awareness, Doritos snack chips pioneered the use of consumer-created content by airing Super Bowl commercials created by fans.

Buzz about the Super Bowl ad competition and the $1 million prize awarded to the winning amateur team generated 1.4 billion media impressions, a measure of the estimated or potential audience for media coverage. Perhaps more important, Doritos sales for the week after the Super Bowl increased by 16 percent over the same week the previous year. Evaluation, the last step of the public relations process, is discussed in Chapter 8. The following sections will discuss ways of doing research.

Research Techniques

When the term *research* is used, people tend to think of *quantitative research*, which uses scientific surveys and complex statistical tabulations. In public relations, however, research techniques also can be as simple as gathering data and information. Although the distinctions between different types of research are not absolute, Table 5.1 helps to sort out some of the options selected by public relations professionals.

In fact, a survey of practitioners by Walter K. Lindenmann, former senior vice president and director of research for Ketchum, found that three-fourths of the respondents described their research techniques as casual and informal rather than scientific and precise, tending to be qualitative, secondary analysis. The research technique cited most often by the respondents was literature searches/database information retrieval.

This technique is called *secondary research*, because it uses existing information in books, magazine articles, electronic databases, and so on. In contrast, *primary research*

PHILIPS

Press Information
July 12, 2006

Hair today, gone tomorrow! Philips Norelco offers guys a more convenient way to trim and shave unwanted body hair

STAMFORD, CONN. - - For some guys, shedding the winter coat means more than finding extra space in the closet. A recent survey commissioned by Philips Norelco and conducted by Opinion Dynamic Corporation revealed that more than 64% of men[1] are more likely to trim and groom their body hair during the warmer spring and summer months. Hearing the call of the wild, Philips Norelco recently introduced Bodygroom, a simple, easy-to-use full-body groomer that is designed to shave everywhere below the chin.

"Men are becoming increasingly conscious of their body hair and especially with the warmer summer months upon us, they're looking for easier ways to trim and shave the hair below their chin," said Arjen Linders, VP Marketing, Philips Norelco. "Until now, there have only been few options for the hairy, but we're hoping to change that by offering a simpler solution in the Philips Norelco Bodygroom."

Among men who already groom their body hair, there is clearly a need for better – and safer options. In fact, more than 72% of the men surveyed indicated that they use a razor blade to remove hair in even the most sensitive places –ouch! To help educate guys and provide useful information on an otherwise taboo topic, Philips Norelco Bodygroom launched www.shaveeverywhere.com – a fun Web site that features an unforgettable character who's not afraid to talk about the perks of a well-groomed body. Proof that men are looking for advice on a better way to groom, the site has drawn more than one million unique visitors in the first month.

---

[1] National telephone survey of 500 men ages 24-54 conducted by Opinion Dynamics Corporation in April 2006.

Philips Norelco News Release

This first page shows the results of a telephone survey about how men feel about body hair. The survey was a news "hook" to get media attention for its new product, BodyGroom, but the news release followed proper research protocols by providing information about the survey and how it was conducted. See the footnote at the bottom of the page. Also, on the second page (not shown), the company provided a seven-line description of the research methodology and also a five-line profile of the survey organization, Opinion Dynamics Corporation.

Table 5.1	Qualitative and Quantitative versus Primary and Secondary Research	
	QUALITATIVE RESEARCH Non-numerical research to seek insights	QUANTITATIVE RESEARCH Numerically based research with larger samples of respondents
PRIMARY Data collected by the professional	For example, professional conducts interviews or focus groups	For example, professional conducts large national survey
SECONDARY Data collected previously by others	For example, professional carefully reads news coverage or transcripts	For example, professional analyzes statistical data from General Social Survey

> For public relations research to provide support and assistance to the strategic planning and program development process, a mix of both qualitative and quantitative research is preferable.
>
> *Walter K. Lindenmann, specialist in public relations research and measurement*

uses new and original information that is generated through a research project and is directed to answer a specific question. Some examples of primary research methods include in-depth interviews, focus groups, surveys, and observation of behavior.

Another way of categorizing research is by distinguishing between *qualitative* and *quantitative* research. Lindenmann's determinations of the basic differences between qualitative and quantitative research appear in Table 5.2. In general, qualitative research affords the researcher rich insights and understanding of a situation or a target public, but does not use numerical data. It also provides "red flags" or warnings when strong or adverse responses occur. These responses may not be generalizable, but they may provide the practitioner with an early warning. Quantitative research is often more expensive and complicated, but it gives the researcher greater ability to generalize to large populations. If enormous amounts of money are to be spent on a national campaign, an investment in quantitative research may be appropriate.

The following sections briefly describe the three broad, and somewhat overlapping, approaches to research. They are (1) secondary research, (2) qualitative research, and (3) quantitative research based on scientific sampling.

Table 5.2	Qualitative versus Quantitative Research
QUALITATIVE RESEARCH	QUANTITATIVE RESEARCH
"Soft" data	"Hard" data
Usually uses open-ended questions, unstructured	Usually uses close-ended questions, requires forced choices, highly structured
Exploratory in nature; probing, fishing-expedition type of research	Descriptive or explanatory type of research
Usually valid, but not reliable	Usually valid and reliable
Rarely projectable to larger audiences	Usually projectable to larger audiences
Generally uses nonrandom samples	Generally uses random samples
Examples: Focus groups; one-on-one, in-depth interviews; observation; participation; role-playing studies; convenience polling	Examples: Telephone polls, mailed surveys, mall intercept studies, face-to-face interviews, shared cost, or omnibus studies; panel studies

on the job

on the job

INSIGHTS

Rules for Publicizing Surveys and Polls

The Council of American Survey Research Organizations (CASRO), a nonprofit national trade organization of more than 150 survey research companies, states that survey findings released to the public should contain the following information:

- The sponsor of the study
- The name of the research company conducting the study
- A description of the study's objectives

- A description of the sample, including the size of the sample and the population to which the results are intended to be generalized
- The dates of data collection
- The exact wording of the questions asked
- Any information that the researcher believes is relevant to help the public make a fair assessment of the results

In addition, CASRO recommends that other information be readily available in case anyone asks for it. This information includes the following: (1) the type of survey conducted, (2) the methods used to select the survey sample, (3) how the respondents were screened, and (4) the procedure for data coding and analysis.

Secondary Research

When a public relations professional analyzes data of any sort—whether numerical or textual in nature—that was originally collected by someone else, it is considered secondary research. Techniques range from archival research in an organization's files to reference books, computer databases, and online searches.

Archival Research

Robert Kendall, in his book *Public Relations Campaign Strategies*, terms the process of researching organizational materials *archival research*. Such materials may include an organization's policy statements, speeches by key executives, past issues of employee newsletters and magazines, reports on past public relations and marketing efforts, and news clippings. Marketing statistics, in particular, often provide baseline data that newly hired public relations firms can use to launch a new product or boost awareness and sales of an existing product or service. Archival research also is a major component in audits that are intended to determine how an organization communicates to its internal and external publics.

Library and Online Databases

Reference books, academic journals, and trade publications are in every city or university library. Online databases such as ProQuest, Factiva, and LexisNexis contain abstracts or full text of thousands, or even millions, of articles.

Some common reference sources used by public relations professionals include the *Statistical Abstract of the United States* (http://www.census.gov/statab/www/), which summarizes census information; the Gallup Poll (http://poll.gallup.com/), which provides an index of public opinion on a variety of issues; and *Simmons Study Media and Markets*, an extensive annual survey of households on their product usage by brand and exposure to various media.

Literature searches, the most often used informal research method in public relations, can tap into an estimated 1,500 electronic databases that store an enormous amount of current and historical information.

Public relations departments and firms use online databases to:

- Research facts to support a proposed project or campaign that requires top management approval
- Keep up-to-date with news about clients and their competitors
- Track an organization's media campaigns and competitors' press announcements
- Locate a special quote or impressive statistic for a speech or report
- Track press and business reaction to an organization's latest actions
- Locate an expert who can provide advice on an issue or a possible strategy
- Keep top management apprised of current business trends and issues
- Learn about the demographics and attitudes of target publics

Online databases are available on a subscription basis and usually charge by the number of minutes the service is in use.

The following are some of the online databases commonly used in public relations:

- *Burrelle's Broadcast Database* contains the full-text transcripts of radio and television programs within 24 hours after they are transmitted. Sources include ABC, NBC, CBS, CNN, National Public Radio, and selected syndicated programs.
- *Dow Jones Factiva News/Retrieval* electronically transmits up-to-the-second global coverage of business news, economic indicators, and industry and market data.
- *LexisNexis* includes millions of full-text articles from magazines, newspapers, and news services including the full text of the *New York Times* and the *Washington Post*.

Information delivery systems now seem to be virtually limitless in number and form. Magazines (zinio.com) or newspapers (pressdisplay.com and newsstand.com) provide products that are formatted like their print counterparts, but also include online links and video. Smart phones feature free or moderately priced applications that allow access to quality news sources, such as the *New York Times*, *USA Today*, CNN Mobile, World News Feed, and many others. These services make the work of monitoring news and trends easier for on-the-go professionals. This wide array of information resources enables public relations practitioners to be current and knowledgeable about their own organization and its place in the larger world.

The World Wide Web

The Internet is a powerful research tool for the public relations practitioner. Any number of corporations, nonprofits, trade groups, special interest groups, foundations, universities, think tanks, and government agencies post reams of data on the Internet, usually in the form of home pages on the World Wide Web.

Online search engines are essential for finding information on the Internet. Search engines such as Google also have become locations for sharing expertise and problem-solving skills regarding a wide array of topics. In the Google Groups section of the Google website (www.groups.google.com), helpful information can be found on everything from recreation to business to the arts.

Researchers can use specialized search engines or search tools to locate audio and video content or content of topical interest, such as sports or business news. Reviews and directories of search engines are available at searchenginewatch.com. Public relations professionals should visit such sites frequently to stay current on search engines.

Researchers can use profession-specific social media such as PROpenMic.org and newsgroups such as PRFORUM, a newsgroup dedicated to public relations topics, to request information from others. Discussion groups and blogs are increasingly common sources of information for public relations practitioners. There are several Yahoo!-based PR discussion groups—NYCPublicRelationsGroup, SmallPRAgencyPros, PRBytes, PRMindshare, PRQuorum, and YoungPRPros are examples.

Professional organizations such as the Public Relations Society of America and the International Association of Business Communicators have members-only discussion groups, PRCOnline and MemberSpeak, respectively. Blogs including briansolis.com examine PR business trends. IABC has blogs addressing branding, employee communications, measurement, and media relations compiled in the IABC Exchange (http://x.iabc.com/available-exchange-sites/). For more sites, see the Insights box below.

Mattel Toys, for example, saw a rapid increase in searches about toy safety after announcing a major recall of toys made in China. Such an increase told Mattel's

on the job

INSIGHTS

Surfing the Internet

An Internet search engine can help inform public relations campaign development by making a wealth of data immediately available.

Helpful sites for public relations professionals:

- *Statistical Abstract of the United States*: http://www.census.gov/compendia/statab/
- The PR Survey Observer: www.clientize.com/home.asp
- Bureau of Labor Statistics: www.bls.gov

- Environmental News Network: www.enn.com
- A list of home pages of various public relations firms: www.prfirms.org
- International Association of Business Communicators (IABC): www.iabc.com
- Public Relations Society of America (PRSA): www.prsa.org

- Business Wire (hyperlinks to corporate home pages): http://www.businesswire.com/portal/site/home/
- Zinio Magazine Reader: www.zinio.com
- NewsStand, Inc.: www.home.newsstand.com
- Vanderbilt Television News Archive: tvnews.vanderbilt.edu/

public relations staff that toy safety was high on the public's agenda and that the company should be aggressive in communicating its commitment to fix the problem. After the movie *Blood Diamond* arrived in theaters, the diamond industry no doubt used monitoring software to track searches about the source of diamonds. Monitoring indicated that the diamond issue was creating buzz among the public and that the diamond industry should proactively communicate its side of the story. More information about the Internet is in Chapter 13.

Google Trends is one popular monitoring service that reports how often selected words and topics have been used in Web searches. Google Trends also offers "Hot Trends," which is a snapshot of the top 40 fastest-rising search queries in the United States.

Qualitative Research

A great deal of public relations research is qualitative, relying less on numbers and statistics and more on interpretation of text such as editorial pages or focus group transcripts for themes or insights; such research is good for probing attitudes and perceptions, assessing penetration of messages, and testing the clarity and effectiveness of materials. This section explores five qualitative research techniques: (1) content analysis, (2) interviews, (3) focus groups, (4) copy testing, and (5) ethnographic techniques.

Content Analysis

Content analysis is the systematic and objective counting or categorizing of information. In public relations, content analysis is often used to measure the amount of media coverage and the content of that coverage. This research method ranges from relatively informal to quite scientific in terms of random sampling and establishing specific subject categories.

Professionals regularly analyze news stories about an organization to document themes and general conclusions about media coverage that might signal important issues needing attention. See Chapter 10 for a discussion of issues management. Content analysis can help to determine whether a need exists for additional public relations efforts.

By analyzing the media coverage given to an organization's competitors, a public relations professional can learn about the competition's marketing strategies, strengths, and weaknesses. The results often help shape an organization's marketing, advertising, and public relations programs to gain a bigger share of media attention.

At a basic level, a researcher can assemble news clips and count the number of column inches or minutes of broadcast time. Don Stacks, University of Miami professor and author of *Primer of Public Relations Research*, writes that content analysis "is particularly appropriate for the analysis of documents, speeches, media releases, video content and scripts, interviews, and focus groups. The key to content analysis is that it is done objectively..., and content is treated systematically..."

Meaningful content analysis that enables public relations departments to plan responsive communication should include factors such as (1) the percentage of favorable, neutral, and negative mentions about the company or its product or service; (2) the overall tone of the article or broadcast mention; and (3) the percentage of articles that contain key message points that the organization wants to communicate. Dr. David Michaelson of Echo Research noted at a recent Measurement Summit sponsored by the Institute for Public Relations that his clients worldwide do care about favorability, but frequently are at least as concerned with accuracy, regardless of the tone of the news coverage. Presence of a company's key messages goes a long way toward the judgment that coverage is indeed accurate.

Because Internet chat groups and blogs, as well as letters and phone calls to an organization, provide good feedback about problems with the organization's policies and services, they can be vital sources of current opinion about performance and reputation. A pattern of blog postings, letters, and phone calls pointing out a problem is often evidence that the organization needs to address the situation. A number of companies, such as Carma International, Cymfony, and VMS, can slice and dice media data in any number of ways for their clients. Research firm KD Paine and Partners delivers content analysis on a custom-designed webpage for the client. Called a *Dashboard*, clients can see at a glance how they are being covered in traditional and new media.

Interviews

As with content analysis, interviews can be conducted in several different ways. Almost everyone talks to colleagues on a daily basis and calls other organizations to gather information. In fact, public relations personnel faced with solving a particular problem often "interview" other public relations professionals for ideas and suggestions.

If information is needed on public opinions and attitudes, many public relations firms will conduct short interviews with people in a shopping mall or at a meeting. This kind of interview is called an *intercept interview*, because people are literally intercepted in public places and asked their opinions. It is also called a *convenience poll* because it's relatively convenient to stand in a mall and talk to people.

The intercept interview is considered by researchers to be highly unscientific and unreliable, but it does give an organization some sense of current thinking or exposure to certain key messages. For example, a health group wanted to find out whether the public was actually receiving and retaining crucial aspects of its message. To gather such information, intercept interviews were conducted with 300 adults at six malls. Both unaided and aided recall questions were asked, to assess the overall impact of the publicity.

Intercept interviews last only 2 to 5 minutes. At other times, the best approach is to do in-depth interviews to get more comprehensive information. Major fund-raising projects by charitable groups, for example, often require in-depth interviews of community

Public Opinion Survey

Interviews, often conducted by researchers on the street or in shopping malls, help public relations practitioners target audiences they wish to reach and to shape their messages.

on the job

A MULTICULTURAL WORLD

Reaching a Diverse Audience about Electric Rates

How do you reach an audience when almost 40 percent of your audience is illiterate, 20 percent live below the poverty line, and many speak a language other than English? That's exactly what Dittus Communications faced—not in a developing nation, but in Washington, D.C.

The challenge was legislation passed by the city council that deregulated electricity so that residents could choose service from several competing suppliers instead of just one company having a monopoly. A Customer Education Advisory Board—a partnership of government, local utility, and consumer advocacy groups—was formed

and given the assignment of implementing a two-year public education campaign to inform D.C. residents about their electricity supply choices.

Dittus Communications started with a literature search to gain information about the demographic profile of D.C. residents. Personal interviews were then conducted with city officials and leaders of local nonprofit and faith-based organizations to gain insight into the best ways to reach the population. One key finding was that messages had to be simple and direct, and feature one fact at a time. It was also necessary to have multiple communication tools that could be cus-

tomized for hard-to-reach audiences. To reach the illiterate audience, for example, radio announcements and talks at community and faith-based organizations were used.

Ongoing research tracking the residents' awareness of electricity choices found that women were more interested in the topic than men, so additional female models were used in the campaign's advertising. Ultimately, the award-winning campaign helped increase resident confidence about making electricity choices. Almost 45 percent of the population felt more capable of decision making than when the effort had begun.

and business opinion leaders. The success of any major fund drive, those seeking $500,000 or more, depends on the support of key leaders and wealthy individuals.

This more in-depth approach is called *purposive interviewing*, because the interviewees are carefully selected based on their expertise, influence, or leadership in the community. For example, the Greater Durham, North Carolina, chamber of commerce interviewed 50 "movers and shakers" to determine support for an extensive image-building and economic development program. See the Multicultural box above about how interviews with community leaders in Washington, D.C., helped plan an information campaign.

Focus Groups

A good alternative to individual interviews is the *focus group*. The focus group technique is widely used in advertising, marketing, and public relations to help identify attitudes and motivations of important publics. Another purpose of focus groups is to formulate or pretest message themes and communication strategies before launching a full campaign.

Focus groups usually consist of 8 to 12 people who represent the characteristics of the target audience, such as employees, consumers, or community residents. During the session, a trained facilitator uses nondirective interviewing techniques that encourage group members to talk freely about a topic or give candid reactions to suggested message themes. The setting is usually a conference room, and the discussion is informal. A focus group may last one or two hours, depending on the subject matter.

A focus group, by definition, is an informal research procedure that develops qualitative information rather than hard data. Results should not be summarized by percentages or even projected onto an entire population because this accords a level of precision not supported by the method.

Nevertheless, focus groups are useful in identifying the range of attitudes and opinions among the participants. For example, the opinion of several focus group participants that a proposed slogan or logo is off-color and in bad taste may not be generalizable to large populations, but it raises a red flag that communication staff should go back to the drawing board. Such insights can help an organization structure its messages or, on another level, formulate hypotheses and questions for a quantitative research survey.

Increasingly, focus groups are being conducted online. The online technique can be as simple as posing a question to a chat or interest group online. Researchers also are using more formal selection processes to invite far-flung participants to meet in a prearranged virtual space. In the coming years, techniques and services will be well developed for cost-effective, online focus group research.

Although highly informal, Domino's Pizza conducted an online focus group regarding its bold move to completely change the recipe for its pizza—crust, cheese and sauce. In national taste tests, Domino's inhabited the basement with Chuck E. Cheese. Domino's canvassed food bloggers and tweeters to respond in real time as they tasted the new pizza and to comment live on Domino's website about the new formula. This daring move reflected Domino's confidence in the new recipe as it conducted an online focus group with the whole world watching. Opportunities for publicity and for brand advertising related to the recipe change made the uncontrolled research process a gamble worth taking.

Copy Testing

All too often, organizations fail to communicate effectively because they produce and distribute materials that the target audience can't understand. In many cases, the material is written above the educational level of the audience. To avoid this problem, representatives of the target audience should be asked to read or view the material in draft form before it is mass-produced and distributed. This can be done one on one or in a small-group setting.

In health public relations, readability is crucial to enhancing health literacy so that individuals can make smart health decisions. (To see how one of the authors works to improve health literacy, go to http://i-shd.missouri.edu/.) A brochure about employee medical benefits or pension plans, for example, should be pretested with rank-and-file employees for readability. Executives and lawyers who must approve the copy may understand the material, but a worker with a high school education might find the material difficult to follow.

Another approach to determine the degree of difficulty of the material is to apply a readability formula to the draft copy. Fog, Flesch Reading Ease, and similar techniques relate the number of words and syllables per sentence or passage with reading level. Highly complex sentences and multisyllabic words require an audience with a college education. One readily available software tool for assessing readability is Microsoft Word.

Two examples of how to test copy using Internet sources are Web surveys and Wikis. Web survey systems such as Survey Artisan (www.surveyartisan.com) allow attachment of video or photo files that can be critiqued by a target audience across many locations. A less sophisticated but equally effective way to test copy is simply to attach the copy to an e-mail and provide a link to an online survey. Similarly, photos or videos can be tested through secure Flickr or YouTube sharing communities. A Wiki is a website that allows users to easily edit content; these sites provide a way for clients or audience members to critique and correct copy, essentially turning audience members into copy collaborators.

Ethnographic Techniques

Public relations often takes a page from anthropology to conduct research. One technique is observation of individual or group behavior. One director of public relations, for example, wanted to know how effective bulletin boards were in terms of informing employees in an industrial plant, so he stationed staff near bulletin boards to record how many employees actually stopped and read something off the board. In another situation, a public relations representative sat in a coffee house for most of one day to gain insights about the types of customers who came in, how much they spent, and how long they stayed.

On occasion, role-playing can be helpful for gaining insights into the strengths and weaknesses of an organization. One public relations professional with a college as a client had his daughter and several other young adults in the area apply to the university just to see how the college compared with others in terms of handling prospective students. He also got feedback from his daughter about how well she was treated in the process.

An amusing example is recounted in Ted Turner's autobiography, *Call Me Ted*. The founder of CNN and owner of the Atlanta Braves baseball team faced an internal communication problem after his purchase of the Braves—he knew little about baseball. Turner sent a company executive to pose as a player during spring training. The future media magnate learned about the game and the mental state of his newly acquired team through nightly dinners with his informant for three weeks. Ethical considerations often come into play with undisclosed participant observations such as this, but the team found the gambit hilarious and considered their new owner clever and resourceful. The executive planted on the team actually received a minor league contract—which he turned down.

Quantitative Research

The research techniques discussed thus far can provide good insights to public relations personnel and help them formulate effective programs. Many involve a thoughtful review of existing materials or careful listening in one form or another to small numbers of individuals. Increasingly, however, public relations professionals need to conduct polls and surveys using highly precise, scientific sampling methods. Such sampling is based on two important factors: randomness to ensure that the subject pool is not biased and a large number of respondents to ensure that results can be generalized to the entire population being studied. See the PR Casebook at the end of the chapter about a campaign based on a random survey. Social science research can be costly, but when the stakes are high for an organization, the following social scientific processes are often worth the effort and expense.

Random Sampling

Effective polls and surveys require a random sample. In statistics, this means that everyone in the targeted audience (as defined by the researcher) has an equal or known chance of being selected for the survey. This is also called a probability sample.

In contrast, a nonprobability survey is not random at all. Improper sampling can lead to misleading results. The most precise random sample is generated from lists that have the name of every person in the target audience. This is simple if the researcher is conducting a random survey of an organization's employees or members, because the researcher can randomly select, for example, every 25th name on a list. To avoid patterns in the lists based on rank or employee category, the researcher should choose large intervals between selected names so that he or she makes numerous passes through the list. Computerized lists often allow for random selection of names.

The distinction between probability and nonprobability samples can be illustrated with two different approaches to Web-based surveys. When ESPN invites viewers of *Sports Central* to vote among five NFL teams as the best bet to win the Super Bowl, the response can be enormous—but is unscientific. For one thing, fans of a team can vote repeatedly.

By contrast, a doctoral student at the University of Missouri obtained the membership list of the Health Acadamy of PRSA. She then randomly drew a sample of members, assigned a unique identification number to each respondent to allow only one visit to the website, and e-mailed them an invitation to complete the Web-based survey. Respondents had an equal and known chance of being included, making the results of the survey representative of Health Academy members. The point is that Web-based surveys run the gamut from trivial popularity polls to rigorously drawn surveys of important respondents.

Another common method to ensure representation is to draw a random sample that matches the statistical characteristics of the audience. This is called quota sampling. Human resource departments usually have breakdowns of employees by job classification, and it is relatively easy to proportion a sample accordingly. For example, if 42 percent of a company's employees work on the assembly line, then 42 percent of the sample should be assembly-line workers. A quota sample can be drawn on any number of demographic factors—age, sex, religion, race, income—depending on the purpose of the survey.

Random sampling becomes more difficult when comprehensive lists are not available. In those cases, researchers surveying the general population often use telephone directories or customer lists to select respondents at random. A more rigorous technique employs random, computerized generation of telephone numbers; this process ensures that both new and unlisted numbers are included in the sample.

A travel company used this *random digit dialing* (RDD) method for a nationwide telephone survey of 1,000 adult Americans to determine whether the hurricane that had devastated the island of Kauai affected vacation plans to visit the Hawaiian islands not struck by the hurricane. On the basis of the results, the travel company restructured its advertising and public relations messages to emphasize that resorts on the other islands were open for business as usual.

Sample Size

In any probability study, sample size is always a big question. National polling firms usually sample 1,000 to 1,500 people and get a highly accurate idea of what the U.S. adult population is thinking. The average national poll samples 1,500 people, and the margin of error is within three percentage points 95 percent of the time. In other words, 19 out of 20 times the same questionnaire is administered, the results should be within the same three percentage points and reflect the whole population accurately.

In public relations, the primary purpose of poll data is to get indications of attitudes and opinions, not to predict elections. Therefore, it is not usually necessary or practical to do a scientific sampling of 1,500 people. A sample of 250 to 500 will give relatively accurate data—with a 5 or 6 percent variance—that will help determine general public attitudes and opinions. A sample of about 100 people, accurately drawn according to probability guidelines, will include about a 10 percent margin of error.

This percentage of error would be acceptable if a public relations person, for example, asked employees what they want to read in the company magazine. Sixty percent may indicate that they would like to see more news about opportunities for promotion. If only 100 employees were properly surveyed, it really doesn't matter whether the actual percentage is 50 or 70 percent. The large percentage, in either case, would be sufficient to justify an increase in news stories about advancement opportunities.

This is also true in ascertaining community attitudes. If a survey of 100 or fewer citizens indicates that only 25 percent believe that a certain organization is a good community citizen, it really doesn't matter whether the result is truly 15 or 35 percent. The main point is that the organization must take immediate steps to improve its performance.

One problem with many Web surveys, which will be discussed in more detail shortly, is that the sample size can't be determined in advance because access to the

on the job

ETHICS

Sex and Alcohol: The AMA's News Release

The American Medical Association (AMA) wanted to call public attention to the issue of "risky" behavior by college students during spring break. The AMA's strategy was to commission a survey of female college students so that it would have some "facts" to demonstrate the seriousness of the issue.

The resulting news release stated that its survey of 644 college women and graduates aged 17 to 35 showed troubling findings about drinking habits on spring break trips. For instance, 92 percent of respondents said it was easy to get alcohol on these trips. The news release also stated, "One in five respondents regretted the sexual activity they engaged in during spring break, and 12

percent felt forced or pressured into sex." Because of the topic, which included sex, the Associated Press moved the story and many media outlets reported the survey results.

What the news release didn't say was that the survey was less than scientific. It was an online survey in which respondents self-selected themselves to participate. In other words, the survey was not a random or representative sample of female college students. The news release also didn't mention that a quarter of the respondents had never gone on a spring break trip, so their opinions were actually secondhand impressions or perceptions of what occurs during spring break.

Carl Bialik, who writes a column for the *Wall Street Journal* titled "The Numbers Guy," called the AMA about the validity of the survey. He was told by an AMA spokesperson, "We used the poll mostly to bring national attention to the issue." What do you think of this answer? Was the news release misleading? Do you think sending out news releases reporting survey results based on non-scientific research methods is ethical? The news release did accomplish the objective of getting "national attention," so does the end justify the means?

PEARSON
my**communication**lab

survey is not limited or controlled. As a result, such surveys lack random selection and should be interpreted with caution. Reporting the results of such surveys often raises some ethical issues. See the Ethics box on page 134.

Questionnaire Construction

Although correct sampling is important in gaining accurate results, pollsters generally acknowledge that sampling error may be far less important than the errors that result from the wording and order of questions in a survey and even the timing of a survey.

Carefully Consider Wording

Wording the questions on a questionnaire is a time-consuming process, and it is not unusual for a questionnaire to go through multiple drafts to achieve maximum clarity. The question "Is it a good idea to limit alcohol consumption on college campuses?" differs from "Do you think campus alcohol prohibitions will curtail drinking on campus?" On first glance, the two questions seem to be asking the same thing. On closer examination, however, one realizes that a respondent could easily answer "yes" to the first question and "no" to the second.

The first question asks whether limiting student drinking is a good idea. The second asks whether people think it will curtail drinking. A third question that might elicit a different response would be "Do you think that a policy curtailing drinking on campus would work?" Thus, the questions emphasize three different aspects of the problem. The first stresses the value of an idea, the second explores a possible effect, and the third examines the practicality of a proposed solution. Research shows that people often think something is a good idea, but do not think it would work. Another related problem is how respondents might interpret the words "limit" and "curtail." To some, these words may refer to a total ban on alcohol, including adult consumption at tailgate locations before football games, whereas others may think they suggest that alcohol should be kept away from minors or all students of any age. It's simply a matter of semantics, which is a good area of study for aspiring public relations professionals.

Avoid Loaded Questions

Some organizations engage in what is called *advocacy research*. They send out surveys with questions that use highly charged words to elicit an emotional reaction from the respondent. Such questions are considered "loaded" because they are intentionally skewed to generate a predictable response. Such surveys often are done in the arena of politics and public policy debate.

Republican Party pollsters, for example, asked respondents, "Do you support the creation of a national health insurance plan that would be administered by bureaucrats in Washington, D.C.?" Not surprisingly, most respondents want medical professionals, not the stereotypically negative bureaucrat making health decisions. Interestingly, during the health care debate, President Obama used the term "health insurance bureaucrats" to counter the stereotype that indifferent functionaries inhabit only federal offices. Another example of a loaded question is one created by the American Civil Liberties Union (ACLU), which asked respondents whether they agreed with the statement "I believe that the President does not need to use unauthorized and illegal powers to keep us safe, that warrantless spying on Americans is unnecessary, and illegal and that, in America, no one—including the President—is above the law."

Public relations practitioners have a professional obligation to avoid using the rubric of "surveys" if the objective is really advocacy research. Such "surveys" are misleading and tarnish the reputation of legitimate survey research.

Consider Timing and Context

Responses to survey questions are influenced by events, and this should be taken into consideration when reviewing the results of a survey. Consequently, polls and surveys should be conducted when the organization isn't in the news or connected to a significant event that may influence public opinion. In a neutral context, a more valid survey can be conducted about an organization's reputation, products, or services.

Large organizations, such as Exxon/Mobil, General Electric, and Microsoft, counterbalance the effects of one-time events—huge profit reports, lavish CEO salary, or a crippling computer virus, for example—through regular monitoring of media coverage, Internet discussion groups, blogs, and measurements of brand awareness. This technique, called *benchmarking*, is done by a number of companies who use software programs to track and monitor a client's reputation almost on a daily basis. See Chapter 8 on evaluation for more details.

Avoid the Politically Correct Answer

Another problem with questionnaire design involves questions that tend to elicit the "correct" response. This is also called a *courtesy bias*. In such a situation, respondents often choose answers that they think are the "politically correct" answers that the sponsor of the survey wants to hear or that reflect favorably on them as good workers or citizens. For example, surveys show that more than 80 percent of Americans consider themselves "environmentalists." As skeptics point out, however, would anyone admit that he or she is not concerned about the environment?

Those conducting employee surveys also fall into the "courtesy" trap by posing such questions as "How much of each newsletter do you read?" or "How well do you like the column by the president?" Employees may never read the newsletter or think that the president's column is ridiculous, but they know the "correct" answer. Researchers try to avoid politically correct answers by making questionnaires confidential and by promising anonymity to the people who are surveyed. Because employees often perceive the public relations department to be part of management, it is often best to employ an outside research firm to conduct employee surveys to ensure more honest answers.

Give a Range of Possible Answers

Answer categories also can skew a questionnaire. It is important that the provided answer choices cover a range of opinions. Several years ago, a national polling organization asked the question "How much confidence do you have in business corporations?" but provided only the following answer categories: (a) a great deal, (b) only some, and (c) none at all. A large gap exists between "a great deal" and the next category, "only some."

Such categories invariably skew the results to show very little confidence in business. A better list of answers might have been (a) a great deal, (b) quite a lot, (c) some,

on the job

INSIGHTS

Questionnaire Guidelines

The following are some general guidelines for the construction of questionnaires:

- Determine the type of information that is needed and in what detail.

- State the objectives of the survey in writing.

- Decide which group(s) will receive the questionnaire.

- Decide on the size of the sample.

- State the purpose of the survey and guarantee anonymity.

- Use closed-end (multiple-choice) answers as often as possible. Respondents find it easier and less time-consuming to select answers than to compose their own.

- Design the questionnaire in such a way that answers can be easily coded for statistical analysis.

- Strive to make the questionnaire fewer than 25 questions. Long questionnaires put people off and reduce the number of responses.

- Use categories when asking questions about education, age, and income. People are more willing to answer when a range is given. For example, "What best describes your age? (a) Under 25, (b) 26 to 40," and so on.

- Use simple, familiar words. Readability should be appropriate for the group being sampled.

- Avoid ambiguous words and phrases that may confuse the respondents.

- Remember to consider the context and placement of questions. A question earlier in the questionnaire might influence the response to a later question.

- Provide space at the end of the questionnaire for respondents' comments. This allows them to provide additional information that may not have been covered in the main body of the questionnaire.

- Pretest the questions with representatives of the target audience for understanding and possible bias. Their feedback will help improve the final draft.

(d) very little, and (e) none. Another approach is to use such categories as (a) above average, (b) average, and (c) below average. The psychological distance between the three choices is equal, and there is less room for a respondent's interpretation of what "quite a lot" means.

In general, "yes or no" questions are not very good for examining respondents' perceptions and attitudes. An answer of "yes" or "no" provides little feedback on the strength or weakness of a respondent's opinion. A question such as "Do you agree with the company's policy of requiring drug testing for all new employees?" can be answered by "yes" or "no," but more useful information would be obtained by setting up a Likert-type scale—(a) strongly agree, (b) agree, (c) undecided, (d) disagree, and (e) strongly disagree. These types of answers enable the surveyor to probe the depth of feeling among respondents and may serve as guidelines for management in making major changes or just fine-tuning the existing policy.

Another way of designing a numeric scale to pinpoint a respondent's beliefs or attitudes is to use a 5-point scale. Such a question might say, "How would you evaluate the company's efforts to keep you informed about job benefits? Please circle one of the following numbers" ("1" being a low rating and "5" being a high rating).

The advantage of numeric scales is that medians and means can be calculated. In the previous example, the average from all respondents might be 4.25, which indicates that employees think the company does keep them informed about job benefits, but that there is still room for communication improvement. See the Insights box on page 137 that gives questionnaire guidelines.

How to Reach Respondents

A questionnaire is only as good as the delivery system that gets it to respondents. This section presents the pros and cons of (1) mail questionnaires, (2) telephone surveys, (3) personal interviews, (4) omnibus surveys, and (5) Web and e-mail surveys.

Mailed Questionnaires

Questionnaires may be distributed in a variety of settings. They may be handed out at a manufacturing plant, at a county fair, or even in a bank lobby. Historically, most survey questionnaires were mailed to respondents to control costs and to ensure that the right person got the survey. With care, these advantages can be achieved with e-mail and Web-based survey-collection techniques. Because practitioners find the Internet approach convenient and quicker, mailed questionnaires are used less often than in the recent past.

Mailed questionnaires suffer from low response rates, as low as 1 to 2 percent when mailed to the general public. Better response is garnered when an organization is known and trusted by the survey subjects, but may increase only to 20–30 percent. These response rates threaten the generalizability of the results. To increase response rates, researchers should keep the following suggestions in mind:

- Include a stamped, self-addressed return envelope.
- Personally sign a note explaining the importance of the survey.
- Provide an incentive.
- Use first-class mail.
- Mail a reminder postcard.
- Do a second mailing.

Telephone Surveys

Surveys by telephone, particularly those that are locally based, are used extensively by research firms. The telephone survey has four major advantages: (1) The feedback is immediate, (2) the telephone is a more personal form of communication, (3) it's less intrusive than interviewers going door to door, and (4) the response rate, if the survey is short and handled by skilled phone interviewers, can regularly reach 60 percent.

The major disadvantage of telephone surveys is the difficulty in getting access to telephone numbers. In many urban areas, one-third to one-half of all numbers are unlisted. The greater challenge is the shift away from landline telephone service in homes to individual cell phones within the residence. Because cell phones are portable, area codes no longer reflect place of residence, which can be crucial for surveys intended only for current residents of a geographical area, such as voters in a state election. Although researchers can let a computer program, through random dialing, pick numbers that will include unlisted numbers, generating random phone numbers that include cell phones means unwanted calls to the owner at his or her expense.

Another barrier is convincing respondents that a legitimate poll or survey is being taken. Far too many salespeople, and even charitable organizations, attempt to sell goods or get donations by posing as researchers. To the relief of phone survey companies, genuine surveys are not blocked by the do-not-call registration that enables citizens to be blocked from marketing and solicitation calls.

Personal Interviews

The personal interview is the most expensive form of research because it requires trained staff and travel. If travel within a city is involved, a trained interviewer may be able to interview only 8 to 10 people a day, and salaries and transportation costs make it expensive. Considerable advance work is required to select and arrange interview appointments. Such interviews, taking 20 minutes to an hour, are usually much more intensive and representative than the mall-intercept interviews that occur when an interviewer stops mall shoppers to record a few quick answers on a clipboard.

Omnibus or Piggyback Surveys

The word *omnibus* means something that serves several purposes. In survey research, it means that an organization buys one or two questions in a national survey conducted by a national polling firm such as Gallup or Harris. For example, General Mills may place one or two questions in a large, professionally conducted survey that asks respondents what professional athlete they most admire, as a way to find new endorsers for its breakfast foods. In the same survey, the American Cancer Society may place a question to find out what percentage of women know the common symptoms of ovarian cancer. If awareness is low, such a finding shows that a public information campaign is needed.

> Online surveys are easier and less intrusive than a phone call.
>
> *Giselle Lederman, survey methodologist for* Zoomerang

Web and E-Mail Surveys

The newest way to reach respondents is through the Internet. One such method is to post a questionnaire on an organization's website and ask visitors to complete it online. The advantage of this is that once the visitor completes the survey, his or her response is immediately available and the results can be added to a running tabulation of results.

A good example of an online research survey is one that Church & Dwight, the maker of Trojan Condoms, conducted before it launched its new Elexa line of condoms and sexual health products, including a vibrating ring targeting women. The online survey, aimed at women ages 18 to 59, was conducted to understand "women's sexual journeys." The responses enabled the company to position the new product line through a research report called the "Elexa Study of Women and Desire," which, of course, generated a great deal of media coverage.

As *PRWeek* pointed out, "What lifestyle reporter doesn't want to know that 'American women want great sex.'" The survey found, for example, that "84% of women

PRCasebook

Research Vital for Formulating Campaign Messages

Public relations programs and campaigns always involve making decisions about the essence and content of core messages that will resonate with the target audience. And the only way to get it "right" is through research.

The following are two examples of how public relations firms used research to determine the core messages of a campaign:

U.S. Department of Defense

Research can be used not only in the work leading up to a campaign, but also throughout a campaign's continuing stages. Fleishman-Hillard, for example, was engaged by the Department of Defense (DoD) to organize a campaign to combat binge drinking in the military. The catalyst for the campaign was a survey by the DoD that indicated that 54 percent of active-duty military personnel between the ages of 18 and 25 were binge drinking—consuming five or more drinks in one sitting at least once in the previous 30 days.

Fleishman conducted three different focus groups with military personnel. The first one tested which message themes would be most effective. A second focus group was conducted to test the "That Guy" concept, which was based on not being "that guy" who loses control after a night of partying. According to *PRWeek*, "The team learned that the long-term consequences of binge drinking, like poor health, didn't resonate as well as short-term ones, like embarrassment, spending too much, or not getting the girl."

Based on this research, messages were formulated for an interactive website (www.ThatGuy.com). One message, showing a guy passed out under a urinal, had the caption "Reason #76 Not to be That Guy: Toilet Paper Does Not Make a Good Pillow." A third focus group was held during the campaign to make sure the message was on target. Jennifer Quermann, SVP at Fleishman-Hillard, told *PRWeek*,

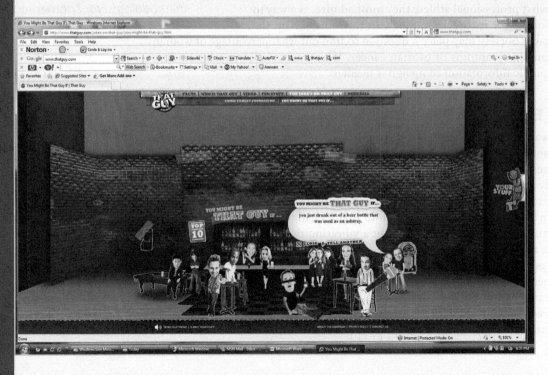

"Some of these jokes are edgy and we can say, this is how these guys are talking. This is what matters to them."

Haagen-Dazs

The ice cream company employed Ketchum Public Affairs to help develop congressional testimony and a public affairs campaign about America's declining honey bee population. Making the case for why the public should care about such an arcane subject was important to Haagen-Dazs because bees are crucial to pollinating many food ingredients, such as berries used in ice cream.

Ketchum first conducted secondary research of media coverage about the declining bee population and found that most of the congressional testimony to date was scientific data that didn't translate very well in terms of raising public concern. The firm also interviewed a number of agricultural reporters to get their perspectives on how they viewed the issue. What Ketchum found was that the status of bees could affect the cost of many food items for the American consumer. This conclusion was reinforced by a few questions on a consumer "omnibus" survey by Harris polling that showed consumers had never before made the connection between bees and food prices.

The research helped validate the planned messaging about bees and food prices, which also helped Haagen-Dazs position itself as an advocate creating bee-friendly habitats and supporting bee research. Sales of its ice cream products also increased, and media coverage about the ice cream maker's efforts to save the bees surpassed 273 million impressions.

agree that a good sex life is part of a healthy life," and "76% say that, at the request of a partner, they have tried something new sexually that they have enjoyed." Cassandra Johnson, a product manager for Elexa, told *PRWeek*, "We were expecting that the research would help refine the voice of the campaign and key messages, and give us something thought-provoking to say to the media and to women about female sexuality."

Because the survey employed a convenience sample consisting of those who visited the site and volunteered to respond, results are suspect in terms of generalizability. But as "main event research" intended to be newsworthy and stimulating, the research was a great success.

Researchers use several methods to attract respondents to a website, including (1) banner ads announcing the survey on other websites or online networks, (2) sending e-mail invitations to members of the target audience, (3) telephoning individuals with an invitation to participate, and (4) sending a postcard.

The major disadvantage of a Web survey is that it is difficult to know the exact characteristics of the respondents, because a website is accessible to virtually anyone with a computer and an Internet connection. It is also very important to prevent repeated participation by the same respondent by identifying the unique identifying number of the computer (called the IP address) and allowing only one submission. One of the biggest problems for online surveys is the low response rate due to the impersonal nature of the survey and the ease of exiting the survey's website with a single mouse click. For this reason, many online surveys begin with the most crucial questions.

If reaching a specific audience is important, another approach is an e-mail survey that is sent to a list of known respondents, as was described earlier in this chapter for the study of Health Academy members of PRSA. Organizations can compile e-mail lists of clients or customers or purchase e-mail address lists from a variety of sources. Full-service Web survey companies target populations, collect responses, and deliver data to the client. The costs of such surveys can be low if an online survey service such as freeonlinesurveys.com—more of a do-it-yourself service—is used. Zoomerang (info.zoomerang.com) and Harris Interactive recruit and maintain pools of respondents to fit profiles that clients want to survey. Gender, income, and political persuasion are examples of characteristics that can be selected for Web survey purposes.

As in all research methods, there are advantages and disadvantages of using Web and e-mail surveys. The three major advantages are that (1) large samples are generated in a short amount of time, (2) they are more economical than even mailed questionnaires or phone interviews, and (3) data can be analyzed continually. The three major disadvantages are (1) respondents are usually self-selected, (2) there is no control over the size of the sample or selection of respondents, and (3) probability sampling is not achievable.

Summary

The Importance of Research

Research is the basic groundwork of any public relations program. It involves the gathering and interpretation of information. Research is used in every phase of a communications program.

Secondary Research

Secondary research often begins by doing archival research, which reviews an organization's data on sales, profile of customers, and so on. Another source is information from library and online databases. Search engines such as Google, MSN, and Yahoo! allow practically everyone to find information and statistics on the Internet and the World Wide Web. Thus, the often-heard expression "Let's Google it."

Qualitative Research

The value of this technique is that it gains insights into how individuals behave, think, and make decisions. It's also used to ascertain whether key messages were communicated by the media. The primary techniques are (1) content analysis, (2) interviews, (3) focus groups, (4) copy testing, and (5) ethnographic observation and role-playing.

Quantitative Research

This kind of research demands scientific rigor and proper sampling procedures so that information will be representative of the general population. Random sampling gives everyone in the target audience the chance to be in the sample. Sample size determines the margin of error in the statistical findings.

Questionnaire Construction

There are many factors to consider when designing a questionnaire, including wording, biased questions, politically correct answers, and answer categories. There are also a number of guidelines, such as deciding what you want to find out, keeping the questionnaire relatively short, defining the target audience, and selecting the appropriate sample size.

How to Reach Respondents

Survey respondents may be reached by mail, telephone, personal interviews, and omnibus surveys. Increasingly, surveys are being done via the Web and e-mail.

Case Activity   Conducting Research at Precision Control

Universal Precision Control Corporation is located in a Midwestern city of 500,000 people. At 6,000 employees, it is one of the largest employers in the county, and the company has been at its present location for the past 50 years, where it started making thermostats in the founder's garage. Despite this record, there are rumblings within the workforce that the company is planning to move its operations to Mexico. Top management is adamant that Universal is not leaving the United States. Even so, the personnel department reports that, based on a stack of notes collected from Comment boxes in break rooms and the cafeteria, employee morale is low.

The director of public relations has been asked to prepare a new internal communication plan for the coming fiscal year to address employees' worry that they cannot count on a future at Universal. She recommends that the company first conduct research to determine exactly what employees know and feel about the future of the company during these trying economic times. Her main argument is that the Comment box is not the best source of intelligence about the workforce. Furthermore, the sporadic comments don't distinguish among executives, managers, support staff, and line workers.

As a recently trained public relations graduate, you are placed in charge of the research program over the next several months. What kind of secondary research would you do?

What qualitative and quantitative research would you recommend? The idea is to get some hard data on which to base an employee relations campaign that will drive home that Universal is staying put. Your boss wants variations on the core message that Universal is staying to be designed for various segments of the workforce, from the executive suite to the factory line.

Questions   For Review and Discussion

1. Why is research important to public relations work?
2. What questions should a person ask before planning a research project?
3. Identify at least five ways that research is used in public relations.
4. How can survey research be used as a publicity tool?
5. List at least five informal research methods.
6. What are online databases? How are they used by public relations professionals?
7. How can the Internet and World Wide Web be used as research tools?
8. What is the procedure for organizing and conducting a focus group? What are the pros and cons of using focus groups?
9. What is an intercept interview?
10. What is the difference between probability (random) and nonprobability samples?
11. What guidelines should be followed when releasing the results of a survey to the media and the public?
12. What percentage margin of error is associated with various sample sizes? What size samples are usually adequate for public relations work?
13. Identify at least five guidelines that should be followed when preparing a questionnaire.
14. What are the pros and cons of each of the following: mail questionnaires, telephone surveys, personal interviews, piggyback surveys, and Web surveys?

Media Resources

Clary, S. (2008, January). You are what you know: Research for campaign success. *Public Relations Tactics*, 19.

Garcia, T. (2008, February 4). Keys to a good start: Research is essential in the development of a good campaign, offering useful information to be used during the launch and beyond. *PRWeek*, 13.

Holland, R. J. (2009, July 2). Ask the right questions to get useful survey data. Ragan.com.

McKenna, T. (2008, July 28). The right message: Research is essential to crafting a public affairs campaign that will truly resonate with target audiences. *PRWeek*, 17.

Paine, K. D. (2007). *Measuring public relationships: The data-driven guide to success.* Berlin, NH: KD Paine & Partners.

Stacks, D. W. (2010). *Primer of public relations research.* New York, NY: Guilford Press.

Vahouny, K. (2009, August). Get started on your communication audit. *Communication World*, 35–37.

PEARSON
my**communication**lab

Career Explorations. Interview with Larry Patrick: President Patrick Communications.

6

Program Planning

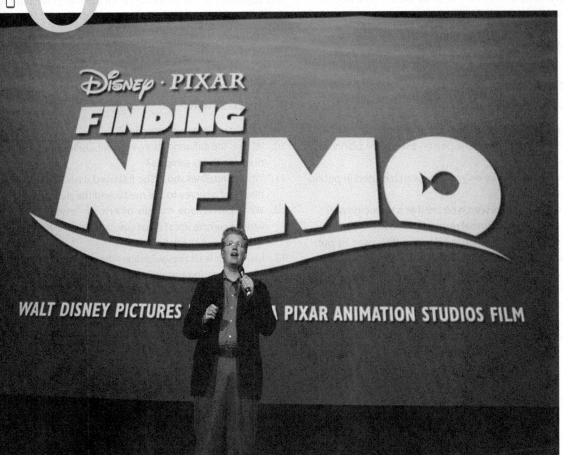

After reading this chapter, you will be able to:

Understand the value of the planning process

Identify the elements of a plan

Describe two approaches to planning

Provide a rationale for including each element of a plan

Describe the essentials of each element of a plan

The Value of Planning

The second step of the public relations process, following research, is program planning. In the RACE acronym mentioned in Chapter 1, this step was labeled "Action" because the organization starts making plans to do something about an issue or situation. Before any public relations activity can be implemented, it is essential that considerable thought be given to what should be done and in what sequence to accomplish the organization's objectives.

A good public relations program should be an effective strategy to support an organization's business, marketing, and communication objectives. Jim Lukaszewski, a veteran public relations counselor, adds, "Strategy is a unique mixture of mental energy, injected into an organization through communication, which results in behavior that achieves organizational objectives."

In other words, public relations planning should be strategic. As Glen Broom and David Dozier say in their text *Using Public Relations Research*, "Strategic planning is deciding where you want to be in the future (the goal) and how to get there (the strategies). It sets the organization's direction proactively, avoiding 'drift' and routine repetition of activities." A practitioner must think about a situation, analyze what can be done about it, creatively conceptualize the appropriate strategies and tactics, and determine how the results will be measured. Planning also involves the coordination of multiple methods—social media, news releases, special events, Web pages, press kits, news conferences, media interviews, brochures, newsletters, speeches, advocacy ads, and so on—to achieve specific results.

Systematic and strategic planning prevents haphazard, ineffective communication. Having a blueprint of what is to be done and how it will be executed makes programs more effective and public relations more valuable to the organization.

> A program plan is the formal, written presentation of your research findings and program recommendations for strategy, tactics, and evaluation.
>
> *Ronald Smith, author of* Strategic Planning for Public Relations

Approaches to Planning

Planning is like putting together a jigsaw puzzle. Research, which was discussed in Chapter 5, provides the various pieces. Next, it is necessary to arrange the pieces so that a coherent design, or picture, emerges. The best planning is systematic, that is, gathering information, analyzing it, and creatively applying it for the specific purpose of attaining an objective.

This section presents two approaches to planning. In both cases, the emphasis is on asking and answering questions to generate a roadmap for success.

Management by Objective

One popular approach to planning is a process called *management by objective* (MBO). MBO provides focus and direction for formulating strategy to achieve specific organizational objectives. According to Robert E. Simmons, author of *Communication Campaign Management*, the use of MBO in planning ensures the "production of relevant messages and establishes criteria against which campaign results can be measured."

> Planning is important because a plan is the instrument used to propose and obtain approvals, a mechanism for monitoring and evaluating and a product that distinguishes true public relations professionals.
>
> *Thomas R. Hagley, author of* Writing Winning Proposals: PR Cases

on the job

INSIGHTS

Wii Fit Gets America Moving

Lukewarm response greeted the Wii Fit debut in 2007, posing a major challenge for Nintendo to build buzz for a video game that looked like a bathroom scale. Working with GolinHarris, Nintendo used a carefully orchestrated public relations campaign to reach three target audiences through major media coverage:

1. Parents over the age of 35
2. Health-conscious consumers
3. Both casual and core gamers

Strategy for the campaign stressed the fun and fitness that the game can provide. Credibility for Wii Fit as an exercise device was driven by partnering with the American Heart Association to offer consumers free tryouts, which research showed would boost sales.

Media interviews with the creator of the game and online interviews with the company president were complemented by personal trainers delivering Wii Fits to several key media outlets, which resulted in coverage by publications including *People* and *Vanity Fair*. Three morning shows—*Today*, *Good Morning America*, and *The Early Show*, as well as the *Ellen DeGeneres Show*—had on-air demos. A *Saturday Night Live* parody helped Wii Fit enter the pop culture dialogue.

Trainers demonstrate wii at an event in Central Park that raised money for the American Heart Association.

Overall, nearly 2,000 publications featured a Wii Fit, with media impressions reaching more than 2 billion, most of which included key messages about how to use the product and how to have fun while getting some exercise.

The well-received launch event took place in New York's Central Park, where $5 was donated to the American Heart Association for every person who got onboard.

Converting information dissemination into purchasing behavior is the ultimate test of a product launch: Wii Fit sold out at the Nintendo world store on launch day and Nintendo reported that the introduction was among the most successful launches in company history. The campaign "turned the product into a phenomenon, a sensation, and it achieved broad ubiquity," said one *PRWeek* judge.

Source: PRWeek Awards 2009.

mycommunicationlab

In their book *Public Relations Management by Objectives*, Norman R. Nager and T. Harrell Allen discuss nine basic MBO steps that can help a practitioner conceptualize everything from a simple news release to a multifaceted communication program. The steps can serve as a planning checklist that provides the basis for strategic planning.

1. **Client/employer objectives.** What is the purpose of the communication, and how does it promote or achieve the objectives of the organization? A specific objective such as "to make 40% of television buyers aware of the product's #1 *Consumer Reports* rating" is more meaningful than "to make people aware of the product."

2. **Audience/publics.** Who exactly should be reached with the message, and how can that audience help achieve the organization's objectives? What are the characteristics of the audience, and how can demographic information be used to structure the message? The primary audience for a campaign to encourage carpooling consists of people who belong to environmental groups and commute long distances, not the general public.

3. **Audience objectives.** What is it that the audience wants to know, and how can the message be tailored to audience self-interest? Consumers are more interested in how a new tablet computer will increase their productivity than in how it works.

4. **Media channels.** What is the appropriate channel for reaching the audience, and how can multiple channels such as news media, brochures, special events, and Twitter reinforce the message among key publics? A news release or an ad may be good for making consumers aware of a new product, but a posting on a popular consumer website may be better for conveying more credible consumer information about the product.

5. **Media channel objectives.** What is the media gatekeeper looking for in a news angle, and why would a particular publication be interested in the information? A community newspaper is primarily interested in a story with a local angle. A television station is interested in stories that have good visuals and emotional impact.

6. **Sources and questions.** What primary and secondary sources of information are required to provide a factual base for the message? What experts should be interviewed? What archival, secondary, and primary research should be conducted? A quote from a project engineer about a new technology is better than a quote from the marketing vice president. A survey, properly conducted, might be best for media interest if there's an interesting statistic or finding.

7. **Communication strategies.** What environmental factors will affect the dissemination and acceptance of the message? Are the target publics hostile or favorably disposed to the message? What other events or pieces of information negate or reinforce the message? A campaign to conserve water is more salient if there has been a recent drought.

8. **Essence of the message.** What is the planned communication impact on the audience? Is the message designed merely to inform, or is it designed to change attitudes and behaviors? Telling people about the dangers of global warming is different from telling people what they can do about it.

9. **Nonverbal support.** How can photographs, graphs, films, and artwork clarify and visually enhance the written message? Bar graphs or pie charts are easier to understand than columns of numbers.

A Strategic Planning Model

By working through the checklist adapted from Nager and Allen's book, a practitioner has in place the general building blocks for planning. These building blocks serve as background to create a specific plan. Ketchum offers more specific questions in its "Strategic Planning Model for Public Relations." Its organizational model makes sense to professionals and clients alike, moving both parties toward the clear situation analysis needed to make planning relevant to the client's overall objectives. As Larry Werner, executive vice president of Ketchum, points out, "No longer are we simply in the business of putting press releases out; we're in the business of solving business problems through communications." See the Insights box on page 146 for an example of Nintendo's strategies to promote its Wii Fit game device.

Facts

- **Category facts.** What are recent industry trends?
- **Product/service issues.** What are the significant characteristics of the product, service, or issue?
- **Competitive facts.** Who are the competitors, and what are their competitive strengths, similarities, and differences?
- **Customer facts.** Who uses the product and why?

Goals

- **Business objectives.** What are the company's business objectives? What is the time frame?
- **Role of public relations.** How does public relations fit into the marketing mix?
- **Sources of new business.** What sectors will produce growth?

Audience

- **Target audiences.** Who are the target audiences? What are their "hot" buttons?
- **Current mindset.** How do audiences feel about the product, service, or issue?
- **Desired mindset.** How do we want them to feel?

Key Message

- **Main point.** What one key message must be conveyed to change or reinforce mindsets?

Each of the many planning processes has its strengths and weaknesses. The culture of the organization as well as the wants and needs of upper management will often give a public relations professional the best indication of which planning approach to adopt. For example, executives who take a bottom-line orientation concerning performance will likely prefer the Ketchum approach to strategic planning. These various approaches to planning lead to the next important step—the writing of a strategic public relations plan. The next section explains the elements of such a plan.

Elements of a Program Plan

A public relations program plan identifies what is to be done, why, and how to accomplish it. By preparing such a plan, either as a brief outline or as an extensive document, the practitioner can make certain that all the elements have been properly considered and that everyone involved understands the "big picture."

It is common practice for public relations firms to prepare a program plan for client approval and possible modification before implementing a public relations campaign. At that time, both the public relations firm and the client reach a mutual understanding of the campaign's objectives and how to accomplish them. Public relations departments of organizations also map out a particular campaign or show the department's plans for the coming year.

Although there can be some variation, public relations plans include eight basic elements:

1. Situation
2. Objectives
3. Audience
4. Strategy
5. Tactics
6. Calendar/timetable
7. Budget
8. Evaluation

The following is a brief description of the various components of a public relations plan and also gives some examples from campaigns receiving PRSA Silver Anvil awards. In addition, the PR Casebook on page 150 gives a real-world example of how public relations firm Fleishman-Hillard implemented a program for its client, United Parcel Service (UPS).

Situation

Valid objectives cannot be set without a clear understanding of the situation that led to the conclusion that a public relations program is needed. Three traditional situations often prompt a public relations program: (1) The organization must conduct a remedial program to overcome a problem or negative situation; (2) the organization needs to conduct a specific, one-time project to launch a new product or service; or (3) the organization wants to reinforce an ongoing effort to preserve its reputation and public support.

Loss of market share and declining sales often require a remedial program. The Butterfinger candy bar brand, for example, was highly popular over its 80-year history, but lost consumer loyalty and store shelf space in recent years because of competition and the proliferation of candy options in convenience stores. Butterfinger brand was considered venerable but out of date, especially for the target market of candy-loving 20- to 27-year-old males. The campaign name, "The Finger," employed a double-entendre that would likely appeal to this group. This campaign will be discussed in subsequent sections. Another example is Sunkist Growers. One impetus for its program was a decline in the purchase of Sunkist lemons as competition increased from foreign imports.

Specific, one-time events often lead to public relations programs. One such campaign was sponsored by Humana Healthcare during the democratic and republican presidential conventions to showcase the health benefits of outdoor activity. The bike-sharing program enabled conventioneers to get around on 1,000 bikes for fresh air, exercise, and environmental benefits to the host cities. The introduction of Microsoft's Windows 7 operating system was also a one-time event; it required a program plan that covered many months of prelaunch activities.

In the third situation, program plans are initiated to reinforce corporate reputation or to preserve customer loyalty or public support. The Denny's restaurant chain

PRCasebook

Going Green Is the New Color of UPS

A public relations plan contains eight basic elements. The following is an outline of a plan that United Parcel Service (UPS) and its public relations firm, Fleishman-Hillard, developed to educate the public about its efforts to reduce its carbon footprint and also to highlight its efficient use of new environmental technologies in its delivery operations.

Situation

UPS delivers 15.5 million packages worldwide every day. To do so, UPS operates about 99,000 vehicles and logs 2 billion miles per year. Because of the huge carbon footprint left by such a fleet, shipping customers often ask for data about emissions linked to package delivery. UPS tracks such data and wanted to communicate its commitment to doing all it can to limit its environmental impact.

Objectives

Research found that customer requests for data about UPS's carbon footprint had increased 243 percent in a single quarter, which led to the following objectives:

- "Position UPS as a company committed to environmental responsibility by showcasing initiatives with positive environmental impacts that are measurable."

- "Highlight the technologies UPS employs to be more efficient and reduce its environmental impact."

Target Audience

Current and prospective customers, investors, and public officials were among UPS's target publics.

Strategies

UPS and Fleishman-Hillard decided the strategy would be to identify "proof points" regarding UPS's efforts to minimize its environmental impact and to develop stories around these points that were remarkable enough to trump other corporate "green stories."

Tactics

On Earth Day, they pitched a story about UPS's high-tech routing system, which helps drivers avoid making left turns, thus reducing emissions. In its PRSA Silver Anvil summary, UPS reported, "The key is minimizing left turns, which require drivers to idle at intersections to wait for traffic to pass, burning excess fuel and generating excess emissions." Their press materials included statistics such as that the policy reduces emissions by 32,000 metric tons of CO_2 (equal to the annual output of 5,200 automobiles).

When UPS placed the world's largest order for hybrid vehicles, press coverage was actively pursued. Similarly, UPS announced a new paperless invoice system to save paper and make global invoicing easier. Many other activities were aggressively pitched to the media in this media relations campaign.

Calendar

The program consisted of nine major announcements to the press over the course of one year.

Budget

The budget for the campaign was undisclosed.

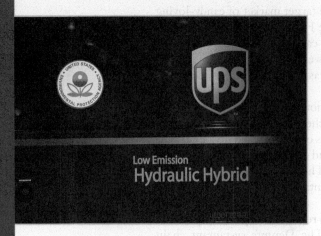

Low Emission
Hydraulic Hybrid

Evaluation

Evaluation consisted of counting impressions (the potential number of people who saw or heard the stories) and identifying prestige media placements. The left-turn story generated 76.9 million impressions, appearing twice in *Parade* magazine, on CBS's *Early Show*, and in *USA Today*. The hybrid vehicle order story was printed in the *Wall Street Journal* and in *USA Today*, and was picked up by the Associated Press, earning 7.8 million impressions. The paperless invoice story was distributed by Reuters and the AP and garnered 3.7 million impressions.

hearkened back to its roots as a cool late-night destination for young people, much as it had been in an earlier era.

In a program plan, relevant research often is included as part of the situation. In the case of Sunkist, it was documented that the brand was losing market share to less expensive lemon imports. For the Nintendo Wii Fit, research indicated that the video game device reminded potential consumers of an unappealing bathroom scale. For the Butterfinger candy bar, the demographics of prospective users uncovered through research pointed to young adult men who feel there is no such thing as too much fun in life and who seek instant gratification and act on it.

Objectives

Once the situation or problem is understood, the next step is to establish objectives for the program. A stated objective should be evaluated by asking: (1) Does it really address the situation? (2) Is it realistic and achievable? (3) Can success be measured in meaningful terms?

An objective is usually stated in terms of program outcomes rather than communication outputs such as news releases created. Or, put another way, objectives should not be the "means" but the "end." A poor objective, for example, is to "generate publicity for a new product." Publicity is not an "end" in itself. The actual objective is to "create consumer awareness of specific product features."

> Before goals and tactics are drafted, PR directors must thoroughly understand their organization's business plan.
>
> *David B. Oates, a Stalwart Communications executive, San Diego*

Butterfinger conducted a successful campaign to increase its sales to young males.

This is accomplished by such tactics as news releases, special events, and even a YouTube video.

It is particularly important that public relations objectives complement and reinforce the organization's objectives. Professor David Dozier of San Diego State University expressed the point well in a *Public Relations Review* article: "The prudent and strategic selection of public relations goals and objectives linked to organizational survival and growth serves to justify the public relations program as a viable management activity."

Basically, objectives are either informational or motivational.

Informational Objectives   Many public relations plans are designed primarily to expose audiences to information through key message points and to increase awareness of an issue, an event, or a product. The five objectives of public relations activity will be discussed in Chapter 7. The first two of these—message exposure and accurate dissemination of messages—are the most common.

The following are some examples of informational objectives:

- **Butterfinger:** "Create national buzz and awareness for Butterfinger by securing 5.5 million media impressions for our program and increasing overall interest in the brand."
- **Denny's:** "Execute a multi-tiered communication program. . . ."
- **Air New Zealand Pink:** "Raise brand awareness of Air New Zealand's unique kiwi service amongst the GLBT [Gay Lesbian Bisexual Transsexual] community."

One difficulty with informational objectives is measuring how well a particular objective has been achieved. Public awareness and the extent of education that takes place are somewhat abstract and difficult to quantify. Some novices try to quantify informational objectives by stating something like "Increase awareness 30 percent." That's very difficult to prove unless an organization has solid baseline research determining the awareness level of the target audience before the campaign was launched and another scientific sample after the campaign to measure any differences in the audience's knowledge or perceptions.

Another approach that many organizations and public relations firms take is to infer that "awareness" or "education" occurred because many media placements were obtained. In reality, message exposure doesn't necessarily lead to increased public awareness. First the message must be viewed or read and then the audience must actually internalize the message for it to have any real impact on knowledge or attitude, much less on behavior. (See Chapter 7 for more on information processing.)

Motivational Objectives   Although changing attitudes and influencing behavior are difficult to accomplish in a public relations campaign, motivational objectives are much easier to measure than informational ones. That's because the former are bottom-line-oriented and based on clearly measurable results that can be quantified. This is true whether the objective is an increase in product sales, a sellout crowd for a theatrical performance, expanded donations to a charitable agency, or a targeted number of media placements regarding the product, service, or issue.

The following are some examples of motivational objectives:

- **Butterfinger:** "Drive trial of Butterfinger with 20-something-year-old guys by securing a convenience store partner for a product giveaway."

- **AT&T U-verse (TV, high-speed Internet, and digital home phone service):** "Double the number of U-verse media stories in the second half of 2008 versus the first half."
- **Doritos:** "Drive consumer engagement in contest via submissions and video views on program website."

Although many public relations programs specify an increased number or percentage as a target, others don't. That increase, of course, could be minimal and still meet the objective of the campaign. Objective setting is the joint responsibility of the public relations firm and the client. Both sides have to keep in mind that the objectives, as already mentioned, must be realistic, achievable, and measurable in some way. Chapter 8 further discusses measurement and evaluation.

Audience

Public relations programs should be directed toward specific and defined audiences or publics. Although some campaigns are directed to a general public, such instances are the exception. Even the word-of-mouth campaign for Clorox Anywhere bleach, a variant of a common household item, was specifically targeted to moms with children under six who are active in the community.

In other words, public relations practitioners target specific publics within the general public. This is done through market research that can identify key publics by such demographics as age, income, social strata, zip code, education, and existing ownership or consumption of specific products. For example, market research told Doritos that their target consumer is between the ages of 16 and 24, and is a member of a technology savvy group that has mastered multitasking with media. The Internet is the second most consumed medium by this group, and they spend approximately three hours online per day.

In many cases, the product or service often self-defines a specific audience. Take, for example, Novartis Animal Health US, which launched a campaign to promote its new drug for older dogs with arthritis. The target audience was not the general public, but dog owners (skewed toward women 18 to 54 with household incomes of $40,000+) who regularly provide health care for their pets. A second primary audience was veterinarians, who would be prescribing the drug. The audience for a water-conservation campaign in Australia, described in the Multicultural World box on page 155, was focused on homeowners living in Queensland.

The following are examples of how other organizations have defined target audiences.

- **AT&T U-verse:** "Existing and potential customers"; "National, local, industry, and online media"; "Internal audiences"
- **Doritos:** "Core: 16- to 24-year-olds; broader: 18- to 45-year-olds"
- **Butterfinger:** "The target audience for Butterfinger is guys 20 to 27 years old, with a 'sweet spot' of the 24-year-old males. . . . More often than not, what they like is clever and irreverent humor, and being able to share their favorite examples of this with their friends."

Many campaigns have multiple audiences, depending on the objectives of the campaign. Tyson Foods used public relations to promote its "Powering the Fight Against Hunger," which donated its products through local charitable agencies to fight hunger. Its target publics were (1) grocery retailers, (2) general consumers of

Tyson products, (3) key business and civic leaders in local communities, (4) Tyson team members in markets throughout the country, and (5) hunger relief and other direct service agencies.

Some organizations and public relations firms identify the media as a "public." On occasion, in programs that seek media endorsements or that try to change how the media report on an organization or an issue, editors and reporters can become a legitimate "public." In general, however, mass media outlets fall in the category of a means to an end, channels to reach defined audiences that need to be informed, persuaded, and motivated.

A better approach, if the campaign is primarily designed to generate media coverage, is to have two categories. Rosetta Stone, the language software company, listed consumers segmented by various demographics as "target publics." It also listed national daily newspapers, travel-leisure and in-flight magazines, national syndicated writers and columnists, and online media as "target media." The demographics of the "target audience" basically determines the characteristics of the "target media."

A thorough understanding of the primary and secondary publics is key to accomplishing a program's objectives. Such knowledge also sharpens selection of appropriate strategies and tactics to reach defined audiences. Cost is a driving force for narrowing the audience; spending large sums to reach members of the general public on matters in which they have no stake or interest is nonproductive and a waste of money.

Strategy

A strategy describes how and why campaign components will achieve objectives. A strategy provides guidelines and key message themes for the overall program, and also offers a rationale for the actions and program components that are planned. A single strategy may be outlined or a program may have several strategies, depending on the objectives and the designated audiences.

With the motto "Go big or go home," Doritos made a strategic gamble so daring that Las Vegas bookies accepted bets on whether it would pay off. The company gave fans complete creative control of the brand and dangled a reward so sweet it motivated avid consumer and media engagement. Among the strategies were:

1. Invite America to develop Doritos Super Bowl ads and award the winning creator with $1 million.
2. Implement a two-pronged media outreach approach to simultaneously reach Doritos' core target audience and likely ad competition entrants and maintain ongoing coverage in mainstream news outlets.

Key Messages   Public relations plans, as part of the strategy, often contain a listing of key messages that the campaign wants to get across to the target audiences and the media. In the case of Go Red for Women, a national awareness campaign for heart disease in women, the three key messages were:

1. Heart disease is the number-one killer of women.
2. Take the Go Red Heart Checkup to find out your personal risk for heart disease.
3. Spread the national rallying cry to "Share Your Untold Story of the Heart."

A New Frontier for Strategy   One of the tendencies in human nature that is shared among public relations professionals is a blind faith in common sense as well as a tendency to use a "same-old, same-old" approach to strategies.

on the job

A MULTICULTURAL WORLD

Australians Adopt the Four-Minute Shower

How do you convince home-owners to use less water? That was the question confronting the Queensland Water Commission because several years of drought had placed the available water supply at serious risk.

The solution was a well-planned campaign to target indoor water consumption in homes, since restrictions had already been placed on outdoor water use. Basic research showed that showers accounted for 33 percent of residential use, and the average shower time was seven minutes. Consequently, a key campaign message was "Shower for four minutes or less." If everyone did this, billions of liters of water could be saved.

The campaign strategy had several components: (1) partnerships with news outlets to get their support and endorsement; (2) partnerships with local water companies and local governments to deliver complementary messages; (3) direct mail to 1.1 million households, which included a shower timer and a booklet; (4) a campaign website (www.target140.com.au); (5) distribution of materials such as brochures, fact sheets, and posters; and (6) a mass media advertising campaign to reinforce key messages.

The result was that indoor water consumption dropped to the target goal of 140 liters or less per day per person, and that 95 percent of residents were saving water in their homes and taking shorter showers. In a follow-up survey, 90 percent of the respondents agreed that water scarcity is here to stay and that changes in water consumption have to be for the long term.

The campaign received a Golden Globe award in 2009 from the International Public Relations Association (IPRA), and it was noted that "Target 140 serves as a national and international model for using attitudinal and behavioural changes to achieve water conservation. . . ."

Both of these are probably wise instincts in general. However, from the perspective of upper management, commonsensical, clichéd counsel on communication strategy may appear less rigorous and less valuable than comparable counsel from legal professionals who bring case law to bear on questions or counsel from consulting engineers who bring materials science to their recommendations to management. Over the last several decades, a large body of social science research has developed to provide better understanding of how communication works and what effect it has on audiences.

The next frontier for the field of public relations, and for students entering the profession now, should be to embrace theories of communication as a basis for strategy recommendations. (See Chapters 9 and 10 for an introduction to many of the social science breakthroughs that can provide a sound basis for strategy development.)

Tactics

Tactics, in contrast to strategies, are the nuts-and-bolts part of the plan. They describe the specific activities that put each strategy into operation and help to achieve the stated objectives. In the public relations field, the implementation of various tactics is the most visible part of any plan. Tactics use various methods to reach target audiences with key messages. Chapters 13 through 16 discuss tactical communication tools in greater detail. To help the reader better understand the difference between strategies and tactics, several tactics of the Butterfinger campaign plan are nested under the strategy that drove the campaign:

> **Strategy:** Carry off an April Fool's prank nationwide that would appeal to the irreverent sense of humor of the young male target market by "punking" journalists all across the country.

> **Tactics:** (1) Establish a media relations campaign that would convince journalists that the Nestlé corporation had actually renamed its famous candy bar "The Finger"; (2) create a consumer website, thefingerbar.com; (3) create actual Finger bars to send to media outlets, along with video of The Finger assembly line.

Strategy establishes why something is being done and why it will work for the purposes of the campaign. But it is in the tactics that the job gets done, such as the difficult task of actually creating and distributing bogus Finger bars to reporters and editors.

Conceiving tactics requires a lot of creativity, which is often accomplished through a brainstorming session that can generate any number of ideas from the practical to the impractical. The goal is to generate many ideas that are innovative and unusual, but grounded in the objectives of the program.

> A tactic is a public relations action designed to have a particular effect on an organization's relationship with a particular public.
>
> *David Guth and Charles Marsh,*
> *authors of* Public Relations:
> A Values-Driven Approach

Calendar/Timetable

The next step is to determine a timetable for the campaign or program. Depending on the objectives and complexity of the program plan, a campaign may last less than three months. Other programs may take more than a year to implement all the strategies and tactics required to accomplish program objectives. The following are three aspects of establishing a calendar and timetable for a program.

The Timing of a Campaign   Program planning should take into account when key messages are most meaningful to the intended audience. A campaign to encourage carpooling, for example, might be more successful if it follows a major price increase in gasoline or a government report that traffic congestion has reached gridlock proportions. Continuing news coverage and public concern about an issue or event also trigger public relations campaigns. Toyota, for example, launched campaigns to emphasize what the company was doing to ensure the safety of its vehicles after the company was rocked by massive recalls in 2010.

Some subjects are seasonal. The Butterfinger spoof of the media would have made little sense if done in mid-July. More importantly, not only did renaming a staid candy brand "The Finger" work best as an April Fool's trick on the media, but it was also done in the season when such shenanigans are forgiven. Charitable agencies, such as Second Harvest, gear their campaigns around Thanksgiving and Christmas, when there is increased interest in helping the unfortunate.

Other kinds of campaigns depend less on environmental or seasonal context. For example, Home Instead Senior Care Service promotes its 40–70 rule year-round (children in their forties need to talk to their parents in their seventies about long-term care year-round). Similarly, the launch of the Denny's Allnighter Rockstar Menu was not tied to a season; any time of the year is a great time for 18- to 34-year-olds to hang out at Denny's late into the night. See the Ethics box below for a campaign prompted by a period of high oil prices.

on the job

ETHICS

Grassroots Environmentalism: Conflict of Interest or a Win-Win?

In response to record-high oil prices that were driving airlines into bankruptcy, a coalition of business and labor groups formed a grassroots campaign against oil speculation in commodity-trading markets. Two weeks of intense strategic planning resulted in a movement called SOS Now (Stop Oil Speculation Now). The plan included impressive tactics:

- Broad coalition building
- Clear, multilingual website
- Airline Frequent Flier Call to Action
- Grassroots advocacy to Congress
- Coalition media toolkit
- Coalition press conference
- Congressional information packets

The campaign succeeded in building congressional interest in regulatory action, resulting in investors pulling $39 billion from commodity markets during the first seven weeks of the campaign. Public opinion polls taken before and during the campaign showed a jump from 6 percent to 50 percent against speculative oil trading. Although planning, execution, and outcomes of the campaign were impressive, several ethical questions need to be considered.

- The SOS campaign was motivated by skyrocketing fuel costs but didn't make it clear that SOS was instigated primarily by the airline industry. Is this really a grassroots movement? Is it ethical, according to PRSA ethical guidelines, to create such coalitions, which might also be called false-front organizations? What is needed for such movements to be ethical?

- Would it be ethical for the American Petroleum Institute (API) to undertake a similar campaign opposing SOS, based on API's conviction that free markets should exist and that the only way to ensure oil exploration and production is healthy oil markets, with strong oil prices responding to supply and demand pressures?

- Environmental activists argue that high fuel prices are good for the environment because they curtail wasteful travel. Would such groups be doing the right thing to argue for oil speculation?

The point may be that in a free society, pluralistic voices often arise on opposing sides of an issue. (See Chapter 10 for explication of the idea of a wrangle of voices in the marketplace of ideas and that there is no single worldview or "truth.") The key may be to work for an organization that one personally believes in, whether, in this case, that is the airline, the petroleum, or the environmental group.

Source: PRSA Silver Anvil Award, 2009.

Scheduling of Tactics   The second aspect of timing is the scheduling and sequencing of various tactics or activities. A typical pattern is to concentrate the most effort at the beginning of a campaign, when a number of tactics are implemented. The launch phase of a campaign, much like that of a rocket, requires a burst of activity just to break the awareness barrier. After the campaign has achieved orbit, however, less energy and fewer activities are required to maintain momentum.

Public relations campaigns often are the first stage of an integrated marketing communications program. Once public relations has created awareness and customer anticipation of a new product, the second stage may be a marketing and advertising campaign. A good example is the iPad, Apple's entrant in the tablet computer category, which generated thousands of news stories before it was available for purchase. Ads for the device didn't appear until several months after the launch of the new product. Apple kept buzz about the product going by rolling out new versions, dropping prices of earlier versions, and promoting the app store, the nifty applications for the iPad developed by inventive third-party programmers.

Compiling a Calendar   An integral part of timing is advance planning. A video news release, a press kit, or a brochure often takes weeks or months to prepare. Arrangements for special events also take considerable time. Practitioners must thus take into account the deadlines of publications. Monthly periodicals, for example, frequently need information several months before publication. A popular talk show may book guests three or four months in advance.

The public relations professional must think ahead to make things happen in the right sequence at the right time. One way to achieve this goal is to compile timelines and charts that list the necessary steps and their required completion dates. Calendars and timelines take various forms. One simple method is to post activities for each day on a large monthly calendar that indicates who has responsibility for a particular task. Gantt charts are popular for scheduling purposes and can be formatted easily using such programs as Microsoft Excel. See Figure 6.1 for a simplified example of a Gantt chart. Such charts can track when a media kit must be written, designed, and turned over to a printer, all with a timely date of final delivery.

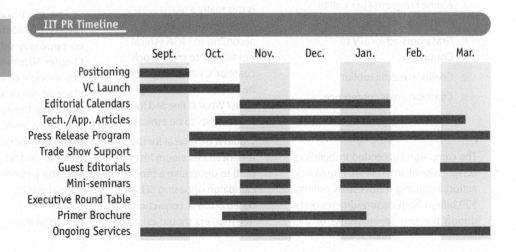

Figure 6.1
A Typical Gantt Chart

IIT PR Timeline

	Sept.	Oct.	Nov.	Dec.	Jan.	Feb.	Mar.
Positioning							
VC Launch							
Editorial Calendars							
Tech./App. Articles							
Press Release Program							
Trade Show Support							
Guest Editorials							
Mini-seminars							
Executive Round Table							
Primer Brochure							
Ongoing Services							

Budget

No program plan is complete without a budget. Both clients and employers ask, "How much will this program cost?" In many cases, the reverse approach is taken, in which organizations establish an amount they can afford and then ask the public relations staff or firm to write a program plan that reflects the amount allocated. The range of total costs shown below is based either on the needs of the campaign or on the amount available from the client:

- **Scripps Workforce Communication Program:** $150,000 for collateral, design, printing, mailing and personnel
- **SanDisk's launch of its Extreme Pro flash memory card:** $300,000
- **Frito-Lay's Change the Oil:** $1.7 million to cover a three-phase campaign
- **Miller Brewing "Take Back the High Life" marketing campaign:** $80,000
- **Blockbuster Total Access:** $300,000, exclusive of the celebrity-appearance fee
- **Tyson's Fight Against Hunger:** $110,000; another $300,000 was financial support to charitable agencies, and another $2.3 million worth of products were donated

A budget is often divided into two categories: (1) staff time and (2) out-of-pocket expenses. The latter often goes by the acronym *OOP* and includes such collateral material as news releases, media kits, brochures, video news releases (VNRs), transportation, Web programming, and even video production. Staff and administrative time usually takes the lion's share, as much as 70 percent, of any public relations budget. Information about how public relations firms charge fees was presented in Chapter 4.

One method of budgeting is to use two columns. The left column lists the staff cost for writing a pamphlet or compiling a press kit. The right column lists the actual OOP expense for having the pamphlet or press kit designed, printed, and delivered. Internal public relations staffs, whose members are on the payroll, often complete only the OOP expenses. It is good practice to allocate about 10 percent of the budget for contingencies or unexpected costs.

Evaluation

The evaluation element of a plan relates directly back to the stated objectives of the program. As discussed earlier, objectives must be measurable in some way to show clients and employers that the program accomplished its purpose. Consequently, it's important to have a good idea of what metrics you will use to evaluate whether the plan's objectives have been met. Again, evaluation criteria should be realistic, credible, and specific. The evaluation section of a program plan should restate the objectives and then name the evaluation methods to be used.

Evaluation of an informational objective often entails a compilation of news clips and an analysis of how often key message points were mentioned. Other methods might be to determine how many brochures were distributed or the estimated number of viewers who saw a video news release. Motivational objectives often are measured and evaluated by increases in sales or market share, by the number of people who called an 800 number for more information, or by benchmark surveys that measure people's perceptions before and after a campaign.

Evaluation and measurement techniques are thoroughly discussed in Chapter 8, with reference to many of the campaigns mentioned in this chapter. To give the reader some idea of how campaign success is evaluated, however, the Denny's Allnighter campaign evaluation is summarized below by highlighting how each campaign objective was met. The campaign, conducted by Fleishman-Hillard public relations, received a 2009 Silver Anvil award from PRSA in the category of Marketing Consumer Products. See the Insights box below for key values in effective plans.

- **Objective 1: Create Denny's brand relevance among the target 18- to 34-year-old audience by recapturing Denny's brand heritage of association with music.**
  - Media highlights included *The Daily Show with Jon Stewart*, "MTV News," *The Daily Buzz*, perezhilton.com, vibe.com.
  - Denny's Rockstar menu cited in *USA Today* 2008 cover story, "Test Your Pop-Culture Prowess."
- **Objective 2: Increase late-night menu trial and sales.**
  - Denny's Allnighter program increased late-night guest counts, check averages, and overall sales.
  - The new menu items have become the dominant portion of sales during late night.
- **Objective 3: Execute a multi-tiered communications program that delivers immediate launch impact and sustained support for the initiative.**
  - Online impressions at dennyallnighter.com totaled 3 million in the launch phase.
  - During launch week alone, the website recorded nearly 1,000,000 page views.
  - Media impact in 2008 included 215 insertions, with over 167 million impressions.

The next chapter discusses the third element of the public relations process, communication, which basically deals with the implementation and execution of a program plan.

on the job

INSIGHTS

The "Big Picture" of Program Planning

The eight elements of a program plan are important for structuring an effective campaign, but the perspective of the "bigger picture" should also be kept in mind. Michael Morley, president of his own consulting firm in New York City, gives four personal guideposts " . . . that [have] served me well over the years when embarking on every public relations initiative." They are:

- The idea is more important than the message.
- The message is more important than the medium.
- The individual is more important than the audience.
- Thinking and acting locally are the only sound building blocks of a global strategy.

Source: Michael Morley, Atlas Award presentation at the 2009 PRSA International Conference, San Diego, CA.

PEARSON **mycommunication**lab

Summary

The Value of Planning

After research is done, the next step in the public relations process is planning a program or campaign to accomplish organizational objectives. Such planning must be strategic, creative, and pay close attention to reaching key audiences. A program's objectives can be purely informational to create awareness, or more motivational to actually increase participation or sales.

Approaches to Planning

One classic approach is the management by objective (MBO) model, which systematically categorizes objectives, communication strategies, audiences, and the essence of the message. Public relations firms often have their own planning model, which often includes market research, demographic segmentation of target audiences, and establishment of key messages.

Elements of a Program Plan

A program plan is either a brief outline or an extensive document identifying what is to be done and how. Public relations firms prepare these for client approval, and there is joint consultation about budgets, strategies, and tactical communication tools. A public relations plan, at minimum, should contain eight elements: situation, objectives, audience, strategy, tactics, calendar or timeline, budget, and evaluation.

Case Activity   A Plan for Sunshine Cafe

Sunshine Cafe, a chain of coffee houses, conducted market research and found that college students would be an excellent audience for its product and services. To this end, Sunshine Cafe has contacted your public relations firm and asked you to develop a comprehensive plan that does two things: (1) creates brand awareness among college students

and (2) increases walk-in business at their local stores in college towns.

Using the eight-point planning outline described in this chapter, write a public relations program for Sunshine Cafe. You should consider a variety of communication tools, including campus events. No money has been allocated for advertising.

Questions   for Review and Discussion

1. Why is planning so important in the public relations process?
2. What is MBO, and how can it be applied to public relations planning?
3. Explain the difference between an informational objective and a motivational objective.
4. Should a practitioner define an audience as the "general public"? Why or why not?
5. What is the difference between a strategy and a tactic?
6. Why are timing and scheduling so important in a public relations campaign?
7. Why is evaluation of a campaign linked to the program's objectives?

Media Resources

Auffermann, K. (2009, Fall). RIP mass media: Why ad guru Bob Garfield thinks PR will survive. *The Strategist*, 25–28.

Hagley, T. R. (2009). *Writing winning proposals: PR cases*. San Diego, CA: Cognella.

Hazley, G. (2009, December). College football fattens PR playbook. *O'Dwyer's PR Report*, 1, 11.

Henkel, D., & Niehaus, R. (2009, December). *Time management: How a negative cover story spurred positive messaging. *Public Relations Tactics*, 4.

Silver Anvil Award summaries for 2009. (2009). Retrieved from www.prsa.org

Smith, R. D. (2005). *Strategic planning for public relations* (2nd ed.). Mahwah, NJ: Lawrence Erlbaum.

Wilson, L., & Ogden, J. (2008). *Strategic communications planning for effective public relations and marketing* (5th ed.). Dubuque, IA: Kendall Hunt.

Communication

Steve Jobs is a charismatic communicator for Apple's new products.

After reading this chapter, you will be able to:

Understand the role of effective communication in the public relations process

Identify the characteristics of various media channels

Be familiar with the communication objectives of a campaign

Recognize the components of how audiences receive messages and process them

Understand the five stages of how individuals adopt a new product or idea

The Goals of Communication

The third step in the public relations process, after research and planning, is *communication*. This step, also called *execution*, is the most visible part of public relations work.

Implementing the Plan

In a public relations program, as pointed out in Chapter 6, communication is the implementation of a decision, the process and the means by which objectives are achieved. A program's strategies and tactics may take the form of news releases, news conferences, special events, social media such as Facebook and Twitter, speeches, webcasts, rallies, posters, and even word of mouth.

The goals of the communication process are to inform, persuade, motivate, or achieve mutual understanding. To be an effective communicator, a person must have basic knowledge of (1) what constitutes communication and how people receive messages, (2) how people process information and change their perceptions, and (3) what kinds of media and communication tools are most appropriate for a particular message.

Concerning the last point, Kirk Hallahan of Colorado State University notes that today's communication revolution has given public relations professionals a full range of communication tools and media, and the traditional approach of simply obtaining publicity in the mass media—newspapers, magazines, radio, and television—is no longer sufficient, if it ever was. He writes:

> PR program planners need to reexamine their traditional approaches to the practice and think about media broadly and strategically. PR media planners must now address some of the same questions that confront advisers. What media best meet a program's objectives? How can media be combined to enhance program effectiveness? What media are most efficient to reach key audiences?

Hallahan's concept of an integrated public relations media model, which outlines five categories of media, is shown in Table 7.1. Another model worth noting is one used by Hewlett-Packard (HP). Shown in Figure 7.1 on page 166 is a message-based communications spectrum that includes programs, audiences, and various communication vehicles. Many of these media are discussed in Chapters 13–16.

A Public Relations Perspective

A number of variables must be considered when planning a message on behalf of an employer or client. Patrick Jackson, who was editor of *pr reporter* and a senior counselor before his death, believed that the communicator should ask whether the proposed message is (1) appropriate, (2) meaningful, (3) memorable, (4) understandable, and (5) believable to the prospective recipient. According to Jackson, "Many a wrongly directed or unnecessary communication has been corrected or dropped by using a screen like this."

In addition to examining the proposed content, a communicator should determine exactly what objective is being sought by means of the communication. James Grunig, professor emeritus of public relations at the University of Maryland, lists five possible objectives for a communicator:

Table 7.1   An Integrated Public Relations Media Model

The variety and scope of media and communication tools available to public relations professionals runs the spectrum from mass media (public media) to one-on-one communication (interpersonal communication). Here, in chart form, is a concept developed by Professor Kirk Hallahan at Colorado State University.

← Mass Communication

High tech, Perceptually Based,
Low Social Presence, Asynchronous

Personalized Communication →

Low tech, Experientially Based,
High Social Presence, Synchronous

PUBLIC MEDIA	CONTROLLED MEDIA	INTERACTIVE MEDIA	EVENTS	ONE-ON-ONE
Key Uses in a Communication Program				
Build awareness; Enhance credibility	Promotion; Provide detailed information	Respond to queries; Exchange information; Engage users	Motivate participants; Reinforce existing beliefs, attitudes	Obtain commitments; Negotiation, resolution of problems
Principal Examples of Media				
Publicity/advertising/ advertorials/product placements in	Brochures	E-mail, instant, text and microblog messages	Meetings/conferences	Personal visits/lobbying
	Newsletters		Speeches/presentations	Correspondence
Newspapers	Sponsored magazines	E-newsletters, e-zines	Government or judicial testimony	Telephone calls
Magazines	Annual reports	Automated telephone call systems	Trade shows, exhibitions	
Radio	Books		Demonstrations/rallies	
Television	Direct mail	Web sites, blogs	Sponsored events	
		Vodcasts/podcasts	Observances/anniversaries	
Paid advertising	Exhibits and displays	Games	Contests/sweepstakes	
Transit media	Point-of-purchase support	Web conferences, webinars, webcasts	Recognition award programs	
Out-of-home media (Billboards, posters, electronic displays)	DVDs/Videobrochures	Information kiosks		
Directories	Statement inserts	Internets and extranets	(Often supported with multi-media presentations)	
Venue signage	Other collateral or printed ephemera	Social networking sites		
Movie theater trailers, advertising	Advertising specialties	Forums (chats, groups)		
		Media sharing sites		
		Paid text/display click-through advertising		

1. **Message exposure.** Public relations personnel provide materials to the mass media and disseminate other messages through controlled media such as newsletters and the organization's websites. Intended audiences are exposed to the message in various forms.

2. **Accurate dissemination of the message.** The basic information, often filtered by journalists, editors, and bloggers, remains intact as it is transmitted through various channels.

3. **Acceptance of the message.** Based on its view of reality, the audience not only retains the message, but accepts it as valid.

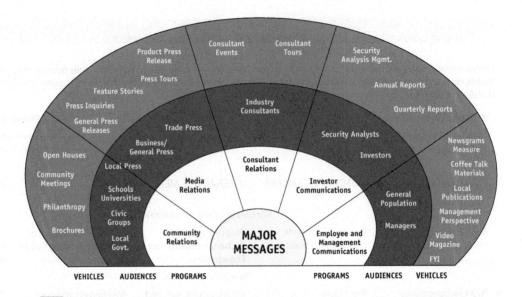

VEHICLES   AUDIENCES   PROGRAMS   PROGRAMS   AUDIENCES   VEHICLES

Figure 7.1   HP's Message-Based Communications Spectrum

A variety of communication vehicles, audiences, and programs must be considered when an organization wants to communicate key messages. This chart, developed by Roy Verley when he was VP of corporate communications at Hewlett-Packard (HP), shows the multiple aspects.

4. **Attitude change.** The audience not only believes the message, but makes a verbal or mental commitment to change behavior as a result of the message.

5. **Change in overt behavior.** Members of the audience actually change their current behavior or purchase the product and use it.

Grunig says that most public relations experts usually aim for the first two objectives: exposure to the message and accurate dissemination. The last three objectives depend in large part on a mix of variables—predisposition to the message, peer reinforcement, feasibility of the suggested action, and environmental context, to name a few. The first two objectives are easier to accomplish than attitude change (see Chapter 9).

Although the communicator cannot always control the outcome of a message, researchers recognize that effective dissemination is the beginning of the process that leads to opinion change and adoption of products or services. Therefore, it is important to review all components of the communication process.

David Therkelsen, former CEO of the American Red Cross in St. Paul, Minnesota, and now executive director of the Crisis Connection in Minneapolis, succinctly outlines the process:

> To be successful, a message must be received by the intended individual or audience. It must get the audience's attention. It must be understood. It must be believed. It must be remembered. And ultimately, in some fashion, it must be acted upon. Failure to accomplish any of these tasks means the entire message fails.

Therkelsen appropriately places the emphasis on the audience and what it does with the message. The following sections elaborate on the six elements he enumerates: (1) receiving the message, (2) paying attention to the message, (3) understanding the message, (4) believing the message, (5) remembering the message, and (6) acting on the message.

Receiving the Message

There are numerous communication models that explain how a message moves from the sender to the recipient. Some are quite complex, attempting to incorporate an almost infinite number of events, ideas, objects, and people that interact among the message, channel, and receiver.

Five Communication Elements

The evolution of communication models is best illustrated by Figure 7.2. Wilbur Schramm, a pioneer in communication theory, first conceptualized a one-way linear model that shows the five basic elements of source, encoder, signal, decoder, and destination. The model emphasizes that both the source and the receiver continually encode, interpret, decode, transmit, and receive information.

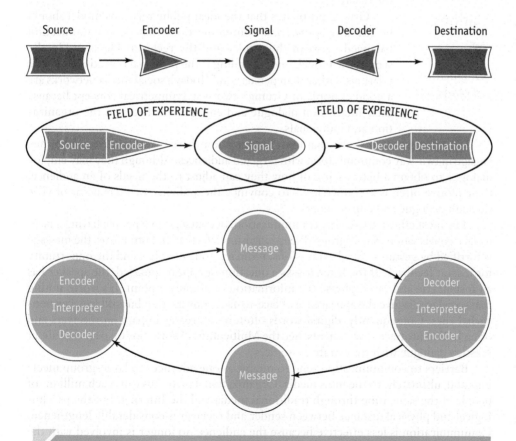

Source   Encoder   Signal   Decoder   Destination

FIELD OF EXPERIENCE   FIELD OF EXPERIENCE

Source Encoder → Signal → Decoder Destination

Message

Encoder / Interpreter / Decoder

Decoder / Interpreter / Encoder

Message

Figure 7.2   Schramm's Communication Models

These three models, formulated by Wilbur Schramm, show the evolution of our thinking about communication toward the current emphasis on an interactive process between a sender and a receiver. Effective communication takes place within a sphere of "shared experience."

The second model developed by Schramm takes into consideration the idea that communication occurs only if both the sender and the receiver have a field of shared experience, such as a common language and similar educational levels. Ultimately, Schramm developed a third model, which incorporates the concept that there is constant feedback between the source and the receiver in a continual loop.

The loop process also is integral to models that show the public relations process of research, planning, communication, and evaluation. This concept was illustrated in Chapter 1, which showed public relations as a cyclical process. Communication to internal and external audiences produces feedback that is taken into consideration during research, the first step, and evaluation, the fourth step. In this way, the structure and dissemination of messages are continuously refined for maximum effectiveness.

The Importance of Two-Way Communication

> In the symmetric model, understanding is the principal objective of public relations, rather than persuasion.
>
> *James E. Grunig, professor emeritus, University of Maryland*

Another way to think of feedback is as two-way communication. One-way communication, from sender to receiver, only disseminates information. Such a monologue is less effective than two-way communication, which establishes a dialogue between the sender and the receiver.

Grunig postulates that the ideal public relations model should be *two-way symmetrical* communication, that is, communication balanced between the sender and the receiver. He says: "In the symmetric model, understanding is the principal objective of public relations, rather than persuasion." Today's social media networks are a good example of Grunig's two-way symmetrical concept because their focus is on dialogue and engagement between the organization and individuals.

In reality, research shows that most organizations have mixed motives when they engage in two-way communication with targeted audiences. Although they may employ dialogue to obtain a better sense of how they can adjust to the needs of an audience, their motive often is asymmetrical—to convince the audience of their point of view through dialogue and engagement.

The most effective two-way communication, of course, is two people having a face-to-face conversation. Small-group discussion also is effective. In both forms, the message is fortified by gestures, facial expressions, intimacy, tone of voice, and the opportunity for instant feedback. If the listener asks a question or appears puzzled, the speaker has an instant cue and can rephrase the information or amplify a point. It's worth noting that social media give the appearance of face-to-face conversation but still lack key nonverbal cues. Consequently, digital words often have greater impact on receivers and often lead to protracted arguments. See the Multicultural World box on page 169 about Nestlé's dialogue with some irate customers.

Barriers to communication tend to mount as one advances to large-group meetings and, ultimately, to the mass media. Organizational materials can reach millions of people at the same time through traditional media and the Internet, but the psychological and physical distance between sender and receiver is considerably lengthened. Communication is less effective because the audience no longer is involved with the source. No immediate feedback may be possible, and the message may undergo distortion as it is edited and revised by journalists and editors in traditional mass media outlets.

on the job

A MULTICULTURAL WORLD

It's a Small, Two-Way World

According to Andy Beaupre, CEO of the eponymous Beaupre public relations agency, Nestlé Foods offers seven important lessons for any company wanting to use social media to engage in meaningful communication with key audiences. Lessons learned clearly also showcase the value of genuine, two-way communication in a world made tiny by the Internet and social media. The case also reinforces recommendations made on page 168 by Dr. James E. Grunig. Beaupre states: "If a company still doesn't 'get' how social media has changed the rules of branding by empowering consumers, look no further than the ongoing Nestlé firestorm."

Nestlé endured a contracted conflict with Greenpeace over Nestlé's ongoing use of palm oil in its food products. Greenpeace argues that palm oil is linked to environmental harm, including deforestation, greenhouse gas emissions, and endangered species loss. For a potentially upsetting but powerful video from Greenpeace, go to the site playing the video after Nestlé forced YouTube to pull the piece: http://vimeo.com/10236827.

According to *CNET News*'s blog called *The Social*, Nestlé created a backlash and a "twitstorm" of negative reaction on Facebook and Twitter by taking sharp action against a flood of comments to the Nestlé Facebook page inspired and orchestrated by

Greenpeace. Greenpeace encouraged individuals to create satirical slogans using Nestlé food logos as profile photos. Nestlé responded with a sharp warning about copyright violation for altering logos and rude comments to its social media critics as the furor built momentum. Typical responses from the global community, concerned about rain forest habitat and orangutan decimation, included:

Thanks, you are doing a far better job than we could ever achieve in destroying your brand.

It's not okay for people to use altered versions of your logos, but it's okay for you to alter the face of Indonesian rainforests? Wow!

I would like to enjoy my Kit Kats without feeling responsible for rainforest destruction and orangutan deaths.

Writing for *CNET*, Caroline McCarthy summed up the situation with a word of caution for public relations practitioners using social media:

Putting aside all judgment on who's right and who's wrong in this situation, we are seeing the dark side of the Facebook fan page: what was intended to be an open way for fans to show their support was turned into a billboard of outrage on behalf of critics, and with the company representative in obvious panic over how to tame the mob. It's rare that public oppo-

sition will reach a truly uncontrollable level, but when it does, it's ugly. . . . But this is the first time that we've seen such a massive blow-up in the comments of a Facebook fan page. Right now, the Facebook page is one of the hottest digital marketing tools out there, and brands hearing about the Nestlé debacle are also seeing the downsides of operating such a public forum to welcome consumer comments. Whether this will be remembered as a single badly mismanaged user backlash or a pratfall of social media marketing in general has yet to be seen.

Beaupre notes that Nestlé was clueless about the power shift enabled by social media and acted in an old-school, authoritarian, "we own the brand" way.

Vital lessons from the Nestlé debacle are offered by Beaupre for professional communicators advising their execs or clients:

1. **Before diving into social media,** make sure key decision makers truly "get" how the game is played. It's not a press release.

2. **Make sure they understand** that tools like Facebook, Twitter, and LinkedIn aren't one-way vehicles (where the brand dominates the message), but an invitation to a never-ending dance with constantly changing partners, some of whom are never your friend.

(continued)

3. **Don't use social media unless the brand** is willing to take the risk of *jumping off the cliff*, giving up control to customers and consumers who will express their viewpoints, both positive and negative.

4. **If your company or client wants to control the message,** then social media isn't the right choice. Look at how Nestlé tried to tell people not to post their logos. Imposing controls on participants will only incur their wrath.

5. **Creating LinkedIn, Facebook, and Twitter accounts is just the first step.** The goal isn't to Tweet or post, but to build an active community and an authentic two-way relationship based on trust. It's easy to get started in social media, but time-consuming and challenging to remain engaged and build a following.

6. **Remember** that even if your company or client decides not to engage in social media, that won't stop rants, rebellion, and revolution. People will find a way to express themselves and let it be known they're disturbed, upset, confused, or disappointed. The train has left the station—be prepared.

7. **As we've learned from Nestlé** (and many others), people don't want to be scammed, ignored, or mistreated. It *will* come back to bite you. So if your exec or client wants social media to become a positive tool, the brand must be a concerned good listener prepared to take action to correct situations that aren't right.

By the way, Nestlé ultimately dropped the palm oil supplier.

PEARSON
mycommunicationlab

Paying Attention to the Message

Who says what, in which channel, to whom, with what effect?

Sociologist Harold Lasswell

Sociologist Harold Lasswell has defined the act of communication as "Who says what, in which channel, to whom, with what effect?"

Although in public relations much emphasis is given to the formation and dissemination of messages, this effort is wasted if the audience pays no attention. The axiom of Walt Seifert, pioneering professor of public relations at Ohio State University, holds true today: "Dissemination does not equal publication, and publication does not equal absorption and action." In other words, "All who receive it won't publish it, and all who read or hear it won't understand or act upon it."

Some Theoretical Perspectives

Seifert and social psychologists recognize that the majority of an audience at any given time is not particularly interested in a message or in adopting an idea. This doesn't mean, however, that audiences are merely passive receivers of information. Werner Severin and James Tankard, in their text *Communication Theories*, quote one researcher as saying:

The communicator's audience is not a passive recipient—it cannot be regarded as a lump of clay to be molded by the master propagandist. Rather, the audience is made up of individuals who demand something from the communication to which they are exposed, and who select those that are likely to be useful to them.

This is called the *media uses and gratification theory* of communication. Its basic premise is that the communication process is interactive. The communicator wants to inform and even persuade; the recipient wants to be entertained, informed, or alerted to opportunities that can fulfill individual needs. Later theoretical versions compare uses and gratifications sought with those achieved. This emphasizes that a professional can communicate with an eye toward what is sought by an audience and then assess what the audience felt it achieved by reading or viewing the public relations message.

In other words, audiences come to messages for very different reasons. People use mass media for such purposes as (1) surveillance of the environment to find out what is happening, locally or even globally, that has some impact on them; (2) entertainment and diversion; (3) reinforcement of their opinions and predispositions; and (4) decision making about buying a product or service.

The media uses and gratification theory assumes that people make highly intelligent choices about which messages require their attention and fulfill their needs. If this is true, as research indicates it is, the public relations communicator must tailor messages that focus on getting the audience's attention.

One approach is to understand the mental state of the intended audience. Grunig and Hunt, in *Managing Public Relations*, suggest that communication strategies be designed to attract the attention of two kinds of audiences: those who passively process information and those who actively seek information.

Passive Audiences   Individuals in this category pay attention to a message only because it is entertaining and offers a diversion. Passive audiences use communication channels such as billboards or radio spots that they can briefly notice while they are doing something else.

For this reason, passive audiences need messages that have style and creativity. The person must be lured by photos, illustrations, and catchy slogans into processing information. Press agentry, the dramatic picture, the use of celebrities, radio and television announcements, and events featuring entertainment can make passive audiences aware of a message. The objectives of a communication, therefore, are simply exposure to and accurate dissemination of a message. In most public relations campaigns, communications are designed to reach primarily passive audiences. See the Insights box on page 172 about Gillette's effort to convince young men to shave more often.

Active Audiences   A communicator's approach to audiences that actively seek information is different. These people are already interested and engaged, and are in search of more sophisticated, supplemental information. An example is the person who has already determined that further health care reform is needed and begins actively seeking more detailed information by visiting health policy websites and reading in-depth newspaper and magazine articles about single-payer health systems. A person actively seeking information may attend a talk or begin following experts on Twitter who offer useful arguments and links to fellow advocates of a shared policy position.

At any given time, of course, the intended audience has both passive and active information seekers in it. It is important, therefore, that multiple messages and a variety of communication tools be used in a full-fledged information campaign so that both passive and active audiences can be effectively reached.

The Concept of Triggering Events   Public relations practitioners should spend more time thinking about what behaviors they are trying to motivate in target publics than about what information they are communicating to those publics. Professionals should build triggering events into their planning to cause people to act on their latent willingness to behave in a certain way.

A triggering event, for example, might be rapid response to a natural disaster such as the H1N1 flu epidemic, which threatened the well-being of millions worldwide. Although this was not planned, it was the catalyst for thousands of people to act on their latent readiness to take care of themselves and their loved ones through frequent

on the job
INSIGHTS

Women Mobilize Against Scruffy-Faced Men

The unshaven look remains in fashion these days for men, ranging from fashion models to celebrities to the average guy who wants to look "cool." So what is a razor manufacturer committed to the clean-shaven look to do?

Gillette and its public relations firm, Porter Novelli, decided that something had to be done after research indicated that shaving frequency was on the decline among younger men. The research also indicated, however, that only 3 percent of the women surveyed prefer scruffy men. That piece of information became the centerpiece of a campaign to leverage the influence that women exert in their partners' grooming decisions to create greater support for the clean-shaven look.

The challenge, however, was how to create a campaign that would make men pay attention to the message. The creative solution was a somewhat edgy promotional event designed primarily to generate widespread media coverage. The company created a tongue-in-cheek protest group called the National Organization of Social Crusaders Repulsed by Unshaven Faces (NoScruf), whose "members" were women who vowed to stop shaving until their men started doing so. The ultimatum given to guys was "Lose the scruff or lose the girl."

The "movement" began online at *NoScruf.org*, which featured deliber-

No Scruff

Gillette's staged rally for clean-shaven men was a highly visual event that attracted media attention.

ately amateurish graphics and humorous streaming videos that reinforced the idea of a grassroots campaign. The website featured news reports and video clips. In one video titled "In Your Dreams, Stubble Boy," a scruffy young man gets a glimpse of what the world would be like if women stopped shaving.

The site also featured two female celebrities as "founders" of the NoScruf movement: Kelly Monaco, the first winner of *Dancing with the Stars* and now a television actor, and Brooke Burke, widely known as a swimsuit model and ranked in men's magazines as one of the sexiest women in the

world. According to one news release, Monaco said, "We at NoScruf have a message for scruffy guys out there who want to get close to us: 'In your dreams, stubble boy!'"

The two female celebrities were also on hand at a protest rally staged in New York's Herald Square. They led a group of 50 attractive young women in NoScruf-branded T-shirts who proudly sported fake unshaven underarm hair and placards reading, "We Won't Shave Until You Do." The protest rally seemed so real that even a CNN producer on his way to work called in a news crew to cover it. The rally was also featured on *Today* and generated coverage in other major cities. According to Porter Novelli, "The humor, incongruous make-up and celebrity presence collectively translated into uniformly favorable coverage. The core message that women are hugely dissatisfied with their scruffy boyfriends was reinforced repeatedly."

As a result of media covering the protest rally, the NoScruf website received more than 2 million hits, with 65,000 unique visitors in 24 hours. The short video "In Your Dreams, Stubble Boy" was viewed more than 7 million times.

hand washing and revised sneezing practices—into the shirt sleeve, not the hand. The H1N1 trigger was a boon to companies selling hand-disinfectant gels. However, a triggering event doesn't have to be a disaster or a crisis; it can also be the launch of a new product such as the iPad or a new vampire novel. In either case, the "event" was the catalyst for people to engage with others about a shared interest.

Other Attention-Getting Concepts

Communicators should think in terms of the five senses: sight, hearing, smell, touch, and taste. Motion media such as television, animation, games, virtual reality, and videos are the most effective and the most popular modes of communication today for an audience expecting a full sensual experience, with 3-D sight, sound, color, movement, and engagement. Radio, on the other hand, relies on only the sense of hearing. Print media, although capable of communicating a large amount of information in great detail, rely only on sight.

Individuals learn through all five senses, but psychologists estimate that 83 percent of learning is accomplished through sight. Hearing accounts for 11 percent. Fifty percent of what individuals retain consists of what they see and hear. For this reason, speakers often use visual aids.

These figures have obvious implications for the public relations practitioner. Any communication strategy should, if possible, include vehicles of communication designed to tap the senses of sight or hearing or a combination of the two. In other words, a variety of communication tools is needed, including news releases, publicity photos, special events, YouTube videos, billboards, newsletters, radio announcements, video news releases, media interviews, and news conferences. This multiple approach not only assists learning and retention, it also provides repetition of a message in a variety of forms that accommodate audience needs.

Other research suggests that audience attention can be engaged if the communicator raises a "need" level first. The idea is to "hook" an audience's attention by beginning the message with something that will make its members' lives easier or benefit them in some way. An example is the message from the Census Bureau emphasizing that everyone counts in America and urging people to complete the simple census form so that government resources get distributed fairly. Public relations writers also should be aware that audience attention is highest at the beginning of a message. Thus, it is wise to state the major point at the beginning, give details in the middle, and end with a summary of the message.

Another technique to garner audience attention is to begin a message with a statement that reflects audience values and predispositions. This is called channeling (see Chapter 9). According to social science research, people pay attention to messages that reinforce their predispositions.

Prior knowledge and interest also make people pay more attention to messages. If a message taps current events or issues of public concern already in the news, there is an increased chance that the audience will pay attention.

Understanding the Message

Communication is the act of transmitting information, ideas, and attitudes from one person to another. Communication can take place, however, only if the sender and receiver have a common understanding of the symbols being used. This is Schramm's concept of "field of experience," shown in Figure 7.2 on page 167.

Effective Use of Language

Words are the most common symbols. The degree to which two people understand each other is heavily dependent on their common knowledge of word symbols. Anyone who has traveled abroad can readily attest that very little communication occurs between two people who speak different languages. Even signs translated into English for tourists often lead to some confusing and amusing messages. A brochure for a Japanese hotel, for example, said, "In our hotel, you will be well fed and agreeably drunk. In every room there is a large window offering delightful prospects."

Even if sender and receiver speak the same language and live in the same country, the effectiveness of their communication depends on such factors as education, social class, regional differences, nationality, and cultural background.

Employee communication specialists are particularly aware of such differences as a multicultural workforce becomes the norm for most organizations. One major factor is the impact of a global economy in which multinational organizations employ culturally diverse workforces in the countries where they operate. One study says that 85 percent of new entrants into the American workforce are now white women, immigrants, African Americans, Hispanics, and Asians. For many of these workers, English will be a second language.

These statistical trends will require communicators to be better informed about cultural differences and conflicting values in order to find common ground and build bridges between various groups. At the same time, a major task will be to communicate in clear and simple terms. National studies show that 42 million American adults fall within the lowest category of literacy, with one in eight employees reading at no better than a fourth-grade level. Delivering usable information to these citizens is a challenge and a problem. For example, Health Literacy Missouri (www.healthliteracymissouri.org) points out that errors, confusion, and miscommunication due to low health literacy result in tragic human costs as well as billions of dollars annually.

Writing for Clarity

The nature of the audience and its literacy level are important considerations for any communicator. The key is to produce messages that match, in content and structure, the characteristics of the audience.

The Illinois Public Health Department had the right idea when it commissioned a song in rap-music style as one way to inform low-income, poorly educated groups about the dangers of AIDS. The words and music of the "Condom Rag," however, were offensive to elected officials, who cancelled the song.

This example poses the classic dilemma for the expert communicator: Should the message be produced for supervisors, whose backgrounds and education levels may be totally different from those of the intended audience, or should it be produced with the audience in mind? The obvious answer is the latter, but it is often difficult to convince management of this. One solution is to copy-test all public relations materials on the target audience. This helps convince management—and communicators—that what they like isn't necessarily what the audience wants, needs, or understands.

Another approach is to apply readability and comprehension formulas to materials before they are produced and disseminated. Learning theory makes the case: The simpler the piece of writing, the easier it will be for audiences to understand.

The most widely known readability formula is by Rudolph Flesch. Another is by Barr, Jenkins, and Peterson. Both are based on average sentence length and the number of one-syllable words per 100 words. If a randomly selected sample of 100 words contains 4.2 sentences and 142 syllables, it is ranked at about the ninth-grade level. This is the level for which most news releases and daily newspapers strive. In other words, long, complex sentences (more than 19 words) and multisyllabic words (for example, "compensation" instead of "pay") reduce comprehension for the average reader.

The Cloze procedure, developed by William Taylor, also tests comprehension. The concept comes from the idea of closure, or the human tendency to complete a familiar but incomplete pattern. In the Cloze procedure, copy is tested for comprehension and redundancy by having test subjects read sentences in which words have been removed. The subjects' ability to fill in the missing words determines whether the pattern of words is familiar and people can understand the message.

If these formulas sound like too much work, Microsoft Word has a built-in readability testing function, making it relatively easy to test any message for clarity.

Audience understanding and comprehension also can be increased by applying some of the following concepts.

Use Symbols, Acronyms, and Slogans Clarity and simplicity of message are enhanced by the use of symbols, acronyms, and slogans. Each is a form of shorthand that quickly conceptualizes an idea and travels through extended lines of communication.

The world is full of symbols. Corporate symbols such as the Mercedes Benz star, the Nike swoosh, and the multicolored, now holographic, apple of Apple Computer are known throughout the world. The concept is called *branding*, and corporations invest considerable time and money in public relations to support their names and logos as symbols of quality and service. Audio symbols such as the NFL theme or Windows' musical chord when a computer boots up are recognized, as are colors such as Coca-Cola red or McDonald's gold.

A symbol should be unique, memorable, widely recognized, and appropriate. Organizations spend considerable time and energy searching for unique symbols that convey the essence of what they are or what they hope to become. Considerable amounts of money are then spent on publicizing the symbols and creating meanings for them.

Acronyms are shorthand for conveying information. An acronym is a word formed from the initial letters of other words. The Group Against Smokers' Pollution goes by the acronym GASP; Juvenile Opportunities in Business becomes JOB. And the National Organization for Women has the acronym NOW, which says a great deal about its political priorities.

In many cases, the acronym—because it is short and simple—becomes the common name. The mass media continually use the term *AIDS* instead of *Acquired Immune Deficiency Syndrome*. And *UNESCO* is easier to write and say than *United Nations Educational, Scientific, and Cultural Organization*. A corporation often adopts its acronym as its official, trademarked name. Thus, we now have IBM instead of International Business Machines and FedEx instead of Federal Express. In the nonprofit sector the American Association of Retired People now uses AARP as its official name.

Slogans help condense a concept and motivate a movement. Presidential candidate Barack Obama's secondary slogan, "Yes we can," was infectious for its optimism. It has been adapted as "Yes we did" since his election to celebrate victories such as passage of health care reform.

> Our business is infested with idiots who try to impress by using pretentious jargon.
>
> *David Ogilvy, a legend in the advertising industry*

Avoid Jargon   One source of blocked communication is technical and bureaucratic jargon. Social scientists call it *semantic noise* when such language is delivered to a general audience. Jargon interferes with the message and impedes the receiver's ability to understand it. Reporters and editors reject jargon in news releases or pitches because the average reader or listener doesn't recognize terms that are unique to a particular industry. Cell phone executives, for example, may talk about "attenuation rates," which means little or nothing to the average person. And even the public relations field has terms that the average person probably doesn't know, such as "mug shot" or "VNR."

Avoid Clichés and Hype Words   You can ruin the credibility and believability of your message by using exaggerated words and phrases. Companies often describe their products as "first of its kind," "unique," "a major breakthrough," and even "revolutionary," which tends to raise suspicion among journalists and the public.

Factiva, a media-monitoring company, analyzed about 14,000 articles in business publications to compile a chart of frequently used hype words. Leading the list was the term *next generation*. Other most frequently used words, in descending order, were *robust, flexible, world class, easy to use,* and *cutting edge*. A list of other overused hype words in digital news releases is in the Insights box on page 177.

Avoid Euphemisms   According to Frank Grazian, founding editor of *Communication Briefings*, a *euphemism* is "an inoffensive word or phrase that is less direct and less distasteful than the one that represents reality."

Public relations personnel should use positive, favorable words to convey a message, but they have an ethical responsibility not to use words that hide information, mislead, or offend. Probably little danger exists in saying a person is *hearing impaired* instead of *deaf*. Some euphemisms can even cause amusement, such as when car mechanics become *automotive internists*, and luxury cars are called *preowned* on the used-car lot.

More dangerous are euphemisms that actually alter the meaning or impact of a word or concept. Writers call this *doublespeak*—words that pretend to communicate but really do not. Governments are famous for doublespeak. In Afghanistan, the U.S. military sometimes describe civilian casualties and destruction as "collateral damage." A government economist once called a recession "a meaningful downturn in aggregate output."

Corporations also use euphemisms and doublespeak to hide unfavorable news. Reducing the number of employees, for example, is often called *right-sizing, skill-mix adjustment,* or *career assignment and relocation*. An airline once called the crash of one of its planes as "the involuntary conversion of a 727."

Using euphemisms to hide or mislead is obviously contrary to professional public relations standards and the public interest. As William Lutz writes in *Public Relations Quarterly*, "Such language breeds suspicion, cynicism, distrust, and, ultimately, hostility."

on the job

INSIGHTS

Hit Parade of Overused Words in News Releases

Author and viral marketing specialist David Meerman Scott analyzed 711,000 news releases to determine the most commonly used gobbledygook words and phrases. The following is a list of the top 25 words and phrases in rank order of excessive use:

Innovate

Pleased to

Unique

Focused on

Leading provider
Commitment
Partnership
New and improved
Leverage
120 perent
Cost effective
Next generation
110 percent
Flexible
World class

Robust
High performance
Scalability
Proud to
Optimize
Outcomes
In terms of
Value added
Easy to use
Metrics

Avoid Discriminatory Language   In today's world, effective communication also means nondiscriminatory communication. Public relations personnel should double-check every message to eliminate undesirable gender, racial, and ethnic connotations. See the Insights box on page 179 about social media divas to explore gender roles in public relations.

With regard to gender, it is unnecessary to write about something as being *man-made* when a word such as *synthetic* or *artificial* is just as good. Companies no longer have *manpower*, but rather *employees*, *personnel*, and *workers*. Most civic organizations have *chairpersons* now, and cities have *firefighters* instead of *firemen* and *police officers* instead of *policemen*. Airlines, of course, have *flight attendants*, not *stewardesses*. It also is considered sexist to write about a woman's physical characteristics or clothing, particularly if similar comments would not be made about a man.

As a general rule, you should not identify any individual by ethnic background or sexual orientation. It may, however, be appropriate in some situations to provide context. It is newsworthy, for example, when a major corporation hires an African American woman to be its CEO. In any case, you should be aware of what terms are acceptable. The term *black*, for example, is widely used and even preferred by a large percentage of the black population, according to the U.S. Bureau of Labor Statistics. A smaller percentage prefers *African American* and *Afro American*. Headlines almost always use *black* because it is short.

Although preferences change, today's writers use *Asian American* or even a more specific designation such as *Chinese American* because Asia has multiple ethnic groups. The term *Oriental* is no longer acceptable in any situation. *Hispanic* is now more acceptable than the politically charged *Spanish-speaking*. The term *Latino*, however, raises some controversy; some women say that it is sexist because the "o" in Spanish is masculine.

Believing the Message

One key variable in the communication process, discussed further in Chapter 9, is *source credibility*. Do members of the audience perceive the source as knowledgeable and expert on the subject? Do they perceive the source as honest and objective or as representing a special interest? For example, audiences ascribe lower credibility to statements in an advertisement than to the same information contained in a news article, because news articles are selected by media gatekeepers with little vested interest in the product.

Source credibility is a problem for any organizational spokesperson because the public already has a bias. In one study conducted for the GCI Group, Opinion Research Corporation found that more than half of Americans surveyed are likely to believe that a large company is probably guilty of some wrongdoing if it is being investigated by a government agency or if a major lawsuit is filed against the company. At the same time, only one-third would trust the statements of a large company.

The problem of source credibility is the main reason that organizations, whenever possible, use respected outside experts or celebrities as representatives to convey their messages.

The *sleeper effect* also influences source credibility. This concept was developed by Carl Hovland, who stated: "There is decreased tendency over time to reject the material presented by an untrustworthy source." In other words, even if organizations are perceived initially as not being very credible sources, people may retain the information and eventually separate the source from the opinion. On the other hand, studies show that audiences register more constant opinion change if they perceive the source to be highly credible in the first place.

A second variable in believability is the *context* of the message. Action (performance) speaks louder than a stack of news releases. A bank may spend thousands of dollars on a promotion campaign with the slogan "Your Friendly Bank—Where Service Counts," but the effort is wasted if public relations efforts do not build a culture of caring among bank employees.

Incompatible rhetoric and actions can be somewhat amusing at times. At a press briefing about the importance of "buying American," the U.S. Chamber of Commerce passed out commemorative coffee mugs marked in small print on the bottom, "Made in China."

Another barrier to the believability of messages is the audience's *predispositions*. This problem brings to mind the old saying, "Don't confuse me with the facts, my mind is already made up." In this case, Leon Festinger's theory of *cognitive dissonance* should be understood. In essence, it says that people will not believe a message contrary to their predispositions unless the communicator can introduce information that causes them to question their beliefs.

Dissonance can be created in at least three ways. First, make the public aware that circumstances have changed. Oil companies, for example, say the era of cheap gasoline is over because a rising middle class in such nations as India and China also have cars and are now competing with U.S. drivers for the available supply. Second, give information about new developments. Public perceptions about China making unsafe toys somewhat changed when Mattel finally admitted that it had recalled 18 million toys because of design flaws instead of manufacturing problems. A third approach is to use an unexpected

on the job

INSIGHTS

Are Women Better at Social Media Public Relations than Men?

This question may be well worth discussing in the public relations classroom, not to arrive at a definitive answer about women and social media but to wrestle with the question of whether we can or should generalize about gender-based skill sets in public relations. The challenges and opportunities posed by social media undoubtedly require a special set of skills, whether they reside only in the female majority of public relations professionals or equally in the male minority in the field. One thing is certain: Women with admirable track records in online and social media are earning well-deserved time in the limelight as speakers and seminar presenters. For example, the public relations field. The challenges and opportunities posed by social media undoubtedly require a special set of skills, whether they reside only in the female majority of public relations professionals or equally in the male minority in the trade publication *Bulldog Reporter* sponsored a recent PR University Audio Conference entitled "Social Media Divas On Digital PR: Top-Ranked Women Online Gurus Reveal 10 Best Social Media Tools And Practices For PR." These so-called divas are accomplished bloggers, managers, and executives who make decisions every day about how best to use the many choices covered in this chapter to achieve communication objectives. Several questions come to mind:

- Should terms like *diva* be used for public relations professionals who happen to be women, or is this just a fun way to promote a webinar?

- Are women uniquely equipped, in general, to handle the communication tactics of the field—to produce nice materials or to relate well to others online?

- Is such a description demeaning or a selling point for female job applicants to use?

- Does praising women for what they bring to the field turn out to be "damning with faint praise" by precluding other managerial opportunities for women?

- Is the truism that "men manage and women create" no longer true?

Women Divas

Women are prominent across the public relations field today, but never more so than in the social media and Web development areas of the profession.

YouTube promo of the Divas: http://www.youtube.com/watch?v= YogX9sAL4s0 Link to On-Demand Access to the Audio conference at Bulldogreporter.com: http://www.bull dogreporter.com

Creating Dissonance

Executives from five major oil companies had to convince Congress that off-shore oil drilling is safe and is in the best interest of the American people.

spokesperson. Chevron, for example, sought to overcome opposition to its oil-exploration policies by getting endorsements from several respected leaders in the conservation movement.

Involvement is another important predisposition that impacts how audience members process messages. Involvement can be described in simple terms as interest or concern for an issue or a product. Those with a higher level of involvement often process persuasive messages with greater attention to evidence and to logical argument, whereas those with a low level of involvement with the topic are impressed more by incidental cues, such as an attractive spokesperson, humor, or the number of arguments given. The public relations professional can use the involvement concept to devise messages that focus more on "what is said," for high-involvement audiences, and more on "who says it," for low-involvement audiences.

Remembering the Message

For several reasons, many messages prepared by public relations personnel are repeated extensively:

- Repetition is necessary because not all members of the target audience see or hear the message at the same time. Not everyone reads the newspaper on a particular day, watches the same television news program, or regularly reads the same blog.

- Repetition reminds the audience, so there is less chance of a failure to remember the message. If a source has high credibility, repetition prevents erosion of opinion change.

- Repetition helps the audience remember the message itself. Studies have shown that advertising is quickly forgotten if not repeated constantly.

- Repetition can lead to improved learning and increase the chance of penetrating audience indifference or resistance.

Researchers say that repetition, or *redundancy*, also is necessary to offset the "noise" surrounding a message. People often hear or see messages in an environment filled with distractions—a baby crying, the conversations of family members or office staff, a barking dog—or even while daydreaming or thinking of other things.

Consequently, communicators often build repetition into a message. Key points may be mentioned at the beginning and then summarized at the end. If the source is asking the receiver to seek more information, the telephone number or Web address must be repeated several times. Such precautions also fight *entropy*, which means that messages continually lose information as media channels and people process the information and pass it on to others. In one study about employee communication, for example, it was found that rank-and-file workers got only 20 percent of a message that had passed through four levels of managers.

The key to effective communication and retention of the message is to convey information in a variety of ways, using multiple communication channels. This helps people remember the message as they receive it through different media and extends the message to both passive and active audiences.

Acting on the Message

The ultimate purpose of any message is to have an effect on the recipient. Public relations personnel communicate messages on behalf of organizations to change perceptions, attitudes, opinions, or behavior in some way. Marketing communication, in particular, has the objective of convincing people to buy goods and services.

> Communicators must have a thorough understanding of their audiences, and they must stay very current with the media being used by those audiences.
>
> *Jerry Swerling, director of the Strategic Public Relations Center at USC Annenberg*

The Five-Stage Adoption Process

Getting people to act on a message is not a simple process. In fact, research shows that it can be a somewhat lengthy and complex procedure that depends on a number of intervening influences. One key to understanding how people accept new ideas or products is to analyze the adoption process. The five stages are summarized as follows:

1. **Awareness.** A person becomes aware of an idea or a new product, often by means of an advertisement, a news story in a newspaper, a mention on the nightly news, or a posting in a chat group.

2. **Interest.** The individual seeks more information about the idea or the product, perhaps by ordering a brochure, reading an in-depth article in a newspaper or magazine, or doing a Google search.

3. **Evaluation.** The person evaluates the idea or the product on the basis of how it meets specific needs and wants. Feedback from friends and family is part of this process.

4. **Trial.** Next, the person tries the product or the idea on an experimental basis by using a sample, witnessing a demonstration, or making qualifying statements such as, "I read. . . ."

5. **Adoption.** The individual begins to use the product on a regular basis or integrates the idea into his or her belief system. The "I read . . ." becomes "I think . . ." if peers provide support and reinforcement of the idea.

Figure 7.3 is a more sophisticated concept that describes the five-step adoption process in terms of *knowledge, persuasion, decision, implementation,* and *confirmation.* The *evaluation* stage, for example, is called the *decision* stage in the chart formatted by Everett Rogers in his book *Diffusion of Innovation*. He notes that at least five factors influence a person's evaluation of a product or an idea.

1. **Relative advantage.** The degree to which an innovation is perceived as better than the idea it replaces.

2. **Compatibility.** The degree to which an innovation is perceived as being consistent with the existing values, experiences, and needs of potential adopters.

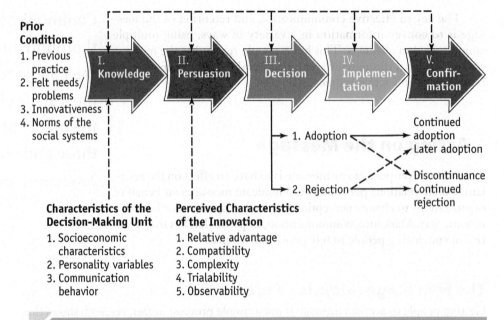

Prior Conditions
1. Previous practice
2. Felt needs/ problems
3. Innovativeness
4. Norms of the social systems

Characteristics of the Decision-Making Unit
1. Socioeconomic characteristics
2. Personality variables
3. Communication behavior

Perceived Characteristics of the Innovation
1. Relative advantage
2. Compatibility
3. Complexity
4. Trialability
5. Observability

> **Figure 7.3   Adoption Model**
>
> This graph shows the steps through which an individual or other decision-making unit goes in the innovation-decision process from first knowledge of an innovation to the decision to adopt it, followed by implementation of the new idea and confirmation of the new decision.

3. **Complexity.** The degree to which an innovation is perceived as difficult to understand and use.

4. **Trialability.** The degree to which an innovation may be experienced on a limited basis.

5. **Observability.** The degree to which the results of an innovation are visible to others.

The communicator should be aware of these factors and attempt to implement communication strategies that will overcome as many of them as possible. Repeating a message in various ways, reducing its complexity, taking into account competing messages, and structuring the message to meet the needs of the audience are ways to do this.

It's also important to understand that a person does not necessarily go through all five stages with any given idea or product. The process may be terminated after any step. In fact, the process is like a large funnel. Although many are made aware of an idea or a product, only a few will ultimately adopt it.

The Time Factor

Another aspect that confuses people is the amount of time needed to adopt a new idea or product. Depending on the individual and the situation, the entire adoption process can take place almost instantly if the result is of minor consequence or requires low-level commitment. Buying a new brand of soft drink or bar of soap is relatively inexpensive and often done on impulse. On the other hand, deciding to buy a new car or vote for a particular candidate may involve an adoption process that takes several weeks or months.

Rogers's research shows that people approach innovation in different ways, depending on their personality traits and the risk involved. There are five levels:

- **Innovators:** Individuals who are venturesome and eager to try new ideas.
- **Early Adopters:** Savvy individuals who keep up with new ideas and new products, often the opinion leaders for their friends and colleagues.
- **Early Majority:** Individuals who take a deliberate, pragmatic approach to adopting ideas.
- **Late Majority:** Individuals who are often skeptical and somewhat resistant but eventually bow to peer pressure.
- **Laggards:** Individuals who are very traditional and the last group to adopt a new idea or product.

Psychographics, discussed in Chapter 9, can often help communicators segment audiences that have "Innovator" or "Early Adopter" characteristics and would be predisposed to adopting new ideas. See the PR Casebook on page 184 about the early adopters of Apple's new iPad.

How Decisions Are Influenced

Of particular interest to public relations people is the primary source of information at each step in the adoption process.

Awareness Stage   Mass media vehicles such as advertising, short news articles, feature stories, and radio and television news announcements are the most influential, with support from eWOM and websites. A news article or a television announcement makes people aware of an idea, event, or new product. They also are made aware through such vehicles as direct mail, office memos, simple brochures, and online news sites.

Interest Stage   There is reliance on mass media vehicles, but individuals actively seek information on the Web and pay attention to longer, in-depth articles. They rely more on detailed brochures, specialized publications, small-group seminars, websites, and meetings to provide details.

Evaluation, Trial, and Adoption Stages   Personal experience, group norms, and opinions of family and friends become more influential than mass media. Also influential is personal contact and conversation with individuals who are perceived as credible sources and experts. Feedback, negative or positive, may determine adoption. For this reason, word-of-mouth public relations and viral marketing campaigns can be crucial at this stage.

Word-of-Mouth Campaigns

The influence of peers and colleagues in the adoption process has been known for years. Now, word of mouth (WOM) has been institutionalized by a number of organizations to reach consumers and other audiences through their friends and colleagues. Procter & Gamble (P&G) was an early pioneer in the field. Its Tremor Division, for example, enlisted 225,000 teenagers to tell their friends about brands such as Herbal Essences and Old Spice. P&G has also

It's interesting to find that as much time as we spend online, we still prefer a personal recommendation from someone we know and trust.

Chris Haack of Mintel

PRCasebook

Apple's iPad Exploits Early Adoption Buzz

Once Apple's iPad actually reached the market, the debates in the blogosphere began. Is the iPad nothing more than a better Kindle-style e-book reader? Is it a glorified iPhone—but, um, without any phone functions? Is it too big for men to carry without a man-purse?

And speaking of gender roles, does Apple's product-naming team have a tin ear when it comes to the perspective of women and feminine products? Is it a revolutionary form factor putting us on the verge of the demise of the laptop computer?

Pontificating aside, the product launch was another tour de force for the Apple marketing and public relations team, showcasing the diffusion of the innovation process. Apple's deft use of long-lead, slow-developing rumors of a new product, followed by a formal announcement in January, was followed by a full suite of communication tools such as:

Promoting the iPad

Apple counts on early adopters to generate buzz and media coverage.

- Executive interviews
- Online demos
- Advertisements
- Special events
- Blog posts
- Product placement in the ABC comedy *Modern Family* (http://www.youtube.com/watch?v=RBJW1mT613s)
- E-mail exchanges by Apple CEO Steve Jobs to questions from enthusiasts

The company built a buzz among prospective buyers, dubbed *icultists*, of its newest product, the iPad. Also known as *innovators* and *early adopters* in the diffusion of innovation theory, Apple's hard-core fans respond with a frenzy to orchestrated communication components and the chance at first-generation electronics. As Ross Rubin, a wireless expert at a research firm, told a newspaper reporter, "It's an 'early-adopter' product for those who really care about getting the latest, snazziest technology product and those who care about brands." Other characteristics, according to Bob Wallace, writing in the *New York Times*

magazine about "iPad Envy," are vanity, desire for status, and higher-than-average income.

Innovators or early adopters are particularly important publics for public relations and marketing experts because they are the vanguard who help form public opinion about an issue or a new product. They are also considered the "experts" among their friends and peers on a particular product, and through word of mouth, a product can soar in sales or take a nosedive. These individuals also are known as *influencers* or *catalysts*.

Although the technophiles are the most influential in terms of a product such as the iPad, there are also the *iconverts*, who play an important role in influencing their peers. Having the new iPad, for example, gives these less savvy individuals status among their peers even though they aren't truly icultists.

Skilled public relations can drive buzz about any new product, but electronic products tend to benefit from the excitement generated through electronic word of mouth (eWOM). To that end, Apple kept consumer, media, and blogger interest in the iPad at high levels in the months before the launch by being somewhat secretive. Even Apple store managers did not see or hold an iPad until one hour before sales began April 3, 2010.

> ## I don't know what drives me—I just know I want it.
>
> *An early adopter who preordered an iPad*

This, in turn, fueled intense speculation about its exact features, its cost, and even how many would be available on the first day of sales. In addition, Apple kept the wraps on the whole project while not denying the rumors that Apple was building an e-book reader to rival the Amazon Kindle. By agreement with Apple, product reviews by a few privileged tech journalists were not published until the day that all those early adopters could take possession of their latest Apple gadget.

The tension between extensive communication components and absolute secrecy about the product itself did indeed build buzz. Apple's iPad sales reached nearly half a million units in the first week, partly driven by the 3.5 million apps available at launch thanks to iPhone compatibility. Only time will tell whether the iPad eventually attracts others in the diffusion-of-innovation process—the early majority, the late majority, and eventually the laggards, who are the last to adopt anything.

PEARSON
mycommunicationlab

---

signed up about 500,000 mothers to receive coupons and sample products, in the hope that these women will tell their friends and colleagues about the products.

The popularity of WOM is based on recent research that reinforces the classic theory of adoption articulated by Everett Rogers and others many years ago. One recent study by Mintel, a research firm, found that even Internet users find that "real friends" are more influential in the decision to buy a product than "online friends." Sixty percent said the source of product recommendations came from friends, relatives, or spouses. Only 10 percent listed a blogger or a chat room as influential in their buying decision. "It's interesting to find that as much time as we spend online, we still prefer a personal recommendation from someone we know and trust," commented Chris Haack of Mintel. One recent study, for example, found that 72 percent of consumers are influenced by their own experience, and another 56 percent by friends and family.

Other studies have found that a key factor in WOM is to identify and reach *opinion leaders*, who are also known as *influentials* or *catalysts*. Opinion leaders and their characteristics are discussed more thoroughly in Chapter 9, but a study by the Keller Fay Group and Manning Selvage & Lee found that conversation catalysts (either online or in person) average about 200 weekly word-of-mouth conversations, and a large percentage of these conversations mention various products and brands.

An example of a successful WOM marketing campaign is one by U.K. pet food maker Masterfoods. The company identified 10,000 consumers likely to generate positive word-of-mouth reports to others if they liked the product, Whiskas Oh So. These "influencers" were then mailed free samples and coupons to pass on to family and friends. Sales of the product among those who received WOM recommendations and coupons from their friends *were 11 times higher than from consumers who didn't receive any information or coupons from a family member or friend. In other situations, WOM campaigns have raised some ethical concerns. See the Ethics box on page 186.

> ## The new strategy for manufacturers is to engage customers to do the talking for them, and then amplify the customer's voice within their own site and through multiple channel marketing strategies.
>
> *Sam Ecker, Chief Marketing Officer, Bazaarrvoice*

on the job

ETHICS

eWOM Poses Ethical Challenges

lectronic word-of-mouth (eWOM) tactics are now a major communication tool in marketing and increasingly in public relations campaigns. The basic principle is that friends and peers are more influential than traditional tactics in changing opinions and motivating people to try new products.

Such campaigns, however, have generated some controversy. Some say it's a form of "stealth" communication because the public isn't told that the hired actor or "peer" is being rewarded to spread the word about a product or a social position. Faking word-of-mouth endorsements of products or ideas can be done easily with immediate rewards such as coupons or free products from secret sponsors.

A campaign can be developed without disclosing who is actually behind it. Stop Oil Speculation Now (see page 157 in Chapter 6) fought high oil and fuel prices with aggressive communication about everything except the funders of the campaign—in *PRWeek's* words, "making it appear to be a true grassroots effort." However, airlines and unions were actually sponsors as part

of efforts to save companies and jobs.

What do you think? Do word-of-mouth campaigns such as those just described cross the ethical line? The Word of Mouth Marketing Association (www.womma.org), for example, has a code of ethics requiring transparency and full disclosure. Online standards call for transparency regarding the sponsor of a communication, accuracy of information, and protection of confidential information. Although eWOM works well for marketing efforts, it can also be a powerful tool for corporations and activist groups.

■ The Tea Party, a conservative movement dedicated to reduced government, gained momentum through its word-of-mouth campaign to defeat health care reform. The effort failed, but the large turnouts at protest events were notable.

■ In response, a progressive movement called the Coffee Party used a combination of

> ## Word of mouth will only work if it's based on a platform of ethics.
>
> *Andy Sernovitz, CEO of the Word of Mouth Marketing Association (WOMMA)*

mass media and viral efforts to execute its own eWOM strategies.

■ Edelman Public Relations created a blog on behalf of Wal-Mart to counter some of the accusations made by Walmartwatch.com.

The PRSA code mentions that public relations firms should disclose "any existing or potential conflicts of interest," but that primarily applies to clients—not eWOM campaigns. If you decided to use eWOM strategies in a public relations program, what ethical guidelines would you adopt? Or do you hold the view that as long as everyone is free to make his or her case in the court of public opinion, little oversight is needed?

Summary

The Goals of Communication

■ Communication, also called *execution*, is the third step in the public relations process.

■ The five possible objectives in a public relations campaign are (1) message exposure, (2) accurate dissemination of

the message, (3) acceptance of the message, (4) attitude change, and (5) change in overt behavior.

■ Many campaigns strive to accomplish only the first two objectives: message exposure and accurate dissemination of the message.

- The six components of effective communication for audiences are (1) receiving the message, (2) paying attention to the message, (3) understanding the message, (4) believing the message, (5) remembering the message, and (6) acting on the message.

Receiving the Message

- Most communication models have five basic elements: (1) source, (2) encoder, (3) signal, (4) decoder, and (5) destination.
- Effective communication requires the sender and the receiver to have a field of shared experience.
- Most modern models emphasize communication as a loop process that involves constant feedback and two-way communication.
- The larger the audience, the greater the number of barriers to communication.

Paying Attention to the Message

- Because audiences have different approaches to receiving messages, communicators must tailor the message to get the recipients' attention.
- Messages for passive audiences must have style and creativity, whereas messages for an audience actively seeking information must have more informative content.
- Effective communication of a message requires the use of multiple media channels.

Understanding the Message

- The most basic element of understanding between communicator and audience is a common language. This is becoming a greater issue with the emphasis on multiculturalism.

- Public relations practitioners must consider their audiences and style their language appropriately, taking into consideration literacy levels, clarity and simplicity of language, and avoidance of discriminatory or offensive language.

Believing the Message

- Key variables in believability include source credibility, context, and the audience's predispositions, especially their level of involvement.

Remembering the Message

- Messages are often repeated extensively to reach all members of the target audience and to help them remember and enhance their learning.
- One way to do this is to convey information in several ways, through a variety of channels.

Acting on the Message

- The five steps in the acceptance of new ideas or products are awareness, interest, evaluation, trial, and adoption.
- The adoption process is affected by relative advantage, compatibility, complexity, trialability, and observability.
- The time needed to adopt a new idea or product can be affected by the importance of the decision as well as by the personality of the person receiving the message.
- Word-of-mouth (WOM) campaigns are increasingly being used to take advantage of peer influence in the persuasion process.

Case Activity   Combatting AIDS in Africa

Billions of U.S. dollars have been allocated to treating HIV-AIDS around the world. As a specialist in communication planning for rural areas of South Africa, outline the variety of communication strategies and tactics you would use to increase patient participation in weekly anti-retroviral treatments (ART) available at free clinics.

You know that traditional healers are credible and influential health advisors in their villages, but in some ways they feel they compete against government programs for clients. Also take into consideration that cell phones in South Africa are a leapfrog technology and that healers rely on smartphones to run their business. Using this chapter as a guide, how would you engage healers as change agents to provide rural people with decades of relatively healthy life using regular ART treatment?

Questions   **For Review and Discussion**

1. What are the five basic elements of a communication model?

2. Why is two-way communication (feedback) an important aspect of effective communication?

3. What are the advantages and disadvantages, from a communication standpoint, of reaching the audience through mass media channels?

4. What kinds of messages and communication channels would you use for a passive audience? An active, information-seeking audience?

5. Why is it necessary to use a variety of messages and communication channels in a public relations program?

6. Why is it important to write with clarity and simplicity? How can symbols, acronyms, and slogans help?

7. Why is it important to build repetition into a message?

8. Explain the five steps of the adoption process. What are some of the factors that affect the adoption of an idea or product?

9. What is WOM? Why are many organizations now using it as a major strategy for marketing and public relations campaigns?

Media Resources

Beardsley, J. (2006, Spring). Get smart: Using the right word at the right time. *The Strategist*, 29–31.

Decker, S., & Bockius, C. (2010). Driving channel sales with user generated marketing: A new manufacturer strategy to acquire and amplify online word of mouth. White Paper, *PRWeek Online*.

DeVito, J. (2007). Essentials of human communication (6th ed.). Boston, MA: Allyn & Bacon.

Horn, T. H., & Neff, B. D. (2007). *Public relations: From theory to practice*. Boston, MA: Allyn & Bacon.

McCarthy, C. (2010, March 19). Nestlé mess shows sticky side of Face book pages. *CNET News, The Social*. Retrieved from http://news.cnet.com/8301-13577_3-20000805-36.html

Toth, E. L. (2009). The case for pluralistic studies of public relations. In R. L. Heath, E. L. Toth, & D. Waymer (Eds.), *Rhetorical and critical approaches to public relations II* (pp. 48–60). Madison, NY: Routledge.

Vranica, S. (2007, July 10). Laughing all the way to the bank: Viral marketers count on consumers to pass the word. *Wall Street Journal*, p. R4.

Evaluation

After reading this chapter, you will be able to:

Understand the purpose of evaluation

Know the key elements of objectives

Distinguish the measurement of different communication components

The Purpose of Evaluation

The fourth step of the public relations process is evaluation. It is the measurement of results against established objectives set during the planning process discussed in Chapter 6.

> We are talking about an orderly evaluation of our progress in attaining the specific objectives of our public relations plan. We are learning what we did right, what we did wrong, how much progress we've made and, most importantly, how we can do it better next time.
>
> *Frank Wylie, emeritus professor at California State University in Long Beach*

Evaluation is well described by Professor James Bissland, formerly of Bowling Green State University. He defines it as "the systematic assessment of a program and its results. It is a means for practitioners to offer accountability to clients—and to themselves." Evaluation provides the opportunity to learn what was done right and what was done wrong, both as a look backward at performance and as a look forward at the improvement of performance.

The desire to do a better job next time is a major reason for evaluating public relations efforts, but another, equally important reason is the widespread adoption of the management-by-objectives system by clients and employers of public relations personnel. They want to know whether the money, time, and effort expended on public relations are well spent and contribute to the realization of an organizational objective, such as attendance at an open house, product sales, or increased awareness of obesity in children.

Objectives: A Prerequisite for Evaluation

Before any public relations program can be properly evaluated, it is important to have a clearly established set of measurable objectives. These should be part of the program plan (discussed in Chapter 6), but first some points need to be reviewed.

■ Public relations personnel and management should agree on the criteria that will be used to evaluate success in attaining objectives. A Ketchum monograph simply states, "Write the most precise, most results-oriented objectives you can that are realistic, credible, measurable, and compatible with the client's demands on public relations."

■ Don't wait until the end of the public relations program to determine how it will be evaluated. Albert L. Schweitzer at Fleishman-Hillard public relations in St. Louis makes the point: "Evaluating impact/results starts in the planning stage. You break down the problem into measurable goals and objectives, then after implementing the program, you measure the results against goals."

> Write the most precise, most results-oriented objectives you can that are realistic, credible, measurable, and compatible with the client's demands on public relations.
>
> *Agency monograph, Ketchum Public Relations*

■ If an objective is informational, measurement techniques must show how successfully information was communicated to target audiences. Such techniques fall under the rubrics of "message dissemination" and "audience exposure," but they do not measure the effect on attitudes or overt behavior and action.

■ Motivational objectives are more difficult to accomplish. If the objective is to increase sales or market share, it is important to show that public relations efforts, rather than advertising or other marketing strategies, caused the increase. Or, if the

PRCasebook

Coco Key Staycation Achieves Measurable Objectives

With travel costs on the rise, many budget-conscious families are opting to replace the traditional weeklong vacation with the "staycation," where they have fun while staying at home. One way to have some fun at minimal expense and without becoming road warriors is the indoor water park. Coco Key Properties launched "The Ultimate Vacation Challenge" by inviting consumers to submit an essay about their past vacations and why they needed to escape to a tropical paradise—close at hand. The challenge increased awareness for the Coco chain of 10 hotel/water park resorts, in addition to bringing in over $200,000 of incremental revenue to the water resort properties.

Communication strategies such as media placements, direct mail, and viral e-mails drove consumers to Coco Key's website and encouraged them to submit their essays online. One winner was selected for each Coco Key property, and those winners received a prize package worth $1,000, which included a two-night stay for a family of four along with VIP treatment.

The goal: Coco Key, just over a year old with seven properties at the time, wanted to build brand and product name recognition while bringing in incremental revenue around the staycation concept. The execution of the communication program included media relations efforts, a website–based

Measuring Success

The Coco Key company evaluated its public relations efforts by tracking message exposure and the resulting increase in business at its resort properties.

national contest, and involvement of employees and associates of Coco Key properties. Measurable objectives were an exemplary element of the communication plan developed by Coco Key. By making the objectives specific with numerical measures, evaluation of the overall communication program was detailed and rigorous.

Because objectives were well crafted, the following outcomes greatly impressed judges of the Public Relations Society of America, who awarded Coco Key with a 2009 Silver Anvil. Here are measurement highlights from the submission to PRSA.

- **Objective #1:** Achieve 20 to 40 media placements. Result: The vacation message garnered 62 million impressions in 155 media placements. The Boston property even secured placements in all media areas including television, radio, print, and online.

- **Objective #2:** Secure 300 to 500 entries. Result: Coco Key received a total of 813 contest entries, surpassing its goal. All properties also exceeded the minimum goal for a particular location.

- **Objective #3:** Increase online traffic by 5 to 10 percent. Result: Online traffic increased significantly, with a total of 12,000 overall page views, 9,000 of those unique page views. Web traffic was up over the previous July by more than 80 percent.

- **Objective #4:** Add 300 new e-mail addresses of prospective customers. Result: Over 500 new consumers opted in.

- **Objective #5:** Bring in $200,000 in income and revenue. Result: More than 925 new packages were secured, for a total estimated package revenue of $206,000

Although the campaign itself was a very sound public relations effort, the truly exemplary feature of the campaign was its ability to drive home to upper management the return on investment of the campaign through a combination of informational and motivational objectives of true value to the company.

objective is to change attitudes or opinions, research should be done before and after the public relations activity to measure the percentage of change.

Although objectives may vary, the following checklist contains the basic evaluation questions that any practitioner should ask:

- Was the activity or program adequately planned?
- Did the recipients of the message understand it?
- How could the program strategy have been more effective?
- Were all primary and secondary audiences reached?
- Was the desired organizational objective achieved?
- What unforeseen circumstances affected the success of the program or activity?
- Did the program or activity fall within the budget set for it?
- What steps can be taken to improve the success of similar future activities?

Current Status of Measurement and Evaluation

Public relations professionals have made considerable progress in evaluation and measurement, the ability to tell clients and employers exactly what has been accomplished. Sophisticated software programs and techniques are being used, including computerized news clip analysis, survey sampling, quasi-experimental designs in which the audience is divided into groups that see different aspects of a public relations campaign, and attempts to correlate efforts directly with sales.

> If you have not carved off at least 10 percent of your budget to measure your impact, you're flying blind, and you have no way of proving your value.
>
> *Mark Stouse, director of worldwide communications for BMC*

Today, the trend toward more systematic evaluation is well established. Katherine Paine, founder of her own public relations measurement firm, says that the percentage of a public relations budget devoted to measurement and evaluation was about 1 percent in the 1990s, but is now closer to 5 percent. A 2010 study by the USC Annenberg Strategic Public Relations Center found about the same percentage; the average corporation devotes only 4 to 5 percent of its total public relations budget to evaluation and measurement. Advocates say measurement should be at least 10 percent of budget because there is constant pressure on public relations departments to justify their budgets and prove their value to the bottom line.

Some practitioners maintain that public relations is more art than science and is thus extremely difficult to measure. Walter K. Lindenmann, a former senior vice president and director of research at Ketchum, takes a more optimistic view. He wrote in *Public Relations Quarterly*: "Let's get something straight right off the bat. First, it is possible to measure public relations effectiveness....Second, measuring public relations effectiveness does not have to be either unbelievably expensive or laboriously time-consuming." The Institute for Public Relations (www.instituteforpr.org) also takes the view that public relations effectiveness can be systematically evaluated. It has commissioned a number of papers and research studies about measurement over the past 20 years, and about 75 of these papers are available free of charge on its website. The Institute's slogan captures the essence of its mission: "The science beneath the art of public relations."

Lindenmann suggests that public relations personnel use a mix of evaluation techniques, many borrowed from advertising and marketing, to provide more complete

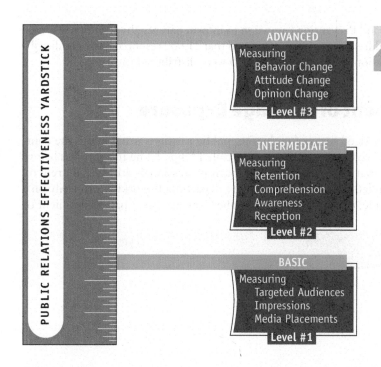

PUBLIC RELATIONS EFFECTIVENESS YARDSTICK

ADVANCED
Measuring
  Behavior Change
  Attitude Change
  Opinion Change
Level #3

INTERMEDIATE
Measuring
  Retention
  Comprehension
  Awareness
  Reception
Level #2

BASIC
Measuring
  Targeted Audiences
  Impressions
  Media Placements
Level #1

Figure 8.1 Public Relations Effectiveness Yardstick

Evaluation goals for public relations programs can be grouped at three levels of measurement, as shown in this chart.

Source: Ketchum, New York, published in *Public Relations Quarterly.*

evaluation. In addition, he notes that there are at least three levels of measurement and evaluation (see Figure 8.1).

On the most basic level are compilations of message distribution and media placement. The second level, which requires more sophisticated techniques, deals with the measurement of audience awareness, comprehension, and retention of the message. The most advanced level is the measurement of changes in attitudes, opinions, and behavior.

The following sections outline the most widely used methods for evaluating public relations efforts. These include measurement of (1) production, (2) message exposure, (3) audience awareness, (4) audience attitudes, and (5) audience action. Supplemental activities such as communication audits, readability tests, event evaluation, and split messages also are discussed. In most cases, a skilled practitioner will use a combination of methods to evaluate the effectiveness of a program.

Measurement of Production

One elementary form of evaluation is simply to count how many news releases, feature stories, photos, guest editorials, blog postings, and the like, are produced in a given period of time. This kind of evaluation is supposed to give management an idea of a staff's productivity and output. Public relations professionals, however, do not believe that this evaluation is very meaningful, because it emphasizes quantity instead of quality. In most cases, it's more cost effective to write fewer news releases and spend more time on the few that really are newsworthy. It also could be more valuable to the organization for a staff person to spend five weeks working to place an article in the *Wall Street Journal* than to write 29 routine personnel releases.

Closely allied to the production of publicity materials is their distribution. Thus, a public relations department might report, for instance, that a total of 756 news releases were sent to 819 daily newspapers, 250 weeklies, and 137 trade magazines within one year or that 230 messages were posted on the organization's blog. A Centers for Disease Control and Prevention campaign to inform parents about the early symptoms of autism in children, for example, reported that 21,000 resource kits were distributed to health professionals and another 60,000 were distributed to parents.

Measurement of Message Exposure

The most widely practiced form of evaluating public relations programs is the compilation of print and broadcast mentions, often called "clips." The Insights box below, for example, shows that both U.S. and European professionals still heavily rely on "clippings." Public relations firms and company departments working primarily on a local basis, for example, often have a staff member scan area newspapers for client or

on the job

INSIGHTS

Effectiveness of Measurement Tools

BenchPoint, a measurement firm, conducted a global survey of public relations and communications professionals for the first European Measurement Summit in Berlin, which was held in June 2009. The respondents, coming primarily from Europe and the United States, ranked the effectiveness of the measurement tools they use to monitor the public relations initiatives in their firms and departments. As illustrated in Figure 8.2, respondents ranked " clippings" first in effectiveness but using advertising equivalency ranked eleventh.

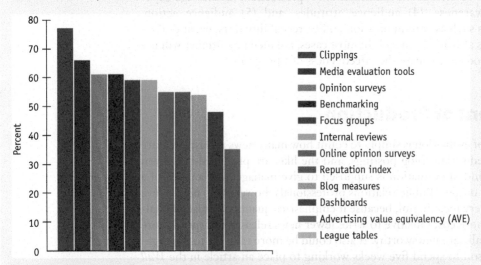

Figure 8.2 Benchpoint's Survey Data

product mentions. Large companies with regional, national, or even international outreach usually retain monitoring services to scan large numbers of publications. It's also possible to have such services monitor television newscasts in major markets, local and national talk shows, Internet chat groups, podcasts, and even blogs.

Burrelles/Luce, for example, monitors 40 million blogs and Internet forums, 16,054 Web news sources, 10,355 daily and nondaily newspapers, 7,893 magazines and trade journals, and 926 TV and cable stations. Another monitoring service, National Aircheck, is able to search almost 8,000 hours of news talk radio each week. Robb Wexler, president of the firm, told *O'Dwyer's PR Report*, "We should be able to tell someone within 10 to 15 minutes where and when they're being talked about."

The result of all this electronic research is the ability for the organization or its public relations firm to do a fairly accurate count of how many media stories are generated by the program or campaign. The Denny's Allnighter Rockstar Menu Launch, mentioned in Chapter 6, generated 215 stories in print, broadcast, and online placements. The number of media placements, however, is just the first level of assessing the exposure of the message to potential audiences.

> We should be able to tell someone within 10 to 15 minutes where and when they're being talked about.
>
> *Robb Wexler, National Aircheck media-monitoring service*

on the job

INSIGHTS

Measuring Effectiveness on the Web

Blogs, chat groups, and online publications can also be monitored using the metric of visits to a site, but such data are less valuable than the content and tone of what is being said. Consequently, public relations professionals use free online sites such as Technorati, Blogpulse, and Google Alerts to compile mentions regarding the organization or client. All this information can be received free of charge on a daily basis via RSS feeds or by paying such companies as Converseon, Visible Technologies, or *Kalivo.com* to monitor the entire Internet for relevant content delivered in a daily report. *Kalivo.com*,

for example, combines a variety of search techniques such as RSS, search engine optimization (SEO), and blog interfaces to track everything said anywhere in the blogosphere or on websites. Rod Amis, writing in *Public Relations Tactics*, says, "Think of it as a digital clipping service that runs on autopilot."

Monitoring blogs and chat groups is increasingly important in issues management. It provides direct feedback about what people are thinking, and what rumors are circulating about the organization. While the people expressing their views may not represent the opinion of the majority, their

comments often give organizations a "wake-up call" about potential problems and issues.

The metrics of measurement are now available and improving by the month at social networking sites. MySpace, for example, is now compiling data on visits to community pages, time spent there, and whether visitors watched a video or embedded a piece of content into their pages. It is even tracking the pass-along rate for materials and the demographic and psychologic information for "friends" of an organization or brand.

YouTube also has improved its ability to provide more data beyond just

(continued)

the number of viewers and how many times a video has been downloaded. A feature called YouTube Insight gives account holders who have uploaded videos to the site a range of statistics, charts, and maps about their audience. The data available through Insight include age, gender, and geographic location as well as the identities of the Internet sites that viewers came from and where they went after watching a video. Insight product manager Tracy Chan told the *Los Angeles Times*, "Marketers and advertisers use the data to decide how to target their next round of ads or where bands should tour." She was referring to Weezer, an alternative rock band that found out that 2.2 million watched their YouTube video, but that 65 percent of the audience were men under 18 and between ages 35 and 45.

Other metrics on the Internet are more difficult to quantify. Social network sites, for example, are all about listening, participating, and engaging the audience, rather than necessarily delivering key messages. Ed Terpen-

ing, VP of social media at Wells Fargo, told a Dow Jones seminar, "We care a lot about participation and engagement. That's our No. 1 metric."

One dimension is called the "conversation index," which is the ratio between blog posts and comments. It helps measure whether a blogger is doing a lot of writing with very little response from readers, or whether the audience is engaged and contributing to the conversation. Obviously, blogs that generate a lot of "conversation" are more important to organizations in terms of feedback and dialogue.

Another metric that is somewhat difficult to quantify is the tone of the conversation; is it positive, hostile, or neutral? Some experts say this is too simplistic since it doesn't take into consideration whether someone is being sarcastic. Tone can be misconstrued by analysis that evaluates language too literally. Nevertheless, such information generally helps organizations respond to concerns raised by key publics such as consumers. Other forms of measurement are (1) engagement, such as time

spent with the site and whether visitors downloaded materials; (2) word-of-mouth impact; and (3) search engine visibility.

In sum, the ability to measure the effectiveness of social media is continuing to evolve. The four challenges, highlighted by Tonya Garcia in *PRWeek*, are:

1. **The human factor.** Metrics such as tone require a human touch, which is slower than computers and sometimes prone to error.

2. **The language barrier.** The Internet is international and engagement occurs cross-border, creating a need for multilingual analysts.

3. **The need for a new model.** Many try to measure social media using traditional media metrics, which can provide little value.

4. **The blogger effect.** It's tough to decipher the strong feeling and sarcasm usually projected by this group.

Media Impressions

In addition to the number of media placements, public relations departments and firms report how many people may have been exposed to the message. These numbers are referred to as *media impressions*, the potential audience reached by a periodical, a broadcast program, or a website.

If, for example, a story about an organization appears in a local daily that has a circulation of 130,000, the media impressions are 130,000. If another story is published the next day, this counts as 130,000 more impressions. Estimated audiences for radio and television programs, certified by auditing organizations, also are used to compile media impressions. Thus, if there's even a brief mention of a new product or service on *Today*, for example, this might constitute 20 million impressions, if that is the audited size of the audience that regularly watches the program.

Some firms inflate the number of "impressions" by also estimating the number of people who are not actual subscribers, but who may read a newspaper because it's delivered to the office or home. So instead of 130,000 impressions, it would be 520,000 impressions if it was estimated that four additional individuals had access to the newspaper. The Denny's menu launch, for example, claimed that its 215 stories generated more than 167 million impressions, but this figure seems to indicate an optimal projection of audience size and exposure to the story.

A regional or national news story can generate millions of impressions by simple multiplication of each placement by the circulation or audience of each medium. The Doritos Super Bowl advertising competition generated more than 600 million impressions. The breakdown, in part, included:

- 25 national print/wire features
- 108 national TV and radio segments
- More than 360 online news stories
- More than 2,200 local TV/radio mentions

Media impressions are commonly used in advertising to document the breadth of penetration of a particular message. Such figures give a rough estimate of how many people are potentially exposed to a message. They don't, however, document how many people actually read or heard the stories and, more important, how many absorbed or acted on the information. Other techniques needed for this kind of evaluation are discussed later in this chapter.

Tracking Internet Visitors

Measuring the reach and effectiveness of messages on the Internet is getting more sophisticated by the month. One cyberspace version of media impressions, used for some years, is the number of people reached via an organization's webpage. Each instance of a person accessing a site is called a **hit** or a **visit**. See also the Insights box on page 195, which details online measurement efforts, and the Multicultural World box about World Water Day on page 198, which shows the techniques in action.

In a national campaign to increase awareness of autism, for example, the Centers for Disease Control and Prevention reported 540,000 unique visitors and more than 50,000 materials downloaded from its website. Even a campaign by the National Potato Board did pretty well. Its Mr. Potato Head site attracted almost 10,000 visitors, who spent an average of 5.5 minutes at the site, reviewing an average of 6.6 pages, about the health benefits of potatoes.

Additional information about users is often gathered by asking them to answer some demographic questions before they use the site or as they leave it. For best results, offer free software or something similar that must be mailed to users; this entices people to give their names and addresses. Marketers, for example, use this technique to compile databases of potential customers.

> Targeted outreach affects web traffic. That's the gold standard of how to develop our measurement program.
>
> *Sbonali Burke, VP of media for ASPCA, as quoted in* PRWeek

Advertising Value Equivalency (AVE)

Another standard approach is to calculate the monetary value of message exposure. In fact, a global survey by Benchpoint, cosponsored by the Institute for Public Relations and international partners, found that AVE was the third most used measurement method although it only ranked eleventh in effectiveness. This is typically done by converting stories in regular news columns or on the air into equivalent advertising costs. In other words, a five-inch article in a trade magazine that charges $100 per column inch for advertising would be worth $500 in publicity value. The Doritos Super Bowl

on the job

A MULTICULTURAL WORLD

YouTube Videos Promote World Water Day

Public relations agency Weber Shandwick (WS) and Population Services International (PSI) combined forces to create a social media campaign that capitalizes on the emotional power of video. World Water Day Viral Video Series set out to open eyes to the heartbreaking reality of water-related disease as a major cause of death worldwide for children.

PSI wanted socially and environmentally conscious Americans to know that unsafe drinking water often leads to sudden death and devastating illness for children in developing countries. The online public service announcement (PSA) video series informed people of the simple, cheap solutions to the problem.

The team knew that the key to generating strong viewership of the online PSA videos was telling a compelling story, so it enlisted Good, an integrated media company, to help build a strong narrative. From here, the team took an unconventional approach and drew upon existing footage from iconic Hollywood moments, including scenes from *Cool Hand Luke* and *Psycho*. In one video, children are seen sliding down a chute of the popular toy Crocodile Mile, but landing in sludgy, contaminated water.

To generate buzz leading up to World Water Day, WS conducted a staggered rollout. Prior to the videos'

launch, content editors at YouTube got a sneak peak to stimulate their interest in a home page exclusive. The first four videos launched in March 2010 on PSI's partner sites, YouTube, Facebook, MySpace, MTVThink, and Twitter.

Within 10 days of launching, total video views exceeded 1 million. The video *Transparency* was featured as a YouTube home page exclusive and generated 600,000 views in its first three days. The top-viewed video, *Psycho*, was YouTube's most viewed video in its nonprofit and activism category.

The viewer feedback showed that the videos raised awareness and interest in helping the cause.

The cause was good.

The delivery channel capitalized on the reach of social media.

And the narrative was compelling.

The tagline under PSI's logo states: "Healthy Lives. Measurable Results." But could the sponsors be certain that money was well spent on public relations based only on the measurement of media exposure and anecdotal praise from viewers? Using the measurement guidelines from this chapter, what would you recommend to Population Services International that would enhance substantive evaluation of these sorts of communication programs in the future?

Source: PRWeek Awards 2010, www.prweekus .com/awards http://www.psi.org/our-work /measurable-results

campaign, mentioned above, claimed that the news coverage was comparable to $40 million in paid advertising.

Some practitioners even take the approach of calculating the cost of advertising for the same amount of space and then multiplying that total three to six times to reflect the common belief that a news story has greater credibility than an advertisement. Research It has consistently found greater memorability for publicity than for the same message presented as advertising. But several mitigating factors argue against using a multiplier. For one, there is no empirical evidence to support any multiple factor. Professor Don Stacks at the University of Miami has conducted several research studies about AVE and concluded, "We failed to find the existence of a multiplier." Other professionals, not using systematic research, have come to the same conclusion.

Such multipliers imply a level of precision that cannot be justified, given the complexity of the comparison between publicity and advertising. For example, one reason why the two can't be compared is the fundamental difference between advertising and publicity. Advertising copy is directly controlled by the organization and can be oriented to specific objectives. The organization also controls the size and placement of the message. News mentions, on the other hand, are determined by media gatekeepers and can be negative, neutral, or positive. In addition, a news release can be edited to the point that key corporate messages are deleted. In other words, the organization can't control size, placement, or content.

It thus becomes a question of what is being measured. Should an article be counted as equivalent advertising space if it is negative? It also is questionable whether a 15-inch article that mentions the organization only once among six other organizations is comparable to the same amount of advertising space. There are, however, defenders of the AVE approach to evaluation. Some argue that such metrics help corporate management put a value on public relations. Others say it helps marketing executives decide how to split resources between public relations and marketing. Even Mark Weiner, president of measuring firm Delahaye, says, "So what's bad about ad values? If it works for some people, who's to say that they're unequivocally wrong or unprofessional even if we believe that better methods exist." See the Ethics box on page 200 for an ethical dilemma regarding AVEs.

One promising new direction for assessing advertising equivalency is outlined in a monograph from the Institute for Public Relations. The proposed Weighted Media Cost method measures the cost of media space or time as a means to evaluate "the *news medium itself* in which a story resides, similar to the way the cost of real estate impacts the overall value of a house." Garnering media coverage in the better media neighborhoods, so to speak, equates with greater success in achieving campaign objectives. Instead of calculating a contentious dollar value for media coverage, the weighted media cost presents an estimate of the quality of the media neighborhood where media placements reside.

In summary, the **dollar-value** approach to measuring publicity effectiveness should be used judiciously, as reflected by the limited use of such metrics in PRSA Silver Anvil award entries. A more defensible dollar evaluation can be made for messages such as public service announcements (PSAs) on radio or television, which are controlled by the creator much like a paid commercial would be. Johnson & Johnson, for example, conducted a Safe Pools for Safe Kids campaign and reported, "There was more than $2 million worth of free advertising including more than 1,000 TV spots from Turner Broadcasting's efforts."

The most important concern is that AVEs concentrate on outputs, not outcomes. AVE tends to relegate public relations to a media relations function, which diminishes the role of public relations' strategic counsel to upper management when decisions are made, not just when they are publicized. At the same time, equating publicity with advertising rates for comparable space does not engender good media relations. The

Once you start comparing a PR placement to an ad, that raises a whole spectrum of issues.

Don Bartholomew, director of research at MWW Group

on the job
ETHICS

The New Math: Ad Rates versus News Coverage

You've been hired as an intern at a public relations firm for the summer. One of your duties is to go through recent issues of trade magazines and clip any article in which the name of a client appears. You are then asked to look up advertising rates for these publications and calculate what the comparable space in advertising would cost. The public relations firm routinely triples the ad cost because a news story is more "valuable" than an ad.

The idea, says the account supervisor, is to count entire articles even if the client's name is mentioned only once. "The client is impressed with big numbers," she says, "so count anything you can find, get the actual ad cost, and then triple it." You ask whether you should also try to judge whether the coverage is favorable or not. Your supervisor says that all the client really wants is to be visible—and besides, it takes too much time to decide what is favorable or unfavorable coverage.

Does AVE raise any ethical concerns on your part? Why or why not? How would you handle the assignment? Would you be inclined to suggest to your boss that Weighted Media Equivalency might be worth considering?

technique reinforces the opinion of many media gatekeepers that all news releases are just attempts to get free advertising.

Systematic Tracking

As noted earlier, message exposure traditionally has been measured by sheer bulk. New advances in computer software and databases, however, now make it possible to track media placements in a more sophisticated way.

Computer software and databases can now be used to analyze the content of media placements by such variables as market penetration, type of publication, tone of coverage, sources quoted, and mention of key copy points. Ketchum, for example, can build up to 40 variables into its computer program, including the tracking of reporter bylines to determine whether a journalist is predisposed negatively or positively to the client's key messages.

Specialty measurement firms such as Vocus, Cymfony, VMS, and Factiva do extensive analysis for a variety of clients on a number of metrics such as (1) analysis of coverage telling how a company's news coverage compares with that of the competition, (2) share of voice in terms of what percentage of overall coverage about an industry or subject focuses on the client company, (3) tone showing whether the slant of coverage is positive or negative, (4) percentage of time that stories mention key messages, and (5) analysis of what third-party experts, consumers, and bloggers say about the organization. See Figure 8.3 for sample charts Vocus, a measurement firm, compiled on the athletic shoe industry for use in this textbook.

Systematic monitoring can provide a baseline to determine whether an organization's publicity efforts paid off in terms of placements and mention of key messages. Essentially, a baseline study is a measurement of audience response (awareness, understanding, or attitudes and opinions) before, during, and after a public relations campaign. Baseline studies can graphically show the percentage

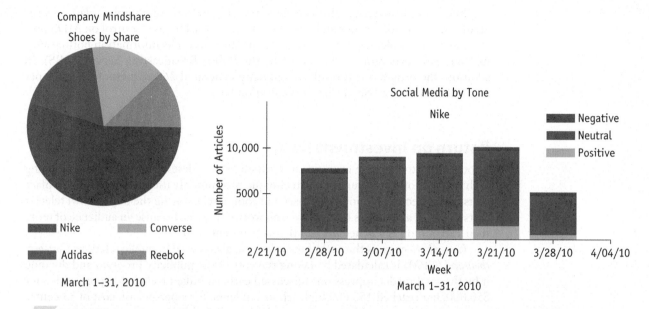

Figure 8.3 Measuring Results in the Athletic Shoe Industry

Public relations software and research firms are able to capture enormous amounts of data over time, which are then encapsulated in graphics that inform evaluation of measurable objectives. For example, if Nike had set the objective of leading the top four shoe manufacturers in share of media mentions, the Company Mindshare chart would demonstrate success at a glance. If the objective were to hold negative comments to a minimum among bloggers and tweeters, the Social Media by Tone chart would show a small red band of negative comments compared to the large sections of neutral and positive comments.

difference in measured audience performance as a result of public relations campaign components.

For example, the Johnson & Johnson public service campaign to increase parental awareness of dangers to children in swimming pools used a baseline survey by Harris Interactive before its campaign. Post-campaign research found that awareness of pool-drain hazards increased from 26 percent to 32 percent.

Another form of analysis compares the number of news releases sent with the number actually published and in what kinds of periodicals. Such analysis often helps a public relations department determine what kinds of publicity are most effective and earn the most return on investment (ROI).

> The world doesn't need more data. What it needs is analyzed data.
>
> *Katharine Paine, president of KD Paine & Partners*

Requests and 800 Numbers

Another measure of media exposure is to compile the number of requests for more information. A story in a newspaper or a company spokesperson on a broadcast often tells people where they can get more information about a subject.

In many cases, a toll-free 800 number is provided. Dayton Hudson Corporation, owner of several department store chains, once used a toll-free hotline number as part of its "Child Care Aware" program to help educate parents about quality child care and how to get it. In a six-month period, 19,000 calls were received from people seeking advice and copies of a brochure.

Requests for materials also can show the effectiveness of a public relations program. An information program by the U.S. Centers for Disease Control on AIDS prevention, for example, received nearly 2,000 phone calls on its information hotline after its "Safe Sex" program was broadcast by the Public Broadcasting Service (PBS). In addition, the program and resulting publicity generated 260 requests for videotapes and 400 requests for "Smart Sex" organization kits.

Return on Investment (ROI)

Another way to evaluate exposure to a message is to determine the cost of reaching each member of the audience. The technique is commonly used in advertising to place costs in perspective. Although a 30-second commercial during the Super Bowl telecast costs millions, advertisers believe it is well worth the price because an audience of more than 150 million is reached for less than a half-cent each.

Cost-effectiveness, as this technique is known, also is used in public relations. *Cost-per-thousand* (CPM) is calculated by taking the cost of the publicity program and dividing it by the total media impressions (discussed earlier). Nike produced a sports video for $50,000, but reached 150,000 high school students, for a per-person cost of 33 cents.

> It was clear to us that you can't go and ask for money . . . unless you can show a return. You can't show a return unless you have measurement.
>
> *Valerie M. Cunningham, VP of corporate marketing for Xerox*

Many professionals also call this *ROI*, or *return on investment*. In other words, if an organization spends $500,000 on a campaign that results in a $20 million increase in sales, the ROI is 40 times the cost. Increasingly, public relations professionals are measuring public relations in terms of (1) what sales or revenues are generated, and (2) how much they have saved the company in terms of avoiding a crisis or litigation. One measuring firm, CCW, gave an example in an advertisement for its services: If public relations contributes just 3.5 percent to a major airline's stock price in terms of reputation management, the impact on the company's market value would be $400 million. The Doritos team estimated total impressions at 40 million, which they noted was 13 times the cost of a Super Bowl spot. By creating a competition with all of the attention in the media surrounding the entries as well as the interesting stories about winning ads, this strategy offers a much higher return on investment than the purchase of a single ad during the football game.

Measurement of Audience Awareness

Thus far, techniques of measuring audience exposure and accurate dissemination have been discussed. A higher level of evaluation is needed to determine whether the audience actually became aware of the message and understood it.

Walter Lindenmann calls this the second level of public relations evaluation. He notes:

> At this level, public relations practitioners measure whether target audience groups actually received the messages directed at them: whether they paid attention to those messages, whether they understood the messages, and whether they have retained those messages in any shape or form.

The tools of survey research are needed to answer such questions. Members of the target audience must be asked about the message and what they remember about it.

Public awareness of which organization sponsors an event also is important. The internationally recognized advocacy group Health Literacy Missouri conducts annual surveys of media in the state to assess awareness of the organization, but, more importantly, of health literacy as a crucial factor in the health and well-being of everyday citizens.

Measuring audience awareness and comprehension with *day-after recall* offers a credible metric for evaluating the impact of a campaign component. Participants are asked to view a specific television program or read a particular news story. The next day, they are interviewed to find out which messages they remember.

Ketchum, on behalf of the California Prune Board, used this technique to determine whether a 15-city media tour was conveying the key message that prunes are a high-fiber food source. Forty women in Detroit considered likely to watch daytime television shows were asked to view a program on which a Prune Board spokesperson appeared. The day after the program, Ketchum asked the women questions about the show, including their knowledge of the fiber content of prunes. Ninety-three percent remembered the Prune Board spokesperson, and 65 percent, on an unaided basis, named prunes as a high-fiber food source. See the Insights box on page 204 for an example of measurement by the CDC of awareness of a health issue.

Measurement of Audience Attitudes

Closely related to audience awareness and understanding of a message are changes in an audience's perceptions and attitudes, which can be evaluated using pre- and post-measurements of attitudes. A number of intervening variables may account for changes in attitude, of course, but statistical analysis of variance can help pinpoint how much the change is attributable to public relations efforts. Advanced evaluation designs can even control for the effect of all the measurement, which has its own impact on audiences.

The insurance company Prudential Financial regularly conducts baseline studies. One survey found that the company scored high in respondent familiarity, but achieved only a 29 percent favorable rating in fulfilling its corporate social responsibilities. As a result, the company launched The Prudential Spirit of Community Awards program, the United States' largest youth-recognition program based exclusively on volunteer community service. The value of the baseline survey is underscored by Frank R. Stansberry, former manager of guest affairs for Coca-Cola, who said, "The only way to determine if communications are making an impact is by pre- and posttest research. The first survey measures the status quo. The second one will demonstrate any change and the direction of that change."

Measurement of Audience Action

The ultimate objective of any public relations effort, as has been pointed out, is to accomplish organizational objectives. As David Dozier of San Diego State University aptly points out, "The outcome of a successful public relations program is not a hefty stack of news stories. . . . Communication is important only in the effects it achieves among publics."

The objective of an amateur theater group is not to get media publicity; the objective is to sell tickets. The objective of an environmental organization such as Greenpeace is not to get publicity on behalf of whales, but to motivate the public to (1) write elected officials, (2) send donations for its preservation efforts, and (3) get protective legislation passed that actually saves whales.

on the job

INSIGHTS

Amount of Awareness Measured in a Health Campaign

The Centers for Disease Control (CDC) had a problem. Parents were increasingly contacting the U.S. health agency expressing concern about MRSA, a potentially life-threatening staph bacteria, that particularly affects children. Porter Novelli public relations was retained to organize an awareness campaign to educate parents about the signs and symptoms of MRSA, when to seek treatment, and how to prevent its spread. Focus groups and other survey databases indicated that the campaign should be directed at moms, primarily low-income and African American women.

The campaign was launched at the beginning of the school year. Among the tactics used were satellite media tours (SMTs), mat releases, public service announcements (PSAs), and CDC's MySpace page. Messages were also included in Lysol's "Looking After You and Your Child" booklet, distributed to 1 million households. Information was also distributed through health care professionals and school parent associations. The SMT reached about 2.1 million people, the mat release reached about 500,000 people, and the PSAs were aired on more than 200 radio stations. Such figures measured exposure to the message, but they didn't answer the question of whether awareness among moms increased.

Consequently, the CDC and Porter Novelli also conducted post-campaign surveys with the target audience. The research showed that 4 in 10 moms had heard of the campaign, and they were more likely to know the symptoms. Twice as many moms who were aware of the campaign also knew when to seek treatment. According to a summary in *PRWeek*, which named the campaign as the best use of research/measurement in its 2010 annual awards, " . . . knowledge among African American moms increased, with those knowing the signs and when to seek treatment up from 18 percent to 25 percent, and those knowing about prevention up from 64 percent to 72 percent."

A CHILD'S FIRST LINE OF DEFENSE
AGAINST MRSA:
A WELL-INFORMED MOM.

MRSA is methicillin-resistant *Staphylococcus aureus*, a potentially dangerous type of staph bacteria that is resistant to certain antibiotics and may cause skin and other infections. What are the signs and symptoms of an MRSA skin infection? It usually starts as a bump or infected area on the skin that appears red or swollen, has pus, is warm to the touch, or just looks infected. If you or someone in your family experiences these signs and symptoms, cover the area with a bandage and contact your healthcare professional. It is especially important to contact your healthcare professional if signs and symptoms of an MRSA skin infection are accompanied by a fever.

Similarly, the ultimate objective of a company is to sell its products and services, not get 200 million media impressions. See the Insights box below for more information about linking sales to measurements. Although the immediate objective of many public relations campaigns is to raise awareness driven by the number of media placements and impressions, such campaigns should be seen in the context of the adoption theory that was described in Chapter 7 and in that chapter's iPad Casebook. In other words, raising awareness and raising interest are the first two steps of the five-step process to ultimately motivate people to adopt an idea, vote for a candidate, use a service, or buy a product.

Thus, public relations efforts ultimately are evaluated on how they help an organization achieve its objectives. For example, the airline- and union-backed Stop Oil Speculation Now campaign did not tout its media coverage or its website hits as much as it focused on "bottom-line" outcomes:

- Investors pulled $39 billion out of the commodities market, where oil speculation was rampant.
- Oil prices dropped 35 percent as a consequence.
- Lower fuel costs helped the airline industry return to profitability.
- Members of Congress repeated campaign messages during floor debate.

> The outcome of a successful public relations program is not a hefty stack of news stories. . . . Communication is important only in the effects it achieves among publics.
>
> *Dr. David Dozier, professor,*
> *San Diego State University*

on the job

INSIGHTS

Sales: For Many Companies, This Is the Ultimate Evaluation

In the corporate world, one behavioral outcome of company performance is almost always measured daily and with great precision. It is sales of products and services. Sabrina Horn calls for a shift in thinking about the role of public relations in driving sales figures: "To those outside marketing, public relations is frequently misunderstood as nothing more than a tactical press release machine. Unfortunately, PR is often an afterthought to strategic planning."

By being involved in the strategic plan, the role of public relations can be broader, and objectives that are clearly linked to sales can be set, for example, "Increase sales leads by 50 percent in financial services through precision public relations efforts targeted at the new customer base." It is essential to then plan strategies that can help achieve this objective and, finally, to devise measures that evaluate their impact on sales performance.

With early participation in the planning process and some clever techniques, it is possible for public relations to contribute to the sales figures that are already being captured by the company.

BUSINESS GOAL	PR STRATEGY	MEASUREMENT TOOLS
Increase sales leads by 50 percent in financial services for new customers.	Product launches, including tours, press releases, a customer testimonial program, direct mail of CD-ROMs presenting services, and repeated urging of new, prospective customers to call the toll-free number and ask for Operator 39 to receive special discounts.	1. Telemarketing staff maps source of incoming calls back to articles published as the result of press releases. 2. Sales-lead tracking system is programmed to track callers' requests for Operator 39—the marker for the public relations effort.

Measurement of Supplemental Activities

Other forms of measurement can be used in public relations activities. This section discusses (1) communication audits, (2) pilot tests and split messages, (3) meeting and event attendance, and (4) newsletter readership.

Communication Audits

The entire communication activity of an organization should be evaluated at least once a year to make sure that every primary and secondary public is receiving appropriate messages. David Hilton-Barber, a past president of the Public Relations Institute of South Africa (PRISA), once wrote: "The most important reasons for an audit are to help establish communication goals and objectives, to evaluate long-term programs, to identify strengths and weaknesses, and to point up any areas which require increased activity."

A communication audit, as an assessment of an organization's entire communications program, could include the following:

- Analysis of all communication activities
- Informal interviews with rank-and-file employees, middle management, and top executives
- Informal interviews with community leaders, media gatekeepers, consumers, distributors, and other influential persons in the industry

A number of research techniques, as outlined in Chapter 5, can be used during a communication audit, including mail and telephone surveys, focus groups, and so forth. The important point is that the communications of an organization should be analyzed from every possible angle, with the input of as many publics as possible.

Pilot Tests and Split Messages

Evaluation is important even before a public relations effort is launched. If exposure to a message is to be maximized, it is wise to pretest it with a sample group from the targeted audience. Do its members easily understand the message? Do they accept the message? Does the message motivate them to adopt a new idea or product?

A variation of pretesting is the *pilot test*. Before going national with a public relations message, companies often test the message and key copy points in selected cities to learn how the media accept the message and how the public reacts. This approach is quite common in marketing public relations because it limits costs and enables the company to revamp or fine-tune the message for maximum exposure. In the new media landscape, with numerous controlled media such as Web and social media platforms, piloting also allows the company to switch channels of dissemination if the original media channels are not exposing the message to the proper audiences.

The *split-message* approach is common in direct mail and direct e-mail campaigns. Two or three different appeals may be prepared by a charitable organization and sent to different audience segments. The response rate is then monitored (perhaps the amount of donations is totaled) to learn what messages and graphics seemed to be the most effective.

Meeting and Event Attendance

Audience awareness is often evaluated by attendance at an event. The New York Public Library centennial day celebration, for example, attracted a crowd of 10,000 for a sound-and-laser show and speeches. In addition, 20,000 visitors came to the library on the designated centennial day and more than 200,000 people from around the world visited the library's exhibitions during the year-long celebration.

Such data provide information about the number of people exposed to a message, but don't answer the more crucial question of what the audience took away from the meeting.

Public relations people often get an informal sense of an audience's attitudes by its behavior. A standing ovation, spontaneous applause, complimentary remarks as people leave, and even the expressions on people's faces provide clues as to how a meeting was received. On the other hand, if people are not responsive, if they ask questions about subjects supposedly explained, or if they express doubts or antagonism, the meeting can be considered only partly successful.

Public relations practitioners use a number of information methods to evaluate the success of a meeting, but they also employ more systematic methods. The most common technique is providing an evaluation sheet for participants to fill out at the end of the meeting. Hiring independent evaluators is money well spent for major conferences or annual meetings.

A simple form asking people to rate such items as location, costs, facilities, and program on a 1 to 5 scale (1 being the best) can be used. Other forms may ask people to rate aspects of a conference or meeting as (1) excellent, (2) good, (3) average, (4) poor, or (5) very poor.

Evaluation forms also determine how people heard about the program and what suggestions they have for future meetings. Another approach is to ask attendees whether they heard or believed the key messages of a spokesperson's presentation and whether they would like to receive any follow-up information from the sponsoring organization.

Tracking Success

Measuring the success of Moscow's Avon Breast Cancer Walk will include a number of factors such as the number of walkers who take part and the financial success.

Newsletter Readership

Editors of newsletters, e-newsletters, and internal communication tools such as company magazines should evaluate readership annually. Such an evaluation can help ascertain (1) reader perceptions, (2) the degree to which stories are balanced, (3) the kinds of stories that have high reader interest, (4) additional topics that should be covered, (5) the credibility of the publication, and (6) the extent to which the newsletter is meeting organizational objectives.

Note that systematic evaluation is not based on whether all the copies of a newsletter have been distributed or picked up. This information doesn't tell the editor what the audience actually read, retained, or acted upon.

Materials can be evaluated in a number of ways. The methods include (1) content analysis, (2) readership-interest surveys, (3) readership recall of articles actually read, and (4) the use of advisory boards.

Content Analysis   Based on a representative sample of past issues, stories may be categorized under general headings such as (1) management announcements, (2) new product developments, (3) new personnel and retirements, (4) features about employees, (5) corporate finances, (6) news of departments and divisions, and (7) job-related information.

Such a systematic analysis will show what percentage of the publication is devoted to each category. It may be found that one division rarely is covered in the employee newsletter or that management pronouncements tend to dominate the entire publication. Given the content-analysis findings, editors have an empirical basis on which to shift the content.

Readership-Interest Surveys   The purpose of these surveys is to get feedback about the types of stories employees are most interested in reading. The most common survey method is simply to provide a long list of generic story topics and have employees rate each as (1) important, (2) somewhat important, or (3) not important. The International Association of Business Communicators (IABC) conducted such a survey on behalf of several dozen companies and found that readers were not very interested in "personals" about other employees (birthdays, anniversaries, and the like).

A readership-interest survey becomes even more valuable when it is compared with the content analysis of a publication. Substantial differences signal a possible need for changes in the editorial content.

Article Recall   One effective readership survey involves trained interviewers asking a sample of employees what they have read in the latest issue of the publication. Employees are shown the publication page by page and asked to indicate which articles they have read. As a check on the tendency of employees to report that they have read everything, interviewers also ask them (1) how much of each article they have read and (2) what the articles were about. The results are then content-analyzed to determine which kinds of articles have the most readership.

Advisory Boards   Periodic feedback and evaluation can be provided by organizing an employee advisory board that meets several times a year to discuss the direction and content of the publication. This is a useful technique because it expands the editor's feedback network and elicits comments that employees might be hesitant to tell the editor face-to-face. A variation of the advisory board method is to occasionally invite a sampling of employees to meet and discuss the publication or website.

Summary

The Purpose of Evaluation

■ Evaluation is the measurement of results against objectives.

■ One major purpose of evaluation is to do a better job of planning future programs.

Objectives: A Prerequisite for Evaluation

■ Objectives should be part of any program plan.

■ There must be agreed-upon criteria used to evaluate success in obtaining these objectives.

Current Status of Measurement and Evaluation

■ Studies indicate that about 4 or 5 percent of a typical public relations budget is allocated to evaluations and measurement.

■ On the most basic level, practitioners can measure message distribution and media placements. The second level is measurement of audience awareness, comprehension, and retention. The most advanced level is the measurement of changes in attitudes, opinions, and behaviors.

Measurement of Production

■ The most elementary form of measurement is a tabulation of how many news releases, brochures, annual reports, and so on, are distributed in a single year.

■ Measurement of production gives management an idea of a staff's productivity and output.

Measurement of Message Exposure

■ Several criteria can be used to measure message exposure, including the compilation of media placements in print, broadcast, and Internet media.

■ One common method is calculating media impressions, which the potential audience reached with a message. Advertising value equivalency, commonly called AVE, is calculated by converting news stories to the cost of a comparable amount of paid space.

■ More sophisticated methods include systematic tracking using software and databases to find out such information as tone of coverage, percentage of key messages used, and percentage of coverage related to that of the competition.

■ Sometimes, exposure is evaluated by determining how much it cost to reach each member of the target audience.

Measurement of Audience Awareness

■ The next level of evaluation is whether the audience became aware of and understood the message.

■ Audience awareness can be measured through survey research, which, by having the audience engage in unaided recall, can determine whether the audience understood and remembered the message.

Measurement of Audience Attitudes

■ Changes in audience attitudes can be evaluated through a baseline or benchmark study, which measures awareness and opinions before, during, and after a public relations campaign.

Measurement of Audience Action

■ Ultimately, public relations campaigns are evaluated based on how they help an organization achieve its objectives through changing audience behavior, whether that involves sales, fund-raising, or the election of a candidate.

Measurement of Supplemental Activities

■ A yearly communication audit helps ensure that all publics are receiving appropriate messages. Several techniques, such as pilot tests and split messages, can be used to pretest a public relations effort.

■ Meeting and event attendance can be measured both by the number of attendees and by their behavior, which is an indicator of their acceptance of a message.

■ Newsletter readership can be evaluated by content analysis, interest surveys, and article recall.

Case Activity   Evaluating the Success of Ridesharing

The Ohio Department of Transportation, with 17 rideshare groups, is planning a Rideshare Week. The objective is to increase participation in carpooling and the use of mass transit during this special week. A long-term objective, of course, is to increase the number of people who use carpools or mass transit on a regular basis.

Your public relations firm has been retained to promote Ohio Rideshare Week. Your campaign will include a news conference with the governor encouraging participation, press kits, news releases, interviews on broadcast talk shows, special events, and distribution of Rideshare information booklets at major businesses.

What methods would you use to evaluate the effectiveness of your public relations efforts on behalf of Ohio's Rideshare Week?

Questions   For Review and Discussion

1. What is the role of stated objectives in evaluating public relations programs?
2. What are some general types of evaluation questions that a person should ask about a program?
3. List four ways that publicity activity is evaluated. What, if any, are the drawbacks of each one?
4. Do you think news stories about a product or service should be evaluated in terms of comparable advertising costs? Why or why not?
5. What are the advantages of systematic tracking and content analysis of news clippings?
6. How are pilot tests and split messages used to determine the suitability of a message?
7. How does measurement of message exposure differ from measurement of audience comprehension of the message?
8. What is a communication audit?
9. What methods can be used to evaluate a company newsletter or magazine?

Media Resources

Bialik, C. (2010, February 20). Dot-complicated: Measuring traffic on the web. *Wall Street Journal*. Retrieved from http://online.wsj.com

Elrick, M. (2009, May–June). Measuring to demonstrate value in a tough economy. *Communication World*, 16–20.

Hagley, T. R. (2009). *Writing winning proposals: PR cases.* San Diego, CA: Cognella.

Iacona, E. (2007, March 19). Measuring the value of AVEs. *PRWeek*, 13.

Jeffrey, A., Jeffries-Fox, B., & Rawlins, B. L. (2010). *A new paradigm for media analysis: Weighted media cost* [Monograph]. Retrieved from Institute for Public Relations Research website: http://www.instituteforpr.org/ipr _info/a_new_paradigm_for_media_analysis_weighted _media_cost/

Lindenmann, W. K. Guidelines and standards for measuring and evaluating PR effectiveness. Retrieved from Institute for Public Relations website: www.instituteforpr.com.

Paine, K. (2010, February). Six indicators of hope in PR measurement. *The RaganReport*, 19–20.

PR measurement lumbers into the digital age. (2010, March 22). Retrieved from *PRNews Online* website: http://www.prnewsonline.com/news/

Sinickas, A. (2009, July 15). *Measure your ROI—fast!!!* Retrieved from www.ragan.com

Stacks, D. (2007, April 23). Multiplier or not: PR on par with ads. *PRWeek*, 8.

Warren, C. (2009, October 27). *How to measure social media ROI.* Retrieved from http://mashable.com/2009/10/27

Wright, A. (2009, August 24). Mining the web for feelings, not facts. *New York Times*, pp. B1, B7.

Public Opinion and Persuasion

George Clooney as a catalyst for change—an opinion leader.

After reading this chapter you will be able to:

Understand the implications of public opinion for public relations

Explain the crucial role of opinion leaders in public discourse

Describe key theories explaining the role of mass media

Understand the pervasive role of persuasion in modern life

Enumerate key factors in persuasion

Identify major considerations in conducting ethical persuasive campaigns

What Is Public Opinion?

Americans talk about public opinion as if it were a monolithic entity overshadowing the entire landscape. Editorial cartoonists humanize it in the form of John or Jane Q. Public, characters who symbolize what people think about any given issue. The reality is that public opinion is somewhat elusive and extremely difficult to measure at any given moment.

In fact, to continue the metaphor, public opinion is a number of monoliths perceived by John and Jane Q. Public, all existing at the same time. Few issues create unanimity of thought among the population, and public opinion on any issue is split in several directions. It also may come as a surprise to note that only a small number of people at any given time take part in public opinion formation on a specific issue. But once people and the media begin to speak of public opinion on an issue as an accomplished fact, it can take on its own momentum. According to Elisabeth Noelle-Neumann's spiral-of-silence theory, public opinion can be an almost tangible force on people's thinking. Noelle-Neumann defines *public opinion* as opinions on controversial issues that one can express in public without isolating oneself. This implies the element of conformity that perceived public opinion can impose on individuals who want to avoid alienation.

There are two reasons for the profound influence of vocal segments of society and public opinion momentum. First, psychologists have found that the public tends to be passive. It is often assumed that a small vocal group represents the attitude of the public, when in reality, it is more accurate to say that the majority of the people are apathetic because an issue doesn't interest or affect them. Thus, "public" opposition to such issues as nuclear power, gay marriage, abortion, and gun control may really be the view of a small but significant number of concerned people.

Second, one issue may engage the attention of one part of the population, whereas another arouses the interest of another segment. Parents, for example, may form public opinion on the need for improved secondary education, whereas senior citizens constitute the bulk of public opinion on the need to close the unfair "donut hole" in Medicare coverage of prescription drugs.

These two examples illustrate the most common definition of *public opinion*: "Public opinion is the sum of individual opinions on an issue affecting those individuals." Another popular definition states: "Public opinion is a collection of views held by persons interested in the subject." Thus, a person unaffected by or uninterested in (and perhaps unaware of) an issue does not contribute to public opinion on the subject.

Inherent in these definitions is the concept of *self-interest*. The following statements appear in public opinion research:

- Public opinion is the collective expression of opinion of many individuals bound into a group by common aims, aspirations, needs, and ideals.

- People who are interested in or who have a vested or self-interest in an issue—or who can be affected by the outcome of the issue—form public opinion on that particular item.

- Psychologically, opinion basically is determined by self-interest. Events, words, or other stimuli affect opinion only insofar as their relationship to self-interest or a general concern is apparent.

- Opinion does not remain aroused for a long period of time unless people feel their self-interest is acutely involved or unless opinion—aroused by words—is sustained by events.

- Once self-interest is involved, opinion is not easily changed.

Research studies also emphasize the importance of *events* in the formation of public opinion. Social scientists, for example, have made the following generalizations:

- Opinion is highly sensitive to events that have an impact on the public at large or a particular segment of the public.

- By and large, public opinion does not anticipate events. It only reacts to them.

- Events trigger formation of public opinion. Unless people are aware of an issue, they are not likely to be concerned or have an opinion about it. Awareness and discussion lead to crystallizing of opinions and often a consensus among the public.

- Events of unusual magnitude are likely to swing public opinion temporarily from one extreme to another. Opinion does not stabilize until the implication of the event is seen with some perspective. The terrorist attacks on the World Trade Center and the Pentagon on 9/11 are perhaps the most galvanizing events in the new century to swing public opinion, including media opinion at the time, regarding external threats to safety and security. The groundswell of militant public opinion probably served as the driving force for the U.S. invasion of Afghanistan and Iraq.

People also have more opinions, and are able to form them more easily, with respect to goals rather than with respect to the methods necessary to reach those goals. For example, according to polls, there is fairly strong public opinion for preventing a Wall Street collapse from ever happening again. However, there is little agreement on how to do this. One group calls for criminal prosecutions of bankers and traders, another endorses breaking up huge financial corporations that are "too large to fail," while others called for stringent reform of regulations, and still others simply say let the free market run its course.

Opinion Leaders as Catalysts

Public opinion on an issue may have its roots in self-interest or in events, but the primary catalyst is public discussion. Only in this way does opinion begin to crystallize to the extent that pollsters can measure it.

Serving as catalysts for the formation of public opinion are people who are knowledgeable and articulate about specific issues. They are called *opinion leaders*. Sociologists describe them as:

1. highly interested in a subject or issue.

2. better informed on an issue than the average person.

3. avid consumers of mass media.

4. early adopters of new ideas.

5. good organizers who can get other people to take action.

The Health Care Debate

An individual's opinion on an issue or controversy may not always be logical or consistent, but it reflects strongly held beliefs.

Types of Leaders

Sociologists traditionally have defined two types of leaders. First are the *formal opinion leaders*, so called because of their positions as elected officials, presidents of companies, or heads of membership groups. News reporters often ask them for statements when a specific issue relates to their areas of responsibility or concern. People in formal leadership positions also are called *power leaders*.

Second are the *informal opinion leaders*, those who have clout with peers because of some special characteristic. They may be role models who are admired and emulated or opinion leaders who can exert peer pressure on others to go along with something. In general, informal opinion leaders exert considerable influence on their peer groups by being highly informed, articulate, and credible on particular issues. Both formal and informal opinion leaders play a major role in the life cycle of public opinion, which is discussed in the Insights box on page 215.

The Irish singer Bono is a current example of an informal leader who has had a great impact on public opinion regarding issues such as world hunger and poverty (see

The Life Cycle of Public Opinion

Public opinion and persuasion are important catalysts in the formation of a public issue and its ultimate resolution. The natural evolution of an issue involves five stages:

1.   **Definition of the issue.** Activist and special interest groups raise an issue, perhaps a protest about the environmental dangers of offshore oil drilling. These groups have no formal power but serve as "agenda stimuli" for the media that cover controversy and conflict. Visual opportunities for television coverage occur when activists hold rallies and demonstrations.

2.   **Involvement of opinion leaders.** Through media coverage, the issue is put on the public agenda and people become aware of it. Opinion leaders begin to discuss the issue and perhaps see it as being symbolic of broader environmental issues. According to research in *Roper Reports*, 10 to 12 percent of the population that the magazine calls "The Influentials" drive public opinion and consumer trends.

3.   **Public awareness.** As public awareness grows, the issue becomes a matter of public discussion and debate, garnering extensive media coverage. The issue is simplified by the media into "them versus us." Suggested solutions tend to be at either end of the spectrum.

4.   **Government/regulatory involvement.** Public consensus begins to build for a resolution as government/regulatory involvement occurs. Large groups identify with some side of the issue. Demand grows for government to act.

5.   **Resolution.** The resolution stage begins as people with authority (elected officials) draft legislation or interpret existing rules and regulations to make a statement. A decision is made to protect the scenic areas or to reach a compromise with advocates of development. If some groups remain unhappy, however, the cycle may repeat itself.

Chapter 21 for the unintended consequences of celebrity fund-raising such as Bono's high-profile efforts). Actor George Clooney has emerged as another opinion leader on a wide range of social issues. Although many Americans find his ideas about the political process controversial, Clooney's advocacy to end genocide in strife-torn countries is widely accepted.

People seldom make a decision on their own but are influenced by their friends, parents, educators, supervisors, church leaders, physicians, public officials, movie stars or singers, and the media in general when deciding to vote for a president or a city mayor, or to purchase a car or even toothpaste. Public relations professionals attempt to influence these leaders just as they seek to influence the public at large.

For example, those seeking stronger laws requiring helmets for motorcyclists are making use of statistics about increased motorcycle fatalities, but are likely holding sway in shifting public opinion by pointing to the highly publicized motorcycle accident of NFL star Ben Roethlisberger. According to *USA Today*, proponents of motorcycle helmets were galvanized to speak out when the Pittsburgh Steelers quarterback broke facial bones in a collision with a car in which Roethlisberger wasn't wearing a helmet.

Of course, Roethlisberger's crude and lascivious behavior in the Georgia bar with a 20-year-old coed has made him a far less sympathetic figure today and a poor choice as a spokesman for any worthy cause. Time will tell whether the incident will hamper his professional career beyond the six-game suspension handed out by the league.

A survey of 20,000 Americans by the Roper Organization found that only 10 to 12 percent of the general public are opinion leaders. These "influentials," those whom other people seek out for advice, fit the profile of:

1. Being active in the community
2. Having a college degree
3. Earning a relatively high income
4. Regularly reading newspapers and magazines
5. Actively participating in recreational activities
6. Showing environmental concern by recycling

Regis McKenna, the marketing communications expert responsible for the original launch of the Apple Macintosh, likes to think of opinion leaders as luminaries because "There are about 20 to 30 key people in every industry who have major influence on trends, standards, and an organization's reputation." He also knows that journalists seek quotes from the key opinion leaders in an industry whenever a new product is introduced.

The Flow of Opinion

Many public relations campaigns, particularly those in the public affairs area, concentrate on identifying and reaching key opinion leaders, who are pivotal to the success or failure of an idea or project. In the 1940s, sociologists Elihu Katz and Paul Lazarsfeld discovered the importance of opinion leaders during their study of how people choose candidates in an election. They found that the mass media have minimal influence on electoral choices, but that voters do rely on person-to-person communication with formal and informal opinion leaders.

These findings became known as the *two-step flow theory* of communication, a model that remains central to public relations strategy 60 years later, in a world the theorists would hardly recognize. Although later research confirmed that it is really a multiple-step flow, the basic idea remains intact: Public opinion is formed by the views of people who have taken the time to sift information, evaluate it, and form an opinion that they express to others.

The *multiple-step flow model* starts with opinion makers, who derive large amounts of information from the mass media and other sources and then share that information with the "attentive public." The latter are interested in the issue but rely on opinion leaders to provide synthesized information and interpretation. The "inattentive public" is unaware of or uninterested in the issue and remains outside the opinion-formation process. The multiple-step flow theory, however, means that some members of the inattentive public eventually will become interested in or at least aware of the issue.

Another variation of the two-step model is *N-step theory*. Individuals are seldom influenced by only one opinion leader but interact with different leaders around one issue. For example, patients can seek information from their primary-care physician but may also turn to any individual in a close relationship, such as parents or children, when making a medical decision.

Mass media effects are limited by personal influences. Diffusion of innovation theory, discussed in Chapter 7, explains that individuals adopt new ideas or products through the five stages of awareness, interest, trial, evaluation, and adoption. According to Everett Rogers, author of *Diffusion of Innovations*, individuals are often influenced by media in the first two steps, but by friends and family members in the third and fourth steps. And each individual is the decision maker who will adopt a new idea or product and reach the final step.

The Role of Mass Media

Public relations personnel reach opinion leaders and other key publics via the mass media—radio, television, newspapers, and magazines. The term *mass media*, also called traditional media when contrasted with online media, implies that information from a public relations source can be efficiently and rapidly disseminated to literally millions of people.

Although journalists often argue that they rarely use public relations materials, one has only to look at the daily newspaper to see the quote from the press officer at the sheriff's department, the article on a new computer product, the statistics from the local real estate board, or even the after-game interview with the winning quarterback. In almost all cases, a public relations source at the organization provided the information or arranged the interview. Indeed, Oscar H. Gandy Jr., of the University of Pennsylvania, says that up to 50 percent of what the media carry comes from public relations sources in the form of "information subsidies." A more recent study by professors and students at the University of Technology in Sydney (UTS) found that 55 percent of the stories in leading Australian dailies come from public relations sources.

> Few professions have so many skilled and talented individuals contributing to the thoughts, actions, and policies of our nation.
>
> *Elizabeth L. Toth and Robert L. Heath,* authors of Rhetorical and Critical Approaches to Public Relations

Gandy and other theorists have concluded that public relations people—via the mass media—are major players in forming public opinion because they often provide the mass media with the information in the first place. This opinion also is echoed by Elizabeth L. Toth and Robert L. Heath, authors of *Rhetorical and Critical Approaches to Public Relations.* They say, "Few professions have so many skilled and talented individuals contributing to the thoughts, actions, and policies of our nation."

To better understand how public relations people inform the public and shape public opinion via the mass media, it is necessary to review briefly several theories about mass media effects.

Agenda-Setting Theory

One of the early theories, pioneered by Max McCombs and Don Shaw, contends that media content sets the agenda for public discussion. People tend to talk about what they see or hear on the 6 o'clock news or read on the front page of the newspaper. Media, through the selection of stories and headlines, tell the public what to think about, although not necessarily what to think.

Social scientist Joseph Klapper calls this the *limited-effects model* of mass media. He postulates, "Mass media ordinarily does not serve as a necessary and sufficient cause for audience effects, but rather functions among and through a nexus of mediating factors and influence." Such factors may include the way that opinion leaders analyze and interpret the information provided by the mass media.

More recently, Professor Wayne Wanta at Oklahoma State University and others have explored second-level agenda-setting effects, finding evidence that the media not only set an agenda, but also convey a set of attributes about the subject of the news. These positive or negative attributes are remembered and color public opinion. For example, a plethora of news stories regarding the actions of cool-headed Sully Sullenberger, who deftly set down his airliner in New York's Hudson River, raised respect for the pilots of the thousands of aircraft who make safe trips every day.

From a public relations standpoint, even getting a subject on the media agenda is an accomplishment that advances organizational goals. Sales of Apple's iPad rose as the media reported its success and the public became aware of this "hot" item. Research is under way to document how public relations efforts can build the media agenda, and thus affect public opinion. Research evidence from scholars such as Patricia Curtin, Qi Qiu, and Spiro Khiousis suggests that public relations effort does contribute to the creation of news media agendas. Agenda-building research will continue to explore and empirically document how public relations sets the agenda that the media then adopt, ultimately impacting what audiences think about, if not what they think.

Media-Dependency Theory

Although the agenda-setting function of the media is generally valid, other research indicates that mass media can have a "moderate" or even a "powerful" effect on the formation of opinions and attitudes. When people have no prior information or attitude disposition regarding a subject, the mass media play a role in telling people what to think.

Mass media effects also are increased when people cannot verify information through personal experience or knowledge but are highly dependent on the media for that verification. This tendency is particularly evident in crisis situations, which also often leave reporter and editor dependent on official spokespersons for information as the story breaks. Therefore, if much of this crucial initial information comes from official spokespersons of organizations, it's an opportunity for public relations to shape the tone and content of a story, that is, to put a particular emphasis on the story. In sum, media dependency often occurs when the media are, in turn, quite dependent on public relations sources.

Framing Theory

The term *framing* has a long history in mass media research. Traditionally, framing was related to journalists and how they selected certain facts, themes, treatments, and even words to "frame" a story. According to researchers Julie L. Andsager at the University of Iowa and Angela Powers at Northern Illinois University, "Mass media scholars have long argued that it is important to understand the ways in which journalistic framing of issues occurs because such framing impacts public understanding and, consequently, policy formation." For example, how media frame the debate over health care and the role of HMOs often plays a major role in public perceptions of the problem. See the Ethics box on page 219 about the ethics of framing bottled water as an environmental problem.

ETHICS

Who Is Framing Bottled Water?: Answer: Who Isn't?

The average American drinks 28.5 gallons of bottled water per year. At the same time, the United States has plenty of safe, clean tap water—as opposed to the United Nations' estimate that 1.1 billion people around the globe lack safe drinking water.

The producers of bottled water are quite pleased with the expanding $11 billion American market for bottled water, but various environmental groups are starting to frame drinking bottled water as ecologically incorrect. And to compound the problem, the bottled water industry faces the challenge of dealing not only with conflict with activist groups, but with competition in the marketplace.

Some of the competition comes from companies (such as Brita) that promote the attachment of a water filter on a faucet for tap water. Other competition comes from companies (such as Nalgene or SIGG) that promote the use of their reusable water containers. Tappening, one company that manufactures reusable containers, has even placed ads directly attacking bottled water. One ad made the claim that "Bottled water makes acid rain fall on playgrounds." Brita, not to be outdone, has used photos in its ads of oil running out of people's mouths above the caption, "Last year, 16 million

gallons of oil were consumed to make plastic water bottles."

Conflict comes from various environmental groups, who state that drinking bottled water is environmentally unfriendly. These groups explain that plastic bottles generate greenhouse gases, fill landfills, and contribute to large carbon footprints because they are shipped from such exotic places as Fiji and Iceland. Corporate Advocacy International has even launched a Think Outside the Bottle campaign to persuade people that drinking bottled water is an act of environmental irresponsibility in an era of global warming.

They argue that all those plastic bottles are made with oil, and less than a quarter of them are ever recycled. The result is about a billion pounds (900 million kilograms) clogging landfills. There's also the creation of greenhouse gases (the major cause of global warming) produced by the transport of bottled water from distant locations. *Time* magazine, for example, calculated that a case of Fiji water produces nearly

seven pounds of greenhouses gases on its 5,500-mile trip from the South Pacific to Los Angeles.

> An entire generation is growing up thinking they have to get their water out of a bottle.
>
> *Gigi Kellett, director of the "Think Outside the Bottle" campaign*

(continued)

The bottled water industry is clearly under attack from its competition and environmental groups. In fact, partially as a result of the economic recession in 2009 and campaigns such as those mounted by Brita and Tappening, sales of bottled water declined almost 10 percent that year. The main question, of course, is whether the industry can change consumers' perceptions and reverse the shift from bottled water to tap water. The bottled water industry, which is represented by trade groups such as the International Bottled Water Association and the Natural Hydration Council, insists that its critics are being unfair. Jeremy Clarke, director of the Natural Hydration Council, counters their claims by saying, "Bottled water is the cheapest, greenest, healthiest drink on the shelf. It's a packaged product and must be understood in that context." Joseph Doss, the chief executive of the International Bottled Water Association, chimes in, "In the marketplace, bottled water considers its competition to be soft drinks, soda, juices, and teas. Pitting bottled water versus tap water just doesn't seem like a useful exercise."

What do you think? Is the bottled water industry being unjustly criticized? If you were public relations counsel for Aquafina or Dasani, do you think framing bottled water as the "healthiest drink on the shelf" is a good strategy for conflict management? Or would you develop a different strategy for justifying the existence of bottled water? Would your marketing department protest a message that implies it's best to drink tap water, but when you need bottled fluids, choose water?

> ... public relations professionals fundamentally operate as frame strategists, who strive to determine how situations, attributes, choices, actions, issues, and the responsibility should be posed to achieve a favorable objective. Framing decisions are perhaps the most important strategic choices made in a public relations effort.
>
> *Kirk Hallahan, Colorado State University*

Dietram Scheufele at the University of Wisconsin–Madison suggests that there are two types of framing: media framing and audience framing. He argues that framing is a continuous process and that the behavioral, attitudinal, cognitive, and affective states of individuals are also involved in how they interpret issues. For example, voters in Florida may be less likely to respond favorably to a story about increased school funding than voters in Georgia, which has a younger population and many parents of school-aged children. However, a range of variables, beliefs, and attitudes simultaneously affect how individuals interpret an issue.

Political science Professors Shanto Iyengar and Donald Kinder focus on the media's power to prime people in a more subtle but significant form of persuasive effect. They note how public relations professionals working for political campaigns seek to emphasize considerations that will help voters decide in their favor, often enlisting the expertise of a popular leader, and to downplay the considerations that will hurt their cause or candidate. Ultimately, the goal is to encourage voters to change the basis on which they make decisions about voting rather than to simply change their choices about a given candidate or issue.

Using this approach, Senator Hillary Clinton sought to frame her democratic nomination for president as inevitable. However, huge fund-raising gains and early primary successes by Senator Barak Obama destroyed that frame, as news media enlivened their coverage by framing him as the hard-charging upstart who ran away from the field to win the democratic nomination—framing political campaigns as a "horse race" is a common theme used by the media.

Conflict Theory

The process of public discourse is often rooted in conflict. Social scientists and legal scholars define conflict as any situation in which two or more individuals, groups, organizations, or communities perceive a divergence of interests. Conflict theory offers insight into differences among individuals or groups and explains conflicting interests, goals, values, or desires. Public opinion often reflects such different, or even conflicting, views, attitudes, and behaviors.

According to conflict resolution scholars Morton Deutsch and Peter Colman, conflict in the public arena does not necessarily yield negative outcomes but creates a constructive process that builds toward consensus. Indeed, conflict or consensus is an actual theme of court opinions, which regulate and help ensure social stability and peaceful change within a democratic society. Conflict itself is an inherent constraint within social structures. Controversies often serve to shape public opinion intensively and extensively. Public relations professionals frequently have the challenging role of trying to minimize or resolve controversy in conflict situations. See the Multicultural World box below about Google's conflict with the government of China over Internet censorship.

on the job

A MULTICULTURAL WORLD

Google Gets Back to Doing No Evil

A company operating in multiple countries has many public relations challenges because of different cultures, values, norms, regulations, and laws. The court of public opinion back home is also factor, which Google found out when it agreed to obey China's extensive Internet censorship regulations in order to enter the lucrative Chinese market.

The life cycle of public opinion (see page 215) started almost immediately. Human rights organizations and advocates of an Internet free from government control immediately cried foul, saying that Google's self-professed value of "Do No Evil" was a sham.

Protesters lined up outside Google's New York headquarters to complain that Google was "selling out" by agreeing to Beijing's directive that it censor search results in China, which meant censoring searches for such terms as *Tiananmen Square*, *Tibet*, *the Dalai Lama*, and *Taiwan*.

The statements and rallies by protest groups, of course, were covered by the traditional media and blogs, which helped set the agenda for public debate. In general, public opinion was negative and Google suffered damage to its reputation. Sergey Brin, cofounder of Google, justified the China business in 2006, saying, "We felt that perhaps we could compromise

our principles but provide ultimately more information to the Chinese and be a more effective service and perhaps make a difference."

Fast-forward to 2010, when Google announced that it would no longer censor its searches in China and would move its operations to Hong Kong. The straw that broke the camel's back, so to speak, was Chinese hackers who stole some of the company's proprietary computer code and tried to spy on Chinese activists' e-mails. Brin told the *Wall Street Journal*, "Ultimately, I guess it is where your threshold of discomfort is, so we obviously as a company crossed that threshold of discomfort."

(continued)

Google's action delighted human rights activists, and the media framed the story as a principled company fighting back against a nation's draconian censorship laws. A reporter for the *Financial Times* wrote, "Taking a stand now could help to burnish some of the idealism traditionally attached to its brand and reinforce the goodwill of advertisers and users." Other experts commented that the company's stand would also help its image among government regulators who oversee antitrust and monopoly issues.

Other pundits, however, say Google's decision was based less on ethics and more on making a practical business decision. Its share of the Chinese search market was only 20 percent and generated less than 2 percent of its worldwide revenues. At the same time, the Chinese government was already making it difficult for foreign companies to compete with local Internet search firms such as Baidu, which already had 60 percent of the market.

What do you think? Even if Google did withdraw from China for business reasons, was it a good public relations strategy to frame the decision as an ethics issue? Why or why not?

> It is a lose-lose situation. Google has lost the Chinese market; and the incident has made China's already bad international image even worse.
>
> *A blogger quoted on FTChinese.com*

Google Headquarters in Beijing

At other times public relations practitioners may generate or promote controversy to rouse key publics. The Western Fuels Association, for example, hired Jack Bonner to manufacture a "grassroots" public relations campaign between 1997 and 2001. The website www.globalwarmingcost.org posed as an informational site, but surreptitiously generated e-mails, signed by those who answered questions about their heating costs, and sent them to congressional representatives supporting the Western Fuels Association's views.

Mass media play a role in the unfolding of a conflict and serve to promote public debate by engaging widespread public involvement, a process known as *escalation*. The media may also enable parties to de-escalate the conflict by working out the conflict in public fora. But in an era of 24-hour news, communication between parties via talk shows and endless news segments does more harm than good, as the same arguments are stridently repeated and nonnegotiable positions are formed. The role of the media should instead be to interpret the issue, deliver the position of the opposing party, and even suggest avenues for resolution. George Will's "The Last Word" columns and Fareed Zakaria's editorials in *Newsweek* provide excellent examples of media's ability to interpret competing positions and offer avenues for resolution. A good example is the debate on national health care reform, which is outlined in the PR Casebook on page 223.

PRCasebook

Health Care Reform at the Crossroads

In October 2009, the fate of President Barack Obama's health care reform was hanging in the balance. Reform had been favored by more than half of the country when it was announced earlier in the year by President Obama and Democrats in Congress. But by the spring, support had eroded following a series of town hall meetings dominated by conservative constituents.

These critics garnered headlines, railing about government takeover of health care, reduced freedom of choice, and the now notorious specter of government "death panels." Public opinion was divided sharply; individuals who were polled sometimes even appeared to be divided against themselves. For example, an ABC/*Washington Post* poll found in July 2009 that 57 percent of U.S. adults were unhappy with the current health care system, but 83 percent were satisfied with the care that they themselves received. More strikingly, according to a *New York Times*/CBS News poll, 72 percent favored a public option, but 63 percent had serious reservations about the negative effects of government intervention in the health care system.

Americans may feel that we have seen this movie before. In 1993, President Bill Clinton announced a sweeping plan to provide universal health insurance coverage for all Americans. The proposal had astonishing public support. But within a year—after the insurance

and pharmaceutical companies had mounted a relentless and highly successful public relations campaign against the plan—reform was quietly pronounced dead on arrival at the floor of the Senate.

Will Obama's initiative suffer the same fate as Clinton's? Part of the problem for the president and his allies was that the proposed 2009 health care legislation was enormously complex and that proponents failed to offer a clear message for why it should be adopted. Opposition groups such as FreedomWorks and Americans for Prosperity dominated news coverage by offering a few simple messages appealing to fear and encouraging public demonstrations. Like Bill Clinton, President Obama tends to shift messages and become caught up in details. In fact, not until July 2009 did Obama make a strong, direct, and emotional appeal in his message for passage of health care reform legislation.

Yet important differences emerged between 1994 and 2009. President Obama managed to win the support of groups representing the pharmaceutical industry (Pharmaceutical Researchers and Manufacturers of America [PhRMA] and Pharmaceutical Industry Labor–Management Association [PILMA]) that had been opposed to reform 15 years earlier.

While opposition groups dominated the debate in 1994, this time around pro-reform groups (such as the Center for Economic and Social Rights and Physicians for a National Health Program) have spent nearly as much on public relations as their opponents. Interestingly, grassroots initiatives, supported by social media formats such as Facebook and Twitter, introduced an important facet to the debate, serving to multiply the effect of traditional news platforms.

How has public opinion in the case of health care reform been informed by interest groups and mass media coverage?

In what ways has public opinion been divided on the health care reform proposal?

What persuasion techniques have proponents and opponents of health care reform used to present their messages?

Conflict is inherent in how a reporter frames most issues. A reporter's story on a conflict can be the sole information available to an audience. For example, an investigative reporter with special access to information about a controversial secret program at the Pentagon may represent the only perspective seen by the public. How that reporter frames the conflict can bias the public in favor of one party, or one solution, over another.

Because the media are so crucial not only in presenting and explaining conflicts but also in keeping them from escalating, it is necessary for the parties and public relations practitioners involved to know how to work effectively with the media. Similarly, the media play a central role when public relations professionals want a conflict to escalate, to bring the issue to the fore.

Conflict, as a component of news, ranges from wars to philosophical differences of opinion. Daily news stories and op-ed pieces include people criticizing government agencies or policies, a company's fraud, or celebrity scandals. Given the public's penchant for pleasure in the tribulations of others and voyeurism, it is little wonder that the daily news is filled with stories of conflict and turmoil. All too often, conflict is regarded as more newsworthy than resolution. Details about a volatile political election or corporate malfeasance are far more interesting to the public than the reporting of an amicable settlement or an acquittal.

The media's inclination to focus on tribulation posing as human interest often creates a conflict with sources. To maintain their credibility as objective judges of information, journalists are primed to conflict as part of their strategic approach to dealing with sources, while public relations practitioners, as advocates for favorable coverage, have a tendency to be accommodative or cooperative with reporters, according to researchers Jae-Hwa Shin and Glen T. Cameron. The relationships between public relations professionals and journalists moves on a continuum from conflict to cooperation.

Public relations professionals should understand journalists' orientation to escalate conflict as a means of maintaining balance and independence. Public relations practitioners should also try to transform conflicts in constructive ways. Rather than reporting only from the perspective of a dominant power such as governments and delivering the ideology of media conglomerates, the public interest can best be served by healthy competition among public relations sources and the media. From this perspective, public relations serves as a social force in the ongoing creation of news and news trends or agendas.

The Dominant View of Public Relations

The dominant view of public relations, in fact, is one of persuasive communication actions performed on behalf of clients. Oscar Gandy Jr. notes that "…the primary role of public relations is one of purposeful, self-interested communications." And Edward Bernays, featured in Chapter 2, even called public relations the "engineering" of consent to create "a favorable and positive climate of opinion toward the individual, product, institution or idea which is represented."

To accomplish this goal, public relations personnel use a variety of techniques to reach and influence their audiences. At the same time, persuasion or rhetoric should be considered more than a one-way flow of information, argument, and influence. In the best sense, Toth and Heath say that persuasion should be a dialogue between points of view in the marketplace of public opinion, where any number of persuaders are hawking their wares.

Indeed, persuasion is an integral part of democratic society. It is the freedom of speech used by every individual and organization to influence opinion, understanding, judgment, and action. Consequently, it is important for public relations professionals to master the basic principles of persuasion. See the Insights box below for six basic principles.

Uses of Persuasion

Persuasion is used to (1) change or neutralize hostile opinions, (2) crystallize latent opinions and positive attitudes, and (3) conserve favorable opinions.

The most difficult persuasive task is to turn hostile opinions into favorable ones. There is much truth to the adage "Don't confuse me with the facts; my mind is made up." Once people have decided, for instance, that HMOs are making excessive profits or that a nonprofit agency is wasting public donations, they tend to ignore or disbelieve any contradictory information. Everyone, as Walter Lippmann has described, has pictures in his or her head based on an individual perception of reality. People generalize from personal experience and what peers tell them in person or through blogs and Tweets.

on the job

INSIGHTS

Six Principles of Persuasion

No public relations professional can succeed without mastering the art of persuasion. Robert Cialdini, author of *Influence: Science and Practice*, says there are six basic principles of winning friends and influencing people. The following chart, from a *Harvard Business Review* article, gives the basic principles and an example of each one:

PRINCIPLE	EXAMPLE
Liking: People like those who like them.	At Tupperware parties, guests' fondness for their host influences purchase decisions twice as much as regard for the products does.
Reciprocity: People repay in kind.	When the Disabled American Veterans enclosed free personalized address labels in donation-request envelopes, response rates doubled.
Social Proof: People follow the lead of others.	More New York City residents tried returning a lost wallet after learning that other New Yorkers had tried to do so.
Consistency: People fulfill written, public, and voluntary commitments.	Ninety-two percent of residents of an apartment complex who signed a petition supporting a new recreation center later donated to the cause.
Authority: People defer to experts who provide shortcuts requiring specialized information.	A single *New York Times* expert-opinion news story aired on TV generates a 4 percent shift in U.S. public opinion.
Scarcity: People value what's scarce.	Wholesale beef buyers' orders jumped 600 percent when they received information on a possible beef shortage.

Persuasion is much easier if the message is compatible with a person's general disposition toward a subject. If a person tends to identify Starbucks as a company with a good reputation, he or she may express this feeling by being a loyal customer. Nonprofit agencies usually crystallize the public's latent inclination to aid the less fortunate by asking for donations. Both examples illustrate the reason that organizations strive to have a good reputation—it is translated into sales and donations.

The easiest form of persuasion is communication that reinforces favorable opinions. Public relations people, by providing a steady stream of reinforcing messages, keep the reservoir of goodwill in sound condition. More than one organization has survived a major problem because public esteem for it tended to minimize current difficulties. Continual efforts to maintain the reservoir of goodwill are called *preventive public relations*, and it is the most effective type of public relations.

Persuasion in Negotiation

How parties position themselves before negotiations begin can be crucial to how the give-and-take unfolds. Public relations can play a major role in this positioning. Persuasion is an integral component of the public relations effort to bring parties into ultimate agreement. For example, using persuasion to put your organization on an equal footing with a competitor could lead to the realization that the two parties need to talk. In other words, public relations can be used as a tool leading to the alternative dispute resolution (ADR) process. ADR takes place outside the traditional courtroom and has gained acceptance among public relations professionals, the legal profession, and the public at large. ADR is typically much less expensive and often much more efficient than a traditional lawsuit.

"Public relations, based on the contingency theory, can be viewed as a constructive creator of antecedent conditions for alternative dispute resolution," note researchers Bryan Reber, Fritz Cropp, and Glen Cameron. They illustrate this with a case in which public relations and legal professionals worked cooperatively to negotiate the hostile takeover bid of Conrail Inc. by the Norfolk Southern Corporation in the mid-1990s. Conrail resisted Norfolk Southern's bid to buy the company, favoring a deal tendered by the CSX Corporation that was less favorable to Conrail's stockholders.

With the help of a public relations campaign coordinated by Fleishman-Hillard, Norfolk Southern effectively persuaded their target audiences that their offer was more fiscally sound, preserved competition, and best served shipping clients. The public relations campaign, which helped sway public opinion in Norfolk Southern's favor, facilitated the negotiation process. The three companies reached a mutually beneficial agreement—CSX would purchase Conrail and immediately sell 58 percent of the rail routes and assets to Norfolk Southern.

Formulating Persuasive Messages

Psychologists have found that successful speakers, bloggers, and viral marketers use several persuasion techniques:

- **Yes–yes.** Start with points with which the audience agrees to develop a pattern of "yes" answers. Getting agreement to a basic premise often means that the receiver will agree to the logically developed conclusion.
- **Offer structured choice.** Give choices that force the audience to choose between A and B. College officials may ask audiences, "Do you want to raise taxes or raise

tuition?" Political candidates ask, "Do you want more free enterprise or government telling you what to do?"

- **Seek partial commitment.** Get a commitment for some action on the part of the receiver. This leaves the door open for commitment to other parts of the proposal at a later date. "You don't need to decide on the supplemental insurance plan now, but check out this YouTube video to see how major surgery can exhaust typical deductibles. . . ."

- **Ask for more, settle for less.** Submit a complete public relations program to management, but be prepared to compromise by dropping certain parts of the program. It has become almost a cliché that a department asks for a larger budget than it expects to receive.

A persuasive speech can either be one-sided or offer several sides of an issue, depending on the audience. One-sided speeches are most effective with persons favorable to the message, whereas two-sided speeches are most effective with audiences that might be opposed to the message.

By mentioning all sides of the argument, the speaker accomplishes three objectives. First, the speaker is perceived as having objectivity. This translates into increased credibility and makes the audience less suspicious of the speaker's motives. Second, the speaker is treating the audience as mature, intelligent adults. Third, including counterarguments allows the speaker to control how those arguments are structured. It also deflates opponents who might challenge the speaker by saying, "But you didn't consider. . . ."

Findings from Persuasion Research

Many of the precepts offered in this chapter come from experience and from some level of common sense. Starting with the Office of War Information (see Chapter 2), researchers have also systematically studied persuasion processes. A number of research studies have contributed to persuasion concepts. Here are some precepts from the text *Public Communication Campaigns*, edited by Ronald E. Rice and William J. Paisley, that can be used in public relations practice:

- Positive appeals are generally more effective than negative appeals for retention of the message and actual compliance.

- Radio and television messages tend to be more persuasive than print, but if the message is complex, better comprehension is achieved through print media.

- Strong emotional appeals and fear arousal are most effective when the audience has minimal concern about or interest in the topic.

- High fear appeals are effective only when a readily available action can be taken to eliminate the threat.

- Logical appeals, using facts and figures, are better for highly educated, sophisticated audiences than strong emotional appeals.

- Altruistic need, like self-interest, can be a strong motivator. Men are more willing to get a physical checkup to protect their families than to protect themselves.

- A celebrity or an attractive model is most effective when the audience has low involvement, the theme is simple, and broadcast channels are used. An exciting spokesperson attracts attention to a message that would otherwise be ignored.

Factors in Persuasive Communication

A number of factors are involved in persuasive communication, and the public relations practitioner should be knowledgeable about each one. The following is a brief discussion of (1) audience analysis, (2) source credibility, (3) appeal to self-interest, (4) clarity of message, (5) timing and context, (6) audience participation, (7) suggestions for action, (8) content and structure of messages.

Audience Analysis

Knowledge of audience characteristics such as beliefs, attitudes, concerns, and lifestyles is an essential part of persuasion. It helps the communicator tailor messages that are salient, answer a felt need, and provide a logical course of action.

Basic demographic information, readily available through census data, can help determine an audience's gender, income level, education, ethnic background, and age groupings. Other data, often prepared by marketing departments, give information on a group's buying habits, disposable income, and ways of spending leisure time. In many cases, the nature of the product or service easily defines the audience along the lines of age, gender, and income.

Another audience-analysis tool is *psychographics*. This method attempts to classify people by lifestyle, attitudes, and beliefs. The Values and Lifestyle Program, popularly known as VALS, was developed by SRI International, a research organization in Menlo Park, California. VALS is routinely used in public relations to help communicators structure persuasive messages to different members of the population.

Current audience analysis is moving into new frontiers. Researchers are looking inside the black box, i.e., our brains, to understand how audiences process information. This cutting-edge, information-processing research employs everything from brain scans while subjects view messages, to measurement of smile and frown muscle groups, galvanic skin reaction, and heart rate to better understand how messages are processed and what effects different kinds of message strategies have on audiences. Kirk Hallahan of Colorado State University gives a good model for structuring messages in the Insights box on page 229.

Such audience analysis, coupled with suitably tailored messages in the appropriate media outlets, is the technique of *channeling*. Persuasive messages are more effective when they take into account the audience's lifestyles, beliefs, and concerns.

Source Credibility

A message is more believable to the intended audience if the source has *credibility*. This was Aristotle's concept of *ethos*, mentioned earlier, and it explains why organizations use a variety of spokespeople, depending on the message and the audience.

The California Strawberry Advisory Board, for example, arranged for a home economist to appear on television talk shows to discuss nutrition and to demonstrate easy-to-follow strawberry recipes. The viewers, primarily homemakers, identified with the representative and found her highly credible. By the same token, a manufacturer of sunscreen lotion used a professor of pharmacology and a past president of the State Pharmacy Board to discuss the scientific merits of sunscreen versus suntan lotions.

The concept of motion media (TV, YouTube, virtual reality, games, animation appearing all around us from giant billboards to iPhones in our pockets) mentioned in

on the job

INSIGHTS

Motivation–Ability–Opportunity Model for Enhancing Message Processing

The following chart summarizes the various communication strategies that can be used to reach publics who have little knowledge or interest in a particular issue, product, or service. The object, of course, is to structure persuasive messages that attract their attention.

ENHANCE MOTIVATION	ENHANCE ABILITY	ENHANCE OPPORTUNITY
Attract and encourage audiences to commence, continue processing	***Make it easier to process the message by tapping cognitive resources***	***Structure messages to optimize processing***
Create attractive, likable messages (create affect)	Include background, definitions, explanations	Expend sufficient effort to provide information
Appeal to hedonistic needs (sex, appetite, safety)	Be simple, clear	Repeat messages frequently
Use novel stimuli:	Use advance organizers (e.g., headlines)	Repeat key points within text—in headlines, text, captions, illustrations, etc.
■ Photos	Include synopses	Use longer messages
■ Typography	Combine graphics, text, and narration (dual coding of memory traces)	Include multiple arguments
■ Oversized formats	Use congruent memory cues (same format as original)	Feature "interactive" illustrations, photos
■ Large number of scenes, elements	Label graphics (helps identify which attributes to focus on)	Avoid distractions:
■ Changes in voice, silence, movement		■ Annoying music
Make the most of formal features:	Use specific, concrete (versus abstract) words and images	■ Excessively attractive spokespersons
■ Format size	Include exemplars, models	■ Complex arguments
■ Music	Make comparison with analogies	■ Disorganized layouts
■ Color	Show actions, train audience skills through demonstrations	Allow audiences to control pace of processing
■ Include key points in headlines	Include marks (logos, logotypes, trademarks), slogans, and symbols as continuity devices	Provide sufficient time
Use moderately complex messages		Keep pace lively and avoid audience boredom
Use sources who are credible, attractive, or similar to audience	Appeal to self-schemas (roles, what's important to audience's identity)	
Involve celebrities	Enhance perceptions of self-efficacy to perform tasks	
Enhance relevance to audience—ask them to think about a question	Place messages in conducive environment (priming effects)	
Use stories, anecdotes, or drama to draw audience into action	Frame stories using culturally resonating themes, catchphrases	
Stimulate curiosity: Use humor, metaphors, questions		
Vary language, format, source		
Use multiple, ostensibly independent sources		

Source: K. Hallahan. (2000). Enhancing motivation, ability, and opportunity to process public relations messages. *Public Relations Review, 26*(4), 463–480.

Chapter 8 is particularly relevant here with regard to credibility of UGC (user generated content such as YouTube video and v-logging).

Motion media pose challenges for traditional thinking about source credibility in the new media landscape, where less is known about the source and a more egalitarian approach to sources prevails. Based on an old saying, "Seeing is believing," the veridicality of a message takes on greater importance. As initially introduced by Professor Michael Slater at Ohio State and Professor Donna Rouner at Colorado State, the features of an online story such as production values and quality of the script can accord credibility to the source. This process also diminishes the distinction between a news source and a public relations source for a message, because judgments derive from how well done the story is, not who is doing it.

> Popularization happens when you get credible third parties to speak for your brand, and that is something PR can do extremely well.
>
> *Scott Keogh, chief marketing officer of Audi*

The Three Factors   Source credibility is based on three factors. One is *expertise*. Does the audience perceive the person as an expert on the subject? Companies, for example, use engineers and scientists to answer news conference questions about how an engineering process works or whether an ingredient in the manufacturing process of a product presents a potential hazard.

The second component is *sincerity*. Does the person come across as believing what he or she is saying? Simon Cowell, hypercritical judge on *American Idol*, may not be considered an expert on the countries and recipients of aid from the charity special *Idol Gives Back*, but he does get high ratings for his bristling sincerity.

Is Simon Cowell a Credible Source?

While he may not be known for his expertise or charisma, many people can agree that he is sincere.

The third component, which is even more elusive, is *charisma*. Is the individual attractive, self-assured, and articulate, projecting an image of competence and leadership? Former President Clinton is an excellent example. His commanding presence and polished public speaking make him a charismatic figure and a highly paid speaker. Throughout his leadership in the Haitian earthquake rescue operations, Clinton projected an aura of authenticity and conviction that America should take constructive action to help Haiti rebuild.

Expertise is less important than sincerity and charisma if celebrities are used as spokespersons. Their primary purpose is to call attention to the product or service. Another purpose is to associate the celebrity's popularity with the product. This technique is called *transfer*.

Some kinds of celebrities, however, are more persuasive than others. An Adweek Media/Harris poll, for example, found that celebrity business leaders endorsing a product are more persuasive overall than athletes, television stars, and movie stars. Age, however, is a factor. Business leaders are more persuasive with people over 45 years old while athletes, television stars, and movie stars are more persuasive with people under 45. Former political figures are the least persuasive celebrities among all age groups.

> Anytime an advertiser pins its image to a star, whether an athlete or an actor, it takes a chance that reality won't live up to the story-board.
>
> *Christina White, reporter for the*
> Wall Street Journal

Problems with Celebrities Using celebrities, however, has several possible downsides. One is the increasing number of celebrity endorsements, to the point that the public sometimes can't remember who endorses what. A second problem can be overexposure of a celebrity, such as Michael Jordan or Drew Barrymore, who earn millions of dollars annually from multiple products.

A third problem occurs when an endorser's actions undercut the product or service. And when such a popular celebrity as Tiger Woods falls from grace due to a sexual addiction, the panic of sponsors, criticism of journalists, and desertion of fans is notable. See the PR Casebook about Woods on page 476 in Chapter 18.

A fourth problem is when a celebrity decides to speak out on controversial public issues and even endorses political candidates. Such actions tend to reduce the celebrity's effectiveness as an endorser of products or services because they tend to alienate segments of the consumer public who disagree with their views. One survey, for example, found that a third of the respondents said they would avoid buying products endorsed by celebrities who express political views that they disagree with.

In summary, the use of various sources for credibility depends, in large part, on the type of audience being reached. That is why audience analysis is the first step in formulating persuasive messages. An important component of source credibility, of course, is the concept of trust. Most research shows that a friend's recommendation is the most trusted. The amount of credibility, or trust, that individuals assign to various sources is shown in the Insights box on page 232.

Appeal to Self-Interest

Self-interest was described during an earlier discussion about the formation of public opinion. Publics become involved in issues or pay attention to messages that appeal to their psychological or economic needs.

Charitable organizations don't sell products, but they do need volunteers and donations. This is accomplished by careful structuring of messages that appeal to self-interest.

on the job

INSIGHTS

A Friend's Recommendation Is Most Trusted

Recommendations from personal friends or opinions posted by consumers online are the most trusted form of source credibility according to the Nielsen Global Online Consumer Survey of more than 25,000 Internet consumers in 50 nations. Advertisers and public relations personnel should be encouraged, however, that company websites are trusted by 70 percent of consumers. Here are the results of the Nielsen survey:

FORM OF COMMUNICATION	PERCENT OF RESPONDENTS EXPRESSING "TRUST"
Recommendations from friends	90%
Consumer opinions posted online	70%
Brand websites	70%
Editorial content (Newspaper article)	69%
Brand sponsorships	64%
TV	62%
Newspapers	61%
Magazines	59%
Billboards/Outdoor advertising	55%
Radio	55%
E-mails signed up for	54%
Ads before movies	52%
Search engine result ads	41%
Online video ads	37%
Online banner ads	33%
Text ads on mobile phones	24%

Source: Nielsen Global Online Consumer Survey, April 2009.

A Functional Foods project at the University of Missouri promoted special benefits of berries, broccoli, and soy to diet and lifestyle during cancer recovery.

Based on audience research, oncology nurses expressed a lack of knowledge of nutrition and a desire to shape up their own diet and lifestyle. Appeals for these nurses to order an information kit to share with their patients were promoted first and foremost for the nurses' own edification. Evaluation revealed that once the kits were in hand, the nurses regularly shared recommendations about functional foods with patients during chemotherapy.

Self-interest is powerful, but altruism is not dead. Thousands of people give freely of their time and money to charitable organizations, but unless they receive something in return, they will stop their contributions. The "something in return" may be (1) self-esteem, (2) the opportunity to make a contribution to society, (3) recognition from peers and the community, (4) a sense of belonging, (5) ego gratification, or even (6) a tax deduction. Public relations people understand psychological needs and rewards, and that is why there is constant recognition of volunteers in newsletters and at award banquets. (Further discussion of volunteerism appears in Chapter 21.)

Sociologist Harold Lasswell says that people are motivated by eight basic appeals. They are:

- power
- respect
- well-being
- affection
- wealth
- skill
- enlightenment
- physical and mental vitality

The challenge for public relations personnel, as creators of persuasive messages, is to tailor information to address these appeals. Social scientists have said that success in persuasion largely depends on accurate assessment of audience needs and self-interests.

Clarity of Message

Many messages fail because the audience finds the message unnecessarily complex in content or language. The most persuasive messages are direct, simply expressed, and contain only one primary idea. The management expert Peter Drucker once said, "An innovation, to be effective, has to be simple and it has to be focused. It should do only one thing, otherwise it confuses." The same can be said for the content of any message.

Public relations personnel should always ask two questions: "Will the audience understand the message?" and "What do I want the audience to do with the message?" Although persuasion theory says that people retain information better and form stronger opinions when they are asked to draw their own conclusions, this doesn't negate the importance of explicitly stating what action an audience should take. Is it buy the product, visit a showroom, write a member of Congress, make a $10 donation, or something else?

If an explicit request for action is not part of the message, members of the audience may not understand what is expected of them. Public relations firms, when making a presentation to a potential client, always ask at the end of the presentation to be awarded the account.

> What people in PR have to understand is not only do you have the facts on your side, you have to know how to communicate them.
>
> *Peter Pitts, senior vice president of Manning, Selvage & Lee*

Timing and Context

A message is more persuasive if environmental factors support the message or if the message is received within the context of other messages and situations with which the individual is familiar. These factors are called *timing* and *context*.

Information from a utility on how to conserve energy is more salient if the consumer has just received the January heating bill. A pamphlet on a new stock offering is more effective if it accompanies an investor's dividend check. If a major t-bone collision occurs due to a driver running a red light, a citizens' group lobbying for a red light camera program will get more attention and support.

Political candidates are aware of public concerns and avidly read polls to learn what issues are most important to voters. If the polls indicate that crime and unemployment are key issues, the candidate begins to use these issues—and to offer his or her proposals—in the campaign.

Timing and context also play an important role in achieving publicity in the mass media. Public relations personnel, as pointed out earlier in the text, should read newspapers and watch television news programs to find out what media gatekeepers consider newsworthy. A manufacturer of a locking device for computer files got extensive media coverage about its product simply because its release followed a rash of news stories about thieves' gaining access to bank accounts through computers. Media gatekeepers found the product newsworthy within the context of actual news events.

The value of information and its newsworthiness are based on timing and context. Public relations professionals must immerse themselves in news and public affairs to disseminate information at just the right time.

Audience Participation

Practitioners have known for decades that a change in attitude or reinforcement of beliefs is enhanced by audience involvement and participation. With the onset of widespread social media such as YouTube videos produced by individual amateurs, this sort of user generated content (UGC) can have a beneficial effect on the creator, if not the audience.

For example, health campaigns for teenagers that encourage UGC by the teens about health issues and their solutions can strengthen and reinforce positive attitudes toward healthy lifestyles. Persuasion theorists such as Albert Bandura say that self-efficacy, the belief in one's own capability to persist in attaining health goals, is increased through a process called self-persuasion, which has more powerful and long-lasting effects than traditional persuasive tactics.

Activist groups use participation as a way of helping people actualize their beliefs. Not only do rallies and demonstrations give people a sense of belonging, but the act of participation reinforces their beliefs. The Tea Party Movement for conservative values formed in response to the Wall Street and automaker bailouts and built its momentum through major events that cemented resolve of members.

Suggestions for Action

A principle of persuasion is that people endorse ideas only if the sponsor proposes an action. Recommendations for action must be clear. Public relations practitioners must not only ask people to conserve energy, for instance, but must also furnish detailed data and ideas on how to do so.

A campaign conducted by Pacific Gas & Electric Company provides an example. The utility inaugurated a Zero Interest Program (ZIP) to offer customers a way to implement energy-saving ideas. The program involved several components:

- **Energy kit.** A telephone hotline was established and widely publicized so that interested customers could order an energy kit detailing what the average homeowner could do to reduce energy use.
- **Service bureau.** The company, at no charge, sent representatives to homes to check the efficiency of water heaters and furnaces, measure the amount of insulation, and check doors and windows for drafts.
- **ZIP.** The cost of making a home more energy efficient was funded by zero-interest loans to any qualified customer.

> These days, "spin" is more likely to mean ensuring the story is told in a way that's meaningful to the audience rather than twisting a client's response to an issue to make them look good.
>
> *Shel Holtz, on his blog, "a shel of my former self"*

Content and Structure of Messages

A number of techniques can make a message more persuasive. Writers throughout history have emphasized some information while downplaying or omitting other pieces of information. Thus, they address both the content and the structure of messages.

Expert communicators continue to use a number of devices, including (1) drama, (2) statistics, (3) surveys and polls, (4) examples, (5) testimonials, (6) endorsements, and (7) emotional appeals.

Drama Because everyone likes a good story, the first task of a communicator is to get the audience's attention. This is often called *humanizing* a situation or issue. Relief organizations, in particular, attempt to galvanize public concern and donations through stark, black-and-white photographs of an individual accompanied by emotionally charged descriptions of the person's suffering.

A more mundane use of drama is the *application story*, sent to the trade press. This is sometimes called the *case study technique*, in which a manufacturer prepares an article on how an individual or a company is successfully using the product.

Statistics People are impressed by statistics. Use of numbers can convey objectivity, size, and importance in a credible way that can influence public opinion. Sheer numbers, however, often don't elicit the same emotional response as a good story. That's why the *Wall Street Journal* often starts a major story with the travails of one businessperson or family and then gives overall statistics later in the story. Statistics can also be enlightening when they are related to common things that people understand. In the news release for the largest truck in the world, Caterpillar announced that the bed of the truck is so large that it could haul 4 blue whales, 217 taxicabs, 1,200 grand pianos, and 23,000 Barbie dolls.

Surveys and Polls Airlines and auto manufacturers, in particular, use the results of surveys and polls to show that they are first in "customer satisfaction," "service," and even "leg room" or "cargo space." The most credible surveys are those conducted by independent research organizations, but readers still should read the fine print to see what is being compared and rated.

Examples A statement of opinion can be more persuasive if some examples are given. A school board can often get support for a bond issue by citing examples of how the present facilities are inadequate for student needs. Environmental groups, when they are requesting a city council to establish a greenbelt, tell how other communities have successfully done so. Automakers promote the durability of their vehicles by citing their performance on a test track or in a road race.

Testimonials   These are usually statements by a person who is a satisfied customer. Many ads, for example, feature the average "housewife" raving about the cleaning power of a detergent. Testimonials honoring an individual or organization are often given at banquets and other public events.

Endorsements   An endorsement, unlike a testimonial, is usually given by celebrities who are paid to say nice things about the organization, product, or service. Organizations such as the American Dental Association and the National Safety Council also endorse products and services.

Media endorsements are unpaid and take the form of editorials, reviews, surveys, and news stories. The most direct endorsement is an editorial supporting a political candidate or a community cause. A more indirect "endorsement" is a published, broadcasted, or posted favorable review of a play, a movie, or a restaurant. The media also produce news stories about new products and services that, because of the media's perceived objectivity, are considered a form of third-party endorsement. The idea is that media coverage bestows legitimacy and newsworthiness on a product or service.

Emotional Appeals   Fund-raising letters from nonprofit groups, in particular, use this persuasive device. Appeals to protect animals, for example, often use the emotional appeal of personifying the animal. See the sample letter from the Defenders of Wildlife on page 237.

Emotional appeals are also used in politics. Opponents of President Obama's health care reform, for example, claimed that the government would appoint "death panels" to decide whether sick and elderly people should be euthanatized.

This kind of emotional appeal is called *fear arousal*. Strong statements like this, however, tend to alienate the audience and cause them to tune out the message. Research indicates that a moderate fear arousal, accompanied by a relatively easy solution, is more effective. A moderate fear arousal is: "What would happen if your child were thrown through the windshield in an accident?" The message concludes with the suggestion that a baby, for protection and safety, should be placed in a secured infant seat.

Psychologists say the most effective emotional appeal is one coupled with facts and figures. The emotional appeal attracts audience interest, but logical arguments also are needed for the appeal to be persuasive.

The Limits of Persuasion

The discussion on the previous pages examined ways in which an individual can formulate persuasive messages. The ability to use these techniques often leads to charges that public relations practitioners have great power to influence and manipulate people.

In reality, the effectiveness of persuasive techniques is greatly exaggerated. Persuasion is not an exact science, and no surefire way exists to predict that people will be persuaded to believe a message or act on it. If persuasive techniques were as refined as the critics say, all people might be driving the same make of car, using the same soap, and voting for the same political candidate.

Lonely Planet Images / Getty Images

Dear Friend,

For polar bear cubs like Snowflake, life starts out as a nearly impossible challenge.

Born with her sister Aurora in the frigid darkness of the Arctic winter, Snowflake weighed only about a pound at birth, the size of a cell phone. For months, she and her sister didn't leave the den where they were born, a small cave that their mother had dug in a snow bank. Helpless, they depended on their mother for the essentials of life — her body warmth and her nutrient-rich milk.

Snowflake

Snowflake and her sister will stay with their mother for more than two years. She will feed them, teach them to hunt, and protect them from predators.

With the fierce maternal protection of her mother, cuddly little Snowflake will grow up to become one of the most awesome animals on Earth.

But now, a looming new threat could cut short the lives of precious little polar bear cubs like Snowflake.

You see, the powerful oil lobby and its political allies in Congress are pushing to open Snowflake's home — the Arctic National Wildlife Refuge — to environmentally destructive oil and gas drilling. The Refuge's coastal plain is America's most important on-shore polar bear nursery, and scientist warn that the habitat destruction, pollution and other impacts of the plan could be deadly to the bears.

That's why I'm asking you to please "adopt" a polar bear cub like Snowflake by joining Defenders of Wildlife today with a contribution of $15 or more.

Defenders of Wildlife is helping lead the fight to save America's greatest wildlife sanctuary for Snowflake and the other wild animals that call it home. But to succeed, we urgently need the help of concerned individuals like you to overcome the enormous money and political clout of the oil lobby.

And we must act now — because politicians are already moving to hand over this unique natural treasure to Big Oil. Congressman Don Young (R-Alaska) — who decorates his office with animal skins — has already introduced legislation to allow drilling. The pristine 19 million-acre Arctic Refuge is the last place in North America where Arctic wildlife is fully protected. And the Refuge's coastal plain, often referred to as "America's Serengeti," is the biological heart of this

(over, please)

Defenders of Wildlife • 1101 Fourteenth Street, N.W. • Room 1400 • Washington, D.C. 20005
www.defenders.org • www.kidsplanet.org

Your continued activism is important. Please call your representatives in Washington to let them know you support the preservation of wildlife and its habitat. You can contact them at 202-224-3121. Thank you.

Persuasion by Direct Mail

An eye-catching opening must persuade the recipient to read on rather than to toss the letter aside. Letters such as this have a strong emotional appeal and often stir a reader's high concern for a particular situation. The plight of the polar bear has become a potent symbol of the effects of global warming.

This doesn't happen because several variables intervene in the flow of persuasive messages. Elihu Katz says the two major intervening variables are selectivity and interpersonal relations; these are consistent with the limited-effects model of mass communication.

For purposes of discussion, the limitations on effective persuasive messages can be listed as (1) lack of message penetration, (2) competing messages, (3) self-selection, and (4) self-perception.

Lack of Message Penetration

The diffusion of messages, despite modern communication technologies, is not pervasive. People don't, of course, watch the same television programs, read the same newspapers, or visit the same blogs. There is also the problem of messages being distorted as they pass through traditional media gatekeepers or get interpreted by Tweets, blogs, and other social network interaction. Key message points often are left out or the context of the message is changed.

Competing Messages

In the 1930s, before much was known about the complex process of communication, it was believed that people receive information directly, without any intervening variables. This was called the *bullet theory* or the *hypodermic-needle theory* of communication.

Today, communication experts realize that no message is received in a vacuum. Messages are filtered through a receiver's entire social structure and belief system, which includes the influences of opinion leaders and even acquaintances. Nationality, race, religion, gender, cultural patterns, family, and friends are among the variables that filter and dilute persuasive messages. People receive countless competing and conflicting messages daily. Social scientists say a person usually conforms to the standards of his or her family and friends. Consequently, most people do not believe or act on messages that are contrary to group norms.

Self-Selection

The people most wanted in an audience are often the least likely to be there. Vehement supporters or loyalists frequently ignore information and even facts from the other side. They do so by being selective in the messages they want to hear. They read books, newspaper editorials, and magazine articles and view television programs that support their predispositions. This is why social scientists say that the media are more effective in reinforcing existing attitudes than in changing them.

Self-Perception

Self-perception is the context through which messages are interpreted. People will perceive the same information differently, depending on their predispositions and already formulated opinions. In other words, public relations personnel must take into account the axiom "Perception is reality."

The Ethics of Persuasion

Public relations people, by definition, are advocates of their clients and employers. Their emphasis is on persuasive communication to influence a particular public in some way. At the same time, as Chapter 3 points out, public relations practitioners must conduct their activities in an ethical manner.

The use of persuasive techniques, therefore, calls for some additional guidelines. Professor Richard L. Johannesen of Northern Illinois University, writing in Charles Larson's *Persuasion, Reception and Responsibility*, lists the following ethical criteria for using persuasive devices that every public relations professional should keep in mind:

- Do not use false, fabricated, misrepresented, distorted, or irrelevant evidence to support arguments or claims.
- Do not intentionally use specious, unsupported, or illogical reasoning.
- Do not represent yourself as informed or as an "expert" on a subject when you are not.
- Do not use irrelevant appeals to divert attention or scrutiny from the issue at hand. Among the appeals that commonly serve such a purpose are smear attacks on an opponent's character, appeals to hatred and bigotry, innuendo, and "God" or "devil" terms that cause intense but unreflective positive or negative reactions.
- Do not ask your audience to link your idea or proposal to emotion-laden values, motives, or goals to which it actually is not related.
- Do not deceive your audience by concealing your real purpose, your self-interest, the group you represent, or your position as an advocate of a viewpoint.
- Do not distort, hide, or misrepresent the number, scope, intensity, or undesirable features or consequences.
- Do not use emotional appeals that lack a supporting basis of evidence or reasoning or that would not be accepted if the audience had the time and opportunity to examine the subject itself.
- Do not oversimplify complex situations into simplistic, two-valued, either/or, polar views or choices.
- Do not pretend certainty when tentativeness and degrees of probability are more accurate.
- Do not advocate something in which you do not believe yourself.

It is clear from the preceding list that a public relations professional should be more than a technician or a "hired gun." This raises the issue that public relations personnel often lack the technical and legal expertise to know whether information provided to them by the client or employer is accurate. Robert Heath makes it clear that this lack of expertise doesn't excuse public relations professionals from ethical responsibility. He writes:

> The problem of reporting information that they cannot personally verify does not excuse them from being responsible communicators. Their responsibility is to demand that the most accurate information be provided and the evaluation be the best available.

Persuasive messages require truth, honesty, and candor for two practical reasons. First, Heath says, a message is already suspect because it is advanced on behalf of a client or organization. Second, half-truths and misleading information do not serve the best interests of the public or the organization.

Summary

What Is Public Opinion?

■ Public opinion can be difficult to measure; there are few if any issues on which the public (which is in fact many publics) can be said to have a unanimous opinion.

■ Only a small number of people will have opinions on any given issue.

■ Engaging the interest of a public will involve affecting its self-interest. Publics also react strongly to events.

Opinion Leaders as Catalysts

■ The primary catalyst in the formation of public opinion is public discussion.

■ People who are knowledgeable and articulate on specific issues can be either formal opinion leaders (power leaders) or informal opinion leaders (role models).

■ Opinion "flows" from these leaders to the public, often through the mass media.

The Role of Mass Media

■ Mass media play a major role in setting the agenda for public discussion and debate.

■ People who know little or nothing about a subject depend on mass media for their information and opinions. This is called the media-dependency theory.

■ Framing theory describes how both journalists and public relations personnel promote a particular aspect of an issue or controversy.

■ Journalists often look for conflict in a story; public relations people strive for accommodation and conflict resolution.

The Dominant View of Public Relations

■ The dominant view of public relations is of persuasive communications on behalf of clients.

■ Persuasion can be used to change or neutralize hostile opinions, crystallize latent opinions and positive attitudes, and conserve favorable opinions.

■ Research studies have established many basic concepts of persuasive communication.

Factors in Persuasive Communication

■ Factors involved in persuasion include audience analysis, source credibility, appeal to self-interest, message clarity, timing and context, audience participation, suggestions for action, content and structure of messages, and persuasive speaking.

The Limits of Persuasion

■ Limitations on effective persuasion include lack of message penetration, competing messages, self-selection, and self-perception.

The Ethics of Persuasion

■ Publics will automatically have a level of suspicion because they know the communicator is promoting a client or organization.

■ The interests of that client or organization will not be well served by false or misleading communications.

Case Activity   Persuading People to Support a Cause

One of your family members volunteers in an after-school study program for at-risk children. This local nonprofit is struggling to make its budget numbers and to keep the doors open during these hard economic times. The program, coordinated in a donated space that was formerly a small insurance agency, serves several dozen adorable K–5 children. Over the years, a number of these budding young students have gone on to college.

Your uncle asks you during a Sunday dinner if you could come up with an example or two of how best to appeal to several people in town who are known for their philanthropic giving. This is not a mass appeal and it is not intended necessarily for the media, although you are convincing in your advice that media coverage should be part of the plan. Gather one or two examples either from the local community or from the Web and provide simple, clear annotations for your uncle, explaining why you think these materials use effective persuasion strategies to set the stage for an "ask" to the large local donors.

Questions   **For Review and Discussion**

1. Public opinion is highly influenced by self-interest and events. What are these concepts?
2. What is the importance of opinion leaders in the formation of public opinion?
3. What theories about mass media effects have relevance for public relations?
4. Name the three objectives of persuasion in public relations work. What objective is the most difficult to accomplish?

5. What are three factors involved in source credibility?
6. What are the pros and cons of using celebrities for product endorsements?
7. Why is audience involvement and participation important in persuasion?
8. What techniques can be used to write persuasive messages?
9. What are some of the ethical responsibilities of a person who uses persuasion techniques to influence others?

Media Resources

Berger, B. K., & Reber, B. H. (2006). *Gaining influence in public relations: The role of resistance in practice.* Mahwah, NJ: Erlbaum Associates.

Cialdini, R. B. (2001, October). Harnessing the science of persuasion. *Harvard Business Review,* 72–79.

Grunwald, M. (2009, April 13). How Obama is using the science of change. *Time,* 26–32.

Hallahan, K. (2000). Enhancing motivation, ability, and opportunity to process public relations messages. *Public Relations Review, 26*(4), 463–480.

Hansen-Horn, T., & Neff, B. D. (2007). *Public relations: From theory to practice.* Boston, MA: Allyn & Bacon.

Ihlen, O., van Ruler, B., & Fredriksson, M. (2009). *Public relations and social theory: Key figures and concepts.* Clifton, NJ: Routledge.

Len-Rios, M., Hinnant, A., Park, S. A., Cameron, G. T., Frisby, C. M., & Lee, Y. A. (2009, Summer). Agenda building: Journalists' perceptions of the role of public relations.

Journalism and Mass Communication Quarterly, 86(2), 315–331.

Miller, B. M. (2010). Community stakeholders and marketplace advocacy: A model of advocacy, agenda building and industry approval. *Journal of Public Relations Research, 22*(1), 85–112.

Murphy, P. (2010). The intractability of reputation: Media coverage as a complex system in the case of Martha Stewart. *Journal of Public Relations Research, 22*(2), 209–237.

O'Quinn, K. (2009, February). The elements of persuasion: Three principles that will strengthen any appeal. *Public Relations Tactics,* 20.

Pasadeos, Y., Berger, B., & Renfro, R. B. (2010). Public relations is a maturing discipline: An update on research networks. *Journal of Public Relations Research, 22*(2), 136–158.

Rotolo, A. (2010, May). Beyond friends and followers: Next steps for social media. *Public Relations Tactics, 17*(5), 9.

10

Conflict Management: Dealing with Issues, Risks, and Crises

MR. TOYODA

After reading this chapter you will be able to:

Understand the role of public relations in managing conflict

Describe the two basic principles of strategic conflict management

Identify the four phases of the conflict management life cycle

Understand the issues management process as a key public relations contribution

Explain the relationship between the conflict stance and the communication strategy

Identify important steps to deal with a crisis as it occurs

Define reputation and the role public relations plays in image repair

Strategic Conflict Management

Conflict takes many forms, from warfare between nations to spats between teenagers and their parents. Often, conflicts take place in the marketplace of ideas as opposing groups clash over issues such as gun control, abortion, and immigration reform, or even where Home Depot or Wal-Mart should build a "big-box" store.

Many of these conflicts fall under the purview of public relations. This means that a public relations professional must develop communication strategies and processes *to influence the course of conflicts to the benefit of the organization and, when possible, to the benefit of the organization's many constituents.* Such use of public relations to influence the course of a conflict, and ultimately a crisis, is called *strategic conflict management.* Its key components are:

- Strategic—for the purpose of achieving particular objectives
- Management—planned, deliberate action
- Competition—striving for the same object, position, or prize as others
- Conflict—sharp disagreements or opposition resulting in a direct, overt threat of attack from another entity

This approach to public relations is more assertive than most definitions, which place an emphasis on building mutually beneficial relationships between the organization and its various stakeholders. Indeed, building relationships is a key objective, but it is only one part of what public relations does for organizations. The management of competition and conflict offers relationship building but also more "muscular" public relations. Olympic skier Lindsey Vonn embodies the preparation, strength, and fair play required to compete against others while maintaining cordial relationships.

The point is that public relations plays a key role in enabling both profit and nonprofit organizations to compete for limited resources (customers, volunteers, employees, donations, grants, etc.) and to engage in healthy, honest conflict with others who hold different views of what is best and right for society. Achieving these sorts of objectives increases the value of public relations to the organization. It is how public relations professionals earn influence, which leads to greater recognition by top management, increased respect in the field, and, ultimately, better-paying, more secure positions for public relations professionals.

Although competition and conflict are closely related to each other, this book makes a distinction between the two terms (see Figure 10.1). *Competition*, a pervasive condition in life, occurs when two or more groups or organizations vie for the same resources. In business, these "resources" can be sales, share of market, contracts, employees, and, ultimately, profits. In the nonprofit sector, the competition might be donations, grants, clients, volunteers, and even political influence.

Conflict, on the other hand, occurs when two groups direct their efforts against each other, devising actions and communication that directly or verbally attack the other group. Conflict

Relationship Building

Lindsey Vonn embodies the view of public relations as strong and competitive in spirit, yet not macho or underhanded.

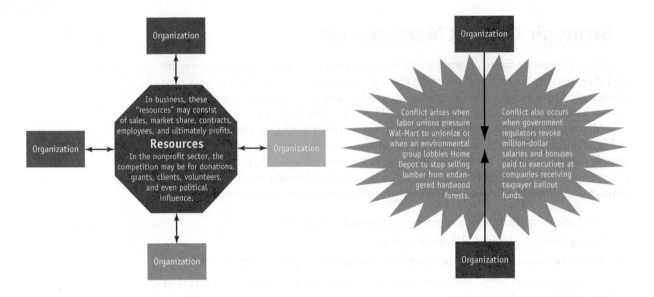

COMPETITION is inevitable and omnipresent. It occurs when two or more groups or organizations vie for the same resources.

CONFLICT occurs when two groups direct their efforts against each other, devising communication and actions that attack.

Figure 10.1 Competition and Conflict

Competition is inevitable and omnipresent. It occurs when two or more groups or organizations vie for the same resources.

arises, for example, when labor unions pressure Wal-Mart to unionize, or when the Sierra Club lobbies Home Depot to stop advertising on *Fox News* because several commentators dismiss global warming, which is inconsistent with Home Depot's green initiatives. It also occurs when government regulators investigate BP's lax standards for fail-safe valves on drilling rigs to prevent deaths and environmental disaster.

Experienced public relations experts, however, are quick to point out that many practitioners will spend most of their professional lives with fairly moderate levels of competition (such as marketing communications) but perhaps have few, if any, situations that involve conflict. For example, the development director for the Audubon Society may be competing to get donations for a new program from the same donors who are being approached for donations by the Sierra Club. The two professionals may be friends and perhaps one was actually the mentor of the other. On the other hand, a more heightened level of competition might exist between public relations professionals at Wal-Mart, Target, and Costco, who compete with each other to increase consumer visibility and retail sales.

Most public relations activity and programs, as already noted, deal with competition between organizations for sales and customers. Conflict, in contrast, deals with attacks and confrontations between organizations and various stakeholders or publics. For example, after the bailout of banks, President Obama appointed a salary czar to supervise compensation packages for executives at banks on the federal dole. The companies pushed back, arguing they would lose top talent if large bonuses were discontinued.

This was met with furor from ordinary citizens suffering from the consequences of the deep recession caused, in part, by the banks. Admittedly, the distinction between competition and conflict is partly a matter of degree, but it is also a matter of focus. In competition, the eye is on the prize—such as sales or political support. In conflict, the eye is on the opposition, on dealing with or initiating threats of some sort or another. In either case, professional practice by this definition is vitally important to organizations. It requires a sense of mission and conviction that:

- your organization's behavior is honorable and defensible.
- your organization is ethical.
- your organization's mission is worthy.
- your advocacy of the organization has integrity.
- your organization works at creating mutual benefits whenever possible.

The last point, striving for mutual benefit, is extremely important. It involves balancing the interests of an employer or client against those of a number of stakeholders. Often, professionals are able to accommodate the interests of both the organization and its various publics. By the same token, an organization may not be able to please all of its publics because there are differences in worldview.

Wal-Mart may please labor unions by paying for more employee benefits, but consumers who like low prices may object. Environmentalists may want to close a steel plant, but the employees and the local community may be the most avid supporters for keeping the plant open despite its pollution problems. Given competing agendas and issues, the public relations professional will need to look first to the needs of the organization and manage the inevitable conflicts that arise.

The Role of Public Relations in Managing Conflict

The influence of public relations on the course of a conflict can involve reducing conflict, as is often the case in crisis management. At other times, conflict is escalated for activist purposes, such as when antiabortion advocates not only picket health clinics but also assault clients, doctors, and nurses. Other strategies are less dramatic, such as oil industry advocates lobbying to open parts of the Alaskan wilderness to exploration, striving to win approval over time from the public—and, ultimately, Congress.

Indeed, conflict management often occurs when a business or industry contends with government regulators or activist groups that seem determined to curtail operations through what the industry considers excessive safety or environmental standards. At the same time, both the regulatory body and the activists engage in their own public relations efforts to make their case against the company.

A good example is the Canadian fur industry, which lobbied the European Union to defeat a seal-product ban because seal is the "ultimate eco-fabric." The Fur Council of Canada says seal hunting is part of the country's historic heritage and, despite claims by activist groups, that the seals are killed in a humane way. Groups in opposition, such as the International Fund for Welfare and the Humane Society of the United States, violently oppose seal hunting and are also using public relations tactics to convince legislators and consumers that the practice is cruel and inhumane. A now

Managing Conflict

In cases like the conflict between seal hunters and the activists who are attempting to ban the practice, effective public relations tactics can mitigate the conflict.

on the job

A MULTICULTURAL WORLD

Managing Conflict: Wal-Mart Wades Into Shrimp Farming

The giant retailer Wal-Mart is committed to environmental sustainability, but is finding that even this admirable goal presents problems in competition and conflict. A good example is how Wal-Mart's sustainable policies are in conflict with about 80 percent of the shrimp farms in Thailand, which are small, family-owned operations.

The conflict started when the retailer decided, as the largest importer of shrimp in the United States, that only shrimp from Wal-Mart-certified Thai farms would be imported. Certification was based on guidelines from the Global Aquaculture Alliance, an international, non-profit trade association dedicated to advancing environmentally and socially responsible aquaculture.

Certification was given for the farmers who did such things as plant trees, remove contaminants from shrimp ponds with filters before discharging the water, and refrain from using antibiotics in the ponds that would endanger other wildlife.

There's only one problem. The vast majority of Thai farmers cannot afford to upgrade their farms and complete the certification process. As a result, Rubicon Resources, a Los Angeles–based supplier of farmed shrimp to Wal-Mart, has stepped in to buy about 150 Thai farms and upgrade them. The effect has been a widening of the gap between the haves and the have-nots in Thai shrimp farming. Thus, the Wal-Mart push for sustainability, although environmentally friendly, also favors U.S. corporate-style farming

in Thailand at the expense of the family-owned farm.

Adding to the conflict are various environmental groups. Although they say Wal-Mart and the Global Aquaculture Alliance are on the right track, they argue that the standards are too low and stop short of significant environmental safeguards because the rules for producers are too vague.

This case illustrates that an organization, even with good intentions, makes policies and decisions that often bring it into conflict with some segment of the population or opposing groups. This is why public relations professionals must be well versed in strategic conflict management and how to deal with multiple publics that are affected in different ways by corporate actions.

---

iconic campaign showing photos of baby seals being clubbed to death, with plenty of red blood visible on white ice, convinced the U.S. Congress to ban all seal products more than 30 years ago. See also the Multicultural World box above about Wal-Mart and Thai shrimp farmers.

Professor Jae-Hwa Shin, at the University of Southern Mississippi, describes this dialogue between multiple parties as the "wrangle in the marketplace of ideas." And much like Olympic skiers striving on the slopes to represent their own interests, this wrangle is inevitable and perfectly acceptable, according to Shin. Sometimes, an organization is able to catch a conflict at an early stage and reduce damage to the organization. However, in other cases, an issue may smolder until it finally becomes a major fire. Toyota had been aware of dangerous acceleration problems well in advance of the crisis in consumer confidence that nearly ruined the automaker. See the PR Casebook on page 266 for more on Toyota's missteps. Dealing with problems early on is not only more efficient, it is also usually the morally right thing to do. The basic concepts of issue and risk management will be discussed shortly.

Unfortunately, most conflict situations are not clear-cut in terms of an ideal solution. In many cases, public relations professionals will not be able to accommodate the concerns of an activist group or a particular public because of many other factors, including the survivability of the organization. KFC, for example, is not going out of the fried chicken business in response to People for the Ethical Treatment of Animals (PETA) picketing stores over treatment of chickens. In such cases, public relations professionals have to make tough calls and advocate strictly on behalf of their organization. How they decide what stand to take is the subject of the next section.

> Public relations practitioners should understand the ... challenges of public relations practice by identifying what constraints they have in their activities and recognizing that their professional qualifications are important assets.
>
> *Jae-Hwa Shin, University of Southern Mississippi*

It Depends—A System for Managing Conflict

A public relations professional or team must determine the stance its organization will take toward each public or stakeholder involved in the conflict situation. Stance then determines strategy—what will be done and why. The stance-driven approach to public relations began with the discovery that virtually all practitioners share an unstated, informal approach to managing conflict and competition: "It depends."

In other words, the stance taken toward publics "depends" on many factors that cause the stance to change in response to changing circumstances. Simply put, the outstanding practitioner monitors for threats, assesses them, arrives at a stance for the organization, and then begins communication efforts from that stance.

Practitioners face a complex set of forces that must be monitored and taken into consideration. One approach is the "threat appraisal" model, which is shown in Figure 10.2. Essentially, a threat to an organization requires an assessment of the demands that threat makes on the organization, as well as what resources are available to deal with the threat. An identified threat, for example, forces the public relations professional to consider two

Figure 10.2   Threat Appraisal Model

The public relations practitioner must consider both situational demands and organizational resources.

Source: Y. Jin & G. T. Cameron. (2007). The effects of threat type and duration on public relations practitioner's cognitive, affective and conative responses to crisis situations. *Journal of Public Relations Research, 19*(3), 256.

major factors. One is *organizational*. Do you have the knowledge, time, finances, and management commitment to combat the threat? The second is *situational*. How do you assess the severity of the danger to the organization? What effort is required from you? Is it a difficult situation with potential for long duration, or is it a relatively simple matter that can be solved fairly quickly? How much is uncertain about the facts or actual situation? Oftentimes, the public relations professional must base decisions on past experience and instinct.

An example of how the threat appraisal model is used in the real world is how McDonald's reacted when the mayor of Bogota, New Jersey, accused the restaurant chain of racism because it posted a billboard in Spanish to advertise its new iced coffee. He said the company was assuming local Latinos didn't speak English. McDonald's and its public relations firm, MWW Group, had to assess the threat to the company's reputation and how the media and the public (particularly the Hispanic public) would react to the charge of racism.

The appraisal indicated that a response was required, but at a localized level. It based its decision, in part, on researching the background and popularity of the mayor among Hispanics. It found that the mayor himself had distributed Spanish-language campaign materials in the past and that he was not particularly popular in the generally democratic Hispanic community because he was a Republican.

McDonald's then prepared its store managers in the tri-state area to handle local media inquiries and also immediately sent backgrounders to editors and reporters about its long history of multicultural programs, including extensive annual scholarship grants to Hispanic students. Many media outlets referenced this information in stories about the controversial billboard, and McDonald's received generally positive coverage. Thus, the issue was short-lived and didn't snowball into a national controversy. Sales of iced coffee even increased 22 percent in the greater New York metro area.

It is important to note that organizations assess threat in different ways. Films about industries are an example. In the case of Leonardo DiCaprio's film *Blood Diamond*, the World Diamond Council spent about $25 million to inform jewelers and consumers that 99 percent of the diamonds on the market are certified as "conflict-free" and that the movie doesn't reflect the current situation in Africa. Michael Moore's new film, *Sicko*, prompted health care organizations and the pharmaceutical industry to mount a major defense against what they considered to be misrepresentations in the film. On the other hand, the food industry has decided that such films as *Fast-Food Nation* are simply movies and don't need any proactive public relations initiatives.

It Depends: Two Basic Principles

When a public relations practitioner is involved in a crisis situation, external and long-term threats lead to the most severe consequences.

Yan Jin, Virginia Commonwealth University

The threat appraisal model, assessing the seriousness of the threat and the resources needed to combat it, is common in the practice of strategic public relations. The model illustrates the "it depends" approach, but there are two other principles that are important.

The first principle is that many factors determine the stance or position of an organization when it comes to dealing with conflict and perceived threats against the organization. The second principle is that the

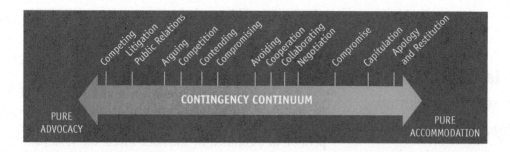

Figure 10.3   Contingency Continuum

This continuum from pure advocacy to pure accommodation forms the foundation for identifying the stance of an organization toward a given public at a given time.

public relations stance for dealing with a particular audience or public is dynamic, that is, it changes as events unfold. This is represented by a continuum of stances from pure advocacy to pure accommodation (see Figure 10.3). These two principles, which form the basis of what is called *contingency theory*, are discussed further in the next sections.

A Matrix of Contingency Factors

Through a series of contingency studies, researchers learned that professionals in public relations recognize dozens of forces and factors that can influence the stance on the continuum from advocacy to accommodation. The public relations approach chosen is contingent on the many factors that professionals must take into account when assessing a threat, although only a few factors will present themselves in most situations. Professionals and scholars thus do not need to memorize the 80+ factors found so far; they simply need to keep a watchful eye for what might move the public relations stance. The factors can be grouped into external factors:

- External threats
- Industry-specific environment
- General political/social environment
- External public's characteristics
- The issue under consideration

  and internal factors:

- General corporate/organizational characteristics
- Characteristics of the public relations department
- Top management characteristics
- Internal threats
- Personality characteristics of internal, involved persons
- Relationship characteristics

A nationwide survey at the University of Missouri of 1,000 members of the Public Relations Society of America (PRSA) explored what variables affect the stance that public relations professionals take, ranging from more advocacy to more accommodation, with a public regarding an issue in order to accomplish organizational goals.

> In times of uncertainty and danger, the organization reverts to denial, ritual, and rigidity and invokes its own version of reality as a basic defense against external evidence or attack.
>
> *Professor Astrid Kersten, LaRoche College*

The survey found that the expertise and experience of the public relations professional play a major role in formulating the proper strategy for dealing with heated competition or a conflict. By the same token, the values and attitudes of top management (known as the *dominant coalition*) also have a great influence on how the organization responds to conflict and threats. Corporate culture also plays a major role, as is illustrated in the PR Casebook on page 266 about Toyota's handling of a major recall.

In fact, Astrid Kersten of LaRoche College in Pittsburgh wrote in a *Public Relations Review* article that an organization's everyday culture and operations highly influence how organizations respond to conflict. She observes, however, that organizations often aren't very realistic in analyzing situations:

> What appears to us as rational and real is determined by the organizational culture we exist within and the economic and political reality that structures that culture. Conflict and crisis often reinforces organizational dysfunction. In times of uncertainty and danger, the organization reverts to denial, ritual, and rigidity and invokes its own version of reality as a basic defense against external evidence or attack.

The Contingency Continuum

The matrix, or list of possible variables, that influences an organization's response is helpful in understanding inputs into the complex decision-making process. Depending on circumstances, the attitudes of top management, and the judgment of public relations professionals, such factors may move the organization toward or away from accommodation of a public.

The range of response can be shown on a continuum from pure advocacy to pure accommodation (see Figure 10.3). Pure advocacy might be described as a hard-nosed stance of completely disagreeing or refuting the arguments, claims, or threats of a competitor or a group concerned about an issue. Later in the chapter, for example, the conflict management of Pepsi, when it was claimed that used syringes were found in cans of its product, is examined. In this case, Pepsi took the stance that such claims were a hoax and stood 100 percent behind its product, resisting suggestions that a product recall was needed.

The other extreme of the continuum is pure accommodation. In this case, the organization agrees with its critics, changes its policies, makes restitution, and even makes a full public apology for its actions. A good example of pure accommodation is that of natural juice company Odwalla. In this case, after it was found that a problem in production caused food poisoning in customers, it immediately issued a product recall, offered to pay all medical expenses of the victims, and made a full apology to the public.

There are other stances along the continuum that an organization can take. Norfolk Southern railroad, for example, used litigation public relations to shift stockholder opinion concerning an offer to take over Conrail. Also, the Vatican is in the middle of the continuum but appears, in 2010, to be shifting more toward accommodation as it copes with ongoing accusations of sexual misconduct by its priests, including some highly placed Catholic leaders. Various archdioceses finally moved from pure advocacy (denial of a problem) to cooperation and negotiation by making restitution to sex abuse victims after their initial resistance. Another part of the continuum is compromise; KFC improved conditions of chickens supplied to its stores as a result of complaints by the animal rights group PETA. See the Ethics box below for a discussion of ethical considerations in the conflict resolution process.

on the job

ETHICS

When to Negotiate, When to Fight

In the field of law, an important specialty that has grown over the last several decades focuses on alternatives to litigation. This conflict resolution, or alternative dispute resolution, movement shares the contingency approach presented in this chapter. Robert Mnookin, author of *Bargaining with the Devil: When to Negotiate, When to Fight* and director of Harvard's Project on Negotiation, exemplifies the "It depends" orientation of the contingency theory in his work guiding countries and corporations through difficult conflict situations.

According to NPR's Guy Raz:

Robert Mnookin has taught hundreds of Harvard Law students how to avoid litigation and pursue negotiated agreements. And yet, for someone who's devoted his career to the idea that you can negotiate your way out of almost anything, Mnookin often suggests that there are certain people you just can't reason with, people you have to fight. And some of those examples are laid out in his new book "Bargaining with the Devil."

Mnookin has developed a bipolar scale similar to the continuum developed by Cameron. The two extremes are a fight/flight response on one end and appeasement on the other. The author draws on decades of experience to delve into the rational and intuitive frames of mind that often cause us to refuse to negotiate, with disastrous consequences.

But it depends; Mnookin also writes about Rudolf Kastner, a leader of the Jewish community in Hungary during the Second World War, who eventually made a deal with the notorious Nazi officer Adolf Eichmann to deliver enormous bribes in exchange for allowing about 1,700 Jews to avoid the Holocaust by fleeing to Switzerland. After the war, a court in Israel actually condemned Kastner, calling him a collaborator, a charge he fought his entire life.

Notably, Mnookin argues the question actually is much more complex and nuanced than simple guilt or innocence:

It's a tragic case. [Kastner] ended up making some very hard decisions. And he concluded that in fact he thought more lives could be saved by attempting to bribe the Nazis than by resistance, which would be impossible because the Jews in Hungary had no arms. He did negotiate over a period of months with Eichmann and he did persuade Eichmann...to let some 1,700 people leave Hungary on a train, which eventually reached Switzerland.

Justice is often backward looking and if you want to make peace, you got to look forward.

Robert Mnookin, director of Harvard Law School's Project on Negotiation

(continued)

Like any good public relations professional, Mnookin calls for lawyers to carefully consider the alternatives, much like those in the contingency theory. He suggests that more often than we'd like, we must negotiate or accommodate adversaries. He says:

> ...there are two reasons, really. One is there are a lot of emotional and psychological and political traps that make you want to avoid negotiation. The other problem is, bargaining

with the devil usually requires giving the devil something he or she wants. And that often doesn't feel very good because you're really on the altar of pragmatism, sacrificing the search for perfect justice.

> Justice is often backward looking and if you want to make peace, you got to look forward.

Applying this logic to strategic management of conflict in public relations, it is often crucial that public

relations people look forward, not backward, and argue with their management to accommodate reporters or publics in spite of the human inclinations to fight or flee.

Do you agree that sometimes we need to bargain with the devil?

Source: R. Mnookin. (2010). *Bargaining with the devil: When to negotiate, when to fight.* New York, NY: Simon & Schuster; and *All things considered.* Retrieved from National Public Radio website: www.npr.org

The key point about the continuum is that it identifies the stance of an organization toward a given public at a given time. It also shows the dynamism of public relations. In many cases, an organization will initially adopt a pure advocacy stance but, as the situation changes, new information comes to light, and public opinion shifts, the stance will change toward more accommodation. A similar continuum is used to portray how organizations respond to a crisis situation, which is discussed on pages 261–262.

The Conflict Management Life Cycle

To best understand the entire conflict management process, it helps to think of it as a life cycle of a problem or issue that professionals must track. Figure 10.4 shows the *Conflict Management Life Cycle*. The life cycle shows the "big picture" of how to manage a conflict. Strategic conflict management can be divided into four general phases,

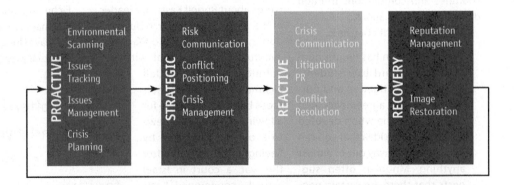

Figure 10.4   Conflict Management Life Cycle

The cycle of conflict depicts the four phases in conflict management experienced by public relations professionals. Typically, events move through time from left to right along the life cycle. At the end of the cycle, the process begins all over again on the left side of the cycle.

but bear in mind that the lines between the phases are not absolute and that some techniques overlap in actual practice. Furthermore, in the exciting world of public relations, busy practitioners may be actively managing different competitive situations as well as conflicts in each of the four phases simultaneously. To better understand the conflict management life cycle, each phase will be briefly explained.

Proactive Phase

The proactive phase includes activities and thought processes that can prevent a conflict from arising or getting out of hand. The first step in the phase is *environmental scanning*—the constant reading, listening, and watching of current affairs with an eye to the organization's interests. As issues emerge, *issues tracking* becomes more focused and systematic through processes such as the daily clipping of news stories. *Issues management* occurs when the organization makes behavioral changes or creates strategic plans in ways that address the emerging issue.

In the proactive phase, well-run organizations will also develop a general *crisis plan* as a first step in preparing for the worst—an issue or an event that has escalated to crisis proportions. Also in the proactive phase, an organization can use a strategy called stealing thunder to disclose its crisis before it is discovered by the media or other interested parties. Studies show that stealing thunder enhances credibility of the organization and decreases the perceived severity of the problem.

Strategic Phase

In the strategic phase, an issue that has become an emerging conflict is identified as needing concerted action by the public relations professional.

Three broad strategies take place in this phase. Through *risk communication*, dangers or threats to people or organizations are conveyed to forestall personal injury, health problems, and environmental damage. This risk communication continues so long as the risk exists or until the risk escalates into a crisis. *Conflict-positioning* strategies enable the organization to position itself favorably in anticipation of actions such as litigation, boycott, adverse legislation, elections, or similar events that will play out in "the court of public opinion." To be prepared for the worst outcome—that is, an issue that resists risk communication efforts and becomes a conflict of crisis proportions—a specific *crisis management plan* is developed for that particular issue.

Reactive Phase

Once the issue or imminent conflict reaches a critical level of impact on the organization, the public relations professional must react to events in the external communication environment as they unfold.

Crisis communications include the implementation of the crisis management plan as well as the hectic, 24/7 efforts to meet the needs of publics such as disaster victims, employees, government officials, and the media. When conflict has emerged but is not careening out of control, *conflict resolution* techniques are used to bring a heated conflict, such as collapsed salary negotiations, to a favorable resolution. The public relations practitioner may employ strategies to assist negotiation or arbitration efforts to resolve the conflict. (See Figure 10.5 on page 261.)

Often, the most intractable conflicts end up in the courts. *Litigation public relations* employs communication strategies and publicity efforts in support of legal actions or trials (see Chapter 12 for details on legal obligations in public relations).

Recovery Phase

In the aftermath of a crisis or a high-profile, heated conflict with a public, the organization should employ strategies to either bolster or repair its reputation in the eyes of key publics.

Reputation management includes systematic research to learn the state of the organization's reputation and then take steps to improve it. As events and conflicts occur, the company responds with actions and communication about those actions. Poorly managed issues, excessive risk imposed on others, and callous responses to a crisis damage an organization's reputation. See the PR Casebook on page 442 in Chapter 17 about BP's response to the Gulf oil spill. When this damage is extreme, *image restoration* strategies can help, provided they include genuine change by the organization.

Processes for Managing the Life Cycle

Not only do public relations practitioners face the challenge of addressing different conflicts in different phases of the life cycle, but no sooner do they deal with a conflict than the cyclical process starts over again for that very same issue. Environmental scanning is resumed to ensure that the conflict does not reemerge as an issue. Although challenging, conflict management is not impossible. Systematic processes described in the next sections of this chapter provide guidance and structure for this highly rewarding role played by public relations professionals in managing competition and conflict. Those processes include (1) issues management, (2) risk communication, (3) crisis management, (4) and reputation management.

Issues Management

Essentially, *issues management* is a proactive and systematic approach to (1) predict problems, (2) anticipate threats, (3) minimize surprises, (4) resolve issues, and (5) prevent crises. Martha Lauzen, a professor at San Diego State University, says that effective issues management requires two-way communications, formal environmental scanning, and active sense-making strategies.

Another definition of issues management has been formulated by Coates, Coates, Jarratt, and Heinz in their book *Issues Management: How You Can Plan, Organize, and Manage for the Future*. They say, "Issues management is the organized activity of identifying emerging trends, concerns, or issues likely to affect an organization in the next few years and developing a wider and more positive range of organizational responses toward the future."

The basic idea behind issues management is *proactive planning*. Philip Gaunt and Jeff Ollenburger, writing in *Public Relations Review*, say, "Issues management is proactive in that it tries to identify issues and influence decisions regarding them before they have a detrimental effect on a corporation." See the Insights box on page 256 for a matrix on how to evaluate an issue's importance.

Gaunt and Ollenburger contrast this approach with crisis management, which is essentially reactive in nature. They note, "Crisis management tends to be more reactive, dealing with an issue after it becomes public knowledge and affects the company." In other words, active planning and prevention through issues management can often mean the difference between a noncrisis and a crisis, or, as one practitioner put it, the difference between little or no news coverage and a page-one headline. This point is particularly relevant because studies have shown that the majority of organizational crises are self-inflicted, because management ignored early warning signs.

The issue of the exploitation of women and children in Third World factories by American companies, for example, simmered for several years before it finally broke into the headlines after a worker activist group publicly accused Nike of using "sweatshop" labor to make its expensive and profitable athletic shoes and apparel.

Such revelations put the entire U.S. garment industry on the defensive. David Birenbaum, a consultant to the garment industry, wrote in the *Wall Street Journal* that the issue of using cheap Third World labor was not really new, but the public reaction to such practices was different. He wrote in the op-ed article:

> What's changed is that for the first time human rights concerns could become a major marketing issue....More and more importers are now considering safety and other conditions in Asian factories. Few can afford not to, because all it takes is one disaster to damage a label's reputation.

All of the publicity and public outrage, however, might have been avoided if the various clothing and athletic shoe manufacturers had paid attention to the concept of issues management.

Public relations counselors W. Howard Chase and Barrie L. Jones were among the first practitioners to specialize in issues management. They defined the process as consisting of five basic steps: (1) issue identification, (2) issue analysis, (3) strategy options, (4) an action plan, and (5) the evaluation of results. The following is a brief description of how these steps could have been used by the garment industry.

Strategy Options

If the company decides that the emerging issue is potentially damaging, the next step is to consider what to do about it. One option might be to set higher standards for foreign contractors seeking the company's business. Another option: Work with human rights groups to monitor possible violations in foreign factories that produce the company's products. A third option might be to establish a new policy that would ensure that Third World workers receive decent pay and health benefits. The pros and cons of each option are weighed against what is most practical and economical for the company.

Action Plan

Once a specific policy has been decided on, the fourth step is to communicate it to all interested publics. These may include consumers, the U.S. Department of Labor, labor unions and worker activist groups, company employees, and the financial community. The action may be an opportunity to use the new policy as a marketing tool among consumers who make buying decisions based on a company's level of social responsibility.

on the job
INSIGHTS

The Issues Management Process

Public relations counselors W. Howard Chase and Barrie L. Jones were among the first practitioners to specialize in issues management. They defined the process as consisting of five basic steps:

Step 1 Issue Identification
Organizations should track the alternative press, mainstream media, online chat groups, and the newsletters of activist groups to learn which issues and concerns are being discussed. Of particular importance is establishing a trend line of coverage.

Step 2 Issue Analysis
Once an emerging issue has been identified, the next step is to assess

its potential impact on and threat to the organization. Another consideration is to determine whether the organization is vulnerable on the issue.

Step 3 Strategy Options
If the company decides that the emerging issue is potentially damaging, it must then consider what to do about it. The pros and cons of each option are weighed against what is most practical and economical for the company.

Step 4 Action Plan
Once a specific policy (stance) has been decided on, the fourth step is to

communicate it to all interested publics.

Step 5 Evaluation
With the new policy in place and communicated, the final step is to evaluate the results. Has news coverage been positive? Is the company being positioned as an industry leader? Have public perceptions of the company and the industry improved? If the company has acted soon enough, perhaps the greatest measurement of success is avoiding the media coverage that occurs when a problem becomes a crisis.

Evaluation

With the new policy in place and communicated, the final step is to evaluate the results. Has news coverage been positive? Have activist groups called off product boycotts? Have the working conditions for women and children in the factories improved? Is the company being positioned as an industry leader? Have public perceptions of the company and the industry improved? If the company has acted soon enough, perhaps the greatest measurement of success is having avoided the media coverage that occurs if the problem becomes a crisis.

Conflict Positioning and Risk Communication

Following upon issues management is conflict positioning. Any verbal or written exchange that attempts to communicate information that positions the organization favorably regarding competition or an anticipated conflict is called *conflict positioning*. Ideally, the public relations professional is not only communicating in a way that positions the organization favorably in the face of competition and imminent conflict, but is also influencing the actual behavior of the organization favorably. For example, facing enormous financial losses and the need to lay off thousands of employees, General Motors announced that it was freezing executive salaries. Doing so reduced the level of criticism for the employee layoffs that followed.

Often, a public relations professional can engage in communication that may reduce risk for affected publics and for his or her employer. Communication regarding risk to public health and safety and the environment are particularly important roles for public relations professionals. (See Chapter 21, "Nonprofits, Health, and Education," for more on health communication as an important risk communication field in public relations.) The risk may be naturally occurring, such as undertows and riptides on beaches that require warning signs and flyers in hotel rooms. Or the risk may be associated with a product, such as over-the-counter drugs or a lawn mower.

Organizations, including large corporations, increasingly engage in risk communication to inform the public of risks such as those surrounding food products, chemical spills, radioactive waste disposal, or the placement of drug-abuse treatment centers or halfway houses in neighborhoods. These issues deserve public notice in fairness to the general populace. Such risks may also result in expensive lawsuits, restrictive legislation, consumer boycotts, and public debate if organizations fail to disclose potential hazards. As is often the case, doing the right thing in conflict management is also the least disruptive in the long run.

Product recalls, in particular, require doing the "right thing." After a six-month-old child suffocated in a crib that had been repaired with duct tape by the parents, the maker of 20 models of Dorel Asia cribs recalled 635,000 units. The company noted the "highly unusual" circumstances of the repair, but also did the right thing at great expense. Dorel Asia's announcement stated, "Hundreds of thousands of Dorel Asia cribs have been properly assembled and used safely without incident." The company emphasized, "At Dorel Asia there is nothing more important than a baby's health and safety." In contrast, RC2, the manufacturer of Thomas trains, recalled 1.5 million of its Chinese-made toys with a single announcement and no follow-up. Company executives didn't answer media inquiries, and crisis experts criticized the company for not assuring customers that it was aggressively addressing the problem. The company also received additional unfavorable international publicity when a *New York Times* reporter wrote several stories about being detained and harassed at RC2's Chinese factory for nine hours when he tried to interview its management. One story was titled "My Time as a Hostage, And I'm a Business Reporter."

Risk communication can minimize adverse effects on publics, but it also often reduces risk—of lawsuits, of damaged morale in the organization, and of diminished reputation—to the organization itself. When risk communication fails, however, the organization often faces a crisis.

Variables Affecting Risk Perceptions

Risk communication researchers have identified several variables that affect public perceptions:

- Risks voluntarily taken tend to be accepted. Smokers have more control over their health situation, for example, than airline passengers do over their safety.
- The more complex a situation, the higher the perception of risk. Disposal of radioactive wastes is more difficult to understand than the dangers of cigarette smoking.

- Familiarity breeds confidence. If the public understands the problem and its factors, it perceives less risk.
- Perception of risk increases when the messages of experts conflict.
- The severity of consequences affects risk perceptions. There is a difference between having a stomachache and getting cancer.

Suzanne Zoda, writing on risk communication in *Communication World*, gives some suggestions to communicators:

- Begin early and initiate a dialogue with publics that might be affected. Do not wait until the opposition marshals its forces. Vital to establishing trust is early contact with anyone who may be concerned or affected.
- Actively solicit and identify people's concerns. Informal discussions, surveys, interviews, and focus groups are effective in evaluating issues and identifying outrage factors.
- Recognize the public as a legitimate partner in the process. Engage interested groups in two-way communication and involve key opinion leaders.
- Address issues of concern, even if they do not directly pertain to the project.
- Anticipate and prepare for hostility. To defuse a situation, use a conflict resolution approach. Identify areas of agreement and work toward common ground.
- Understand the needs of the news media. Provide accurate, timely information and respond promptly to requests.
- Always be honest, even when it hurts.

Crisis Management

In public relations, high-profile events such as accidents, terrorist attacks, disease pandemics, and natural disasters can dwarf even the best conflict positioning and risk management strategies. This is when crisis management takes over. The conflict management process, which includes ongoing issues management and risk communication efforts, is severely tested in crisis situations in which a high degree of uncertainty exists.

Unfortunately, even the most thoughtfully designed conflict management process cannot have a plan in place for every situation. Sometimes, in spite of risk communication to prevent an issue from becoming a major problem, that issue grows into a crisis right before the professional's eyes. At such times, verifiable information about what is happening or has happened may be lacking. This causes people to become more active seekers of information and, as research suggests, more dependent on the media for information to satisfy the human desire for closure.

A crisis situation, in other words, puts a great deal of pressure on organizations to respond with accurate, complete information as quickly as possible. How an organization responds in the first 24 hours, experts say, often determines whether the situation remains an "incident" or becomes a full-blown crisis.

What Is a Crisis?

Kathleen Fearn-Banks, in her book *Crisis Communications: A Casebook Approach*, writes, "A crisis is a major occurrence with a potentially negative outcome affecting the organization, company, or industry, as well as its publics, products, services, or good name."

In other words, an organizational crisis can constitute any number of situations. A *PRWeek* article makes the point:

> Imagine one of these scenarios happening to your company: a product recall; a plane crash; a very public sexual harassment suit; a gunman holding hostages in your office; an *E. coli* bacteria contamination scare; a market crash, along with the worth of your company stock; a labor union strike; a hospital malpractice suit....

Often, management tends to minimize or deny there's a crisis. However, there is a crisis if the organization's stakeholders—customers, vendors, employees, or even local community leaders—perceive the situation to be a crisis. JetBlue's management, for example, didn't particularly think it was a crisis when it cancelled hundreds of flights in the wake of a Valentine's Day snowstorm, which left thousands of passengers stranded for days and even kept passengers sitting on a runway in one plane for 10 hours. The airline failed to keep passengers (let alone employees) informed and didn't even bother to post updates on its website. The result was thousands of irate passengers and a deluge of 5,000 media inquiries, for which the airline was totally unprepared. In terms of agenda-setting and framing theory, as discussed in Chapter 9, the media often frame a situation as a crisis for the organization. And, as more than one pundit has stated, "Perception is reality." See the Insights box on page 260 for some metrics used by a crisis expert to identify a crisis.

Nor are crises always unexpected. One study by the Institute for Crisis Management (www.crisisexperts.com) found that only 14 percent of business crises are unexpected. The remaining 86 percent are what the Institute called "smoldering" crises, in which an organization is aware of a potential business disruption long before the public finds out about it. The study also found that management—or in some cases, mismanagement—causes 78 percent of the crises. In fact, a study by Weber Shandwick public relations with KRC Research found that the top three triggers for a crisis are (1) financial irregularities, (2) unethical behavior, and (3) executive misconduct.

"Most organizations have a crisis plan to deal with sudden crises, like accidents," says Robert B. Irvine, president of the Institute. "However, our data indicates many businesses are denying or ducking serious problems that eventually will ignite and cost them millions of dollars and lost management time." With proper issues management and conflict planning, perhaps many of the smoldering crises could be prevented from bursting into flames.

A Lack of Crisis Planning

Echoing Irvine's thought, another study, by Steven Fink, found that 89 percent of the chief executive officers of *Fortune* 500 companies reported that a business crisis was almost inevitable; however, 50 percent admitted that they did not have a crisis management plan.

This situation has caused Kenneth Myers, a crisis consultant, to write, "If economics is the dismal science, then contingency planning is the abysmal science." As academics Donald Chisholm and Martin Landry have noted, "When people believe that because nothing has gone wrong, nothing will go wrong, they court disaster. There is noise in every system and every design. If this fact is ignored, nature soon reminds us of our folly."

> A quick response is an active response because it tries to fill the vacuum with facts. A slow response allows others to fill the vacuum with speculation and misinformation. But others could be ill-informed or could use the opportunity to attack the organization.
>
> Timothy Coombs, author of *Ongoing Crisis Communications: Planning, Managing, and Responding*

on the job

INSIGHTS

Metrics of Crisis: Building Effective Plans

Crisis public relations guru James Lukaszewski offers a somewhat unusual measurement of what constitutes a crisis: Lukaszewski says that if there are no victims, there is no crisis or potential crisis. On his PRSA blog, he opines:

What's a crisis? A crisis is a people stopping, product stopping, show stopping, reputationally defining or trust busting event that creates victims and/or explosive visibility. The operative word in this definition is the word "victims."

Essentially, the definition is based on a cardinal rule of pickup basketball games: no harm, no foul.

Lukaszewski makes the crucial point that crisis planning is not always well received.

Ninety-five percent of all crises come from what an organization, business or agency does in its normal course of activity every day. This means that it is very likely that there are people who are on duty or nearby who

know what to do when adversity occurs. Therefore, when the boss looks at you askance as you propose something right in the bailiwick of the company and says, "We don't need to prepare for that," and you look surprised or hurt, the boss wonders about you.

All human activity carries some risk and produces some impact—after all, even an innocently sleeping baby is making a tiny contribution of carbon to the atmosphere! PR people who allow their organization to become complacent about daily operations can get caught completely unaware when those routine, daily operations produce victims—Lukaszewski's metric for crisis. He notes, however, that there is a silver lining:

Operational problems and crises are far less likely to damage reputation and credibility. This is just because they are responded to more quickly or more appropriately due to the availability of knowledgeable help.

BUT...

The remaining five percent of crises come from non-operating circumstances . . . . . These circumstances [e.g., employee violence, massive casualties, kidnapping, sexual harassment, criminal behavior] are often highly emotional and there is an unwillingness, fear or great concern about doing anything to resolve them . . . .

Because there is almost no expertise inside organizations to manage these problems the instant they occur, a combination of high-level emotion and fear, coupled with lack of knowledge, causes hesitation, delay, mistakes and significant reputational damage.

Lukaszewski advises that when choosing scenarios for crisis planning, choose mostly from that 5 percent nonoperating category, because the boss' career is more likely to be defined by those circumstances. And when the boss is happy, there's no foul and no harm.

Source: Retrieved from the PRSA blog site: www.comPRehension.org

Many "smoldering" crises could be prevented if professionals used more environmental scanning and issues management leading to the development of a strategic management plan. A common crisis planning technique is rating both the "probability" of a particular crisis and its "impact" on the organization. A fire at a

Mattel toy factory, for example, would probably receive a "2" rating for probability, and a similar score for impact because the company has multiple suppliers. On the other hand, the probability of unsafe products might be a "3" but rank as a "5" in terms of impact on the company because public trust would be eroded and sales would drop.

How to Communicate During a Crisis

Many professionals and books offer good checklists on what to do during a crisis. Figure 10.5 offers a compilation of good suggestions:

Strategies for Responding to Crises

The chart in Figure 10.5 offers sound, practical advice, but recent research has shown that organizations don't respond to a crisis in the same way. Indeed, Timothy W. Coombs postulates that an organization's response may vary on a continuum from defensive to accommodative, which is similar to the contingency continuum explained on page 250. Here is Coombs' list of crisis communication strategies that an organization may use:

- **Attack the accuser.** The party that claims a crisis exists is confronted and its logic and facts are faulted. Sometimes a lawsuit is threatened.
- **Denial.** The organization explains that there is no crisis.

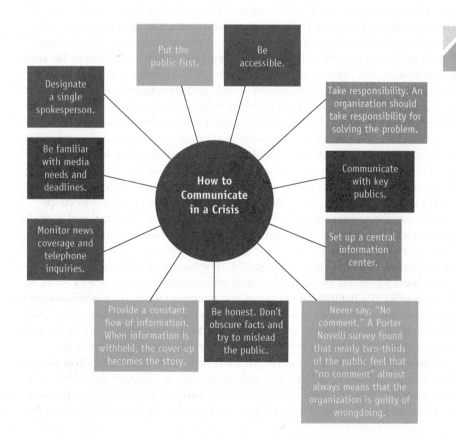

Figure 10.5   How to Communicate in a Crisis

Many professionals offer good advice on what to do during a crisis. Here's a compilation of good suggestions.

- **Excuse.** The organization minimizes its responsibility for the crisis. Any intention to do harm is denied, and the organization says that it had no control over the events that led to the crisis. This strategy is often used when there is a natural disaster or product tampering.

- **Justification.** Crisis is minimized with a statement that no serious damage or injuries resulted. Sometimes, the blame is shifted to the victims, as in the case of the Firestone tire recall. This is often done when a consumer misuses a product or when there is an industrial accident.

- **Ingratiation.** Actions are taken to appease the publics involved. Consumers who complain are given coupons, or the organization makes a donation to a charitable organization. Burlington Industries, for example, gave a large donation to the Humane Society after the discovery that it had imported coats from China with fur collars containing dog fur instead of coyote fur.

- **Corrective action.** Steps are taken to repair the damage from the crisis and to prevent it from happening again.

- **Full apology.** The organization takes responsibility and asks forgiveness. Some compensation of money or aid is often included.

The Coombs typology gives options for crisis communication management that depend on the situation and the stance taken by the organization. He notes that organizations do have to consider more accommodative strategies (ingratiation, corrective action, full apology) if defensive strategies (attack accuser, denial, excuse) are not effective. The more accommodative strategies not only meet immediate crisis communication demands but can help subsequently in repairing an organization's reputation or restoring previous sales levels. He says, "Accommodative strategies emphasize image repair, which is what is needed as image damage worsens. Defensive strategies, such as denial or minimizing, logically become less effective as organizations are viewed as more responsible for the crisis."

Often, however, an organization doesn't adopt an accommodative strategy because of corporate culture and other constraints included in the contingency theory of the conflict management matrix. Organizations do not, and sometimes cannot, engage in two-way communication and accommodative strategies when confronted with a crisis or conflict with a given public. Some variables proscribing accommodation, according to Cameron, include: (1) management's moral conviction that the public is wrong; (2) moral neutrality when two contending publics want the organization to take sides on a policy issue; (3) legal constraints; (4) regulatory constraints such as the FTC or SEC; (5) prohibition by senior management against an accommodative stance; and (6) possible conflict between departments of the organization on what strategies to adopt.

In some cases, the contingency theory contends that the ideal of mutual understanding and accommodation doesn't occur because both sides have staked out highly rigid positions and are not willing to compromise their strong moral positions. (See the Ethics box, "When to Negotiate, When to Fight," on page 251.) For example, it is unlikely that the pro-life and pro-choice forces will ever achieve mutual understanding and accommodation. At other times, conflict is a natural state between competing interests, such as oil interests seeking offshore exploration and environmental groups seeking to block that exploration, especially in light of the BP disaster off the Louisiana coast. Frequently, one's stance and strategies for conflict management entail assessment and balancing of many factors.

It is important to emphasize that not all successful crisis communication strategies are accommodative. Pepsi-Cola was able to mount an effective defensive crisis communication strategy and avoid a recall when a hoax of nationwide proportions created an intense but short-lived crisis for the soft-drink company. (See the Insights box below about classic crisis management campaigns.) On the other hand, the Domino's Pizza PR Casebook in Chapter 13 dramatically showcases that the rapid, thorough accommodation of the concerns of alarmed customers can be highly rewarding for all concerned.

on the job

INSIGHTS

Classic Cases of Crisis Management

The crisis communication strategies outlined by Coombs are useful in evaluating how an organization handles a crisis. Intel, for example, first denied in 1994 that there was a problem with its new Pentium chip. As the crisis deepened and was covered extensively in the mainstream press, Intel tried the strategy of justification, saying that the problem wasn't serious enough to warrant replacing the chips. It also minimized the concerns of end users such as engineers and computer programmers. Only after considerable damage had been done to Intel's reputation, and IBM had suspended orders for the chip, did Intel take corrective action to replace the chips, and Andy Grove, Intel's president, issue a full apology.

Of course, not all crisis communication strategies need to be accommodative to be successful. When a hoax of nationwide proportions created an intense but short-lived crisis for Pepsi-Cola, the soft-drink company was able to mount an effective defensive crisis communication strategy and avoid issuing a recall.

The crisis began when the media reported that a man in Tacoma, Washington, claimed that he had found a syringe inside a can of Diet Pepsi. As the news spread, men and women across the country made similar claims of finding a broken sewing needle, a screw, a bullet, and even a narcotics vial in their Pepsi cans. As a consequence, some people demanded a recall of all Pepsi products—an action that would have had major economic consequences for the company.

Company officials were confident that insertion of foreign objects into cans on high-speed, closely controlled bottling lines was virtually impossible, so they chose to defend their product. The urgent problem, then, was to convince the public that the product was safe, and that any foreign objects found had been inserted after the cans had been opened.

Pepsi officials and their public relations staff employed several strategies. One approach was to attack the accusers. Company officials said the foreign objects probably got into the cans after they were opened, and even explained that many people make such claims just to collect compensation from the company. The company also announced that it would pursue legal action against anyone making

false claims about the integrity of the company's products.

Pepsi also adopted the strategy of denial, saying that there was no crisis. Pepsi President Craig E. Weatherup immediately made appearances on national television programs and gave newspaper interviews to state the company's case that its bottling lines were secure. Helping to convince the public was U.S. Food and Drug Administration Commissioner David Kessler, who said that a recall was not necessary.

These quick actions deflated the public's concern, and polls showed considerable acceptance of Pepsi's contention that the problem was a hoax. A week after the scare had begun, Pepsi ran full-page advertisements with the headline "Pepsi is pleased to announce...Nothing." It stated, "As America now knows, those stories about Diet Pepsi were a hoax...."

The cases highlighted here illustrate one emphasis of contingency theory: No single crisis communication strategy is appropriate for all situations. Indeed, as Coombs indicates, "It is only by understanding the crisis situation that the crisis manager can select the appropriate response for the crisis."

Reputation Management

Reputation is defined as the collective representation of an organization's past performance that describes the firm's ability to deliver valued outcomes to multiple stakeholders. Put in plain terms, reputation is the track record of an organization in the public's mind.

Public relations scholar Lisa Lyon makes the point that reputation, unlike corporate image, is owned by the public. Reputation isn't formed by packaging or slogans. Rather, a good reputation is created and destroyed by everything an organization does, from the way it manages employees to the way it handles conflicts with outside constituents.

The Three Foundations of Reputation

Reputation scholars offer three foundations of reputation: (1) economic performance, (2) social responsiveness, and (3) the ability to deliver valuable outcomes to stakeholders. Public relations plays a role in all three foundations, but professionals who manage conflict effectively will especially enhance the latter two foundations of reputation. The social responsiveness of an organization results from careful issue tracking and effective positioning of the organization. It is further enhanced when risk communication is compelling and persuasive. The ability to make valuable contributions to stakeholders who depend on the organization results in part from fending off threats to the organization that would impair its mission.

Research techniques called *reputation audits* can be used to assess and monitor an organization's reputation. These can be as basic as *Fortune* magazine's list of "Most Admired Companies" (www.fortune.com/fortune/mostadmired) to rigorous global reputation measures, such as the Reputation Quotient offered by the Reputation Institute (www.reputationinstitute.com) in conjunction with Harris Interactive. Of particular interest to public relations professionals is the Media Reputation Index (MRI), which measures the effects of media coverage on corporate reputations. Working with Delahaye Medialink, the project documents the important role of media in reputation management. This relationship is depicted in Figure 10.6.

In addition to tracking and dealing proactively with issues, conveying risks to publics, and managing crises as they arise, public relations practitioners also will be faced with the need to apologize when all efforts to manage conflict have fallen short. The future trust and credibility of the organization are at stake in how well this recovery phase of conflict management is handled.

> Get it right;
> Get it fast;
> Get it out; and
> Get it over.
>
> *Warren Buffett, CEO of Berkshire Hathaway*

The frequent platitude in post-crisis communication is that practitioners should acknowledge failings, apologize, and then put the events in the past as quickly as possible. Warren Buffett, in an interview with CNBC about how a company should deal with a crisis, offered this succinct variation on the stealing thunder strategy: "Get it right; Get it fast; Get it out; and Get it over." Of course, such an approach works best when one has a reputation for integrity and vast charitable generosity such as Mr. Buffett enjoys. What is clear, regardless of track record, is that public relations professionals earn respect by overcoming management's human inclination to obfuscate and stonewall. Stealing thunder rather than letting media break the news does frequently work to advantage.

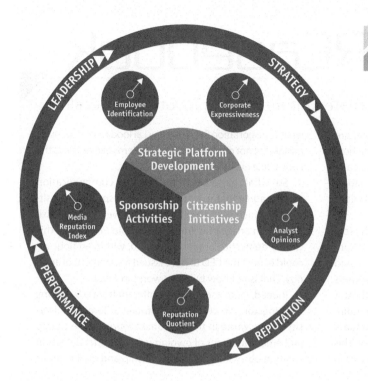

Figure 10.6   The Role of Media in Reputation Management

This diagram shows many of the forces affecting corporate reputation, most notably, how media coverage and performance of an organization impact its reputation and, in return how reputation influences the health of the organization.

However, Lyon has found that apology is not always effective because of the hypocrisy factor. When an organization has a questionable track record (i.e., a bad reputation), the apology may be viewed as insincere and hypocritical. Coombs suggests a relational approach, which assumes that crises are episodes within a larger stakeholder–organization relationship. Applying the contingency theory, considering how stakeholders perceive the situation can help communicators determine which strategy is best to rebuild the stakeholder–organization relationship and restore the organization's reputation.

Image Restoration

Reputation repair and recovery is a long-term process, and the fourth phase in the conflict management life cycle is called the recovery phase. Research by Burson-Marsteller public relations, for example, found that it takes about three years for an organization to recover from a crisis that damaged its reputation. A survey of 685 business influentials also found that quickly disclosing the details of a scandal or corporate misstep should be management's number-one strategy as it begins the process of restoring its reputation.

Other strategies used by executives to recover reputation are, in descending order, (1) make progress/recovery visible, (2) analyze what went wrong, (3) improve governance structure, (4) make the CEO and leadership accessible to the media, (5) fire employees involved in the problem, (6) commit to high corporate citizenship standards, (7) carefully review ethics policies, (8) hire outside auditors for internal audits, and (9) issue an apology from the CEO.

PRCasebook

Corporate Culture Hinders Toyota's Car Recall

Corporate culture, and even a nation's culture, are among the important variables that determine how an organization responds to a crisis. This is clearly illustrated in the case of Toyota, which ultimately had to recall 9 million cars, including 3.2 million in the United States, because of safety defects.

In a matter of weeks from January to February 2010, Toyota's reputation for quality and reliability hit rock bottom when media coverage saturation, the blogosphere, and politicians all criticized Toyota for not telling consumers that there had been a number of incidents in which the gas pedal stuck on Toyota vehicles. A poll by YouGov Brandindex found that Toyota's positive rating of 28 in January plummeted to a minus 17.1 rating by mid-February. This was even lower than the rating of Hummer, which was in second place with a minus 10.7 rating.

In addition, a *USA Today*/Gallup poll found that 55 percent of Americans thought Toyota had failed to respond quickly to potential safety defects. The U.S. Transportation Department agreed, ultimately fining the company $16.4 million for

what Transportation Secretary Ray LaHood called the "huge mistake" of not disclosing safety problems earlier. It was the largest fine ever for a vehicle defect.

So what happened? Most crisis communication experts agree that Toyota was slow to respond to the situation, which made a bad situation even worse. Jesse Toprak, an analyst for *TrueCar.com*, told *PRWeek*, "If this were a domestic company like Ford, within an hour we could expect the CEO to have issued a statement of apology. That is not how business works in Japan."

Indeed, Japanese culture is different from U.S. culture. Jeff Kingston, director of Asian Studies at Temple University Japan, wrote in the *Wall Street Journal*, "The shame and embarrassment of owning up to product defects in a nation obsessed with craftsmanship and quality raises

> ### Japan is still a country where the concept of PR is weak. Companies don't spend on PR, and there are few specialists.
>
> *Tatsumi Tanaka, crisis communications consultant, quoted in the Financial Times*

the bar on disclosure and assuming responsibility. And a high status company like Toyota has much to lose since its corporate face is at stake."

Other experts have noted that Japanese culture has strong elements of deference to authority, employee loyalty, and group harmony. In such a situation, the *Economist* noted, Toyota had

a rigid system of seniority and hierarchy in which people are reluctant to pass bad news up the chain of command, thus keeping information from those who need to hear it in a misguided effort to protect them from losing face. Any attempt to short-circuit the hierarchy is deemed an act of disloyalty and a violation of the traditional consensual corporate culture. The preference for harmony crowds out alternative viewpoints.

The *Economist* further elaborated on the concept of alternative viewpoints. It noted that Toyota, despite being the number-one carmaker in the world since 2008 and getting 70 percent of its revenue from foreign sales, was still operating as if it was a provincial Japanese company. The 29-member board of directors are all Japanese and Toyota insiders, so there is a lack of a broad perspective about the scope of its operations on six continents.

The writer for the *Economist* continued, "If Toyota's board had included, say, a female German boss, a former American senator and a high-flying Hong Kong lawyer, its response to the crisis might have been different." Even the idea of a female on the board of directors of a Japanese company is an alien concept. Notes the *Economist*, "Indeed, there is a greater percentage of women on boards in Kuwait than in Japan."

In other words, Kingston says, corporate culture in Japan tends to be characterized by slow initial response, minimizing the problem, foot dragging on the product recall, poor communication with the public, and little concern for consumers. Another aspect of Japanese culture is a somewhat cozy relationship with big business, government, and the media. While Toyota dominated the headlines elsewhere around the world, the Japanese media tended to downplay the product-defect problem and give minimal coverage to the controversy.

It was in this cultural environment that the president of Toyota, Akio Toyoda, finally gave a news conference a month after the recall had dominated most of the American and European media. The classic approach in crisis communication, if the company is at fault, is to immediately apologize, but Toyoda failed to meet this criterion because he made an apology late in the game and didn't actually take responsibility for the problem.

Toyoda's management style was also at odds regarding disclosure. He was used to a docile Japanese press, so he merely gave a statement and didn't answer reporter questions. That only enraged the foreign media, which then devoted even more coverage to Toyota's problems. By the time Toyoda appeared before a U.S. congressional committee several months later, however, the company had retained five American public relations firms to work on the recall and brief Toyoda on how to handle questions. This time, he came across as more sincere, apologized, and accepted responsibility for fixing all defects.

The Toyota recall caused a major slump in sales, so part of the reputation restoration effort was to get customers back in the salesroom again. To do so, the company offered major discounts, practically interest-free loans, and extended free maintenance plans, which increased sales. Major expenditures were also made on print and television advertising to assure the public that the company was doing everything possible to ensure the safety of its vehicles.

In time, the Toyota recall of 2010 faded from the headlines, but the sobering reality is that it will probably take years for Toyota to regain its reputation for quality and reliability. In 1986, for example, Audi had also gotten extensive coverage on an accelerator problem, and it took 15 years for the company to rebuild its U.S. sales to the level it had achieved before the controversy. And that was even after a government study in 1989 blamed driver errors.

Professor William Benoit of Ohio State University offers a more academic model, with five general strategies for image restoration and a number of substrategies, adding to the options available to the public relations professional when the worst of a crisis has passed:

1. Denial
   - Simple denial—Your organization did not do what it is accused of.
   - Shift the blame—Someone else did it.
2. Evade responsibility
   - Provocation—Your organization was provoked.
   - Defeasibility—Your organization was unable to avoid its actions.
   - Accident—The bad events were an accident.
   - Good intentions—Good intentions went awry.
3. Reduce offensiveness
   - Bolstering—Refer to the organization's clean record and good reputation.
   - Minimization—Reduce the magnitude of negative feelings.

- Differentiation—Distinguish the act from other similar, but more offensive, acts.
- Transcendence—Justify the act by placing it in a more favorable context.
- Attack the accuser—Reduce the credibility of the accusations.
- Compensation—Reduce the perceived severity of the injury.

4. Corrective action—Ensure the prevention or correction of the action.
5. Mortification—Offer a profuse apology.

Benoit's typology for image restoration is somewhat similar to Coombs' list on pages 261–262 about how organizations should respond to a crisis. Both scholars outline a response continuum from defensive (denial and evasion) to accommodation (corrective action and apology).

The image restoration strategy that an organization chooses depends a great deal on the situation, or on what has already been described as the "It depends" concept. If an organization is truly innocent, a simple denial and presentation of the facts is a good strategy. However, not many situations are clear-cut. Consequently, a more common strategy is acknowledging the issue, but making it clear that the situation was an accident or the result of a decision with unintended consequences. Benoit calls this the *strategy of evading responsibility*. Benoit lists six response strategies for *reducing offensiveness*— all the way from bolstering by telling the public about the organization's good record to compensating the victims. Ultimately, the most accommodative response is a profuse apology from the organization to the public and its various stakeholders.

The Benoit and Coombs continuums give a tool chest of possible strategies for dealing with a crisis or beginning image restoration, but it should be noted that a strategy or a combination of strategies may not necessarily restore reputation. A great deal depends on the perceptions of the public and other stakeholders. Do they find the explanation credible? Do they believe the organization is telling the truth? Do they think the organization is acting in the public interest? In many cases, an organization may start out with a defensive strategy, only to find that the situation ultimately demands corrective action or an apology before its reputation can be restored.

Déjà Vu—All Over Again

Empirical evidence from Benoit's work is ongoing, but it appears that image restoration can be an effective final stage in the conflict management process. But to paraphrase Yogi Berra, conflict management is like déjà vu all over again. The best organizations, led by the best public relations professionals, will strive to improve their performance by starting once again along the left side of the conflict management life cycle on page 252, with tasks such as environmental scanning and issues tracking. Issues that are deemed important receive attention for crisis planning and risk communication. When preventive measures fail, the crisis must be handled with the best interests of all parties held in a delicate balance. Reputation then must be given due attention. At all times, the goal is to change organizational behavior in ways that minimize damaging conflict, for the sake of not only the organization, but also its many stakeholders.

Indeed, the true value of public relations and the highest professionalism require that students today also embrace their roles as managers of competition and conflict. Outstanding and successful public relations professionals must serve as more than communication technicians carrying out the tactics of organizing events, writing news releases, handling news conferences, and pitching stories to journalists. They also must take on the responsibilities of managing conflict and weathering the inevitable crises that all organizations face at one time or another.

Summary

Strategic Conflict Management

By defining public relations as strategic management of competition and conflict, a fresh and vigorous approach to public relations is envisioned. Public relations is positioned to earn influence within organizations by focusing on achieving objectives.

The Role of Public Relations in Managing Conflict

Some of the most crucial roles played by public relations professionals involve the strategic management of conflict. The contingency theory argues for a dynamic and multifaceted approach to dealing with conflict in the field.

The Conflict Management Life Cycle

Strategic conflict management can be broadly divided into four phases, with specific techniques and functions falling into each phase. The life cycle emphasizes that conflict management is ongoing and cyclical in nature.

Issues Management

Issues management is a proactive and systematic approach to predicting problems, anticipating threats, minimizing surprises, resolving issues, and preventing crises. The five steps in the issues management process are issue identification, issue analysis, strategy options, an action plan, and the evaluation of results.

Conflict Positioning and Risk Communication

Risk communication attempts to convey information regarding risk to public health and safety and the environment. It involves more than the dissemination of accurate information. The communicator must begin early, identify and address the public's concerns, recognize the public as a legitimate partner, anticipate hostility, respond to the needs of the news media, and always be honest.

Crisis Management

The communications process is severely tested in crisis situations, which can take many forms. A common problem is the lack of crisis management plans even when a crisis is "smoldering."

Reputation Management

One of an organization's most valuable assets is its reputation. This asset is impacted by how the organization deals with conflict, particularly those crises that generate significant media attention. Using research to monitor reputation and making realistic responses after crises have passed can minimize damage to an organization's reputation. More important, returning to the proactive phase of conflict management to improve organizational performance will ultimately improve the organization's reputation.

Case Activity   Gun Control Crossfire at Starbucks

Management often has to take a position or stance in terms of how it deals with a particular conflict. Starbucks is a good example. It found itself in the middle of a debate over whether it would allow customers to carry firearms in its stores.

The debate started when gun advocates, citing the Second Amendment, claimed the right to carry holstered pistols in public places. The "open carry" movement tested its right by staging "meet-ups" at popular places such as Starbucks. Gun control advocates, on the other hand, say the law also gives a business the right to ban weapons from its premises. For example, Wal-Mart, Home Depot, and Peet's Coffee have banned guns from their stores.

Starbucks, however, has taken the position that it allows customers to carry guns in its stores only because it's complying with state laws that allow unconcealed firearms. The company's official statement is "The political, policy, and legal debates around these issues belong in the legislature and courts, not in our stores." It also has a business concern; it has 4,970 stores in the 43 states that have "open carry" laws and doesn't want to alienate gun advocates who are customers.

What Do You Think?

Should Starbucks serve gun-toting customers?

Gun control advocates, however, have petitioned Starbucks to ban firearms and have threatened a boycott. There have already been some incidents of anti-gun picketing at

Starbucks stores. Other observers say that gun-toting customers goes against Starbucks' finely cultivated image of making its stores a "home" where people can relax and socialize. Bob Walker, writing in the *New York Times* magazine, says "...the chain doesn't really sell coffee, it sells an experience."

What do you think of Starbucks' stance or position? Review the concepts given in this chapter of how organizations deal with conflict. If you were public relations counsel for Starbucks, what would you recommend regarding this conflict?

Questions   For Review and Discussion

1. Do you accept the proposition that conflict management is one of the most important functions of public relations? Why or why not?
2. What are the five steps in the issues management process?
3. How can effective issues management prevent organizational crises?
4. Both Exxon and Pepsi used defensive crisis communication strategies. However, one succeeded and the other failed. What factors do you think made the difference?
5. What is risk communication?
6. How would you use the contingency theory of conflict management (the continuum from accommodation to

advocacy) in advising management on a growing conflict situation?
7. Do you think that image restoration is merely a superficial fix or a substantive solution to adverse events? Support your view with some examples from current news stories.
8. Why would lawyers benefit from working closely with public relations counsel? For litigation? For dispute resolution through effective negotiation?
9. Do you think it is ethical for legal counsel to be assisted by public relations expertise?

Media Resources

Arpan, L. M., & Roskos-Ewoldsen, D. R. (2005). Stealing thunder: Analysis of the effects of proactive disclosure of crisis information. *Public Relations Review, 31*(3), 425–433.

Choi, Y., & Lin, Y.-H. (2009). Consumer responses to Mattel product recalls posted on online bulletin boards: Exploring two types of emotion. *Journal of Public Relations Research, 21*(2), 198–207.

Coombs, W. T. (2007). *Crisis management and communications.* Retrieved from Institute for Public Relations Essential Knowledge Project website: www.institute forpr.org

Coombs, W. T., & Holladay, S. J. (2009). Further explorations of post-crisis communication: Effects of media and response strategies on perceptions and intentions. *Public Relations Review, 35,* 1–6.

Donnely, J. (2010, Winter). Sudden impact: The effect of social technologies on reputation management. *Public Relations Strategist, 16*(1), 30–32.

Herman, M. L. (2009, April). A cowboy's guide to crisis management: Common-sense advice." *Public Relations Tactics,* 15.

Hwang, S., & Cameron, G. T. (2009). The estimation of a corporate crisis communication. *Public Relations Review, 35*(2), 136–138.

Jin, Y. (2009). The effects of public's cognitive appraisal of emotions in crises on crisis coping and strategy assessment. *Public Relations Review, 35,* 310–313.

Kim, J. R., & Kim, J.-N. (2010). A theoretical perspective on "Fear" as an organizational motivator for initiating public relations activities. *Public Relations Review, 36*(2), 184–186.

Kolek, J. (2009, Summer). Managing a crisis—and becoming a stronger organization. *The Strategist,* 36–38.

Lukaszewski, J. E. (2010, April 23). Metrics of crisis: Building effective plans [weblog message]. Retrieved from www.comPRehension.org

Mnookin, R. (2010). *Bargaining with the devil: When to negotiate, when to fight.* New York, NY: Simon & Schuster.

Raz, G. (2010, February 13). *When negotiating with a "devil" is the best course.* Retrieved from www.npr.org

Tinker, T. L., Dumlao, M., & McLaughlin, G. (2009, Summer). Effective social media strategies during times of crisis. *The Strategist,* 25–27.

PEARSON
mycommunicationlab

The Pearson Public Relations Podcast. "Crisis PR: Jack in the Box."

Reaching Diverse Audiences

After reading this chapter, you will be able to:

Understand the diversity of audiences in the United States

Gain insights on how to communicate with diverse audiences

Be familiar with the cultural values of Hispanic, black, and Asian audiences

Learn about public relations campaigns directed to specific audiences

Understand the characteristics of various age and lifestyle groups

A Multicultural Nation

If the audience on which public relations practitioners focus their messages were a monolithic whole, their work would be far easier—and far less stimulating. The audience, in fact, is just the opposite: It is a complex intermingling of groups with diverse cultural, ethnic, religious, and economic attributes that public relations professionals must understand and deal with every day.

Indeed, diversity is the most significant aspect of the mass audience in the United States. Today minorities constitute a third of the U.S. population, and the U.S. Census Bureau projects that they will constitute the majority of the total population by 2042. There are also major differences in geography, history, and economy among regions of the sprawling country; ranchers in Montana have different attitudes than residents in the heavily populated Eastern seaboard cities. Yet people in the two areas do have national interests in common. Ethnicity, generational differences, and socioeconomic status also shape the audience segments that public relations practitioners must address when planning a program or campaign.

For example, the American Heart Association (AHA) provides resources aimed at African American and Latino populations that reflect differences in culture for each that impact compliance with diet and lifestyle to ensure a healthy heart. The Power to End Stroke movement targets African Americans with a strategy to increase a sense of self-efficacy or personal empowerment over one's own health outcomes. Soul Food Recipes, an AHA-supported publication, facilitates healthy eating habits that reduce the risk of stroke.

Many product launches and other public relations campaigns also target specific audiences. McDonald's, for example, promoted its new McCafé espresso-based drinks to the African American community in Chicago. In another campaign, the fast-food chain sponsored a traveling exhibit with Latin music artifacts that led up to its sponsorship of the Latin Grammy Awards in Houston. Allstate Insurance kicked off a "Give Back" day on Martin Luther King's birthday to encourage more volunteerism in the black community. And Subaru reached out to the Asian community in the San Francisco Bay area by partnering with the Asian Foundation to encourage Asian Americans to get tested for Hepatitis B, a condition for which the group is at high risk.

> All marketing efforts are wasted if they aren't culturally competent.
>
> *Michael Soon Lee, president of EthnoConnect*

Such ethnic campaigns, however, are only one aspect of reaching diverse audiences. Public relations campaigns are also designed to reach specific audiences that are defined by age, gender, income, and lifestyle. Technology is often used to segment the mass audience and compile related valuable information about target audiences. Geographic and social statistics found in Census Bureau reports provide a rich foundation. Much of these data can be broken down by census tract and zip code. Data on automobile registrations, voter registrations, sales figures, mailing lists, and church and organization membership also can be merged into computer databases.

One marketing research organization, Claritas Inc., has divided the Chicago metropolitan area into 62 lifestyle clusters. It has also assigned a name to each cluster; for example, "Boomers & Babies," whose buying habits, Claritas says, include "rent more than five videos a month, buy children frozen dinners, read parenting magazines."

The Internet and other related technologies also enable public relations efforts to be more efficient and effective in reaching diverse audiences, but they also require greater cultural literacy among public relations professionals to plan campaigns that are tailored to specific audiences and their particular lifestyles. An integral part of this planning is understanding what media channels are most appropriate for reaching a particular public.

The following sections will explore these aspects by providing information about (1) ethnically diverse audiences, (2) age group audiences, and (3) gender/lifestyle audiences.

Reaching Ethnic Audiences

Historically, the United States has welcomed millions of immigrants and assimilated them into the cultural mainstream. They bring a bubbling mixture of personal values, habits, and perceptions that are absorbed slowly, sometimes reluctantly. The question of assimilation somewhat pertains to all immigrant groups, whether they are from Ireland, Poland, Cuba, or the Philippines. It also pertains to two minorities that have a long history in the United States: African Americans and Native Americans. This diversity is a great strength of the United States, but also a source of friction and, at times, negative stereotyping.

Recently, the easily identifiable ethnic groups—primarily Hispanics, African Americans, and Asian Americans—have been growing faster than the general population, with nonwhite ethnic groups now comprising a majority in some states, including California. According to the U.S. Census Bureau, Hispanics and African Americans now constitute about 15 percent and 13 percent of the U.S. population, respectively, for a total of 28 percent. Whites are 66 percent, and Asian Americans and Native Americans comprise the remaining percent. According to the Census Bureau, even greater changes will occur by 2050. Notably, Hispanics will comprise nearly 30 percent of the U.S. population. (See Figure 11.1.)

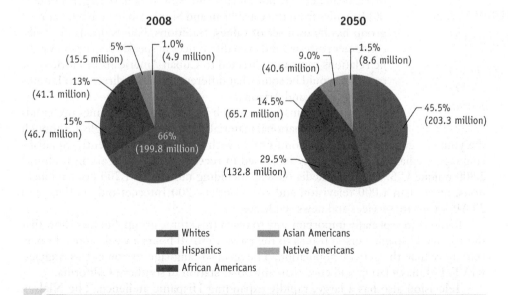

Figure 11.1   Projected Demographic Shifts in the U.S. Population: 2008 to 2050

Source: U.S. Census Bureau.

Such statistics place a strong focus on diversity and multiculturalism in the workplace (internal publics) as well as how public relations and marketing experts communicate with these groups as citizens and consumers. The stakes are high. In terms of disposable income, significant amounts of money are involved. The discretionary income of Hispanics is the highest among minority groups. It is now almost $900 billion and is estimated to be at least $1.2 trillion by 2012. African American buying power is an estimated $800 billion. Asian Americans have about $600 billion in discretionary income, whereas Native Americans—the smallest of the four minority groups—have about $53 billion in buying power, according to the Selig Center for Economic Development at the University of Georgia.

Hispanics

The Hispanic/Latino population is the largest and fastest-growing demographic group in the United States. There are currently about 46 million, making up nearly one in six residents. By 2050, the U.S. Census Bureau estimates that the Hispanic population will be more than 130 million. As a result, public relations campaigns are increasingly focused on reaching this important buying public. Colgate, for example, has targeted mothers in its "El Mes de la Salud Cucal" campaign to promote oral health because the company recognized the importance of maternal influence in Hispanic culture. Heineken's recent "Demuestra Quein Eres" ("Give Yourself a Good Name") Mural Arts Series tapped into Latino cultural pride and male emphasis on establishing reputation.

> In the 2010 census, we'll see confirmation of a shift from Hispanic consumers who are first generation, where Spanish is the dominant language, to second generation, bilingual, bicultural consumers. It totally transforms how we market.
>
> *Cynthia McFarlane, chair of Publicis Groupe's Conill, a Latino agency, in* Brandweek

It's simplistic, however, to think of the Hispanic public as a single entity. First, they represent the heritage of more than 20 nations, ranging from Spain to Mexico, the Caribbean, and South America. On a national basis, about two-thirds of the Hispanic population is of Mexican heritage but Florida and New York have larger numbers of Hispanics from the Caribbean and South America. Each national group has its own set of values, traditions, beliefs, foods, festivals, consumer patterns, and even differences in speaking Spanish. A public relations campaign directed to Cuban Americans in Florida, for example, would be somewhat different from one directed to Latinos living in Texas and Arizona.

In general, market research indicates that Hispanics prefer ads and other informational materials in Spanish over English, although the younger generation is more comfortable with English. Consequently, Spanish-language media have dramatically increased in recent years. There are now almost 2,500 unique U.S. Hispanic media outlets, including more than 1,200 print publications, more than 1,000 television and radio outlets, 200 Internet-only outlets, and 20 AP-style wire services and news syndicates.

Radio is an especially important way to reach this ethnic group. Surveys show that the average Hispanic person listens to the radio 26 to 30 hours a week, about 13 percent more than the general population. The Spanish-language station in Los Angeles, KLVE-FM, has a larger audience than any other station in southern California.

Television also has a large, rapidly expanding Hispanic audience. The Nielsen rating service estimated that the number of Hispanic households rose by 4.3 percent in 2008–2009. Univision, the predominant Spanish-language TV network, claims to reach three-fourths of Hispanic viewers. Univision consistently has ranked fourth or fifth among all broadcast networks in the 18–34 demographic, according to Nielsen's

E.R.A.S.E.

This poster, in Spanish, was used by Fleishman-Hillard public relations during its campaign with New York City schools to raise awareness among students and their parents about the symptoms of asthma. In English, the poster is titled "Asthma Alert: Does your child have asthma?"

National Television Index. The Spanish-language TV network Telemundo is also making impressive market share gains. Indeed, the Pew Hispanic Center found that nearly all Hispanics (91 percent) have access to Spanish-language television stations at home and that even highly assimilated Latinos (46 percent) watch Spanish-language programming. The Pew study concludes that Spanish-language TV is an opportunity to reach across the assimilation spectrum.

Hispanic audiences, particularly the younger generation, have also turned to online sources. In fact, Matthew Robson of Morgan Stanley bank states, "There is no statistical difference between Hispanic youth and the general youth population in relation to their heavy use of social media like Facebook." As a result, the use of social marketing and networks among Latinos has expanded. For example, American Airlines used Twitter and Facebook to promote its AA Advantage program to Hispanic audiences in the United States. Fleishman-Hillard is working with the Boy Scouts of the United States to create bilingual social media components on *Scouting.org* to "reintroduce Scouting to America."

It is important, however, to understand that traditional and online media need more than news releases and features translated into Spanish. The messages must also be relevant to the audience, with themes important to the audience such as family, education, and health.

African Americans

There are more than 40 million African Americans, according to the U.S Census Bureau, and they have the longest history in the United States as a minority group. But they are not necessarily a homogeneous group. One distinction is their geographical origin. One group are citizens whose African relatives were first brought to this country in the 1800s as slaves. A second, more recent group are blacks with Hispanic or Caribbean origin, who tend to self-identify as Hispanic. The terms "African American" and "black" are often used interchangeably in marketing and public relations contexts.

Another distinction is income level. In recent years, the number of black households with $75,000+ income has risen to about 2.5 million. "The world is now a different place for the affluent African American demographic," said Len Burnett, cofounder of specialty magazine *Uptown*. "Luxury brands understand the importance of niche shoppers with disposable income and Uptown delivers them efficiently." Other marketing research found that affluent blacks are more likely than other consumers to spend money on fashionable dress, toiletries, cosmetics, and cruise vacations. See the Insights box on page 278 about Royal Caribbean's outreach to the black community.

The Urban Market is often associated with African Americans even though it is not necessarily urban nor restricted to people of African descent. Rather, the Urban Market is defined by fashion trends set by hip-hop music stars, and extends principally to members of Generations X and Y of all ethnic backgrounds. Nevertheless, 40 percent of African Americans live in the 10 largest U.S. cities, mostly in the South and Mid-Atlantic regions.

Public relations professionals, however, need to ensure that programs and product packaging don't reinforce negative stereotypes. A good example of racial insensitivity was the traditional figure of Aunt Jemima on packages of Quaker Oats food products. Her image was widely regarded in the black community as a patronizing stereotype. To change this perception, Quaker Oats cooperated with the National Council of Negro Women to honor outstanding African American women in local communities, who then competed for a national award. At the local award breakfasts, all food served was Aunt Jemima brands, and Quaker Oats officials participated in the programs. The project generated an atmosphere of mutual understanding.

The black media are less extensive than Hispanic media. Two possible reasons are that African Americans have a longer history in the United States and that English is their native language, as opposed to media that use Spanish or an Asian language such as Chinese to serve their audiences. Currently, there are only about 175 black newspapers in the United States, but the Black Entertainment Television Network has a large national audience, as do such magazines as *Ebony* and *Essence*. Business Wire's "Black PR Wire" lists more than a thousand black-owned publications and journalists.

Asian Americans

In general, Asian Americans are the most affluent and well-educated minority group. Of the almost 16 million Asians in the United States, two-thirds of the adults have at least a bachelor's degree and 20 percent have a master's degree or higher. In addition, the median household income is over $65,000. For Indian-Asian Americans, many of whom work in the high-technology industry, the median family income is $69,000, according to the U.S. Census Bureau.

Asian Americans, however, are just as diverse as Hispanics. Indeed, there are 17 major Asian groups, each of which has its own language and culture. India, with a population of more than 1 billion, is a totally different culture from that of Thailand or China. There are even generational differences within each group. For example, the lifestyles, values, and interests of fourth-generation Korean Americans in Los Angeles are dramatically different from those of Koreans who have recently arrived in the United States.

Thus, the practitioner must define the audience with particular care and sensitivity, taking into account race but increasingly also considering the cultural and ethnic self-identity of many target audience segments. Citizens of Indian descent, for example, often prefer to call themselves Indian Americans because they feel their culture and long history as a civilization are unique.

Indian Americans, for example, prefer English to receive information, but public relations professionals should use cultural cues such as a few Hindi words, music, or images. Other tips for effectively reaching Indian Americans include: (1) using messages related to India because most citizens maintain close ties with their heritage and relatives back in India, (2) emphasizing family relationships, and (3) harnessing online media because the majority of Indian Americans spend time researching products online and 40 percent visit social networks.

The Asian American press, because of language diversity and culture, is fairly numerous but highly concentrated. California, for example, is home to 70 percent of the nation's more than 650 Asian American–focused television channels, radio stations, and newspapers. Common languages used include Chinese, Vietnamese, Korean, and Hindi. For example, television newscasts on KTSF reach 82,000 Cantonese speakers each night in the area around San Francisco, a region where almost 20 percent of the population is Asian.

Understanding Ethnic Values

Although the sensitive communicator needs to take into consideration the differences in nationality, language, generations, and cultural values, there are some general guidelines. Fernando Figueredo, head of the multicultural practice for Porter Novelli, says there are some unique characteristics shared by the top three minority groups—Hispanics, African Americans, and Asian Americans.

Figueredo, writing in *The Strategist*, says, "These include a deep family network with a strong mother or father figure, music, food, religion, and strong bonds between friends and family." He also says that multicultural consumers tend to be more loyal to brands that make an attempt to reach them in ways that are culturally relevant. He continues, "Whether through advertising, in-store promotions, or special festivals and events, reaching consumers in their culture has a strong impact on new and repeat purchases."

> We're trying to get the U.S. Hispanic consumer to not only honor their family and friends, but showcase the cultural beauty of the Latin Community.
>
> *Vincent Young, director of brand marketing for Kodak, in an interview with PRWeek*

A strong community relations program is one way to effectively reach ethnic audiences. Indeed, many major corporations such as McDonald's, Coke, and Pepsi have spent considerable money and time developing community-based programs. In terms of product promotion, Kodak teamed up with Yahoo en Espanol for a campaign titled "Muestra Tu Herencia" ("Show Your Heritage"), which encouraged Hispanics to share photos displaying their heritage online. Kodak created an online mosaic of the images and, for each one uploaded, donated $2 to the Hispanic College Fund. See also the Insights box on page 278 on an African American art auction sponsored by Royal Caribbean Cruises.

State Farm is a good example of a company tailoring public relations programs for specific audiences. To reach Hispanics, the insurance company partnered with the Univision network on Web novellas that feature messages about being there for friends and family. For Asian Americans, the company provided online video contests through social media. For the black community, it promoted "The 50 Million Pound Challenge" with fitness expert Dr. Ian Smith as the spokesperson. A website and blogs were used to build an online community.

on the job

INSIGHTS

A Cruise Ship Line Builds Brand Identity with African Americans

African Americans are traveling in greater numbers and the competition for their business is intense. Royal Caribbean International, working with Fleishman-Hillard public relations, decided on a cause-marketing strategy that would benefit the local community.

The format was a free, live art auction series held on docked cruise ships in Los Angeles, Baltimore, and Miami. It showcased art donated by nationally acclaimed African American artists, and all proceeds supported summer art programs for African American teens in those cities.

The auctions generated more than $20,000 for local art programs and, at the same time, generated extensive coverage in the African American media. In terms of establishing brand awareness, 95 percent of the attendees said they were likely to

Cause Marketing

A work by an African American artist that was part of the Royal Caribbean's art auction to benefit local art programs for black teenagers.

take a Royal Caribbean cruise. Other African American groups also have inquired about holding charitable events aboard the ships.

Other companies, such as Allstate and American Airlines, have sponsored community-based events during the Asian Lunar New Year celebration that is significant for many Asian cultures. "Marketing to Asians during the Lunar New Year is one of the most important mechanisms for PR pros to recognize, show respect for, and strengthen brand relationships with Asian consumers," says Saul Girlin, executive vice president of K&L marketing services.

Figueredo gives five basic concepts that should be considered when developing a communications campaign for multicultural consumers:

1. Organize a team with an inherent understanding of the customs and values of the various demographic groups you are trying to reach.

2. Understand that consumers of diverse cultural backgrounds respond better to messages that are culturally relevant.

3. Remember that consumers of diverse cultural backgrounds are extremely loyal and once your products and services become part of their lives, there is a very good chance you will keep them.

4. Use the primary language of the audience. A large portion of your target audience prefers to communicate in their primary language, even if they also have strong English skills.

5. Use spokespersons that represent the audience. The spokesperson must be able to be a good communicator and be sensitive to the issues that are important to the audience.

Although this book has emphasized the three major minority groups, it should be noted that there are any number of other ethnic communities in the United States that add to the diversity of the population. The *Gale Directory*, for example, lists publications in 48 languages other than English.

Reaching Diverse Age Groups

As the demographic makeup of the United States continues to change, three major age groups deserve special attention. They are youth and young adults, baby boomers, and seniors. The following is a brief snapshot of each group.

The Millennial Generation

Individuals born after 1980 are now called the Millennial Generation because many of them entered the workforce at the start of the 21st century. This generation has also been called the Y Generation because the previous generation, born between 1964 and 1980, is called the X Generation by sociologists and other pundits.

Public relations professionals recognize the importance of the youth market. Children, teenagers, and college students represent an important demographic to marketers because they influence their parents' buying decisions, have their own purchasing power, and are becoming adult consumers. According to the consumer market research company Packaged Facts, today's youth market (15- to 24-year-olds) has over $350 billion of purchasing power.

In a *pr reporter* article, Marianne Friese of Ketchum succinctly stated the importance of the youth audience: "They rival the baby boom in sheer size and their global purchasing power is enormous." Today's children have greater autonomy and decision-making power within the family than in previous generations.

Because they are such voracious consumers of digital media, some pundits have labeled today's youth audience as the *E-Generation*. The Nielsen Company, for example, says that the average mobile teen racks up about 3,000 phone calls and texts a month. In addition, the Pew Research Center found that (1) 95 percent of millennials use a cell phone, (2) 75 percent have posted a profile to a social networking site, and (3) 20 percent have posted a video of themselves online. See the Ethics box on page 280 about how these actions may impact their future employment. The Fortino Group (Pittsburgh) projects that the millennial generation will spend 23 years online. Spending one-third of their lives online will have interesting impacts:

> Today's teenagers, part of the generation of people who have never experienced communication in a world without the Internet, are self-taught masters of social technology and can seamlessly weave this social media Web into their lives.
>
> *Position paper, EURO RSCG Worldwide PR*

- They will spend equal time interacting with friends online and in person.
- Initial interaction online will precede most dating and marriages.
- They will spend more time online than in interaction with parents by tenfold.
- They will be more reserved in social skills.
- They will be savvy and skeptical about online identities such as chat participants.

on the job

ETHICS

Millennials: Will They Give Up Social Networking for a Job?

According to surveys, most teenagers, and even college students, are somewhat addicted to online social networking. In fact, one study found that 70 percent of teenagers participate in social networking for an hour or more on a daily basis. Other surveys say teenagers place about 3,000 phone calls and texts per month.

In sum, social networking has become so central to teens' lifestyles that 60 percent of teens surveyed in the 2009 Junior Achievement/ Deloitte Teen Ethics Survey said they would consider their inability to access networking sites during working hours a deal-breaker in considering a job offer. According to the survey researchers, "This comes as many organizations have begun implementing policies that limit access to social networks during the work day due to concern about unethical usage, such as time theft, spreading rumors about co-workers, and leaking proprietary information, among other reasons."

Such policies, of course, raise some interesting issues as recent high school and college graduates enter the workforce. One key issue is the matter of ethical sensitivity to the perceptions and expectations of others such as employers. The Junior Achievement/Deloitte survey found that teenagers rarely consider the impact of their postings. There is the additional problem of young people who think there is nothing wrong with talking on their cell phones, texting, and even checking their e-mail while they are with friends or sitting at the family dinner table. How will this translate to the workforce when, for example, they start texting and surfing the Net while their boss is conducting a staff meeting?

Ainar D. Aijala, global managing partner of Deloitte Touche, says, "From an employer's perspective, it's clear that organizations need enhanced training and communication relative to social networking. This is particularly the case when more than half of the future talent pool feels so strongly about social networking that their ability to access those sites would play into the decision to take a job."

Do you think employers are justified to restrict online social networking while at work? Would you decline a job offer if the employer blocked Facebook and other social networking sites during working hours? Should employers give employees training about the ethical use of social networking sites? What are the ethical responsibilities of the employee?

- They will not tolerate print forms, slow application processes, or archaic systems.

Millennials value relationships and trust. In a survey of 1,200 teens worldwide, Ketchum's Global Brand Marketing Practice found:

- Parents still rule when it comes to advice about careers and drugs, and even for product decisions.
- Trust in information is derived from relationships.
- The top five sources of advice are parents, doctors, clergy, friends, and teachers.
- As avid and skilled Internet users, millennials remain savvy about unfiltered and unpoliced content.
- Teens also recognize the credibility of editorial content compared to ads and even public service announcements, with television being the most trusted medium for them.
- Publicity for products and issues will include millennials, whether messages are directed at them or at those to whom they look for advice. See the Insights box on page 282 for a campaign by 7-Eleven.

Baby Boomers

This age group, born between 1946 and 1964, represents the tidal wave of Americans born after World War II, when thousands of GIs returned home and started raising families. Today, as a large percentage of these men and women begin to add a "6" to their birthdays, they comprise a market of 78 million people, or about 24 percent of the U.S. population. They have about $3 trillion in buying power, include many of the country's current business and political leaders, and are active users of the Internet.

Baby boomers, unlike their parents' generation, grew up in an age of prosperity and continue to have few qualms about spending on consumer goods instead of saving for retirement, although the economic recession of 2009 changed many of their spending habits. Because of their wealth and numbers, many corporations and non-profit groups have taken a keen interest in reaching this market. Toyota, for example, has promoted its Highlander by tailoring communications to baby boomers who now have "empty nests" because their children are in college or have already established their own careers. One ad, for example, emphasizes the message "For your newfound freedom."

> The boomers offer an audience that has assets, not allowances.
>
> *Henry Schleiff, president of Hallmark Channels*

The oldest boomers will turn 65 in 2011 and are starting to share many of the same concerns as their immediate elders, the seniors, who will be discussed next. In other words, they are naturally concerned about health care, insurance, retirement planning, personal investing, and other issues. But it should also be remembered that about 60 percent of the beer and carbonated beverages in the country are purchased by boomers. Companies such as Procter & Gamble and L'Oreal Paris are also seeing the demand for new products that cater to mature adults who lead active lifestyles and want to look vibrant and healthy, not necessarily younger.

Even the Centers for Disease Control and Prevention (CDC) is tailoring its public service announcements to boomers. One public service announcement (PSA) about colorectal cancer, the second-leading cancer killer in the United States, targeted the

on the job
INSIGHTS

Youth Urged to Drink Coffee, Support a Cause

Today's youth tend to prefer cold beverages and snacks, but 7-Eleven stores started a campaign designed to make them fans of the chain's coffee. The idea was to introduce limited-edition 20-ounce cups designed by entertainment and sports celebrities. Proceeds from the cups would go to the celebrities' charities of choice, and 7-Eleven was prepared to donate up to $300,000 for each charity, depending on cup sales.

"What we really understand about millennials is their interest in community relations," said Rita Bargerhuff, chief marketing officer of 7-Eleven, in an interview with *PRWeek*. She continued, "This program looked like a winner because it tied charitable giving to celebrities—two hot buttons for

millennials. Plus it ties back to our coffee business."

Ketchum communications was used to design an integrated campaign, mostly using Twitter and Facebook channels to create awareness. The featured celebrities on the cups,

for example, were asked to Tweet about the campaign to their followers. Ketchum also conducted media outreach to local and national newspapers and broadcast stations. One tactic was to deliver samples of the celebrity cups to local radio station DJs.

50+ age group with a message about being around for their children and grandchildren. Patricia Cook, vice president of Ogilvy Public Relations Worldwide, who produced the PSA for the CDC, told *PRWeek*, "The idea of being there for your children and grandchildren is powerful. Messages about how to stay healthy and enjoy life as long as possible were found to be important to the over 50 age group."

Baby boomers, as a result of growing up in the 1960s and 1970s, also tend to be what one writer describes as a "rather active, socially conscious bunch." Catherine Welker of Strauss Radio Strategies told *PRWeek*, "Many are parents, voters, retirees, and potentially have disposable income. This is a generation most likely to get involved in a cause." According to the U.S. Census Bureau, about 60 million baby boomers have already reached the age of 55; they are rapidly becoming the new seniors.

Seniors

This group frequently is defined as men and women 65 years or older, although some sociologists and marketing experts, including the American Association of Retired Persons (AARP), include everyone over age 50. However, a typical 50-year-old in good health and working full-time usually doesn't quite see himself or herself as a "senior."

Medical advances have improved life expectancy to the point that today, almost 36.3 million Americans are age 65 or older (12 percent of the population), according to the U.S. Census Bureau. A heavy upsurge in the senior population will occur in 2011, when the post–World War II baby boomers begin to reach age 65. These older citizens form an important opinion group and a consumer market with special interests.

When appealing to seniors, public relations people should try to ignore the stereotypes of "old folks" so often depicted in the movies and television. Some 80-year-old women sit in rocking chairs, knitting or snoozing, but others cheer and boo ardently while watching professional basketball on television. Nor are all grandfathers crotchety complainers with quavering voices or kindly patriarchs who fly kites with their grandsons. As many differences in personality, interest, financial status, and living styles exist in the older audience as among their young-adult grandchildren.

Public relations practitioners should remember these characteristics of seniors:

- With the perspective of long experience, they often are less easily convinced than young adults, demand value in the things they buy, and pay little attention to fads.

- They vote in greater numbers than their juniors and are more intense readers of newspapers and magazines. Retirees also watch television heavily.

- They form an excellent source of volunteers for social, health, and cultural organizations because they have time and often are looking for something to do.

- They are extremely health-conscious, out of self-interest, and want to know about medical developments. A Census Bureau study showed that most people over age 65 say they are in good health; not until their mid-80s do they frequently need assistance in daily living.

Financially, the elderly are better off than the stereotypes suggest. The poverty rate among older Americans (9.8 percent) is slightly below that of the population at large (12.5 percent). The Census Bureau found that people ages 65 to 74 have more discretionary income than any other group, with median assets of $108,885. A large percentage own their own homes without a mortgage, and they hold 70 percent of the country's assets.

Although they are poor customers for household goods, they eat out frequently and do much gift buying. They travel frequently. In fact, seniors account for about 80 percent of commercial vacation travel, especially cruises. All public relations personnel working in the restaurant, travel, and tourism industries should be particularly cognizant of this audience and how to effectively communicate with them. Even toy companies find seniors a lucrative market because grandparents tend to spoil their grandchildren.

In terms of media consumption, seniors do spend 30 percent more time watching TV and 25 percent more time reading a daily newspaper than the average U.S. adult, according to the Center for Media Research. But they are also becoming more active on the Internet; almost 20 million regularly go online to check their e-mail, download maps, check the weather, and pay bills. Facebook even reports that the fastest-growing demographic for new members is the over-55 group, as seniors connect with their children and grandchildren.

Gender/Lifestyle Audiences

Women

Diversity also includes gender. Women of all nationalities and ethnic groups have always been an important audience for such corporations as Procter & Gamble that manufacture numerous household products.

Indeed, Ketchum communications makes the point, "Today's women hold an overwhelming share of consumer purchasing influence, making more than 80 percent of household purchase decisions, and spending over $3.3 trillion annually." Given these statistics, it is no surprise that women are also emerging as "influentials" in a variety of campaigns for a spectrum of companies.

The Ketchum research, conducted by the University of Southern California's Annenberg Strategic Public Relations Centre, also found that women aged 25 to 54 are not only "super consumers" but are much faster than men to embrace some new media, such as social networking sites, and also to use corporate websites.

Other research studies have identified a segment called "supermoms" in terms of opinion leadership and word-of-mouth influence. These women, about 5.4 percent of mothers, have such characteristics as (1) they have at least 75 friends with whom they keep in touch, (2) they give their friends advice on what to buy and restaurants to try, (3) they spend at least nine hours a week on the Internet, and (4) they participate in online chats and discussions. Given these data, companies such as Procter & Gamble and Georgia Pacific's Dixie Brand have used these supermoms to find out their opinions and also to have them sample new products, with the idea that their word-of-mouth influence will motivate other women to buy the product.

> More seminars and workshops are focusing on the fact that diversity in the workplace isn't just about race or gender, it's also about age.
>
> *Jeffrey Zaslow, reporter for the* Wall Street Journal

Companies have also been paying attention to what have been called "mommy bloggers." Campbell Soup Company, for example, invited 11 mom bloggers to corporate headquarters to start a dialogue about the company's policies and products. Other companies, such as Graco, have also engaged in dialogue with mom bloggers and even started their own mommy blogs and branded Twitter accounts.

The research also found that three-fourths of the supermoms are employed outside the home. In fact, women now constitute 50 percent of the American workforce. But women in the workplace are also a diverse group, with differing ideas about work ethics, dress codes, and putting in long hours.

Sociologists say that, for the first time, there are actually four generations of women (and men) in the workplace, which often requires some management sensitivity and diversity training. Baby boomers and seniors, for example, often have a different work ethic than Generation X and Y women, who seem to be less committed to working long hours or making the extra effort. There's also a generational gap in terms of dress codes. Younger women prefer to dress more casually and to some, more provocatively, which upsets the baby boomers and seniors, who grew up with a more formal dress code.

The Gay/Lesbian Community

The gay community is now a mainstream demographic. According to a yearly census conducted by Jeff Garber, president of OpusComm Group, the SI Newhouse School of Public Communications at Syracuse University, and Scarborough Research, between

22 and 30 million gay, lesbian, bisexual, and transgendered people (GLBT) live in the United States, or about 8 percent of the population. Their per capita buying power, however, is estimated at $45,300 per year and they tend to be highly educated.

> LBGT consumers are very vigilant about companies and what their policies are and how they understand the LGBT consumers.
>
> *Howard Buford, CEO of PrimeAccess*

According to Garber, the gay community has high brand loyalty. A research study by marketing agency Prime Access and PlanetOut, for example, found that more than two-thirds of GLBT consumers said they are more likely to buy products from a company perceived to be gay-friendly. They tend to purchase products that target advertisements to gay consumers and support gay issues. Subaru pioneered gay-specific advertising in 1996 with a campaign targeting lesbian consumers using gay tennis star Martina Navratilova as a spokesperson. The Internet travel site Orbitz, Absolut Vodka, and Ford have also concentrated on attracting gay audiences.

The Greater Philadelphia Tourism Marketing Corporation (GPTMC) tapped into gay buying power when it decided to launch a "Get Your History Straight and Your Nightlife Gay" campaign in order to generate more tourism for the city. It produced a 36-page trip planner for gays. Gay and lesbian media and travel professionals were contacted, news releases were sent to gay/lesbian publications, and two familiarization trips for journalists were conducted. The campaign got widespread coverage in the gay and mainstream press, including the *Daily Show with Jon Stewart*. The campaign's website usage increased 1,000 percent, and more than 1,000 hotel packages were sold. For another example of a gay campaign, see the PR Casebook on page 286.

Media targeted to gay and lesbian consumers have grown over the last two decades. Magazines such as *Out* and *Advocate*, and the cable network Logo, focus exclusively on gay themes. Mainstream television shows featuring gay themes, such as *Will & Grace* and *Queer Eye for the Straight Guy*, and the 2005 film *Brokeback Mountain* have attracted gay and straight audiences alike.

In a more recent development, gays are being incorporated into mainstream commercials. Unilever, for example, hired three actors to play a girl's best gay friends in a campaign to introduce Sunsilk shampoo to the United States. They were positioned as style experts who wrote advice columns in magazines such as *Cosmopolitan* diagnosing consumers' hair problems.

Religious Groups

The United States is predominantly a Christian nation, but there is a great deal of diversity among various religious groups. Catholics constitute the largest single group, with about 70 million followers, making the United States the fourth largest Catholic nation in the world. Other large denominations include the Southern Baptist Convention, with 16 million members, and the United Methodist Church, with 8 million followers. There are, however, other major religions represented. For instance, there are about 6 million Jews and about 2.5 million Muslims living in the United States.

Christian Evangelicals Members of religious groups express a great deal of diversity in terms of attitudes and opinions about a variety of topics, but a highly visible element is the evangelical Christian right. In general, they have strong opinions about preserving traditional family values, supporting prayer in public schools, and voting for conservative politicians. They typically are opposed to civil rights for gays and

PRCasebook

Getting the Word Out on Gay Tourism

According to the International Gay and Lesbian Travel Association (IGLTA), the gay tourism market tops $645 billion per year in the United States. More than 75 cities and several states sponsor public relations efforts to encourage GLBT (gay, lesbian, bisexual, and transgendered) people to visit. New York City, for example, launched "The Rainbow Pilgrimage," a campaign to promote GLBT travel. The initiative commemorated the 40th anniversary of the Stonewall Riots, the beginning of the gay rights movement in New York.

The IGLTA promoted GLBT Pride events in more than a dozen cities between August and November 2009. Pride events, they note, are defined by the Human Right Campaign as providing community members the "unique opportunity to celebrate and mobilize around key issues." In 2008–2009, a key issue was same-sex marriage. Although voters in California defeated Proposition 8, which would have legalized gay marriage, several states such as Maine, Vermont, and Iowa passed amendments in favor of same-sex unions. Vermont has been particularly active in promoting the state as a destination for GLBT travel. The Vermont Gay Tourist Association stresses how the state not only offers "picturesque and idyllic places to celebrate a honeymoon," but that "even the older generations don't bat an eyelid at queer couples walking hand in hand into local shops and restaurants."

Yet not all residents or politicians are as eager to have their state known as a destination of GLBT couples. When a poster announcing, "South Carolina is so Gay!" was posted in an Underground station during London's Gay Pride Week, the "low-level" staffer in the South Carolina Department of Parks, Recreations, and Tourism who'd signed off on the initiative was fired. Now disgraced Governor Mark Sanford labeled the posters "inappropriate." State Representative David Thomas worried that taxpayers would be "irate" to learn that tax dollars had been used to promote homosexuality. "We're so gay?" Charleston resident Ventphis Stafford asked rhetorically. "Nah. Wrong state. Go to California." Given the size of the market, however, one wonders whether Thomas, Stafford, or the head of the South Carolina Department of Tourism would be so quick to deny the influx of dollars, euros, or pounds brought the state by GLBT couples.

- Why should organizations pay attention to niche markets such as the GLBT community?
- How can messages that target a niche market avoid backlash or reinforcement of stereotypes?
- What would be some public relations strategies to effectively reach these emerging gender and lifestyle audiences?

PEARSON
mycommunicationlab

lesbians, sex education in the schools, and abortion. Movies such as *The Passion of the Christ* and *The DaVinci Code* have served as a focal point around which such groups have expressed their disapproval through rallies and protests outside theaters. Such groups also express themselves by calling for boycotts of companies who have benefits for same-sex partners or make donations to Planned Parenthood. Disney theme parks and cruise ships, for example, have also generated their wrath by providing same-sex partner benefits and offering gay marriage packages.

The Jewish Community   This audience, which has a long history of fighting against discrimination of any kind, tends to be more liberal on social issues. Jews strongly supported the civil rights movement in the 1960s and tend to vote for Democratic Party candidates. In the 2008 presidential election, for example, almost 80 percent of the Jewish community voted for Barack Obama. The Jewish community also has a reputation for being well organized, active in political fund-raising, and influential on pending legislation. The American Israel Public Affairs Committee (AIPAC), for example, is considered one of the most powerful lobbying groups in Washington, D.C. It has a record of successfully promoting legislation and influencing foreign policy favorable to Israel's national interest.

The Muslim Community   An increasingly visible group in the United States is the Muslim population, which now numbers more than 2.5 million individuals. There is a stereotype that all Muslims come from the Middle East, but the reality is that Muslims represent a variety of ethnic groups and come from a variety of nations, including those in Asia, Europe, and parts of Africa.

Companies are now recognizing the spending power of the Muslim population, which is estimated to be about $200 billion. Best Buy, for example, wished its Muslim consumers "Happy Eid-al-Adha" in its advertising and promotions, although it got criticism from some of its other customers. And Western Union focused a public relations campaign around the celebration of Ramadan. The company hosted a "Fly Home" contest where Western Union customers from the Middle East and Pakistan could win airplane tickets. "Ramadan is one of the key sending periods for our customers," explained Maher Kayali, marketing manager for Western Union in the Middle East and Pakistan. See the Multicultural World box on page 288 for a campaign aimed at Muslim women in Pakistan. Because a large Muslim population is in the Detroit area, McDonald's restaurants there now offer halal chicken McNuggets.

In sum, public relations professionals must be attuned to the sensitivities of religious groups and be prepared to engage in conflict management. How would you handle, for example, a threat by a conservative Christian group to boycott your company's products because the company offers same-sex health benefits to employees? Or what would you do to ensure that Jewish employees can fully participate in Passover and other Holy Days? How would you accommodate Muslim employees who, as part of their religion, pray to Mecca five times a day? It is an increasingly diverse marketplace in which public relations staffs must walk a tightrope in attempting to serve varied and often conflicting religious audiences.

The Disability Community

The disability community, like all other groups, is very diverse. There are those who are in wheelchairs, blind, or deaf, but there also are people who have learning, behavioral, or speech disabilities. Many recognize they are disabled, but others—such as aging baby boomers—are often in denial that their hearing, eyesight, or mobility is gradually diminishing.

Although disabled individuals are only a fraction of the total population, public relations practitioners should be sensitive to their needs and how to effectively communicate with them. Often, one feels uncomfortable around the disabled. As Barbara Bianchi-Kai, a specialist in disability marketing, writes in *The Strategist*, "We're afraid of offending the person through our actions or our language choices."

She goes on to say that it's okay to use the word *deaf* instead of *hearing impaired*, but that it's more proper to use *mobility impaired* or *physically disabled*, than *handicapped*, for people who have difficulty moving. It's not okay to use such terms as *crippled*.

As in any communication, language and the medium are key elements. Many deaf people, for example, use American Sign Language (ASL) as their first language. If you can't communicate in ASL, it's best to produce brochures, newsletters, and specialized

on the job

A MULTICULTURAL WORLD

Women as a Special Audience: Breast Cancer Awareness in Pakistan

The Women's Empowerment Group, a non-governmental organization (NGO) in Pakistan, had a major public relations challenge. Statistics showed that the country had the highest rate of breast cancer of any Asian nation. However, Pakistan's conservative Muslim society made public discussion of anything related to women's breasts a very sensitive topic. Indeed, the majority of Pakistani women were reluctant to be examined by doctors because of shyness and social customs.

Given this situation, the Women's Empowerment Group

sought to break the taboos by first enlisting the support of the prime minister's wife to launch the first-ever nationwide Breast Cancer Awareness Campaign. Its primary objectives were to (1) make breast cancer an acceptable topic in the public domain of Pakistan, (2) create widespread awareness about breast cancer among urban and rural women, and (3) promote understanding and the practice of self-examination.

The tactics used included: (1) distribution, through utility bills, health clinics, and women's colleges, of easy-to-read brochures; (2) the placement of news releases, articles, and interviews in the press; (3) establishment of a bilingual, interactive website where women could get information and exchange information; (4) live discussion programs on FM radio and national television; (5) establishment of support groups; and (6) seminars and workshops for women's groups in various cities.

Because of the prominent spokespersons and the distribution of culturally sensitive promotional materials, the campaign was able to overcome the constraints of a conservative Islamic society and make breast cancer part of the national health agenda. Several governmental ministries became partners in the campaign for breast cancer awareness, and the Ministry of Health in Punjab even started a pilot project to train 3,700 local health volunteers to teach breast self-examination to women. Extensive coverage about the campaign and breast cancer appeared in local print, broadcast, and electronic media. International news outlets, such as the BBC, also covered the story.

webpages that are graphics-heavy and text-light. Sight-impaired individuals, on the other hand, not only require bold graphics but at least 18-point type in all printed materials.

Bianchi-Kai says the best medium to reach a variety of disability groups at the same time is television. Closed-captioning makes television accessible to deaf people, and those with speech or mobility disabilities are also easily reached.

The crafting of key messages is important. Many people, particularly those who are aging, don't know or are unwilling to admit that they have a disability such as hearing loss. For such audiences, the message has to be about innovation and making life easier instead of about buying a hearing aid out of necessity.

Summary

A Multicultural Nation

- Audiences are not monolithic. They are a complex mingling of groups with diverse cultural, ethnic, religious, and economic attributes.

- The demographics of the United States are becoming more multicultural. Minorities, by 2050, will constitute the majority of the U.S. population.

- Through technology and research, it's now possible to segment audiences a number of ways that help the public relations communicator understand the characteristics of the audience and how to best communicate with them.

- Public relations professionals will need to be more culturally literate to understand and communicate with diverse audiences.

Reaching Ethnic Audiences

- The three major ethnic groups in the country are Hispanics, African Americans, and Asian Americans.

- Each group has its own cultural values that must be understood by professional communicators.

- In general, the various ethnic groups are strongly family-oriented and community-minded.

- The ethnic media in the country are rapidly developing, and there are many Spanish-speaking media outlets.

- In conducting campaigns for the Hispanic audience, Spanish is often the preferred language even though the younger generation is increasingly bilingual.

Reaching Diverse Age Groups

- Audiences are generational and each has different values, interests, and needs.

- Public relations practitioners must understand youth audiences as well as the coming tidal wave of baby boomers reaching retirement. Baby boomers and seniors tend to be relatively affluent and constitute the majority of the travel and tourism business.

- Each group, however, prefers to receive information via different media channels.

- Although youths prefer information online and via cell phones, seniors still prefer traditional media such as daily newspapers and television news.

Gender/Lifestyle Audiences

- Women are a major and influential audience. They constitute 50 percent of the workforce, spend most of the family's disposable income, and are more heavily involved in social networking, including blogging.

- The gay/lesbian community is relatively affluent and well educated, and marketing/public relations programs are increasingly directed to them.

- Religious groups run the spectrum from conservative to somewhat liberal. The Christian Right is highly vocal, but the Jewish and Muslim communities are also important audiences.

- Communicating with the disability community requires sensitivity and specialized tactics such as brochures with large type or captioning on videos.

Case Activity   A Campaign Directed to Hispanic Women

The latest innovation in sun care protection is spray-on sunscreens, which come in an ozone-free canister that sprays a clear mist that coats the skin without any rubbing. Dermatologists say the spray-on sunscreen offers the same protection as lotions. They also have the additional advantage of being easy to apply, which means that individuals will be more likely to coat every part of the body rather than just dab a little lotion on the arms, nose, or shoulders.

Banana Boat brand is currently marketing its Ultra-Mist sunblock, but it's interested in developing a tailored campaign directly oriented to Hispanic women aged 18 to 25. Market research indicates that this group is particularly interested in products that help them maintain a lighter skin tone, which is preferred in traditional Hispanic culture.

Banana Boat retains your public relations firm to develop a public relations program that will effectively build awareness and visibility for its Ultra-Mist product in the Hispanic community. What would you do in terms of using ethnic media? What about traditional media? What kinds of events or promotions would you plan? How would you use websites, blogs, and other social networks such as Facebook or even Twitter? Your proposal should be PR-focused; there is no budget for paid advertising.

Questions   For Review and Discussion

1. Public relations practitioners are cautioned not to think of audiences as monolithic, but as very diverse. Why?
2. How can technology be used to segment audiences?
3. What are some guidelines for developing a communications campaign for multicultural audiences?
4. What is the fastest-growing ethnic group in the United States?
5. How do you think the various changes in the racial and ethnic makeup of the United States will impact the future practice of public relations?
6. What are some of the cultural values of such groups as Hispanics, African Americans, and Asian Americans?
7. Describe some of the ethnic media that reach a Hispanic audience.
8. What are some characteristics of millennials, also called Generation Y?
9. What is the baby boomer generation, and what are some of this group's characteristics?
10. Why is the senior audience so important? What are some characteristics of this audience?
11. Why are women considered an important audience for public relations and marketing personnel?
12. What are some characteristics of the gay/lesbian community?
13. In what ways can Christian conservatives impact a company's policies and product sales?

Media Resources

Baar, A. (2008, May 15). Targeting gays, lesbians is a win-win, new survey shows. Retrieved from *MediaPost Publications* website: www.publications.mediapost.com

Elliott, S. (2009, April 20). The older audience is looking better than ever. *New York Times*. Retrieved from www.nytimes.com

Ford, R. L. (2008, October). Celebrate Hispanic heritage month by learning the facts. *Public Relations Tactics*, 6.

Ford, R. L. (2009, June). Reaching out to the Asian-Indian population. *Public Relations Tactics*, 6.

Ford, R. L. (2009, July). Every day could be considered Mother's Day in public relations. *Public Relations Tactics*, 6.

Henry, D. (2009, July). Lost in translation: Reaching Hispanic audiences through mobile communications. *Public Relations Tactics*, 17.

Hupp, W. (2008, February 5). The misunderstood generation: Marketers fail to understand baby boomers. *Advertising Age*. Retrieved from www.adage.com

Kornecki, B. (2008, Spring). In defense of millennials: A contrarian view from a baby boomer. *The Strategist*, 29–31.

Krietsch, B. (2009, March 30). The mom factor: Using social media to reach them. *PRWeek*, 13.

Maul, K.(2009, November). Brands focus on social media to target multicultural groups. *PRWeek*, 18.

McQuire, C. (2009, March 23). On-the-go solutions for reaching teens. *PRWeek,* 14.

O'Hara, K. (2009, October). Using social media to connect with Hispanic audiences. *Public Relations Tactics,* 6.

O'Leary, N. (2009, November 2). Hispanic market is set to soar. *Brandweek.* Retrieved from www.brandweek.com

Skriloff, L. (2009, June). The case for multicultural communications. *O'Dwyer's PR Report,* 8–9.

Toth, E. L. (2009). Diversity and public relations practice: Essential knowledge project. Retrieved from Institute for Public Relations website: www.instituteforpr.org

Tumminello, M. (2009, June). Profits, opportunities and trends in gay marketing. *O'Dwyer's PR Report,* 12.

Witherspoon, C. (2009, June). Attention to diversity pays in the 2009 market. *O'Dwyer's PR Report,* 14.

12

Public Relations and the Law

Courtney Love was sued for remarks she made on Twitter.

After reading this chapter, you will be able to:

Describe what public relations professionals need to know about defamation, employee and privacy rights, copyright, and trademark laws

Understand the key issues surrounding freedom of speech and public relations

Identify which government agencies regulate the commercial speech used by public relations professionals

Explain how public relations professionals can work effectively with lawyers

A Sampling of Legal Problems

The law and its many ramifications are somewhat abstract to the average person. Many people may have difficulty imagining exactly how public relations personnel can run afoul of the law or generate a lawsuit simply by communicating information. The following are just a few of the many ways that public relations practitioners can get in legal hot water:

■ Cosmetic surgery company Lifestyle Lift paid a $300,000 settlement to the New York State Attorney General's office after being accused of having employees post fake consumer reviews online.

■ The Securities and Exchange Commission (SEC) filed suit against MitoPharm Corporation and its public relations firm for hyping the benefits of MitoPharm's anti-aging and nutritional supplements. The lawsuit alleged that the PR firm had "embarked on an aggressive public relations campaign that centered on the misleading promotion" of products.

■ The Federal Trade Commission (FTC) ruled that two video news releases from King Pharmaceuticals were "false and misleading" because they omitted mention of the risks associated with a painkiller drug and presented misleading claims.

■ American Apparel paid a $5 million settlement to film director Woody Allen for using his image in an advertising campaign and other promotional literature without his permission.

■ Westwood One sued TransMedia and its client Pompano Helicopter for $42 million, alleging that they attempted to injure the radio network's stock prices and reputation through a series of defamatory news releases.

■ A former employee filed a libel suit against office supply company Staples after the firm e-mailed a memo to 1,500 division employees stating that the employee was fired for violating company travel and expense reimbursements policies.

■ A Chicago man who appeared in a video news release for a cholesterol-lowering drug sued for invasion of privacy because the company and video producer hadn't told him the actual purpose of the taping.

■ A San Francisco public relations practitioner who was fired for refusing to write misleading news releases won a lawsuit against his former employer for "unlawful dismissal."

These examples provide some idea of the legal pitfalls that a public relations person may encounter. Many of the charges were eventually dismissed or settled out of court, but the organizations paid dearly for the adverse publicity and the expense of defending themselves.

Public relations personnel must be aware that they can be held legally liable if they provide advice or tacitly support an illegal activity of a client or employer. This area of liability is called *conspiracy*. Although political speech that advocates change in the American system has traditionally been protected, the increased threat of terrorism on American soil has compounded security concerns, and the recruitment of U.S. citizens to engage in illegal activities may bring dangerous constraints on free speech. Serving as webmaster or public relations expert for an activist group has legal implications. See the Multicultural World box on page 294 for more discussion on this issue.

on the job

A MULTICULTURAL WORLD

Jihad Janes: Terrorist Recruitment and the Web

With homegrown terrorism cases emerging in the United States, experts are trying to understand why so many are happening now. One explanation has less to do with religion than with adventure and a sense of belonging. The latest wave of jihadists traveling to Pakistan and elsewhere for training may have been motivated by a sense of jihadi cool. NPR documents the radical shift in message strategy for American audiences:

Recruitment More MTV Than Mosque

. . . . It used to be that jihadi recruitment videos opened with the call to prayer and readings from the Quran. These days, many of them are decidedly less religious. They look more like something that would appear on MTV. If you type "jihadi rap videos" into any Internet search engine, you'll find dozens of videos with thumping bass lines and forced rhymes about beheading non-Muslims and making them pay for the indignities they have leveled against Islam.

Law enforcement officials say English-version videos—which have gone viral on the Internet—are aimed at recruiting Americans for al-Shabab. Experts say slick videos coupled with the wars in Iraq and Afghanistan have made a terrorist recruiter's job easier, particularly here in the United States, where traditionally it had been harder. And for people who might not have even considered becoming a Muslim, much less turning to jihad, signing on can be done with just the click of a mouse.

FBI Director Robert Mueller says the Internet is partly to blame for speeding up the recruitment process. He says the Web now not only radicalizes young Muslims but helps connect them to organizations that launch attacks. Mueller stresses that while jihadi cool may be a different motivation for taking up arms, it isn't necessarily any less lethal. And because these new recruits often are lone wolves who do not fit the profile of secret cell members for Al Qaeda, they pose serious new challenges to Homeland Security.

The Web glamorizes not only jihadi cool and ease of enrollment, but also a sense of belonging. That's what officials think happened with Colleen LaRose, the first self-styled Jihad Jane. They allege that she trolled the Internet while she was housebound caring for her boyfriend's ailing father, and that signing up for a holy war was something that attracted a lonely woman. It gave her something to belong to, officials say.

Without long-standing or direct connections to terrorist organizations or networks, LaRose allegedly tried to recruit militants online, plotted an attack, and was in contact with suspects who were plotting to kill a Swedish cartoonist who had portrayed the Prophet Mohammad as a dog. The Justice Department says she thought her blond hair and blue eyes would allow her to operate undetected in Europe, where she traveled in August, allegedly to carry out the attack.

Support for the Patriot Act's terror surveillance provisions was boosted by the Colleen LaRose case. And many would argue that the jihadi sites incite violence and imminent threat to the United States, categorizing the content as non-speech in Constitutional terms. This would suit the FBI. Janice K. Fedarcyk, special FBI agent, put it this way: "We must use all available technologies and techniques to root out potential threats and stop those who intend to harm us." Unfortunately, surveillance may expand to include U.S. citizens who are enticed by extremists looking to harm Americans who are inflamed by dramatic and inviting jihadi websites.

Does the greater threat from homegrown terrorists enticed and recruited by online content justify greater intrusiveness in monitoring suspicious activity, perhaps even emulating China by shutting down some sites?

Considering the importance of free speech to journalism and public relations, will the public discourse that we call the wrangle in the marketplace of ideas (see Chapter 10) be adversely dampened by arguments that terror recruitment sites can and should be suppressed?

Does the price of freedom of speech include increased terrorist activity

resulting from recruitment of bored or lonely individuals who are incited by Web content?

How could public relations skills be used by Homeland Security to counter recruitment efforts of jihadist websites?

Sources: D. Temple-Raston. (2010, March 25). Jihadi cool: Terrorist recruiters' latest weapon. Retrieved from www.NPR.org; Southern Poverty Law Center, www.splcenter.org; M. Calabresi. (2010. March 11). Why the Jihad Jane case is a win for the Patriot Act. *Time.* Retrieved from www.time.com

A public relations person can be named a coconspirator with other organizational officials if he or she:

- Participates in an illegal action such as bribing a government official or covering up information of vital interest to public health and safety
- Counsels and guides the policy behind an illegal action
- Takes a major personal part in the illegal action
- Helps establish a "front group" whereby the connection to the public relations firm or its clients is kept hidden
- Cooperates in any other way to further an illegal action

These five concepts also apply to public relations firms that create, produce, and distribute materials on behalf of clients. The courts have ruled on more than one occasion that public relations firms cannot hide behind the defense of "the client told me to do it." Public relations firms have a legal responsibility to practice "due diligence" in the type of information and documentation supplied by a client. Regulatory agencies such as the FTC (Federal Trade Commission) have the power under the Lanham Act to file charges against public relations firms that distribute false and misleading information.

Libel and Defamation

Public relations professionals should be thoroughly familiar with the concepts of libel and slander. Such knowledge is crucial if an organization's internal and external communications are to meet legal and regulatory standards with a minimum of legal complications.

Traditionally, *libel* was a printed falsehood and *slander* was an oral statement that was false. Today, as a practical matter, there is little difference in the two, and the courts often use *defamation* as a collective term.

Essentially, defamation is any false statement about a person (or organization) that creates public hatred, contempt, or ridicule, or inflicts injury on reputation. A person filing a defamation suit usually must prove that:

- the false statement was communicated to others through print, broadcast, or electronic means;
- the person was identified or is identifiable;

- there is actual injury in the form of money losses, loss of reputation, or mental suffering; and
- the person making the statement was malicious or negligent.

In general, private citizens have more success winning defamation suits than do public figures or corporations. With public figures—government officials, entertainers, political candidates, and other newsworthy personalities—there is the extra test of whether the libelous statements were made with actual malice (*New York Times v. Sullivan*).

Corporations, to some degree, also are considered "public figures" by the courts for several reasons: (1) They engage in advertising and promotion offering products and services to the public, (2) they are often involved in matters of public controversy and public policy, and (3) they have some degree of access to the media—through regular advertising and news releases—that enables them to respond to and rebut defamatory charges made against them.

This is not to say that corporations don't win lawsuits regarding defamation. A good example is General Motors, which filed a multimillion-dollar defamation suit against NBC after the network's *Dateline* news program carried a story about gas tanks on GM pickup trucks exploding in side-impact collisions.

GM's general counsel, in a news conference, meticulously provided evidence that NBC had inserted toy rocket "igniters" into the gas tanks, understated the vehicle speed at the moment of impact, and wrongly claimed that the fuel tanks could be easily ruptured. Within 24 hours after the suit was filed, NBC caved in. It agreed to air a nine-minute apology on the news program and pay GM $2 million to cover the cost of its investigation.

Increasingly, corporations are also filing defamation suits against bloggers and even individuals who Tweet about their businesses. A woman in Chicago, for example, was slapped with a $50,000 defamation suit after tweeting that a real estate company didn't do anything about her moldy apartment. The company claimed that the Tweet "maliciously and wrongfully published the false and defamatory Tweet on Twitter, thereby allowing the tweet to be distributed throughout the world."

Avoiding Libel Suits

Libel suits can be filed against organizational officials who make libelous accusations during a media interview, send out news releases that make false statements, or injure someone's reputation. For example, some executives have lived to regret losing control during a news conference and calling the leaders of a labor union "a bunch of crooks and compulsive liars." Suits have been filed for calling a news reporter "a pimp for all environmental groups." Such language, although highly quotable and colorful, can provoke legal retaliation.

Accurate information, and a delicate choice of words, must be used in all news releases. For instance, a former employee of the J. Walter Thompson advertising agency claimed she was libeled in an agency news release that stated she had been dismissed because of financial irregularities in the department she headed. Eventually, the $20 million lawsuit was dismissed because the ex-employee couldn't prove that the agency had acted in a "grossly irresponsible manner."

Another potentially dangerous practice is making unflattering comments about the competition's products. Although comparative advertising is the norm in the United States, a company must walk a narrow line between comparison and "trade libel," or "product disparagement." Statements should be truthful, with factual evidence and scientific demonstration available to substantiate them. Companies often charge competitors with overstepping the boundary between "puffery" and "factual representation."

An organization can offer the opinion that a particular product or service is the "best" or "a revolutionary development" if the context clearly shows that the communication is a statement of opinion attributed to someone. Then it is classified as "puffery" and doesn't require factual evidence.

Don Sneed, Tim Wulfemeyer, and Harry Stonecipher, in a *Public Relations Review* article, say that a news release should be written to indicate clearly statements of opinion and statements of fact. They suggest that:

1. opinion statements be accompanied by the facts on which the opinions are based,

2. statements of opinion be clearly labeled as such, and

3. the context of the language surrounding the expression of opinion be reviewed for possible legal implications.

The Fair Comment Defense

Organizations can do much to ensure that their communications avoid materials that could lead to potential lawsuits. By the same token, organizations are somewhat limited in their ability to use legal measures to defend themselves against criticism.

Executives are often incensed when an environmental group includes their corporation on its annual "dirty dozen" polluters or similar lists. Executives are also unhappy when a consumer affairs blogger flatly calls the product a "rip-off."

A corporate reputation may be damaged and product sales may go down, but a defamation case is difficult to win because, as previously mentioned, the accuser must prove actual malice. Also operating is the concept of *fair comment and criticism*.

This defense is used by theater and music critics when they lambaste a play or concert. Fair comment also means that when companies and individuals voluntarily display their wares to the public for sale or consumption, they have no real recourse against criticism done with honest purpose and lack of malicious intent.

A utility company in Indiana, for example, once tried to sue a citizen who had written a letter to a newspaper criticizing the utility for seeking a rate hike. The judge threw the suit out of court, stating that the rate increase was a "matter of public interest and concern" even if the letter writer didn't have all the facts straight.

Invasion of Privacy

An area of law that particularly applies to employees of an organization is *invasion of privacy*. Public relations staff must be particularly sensitive to the issue of privacy in at least four areas:

- Employee communication
- Photo releases
- Product publicity and advertising
- Media inquiries about employees

Employee Communication

It is no longer true, if it ever was, that an organization has an unlimited right to publicize the activities of its employees. In fact, Morton J. Simon, a Philadelphia lawyer and author of *Public Relations Law*, writes, "It should not be assumed that a person's status as an employee waives his right to privacy." Simon correctly points out that a company newsletter or magazine does not enjoy the same First Amendment protection that the news media enjoy when they claim "newsworthiness" and "public interest." A number of court cases, he says, show that company newsletters are considered commercial tools of trade.

This distinction does not impede the effectiveness of newsletters, but it does indicate that editors should try to keep employee stories organization-oriented. Indeed, most lawsuits and complaints are generated by "personals columns" that may invade the privacy of employees. Although a mention that Mary Worth is now a great-grandmother may sound completely innocent, she may consider the information a violation of her privacy. The situation may be further compounded into possible defamation by "cutesy" comments on a website such as Facebook.

In sum, one should avoid anything that might embarrass or subject an employee to ridicule by fellow employees. Here are some guidelines to remember when writing about employee activities:

- Keep the focus on organization-related activities.
- Have employees submit "personals" in writing.
- Double-check all information for accuracy.
- Ask: "Will this embarrass anyone or cause someone to be the butt of jokes?"
- Don't rely on secondhand information; confirm the facts with the person involved.
- Don't include racial or ethnic designations of employees in any articles.

Photo Releases

An organization must have a signed release on file if it wants to use the photographs or comments of its employees and other individuals in product publicity, sales brochures, and advertising. In a new book on public relations law, Parkinson and Parkinson offer straightforward advice about contracts that applies to photo releases: a contract is not binding without some form of compensation. Therefore, an added precaution is to give some financial compensation to make a more binding contract. A second principle is that amicable relationships can change, increasing the importance of clarity and documentation, although not necessarily in legal language. According to Michael and L. Marie Parkinson, authors of *Public Relations Law: A Supplemental Text*, the courts require only that agreements be understandable and do-able for each side.

> If I used my mother in an ad, I'd get her permission—and I almost trust her 100 percent.
>
> *Jerry Della Femina,*
> *advertising executive*

Public relations departments, in addition, should take the precaution of (1) filing all photographs, (2) dating them, and (3) giving the context of the situation. This precludes the use of old photos that could embarrass employees or subject them to ridicule. In other cases, it precludes using photographs of persons who are no longer employed with the company or have died. This method also helps to make certain that a photo taken for the employee newsletter isn't used in an advertisement. If a photo of an employee or customer is used in product publicity, sales brochures, or advertisements, the standard practice is to obtain a signed release.

Product Publicity and Advertising

Chemical Bank of New York unfortunately learned the basics of photo releases the hard way. The bank used pictures of 39 employees in various advertisements designed to "humanize" the bank's image, but the employees maintained that no one had requested permission to use their photos in advertisements. Another problem was that the pictures had been taken up to five years before they began appearing in the series of advertisements.

An attorney for the employees, who sued for $600,000 in damages, said, "The bank took the individuality of these employees and used that individuality to make a profit." The judge agreed and ruled that the bank had violated New York's privacy law. This action is called *misappropriation of personality*. Jerry Della Femina, an advertising executive, succinctly makes the point: Get permission. "If I used my mother in an ad," he said, "I'd get her permission—and I almost trust her 100 percent."

Media Inquiries about Employees

Because press inquiries have the potential to invade an employee's right of privacy, public relations personnel should follow basic guidelines as to what information will be provided on the employee's behalf.

In general, employers should give a news reporter only basic information.

DO PROVIDE:

1. confirmation that the person is an employee,
2. the person's title and job description, and
3. date of beginning employment, or, if applicable, date of termination.

DO NOT PROVIDE EMPLOYEE'S:

1. salary,
2. home address,
3. marital status,
4. number of children,
5. organizational memberships, or
6. job performance.

If a reporter does seek any of this information because of the nature of the story, several principles should be followed. First, as Parkinson and Parkinson clearly establish in their public relations law text, the rights of reporters are often exaggerated to mythic levels, partly by the journalists themselves. In fact, reporters have no greater rights to private information than any other citizen. Second, because the information is private, it should be provided by the employee through arrangement with the public relations person. What the employee chooses to tell the reporter is not then the company's responsibility.

If an organization uses biographical sheets, it is important that they be dated, kept current, and used by permission of the employee. A sheet compiled by an employee five years previously may be hopelessly out of date. This is also true of file photographs taken at the time of a person's employment.

> Here we try to correct some misconceptions about journalists' legal rights, because often journalists try to use those "rights" to coerce information or access from public relations practitioners.
>
> *Parkinson and Parkinson,* Public Relations Law: A Supplemental Text

Although employee privacy remains an important consideration, the trend is toward increased monitoring of employee e-mail by employers, who are concerned about being held liable if an employee posts a racial slur, engages in sexual harassment online, or even transmits sexually explicit jokes that might cause another employee to perceive the workplace as a "hostile" environment. In other words, everyone should assume that any e-mails he or she writes at work are subject to monitoring and that he or she can be fired if the e-mails violate company policy. Further complicating this issue is the fact that government employees may have their e-mails made public if some interested party files a Freedom of Information Act (FOIA) request. E-mails produced by a public employee on a government-owned computer are considered requestable documents under the FOIA.

Other important, and sometimes controversial, aspects of employee free speech include the tension between whistle-blowing and protection of an organization's trade secrets. State and federal laws generally protect the right of employees to "blow the whistle" if an organization is guilty of illegal activity, but the protections are limited and the requirements for the whistle-blower are quite specific. Whistle-blowing can occur in corporate, nonprofit, and government organizations. For example, an employee might blow the whistle on his or her organization by reporting to the Environmental Protection Agency the illegal release of a toxic substance from a manufacturing plant.

Copyright Law

Should a news release be copyrighted? How about a corporate annual report? Can a *New Yorker* cartoon be used in the company magazine without permission? What about reprinting an article from *Fortune* magazine and distributing it to the company's sales staff? Are government reports copyrighted? What about posting a video clip from Comedy Central on the Internet? What constitutes copyright infringement?

These are some of the bothersome questions that a public relations professional should be able to answer. Knowledge of copyright law is important from two perspectives: (1) what organizational materials should be copyrighted and (2) how to utilize the copyrighted materials of others correctly.

In very simple terms, *copyright* means protection of a creative work from unauthorized use. A section of the U.S. copyright law of 1978 states: "Copyright protection subsists . . . in the original works of authorship fixed in any tangible medium of expression now known or later developed." The word *authorship* is defined in seven categories: (1) literary works; (2) musical works; (3) dramatic works; (4) pantomimes and choreographic works; (5) pictorial, graphic, or sculptural works; (6) motion pictures; and (7) sound recordings. The word *fixed* means that the work is sufficiently permanent or stable to permit it to be perceived, reproduced, or otherwise communicated.

The shield of copyright protection was weakened somewhat in 1991, when the U.S. Supreme Court ruled unanimously that directories, computer databases, and other compilations of facts may be copied and republished unless they display "some minimum degree of creativity." The Court stated, "Raw facts may be copied at will."

Thus a copyright does not protect ideas, only the specific ways in which those ideas are expressed. An idea for promoting a product, for example, cannot be copyrighted—but brochures, drawings, news features, animated cartoons, display booths, photographs, recordings, videotapes, corporate symbols, slogans, and the like, that express a particular idea can be copyrighted.

Because much money, effort, time, and creative talent are spent on developing organizational materials, obtaining copyright protection for them is important. By copyrighting materials, a company can prevent its competitors from capitalizing on its creative work or producing a facsimile brochure that may mislead the public.

The law presumes that material produced in some tangible form is copyrighted from the moment it is created. This presumption of copyright is often sufficient to discourage unauthorized use, and the writer or creator of the material has some legal protection if he or she can prove that the material was created before another person claims having created it. In other nations, such as China, copyright is widely abused, although some claim that China is moving toward greater enforcement of copyright as part of its rise to prominence as a global nation-state.

A more formal step, providing full legal protection, is official registration of the copyrighted work within three months after its creation. This process consists of depositing two copies of the manuscript (it is not necessary that it has been published), recording, or artwork with the Copyright Office of the Library of Congress. Registration is not a condition of copyright protection, but it is a prerequisite to an infringement action against unauthorized use by others. The Copyright Term Extension Act, passed in 1998 and reaffirmed by the U.S. Supreme Court (*Eldred v. Ashcroft*) in 2003, protects original material for the life of the creator plus 70 years for individual works and 95 years from publication for copyrights held by corporations.

Fair Use versus Infringement

Public relations people are in the business of gathering information from a variety of sources, so it is important to know where fair use ends and infringement begins. See the Insights box on plagiarism versus copyright infringement on page 302.

Fair use means that part of a copyrighted article may be quoted directly, but the quoted material must be brief in relation to the length of the original work. It may be, for example, only one paragraph of a 750-word article and up to 300 words in a long article or book chapter. Complete attribution of the source must be given regardless of the length of the quotation. If the passage is quoted verbatim, quote marks must be used.

It is important to note, however, that the concept of fair use has distinct limitations if part of the copyrighted material is to be used in advertisements and promotional brochures. In this case, permission is required. It also is important for the original source to approve the context in which the quote is used. A quote out of context often runs into legal trouble if it implies endorsement of a product or service.

The copyright law does allow limited copying of a work for fair use such as criticism, comment, or research. However, in recent years, the courts have considerably narrowed the concept of "fair use" when multiple copies of a copyrighted work are involved.

Atlas Telecom paid a $100,000 settlement after admitting that it had electronically distributed about a dozen telecommunications newsletters to its employees. According to the suit filed by Phillips Publishing, Inc., the company made hundreds of copies by reproducing the newsletters on the in-house database. Distribution can be arranged for a fee with the copyright holder or often by paying a royalty fee to the Copyright Clearance Center (www.copyright.com), which has been established to represent a large number of publishers.

on the job
INSIGHTS

Plagiarism versus Copyright Infringement

Copyright infringement and plagiarism differ. You may be guilty of copyright infringement if you attribute the materials and give the source, but don't get permission from the author or publisher to reproduce the materials.

In the case of plagiarism, the author makes no attempt to attribute the information at all. As the guide for Hamilton College says, "Plagiarism is a form of fraud. You plagiarize if you present other writers' words or ideas as your own." Maurice Isserman, writing in the *Chronicle of Higher Education*, further explains, "Plagiarism substitutes someone else's prowess as explanation for your own efforts."

The Internet has increased the problems of plagiarism because it is quite easy for anyone, from students to college presidents, to cut and paste entire paragraphs (or even pages) into a term paper or speech and claim it as their own creation. Of course, students also can purchase complete term papers online, but that loophole is rapidly shrinking as sophisticated online sites. such as turnitin.com, can scan the entire Internet for other sources that use the same phrases found in a student's research paper. Adding to the confusion is that students regularly share podcasts of class lectures, re-tweets, YouTube, and Veoh video clips, and are encouraged to participate in viral marketing—all of which actually encourages sharing of information or cool stuff without attribution. The same holds true for recording artists who sample music and movie clips in musical genres such as hip-hop. In such cases, copyright may actually be acquired by the studio or the viral marketing firm, but no attribution or credit is given to the originator. A word to the wise: In the classroom, always give clear credit whenever the original work of another is used.

John Barrie, founder of *Turnitin*, told the *Wall Street Journal* that "...85 percent of the cases of plagiarism that we see are straight copies from the Internet—a student uses the Internet like a 1.5 billion-page cut-and-paste encyclopedia." Most universities have very strong rules about plagiarism, and it is not uncommon for students to receive an "F" in a course because of plagiarism. In the business world, stealing someone else's words and expressions of thought is called *theft of intellectual property* and lawsuits are filed.

Government documents (city, county, state, and federal) are in the public domain and cannot be copyrighted. Public relations personnel, under the fair use doctrine, can freely use quotations and statistics from a government document, but care must be exercised to ensure that the material is in context and not misleading. The most common problem occurs when an organization uses a government report as a form of endorsement for its services or products. An airline, for example, might cite a government study showing that it provides the most service to customers, but neglect to state the basis of comparison or other factors.

Photography and Artwork

The copyright law makes it clear that freelance and commercial photographers retain ownership of their work. In other words, a customer who buys a copyrighted photo owns the item itself, but not the right to make additional copies. That right remains with the photographer unless transferred in writing.

In a further extension of this right, the duplication of copyrighted photos is also illegal. This was established in a 1990 U.S. Federal District Court case in which the Professional Photographers of America (PPofA) sued a nationwide photofinishing firm for ignoring copyright notices on pictures sent for additional copies. Photoshop edits and other manipulations of original artwork can also violate copyright provisions.

Freelance photographers generally charge for a picture on the basis of its use. If it is used only once, perhaps for an employee newsletter, the fee is low. If, however, the company wants to use the picture in the corporate annual report or on the company calendar, the fee may be considerably higher. Consequently, it is important for a public relations person to tell the photographer exactly how the picture will be used. Arrangements and fees then can be determined for (1) one-time use, (2) unlimited use, or (3) the payment of royalties every time the picture is used.

The Rights of Freelance Writers

Although the rights of freelance photographers have been established for some years, it was only recently that freelance writers gained more control over the ownership of their work.

In the *Reid* case (*Community for Creative Nonviolence v. Reid*), the U.S. Supreme Court in 1989 set a lasting precedent that writers retain ownership of their work and that purchasers of it gain merely a "license" to reproduce the copyrighted work.

Prior to this ruling, the common practice was to assume that commissioned articles are "work for hire" and that the purchaser owns the copyright. In other words, a magazine could reproduce the article in any number of ways and even sell it to another publication without the writer's permission.

Under the new interpretation, ownership of a writer's work is subject to negotiation and contractual agreement. Writers may agree to assign all copyright rights to the work they have been hired to do or they may give permission only for a specific one-time use.

In a related matter, freelance writers are pressing for additional compensation if an organization puts their work on CD-ROM, online databases, or the Web. They won a major victory in 2001 when the Supreme Court (*New York Times v. Tasini*) ruled that publishers, by making articles accessible through electronic databases, infringe the copyrights of freelance contributors.

Public relations firms and corporate public relations departments are responsible for ensuring compliance with the copyright law. This means that all agreements with a freelance writer must be in writing, the use of the material must be clearly stated, and fair exchange of value must be made. Ideally, public relations personnel should negotiate multiple rights or even complete ownership of the copyright.

Copyright Issues on the Internet

The Internet and World Wide Web raise new issues about the protection of intellectual property. Two issues regarding copyright are (1) the downloading of copyrighted material and (2) the unauthorized uploading of such material.

The Downloading of Material   In general, the same rules apply to cyberspace as to more earthbound methods of expressing and disseminating ideas. Original materials in digital form are still protected by copyright, a precedent first established with legal language delivered by telegraph early in the last century. The fair use limits for materials found on the Internet are essentially the same as the fair use of materials disseminated by any other means.

Related to this is the use of news articles and features that are sent via e-mail or the Web to the clients of clipping services. An organization may use such clips to track its publicity efforts, but it can't distribute the article on its own website or intranet without permission and a royalty payment to the publication where the article appeared.

One national clipping service, Burrelle's, has already reached agreements with more than 300 newspapers to have its customers pay a small royalty fee in exchange for being able to make photocopies of clippings and make greater use of them.

The Uploading of Material   In many cases, owners of copyrighted material have uploaded various kinds of information with the intention of making it freely available. Examples include software, games, and even the entire text of *The Hitchhiker's Guide to the Galaxy*. The problem comes, however, when third parties upload copyrighted material without permission. Consequently, copyright holders are increasingly patrolling the Internet to stop the unauthorized use of material.

A good example is Viacom, which constantly monitors such sites as Google's YouTube for unauthorized postings of video clips from its various television programs on MTV and CBS. Under the 1998 Digital Millennium Copyright Act, Internet businesses such as YouTube are immune from liability for material posted by its users, but are required to take down any infringing material after it is notified by the copyright owner. In one year alone, YouTube removed 230,000 clips at the request of Viacom—which is why a viewer may see a video one day but not be able to see it the next day. The posting of illegal video clips continues to dog the industry, causing a great deal of lobbying for more protective legislation and even major lawsuits. Some other examples:

- Dutton Children's Books threatened a lawsuit against a New Mexico State University student for using Winnie the Pooh illustrations on his home page.
- Corbis Corporation, which has millions of photos for licensing or purchase, threatened legal action against a retirement community for using a photo of an elderly couple on its website without paying the licensing fee.

Copyright Guidelines

A number of points have been discussed about copyright. A public relations person should keep the following in mind:

- Ideas cannot be copyrighted, but the expression of those ideas can be.
- Major public relations materials (brochures, annual reports, videotapes, motion pictures, position papers, and the like) should be copyrighted, if only to prevent unauthorized use by competitors.
- Despite the concept of fair use, any copyrighted material intended directly to advance the sales and profits of an organization should not be used unless permission is given.
- Copyrighted material should not be taken out of context, particularly if it implies endorsement of the organization's services or products.
- Quantity reprints of an article should be ordered from the publisher.
- Permission is required to use segments of television programs or motion pictures.

- Permission must be obtained to use segments of popular songs (written verses or sound recordings) from a recording company.

- Photographers and freelance writers retain the rights to their works. Permission and fees must be negotiated to use works for purposes other than originally agreed on.

- Photographs of current celebrities or those who are now deceased cannot be used for promotion and publicity purposes without permission.

- Permission is required to reprint cartoon characters, such as Snoopy or Garfield. In addition, cartoons and other artwork or illustrations in a publication are copyrighted.

- Government documents are not copyrighted, but caution is necessary if the material is used in a way that implies endorsement of products or services.

- Private letters, or excerpts from them, cannot be published or used in sales and publicity materials without the permission of the letter writer.

- Original material posted on the Internet and the World Wide Web has copyright protection.

- The copyrighted material of others should not be posted on the Internet unless specific permission is granted.

Trademark Law

What do the names Diet Coke, iTunes, Dockers, eBay, Academy Awards, and even Droid have in common? They are all registered trademarks protected by law.

A *trademark* is a word, symbol, or slogan, used singly or in combination, that identifies a product's origin. According to Susan L. Cohen, writing in *Editor & Publisher*'s annual trademark supplement, "It also serves as an indicator of quality, a kind of shorthand for consumers to use in recognizing goods in a complex marketplace." Research indicates, for example, that 53 percent of Americans say brand quality takes precedence over price considerations, making brand identity crucial to commercial success.

The concept of a trademark is nothing new. The ancient Egyptians carved marks into the stones of the pyramids, and the craftsmen of the Middle Ages used guild marks to identify the source and quality of products. What is new, however, is the proliferation of trademarks and service marks in modern society. Coca-Cola may be the world's most recognized trademark, according to some studies, but it is only 1 of over 1 million active trademarks registered with the federal Patent and Trademark Office.

Sports logos and team uniforms constitute one of the largest categories of registered trademarks. A *licensing fee* must be paid before anyone can use logos for commercial products and promotions. Teams in the National Football League (NFL) and the National Basketball Association (NBA) earn more than

Protecting Valuable Trademarks

The National Association of Realtors places ads in consumer magazines to let consumers know there is a difference between a Realtor and a "real estate agent."

$3 billion annually just selling licensed merchandise, and the sale of college and university trademarked goods is rapidly approaching that mark. Schools such as Notre Dame, Michigan, and Ohio State rake in more than $3 million a year in royalties from licensing their logos to be placed on everything from beer mugs to T-shirts. The penalty for not paying a licensing fee is steep. The NFL, during Super Bowl week, typically confiscates about $1 million in bogus goods and files criminal charges against the offending vendors. Even the smallest of encroachments on the trademark of licensed sports images are often pursued. A small South Dakota town whose high school's team mascot was a tiger faced a cease and desist order from a college team because the little high school had copied the design of the tiger used by the Division 1 university.

Hi, I'm Jimmy Winkelmann and I started The South Butt for people like us. The South Butt idea is simple: stay comfortable, relaxed, and always be yourself. Welcome, take a look around, and check out the gear in our store.

Greeting on the South Butt website

Because brand identity is so valuable, a major clothing company took an equally aggressive approach against a whimsical startup making a play on its brand name and logo. South Butt is a small company formed as a spoof on the North Face outdoor clothing brand. With the logo inverted, the new company's name, South Butt, became quite apt as the logo took on an abstract resemblance to that lower anatomical part. North Face threatened and then filed suit, boosting the spoof into a viable company through the viral response of supporters to a South Butt Facebook page. The *Times Online* put it this way: "The North Face, however, sued [the South Butt founder], claiming he had committed copyright infringement. In response, South Butt launched a Facebook challenge to help users figure out the difference between a face and a butt. Thousands of followers signed up, and profits soared." An out-of-court settlement was reached.

For more on excessive legal zeal, see the Insights box on letters to children from lawyers on page 307.

The Protection of Trademarks

There are three basic guidelines regarding the use of trademarks:

- Trademarks are proper adjectives and should be capitalized and followed by a generic noun or phrase (e.g., *Kleenex tissues* or *Rollerblade skates*).

- Trademarks should not be pluralized or used in the possessive form. Saying, "American Express's credit card" is improper.

- Trademarks are never verbs. Saying, "The client FedExed the package" violates the rule.

Organizations adamantly insist on the proper use of their trademarks in order to avoid the problem of the name or slogan becoming generic. Or, to put it another way, a brand name becomes a common noun through general public use. Some trade names that have become generic include *aspirin, thermos, cornflakes, nylon, cellophane,* and *yo-yo*. This means that any company can use these names to describe a product.

Is this a parody of North Face?

on the job

INSIGHTS

Lawyers Could Use Some Help Writing Letters

An eight-year-old boy loved airplanes, so he drew a picture featuring his idea for a new plane and sent it to Boeing. In short order, he got an official, jargon-filled letter from the company's legal department saying it doesn't accept product ideas of any kind. And, also in short order, the father let the world know via Facebook and Twitter that Boeing is an insensitive, uncaring company when it comes to kids.

In another situation, Apple made headlines when it sent a nine-year-old girl a nasty cease-and-desist letter after she had suggested enhancements to the iPod—as part of a class project. Her mother, in a TV news interview, said, "She was very upset. She kind of threw the letter up in the air and ran into her room and slammed the door."

So what gives? Why would a company risk a black eye to its reputation by having its lawyers write jargon-filled letters telling kids in no uncertain terms that the company is not interested in their product ideas? The problem is a legal dilemma. Companies such as Mattel don't accept any product suggestions from outside the company because they don't want litigation down the road when someone claims that the company stole his or her idea without compensation. And the same letter is sent to everyone, whether they are adults or just kids who are simply enthusiastic fans of the company's products.

But, in today's Internet environment, social media guru Shel Holtz notes, ". . . potentially millions of consumers are exposed to the view that companies treat children who love their products and want to share their ideas as litigants." He adds in his blog, "a shel of my former self" (blog.holtz.com), "When everyone in the company is responsible for the company's reputation, the legal department needs to embrace a more human approach to doing its very necessary job."

Boeing, stung by the Internet firestorm launched by the irate father, did apologize to the boy. And a corporate spokesperson told reporters, "We should be taking the opportunity with a child to encourage their interest in airplanes and so we're gonna try to come up with a better letter for children that meets our legal needs but also has more positive words for them." According to Holtz, "From Apple, sadly, no response at all."

In what ways do you think the companies' lawyers and public relations staffs could work together to come up with a better letter for kids? What kind of letter would you propose?

Organizations take the step of designating brand names and slogans with various marks. The registered trademark symbol is a superscript, small capital "R" in a circle: ®. "Registered in U.S. Patent and Trademark Office" and "Reg. U.S. Pat. Off." may also be used. A "TM" in small capital letters indicates a trademark that isn't registered. It represents a company's common-law claim to a right of trademark or a trademark for which registration is pending. For example, 3M™ Post-it® Notes.

A *service mark* is like a trademark, but it designates a service rather than a product, or is a logo. An "SM" in small capitals in a circle—Ⓢ—is the symbol for a registered service mark. If registration is pending, the "SM" should be used without the circle.

These symbols are used in advertising, product labeling, news releases, company brochures, and so on, to let the public and competitors know that a name, slogan, or symbol is protected by law. See the trademark ad from the National Association of

Realtors on page 305 for an example of how organizations publicize their trademarks and service marks.

Public relations practitioners play an important role in protecting the trademarks of their clients They safeguard trademarks and respect other organizational trademarks in the following ways:

- Ensure that company trademarks are capitalized and used properly in all organizational literature and graphics. Lax supervision can cause loss of trademark protection.

- Distribute trademark brochures to editors and reporters and place advertisements in trade publications designating names to be capitalized.

- Educate employees as to what the organization's trademarks are and how to use them correctly.

- Monitor the mass media to make certain that trademarks are used correctly. If they are not, send a gentle reminder.

- Check publications to ensure that other organizations are not infringing on a registered trademark. If they are, the company legal department should protest with letters and threats of possible lawsuits.

- Make sure the trademark is actually being used. A 1988 revision of the Trademark Act no longer permits an organization to hold a name in reserve.

- Ensure that the trademarks of other organizations are correctly used and properly noted.

- Avoid the use of trademarked symbols or cartoon figures in promotional materials without the explicit permission of their owner. In some cases, to be discussed, a licensing fee is required.

The Problem of Trademark Infringement

Today, in a marketplace populated with thousands of businesses and organizations, finding a trademark not already in use is extremely difficult. The task is even more frustrating if a company wants to use a trademark on an international level.

The complexity of finding a new name, coupled with the attempts of many to capitalize on an already known trade name, has spawned a number of lawsuits and complaints claiming trademark infringement. A classic example is Phi Beta Kappa, the academic honor society, which filed a $5 million trademark infringement suit against Compaq Computer Corp. after the company launched a "Phi Beta Compaq" promotion targeted at college students.

Organizations often claim that their registered trademarks are being improperly exploited by others for commercial gain. In many cases, conflicts are settled out of court; in others, the courts have to weigh the evidence and make a decision based on the following:

- Has the defendant used a name as a way of capitalizing on the reputation of another organization's trademark—and does the defendant benefit from the original organization's investment in popularizing its trademark?

- Is there an intent (real or otherwise) to create confusion in the public's mind? Is there an intent to imply a connection between the defendant's product and the item identified by trademark?

- How similar are the two organizations? Are they providing the same kinds of products or services?

- Has the original organization actively protected the trademark by publicizing it and by actually continuing to use it in connection with its products or services?

■ Is the trademark unique? A company with a trademark that simply describes a common product might be in trouble.

Misappropriation of Personality

A form of trademark infringement also can result from the unauthorized use of well-known entertainers, professional athletes, and other public figures in an organization's publicity and advertising materials. A photo of a rock or movie star may make a company's advertising campaign more interesting, but the courts call it "misappropriation of personality" if permission and licensing fees have not been negotiated.

Protecting a Likeness

The image of Michael Jackson is owned by his estate, and a licensing fee must be paid to use his image or music.

Deceased celebrities also are protected. To use a likeness or actual photo of a personality such as Elvis Presley, Marilyn Monroe, or Michael Jackson, the user must pay a licensing fee to an agent representing the family, studio, or estate of the deceased. The Presley estate, almost 30 years after his death, is still the "King," with about $40 million in income annually. The estate of *Peanuts* comic strip creator Charles Schulz collects about $30 million annually. NASCAR icon Dale Earnhardt is in a third-place tie with Beatle John Lennon at $20 million.

Even boxing legend Muhammad Ali made a deal with CKX, Inc., which also owns the rights to the name and likeness of Elvis Presley. The company paid the boxer $50 million for the rights to license his name and likeness. According to the *Wall Street Journal*, Ali's name and image currently generate about $4 million to $7 million annually in licensing fees and endorsements.

The legal doctrine is the *right of publicity*, which gives entertainers, athletes, and other celebrities the sole ability to cash in on their fame. The legal right is loosely akin to a trademark or copyright, and many states have made it a commercial asset that can be inherited by a celebrity's descendents. Legal protection also extends to the use of "sound-alikes" and "look-alikes."

Regulations by Government Agencies

The promotion of products and services, whether through advertising, product publicity, or other techniques, is not protected by the First Amendment. Instead, the courts have traditionally ruled that such activities fall under the doctrine of commercial speech. This means that messages can be regulated by the state in the interest of public health, safety, and consumer protection.

Consequently, the states and the federal government have passed legislation that regulates commercial speech and even restricts it if standards of disclosure, truth, and accuracy are violated. One consequence was the banning of cigarette advertising on television in the 1960s. A more difficult legal question is whether government can completely ban the advertising or promotion of a legally sold product such as cigarettes or alcohol.

Public relations personnel involved in product publicity and the distribution of financial information should be aware of guidelines established by major government agencies such as the Federal Trade Commission (FTC), the Securities and Exchange Commission (SEC), and even the Federal Communications Commission (FCC).

Federal Trade Commission

The Federal Trade Commission has jurisdiction to determine that advertisements are not deceptive or misleading. Public relations personnel should also know that the Commission has jurisdiction over product news releases and other forms of product publicity, such as videos and brochures. The FTC makes it clear that its purview also includes social media such as blogs:

"FTC guidelines state that businesses and reviewers will be liable for any false statements made about a product. If a blogger receives a free sample of skin cream that claims to cure his eczema, for example, the company and the blogger could be held liable for false advertising." See the Ethics box about the Ann Taylor Loft on page 311 for an example of this questionable behavior.

In the eyes of the FTC, both advertisements and product publicity materials are vehicles of commercial trade—and therefore are subject to regulation. In fact, Section 43(a) of the Lanham Act makes it clear that anyone, including public relations personnel, is subject to liability if that person participates in the making or dissemination of a false and misleading representation in any advertising or promotional material. This includes advertising and public relations firms, which also can be held liable for writing, producing, and distributing product publicity materials on behalf of clients.

An example of an FTC complaint is the one filed against Campbell Soup Company for claiming that its soups are low in fat and cholesterol and thus helpful in fighting heart disease. The Commission charged that the claim was deceptive because publicity and advertisements didn't disclose that the soups also are high in sodium, a condition that increases the risk of heart disease.

The Campbell Soup case raises an important aspect of FTC guidelines. Although a publicized fact may be accurate in itself, FTC staff also considers the context or "net impression received by the consumers." In Campbell's case, advertising copywriters and publicists ignored the information about high sodium, which placed an entirely new perspective on the health benefits of the soup.

Hollywood's abuse of endorsements and testimonials to publicize its films also has attracted the scrutiny of the FTC. It was discovered that Sony Pictures had concocted quotes from a fictitious movie critic to publicize four of its films. And 20th Century Fox admitted that it had hired actors to appear in "man on the street" commercials to portray unpaid moviegoers.

More recently, the FTC has been focusing on the marketing of food and beverages to children. The agency subpoenaed 44 food marketers, asking for detailed reports on how much they spend promoting their products to children and adolescents to determine whether more federal regulations might be required.

FTC investigators are always on the lookout for unsubstantiated claims and various forms of misleading or deceptive information. Some of the words in promotional materials that trigger FTC interest are *authentic, certified, cure, custom-made, germ-free, natural, unbreakable, perfect, first-class, exclusive,* and *reliable.*

In recent years, the FTC also has established guidelines for "green" marketing and the use of "low-carb" in advertisements and publicity materials for food products. In 2009, the FTC ruled that anyone who endorses a product, including celebrities and bloggers, must make explicit the compensation received from companies. The FTC guidelines also state that businesses and reviewers (including bloggers) may be held liable for any false statements about a product.

on the job

ETHICS

Ann Taylor Loft Offers Gift Cards to Bloggers

One tactic that Ann Taylor Loft has used to publicize its summer collection was to invite fashion bloggers to a preview. Invitations to a preview are a standard tactic in the fashion industry, but this invitation was unusual because it offered a gift card drawing to bloggers who wrote about the summer collection.

The invitation stated:

Please note all bloggers must post coverage from our event to their blog within 24 hours in order to be eligible. Links to the post must be sent to [address] along with the code on the back of your gift card distributed to you at the event. You will be notified of your gift card amount by February 2. Gift card amounts will vary from $10 to $500.

Such an approach raises ethical questions, including whether the tactic violated the new rules for bloggers enacted by the Federal Trade Commission (FTC) and mentioned in this chapter. Basically, the rules require bloggers to disclose the receipt of merchandise or other freebies that might have influenced their coverage of a product or service.

Jezebel (www.jezebel.com) tracked fashion blogger coverage of the summer collection preview, which was very positive. An example was "The

collection contained everything a woman would need for the weekend or a vacation. . . . Stop by your local Loft anytime starting in May to see the entire collection; you won't be disappointed."

All 31 bloggers, according to the company, took the gift card, the implication being that the most favorable reviewers were rewarded with higher-value cards (up to $500) in the retailer's drawing. At the same time, Jezebel reported that none of the fashion bloggers, except two, disclosed to their readers that they had received a gift card for writing a review.

The blog for the *Los Angeles Times* called the gift card tactic "attempted bribery," but the president of Ann Taylor Loft, Gary Muto, told *PRWeek*, "We don't incentivize the press. We would never do that. They could write whatever they want. Obviously, there's freedom of speech."

What do you think? Was the gift card offer by Ann Taylor Loft an unethical public relations tactic? Or were the fashion bloggers at fault for not disclosing in their postings their receipt of the gift card? Do you think Ann Taylor Loft and the bloggers violated FTC rules? Why or why not?

The following general guidelines, adapted from FTC regulations, should be taken into account when writing product publicity materials:

- Make sure the information is accurate and can be substantiated.
- Stick to the facts. Don't "hype" the product or service by using flowery, nonspecific adjectives and ambiguous claims.
- Make sure celebrities or others who endorse the product actually use it. They should not say anything about the product's properties that cannot be substantiated.
- Watch the language. Don't say "independent research study" when the research was done by the organization's staff.
- Provide proper context for statements and statistics attributed to government agencies. They don't endorse products.
- Describe tests and surveys in sufficient detail so that the consumer understands what was tested and under what conditions.
- Remember that a product is not "new" if only the packaging has been changed or the product is more than six months old.
- When comparing products or services with a competitor's, make certain you can substantiate your claims.
- Avoid misleading and deceptive product demonstrations.

Companies found in violation of FTC guidelines are usually given the opportunity to sign a consent decree. This means that the company admits no wrongdoing but agrees to change its advertising and publicity claims. Companies may also be fined by the FTC or ordered to engage in corrective advertising and publicity.

Securities and Exchange Commission

The megamergers and the IPOs (initial public offerings) of many new companies starting in the 1990s made the Securities and Exchange Commission a common name in the business world. Such complex and enormous deals have also made the practice of investor relations increasingly important. This federal agency closely monitors the financial affairs of publicly traded companies and protects the interests of stockholders.

SEC guidelines on public disclosure and insider trading are particularly relevant to corporate public relations staff members, who must meet those federal requirements. The distribution of misleading information or failure to make a timely disclosure of material information may be the basis of liability under the SEC code. A company may even be liable if, while it satisfies regulations by getting information out, it conveys crucial information in a vague way or buries it deep in the news release.

A good example is Enron, the now defunct Houston-based energy company that became a household word overnight when it became the largest single corporate failure in U.S. history. The company management was charged with a number of SEC violations, including the distribution of misleading news releases about its finances. According to congressional testimony, the company issued a quarterly earnings news release that falsely led investors to believe the company was "on track" to meet strong earnings growth in 2002. Three months later, the company was bankrupt. Later, in criminal trials, Enron's head of investor relations, Mark Koenig, received 18 months for aiding and abetting securities fraud.

The SEC has volumes of regulations, but the three concepts most pertinent to public relations personnel are as follows:

1. **Full information must be given on anything that might materially affect the company's stock.** This includes such things as (1) dividends or their deletion, (2) annual and quarterly earnings, (3) stock splits, (4) mergers or takeovers, (5) major management changes, (6) major product developments, (7) expansion plans, (8) change of business purpose, (9) defaults, (10) proxy materials, (11) disposition of major assets, (12) purchase of own stock, and (13) announcements of major contracts or orders. In a somewhat unusual situation, computer giant HP was investigated by the SEC for not disclosing that a prominent member of the board of directors resigned because he disagreed with the board chair, Patricia Dunn, about a decision to "spy" on other board members to discover possible leaks of proprietary information.

2. **Timely disclosure is essential.** A company must act promptly (within minutes or a few hours) to dispel or confirm rumors that result in unusual market activity or market variations. The most common ways of dispensing such financial information are through electronic news release services, contacting the major international news services (Dow Jones Wire), and bulk emails and faxing.

3. **Insider trading is illegal.** Company officials, including public relations staffs and outside counsel, cannot use inside information to buy and sell company stock. The landmark case on insider trading occurred in 1965, when Texas Gulf Sulphur executives used inside information about an ore strike in Canada to buy stock while at the same time issuing a news release downplaying rumors that a rich find had been made.

The courts are increasingly applying the *mosaic doctrine* to financial information. Maureen Rubin, an attorney and professor at California State University, Northridge, explains that a court may examine all information released by a company, including news releases, to determine whether, taken as a whole, they create an "overall misleading" impression. One such case was *Cytryn v. Cook* (1990), in which a U.S. District Court ruled that the proper test of a company's adequate financial disclosure is not the literal truth of each positive statement, but the overall misleading impression that the statements combine to create in the eyes of potential investors.

As a result of such cases, investor relations personnel must also avoid such practices as:

- Unrealistic sales and earnings reports
- Glowing descriptions of products in the experimental stage
- Announcements of possible mergers or takeovers that are only in the speculation stage
- Free trips for business reporters and offers of stock to financial analysts and editors of financial newsletters
- Omission of unfavorable news and developments
- Leaks of information to selected outsiders and financial columnists
- Dissemination of false rumors about a competitor's financial health

The SEC also has regulations supporting the use of "plain English" in prospectuses and other financial documents. Companies and financial firms are supposed to make information understandable to the average investor by removing sentences littered with lawyerisms such as *aforementioned, hereby, therewith, whereas,* and *hereinafter.* The cover page, summary, and risk factor sections of prospectuses must be clear, concise, and understandable. A SEC booklet gives helpful writing hints such as (1) make sentences short; (2) use *we* and *our*, *you* and *your*; and (3) say it with an active verb. More information about SEC guidelines can be accessed from its website: www.sec.gov/

Fair Disclosure Regulation   In 2000, the SEC issued another regulation related to fair disclosure, known as Reg FD. Although regulations already existed regarding "material disclosure" of information that could affect the price of stock, the new regulation expands the concept by requiring publicly traded companies to broadly disseminate "material" information via a news release, webcast, or SEC filing. According to the SEC, Reg FD is intended to ensure that *all* investors—not just brokerage firms and analysts—receive financial information from a company at the same time.

Sarbanes-Oxley Act   The Sarbanes-Oxley Act was made law in 2002 as a result of the Enron and Worldcom financial scandals. Although the Enron scandal alone cost investors an estimated $90 billion, the devastation was dwarfed by the 2009 collapse of banks, market valuation, and real estate prices. Largely due to regulatory failings combined with ruthless speculation akin to betting, the Act failed to protect consumers. The Obama administration faces the daunting task of bolstering the law and changing the culture on Wall Street. For public relations and investor relations professionals, the admonition that ignorance is no excuse before the law should be the operating principle.

Federal Communications Commission

The FCC historically licensed radio and television stations, allocating frequencies and ensuring that the public airwaves are used in the public interest. Increasingly, the Commission oversees Internet policy. FCC actions directly impact public relations personnel who distribute video news releases (VNRs) on behalf of employers and clients and public relations professionals who facilitate viral spread of copyrighted material on the Web.

The controversy about proper *source attribution* of VNRs by television stations was somewhat discussed in Chapter 3, but political debate still continues about the FCC's ruling that broadcasters must disclose to viewers the origin of video news releases produced by the government or corporations when the material runs on the public airways. The agency didn't specify what form such disclosure should take, but broadcasters argued that the FCC was curtailing their First Amendment rights. FCC Commissioner Jonathan Edelstein disagreed, saying the issue is not one of free speech, but of identifying who is actually speaking. He told the *Washington Post*, "We have a responsibility to tell broadcasters they have to let people know where the material is coming from. Viewers are hoodwinked into thinking it's really a news story when it might be from the government or a big corporation trying to influence the way they think."

The issue of source attribution came about as a result of critics complaining that VNRs produced by the Bush administration and aired as part of local television reports were "government propaganda." In addition, public relations firms came under fire from citizen watchdog groups who said the actual client for a VNR was often obscured. For example, television stations used a VNR that featured two prominent "debunkers" of global warming under the rubric of the "TCS Daily Science Roundtable," which was actually owned by a Republican public relations firm that included Exxon/Mobil as a client.

Both the broadcast and the public relations industries have joined together to call for voluntary controls and disclosure instead of "government intrusion" into the news process. Both industries have also adopted codes of practice (discussed in Chapter 3). Fines have also been levied by the FCC in terms of enforcing regulations concerning indecency on the airwaves. The triggering event was Janet Jackson's "wardrobe malfunction" at the 2004 Super Bowl halftime show when Justin Timberlake ripped off a piece of her black leather top, exposing her right breast for an instant. The "malfunction," of course, garnered more media coverage and public discussion than the game itself. The FCC, however, was not amused; it levied a $550,000 fine on CBS television (a division of Viacom) for airing the incident.

Increasingly, the Internet has become not only a major channel for delivery of content, but also a point of contention as a utility. The FCC has consistently supported Net neutrality; the rules prohibit fiber-optic carriers of general Internet traffic from expediting their own customers' information packets. However, a recent court decision overturned the FCC's position favoring Net neutrality, as reported in the *New York Times*: "A federal appeals court ruled on Tuesday that regulators had limited power over Web traffic under current law. The decision will allow Internet service companies to block or slow specific sites and charge video sites like YouTube to deliver their content faster to users."

Other Federal Regulatory Agencies

Although the FTC and the SEC are the major federal agencies concerned with the content of advertising and publicity materials, public relations professionals should be familiar with the guidelines of two other major agencies: the Food and Drug Administration (FDA) and the Equal Employment Opportunity Commission (EEOC).

The Food and Drug Administration

The FDA oversees the advertising and promotion of prescription drugs, over-the-counter medicines, and cosmetics. Under the federal Food, Drug, and Cosmetic Act, any "person" (which includes advertising and public relations firms) who "causes the misbranding" of products through the dissemination of false and misleading information may be liable.

The FDA has specific guidelines for video, audio, and print news releases on health care topics. First, the release must provide "fair balance" by telling consumers about the risks as well as the benefits of the drug or treatment. Second, the writer must be clear about the limitations of a particular drug or treatment, for example, that it may not help people with certain conditions. Third, a news release or media kit should be accompanied by supplementary product sheets or brochures that give full prescribing information. On television, these rules result in the often-parodied, rapid-fire recitation of caveats and side effects of an advertised drug.

Because prescription drugs have major FDA curbs on advertising and promotion, the drug companies try to sidestep the regulations by publicizing diseases, creating patient advocate groups, and enlisting celebrity spokespersons. Eli Lilly & Co., the maker of Prozac, provides a good example. The company sponsors ads and distributes publicity about depression. And the Glaxo Institute for Digestive Health conducts information campaigns about the fact that stomach pains can be an indication of major problems. Of course, Glaxo also makes the ulcer drug Zantac.

Equal Employment Opportunity Commission

Diversity in the workplace has dramatically increased in recent years, and the EEOC is charged with ensuring that workers are not discriminated against on the basis of their religion, ethnic background, gender, or even their English skills.

> Employers must understand that discriminatory English-only rules can hurt productivity, morale, and ultimately their bottom line.
>
> *Kimberlie Ryan, Denver attorney*

Employers, for example, need to accommodate the religious needs of their employees. The focus has been on Muslims, who pray five times a day and have attire prescribed by their religion, but Jews must also be allowed to be absent from the workplace on various Holy days. At the same time, EEOC guidelines also call for employers to ensure that employees don't express their religious views at work or impose their beliefs on others. In other words, a company's policy about harassment also needs to include wording about religion. For example, Abercrombie & Fitch clothing retailer is facing a $40 million lawsuit for refusing to hire a Muslim applicant for a sales associate position because the applicant intended to wear a head scarf, which the manager said violated the store's "Look Policy." Abercrombie & Fitch consistently adheres to its view that the associates are part of the advertising and image of the store, which overrides liberties that are protected outside the work environment.

The EEOC also gets involved in the contentious issue of language. Federal law doesn't prevent employers from requiring workers to speak only English if it is justified by business necessity or safety concerns, but a blanket policy of English-only can get an employer in trouble if it forbids workers to speak another language during breaks, or if the language spoken doesn't make a difference in the performance of the job. English-only advocates argue that multilingualism in the workplace encourages newcomers to retain their own language and that English speakers feel slighted when fellow workers talk to each other in their native language. On the other hand, Denver attorney Kimberlie Ryan told the *Wall Street Journal*, "This is not about whether people should learn English; it's about not using language as a weapon of harassment."

Being sensitive to the diversity of the workplace, plus a thorough understanding of EEOC guidelines, are requirements for anyone working in employee communications. Public relations personnel often work closely with human resources to offer workshops and educational materials on diversity to educate employees to be more tolerant and understanding of each other. It is much cheaper than a series of lawsuits charging discrimination.

Corporate Speech

The First Amendment to the U.S. Constitution guarantees "freedom of speech," but exactly what speech is protected has been defined by the courts over the past 200 years, and is still being interpreted today. However, there is a well-established doctrine that commercial speech doesn't have the same First Amendment protection as other forms of speech.

Essentially, the government may regulate advertising that is

- false,
- misleading,
- deceptive, or
- promotes unlawful goods and services.

The courts also have ruled that product news releases, brochures, and other promotional vehicles intended to sell a product or service constitute commercial speech.

Another area, however, is what is termed corporate speech. Robert Kerr, author of *The Rights of Corporate Speech: Mobil Oil and the Legal Development of the Voice of Big Business*, defines corporate speech as "media efforts by corporations that seek to affect political outcomes or social climate—in contrast with 'commercial speech,' which promotes products or services." The courts, for the most part, have upheld the right of corporations and other organizations to express their views on public policy, proposed legislation, and a host of other issues that may be of societal or corporate concern. Organizations traditionally did so through op-ed articles, letters to the editor, postings on their website, and even news releases. Some landmark Supreme Court cases helped establish the concept of corporate free speech, starting in 1978. But the most decisive ruling to affirm corporate speech rights was the *Citizen's United* case in 2010. For details, see the Insights box below.

on the job

INSIGHTS

Court Rules Corporations Can Spend Freely on Political Candidates

The Supreme Court decision in the case of *Citizens United v. the Federal Election Commission* has drastically changed the political landscape, which had been mostly unchanged over the past couple of decades. In a 5–4 decision, the nation's highest court ruled in favor of Citizens United, thus setting a precedent that gives corporations the power to provide funding for or against a political candidate. This ruling essentially gives corporations the First Amendment right of free speech.

The case, stemming from conservative activist group Citizens United's dissatisfaction with the previous rules, overturned several precedents and previous court cases that limited corporate power in the political realm. Citizens United sued to stop the Federal Elections Commission from enforcing rules laid forth in the 2002 bipartisan McCain-Feingold Campaign Reform Act. These rules prevented Citizens United from airing a documentary critical of Hillary

Clinton within 30 days of the 2008 primary election. The Supreme Court originally looked at the case from a narrower perspective to determine whether the documentary, *Hillary: The Movie*, should be allowed to be aired and advertised. Later, the Justices announced that they would broaden the case to determine whether they should nullify laws that limit corporate spending on political campaigns.

The landmark decision, seen as providing a bullhorn for corporations, has sent a shockwave across America and sparked both outrage and satisfaction. President Obama stood prominently among those outraged by the decision: "It is a

major victory for big oil, Wall Street banks, health insurance companies and the other powerful interests that

(continued)

marshal their power every day in Washington to drown out the voices of everyday Americans." Others, such as Senator Mitch McConnell, have long advocated that corporations receive First Amendment rights. McConnell praised the Court for its decision to restore ". . . the First Amendment rights of [corporations and unions] by ruling that the Constitution protects their right to express themselves about political candidates and issues up until Election Day."

How do you think a corporation's ability to spend freely in political campaigns will impact activist groups' public relations? Will the decision change public discourse about politics?

Do you agree with Senator McConnell that corporations should have First Amendment rights? After all, corporations represent employees, investors, and retirees with a stake in the decisions politicians make. Or are those stakeholders already able to speak as private citizens?

Do you agree with President Obama that a corporation's ability to spend freely will silence the everyday citizen?

Nike's Free Speech Battle

The Supreme Court became involved with corporate free speech in 2003 when it was petitioned by Nike, the shoe and sports clothes manufacturer, to redress a California Supreme Court decision that had ruled that the company's efforts to explain its labor policies abroad were basically "garden variety commercial speech." The ruling seemed to equate public relations speech about a policy issue with commercial advertising.

> There is a trend toward potential claims, including PR firms, for their role in disseminating a message that is misleading or . . . has omitted material facts.
>
> *Michael Lasky, partner in the New York law firm of Davis & Gilbert*

The case, *Nike v. Kasky*, raised the thorny question of how to deal with the blurred lines that often separate "free speech" and "commercial speech." Marc Kasky, an activist, had sued Nike, claiming that the company had made false and misleading statements that constituted unlawful and deceptive business practices. Nike, on the other hand, claimed that it had the right to express its views and defend itself against allegations by activist groups that it operated sweatshop factories in Asia and paid subpar wages.

The U.S. Supreme Court, however, was less certain about the "commercial" nature of Nike's public relations campaign. It did not make a decision and sent the case back to the California courts. Eugene Volokh, professor of law at UCLA, noted in a *Wall Street Journal* op-ed piece that Justice Stephen Breyer made an important point. According to Volokh, "Because the commercial message (buy our shoes) was mixed with a political message (our political opponents are wrong), and was presented outside a traditional advertising medium, it should have been treated as fully protected."

Employee Speech in the Digital Age

A modern, progressive organization encourages employee comments and even criticisms. Many employee newspapers and e-bulletin boards carry letters to the editor because they breed a healthy atmosphere of two-way communication and make company publications more credible. In an era of digital communications and increased legal litigation, however, organizations are increasingly setting guidelines and monitoring what employees say online. The following is a discussion of employee e-mail, surfing the Internet, blogging, and even guidelines for being an "avatar" on sites such as Second Life.

Employee E-Mail

The monitoring of employee e-mail by management is well established. A survey by Forrester Consulting for Proofpoint, a maker of e-mail security products, found that almost 50 percent of large companies audit outbound e-mail by their employees. Another 32 percent have actually fired an employee within the last year for breaking e-mail rules.

A number of court decisions have reinforced the right of employers to read employees' e-mail. Pillsbury, for example, fired a worker for posting an e-mail message to a colleague calling management "back-stabbing bastards." The employee sued, but the court sided with the company. In another case, Intel got a court injunction against a former employee who complained about the company in e-mails sent to thousands of employees. The Electronic Frontier Foundation, a group devoted to civil liberties in cyberspace, worried about violation of First Amendment rights. The company, however, contended that it wasn't a matter of free speech, but of trespassing on company property.

Employers are increasingly monitoring employee e-mail for two reasons. First, they are concerned about being held liable if an employee posts a racial slur, engages in sexual harassment online, or even transmits sexually explicit jokes that would cause another employee to feel that the workplace is a "hostile" environment. Second, companies are concerned about employee e-mails that may include information that the organization considers proprietary, such as trade secrets, marketing plans, and development of new products, which would give the competition an advantage. In other words, you should assume that any e-mails you write at work are subject to monitoring and that you can be fired if you violate company guidelines.

Surfing the Internet

Employees should also be careful about using the Internet at work. According to a recent survey by the American Management Association (AMA), more than 75 percent of American employers monitor personal Web surfing at work. And more than 25 percent of these companies have fired someone for doing it. Other studies, of course, show that Web surfing at work for personal reasons is done by the majority of employees—and many even think of using the Internet in the same context as using the lowly telephone.

Employers, for their part, are concerned about the loss of productivity when employees sit at their desks watching YouTube videos or updating their Facebook pages. Potential liability, however, is another big factor. Companies can and do get sued for what their employees do online. Office workers accessing porn sites, instant messaging smutty and racial jokes, and posting dubious photos and comments to Facebook invite lawsuits when other workers are offended and file complaints with the Equal Employment Opportunity Commission (EEOC). According to the *Financial Times*, "A New Jersey court found that employers were not just permitted but actually obliged to monitor employee Internet use."

> A New Jersey court found that employers were not just permitted but actually obliged to monitor employee Internet use.
>
> *Patti Waldmeir, columnist for the*
> Financial Times

Employee Blogs

Many organizations now encourage employees to have a blog, as a way of fostering discussion on the Internet and getting informal feedback from the public. In some large companies, even top executives have a blog. In most cases, the blog prominently features their association with the business and gives information (and images) about the employer. As John Elasser, editor of *Public Relations Tactics*, says, "Some of that content may be innocuous; other types may be embarrassing or come back to haunt the company in litigation."

Consequently, it is important for a business to have a clear policy that provides guidelines for what rank-and-file employees, as well as executives, can say or not say on their blogs or in a posting on another blog. The public relations staff often prepares general guidelines and trains employees about such matters as the proper use of corporate trademarks, avoiding unfair criticism of other employees or the competition, using copyrighted material, or even what topics are particularly sensitive because of pending lawsuits or business negotiations. Bloggers also have an obligation to inform readers that they are employees of the organization, not just an interested, average citizen.

Other general rules of netiquette are listed in Chapter 3. In addition, the Electronic Frontier Foundation has a "Legal Guide for Bloggers" at its website, www.eff.org /bloggers/lg

Liability for Sponsored Events

Public relations personnel often focus on the planning and logistics of events. Consequently, they must also take steps to protect their organizations from liability and possible lawsuits associated with those activities.

Plant tours, open houses, and other events should not be undertaken lightly. They require detailed planning by the public relations staff to guarantee the safety and comfort of visitors. Consideration must be given to such factors as possible work disruptions as groups pass through the plant, safety, and the amount of staffing required. Many events call for special logistical planning by the public relations staff. Such precautions will generate goodwill and limit the company's liability. It should be noted, however, that a plaintiff can still collect if negligence on the part of the company can be proved.

Liability insurance is a necessity when any public event is planned because accidents can occur that might result in lawsuits charging the sponsoring organization with negligence. Organizations can purchase comprehensive insurance to cover a variety of events or a specific event. The need for liability insurance also applies to charitable organizations when they sponsor events such as a 10-K run, a bicycle race, or a hot-air balloon race. Participants should sign a release form that protects the organization against liability in case of an accident. Promotional events that use public streets and parks also need permits from the appropriate city departments. For more information about event management, see Chapter 16, "Meetings and Events"

The Attorney/Public Relations Relationship

Litigation is an integral part of today's business environment. In fact, it is estimated that 90 percent of American corporations are dealing with lawsuits at any given time. Indeed, Philip Rudolph, a partner in a Washington, D.C., law firm, is quoted in *PRWeek* as saying, "The bounds of liability are beginning to stretch in ways that traditional lawyering does not address. You see companies being sued by their own customers over the lawful use of a legal product—such as obesity lawsuits brought against McDonald's."

In such an environment, it's important for public relations personnel and lawyers to work together to win not only in the court of law but also in the court of public opinion. Indeed, a survey by Kathy R. Fitzpatrick, a public relations professor now at DePaul University, found that almost 85 percent of the public relations respondents said their relationships with legal counsel are either "excellent" or "good." Researchers at the University of Houston and the University of Missouri, in separate studies, also found that lawyers and public relations practitioners report cooperative relationships.

Winning in the court of public opinion is the responsibility of the public relations professional, and such work is the practice of "litigation public relations." A good example of how this works is Daimler Chrysler's integration of public relations and legal counsel. First, both public relations personnel and legal staff serve on joint committees that review possible litigious situations. Second, when a lawsuit is filed, the integrated team formulates strategies to ensure that key company messages about the lawsuit are distributed to the media and the public.

In one case, even before a Texas trial judge had dismissed a $2 billion product liability suit because attorneys for the plaintiffs had falsified evidence, a Daimler Chrysler team had been on a nationwide media tour to explain the company's side of the case. Resulting headlines were "Chrysler Takes Fight to Lawyers" and "Chrysler Group Puts Texas Lawyers on Trial." In a case in which a jury eventually ruled in favor of Chrysler in a wrongful death suit, the automaker regularly throughout the trial gave its perspective on the case to the media to ensure fair and balanced coverage. For the same purposes, public relations firms specializing in litigation are also retained if a celebrity gets into legal trouble.

The cooperation between lawyers and public relations counsel has been strengthened in recent years by court rulings that conversations between the two can be considered attorney–client privilege if certain conditions are met. For example, U.S. District Court Judge Lewis Kaplan in New York ruled that attorney–client privilege exists if the following five conditions are met. In addition, each point must be checked off, says Kaplan, before the next point can be considered: "(1) confidential communications…(2) between lawyers and PR consultants…(3) hired by the lawyers to assist them in dealing with the media in cases such as this…(4) that are made for the giving or receiving of advice…(5) directed at handling the client's legal problems are protected by the attorney–client privilege." Other legal experts, however, say that attorney–client privilege is better protected if outside legal counsel actually employs a litigation public relations firm as a consultant instead of using internal public relations staff.

PRSA's *Tactics* suggests six "keys to winning in the court of law—and public opinion." They are:

■ Make carefully planned public comment in the earliest stages of a crisis or legal issue.

■ Understand the perspective of lawyers and allow them to review statements when an organization is facing or involved in litigation.

■ Guard against providing information to the other side of the legal case.

■ Counsel and coach the legal team.

■ Build support from other interested parties, such as industry associations or chambers of commerce.

■ Develop a litigation communication team before you need it.

To review how Google is taking a proactive approach to possible litigation, see the PR Casebook on page 322.

PRCasebook

Google Prepares for Possible Litigation

Google is the ultimate success story. It handles about two-thirds of all Internet searches, owns the largest online video site (YouTube), and sold more than $22 billion in advertising in 2008, more than any other media company in the world.

The only problem with such success is that it attracts consumer watchdogs and government regulators who are concerned about monopoly and antitrust issues. Google, however, is not waiting around for lawsuits to be filed.

It has launched an extensive public relations effort with the key message that "Competition is a click away." This is the standard speech of Google's legal counsel as he travels the country to talk with reporters, legal scholars, congressional staff members, industry groups, and, as the *New York Times* reports, "anyone else who might influence public opinion."

Google's concern is that regulators are already scrutinizing its every move as they have done with other giants such as IBM and Microsoft. And government litigation in the United States and Europe could pose a major threat to Google's continued success. In the United States, the Justice Department is already looking at the company's hiring practices, a class-action settlement between Google and authors and publishers, and ties between the Apple and Google boards of directors.

Such attention, of course, generates news coverage, and Google's public relations staff is concerned that a steady stream of headlines about possible antitrust investigations could damage Google's image with consumers who currently have positive feeling about the company. "No company, whether it is Google, Microsoft, or anyone else wants to be portrayed in a negative way," David B. Yoffie, a Harvard business school professor, told the *New York Times*.

Google's key message is that it has plenty of competition and it's a relatively small player in a vast market of multiple media resources. Google's general counsel, for example, makes the point that Microsoft and AT&T are not only much larger than Google but also spend much more money on lobbying.

Consumer Watchdog, an advocacy group, is not convinced. It has its own public relations campaign refuting Google's assertions. And even the competition has joined in. Microsoft public relations personnel, for example, often e-mail reporters offering rebuttals to Google's arguments.

A basic premise of litigation public relations, however, is the importance of being proactive and avoiding any lawsuits in the first place. Google is doing exactly that.

Because the collaboration between lawyers and public relations practitioners is so important, an organization can take a number of steps to ensure that the public relations and legal staffs have a cordial, mutually supportive relationship:

- The public relations and legal staffs should report to the same top executive, who can listen to both sides and decide on a course of action.
- Public relations personnel should know basic legal concepts and regulatory guidelines in order to build trust and credibility with the legal department.
- Both functions should be represented on key committees.
- The organization should have a clearly defined statement of responsibilities for each staff and its relationship to the other. Neither should dominate.
- Periodic consultations should be held during which materials and programs are reviewed.
- The legal staff, as part of its duties, should brief public relations personnel on impending developments in litigation so that press inquiries can be answered in an appropriate manner.

Summary

A Sampling of Legal Problems

■ There are a number of ways that a public relations practitioner may get caught up in a lawsuit or a case with a government regulatory agency.

■ Practitioners may also be held legally liable if they provide advice or support the illegal activity of a client.

Libel and Defamation

■ Libel and slander are often collectively referred to as *defamation*.

■ Defamation involves a false and malicious (or at least negligent) communication with an identifiable subject who is injured by loss of money, by loss of reputation, or through mental suffering.

■ Libel suits can be avoided through the careful use of language.

■ Some offensive communications, such as negative reviews by a theater critic, fall under the "fair comment" defense.

Invasion of Privacy

■ When publishing newsletters, companies cannot assume that a person waives his or her right to privacy just because of his or her status as an employee.

■ Companies must get written permission to publish photos or use employees in advertising materials, and they must be cautious in releasing personal information about employees to the media.

Copyright Law

■ *Copyright* is the protection of creative work from unauthorized use.

■ Published works are by definition copyrighted, and permission must be obtained to reprint such material.

■ The "fair use" doctrine allows limited quotation, as in a book review.

■ Unless a company has a specific contract with a freelance writer, photographer, or artist to produce work that will be exclusively owned by that company (a situation called "work for hire"), the freelancer owns his or her work.

■ New copyright issues have been raised by the popularity of the Internet and the ease of downloading, uploading, and disseminating images and information.

Trademark Law

■ A *trademark* is a word, symbol, or slogan identifying a product's origin that can be registered with the U.S. Patent and Trademark Office.

■ Trademarks are always capitalized and used as adjectives rather than nouns or verbs.

■ Companies vigorously protect trademarks to prevent their becoming common nouns.

■ One form of trademark infringement may be "misappropriation of personality," the use of a celebrity's name or image for advertising purposes without permission.

Regulations by Government Agencies

■ Commercial speech is regulated by the government in the interest of public health and safety, and consumer protection.

■ Regulating agencies include the Federal Trade Commission (FTC), the Securities and Exchange Commission (SEC), the Federal Communications Commission (FCC), the Food and Drug Administration (FDA), and the Equal Employment Opportunity Commission (EEOC).

Corporate Speech

■ Organizations have the right to express their opinions and views about a number of public issues.

■ Federal election rules now allow direct corporate support of candidates for office.

■ However, there is still some blurring of lines between what is considered "commercial speech" and "free speech," as illustrated by the *Nike* case.

Employee Speech in the Digital Age

■ Employees are limited in expressing their opinions within the corporate environment.

■ Employee e-mail and surfing the Internet are subject to monitoring.

■ Employees can be fired (or former employees sued) for revealing trade secrets or harassing fellow employees. Companies can set guidelines for keeping a blog and for participating in virtual online communities such as Second Life.

Liability for Sponsored Events

- Plant tours, open houses, and other promotional events raise liability issues concerning safety and security.

- Liability insurance is a necessity.

- Permits may be required for the use of public streets and parks and for serving food and liquor.

The Attorney/Public Relations Relationship

- A cooperative relationship must exist between public relations personnel and legal counsel to handle today's challenges.

- Both groups should report to the same top executive and be represented on key committees.

- Public relations practitioners should also be aware of legal concepts and regulatory guidelines and receive briefings from the legal staff on impending developments.

- A new practice area is litigation public relations.

Case Activity   Are Exposé Filmmakers Journalists?

Just exactly who is a journalist in the age of social media and online news delivery? Is a person prohibited from tweeting at a College World Series game being denied his journalistic right to let the world know the pitch count in real time? Is someone blogging from a D.C. political soiree for *TMZ.com*, the celebrity gossip and entertainment news site, a journalist? Are credentials warranted for these persons?

The question of credentials gets thornier when the courts are involved, as in the case of Joe Berlinger, director of a documentary film about oil spills in Ecuadorean rain forests. His film, *Crude*, proved inspirational and useful in the Ecuador government's $28 billion lawsuit against Chevron for the

environmental problems it created. To mount its defense, Chevron filed a subpoena for access to the 600 hours of video that were cut from the film. Berlinger fought the subpoena by claiming his First Amendment right as a journalist to protect his sources. A federal judge sided with Chevron and against the director's claim to be an investigative reporter.

As a communication law expert, you should determine which of these two parties, the filmmaker or the oil company, most deserves your expert counsel. For background, start at http//en.wikipedia.org/wiki/Crude_(film). Write a memo justifying your decision to the senior partners in your law firm.

Questions   For Review and Discussion

1. How can a public relations person take precautions to avoid libel suits?

2. What is the concept of fair comment and criticism? Are there any limitations to it?

3. When the media call about an employee, what kinds of information should the public relations person provide?

4. What basic guidelines of copyright law should public relations professionals know about?

5. What rights do freelance photographers and writers have regarding ownership of their works?

6. How do public relations people help an organization protect its trademarks?

7. What is "misappropriation of personality"?

8. What should public relations people know about the regulations of the Federal Trade Commission? The Securities and Exchange Commission?

9. What is the difference between plagiarism and copyright infringement?

10. If an organization is sponsoring an open house or a promotional event, what legal aspects should be considered?

Media Resources

Bernstein, J. L. (2010, April 9). Trial by media—do's and don'ts. Retrieved from managementhelp.org/blogs/crisis-management

Business Wire. (2009, October 15). Fulbright & Jaworski 2009 litigation trends survey: U.S. companies experiencing new litigation wave, anticipate more to come. Retrieved from www.freelibrary.com.

Gower, K. K. (2008). *Legal and ethical considerations for public relations*. Long Grove, IL: Waveland Press.

Han, G., & Zhang, A. (2009). Starbucks is forbidden in the Forbidden City: Blog, circuit of culture and informal public relations campaign in China. *Public Relations Review, 35*(4), 395–401.

Lasky, M. (2009, December 4). Successfully negotiate your agency-client agreement. Retrieved from www.prweekus.com

Lasky, M. (2010, February 5). Avoid employee invasion-of-privacy claims with updated tech guidelines. Retrieved from www.prweekus.com

Moshinsky, B. (2008, April 28). A&O's BlackBerry patent win soured as costs inquest criticizes hours tally. Retrieved from www.thelawyer.com

Parkinson, M. G., & Parkinson, L. M. (2009). *Public relations law: A supplemental text*. New York, NY: Taylor & Francis.

Reber, B., Gower, K., & Robinson, J. (2006). The Internet and litigation public relations. *Journal of Public Relations Research, 18*(1), 23–44.

Reuters. (2010, May 19). Novartis fined $250 million in sex discrimination suit. Retrieved from www.nytimes.com

Schwartz, J., & Itzkoff, D. (2010, May 7). A filmmaker's quest for journalistic protection. Retrieved from www.nytimes.com

Searson, E. M., & Johnson, M. A. (2010). Transparency laws and interactive public relations: An analysis of Latin American government web sites. *Public Relations Review, 36*(2), 120–126.

The Internet
and Social Media

After reading this chapter, you will be able to:

Understand why the Internet is
a communications revolution

Organize and design an effective
website

Be familiar with the mechanics of
doing a webcast

Use social media and networking
as public relations tactics

Know the potential of mobile-enabled
content to reach future audiences

The Internet: Pervasive in Our Lives

Today's college students have grown up with the Internet, and it's difficult for many of them to imagine life without it. Even many of their parents fail to understand that the Internet is a revolutionary concept that has transformed a media system dating back to Gutenberg in the 1400s.

For 500 years, mass media dominated the world's landscape. They had the characteristics of being (1) centralized/top-down, (2) costly in terms of being published (3) staffed by professional gatekeepers known as editors and publishers, and (4) mostly one-way communication with limited feedback channels.

Thanks to the Internet, there are now two spheres of influence, which are constantly interacting with each other. CooperKatz and Company calls them (1) the mediasphere and (2) the blogosphere. The new media system has the characteristics of (1) widespread broadband; (2) cheap/free, easy-to-use online publishing tools; (3) new distribution channels; (4) mobile devices, such as camera phones; and (5) new advertising paradigms. For the first time in history, a medium, the Internet, has literally caused the democratization of information around the world. See Figure 13.1 for a breakdown by region of the world's 1.96 billion users.

The Internet, first created as a tool for academic researchers in the 1960s, came into widespread public use in the 1990s and the rest is history. Indeed, the worldwide adoption of the Internet has taken less time than the growth of any other mass medium. Marc Newman, general manager of Medialink Dallas, says, "Whereas it took nearly 40 years before there were 50 million listeners of radio and 13 years until

> Armed with digital cameras, camera phones, handheld video cameras, podcasts, blogs, and social networks, we've entered the era of citizen journalism and user-generated content.
>
> *Brian Solis and Deirdre Breakenridge, authors of* Putting the Public Back in Public Relations

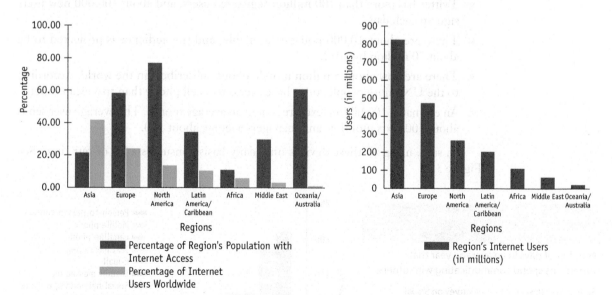

Figure 13.1 Internet Users Around the World

Would you agree or disagree that the Internet has caused the "democratization of information" around the world?

Source: www.internetworldstats.com (as of January 2010).

television reached an audience of 50 million, a mere four years passed before 50 million users were logging on to the Internet since it became widely available."

The growth of the Internet and social networking sites continues at an astounding rate. It's difficult to imagine that today's popular Web brands such as YouTube, Facebook, and Twitter didn't even exist five or six years ago. Consequently, any figures published today regarding the Internet are already out of date. Yet some 2010 stats are worth noting as a reference point.

- The number of Internet users worldwide is estimated to be almost 2 billion people. (See Figure 13.1.)
- U.S. Internet users, on average, spend about 16 hours a week online, up from 8.9 hours in 2006.
- Google, the most popular search engine in the United States, handles about 10 billion search queries a month. The average American visits about 115 domains and 2,500 pages in an average month.
- E-mail is used by 95 percent of Internet users. The average number of e-mails received per person is 13,500 annually.
- The World Wide Web contains 63 billion pages, and there are more than 100 million websites.
- There are an estimated 135 million blogs, and 346 million people around the world read blogs on a regular basis.
- Facebook has more than 500 million active users worldwide and MySpace has about 125 million.
- YouTube has more than 1 billion views per day, and 24 hours of video are being uploaded every minute of the day.
- Twitter has more than 100 million registered users, and about 300,000 new users sign up each day.
- There are about 10,000 podcasts available, and the audience is projected to be about 70 million by 2012.
- There are now about 5 billion mobile phone subscribers in the world. According to the UN, more people today have access to a cell phone than to a clean toilet.
- An estimated 100 billion texts are sent in an average month. The average user sends about 400 texts monthly, and teenagers average about 500.

In sum, using all these devices on a daily basis consumes a lot of our time. See Figure 3.2.

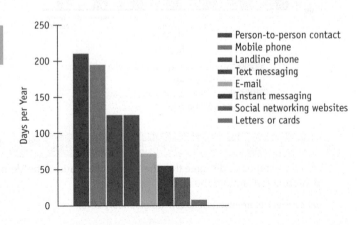

Figure 13.2   Social Interaction in the Internet Age

Number of days in an average year that Americans spend communicating with others.

Source: Pew Research Center survey on Social Isolation and New Technology, 2009.

The World Wide Web

The exponential growth of the World Wide Web is due, in large part, to browsers such as Internet Explorer and search engines such as Google, which have made the World Wide Web accessible to literally billions of people. Here are some characteristics of the Web that enable public relations people to do a better job of distributing a variety of messages:

- Information can be updated quickly without having to reprint brochures and other materials. This is an important element when it comes to major news events and dealing with a crisis.

- It allows interactivity; viewers can ask questions about products or services, download information of value to them, and let the organization know what they think.

- Online readers can dig deeper into subjects that interest them by linking to information provided on other sites, in other articles, and in other sources.

- A great amount of material can be posted. There is no space or time limitation.

- It is a cost-effective way to disseminate information on a global basis to the public and journalists.

- You can reach niche markets and audiences directly without messages being filtered through traditional mass media gatekeepers (editors).

- The media and other users can access details about your organization 24 hours a day from anywhere in the world.

From a public relations standpoint, a website is literally a distribution system in cyberspace. Organizations, for example, use their websites to market products and services and post news releases, corporate backgrounders, product information, position papers, and even photos of key executives or plant locations. The public, as well as media personnel, can access the information, download selected materials into their computers, and even print out hard copies. Websites have also become more interactive, giving public relations professionals valuable feedback from consumers and the general public. See the Insights box on page 330.

In many cases, an organization's website is hyperlinked to other webpages and information sources. A user can thus jump immediately to a related website by clicking the mouse on various icons. Business Wire's website, for example, links to the home pages of various organizations that use its distribution services.

Various surveys indicate that journalists also extensively use websites to retrieve current news releases and other materials. A 2010 survey by Cision and Don Bates of George Washington University, for example, found that corporate websites are ranked number one by journalists as a research tool.

In sum, the Web has become a major source of information for journalists. According to *NetMarketing*, companies are sending out fewer media kits and getting fewer phone inquiries as a result of putting material on websites. As Rick Rudman, president of Capital Hill Software, told *PR Tactics*, "The days of just posting press releases on your website are gone. Today, journalists, investors, all audiences expect to find media kits, photos, annual reports, and multimedia presentations about your organization at your press center."

Marketing communications is also a common objective of organizational websites. All companies, from mom-and-pop businesses to multinational corporations, have websites to sell products and services directly to the public. Apple's website, for example,

on the job
INSIGHTS

Ways that Organizations Use Their Websites

Organizations use their websites in different ways. Here's a sampling:

■ Federal Express uses its website for investor relations. Stock prices, analyses of company performance, the annual report, and other financial information are available.

■ Rutherford Hill Winery in California uses its website to give a video tour of the winery.

■ L. L. Bean has a website that gives a history of the company, shows how it hand-sews its shoes, and lists attractions at 900 state and national parks.

■ Westchester Medical Center posts a virtual encyclopedia of disease and health care information that is freely available to the public. The site also establishes the medical center as a premier medical facility by describing its multiple clinics and medical services.

■ IBM, a global corporation, devotes segments of its website to its activities on various continents. One segment on Africa, for

Health Care Information on the Internet

West Chester Medical Center, located in New York State, has a well-designed website that offers the public a variety of information and services. The site is designed for easy navigation so that visitors can find information about the medical center's treatment centers and also basic health care information.

example, provides pdfs of case studies and short video clips.

■ Starbucks, in an effort to revive its brand, launched a website in which customers can offer the company suggestions about

ordering products and other aspects of its stores. The site was modeled as a social network where users can also post comments on each other's ideas.

was rated by the FT Bowen Craggs Index of Corporate Web Effectiveness as being "too marketing focused" and very poor in the areas of media relations, general contact information, and investor relations (IR).

Other marketing approaches might be page links where potential customers can learn about the organization and its approach to producing environmentally friendly, "green" products. Webpages with a strong marketing emphasis may have several main sections, such as (1) information about the organization and its reputation for service and reliability, (2) a list of product lines, (3) technical support available to customers, (4) information on how to order products or services, and (5) a list of the various services available.

A preliminary step before creating any webpage is to understand the potential audience and their particular needs. Are they accessing the website to find a particular product? Are they primarily investors who are looking for financial information? Or are they looking for employment information? Are they likely to download the material and save documents in print form? Focus groups, personal interviews, and surveys often answer these questions and help the company design a user-friendly site.

The San Diego Convention Center, for example, redesigned its website by forming a customer advisory board of 28 clients that used the facility. Focus groups were held to determine what clients wanted to see in an updated website. According to *PRWeek*, "The Customer Advisory Board feedback enabled SDCC to jettison a great deal of the clutter that plagues many sites and focus on exactly what the target audience wanted. Gone was dense copy and hard-to-navigate pages, replaced by hot links to key portions of the site."

Indeed, paying attention to the needs of the audience helps a company decide exactly what links to list on the home page. Intel's home page, for example, has a list of just three categories: Work, Play, and About Intel. Under each category are index tabs for specific areas. In the Work area, for example, are tabs for Products, Support, Downloads, Online Communities, and Technology. Under the About Intel area are tabs for such items as Corporate History, Executive Biographies, Press Room, and even how to sign up for RSS feeds and Intel newsletters. Indeed, being able to navigate a website with ease is key to its effectiveness. According to *Web Content Report*, "Improved navigation ranks first on nearly every site's priority list. The goal: Fewer required clicks for users to access information because your site loses users at each step in your navigation."

Forrester Research says there are four main reasons why visitors return to a particular website. First and foremost is high-quality content. Then, in descending order, are ease of use, quick downloads, and frequent updates. See the Insights box on page 332 for more tips on designing a website.

> Companies need to remember that a website is the one place they can tell their story in their own words; this is not possible to do in social media.
>
> *David Bowen, senior consultant for Bowen & Craggs*

Making a Website Interactive

A unique characteristic of the Internet and the World Wide Web, which traditional mass media do not offer, is interactivity between the sender and the receiver.

One aspect of interactivity is the "pull" concept. The Web represents the "pull" concept because the user actively searches for sites that can answer specific questions. At the website itself, the user also actively "pulls" information from the various links that are provided. In other words, the user is constantly interacting with the site and "pulling" the information most relevant to him or her. The user thus has total control over what information to call up and how deep to delve into a subject.

In contrast, the concept of "push" is that of information delivered to the user without active participation. Traditional mass media—radio, TV, newspapers, and magazines— are illustrative of the "push" concept, as are news releases that are automatically sent to the media. Another dimension of interactivity is a person's ability to engage in a dialogue with an organization. Many websites, for example, encourage questions and feedback by giving an e-mail address that the user can click on to send a message.

on the job
INSIGHTS

Tips for Designing a Website

Jakob Nielsen, an Internet consultant, gives a list of design elements that increase the usability of virtually all sites (www .useit.com):

- Place your organization's name and logo on every page.

- Provide a "search" tab if the site has more than 100 pages.

- Write straightforward and simple headlines and page titles that clearly explain what the page is about and that will make sense when read out of context in a search engine results listing.

- Structure the page to facilitate scanning and help users ignore large chunks of pages in a single glance. For example, use groupings and subheadings to break a long list into several smaller units.

- Don't cram everything about a product or topic into a single page; use hypertext to structure the content space into a starting page that provides an overview and several secondary pages that each focus on a specific topic.

- Use product photos, but avoid pages with lots of photos. Instead, have a small photo on each of the individual product pages and give the viewer the option of enlarging it for more detail.

- Use link titles to provide users with a preview of where each link will take them, before they have clicked on it.

- Do the same as everybody else. If most big websites do something in a certain way, then follow along, since users will expect things to work the same way on your site.

- Test your design with real users as a reality check. People do things in odd and unexpected ways, so even the most carefully planned project will learn from usability testing.

One successful application of this was a special website set up by the Antwerp Zoo to track the pregnancy of one of its elephants. The first ultrasound was posted on www.baby-olifant.be, and Belgians were asked to suggest names for the baby elephant. They were also kept updated with developments during the pregnancy. Daily news was posted on the site, and further communicated with photos on Flickr and videos on YouTube. A customized Facebook profile picture allowed people to view their faces with an elephant's trunk and the saying, "I'm also waiting for baby K." When labor started, the website carried the birth live as a webcast. More importantly, Antwerp Zoo welcomed 200,000 more paying customers in 2009 than in 2008.

Unfortunately, the ideas of being "interactive" and encouraging feedback are more buzzwords than reality on many websites. According to reporter Thomas E. Weber of the *Wall Street Journal*, "Many big companies invite a dialogue with consumers at their Internet outposts but are ill-prepared to keep up their end of the conversation." He continues, "*The Wall Street Journal* zapped e-mail inquiries to two dozen major corporate Web sites with e-mail capabilities and found many of them decidedly speechless. Nine never responded. Two took three weeks to transmit a reply, while others sent stock responses that failed to address the query. Only three companies adequately answered within a day."

A delayed response to an e-mail query or no response at all damages an organization's reputation and credibility. Ideally, an e-mail query is answered by an organization within 24 hours. Although it is good public relations to solicit feedback from the public, a company should think twice about providing e-mail response forms on its website if it isn't capable of handling the queries.

Managing the Website

An organizational website must serve multiple audiences. Consequently, the overall responsibility of managing the website should lie with the corporate communications department, which is concerned about the needs of multiple stakeholders. One survey of corporate communications and public relations executives by the Institute for Public Relations, for example, found that 70 percent of the respondents believed that an organization's communications/public relations function should manage and control all content on the website.

The reality, however, is that a successful website takes the input and knowledge of several departments. Information Technology (IT), for example, has the technical expertise to create a website. In addition, marketing also plays a major role. Shel Holtz, writing in *Communication World*, says, "As for the Web, electronic commerce falls in the marketing/sales jurisdiction. While communicators can play a role in both these areas, it is highly unusual to expect . . . sales transaction within the communication department."

Consequently, such experts as Holtz say the practical solution is a team approach, where representatives from various departments are equals. Holtz elaborates, "The team should take ownership of responsibility for the intranet or website, since teams work better than a situation in which one department retains control and others are merely subservient to the demands of the controlling group."

The advantage of cross-functional teams is that various members bring different strengths to the table. IT can provide the technical know-how, public relations can share expertise on the formation of messages for various audiences, and marketing can communicate the consumer services available through the site. Even human resources, as a team member, can contribute ideas on how to facilitate and process employment inquiries.

Webcasts

A website is enhanced and supplemented by using webcasts. Indeed, webcasting has become more common as bandwidth has increased and technology has evolved. In fact, one survey found that more than 90 percent of public companies use webcasts for everything from employee training to briefings for financial analysts and news conferences launching a new product. One big advantage is that they save time and money because they eliminate the cost of travel for participants.

In sum, Thomson Financial defines a webcast as "any event, live or archived, which involves the transmission of information from a person or organization to a larger audience over the Internet." The company continues, "Webcasts can be as simple as an audio-only address from a CEO or as elaborate as an audio/video webcast with a PowerPoint slide show presented from multiple locations with follow-up questions from the audience."

A good example of a media-oriented webcast is the one hosted by the Chocolate Manufacturers Association (CMA) and its public relations firm, Fleishman-Hillard. The CMA sponsored a chocolate-tasting webcast for food writers around the country, who also received a "tasting kit" before the event. They could taste various chocolates as they viewed the webcast, which featured experts on chocolate. By having a webcast, the organization doubled attendance from the previous year. Lynn Bragg, CMA president, told *PRWeek*, "It helped us connect with media and build relationships with them in a way that has increased awareness of CMA." The entire budget was about $20,000.

The U.S. Bureau of Engraving and Printing (BEP) also used a webcast news conference for 250 reporters from around the world to launch its newly designed $5 bill. The webcast featured U.S. Treasury, BEP, Federal Reserve, and U.S. Secret Service officials explaining the bill's new security features to prevent counterfeiting. The webcast also helped drive traffic to BEP's website; the site experienced a 1,000 percent increase in visitors, and there were about 100,000 downloads of materials explaining the security features and other characteristics. In addition to the webcast, BEP and its public relations firm, Burson-Marsteller, conducted a satellite media tour with various media outlets and produced podcasts that were archived on the website. Podcasting will be discussed shortly.

In another application, Clarkson University uses webcasts to stream campus events in real time to its alumni and other supporters. One event was a lecture by a Nobel Laureate, Dr. Paul Crutzen, who was visiting the campus to talk about global warming. Another was a "night at the opera" featuring a former opera singer.

The audience for such events may not be very large, but Karen St. Hillaire, director of university communications, thinks their promotional value makes the cost and effort worthwhile. She told *Interactive Public Relations*, "It is our belief that eventually this medium can be one of the most effective media to communicate with our alumni. It's a wonderful way to reach people who cannot be physically present for an event."

The Rise of Social Media

The first generation of the Internet, often called Web 1.0, was primarily based on information being transmitted from supplier to receiver. Although websites still serve that function, the second generation of the Internet (Web 2.0) has become an interactive model in which Web users now have multiple tools to talk to each other in real time. Thus, the term "social media" has now entered the mainstream as what Paul Rand of Ketchum communications calls "one of the most dramatic, if not revolutions, in history."

According to *Wikipedia*, "Social media describes the online technologies and practices that people use to share opinions, insights, experiences, and perspectives with each other." And David Bowen, writing in the *Financial Times*, adds, "Social networks are all about a shift from vertical to horizontal communications on the Web." IDC, a technology consultancy, puts it in more pragmatic terms, saying that 70 percent of all the digital information in world is now created by consumers.

There are various categories of social media. Blogs are now mainstream, but social networks such as MySpace, Facebook, and YouTube are also a major presence in today's world as even more social networks are created almost daily. There is also the rise of Twitter, podcasts, and Wikis, which power conversation between people around the world. This social media conversation is not organized, not controlled, and not on message. Instead, the conversation is vibrant, emergent, fun, compelling, and full of insights. Some experts have even called social networks the world's largest focus group. The *Economist*, for example, noted that "The direct, unfiltered, brutally honest nature of much online discussion is black gold; Texas tea to companies that want to spot trends or find out what customers really think."

The rise of social networks, which exploded in 2007, has also changed the landscape of public relations. This means that public relations, more than ever before, needs to be focused on listening in order to facilitate conversations between organizations and their constituents. One public relations counselor, in a survey conducted by the Institute for Public Relations (IPR), put it this way: "Social media has provided an opportunity to truly put the public back into public relations by providing a mechanism for organizations to engage in real-time, one-on-one conversations with stakeholders." A good example of this is Coca-Cola's Expedition 206, which is highlighted in the Multicultural World box on page 336.

Such conversations, however, can't be controlled, so organizations and their public relations staffs must get used to the idea that everything an organization does is more transparent and fair game for comment. David Pogue, technology columnist for the *New York Times*, thinks this is a valuable concept. He wrote, "When a company embraces the possibilities of Web 2.0, it makes contact with its public in a more casual, less sanitized way that, as a result, is accepted with much less cynicism. Web 2.0 offers a direct, more trusted line of communications than anything that came before it."

The following sections provide a sketch of the most popular social media and how they are being used in public relations activities. There is a discussion of (1) blogs, (2) MySpace and Facebook, (3) YouTube, (4) Flickr, (5) texting, (6) Twitter, (7) Wikis, and (8) podcasts.

> Collectively, the social media—including blogs, social networks, RSS feeds, podcasts, wikis, reviews, bulletin boards, and newsgroups—have the power to support or destroy a brand or reputation. Transparency is the key; but it's risky business and requires a new mindset and toolkit.
>
> *Markovsky Company*

Blogs: Everyone Is a Journalist

Blogs, dating back to 1998, have now become mainstream media in terms of numbers and influence. In the beginning, they were called *weblogs* because they were websites maintained by individuals who wanted to post their commentary and opinions on various topics. Today, the abbreviated term "blog" is commonly used.

Although the vast majority of blogs are still the province of individuals who post their diaries and personal opinions, they are now widely recognized by public relations personnel as an extremely cost-effective way to reach large numbers of people. The format and mechanics of blogs make them attractive for several reasons:

- Almost anyone can create a blog with open-source software. A blog is as ideal for a small business as it is for a large company.
- There are virtually no start-up costs.
- The format and writing are informal, which can give an organization a friendly, youthful human face.
- Links can be made to other blogs and webpages.
- Readers can post comments directly on the blog.
- Material can be updated and changed instantly.

on the job

A MULTICULTURAL WORLD

Coca-Cola Uses Social Media for Global Outreach

How would you like to travel the world courtesy of Coca-Cola? That's exactly what three young people did during 2010 as "Coca-Cola Happiness Ambassadors" who traveled to the 206 nations and territories where Coca-Cola is sold.

The concept of Expedition 206 was designed by Coke's department of social and digital media to connect with young consumers around the world. The first part was setting up a webpage, www .Expedition206.com, and getting the word out via its Facebook fan page and various bloggers. The Coke team then called for online entries from those who wanted to be "ambassadors." Nine were ultimately selected. Fans were then encouraged to vote for the three winners, and this generated several hundred thousand visitors to the website, mostly from outside the United States.

The three winners—Tony, Kelly, and Tono—were announced at Coke's headquarters in Atlanta and conducted interviews via satellite, phone, Skype, and Twitter. The three began their expedition in Madrid on January 1 and, as they traveled to

various nations, they documented their trip through Tweets, videos, photos, and blogs that were aggregated on the Expedition 206 website.

Tony, for example, Tweeted from Puerto Rico, "Left part of my heart in Puerto Rico. Happiness there was heritage, family and celebration. Not a bad combo if you ask me."

The travels of the three ambassadors, however, were not just a tour organized by Coke. Throughout the trip, fans interacted with the trio through the website, acting as virtual travel agents advising them where to go and what to

do in each locale. According to Lindsey Miller, writing in *ragan.com*, "That mindset drives the company's social media strategy. Not only does it embrace the lack of control, but Coca-Cola has put its Facebook page and new social media campaign, Expedition 206, in the public's hands."

Indeed, Coke is unique among global companies because its Facebook page, which has 3 million fans, is the creation of two Hollywood actors who are fans. In any case, Coke gets a lot of attention. Fans have posted more than 65,000 pictures on Flickr and more than 110,000 videos on YouTube. There are also about 2,500 Tweets every day that mention Coke or its other brands.

It's an opportunity to understand social and digital media, how people use it, how to connect with people.

Clyde Tuggle, SVP of public affairs for Coca-Cola

■ Extensive uses of syndication technologies allow aggregation of information from hundreds of blogs at once. An organization can immediately assess what customers and various publics are saying about it.

■ Blogs give an organization an outlet to participate in the online dialogue already going on in other blogs and message boards.

■ They allow organizations to post their own points of view unfettered by the editing process of the traditional media.

Ben King, writing in the *Financial Times*, summarizes the advantages of blogs over traditional websites. He says, "The exchange of links, comments, and trackbacks knits individual blogs into a dense network of mutual reference and endorsement, providing a giant boost in traffic for bloggers who get it right."

Indeed, as already noted, there are about 135 million blogs. Of that number, however, Technorati says only 7.4 million have been updated in the last 120 days. On the other hand, the *Wall Street Journal* estimates that almost 500,000 Americans are now blogging as their primary source of income. Many of these bloggers have garnered a large following because their postings have gained a reputation for credibility and breaking major stories, which are then picked up by the traditional media. One survey by Cison found that 90 percent of journalists turn to blogs for story research.

Susan Balcom Walton, writing in *Public Relations Tactics*, says organizations enter the blogosphere for four reasons:

■ To achieve real-time communication with key stakeholders.

■ To enable passionate, knowledgeable people (employees, executives, customers) to talk about the organization, its products, and its services.

■ To foster conversation among audiences with an affinity for or connection with the organization.

■ To facilitate more interactive communication and encourage audience feedback.

Public relations writers are usually involved in three kinds of blogs: (1) corporate or organizational blogs, (2) employee blogs, and (3) third-party blogs.

Organizational Blogs   A corporate blog, unlike an employee blog, is usually written by an executive and represents the official voice of the organization. In many cases, someone in the public relations department actually writes the blog for the executive. Some corporate blogs are now even being outsourced to public relations firms, but some critics say this is a guaranteed way to ensure that the blog is artificial and full of "execu-babble."

Larry Genkin, publisher of *Blogger and Podcaster* magazine, gives a good description of what a corporate blog should be. He says:

In its best incarnation, corporations will use blogs to become more transparent to their customers, partners, and internally. By encouraging employees to speak their minds, companies will be able to demonstrate their heart and character. Not an easy trick for a faceless entity. This will facilitate stronger relationships and act as "grease in the gears" of a business operation.

An example is how UPS used a corporate blog to connect its employees with its 100th anniversary celebration. It selected 100 outstanding employees from around the world to attend the celebration in Seattle and also to post messages, plus videos of the event, on the corporate blog site for fellow employees. UPS public relations and IT staff helped the employees, many of whom had never blogged before, to produce their posts; as a result, the posts came across as authentic and highly personalized about the employees' experiences attending the celebration.

In another situation, McDonald's started a blog, "Open for Discussion," about its corporate social responsibility (CSR) program. The vice president of CSR, Bob Langert, gave his personal perspective on McDonald's programs, but also invited consumers to engage in dialogue about what the fast-food giant was doing. According to Langert's post, "We want to hear from you because we are always learning and trying to improve. And you can't learn—or improve—without listening."

Although all corporate blogs should provide the opportunity for the public to post comments, it's also important to provide information that the audience can use. This was the approach of Ford & Harrison, a national labor and employment law firm that started a blog to address workplace issues from a legal perspective. The blog, called "That's What She Said," used graphics and humor to explore workplace issues in terms of how much the behavior of the blog's main character would cost companies to defend in real-life lawsuits. This showcased the firm's legal expertise in a user-friendly way, and *PRWeek* noted, "This is pop culture meeting the conservative world of law in a way that sets the blogosphere on fire."

Employee Blogs   Many organizations also encourage their employees to blog. Sun Microsystems, for example, has more than 4,000 employee blogs, or about 15 percent of its workforce. More than half of them, according to the company, are "super-technical" and "project-oriented," which appeal only to fellow computer programmers and engineers. Others, such as those written by the CEO as well as managers in human resources and marketing, are more general in subject matter. Even the company's legal counsel blogs. He opened a recent post with "I really dislike the word compliance" and went on to explain why.

Many organizations are uncomfortable with employee blogs because they are concerned about liability or the possibility that proprietary information will be released. Companies that have a more open system of communication and management believe employee blogs are great sources of feedback, ideas, and employee engagement.

However, companies do need to establish some guidelines for employee blogs. Cisco, for example, tells employees, "If you comment on any aspect of the company's business . . . you must clearly identify yourself as a Cisco employee in your postings and include a disclaimer that the views are your own and not those of Cisco." Dell also expects employees to identify themselves if they do any sort of blogging, social networking, editing of *Wikipedia* entries, or other online activities related to or on behalf of the company.

Steve Cody, managing director of Peppercom public relations, adds several more important points for employee or client blogs: (1) Be transparent about any former, current, or prospective clients being mentioned in the blog; (2) respond in a timely manner to individuals who post comments—pro, con, or indifferent; (3) generate as much original material as possible instead of just commenting on current news events; (4) link only to blog sites that are relevant to your post; and (5) make sure readers know that the blog represents your views and not necessarily those of your employer or client.

Third-Party Blogs   Organizations, in addition to operating their own blogs and providing guidelines for employee blogs, must monitor and respond to the postings on other blog sites. The products and services of organizations are particularly vulnerable to attack and criticism by bloggers, and an unfavorable mention is often multiplied by links to other blogs and search engine indexing.

Roy Vaughn, chair of the PRSA counselor's academy, explains, "Web empowerment has made the consumer king, and it has also made long-standing corporate and individual reputations extremely vulnerable. With Web 2.0, reputations can be made or broken in a nanosecond."

A good example is the 10-day blogstorm that overtook Kryptonite Company, manufacturer of bike locks. A consumer complaint, posted to bike forums and blogs, was that a Bic pen could be used to open a Kryptonite lock. Two days later, videos were posted on blogs showing how to pick the lock. Three days later, the *New York Times* and AP reported the story and it was picked up by the mainstream media. Four days after that, the company was forced to announce a free product exchange that cost it $10 million. See also the PR Casebook on page 343 about Domino's Pizza.

Dell also experienced the wrath of bloggers about its customer service, which caused sales to decline, but the company learned a good lesson. Today, according to the *New York Times*, "It's nearly impossible to find a story or blog entry about Dell that isn't accompanied by a comment from the company." Comcast, a cable giant, also gets its share of consumer complaints on blogs, but it also has stepped up its Internet monitoring and has customer service representatives follow up with anyone who posts a complaint.

Darren Katz, writing in *O'Dwyer's PR Report*, makes the point that "By engaging in online dialogue, companies are showing their customers that they care about their opinions, value their respect, and plan to rightfully earn their repeat business."

Companies should also establish relationships with the most relevant and influential bloggers who are talking about the company. Rick Wion, interactive media director of Golin Harris, told Susan Walton in *Public Relations Tactics*, "Treat them the same as you would any other journalist. In most cases, they will appreciate the recognition. By providing materials directly in a manner that is helpful to bloggers, you can build positive relationships quickly."

A good example is how Weber Shandwick works with about 20 influential food bloggers on behalf of its food industry clients. The public relations firm regularly monitors their posts to find out what the bloggers are saying and which "hot-button" issues they are discussing. This, in turn, allows the firm to build relationships with the bloggers and offer information that they can use in their blogs. Janet Helm, director of the food and nutrition practice at Weber Shandwick, told *PRWeek*, "They are an influential source, and we can't leave them out of the marketing mix."

Making Friends on MySpace and Facebook

There are multiple online social networking communities, including the business-oriented LinkedIn, but MySpace and Facebook established early leads in popularity. Facebook, in 2010, eclipsed MySpace as the most popular site, with 500 million users worldwide, of which 70 percent are outside the United States.

According to the Facebook website, 50 percent of its users log on during any given day, which amounts to more than 500 billion minutes per month. In addition, more than 1 billion photos , and more than 10 million videos, are uploaded to the site each month. And a survey by Student Monitor, a research firm, found that Facebook and beer tied for the most popular "thing" among college students after the iPod. A profile of Facebook is given in Figure 13.3.

The popularity of social networking sites such as Facebook has been noted by advertising, marketing, and public relations professionals, who see such sites as an excellent

Figure 13.3   The Face of Facebook

Source: http://mashable.com/2010/04/05/facebook-us-infographic

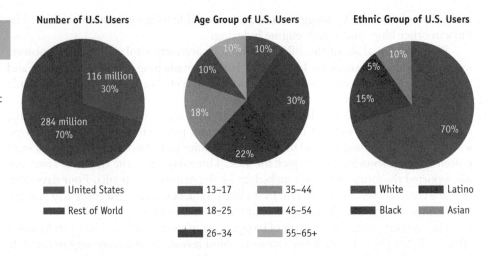

Number of U.S. Users

116 million 30%

284 million 70%

■ United States
■ Rest of World

Age Group of U.S. Users

10% 10%
10%
10% 30%
18%
22%

■ 13–17   ■ 35–44
■ 18–25   ■ 45–54
■ 26–34   ■ 55–65+

Ethnic Group of U.S. Users

10%
5%
15%
70%

■ White   ■ Latino
■ Black   ■ Asian

> We use tools based on their strengths, and each of the entries in the social media space offers its own strengths and weaknesses, possibilities and limitations.
>
> *Shel Holtz, social media guru at an IABC workshop*

opportunity to make "friends" in several ways. A survey of executives by TNS media intelligence/Cymfony, for example, found that marketing and public relations personnel believe networking sites are vital for (1) gaining consumer insights, (2) building brand awareness, and (3) creating customer loyalty.

Accomplishing these objectives, however, takes a great deal of thought and creativity because the public relations professional must shape messages that are relevant and interesting to the company's "friends." This often requires techniques such as humor, short video clips, music, contests, and audience participation. Champion, an apparel manufacturer, established a Facebook group called Champion Fan Zone to generate interest among college students. And even Sarah Palin extensively used her Facebook page to promote her book *Going Rogue*, which highlights her experience as the Republican Party's vice presidential candidate in 2008. According to the *Wall Street Journal*, nearly 1 million people have "friended" her.

Coors has also expanded its traditional advertising and product publicity to embrace social networking sites. One initiative on Facebook enabled visitors (those aged at least 21, of course) to send friends a "Code Blue" alert inviting them to meet up for a Coors Light. They could even use Facebook maps to direct their buddies to the nearest bar. Aaron, one of Coors' almost 2,000 fans, gave the site five stars: "This app is epic. I used it to set up my birthday party and it was so easy to invite everyone."

Another Coors campaign, centered on the Super Bowl, sponsored a contest in which consumers could create video clips and submit them on various networking sites to win prizes. Tim Sproul, a creative director for a Portland, Oregon, advertising agency, told the *New York Times*, "If you have anything to pitch in a social environment, it makes sense to pitch beer. We feel like we're not intrusive in the online experience, we're relevant, by giving people a chance to connect."

Even companies selling luxury goods have discovered the group and business pages of MySpace and Facebook. Cartier, for example, set up a MySpace profile to promote the jewelry in its Love collection. Visitors to the site can do more than look at the jewelry and the high price tags. According to Eric Pfanner, reporting in the *New York Times*, ". . . visitors can also sample music from artists like Lou Reed and Grand National, including several songs with the theme of love that were composed for Cartier. They can watch film clips with a romantic story line. And, of course, they can click on any of those friends' pictures to visit their profiles." Among Cartier's 3,800 friends are Sting, the band Good Charlotte, and Lou Reed.

Research firm Gartner predicts that by 2012, Facebook will be the leader and hub for all social media by developing a framework for the comprehensive, interoperable social Web.

YouTube: King of Video Clips

An extremely popular medium of communication is video clips. According to data from the Nielsen Online Video Census, U.S. Internet users watch more than three hours of online videos in a typical month.

In another study, Nielsen found that YouTube ranked as the second most popular search engine after its parent company, first-place Google. Its monthly video streams total almost 5 billion, compared to second-place Hulu, which has about 700 video streams. In sum, YouTube streams about 40 percent of all online videos.

Most videos are posted by individuals, but organizations are also creating and posting online videos as part of their marketing and public relations outreach to online communities. These communities, in general, are well educated and relatively affluent. In addition, research firms such as Nielsen/NetRatings have found that the 35 to 64 age group constitutes about 50 percent of YouTube's audience. Another large audience is college students; research shows that 95 percent of them regularly view videos online.

Such demographics prompted AirTran Airways to use YouTube to publicize its X-Fares, a stand-by flight program for college students. The airline appealed to students by creating AirTran U, complete with a mascot called Eunice, the AirTran Ewe. The idea was to get students to interact with the brand in a fun way via an online video contest. The airline, according to *PRWeek*, asked students to "Do a little (or big) dance, sing a fight song, chant, or whatever else comes to you." Students could post their videos at *youtube.com/airtranu* to compete for prizes. In addition, AirTran's public relations firm, CKPR, created profiles for Eunice on MySpace, Friendster, and Facebook, which attracted more than 600 friends among the target audience. The EweTube contest attracted 24,000 unique visitors, and Eunice even appeared on NBC's *Today*. The campaign also received *PRWeek*'s award for "Best Use of the Internet/New Media 2008," and one judge commented, "This was really a nice approach to engage the jaded college audience in a brave, clever, and irreverent way."

Humor was also used by H&R Block, a nationwide tax preparation company. Taxes and accounting are not exactly "cool" subjects, but the company wanted to reach younger audiences as it introduced such services as do-it-yourself, online tax preparation. The campaign started in January, the beginning of tax season, with the arrival of Truman Greene on YouTube. According to *Brandweek*, "In a dozen videos, the fictional oddball raves about the joys of online income tax preparation and spoofs popular YouTube shorts (like the precision treadmill routine dancers)." The YouTube videos received more than 556,000

> Embrace online video and watch how creative, genuine, and cool content becomes incredibly viral. Words can carry the message just so far, but video is an opportunity to showcase the product while entertaining viewers.
>
> *Brian Solis and Deirdre Breakenridge, authors of* Putting the Public Back in Public Relations

views, and the company's MySpace page had about 3,300 friends. In all, *Brandweek* reported that awareness of H&R Block's digital products increased 61 percent.

A video parody on YouTube can also be successful in increasing awareness of a product and brand. Smirnoff launched a new iced tea malt beverage on YouTube by creating a two-minute parody of a rap video, titled "Tea Partay." It showed three blond men in polo shirts rapping lines such as "Straight outta Cape Cod, we are keepin' it real." It worked because croquet, yachting, and white men aren't typical rap video imagery. It was viewed more than 500,000 times and created a word-of-mouth buzz as people e-mailed it to friends and colleagues.

Kevin Roddy, creative director of BBH advertising, told the *Wall Street Journal* that the Smirnoff video cost about $200,000 to produce, but it was a good value. A traditional 30-second TV spot costs an average of $350,000 to make, plus the cost of air time—which can run into six figures. He also said, "The client bought into it. They understand that advertising is no longer about talking at someone, it's about engaging with the consumer. To do that, you have to play by different rules. It requires you to be more entertaining." That's good advice for public relations professionals too.

However, not all YouTube videos have to be humorous and entertaining in order to be successful. The United Steelworkers, during a strike against Goodyear Tire & Rubber Co., posted a 30-second video spot on YouTube that showed a photo montage of auto accidents. As a sport-utility vehicle flips over, a question appears on-screen: "What tires do you plan to buy?" The union was making the case against tires made by replacement workers, and the video ranked number 24 on YouTube the day it was posted. Even if there aren't many downloads, organizations believe it's worth the effort because the video may be picked up by a blogger who will repost it and give it new life. Ultimately, it may even attract the attention of traditional media outlets.

On occasion, a YouTube video posted by a third party can do considerable damage to a corporate reputation. Canadian musician Dave Carroll, for example, had a complaint about United Airlines' baggage handlers breaking his guitar. He didn't get any satisfaction from United Airlines, so he composed a video song, "United Breaks Guitars," and posted it on YouTube. The song was an immediate hit and was played more than 3.5 million times over the next several months. This success garnered even more publicity when it became a smash hit on iTunes and when Carroll made guest appearances on every major television network. All the publicity also generated a flood of other customer complaints in the blogosphere about United Airlines. The airline, somewhat belatedly, offered an apology and donated $3,000 to the Thelonious Monk Institute of Jazz. This did nothing, however, to contain the damage to United's reputation.

Flickr: Sharing Photos

If YouTube is the king of videos, Flickr is the queen of photo sharing. The popular site allows individuals to share photos of their vacations, their children's first steps, and even their 21st birthday parties with the rest of the world.

The Flickr site is primarily for personal use, and organizations are strongly discouraged from trying to sell products or services. Public relations personnel, however, do find creative ways to use the social networking aspect of Flickr to build awareness of an organization or brand.

The Monterey Aquarium, for example, encourages the posting of photos taken by visitors at the facility. It even sponsored a photo contest in connection with World Ocean Day. The Aquarium's public relations staff also monitors blogs and if someone posts a good photo from an exhibit, they ask the individual to also post it on the Flickr site. Ken

PRCasebook

Pizza Chain Ambushed by YouTube Video

It wasn't a very happy Easter weekend for Domino's, a national chain of pizza and take-out restaurants. It suffered a major blow to its brand reputation when two employees at a Domino's restaurant in the small town of Conover, North Carolina, were bored one Sunday night and decided to produce a short video of them making a sandwich that violated all health standards.

The disgusting prank video was uploaded to YouTube, and within 24 hours, it was viewed by 500,000 people. In 48 hours, over a million people had viewed it. A number of blogs linked to the video, and then the mainstream media picked up the story.

Domino's, alerted to the video by employees, began to restore its reputation within 48 hours. First, it uploaded a two-minute video to YouTube that featured the company president, Patrick Doyle, saying, "It's not a surprise that this has caused a lot of damage to our brand."

Doyle then apologized for the incident and assured customers that Domino's has high standards of food quality and hygiene. Doyle continued, "Although the individuals in question claim it's a hoax, we are taking this incredibly seriously.... The two team members have been dismissed, and there are felony warrants out for their arrest. The store has been shut down and sanitized from top to bottom. There is nothing more important or sacred to us than our customers' trust."

In addition, the public relations staff of Domino's initiated a number of tactics. These included (1) starting a Twitter account to communicate with customers, (2) placing a "customer care" link about the incident on its corporate webpage to answer consumer concerns, (3) communicating via e-mail with all franchises and employees to keep them informed, (4) conducting interviews with leading bloggers and mainstream media, (5) distributing news releases via electronic news services to media and social network sites, and (6) using its Facebook profile to obtain "friends."

Online surveys indicated that Domino's reputation and brand once again were in the favorable column.

Peterson, communications director, told *Ragan.com*, "We've let some people know that we're interested in using their photos on the aquarium Web site or in other vehicles. That creates great word of mouth, since the photographer will likely tell his or her friends to visit the aquarium Web site—or Flickr group—and see the photo on display."

The Aquarium's example makes the point that social media sites such as Flickr can be used for public relations purposes only if the focus is on generating participation and involvement on the part of consumers and the general public. In all these programs, the organization is basically a facilitator of connecting people to people.

Texting: A Way of Life

Sending text messages via a mobile or cell phone is now pervasive and universal. In fact, *Ragan.com* reports that nearly 75 percent of mobile phone users worldwide send text messages on a daily basis. Text messaging is particularly popular among college students; almost 90 percent of them text on a daily basis, according to the 2009 Vingo Consumer Mobile Messaging Habits Report. Such heavy use, however, raises questions about basic etiquette. See the Ethics box below.

Texting is also used by organizations and public relations staffs to reach employees, customers, and key publics. Shel Holtz, a social media expert, told *Ragan.com* that

on the job
ETHICS

Think Before You Talk, Tweet, or Text

Being "connected" is now part of today's lifestyle for millions of people. In fact, one survey by Harris Interactive and Intel found that 65 percent of the respondents "feel they cannot live without internet access," and 46 percent of the women and 30 percent of the men said that they would rather go without sex for two weeks than give up Internet access for the same length of time.

Such a situation, however, has led to concerns about old-fashioned, basic etiquette. Louise Armstrong, who blogs about basic business etiquette (www.acallforclass.blogspot.com), writes in *Public Relations Tactics*, "The tools may be new but the rules are not. It has never been acceptable to ignore the person who you're with, use profanity in writing, or talk loudly in a crowded elevator."

Yet, in today's world, it's common for people to treat their smartphones or BlackBerry almost as religious touchstones as they talk on the phone in a crowded bus, text and Tweet during a meeting, and even read their e-mail while someone is talking to them. In one example that got media coverage, several New York State politicians pushed for the removal of the senate majority leader after they'd met with him to talk about the budget and he'd spent the entire time reading e-mail on his BlackBerry.

Traditionalists call such behavior rude, but others say that keeping in constant touch is just part of today's lifestyle. However, Armstrong offers some tips about how to improve your personal and professional technology etiquette.

Keep it real. A real person always takes precedent over a device and deserves your full attention.

Be aware of your surroundings. Don't have a cell phone conversation in any place people can't leave. This rules out coffee shops, elevators, airplanes, and bathroom stalls.

Do the crossword puzzle test. Any place that you wouldn't do a crossword puzzle is a place where you shouldn't catch up on e-mails. Think meetings, networking events, and cashier transactions.

Eliminate confusion. The guidelines about using wireless devices during a meeting or event should be announced in advance. Leaders should schedule breaks for people to check their messages.

organizations use three levels of texting. One is the broadcast text, which companies often use to send a brief message to all employees at the same time. The message may be as mundane as reminding people to sign up for the company picnic or as serious as updating employees about a crisis situation.

A second level of texting is by subscription. Users sign up to receive text messages from groups or organizations in much the same way they sign up for RSS feeds to their computer. A reporter, for example, may sign up to receive text messages from a company that he or she covers on a regular basis. The third method, says Holtz, is the "one-off," in which a cell phone user can send a text message to a source to get an answer to a question. The user may text Google, for example, to get the address and phone number of a restaurant. An employee may text HR to get a short answer to a health benefits question. Texting can also be used for fund-raising. See the Insights box below.

on the job

INSIGHTS

Texting Raises Millions for Haiti Earthquake Relief

When an earthquake leveled Haiti, many organizations and nations scrambled to provide relief supplies and cash in the days following the disaster. One successful fund-raising tactic was encouraging Americans to text a donation.

Celebrities, athletes, and First Lady Michelle Obama publicized the option in a YouTube video and a television public service announcement (PSA). The National Football League (NFL) also promoted text donations during its weekend playoff games. The result was about $22 million raised in a few hours for the Red Cross.

Americans who donated used their cell phones to dial 90999, and $10 was billed to their cell phone accounts. The company *mGive.com*

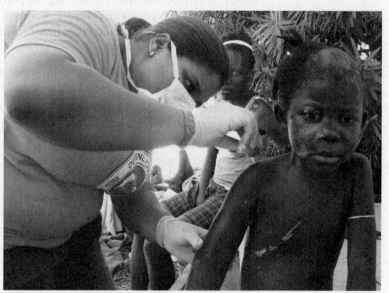

waived text processing fees to set up the program for the Red Cross. Other mobile carriers also pledged to waive fees and forward the money immediately without waiting until customers paid their bills.

A good example of an organization using texting as a communication tool is the South Dakota Office of Tourism. Skiers visiting the state can sign up to receive daily text message alerts about snowfall and weather conditions. E-mail alerts to subscribers were already being used, but sending messages directly to cell phones seemed to be more logical in terms of accessibility. Wanda Goodman, public relations manager at the tourism office, told *Ragan.com*, "It adds a level of convenience for travelers and builds another level of connectivity with potential visitors to the state."

Twitter: The Bluebird of Happiness

Another form of text messaging is Twitter, which became the fastest-growing Web brand by racking up more than 50 million Tweets a day in early 2010. Essentially, it's a social networking and microblogging service that allows users (known as twits) to post messages of up to 140 characters in length on computers and cell phones. Messages and links are displayed on the user's profile page and delivered to other users (called followers) who have signed up for them. Celebrities, for example, have literally millions of followers. Oprah Winfrey started tweeting in April of 2010, and within 15 minutes of her first Tweet, she had 76,000 followers. Four hours later, there were 125,000 followers. See the PR Casebook on page 347 about how the Phoenix Suns have incorporated Twitter into their operations.

Twitter is Web based, so its major advantage over texting is that posts are now indexed by Google and readily available to anyone with Internet access. Twitter, as it matures, is getting more robust. Experts say that one introduced feature, annotations, makes Twitter a possible platform for sharing anything, not just 140 characters of text.

Although some pundits thought Twitter was a fad, it's definitely here to stay. A 2010 survey by Burson-Marsteller found that 65 percent of the Fortune Global 100 companies have active accounts on Twitter. In contrast, only 54 percent have a Facebook page. The following are some examples of how organizations and their public relations staffs use Twitter:

- Qwest Communications, a telecommunications company, uses @TalkToQwest to handle customer questions, concerns, and complaints.
- Starbucks used Twitter messages to refute a rumor that it had stopped donating coffee to troops in Iraq to protest the ongoing U.S. occupation.
- Pepsi used a Twitter post to apologize for an iPhone app telling men how to "score" with categories of women such as "cougars" and "tree-huggers" that was part of an energy drink promotion.
- The presidential campaign of Barack Obama used Twitter to keep campaign volunteers and supporters up-to-date with motivational messages and late-breaking campaign developments.
- Levi's uses a Twitter feed to publicize its global branding campaign, which focuses on the theme of the American pioneer.
- Planned Parenthood has two Twitter accounts, one to answer queries and one to provide basic information about contraception.

Public relations professionals who use Twitter, however, should be aware of some basic guidelines. They include:

- **Think outside the box.** Use Twitter to create ways to engage the public, make the organization stand out, and bring awareness to the brand.

PRCasebook

The Phoenix Suns

Tweeting Is a Slam Dunk

The Phoenix Suns basketball team is one of several in the NBA that have embraced social media as a way to build team visibility and reach out to their fans. The Suns already had an award-winning website, but the popularity of social media encouraged the team to incorporate it into the overall communications strategy. The team started with a proprietary social network, Planet Orange, in 2007 and then added fan pages on Facebook and Twitter. By the end of 2009, the Facebook page had about 60,000 fans and Twitter had about 20,000 followers.

The Suns realized the potential of Twitter (@Suns-Webmaster) when one of its star players, Shaquille O'Neal (THE REAL.SHAQ), joined Twitter in 2008 to counter an imposter and the feed quickly drew more than 2.5 million followers. Jeramie McPeek, the Suns vice president, told Lindsey Miller of *Ragan.com*, "We all fell in love with it for connecting to our fan base. Our fans were not necessarily coming to Suns.Com, but they were pulling up Facebook, MySpace, and YouTube. We need to be in those places; we need to be where the fans are."

Twitter, in particular, has been successful in building communications, interaction, and the fan base.

In terms of communications, the Suns have a main Twitter feed, one run by players and staff, another by the Suns Dancers, and yet another by the Gorilla mascot. For interaction, the Suns ask fans such questions as what music to play at games. Another approach is to have managers and players answer fan questions during a live Twitter chat.

Most important, of course, is building a fan base. The team fills the Twitter feed with exclusive information. According to Miller of *Ragan.com*, this information may be "a live game tweeter, short, funny anecdotes, direct quotes

from practice, 'This date in Suns history' trivia, and even birthday wishes to players and former players."

In general, the team posts practically anything that's interesting, noteworthy, or funny on Twitter because this medium is ideal for frequent, short messages. The Facebook page, on the other hand, has fewer posts, and only very important items are posted.

- **Avoid bulletin board syndrome.** Don't just post announcements and links. Instead, use Twitter to engage in a conversation with your followers.
- **Don't be a "twammer."** Limit the number of Tweets that you post. An excessive number begins to look like spam. Post only important and relevant information.
- **Be committed to updating.** Although you should not post excessive Tweets, it is a good idea to Tweet about something once a day. It keeps your name in front of your followers.

- **Use Twitter in a crisis.** Twitter is an ideal form of communication when there is a crisis or fast-breaking news. It is one of the first steps an organization should take to provide up-to-the-minute details—or reactions—to a crisis.

Wikis: Saving Trees

Interaction between individuals working on a particular project is facilitated by what are known as Wikis. Basically, Wikis are a collection of webpages that enables anyone who accesses them to provide input and even modify their content.

Ward Cunningham, coauthor of *The Wiki Way: Quick Collaboration on the Web*, gives the essence of Wikis:

- They invite all users to edit any page within the website using a basic Web browser.
- They promote meaningful topic associations among different pages.
- They involve visitors in an ongoing process of creation and collaboration.

> Wikis and collaboration is a space we and many people in the industry are using now as opposed to just sticking to dry e-mail.
>
> *Jorand Chanofsky, CEO of Fusion Public Relations*

General Motors, for example, created a Wiki site for its employees and customers as part of its centennial celebration. The site encouraged individuals to contribute first-person experiences—via stories, images, video, and audio—related to the company's history. The advantage of the Wiki was that individuals could comment on other contributions, correct inaccurate information, and even add supplemental information regarding their experiences and viewpoints.

GM originally considered using the standard coffee table book to outline the company's history, but company spokesperson Scot Keller told *MediaPost*, "We felt that a more social, more inclusive approach was appropriate, and the story is best told not by the corporation or media but by men and women who were there." As a spin-off, GM also planned to package various stories and materials for distribution to other social networking communities and websites.

Wikis also are used by public relations departments and firms to keep employees and clients up-to-date on schedules and plans for executing campaigns. Joel Postman, EVP of Eastwick Communications, told *Ragan.com* that the firm's Wiki "allows almost everyone in the agency to set up a well-organized, attractive, customized workspace for any number of tasks. Some of the more popular uses of the wiki are for event management, document version control, and maintenance of standardized documents like client 'boilerplate' and executive bios."

Podcasts: Radio on Steroids

Podcasting was once described by a public relations expert as "radio on steroids." A more standard definition is provided by *Wikipedia*: "A podcast is a digital media file, or a series of such files, that is distributed over the Internet using syndication feeds (RSS) for playback on portable media players and personal computers." Increasingly, podcasts are also produced in a video format. In other words, a podcast can be delivered to users via computers, MP3 players, iPods, and even smartphones.

So who came up with the word "podcast," which the *Oxford American Dictionary* designated as Word of the Year in 2005? According to OneUpWeb, a firm specializing in making podcasts for clients, podcast comes from "pod," as in Apple's iPod, and "cast," as in "broadcast." meaning to transmit for general or public use.

Most podcasts are audio only, but video podcasts are also finding a home on smartphones, websites, YouTube, and other social networking sites. The three major advantages of podcasts for distributing messages are (1) cost-effectiveness, (2) the ability of users to access material on a 24/7 basis, and (3) portability. For example, a person can listen to an audio podcast while driving to work, walking down a mountain trail, or even while gardening. Simply put, podcasts have many of the same advantages as traditional radio.

Organizations use podcasts for a variety of purposes. These may include (1) news about the company, (2) in-depth interviews with executives and other experts, (3) features giving consumer tips about the use of products and services, and (4) training materials for employees. Some examples:

Podcasts
Companies such as Purina are increasingly using podcasts to reach audiences about pet care and, of course, their products.

- Whirlpool produces a podcast series titled "American Family." Topics range from advice and discussions about traveling with kids, weight loss, stroke in women, and even snowmobile safety. Whirlpool, as a policy, never discusses its products within the podcasts but limits mention of the company to the beginning and end of each transmission. The idea is to build customer loyalty and connect with women, the primary audience of Whirlpool. Dan Cook, director of interactive marketing for Whirlpool, told *Ragan.com*, "We cover topics that are important to the life of the everyday consumer. It's an opportunity for us to connect our brand to her."

- Purina, the maker of pet food, has a podcast series that gives advice to pet owners. The series' introduction on the company's website gives the essence of its content: "Is it unusual for a cat to use the toilet? Is your dog bored out of its skull? Can cats and dogs suffer from heart attacks? Get answers to these questions and more in season two of Animal Advice, where veterinarians field questions from pet lovers like you." Some sample titles in the series are "Animal safety during the summer months" and "Itching dogs and cats." See the Purina podcast illustration above.

- Disneyland used podcasts as part of its global campaign to generate interest in the park's 50th anniversary celebration. The content included interesting facts about the park's history, current attractions, and in-depth interviews with employees about their work at the park.

- The University of Pennsylvania's Wharton School produces podcasts that primarily feature insights from professors at the business school regarding current trends and issues.

The equipment needed to produce a podcast is relatively simple. You need only (1) a computer; (2) a good microphone; (3) software such as Audacity to record, edit, and finish audio files; (4) a Web server to store the files in a folder; and (5) a website or a blog that users can access to download the podcast.

The difficult part is creating a podcast that is interesting and relevant to the target audience. A podcast should not be an infomercial or a recitation of an executive's speech. Like radio, a podcast must be informal and conversational. Here are some other tips about podcast content: (1) keep it to less than 15 minutes, (2) use several stories or segments, (3) don't use a script, (4) create an RSS feed, and (5) produce new podcasts on a weekly basis.

The evidence seems to indicate that podcasting will continue to grow as a major tool of communication for public relations professionals. The blog site "eMarketer" predicts that podcast users will grow to 65 million by 2012. And, of those listeners, 25 million will be "active" users who tune in at least once a week.

The Next Generation: Mobile-Enabled Content

The Internet and social media are developing and morphing so rapidly that any crystal ball gazing is somewhat futile. In a few short years, we've seen the mobile phone become universal throughout the world among both the rich and the poor. In addition, users of the Internet call service Skype now total more than 500 million, more than the entire population of the European Union.

Indeed, it's now widely predicted that smartphones and extensive mobile-enabled content will become the major platform for Web access. The movement started with the introduction of the iPhone in 2007, and by 2010, about 40 million had been sold. The price of the iPhone and other smartphones has come down, but the relatively high cost of service plans in the United States continues to somewhat constrict the adoption rate of these phones. In fact, a recent study by the World Economic Forum found that America's level of cell phone adoption ranks below that of 71 other nations.

> By 2013, mobile phones will replace PCs as the most common device for Web access.
>
> *Gartner research firm's "Top Predictions for IT Organizations and Users"*

The increasing number of "apps" available for smartphones will no doubt expand the market in the United States in the near future. In fact, Gartner research found that consumers spent more than $6 billion on mobile applications in 2010. And by 2013, downloads from mobile-application stores worldwide will surpass 21 billion.

Mobile phones already allow users to download videos, surf the Internet at will, receive e-mails and RSS feeds, post comments on blogs, and receive an extensive array of mobile-enabled content. In other nations, mobile phones are being used as virtual credit cards to pay bills and withdraw cash, as files that store a person's medical records, and even as a form of money that allows users to make a purchase by waving the phone over a scanner.

Increasingly, public relations professionals are using apps to reach audiences. Quicken, the financial software firm, is a good example. To reach the 25- to 35-year-old age group, Quicken introduced a budgeting app for the iPhone. Quicken Online Mobile became the number-two finance application in the iTunes application store within three days. News releases will also undergo modification. In the near future, many early adopters will be reading news releases and other materials on a three-inch screen instead of a computer screen.

Indeed, new-generation mobile phones have become portable computers that are as powerful as today's notebooks and netbooks. These phones already have the ability to call up stored online videos, photos, and even PowerPoint presentations. Other popular features are complete map navigation in 3-D format of any location on the planet and interaction with social networks such as Facebook, allowing the user to tell friends exactly where he or she is at any given moment. Web 3.0, coming soon, will respond to spoken commands, thus eliminating the need to tap and click in order to text and call up websites. In other words, access to a world of information and social interaction will be contained in a single device that fits in one's pocket.

Summary

The Internet: Pervasive in Our Lives

- The worldwide adoption of the Internet and the World Wide Web has taken less time than the adoption of any other mass medium in history.

- The Internet is the first major revolution in communication since the invention of the printing press.

- The Internet has democratized information in the respect that nearly anyone can now send and receive vast amounts of information without journalists or editors serving as gatekeepers and mediators of that content.

The World Wide Web

- Public relations practitioners are heavy users of the Internet and the Web. They disseminate information to a variety of audiences and also use the Internet for research.

- The new media, including the Web, have unique characteristics. These include (1) easy updating of material, (2) instant distribution of information, (3) an infinite amount of space for information, and (4) the ability to interact with the audience.

- Webcasting, the streaming of audio and video in real time over a website, is now used by the majority of organizations for everything from news conferences to employee training.

The Rise of Social Media

- The second generation of the Internet, called Web 2.0, has given rise to "social media" in which most of the Internet's content is consumer generated. Web 2.0 provides public relations professionals with the opportunity to participate in social networking sites to get feedback and also to build relationships.

- Blogs have become mainstream in terms of numbers and influence. From a public relations standpoint, there are three kinds of blogs: (1) corporate, (2) employee, and (3) third party.

- MySpace and Facebook are the most popular social networking sites. Increasingly, organizations are establishing a presence on these sites. Public relations materials, however, need to be low key and creative to engage the audience.

- YouTube is the premier social networking site for posting and viewing videos. Organizations are also heavily involved in posting video clips. The clips, however, must be creative, interesting, and somewhat humorous to attract an audience.

- Twitter is now extensively used by organizations to communicate with their customers.

- Texting, Flickr, and Wikis are now part of the public relations toolbox.

- Podcasts are gaining in popularity. They can be either audio or video, but they must provide useful and relevant information in a conversational way.

The Next Generation: Mobile-Enabled Content

- The next generation of the Internet (Web 3.0) will see the further development of smartphones as minicomputers. The cost of mobile-enabled content will go down, which will enable more consumers to send and receive vast amounts of information.

Case Activity   A Social Media Campaign for Yogurt

Happy Valley Yogurt distributes its products nationally and has about 25 percent of the market. It makes a variety of flavors and about 80 percent of its sales come from individual packages of eight ounces. The company has done the standard marketing, advertising, and public relations activities, but your public relations staff believes sales could increase with the use of social media—blogs, MySpace, Facebook, YouTube, Flickr, Twitter, and podcasts—to engage teenagers, college students, and young professionals who are actively accessing social networking sites. Prepare a proposal to management showing how Happy Valley can use social media for fun and profit. You need to consider the special characteristics of these media and what kind of content would be appropriate.

Questions For Review and Discussion

1. In what ways has the Internet completely revolutionized a media system that goes back to Gutenberg in the 1400s?
2. What are some statistics that show how pervasive the Internet has become in today's global society?
3. What are some characteristics of the Web that make it possible for public relations people to do a better job of distributing information?
4. Why is it important for an organization to have a website?
5. One example of Web interactivity is the "pull" and "push" concepts. What's the difference between the two terms?
6. How can a website save an organization money?
7. How can webcasts be used by various organizations?
8. What is the major difference between the first generation of the Internet, Web 1.0, and the second generation of the Internet, Web 2.0?
9. What are the main characteristics of "social media"?
10. In what ways does a corporate blog differ from an organization's website?
11. What are some guidelines for employee blogs?
12. How can Facebook be used in a corporate public relations strategy?
13. What should an organization consider if it is thinking about producing a YouTube video?
14. How can organizations effectively use texting and Wikis?
15. What's the difference between "tweeting" and texting?
16. What makes a good podcast?
17. What role will smartphones play in Web 3.0, the next generation of the Internet?

Media Resources

Bullas, J. (2009, August 17). Nine ways to convince the CEO to use social media and enter the 21st century. Retrieved from Jeffbullas's blog: http://jeffbullas.com/2009/08/17

Daniels, C. (2010, February 23). Fortune global 100 rely on Twitter more than other social media. *PRWeek*. Retrieved from www.prweekus.com

Falkow, S. (2010, April 8). Ten steps for putting Twitter to use as a potent PR tool. Retrieved from www.ragan.com

Giridharadas, A. (2010, April 11). Where a cellphone is still cutting edge. *New York Times*, p. A10.

Johnson, S. (2010, April 22). YouTube turns five. *Chicago Tribune*. Retrieved from www.chicagotribune.com/entertainment

Laker, F. (2010, April 6). What social media will look like in 2012. *Advertising Age*. Retrieved from http://adage.com

Mobile marvels: A special report on telecoms in emerging markets. (2009, September 26). *The Economist*, pp. 3–17.

Ovide, S. (2010, March 12). Hearst jumps into the apps business. *Wall Street Journal*, p. B7.

Porter, J. (2010, February 22). Journalists increase use of social media for story research, new survey finds. Retrieved from www.ragan.com

Postman, J. (2010, January 23). Debunking five social media myths. *Social Media Today*. Retrieved from www.socialmediatoday.com

Solis, B., & Breakenridge, D. (2009). *Putting the public back in public relations*. Upper Saddle River, NJ: Pearson FT Press.

Sudhaman, A. (2010, March 17). When PR goes mobile. *PRWeek*. Retrieved from www.prweek.com/news

Preparing Materials for Mass Media

14 chapter

After reading this chapter, you will be able to:

Write a standard or multimedia news release

Recognize the components of a good publicity photo

Prepare media kits, media advisories, and fact sheets

Use proven techniques to "pitch" a story to a journalist

Understand the structure of an organization's online newsroom

Organize media interviews, news conferences, and media tours

The News Release

The basic news release has been around for centuries in various shapes and forms. Chapter 2, for example, mentioned that the Rosetta Stone of ancient Egypt was basically a publicity release touting a pharaoh's accomplishments. Today's basic version of the news release, commonly referred to as a *press release*, goes back more than a century, when Ivy Lee wrote one for the Pennsylvania Railroad in 1906.

Indeed, the news release continues to be the most commonly used public relations tactic, although the advent of the Internet and social media has changed its basic purpose and format. Some social media gurus have even pronounced the death of the news release. Fuat Kircaali, CEO and publisher of SYS-CON Media, flatly states, "The press release business already belongs to the Stone Age."

But, as Mark Twain is reported to have said, "The news of my death is highly exaggerated." A 2009 poll of corporate communicators by Ragan Communications and PollStream, for example, found that 50 percent of the respondents believed news releases "are as useful as ever." Another third said they are a necessary evil that would not go away anytime soon, primarily due to SEC notification rules. Another survey by Arketi Group of business journalists found that 92 percent of the respondents use news releases for story ideas. "Traditional tools won't go away," says Lauren Fernandez, marketing director of American Mensa. She told *Ragan.com*, "I can't say that something is new and shiny and I'm going to forget everything else. I don't think news releases are dead; most effective brands are using both."

The traditional media rely on basic news releases for two reasons. First, the reality of mass communications today is that reporters and editors spend most of their time processing information, not gathering it. Second, no media enterprise has enough staff to cover every single event in the community. Consequently, a lot of the more routine news in a newspaper is processed from news releases written by public relations practitioners. As one editor of a major daily once said, public relations people are the newspaper's "unpaid reporters."

It must be remembered, however, that a news release is not paid advertising. News reporters and editors have no obligation to use any of the information from a news release in a news story. News releases are judged solely on newsworthiness, timeliness, interest to the readers, and other traditional news values. See the Insights box on page 355 about tips on writing a news release.

Planning a News Release

Before writing any news release, several questions should be answered to give the release direction and purpose. A planning worksheet should be used to answer the following questions:

- What is the key message? This should be expressed in one sentence.
- Who is the primary audience for the release? Is it journalists in traditional media, bloggers, or consumers looking for information via a search engine?
- What does the target audience gain from the product or service? What are the potential benefits and rewards?
- What objective does the release serve? Is it to increase product sales, enhance the organization's reputation, or increase attendance at an event?
- Is a news release the best format for the information?

on the Job

INSIGHTS

Tips On Writing a News Release

Lisa Barbadora, director of public relations and marketing for Schubert Communications, provides the following list of tips for "news-centered" releases in an article by Jerry Walker in *O'Dwyer's PR Report*:

■ Use short, succinct headlines and subheads to highlight main points and pique interest. They should not simply be a repeat of the information in the lead-in paragraph.

■ Don't use generic words such as "the leading provider" or "world-class" to position your company. Be specific, such as "with annual revenues of."

■ Don't describe products using phrases such as "unique" or "total solution." Use specific terms or examples to demonstrate the product's distinctiveness.

■ Use descriptive and creative words to grab an editor's attention, but make sure they are accurate and not exaggerated.

■ Don't highlight the name of your company or product in the headline of a news release if it is not highly recognized. If you are not a household name, focus on the news instead.

■ Tell the news. Focus on how your announcement affects your industry and lead with that rather than overtly promoting your product or company.

■ Critique your writing by asking yourself, "Who cares?" Why should readers be interested in this information?

■ Don't throw everything into a release. Better to break your news into several releases if material is lengthy.

■ Don't use lame quotes. Write like someone is actually talking—eliminate the corporatese that editors love to ignore. Speak with pizzazz to increase your chances of being published.

■ Target your writing. Create two different tailored releases that will go out to different types of media rather than a general release that isn't of great interest to either group.

■ Look for creative ways to tie your announcement in with current news or trends.

■ Write simply. Use contractions, write in active voice, be direct, avoid paired words such as "clear and simple," and incorporate common action-oriented phrases to generate excitement. Sentences should be no longer than 34 words.

■ Follow the *Associated Press Stylebook* and specific publications' editorial standards for dates, technical terms, abbreviations, punctuation, spellings, capitalization, and so on.

■ Don't overdo it. It's important to write colorfully, to focus on small specific details, to include descriptions of people, places, and events—but do not write poetry when you want press.

■ Don't be formulaic in your news release writing. Not every release must start with the name of the company or product. Break out of the mold to attract media attention.

■ Don't expect editors to print your entire release. Important information should be contained in the first two paragraphs.

■ Make it clear how your announcement is relevant for the editors' readers.

These planning questions should also include an ethnical component. See the Ethics box below about two ethical dilemmas. After determining the purpose of the news release, the next step is to structure the content and format.

The Basic Online News Release

The vast majority of news releases today are distributed via e-mail or electronic news services, or are downloaded from an organization's website. The format and content of news releases for distribution via e-mail and the Internet are somewhat different from the traditional double-spaced format that was mailed or faxed only to media outlets. The basic format of an online news release is as follows, which is also illustrated by Figure 14.1.

- Use single spacing.
- Keep the news release to 200 words or less.
- Use the inverted pyramid approach, in which the most important information is first, followed by less important details.
- The top line should give the name of the organization and perhaps its logo.
- The second line should give the date (e.g., April 21, 2010).

on the Job

ETHICS

What to Write ... Or Not Write

A common activity of public relations practitioners is to write news releases on behalf of a client or employer.

At times, the content and choice of words in a news release can be an ethical dilemma. Consider the following two scenarios:

- The president of a small business software company wants to get some publicity and visibility in the business press. He asks you to write a news release announcing that the

company has recently received major contracts from large corporations such as General Electric, AT&T, Starbucks, and Exxon/Mobil. The president then adds, "We only have a contract with AT&T right now, but we've been talking to the other companies, and it's a pretty sure thing that they will sign on." Given this information, would you go ahead and write the news release? Why or why not?

- A top-level executive has been fired by a company for manipulating accounts and claiming more sales for her division than could be documented. The media are calling about the executive's departure, so the president asks you to write a short news release saying that the executive has resigned "to pursue other business opportunities." Would you go ahead and write the news release? Why or why not?

ABIresearch

April 21, 2010 10:01 AM Pacific Daylight Time

United Kingdom, France, India Among Cheapest for Mobile Broadband, According to ABI Research

SINGAPORE--(BUSINESS WIRE)--Where are the best deals for mobile broadband? Comparing mobile data pricing in a number of countries, ABI Research found that the UK, France and India have among the world's lowest prices for mobile broadband plans. In India for example, where 3G mobile broadband services launched in the middle of 2009, an unlimited download plan costs just over US$17 per month.

"ABI Research expects emerging markets with low Internet penetration to price mobile broadband aggressively to drive usage," says ABI Research analyst Bhavya Khanna. "However, in developed markets the widespread use of data dongles has created strains on mobile networks; and one could see data plans change to throttle data consumption."

> "ABI Research expects emerging markets with low Internet penetration to price mobile broadband aggressively to drive usage"

Operators in some countries are already using this approach, limiting data to 5 GB or even as low as 3 GB per month, even for their most expensive plans.

Vice President of Forecasting Jake Saunders, adds, "Another consumer concern is confusing overage charges for data plans: consumers often do not know how many megabytes of data they are downloading. Once again, there is room for innovation here from operators by simplifying overage costs and educating consumers to encourage uptake of such services. For example, operators in Singapore have a fixed "cap" on overage costs per month; ensuring that users do not get 'bill-shock'."

ABI Research's "Mobile Data Pricing Database" (http://www.abiresearch.com/research/1004104) tracks mobile data pricing for both handset use and USB modem across 27 countries worldwide. The database includes information about data pricing plans by carrier, as well as a cross country comparison of the lowest cost plan for downloading 3GB of data.

It is a component of the Mobile Consumer Research Service, (http://www.abiresearch.com/products/service/SE-CMO) which also includes Research Reports, Research Briefs, other Market Data products, ABI Insights, ABI Vendor Matrices, and analyst inquiry support.

ABI Research provides in-depth analysis and quantitative forecasting of emerging trends in global connectivity. From offices in North America, Europe and Asia, ABI Research's worldwide team of experts advise thousands of decision makers through 28 research and advisory services. Est. 1990. For more information visit www.abiresearch.com, or call +1.516.624.2500.

Contacts

ABI Research
Christine Gallen, Tel: +44.203.326.0142
pr@abiresearch.com

Figure 14.1   ABI Online News Release

This news release, distributed by Business Wire on behalf of ABI Research, shows the basic format and components of an online news release.

- The third line should be the headline in boldface with a slightly larger font than the text. This often serves as the subject line in an e-mail, so it should give the key message in 20 words or less. It's also important to include a key word or phrase for search engine optimization (SEO).
- Provide the city of origination at the start of the lead paragraph (e.g., Chicago).
- Write a succinct lead of only two or three sentences that gives the essence of the news release.
- Use a pull quote as part of the news release. This is a quote highlighted in a box that gives a major point about the release.
- Provide links in the news release so that readers can easily click on sites that provide related information.
- The last paragraph should provide basic information about the organization.

- The release should end with the name, telephone number, and e-mail address of the public relations contact person so that a reporter or blogger can easily contact him or her for more information.

B. L. Ochman, writing in *The Strategist*, suggests that public relations personnel "think of the online news release as a teaser to get a reporter or editor to your website for additional information." He makes the following suggestions based on his axiom "Write like you have 10 seconds to make a point. Because online, you do.":

- Use a specific subject line that identifies exactly what the news release is about.
- Make your entire release a maximum of 200 words or less, in five short paragraphs. The idea is brevity so that reporters see the news release on one screen and don't have to scroll.
- Write only two or three short sentences in each of the five paragraphs.
- Use bulleted points to convey key points.
- Above the headline or at the bottom of the release, be sure to provide a contact name, phone number, e-mail address, and URL for additional information.
- Never send a release as an attachment. Journalists, because of possible virus infections, rarely open attachments.

Online releases distributed on a global basis need special sensitivity, as outlined in the Multicultural World box below.

on the Job

A MULTICULTURAL WORLD

Sensitivity Required for Global News Releases

News releases are now distributed internationally, but there are cultural differences, sensitive political issues, and language differences that must be taken into consideration.

In terms of cultural differences, news releases are perceived differently in various nations. In Latin America, for example, editors are highly suspicious of news releases that describe new products or

services as "best," "world-class," or even "cutting edge." In Russia, editors are highly skeptical of anything coming from a U.S. source and won't be interested unless the release is highly oriented to Russia. "Asian general media is more tolerant of technical releases than are Europeans or Latin Americans," according to Colleen Pizarev, PR Newswire's VP of international distribution. A Japanese news release is shown in Figure 14.2.

Political issues are another pitfall. The writer of a news release for the Chinese press, for example, should avoid making any mention of such hot topics as human rights, dissent, freedom, Taiwan, or even refer to the company's commitment to corporate social responsibility (CSR). By the same token, a company sending a news release to the Taiwanese media must be careful not to mention anything about its business

※ 当資料は米国で 3 月 16 日に発表されたプレスリリースの一部抄訳です

PRESS RELEASE

マカフィー株式会社
2010 年 3 月 17 日

マカフィー、クラウド環境の保護に向けて McAfee Cloud Secure プログラムを発表
～クラウドセキュリティ認定サービスと McAfee SECURE テクノロジの組み合わせにより、
SaaS およびクラウドプロバイダーの事業成長を支援～

セキュリティ・テクノロジ専業のリーディングカンパニー、McAfee, Inc.（NYSE: MFE、以下、
マカフィー）は、急成長を続けるクラウド環境を保護する第一歩となる McAfee Cloud Secure（マ
カフィー クラウド セキュア）プログラムを、本日発表しました。

McAfee Cloud Secure プログラムは、SaaS（Software-as-a-Service）およびクラウドプロバイ
ダーがクラウドベースのサービスを導入する際に、妨げとなることが多いセキュリティに関する
不安を払拭し、可視化することを目指しています。初期プログラムでは、大手認定交付ベンダー
が提供するクラウドセキュリティ認定サービスと、マカフィーが提供する自動監査、修復、レポ
ーティング機能が組み合わされています。なお本プログラムは第一弾として、クラウドコンピュ
ーティングサービスの草分けである Amazon Web Services と、SaaS ビジネスのリーディングプ
ロバイダーである SuccessFactors に、導入される予定です。

Figure 14.2 McAfee News Release in Japanese

Global companies need news releases in local languages. This release was prepared by Inoue Public Relations in Tokyo for client McAfee, and distributed to Japanese media.

in China. Another aspect about China is that it has a highly regulated system and all news stories must be government-sanctioned. In other words, news releases can't be distributed directly to media; they first must go through official censorship channels.

Language is another consideration. News releases should be translated into the national language of the country. In India, for example, English is widely used but many organizations also translate news releases into Hindi if they are sending the release to regional and local publications. In Singapore, it's best to have news releases in Chinese and English. Although China now uses simplified Chinese throughout the country, one should be aware that traditional Chinese is still used in Taiwan, Hong Kong, and Macau. Even English-speaking nations have differences in terms of spelling. A news release in the United Kingdom or Australia, for example, should use the Queen's English. This means "organisation" instead of "organization," and "honours" instead of "honors."

Global public relations firms, with offices in many nations, often serve their clients by having local staffs write, translate, and distribute media materials. One key factor, according to *PRWeek* reporter Tanya Lewis, is to adapt a global release by providing local contacts and including quotes from local representatives of the company. Lewis also advises, "Don't use phrases/words that would cause confusion when translated." The number "six," for example, is better than "half dozen."

The Multimedia News Release

The major change in the evolution of the humble news release is the multimedia release, which has also been dubbed the "smart media release" (SMR) and even the *social media news release*. These releases, pioneered by the major electronic distribution services such as Business Wire, PR Newswire, PRWeb, and MarketWire, now make it possible to embed a news release with high-resolution photos/graphics, video, and audio components. A template of a "smart" release is shown in Figure 14.3. In addition, these services have teamed up with search engines such as Google, Yahoo!, and MSN to promote maximum exposure of the news release through search engine optimization (SEO).

Essentially SEO is the process of carefully selecting key words for the news release that make the content easily retrievable. For example, a food company may want to use the term "agricultural biotechnology" in a news release as opposed to "genetic modification," but people will be more likely to use the latter term in a search and will thus completely miss the company's news release.

A search engine looks for certain terms in a document to help it understand how to classify or categorize the content in terms of title, tags, summaries, and hyperlinks. Robert Niles, writing in *OJR: The Online Journalism Review*, adds, "If you're publishing online, Google style (i.e. SEO), always trumps AP style."

Michael Lissauer, executive vice president of Business Wire, told *PRWeek*, "The most important thing to our clients is seeing their news release on these search engines. They know consumers go there. If they write a news release effectively, they can bypass the gatekeepers, the journalists, who always had the opportunity of interpreting the release how they wanted." In other words, the SMR has expanded the audience beyond just the traditional media outlet.

The popularity of social media has also been incorporated into the SMR. A news release will include social media tags so that the content can be circulated through Digg, Technorati, *del.icio.us*, and other social bookmarking sites to increase search engine rankings of the release and also drive targeted traffic to the website. Other links will be to blogs, an organization's newsroom, and even a space where readers can post a comment about the news release.

MarketWire, in particular, has added services to address social media. According to Craig McGuire, writing in *PRWeek*, "The service includes social bookmarks and tags, news channel distribution, audio headline summaries, search-engine-friendly permalinks, social video hosting on Photobucket, photo hosting on YouTube, and more." Paolina Milana, vice president for MarketWire, says "Social media releases are generally formatted so information is easy to scan, utilizing bullets and lists of ready-made quotes instead of dense text." *PRWeek* reporter McGuire gives some tips for using smart news releases that also incorporate social media:

> From press materials to the blog posts that we recommend our clients write, we always keep an eye on SEO because Google is the place where everyone starts these days.
>
> *Todd Defren, principal with Boston-based Shift Communications*

> No matter how much technology you employ to help make your message stand out from the crowd, if the message doesn't resonate, the photos, links, and videos won't help it.
>
> *Michael Pranikoff,* PR Newswire

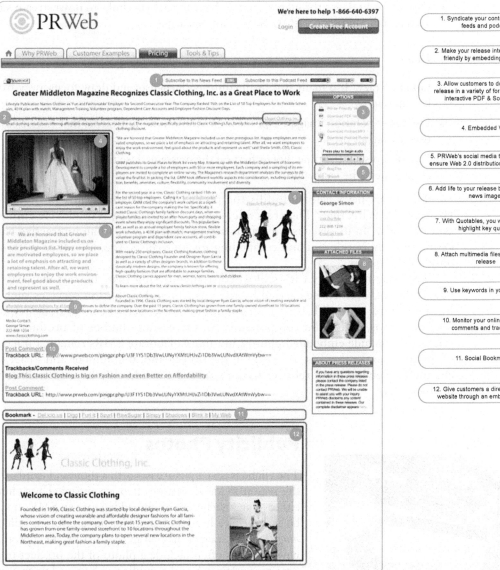

Figure 14.3   PRWeb Smart News Release Template

The components of a "smart" news release are outlined in this graphic prepared by PRWeb, part of the Vocus company. Such multimedia releases are designed for use across a variety of platforms, including traditional media, websites, and social media networks. They also are indexed by search engines such as Google for access by consumers.

Do

■ Include links to pages where multiple instances of your key words/phrases reinforce your message.

■ Place terms in key positions like headlines and first paragraphs.

- Distribute a release through a service that carries hyperlinks to downstream sites such as Yahoo Finance, AOL News, and Netscape.

Don't

- Go link crazy. Too many links will confuse journalists and draw focus away from key messaging.
- Use low-resolution images. Opt for high-resolution multimedia that can be easily used by layout pros.
- Use all tools, all the time. Focus first on the message. Use the bells and whistles to complement the campaign.

The smart news release fulfills the prediction of Manny Ruiz, president of Hispanic PR Wire, that "The press release of the last century is dead." He enthusiastically adds, "In its place is a dynamic service that is more of an interactive marketing tool, more relevant and compelling for journalists; the difference is it's not only for journalists."

This may be true, but it's still worth remembering that the vast majority of news releases, even those carried by the electronic distribution services such as Business Wire, are still basic releases about mundane activities that don't require photos, videos, and audio components. An increasing number of product news releases do include embedded photos, but more elaborate SMRs remain a fraction of the total market because of cost. On the other hand, the number and variety of channels receiving news releases have expanded considerably beyond traditional media outlets.

Samsung Publicity Photo

Product publicity photos must be creative and interesting. A television set isn't very exciting by itself, but several attractive South Korean models around it cause more attention. This photo, distributed by Samsung Electronics, announced its new 3-D high-definition television to the world.

Publicity Photos

The cliché is that a picture is worth a thousand words. For this reason, news releases are often accompanied by a photo, either as an attachment or embedded into an SMR. It may be as basic as a head-and-shoulder picture (often called a *mug shot*) of a person named in the release. New product news releases often include a photo of the product in an attractive setting. See the publicity photo at left that was distributed by Samsung.

Studies show that more people "read" photographs than read articles. The Advertising Research Foundation found that three to four times as many people notice the average one-column photograph as read the average news story. In another study, Wayne Wanta of the University of Missouri found that articles accompanied by photographs are perceived as significantly more important than those without photographs. Even bloggers like photos, as mentioned in the Insights box on page 363.

Like news releases, publicity photos are not published or posted unless they appeal to media gatekeepers who choose the content. Although professional photographers should always be hired to take the photos, public relations practitioners should supervise their work and select the photos that are best suited for media use. Here are some additional suggestions:

Quality Photos must have good contrast and sharp detail so that they reproduce in a variety of formats, including grainy newsprint. Digital photography is the norm, and in many cases editors download digital photos from an organization's website. But a beautiful photo on the computer screen may not come out the same way when it is printed.

Most websites use images at 72 dpi (dots per inch) for fast download, but print publications need photos at 300 dpi in jpeg or gif format. Consequently, electronic news services and corporate online press rooms usually have a protected site that provides high-resolution photos for registered journalists. Photos also are supplied

> The bar has been raised because of digital imagery. For that reason alone, same-old same-old is just not cutting it anymore— and that goes for grip-and-grin. There's always a more visually interesting way to show something than the cliché.
>
> *Suzanne Salvo of Salvo Photography*
> *in* Ragan.com

on the Job
INSIGHTS

Working with "Citizen" Journalists

The most important thing a publicist can do before pitching a blogger is to carefully read his or her blog. In order to begin a conversation with a blogger—and it should be viewed as a conversation, rather than a pitch—it is vital that you are well acquainted with the blogger's opinions and interests. Text 100, a public relations firm, conducted an international survey of 450 bloggers in 2009. The following are some of its findings:

- Blogs have become an influential, mainstream communication channel.

- The most preferred means of contact is via e-mail. Instant messaging is the least welcome.

- Computers, technology, and the Internet are the subjects most blogged about by the respondents.

- Preferred content is news and reviews of new products, opinionated comments, and interviews with key people. Corporate news announcements are of least interest.

- Photographs are the most frequently used content, although many also use video streaming, charts, and graphs. Video and audio podcasts are rarely used.

- Elements of social media releases (SMRs) are frequently used.

- Corporate websites and RSS feeds are the most frequently used sources of content.

PEARSON
mycommunicationlab

to editors on CD or DVD. In general, never send photos as an attachment unless the journalist has specifically requested it.

Subject Matter   A variety of subjects can be used for publicity photos. Trade magazines, weekly newspapers, and organizational newsletters often use the standard "grip-and-grin" photo of a person receiving an award or the CEO shaking hands with a visiting dignitary. These have been a staple of publicity photos for years, and there is no sign that they are going out of fashion despite being tired clichés. Another standard approach is the large-group photograph, which is appropriate for the club newsletter but is never acceptable for a newspaper. A better approach is to take photos of groups of three or four people from the same city and send only that photo to editors in that specific city.

Composition   The best photos are uncluttered. Photo experts recommend (1) tight shots with minimum background; (2) an emphasis on detail, not whole scenes; and (3) limiting wasted space by reducing gaps between individuals or objects. At times, context also is important. Environmental portraits show the subject of the photo in his or her normal surroundings—for example, a research scientist in a lab.

Action   Too many photos are static, with nothing happening except someone looking at the camera. It's better to show people doing something—talking, gesturing, laughing, running, or operating a machine. Action makes the photo interesting. The exception is the standard product photo.

Scale   Another way to add interest is to use scale. Apple, for example, might illustrate its newest iPod by having someone hold the device while surrounded by large stacks of CDs, to show how much music can be stored on it.

Camera Angle   Interesting angles can make the subject of a photo more compelling. Some common methods are shooting upward at a tall building to make it look even taller or shooting an aerial shot to give the viewer an unusual perspective.

Lighting   Professional photographers use a variety of lighting techniques to ensure that the subject is portrayed, quite literally, in the best light. Product photos, for example, always have the light on the product, and the background is usually dark or almost invisible. Background is important. If the executives at a banquet are all wearing dark suits, the photographer shouldn't line them up in front of a dark red curtain because there will be no contrast. Also, outdoor shots require using the sun to advantage.

Color   Today, with digital cameras and flash cards, almost all publicity photos are in color. Daily newspapers, for example, regularly use color publicity photos in the food, business, sports, and travel sections. Publications have differing requirements. Some want photos that can be downloaded via a website; others want a CD, pdf, or even a flash drive. Again, the general rule is to have several formats available and send what the publication or news website needs.

Media Kits

News releases and publicity photos are often included in a *media kit*, which is often referred to as a *press kit*. They are usually prepared for major events and new product launches, and their purpose is to give editors and reporters a variety of information that makes it easier for the reporter to write about the topic. In some ways, the traditional media kit is the print version of today's multimedia news release.

The traditional media kit is a 9 × 12 folder with inside pockets. The contents usually consist of such items as (1) a basic news release; (2) a news feature about the product or service; (3) a fact sheet about the product, organization, or event; (4) photos; (5) bios on the spokesperson or chief executives; (6) a basic brochure; and (7) contact information such as e-mail addresses, phone numbers, and website URLs.

A good example of a well-designed media kit that fit the organization's products and personality was the one Crayola produced to celebrate its 100th anniversary with a 25-city bus tour. The kit was a self-mailer that unfolded into a large, round sheet two feet in diameter that featured artwork done with a rainbow of crayon colors. The kit also included background articles on the history of the company. One piece of interesting trivia: "Since 1903, more than 120 billion crayons have been sold throughout the world. End-to-end they would circle the earth 200 times."

E-Kits

Today, electronic media kits, called EPKs, are the norm and are distributed via e-mail, a website, a CD, or a flash drive. Special events, in particular, often warrant a CD with an attractive cover.

Chicago's Shedd Aquarium used this approach when it mounted an exhibit on lizards. The cover, shown at right, attracted attention, and the CD included a variety of resources for journalists. They included (1) short videos showing lizards in their natural habitat, (2) news releases, (3) fact sheets about the lizards and the exhibit hours, (4) thumbnail sketches of the different lizards on display, and (5) high-resolution photographs. The media kit was a hit. It generated almost 250 print and broadcast stories and helped the Aquarium attract 2.1 million visitors to the exhibit.

EPKs are also posted to organizational websites or to servers so that journalists and bloggers can easily access them. The basic online media kit of SanDisk, for example, includes the following: (1) retail product photos, (2) executive officer photos, (3) trademark information,

Sample Media Kit on CD

Media kits have gone digital, and Shedd Aquarium distributed a CD to local Chicago media to promote a special exhibit on lizards. The CD contained news releases, fact sheets, short videos, and high-resolution photos that both print and broadcast journalists could incorporate into their stories.

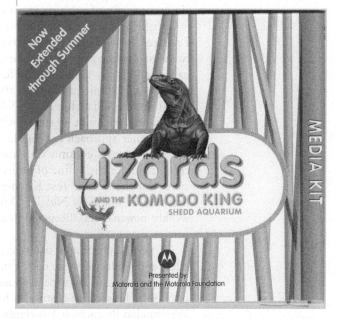

> The days of a thousand press kits are gone. Instead, well-designed online press kits can have an ongoing shelf life with constantly updated content.
>
> *Tom Bucktold, of* Business Wire

(4) industry association links, (5) retail product brochures, and (6) video footage showing the capabilities of its SD cards and other products.

Cost savings for the organization is a big factor. Patrick Pharris, founder of Electronic Media Communications, gave *PR News* a good example. The company developed an Internet media kit for a client that included eight documents, five photos, and a PR Newswire distribution for $4,000, instead of four times that amount for a printed media kit. HP, for a trade show, also used an e-kit that saved the company about $20,000 in printing costs.

Honoring the needs of various publications, however, should always be considered. Sarah Rogers of M45 Marketing Services in Freeport, Illinois, says she needs to consider the smaller newspapers in Illinois and elsewhere. She told *Ragan.com*, "In terms of sending out a media kit, I include paper and electronic versions of everything." Consequently, EPKs probably will never completely replace the traditional media kit.

Mat Releases

A variation of the traditional news release is what is called the *mat feature release*. They were originally called "mat" because they were sent in mat form, ready for the printing press. Today, these materials are distributed in a variety of formats including Word documents, jpegs, and pdfs.

The format of a mat release is somewhat different from the traditional news release because a feature angle is used instead of a lead that gives a key message. They also are in the format of a standing column headline such as *Healthy Eating, Cooking Corner*, or *Vacations of a Lifetime*.

The concept is geared toward providing helpful consumer information and tips about a variety of subjects in an informative way with only a brief mention of the nonprofit or corporation that has distributed the release via firms such as Family Features (www.familyfeatures.com) and the North American Precis Syndicate (www.napsinfo.com). These canned features show up in thousands of weekly newspapers and many dailies in the food, travel, fashion, automotive, and business sections. For example, a recipe feature titled "Chicken and Rice: Always a Winning Combination" distributed by NAPS for Rice-a-Roni generated more than 1,400 newspaper articles in 40 states, with a total readership of 75 million.

Another approach is a regular column that features an expert. Nestlé, for example, distributes a column via Family Features called "Mix it Up With Jenny." The column, under the byline of Jenny Harper, who is identified as a senior culinary specialist for the Nestlé Test Kitchens, offers seasonal recipes that, of course, include ingredients made by Nestlé. One column, distributed in the spring to daily and weekly newspapers, discussed desserts that can be prepared quickly for graduation parties.

A more sophisticated mat release is an entire color page layout that a newspaper can select and publish with no cost. Family Features has pioneered this concept, and a good example is the full-color page about watermelon as a summer treat, which is shown on page 367. This entire feature, offered at no cost to newspapers, was paid for by the Watermelon Promotion Association. Because the feature makes only a passing reference to the sponsor, the entire piece reads like a feature page actually prepared by the newspaper.

Mat services also provide video and audio features to the broadcast industry. Many newspapers, which have reduced staffs, find the features provided by editorial services such as Family Features a cost-effective way to fill space at virtually no cost to them.

Media Alerts and Fact Sheets

On occasion, the public relations staff will send a memo to reporters and editors about a news conference or upcoming event that they may wish to cover. Such memos also are used to let the media know about an interview opportunity with a visiting dignitary or celebrity, or what photo and video possibilities are available. A *media alert* is also referred to as a *media advisory*. Media alerts may be sent with an accompanying news release or by themselves.

The most common format for media alerts is short, bulleted items rather than long paragraphs. A typical one-page advisory might contain the following elements: a one-line headline, a brief paragraph outlining the story idea or event, some of journalism's five Ws and H, and whom to contact for more information. A basic media advisory about the visit of a U.S. cabinet member to New Orleans is shown in Figure 14.4.

Two Kinds of Fact Sheets

Fact sheets are another useful public relations tool. There are two kinds: The first one is basically a summary sheet about the characteristics of a new product that serves as a quick reference for a journalist writing a story. A one-page product fact sheet for Philips Norelco's new Bodygroom shaver, for example, provided such information as (1) ability to remove hair anywhere on the body, (2) chromium steel trimmer blades, (3) three interchangeable attachment combs, (4) 50 minutes of cordless trimming time, and (5) full two-year warranty.

Product fact sheets are often distributed as part of a media kit or with a news release to give supplemental information about a new product.

A second kind of fact sheet, often called a *corporate profile*, is a one-page summary in bulleted list format that gives the basic facts about an organization or a company. It may

09542: All-American Summer Flavor
All materials courtesy of: National Watermelon Promotion Board

To order, download at www.FamilyFeatures.com or contact Media Communications at support@familyfeatures.com or 1-888-824-3337

Sample Mat Release

An innovative approach to the standard mat news release is an entire newspaper page written and designed around a particular theme. This release, distributed by Family Features Editorial Syndicate on behalf of the Watermelon Promotion Board, uses the theme of summer to tell consumers how to select a good melon and enjoy it in several recipes.

April 26, 2010 03:15 AM Pacific Daylight Time

Media Advisory: HHS Secretary Sebelius to Visit St. Thomas Community Health Center in New Orleans

Will tour the facility and participate in press availability with Mayor-elect Mitch Landrieu

WASHINGTON--(BUSINESS WIRE)--On Monday, April 26, U.S. Department of Health and Human Services Secretary Kathleen Sebelius and New Orleans Mayor-elect Mitch Landrieu will visit the St. Thomas Community Health Center in New Orleans, Louisiana. After taking a tour of the facility, she will join the Mayor-elect to discuss the important work being done in the city of New Orleans to provide critical primary care services for area residents. Following the speaking program, there will be an opportunity for questions and answers with members of the media.

Please note that the health center tour will be pooled press.

WHAT: HHS Secretary Sebelius, Mayor-elect Landrieu to Visit St. Thomas Community Heath Center

WHEN: Monday, April 26, 2010
               12:00 PM CT

               Press Pre-set 11:45 AM CT

WHERE: St. Thomas Community Health Center
               1020 Saint Andrew Street
               New Orleans, LA 70130-5022

CONTACT: HHS Press Office   Mary Beth Romig, Transition New Orleans
               (202) 690-6343   (504) 606-8430

Contacts

HHS Press Office
202-690-6343

Figure 14.4   Media Advisory—Health Secretary in New Orleans

Media advisories notify reporters in advance when a dignitary or celebrity will be visiting a local site. They give the basic details of date and time so that media organizations can assign staff to cover the event.

use headings that provide (1) the organization's full name, (2) products or services offered, (3) the organization's annual revenues, (4) the number of employees, (5) the names and one-paragraph biographies of top executives, (6) the markets served, (7) its position in the industry, and (8) any other pertinent details.

The basic corporate profile for Best Buy, for example, starts with a lengthy paragraph about the extent of its operations, its annual revenues, the number of employees, its annual philanthropy to community groups, and its environmental policy. Bullet items follow, giving one-line information on headquarters' address and telephone number; the company's website and stock symbol; the CEO's name; and the name, phone number, and e-mail of the major public relations contact person.

The purpose of a corporate profile is the same as that of the product fact sheet. It provides reporters with a "crib sheet" so that they can verify basic facts, such as the organization's annual revenues or even its product lines, when they are writing a story. Corporate profiles are readily available on news release distribution sites such as Business Wire or on the organization's website in its newsroom link.

The Art of Pitching a Story

Getting the attention of media gatekeepers is difficult because they receive literally thousands of news releases and media kits every week. So, the major question is how to get your story noticed among a virtual rain forest of news releases.

The answer is what is commonly known in the public relations industry as the *pitch*. Some of today's savvy social media practitioners think "pitching" is an archaic concept because it implies one-way communication. They prefer, instead, to use such new buzzwords as "engagement" and "building relationships" with journalists. Some tips about effective media relations are given in the Insights box on page 370. In either case, the objective is to contact journalists and bloggers on a one-to-one basis and convince them that you have a newsworthy story or idea.

Although a pitch can take the form of a note or letter attached to a news release or a media kit, most pitches in today's digital age take the form of a phone call, an e-mail, a text message, or even a Tweet. Blogger Mark Evans advises, "When you're reaching out to a reporter or blogger, it's the two or three introductory paragraphs in an email that play a crucial role in whether they will be intrigued or hit the delete button. If you can capture their attention, they might read the news release to get some more information but in most cases, a reporter or blogger will call or email you to get more information or set up an interview."

Another blogger, David M. Scott, writing in www.webinknow.com, offered what he considers the single most important pitching tip: "Don't pitch your product. Most journalists don't care about products. Instead, tell us how your organization solves problems for customers."

Here are some other basic guidelines for pitching by e-mail:

- Use a succinct subject line that tells the editor what you have to offer; don't try to be cute or gimmicky.

- Keep the message brief, one screen at the most.

- Don't include attachments unless the reporter is expecting you to do so. Many reporters, due to the possibility of virus attacks, never open attachments unless they personally know the source.

- Don't send "blast" e-mails to large numbers of editors. E-mail systems are set up to filter messages with multiple recipients in the "To" and "BCC" fields, a sure sign of spam. If you do send an e-mail to multiple editors, break the list into small groups.

- Send tailored e-mail pitches to specific reporters and editors; the pitch should be relevant to their beats and publications.

- Regularly check the names in your e-mail database to remove redundant recipients.

- Give editors the option of getting off your e-mail list; this will ensure that your list is targeted to those who are interested. By the same token, give editors the opportunity to sign up for regular updates via RSS feeds or from your organization's website. If they cover your industry, they will appreciate it.

- Establish an e-mail relationship. As one reporter said, "The best e-mails come from people I know; I delete e-mails from PR people or agencies I don't recognize."

Pitching is a fine art, however, and public relations personnel must first do some basic research about the publication or broadcast that they want to contact. It's important to know the kinds of stories that a publication usually publishes or what kinds of guests appear on a particular talk show. Knowing a journalist's beat and the kinds of stories he or she has written

> I would argue that relationships and pitches are far more important than social media press releases, and this is what PR practitioners and companies should focus on.
>
> *Mark Evans,*
> www.markevanstech.com

> Media relations specialists should not send out a pitch without knowing the reporters and publications in advance.
>
> *David B. Oates, strategy and planning manager of ContentOne communications*

on the Job

INSIGHTS

Media Relations: How to Get a Date With a Reporter

Working with the media and dating have a lot in common. Jeremy Porter provided "Dating Advice for PR Pros" on http://blog.journalistics.com The following is a summary of his key points.

The Best Pickup Line Is a Basic Introduction

There are many cheesy pickup lines in dating circles, but the most effective pickup line is "Hello, my name is.... In media relations, you should also skip the clever opening line and just let the reporter know who you are and why you are calling.

Don't Seem Too Desperate

Don't give the impression that you're begging for a date, or for the reporter to write a story. You need to create genuine interest and bring something to the relationship. "Avoid being too needy, it doesn't work in either scenario."

Don't Be a Player

"Dates and journalists like exclusivity. If you're playing the field, the other party will lose interest."

Stop Trying to Hook Up

"Don't expect to get everything you want on the first date. If it's the first time you're talking to a journalist, don't expect them to write about the story the first time." Porter continues," Just like dating ... invest the time and energy in building your relationships and you'll get more out of it."

Don't Underestimate Confidence and Humor

"Two of the most attractive qualities in a potential partner are confidence and humor. If you doubt yourself, or come across as boring ... you're not going to get a second date."

Have a Game Plan

"Don't ask for a date and then have no game plan. The same holds true for PR— have a plan. If a journalist agrees to talk to you, make the best use of their time."

Dress to Impress

In dating and media relations, don't dress like a slob. Written and visual materials provided to a journalist should also be accurate, professional, and impressive. If they aren't, your chances of a second "date" are not good.

Have a Friend Set You Up

Use a mutual friend to "set you up" for a date, or with a journalist. A mutual friend can introduce you to a journalist through LinkedIn, Facebook, or Twitter.

Follow Up Is Key to the Second Date

"If you want to build a relationship, you need to follow up after the first date." In the case of a journalist, provide any additional information and ensure that he or she has your contact information.

Manners Matter

"Say please and thank you, be polite. Manners matter in this day and age, and people notice whether or not you have them."

Porter concludes his somewhat tongue-in-cheek advice, "I've seen plenty of desperate people try too hard to win the love and affection of a popular journalist, only to be left sitting alone on Saturday night with no press mentions to speak of. People are people, whether you're trying to date them or get them interested in a story you're pitching."

in the past also is helpful. In addition, reporters are always looking for a topical news hook. The media, for example, express great interest in trends and health issues, so it's also a good idea to relate a particular product or service with something that is already identified as a public concern. A good example of a successful pitch that resulted in a front page story on *USA Today* is discussed in the PR Casebook on page 371.

PRCasebook

A Successful Pitch Pays Dividends

The American Institute for Cancer Research (AICR) had some pretty impressive statistics about cancer, including the fact that excess body fat is responsible for at least 100,000 new cases of cancer every year. The challenge, however, was to get extensive media coverage and raise public awareness.

AICR's public relations firm, MS&L, gave some thought to this and considered having a news conference in Washington, D.C. A better idea, however, was to get a high-profile story in a major publication that would set the agenda for other news outlets. The decision was made to pitch *USA Today*, which has a national readership of 2 million.

USA Today reporter Nanci Hellmich had covered AICR research before, so she was offered the first opportunity to write a story about tying obesity to breast, kidney, and other cancers. Obesity was already in the news, so the essential message was boiled down to three words: fat equals cancer. MS&L staffers provided basic information and also arranged for Hellmich to interview a leading cancer expert at the University of Colorado.

The resulting story ran on the front page of *USA Today* above the fold (prime space) and did indeed trigger widespread follow-up coverage. The AICR report and statistics, for example, were mentioned in more than 340 radio and

television broadcasts, including those of CNN, FOX, NBC, CBS, and ABC.

There were three essential aspects of this successful pitch: (1) MS&L targeted a leading national publication; (2) it contacted a reporter who was already familiar with AICR's work and had written other major health-related stories; and (3) the popular topic of obesity was used as a news hook, which attracted extensive media interest.

The best pitches show a lot of creativity and are successful in grabbing the editor's attention. *Ragan's Media Relations Report* gives some opening lines that generated media interest and resulted in stories:

- "How many students does it take to change a light bulb?" (A pitch about a residence hall maintenance program operated by students on financial aid.)
- "The Man Who Will End iPod Whiplash." (A story about a Sun Microsystems engineer who came up with a new technique for searching for music online.)
- "Wearing Prada Can Be the Devil for Your Spine." (A story about a hospital that found many of the patients there for spinal therapy were women suffering neck and back pain from lugging around oversized purses.)

Tapping into Media Queries

Not all pitches have to be what salespeople term "cold calls." On many occasions, journalists are seeking information and names of people to interview for a particular story. One of the oldest services that match reporter queries with public relations sources is ProfNet, which is operated by PRNewswire. It offers a direct way for public relations pros to list experts in the organizations they represent, and to also be on the alert for a pitching opportunity to meet a reporter's specific needs.

ProfNet is available only on a subscription basis, but two free services that match reporters with public relations sources are Reporter Connection and Help a Reporter Out (HARO), the largest of the two, with 100,000 sources and 29,000 registered journalists, fields more than 200 queries daily. HARO also sends an e-mail out three times a day with a list of reporter queries, as well as urgent source requests, to more than 16,000 followers on Twitter.

Distributing Media Materials

News releases, photos, media kits, and a host of other media materials can be distributed by five major methods: (1) first-class mail, (2) fax, (3) e-mail, (4) electronic wire services, and (5) online newsrooms. The capabilities of e-mail are well known, so this section will focus on two other major distribution methods used today, electronic news services and online newsrooms.

Electronic News Services

Almost all organizations of all sizes now use an electronic wire service to distribute news releases, photos, and advisories. This is particularly true for corporate and financial information that must be released, according to SEC guidelines, to multiple media outlets at exactly the same time.

The two major newswires are Business Wire (www.businesswire.com) and PR Newswire (www.prnewswire.com). Each organization transmits about 20,000 news releases monthly to daily newspapers, broadcast stations, ethnic media, financial networks, and online news services. Other speciality electronic news services include PRWeb, MarketWire, Hispanic PRWire, USAsian Wire, and Black PRWire.

No paper is involved; the release is automatically entered into the appropriate databases and search engines, which can be accessed not only by editors and reporters throughout the world but also by the general public. Editors select releases that are newsworthy to them, write a headline, and then push another key to have it automatically set for publishing or broadcast. Of course, they can easily hit the delete key, too.

Wire services are making the news release more sophisticated. Business Wire, for example, now has "smart" news releases that can be embedded with visuals and audio, as has already been mentioned. A reporter also can click various hyperlinks to get more information and photographs or charts. Tags can also be embedded in news releases that give key words that can be picked up by more than 300 social networks, such as *YouTube.com*, Yahoo!, and Google. According to Craig McGuire, writing in *PRWeek*, "BusinessWire can convert a traditional news release into a search-engine optimized page of Web content that includes photos, graphics, video and multimedia, logo branding, keyword links, formatting, and social media tags." This is best illustrated by Figure 14.5, which shows the various components of a news release from Business Wire.

National distribution of a "smart" release with one photo or file can cost up to $1,000, but a complete "smart" page with multiple pictures and files, and distribution to mobile platforms worldwide, costs about $3,000. On the other hand, a basic 400-word news release transmitted to all major media in the United States is about $700. If the public relations person wants to cover the entire planet (100 nations and 21

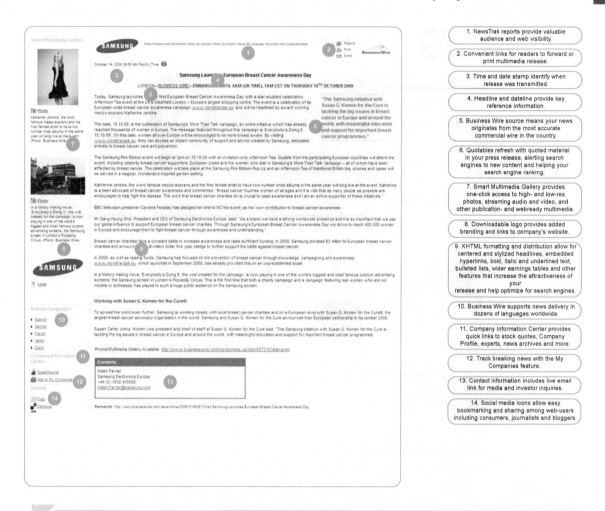

Figure 14.5   Business Wire News Release

The modern news release, distributed via electronic news services, is now embedded with links to photo galleries, social media sites, and other websites. This graphic was prepared by Business Wire in San Francisco exclusively for this textbook.

languages), it's about $8,000. Business Wire also offers mobile news releases, which it says, "makes your news available in multiple languages worldwide, across multiple platforms, including BlackBerry and Droid." In sum, electronic news services provide a cost-effective way to directly reach thousands of media across the nation and even the globe with a single click.

Online Newsrooms

"An online pressroom is the media's front door to the company," writes *PRWeek* reporter Sherri Deatherage Green. Most major organizations have a pressroom or a newsroom as part of their website. With a few clicks, a journalist can access everything from the organization's executive profiles to the most recent news releases. They also can download high-resolution photos and graphics, videos, and background materials such as position papers and annual reports. HP's online newsroom is shown on page 374.

Sample Online Newsroom

Journalists and bloggers rely on company online newsrooms to get up-to-date news about the organization. HP's online newsroom is well designed and includes a variety of materials including news releases, media kits, videos, podcasts, features, executive bios, and product photos.

An online pressroom is the media's front door to the company.

Sherri Deatherage Green,
reporter for PRWeek

An organization often informs journalists via e-mail that a particular item is available on the company's site. Because there are virtually millions of webpages, extra effort must be made to ensure that reporters are aware of the website and what's on it. A good online newsroom, at minimum, should have (1) current and archived news releases; (2) the names, phone numbers, and direct e-mail addresses of public relations contacts; (3) photographs; (4) product information; and (5) an opportunity for journalists to sign up for a daily RSS feed if they regularly cover that particular company or industry.

In today's 24/7 news cycle it's important that a company keep its website up-to-date. Reporters seeking information usually look first at the organization's website and online newsroom. In the case of a major news development or crisis that involves the organization, such as a product recall or a plant explosion, it's also vital that the organization posts updates on an hourly basis.

Surveys have found that journalists go first to an organization's website for information in the case of a crisis. It's also important for the materials posted on the website to be more than just copies of the printed materials. They must be reformatted and offer short summaries, extensive links, and strong visual elements. All documents, however, should have a "printer-friendly" version available.

Other tips, given by *PRWeek*'s Green, are (1) keep the online newsroom content somewhat simple; don't use sophisticated animation that might not be compatible with reporters' computers, (2) make high-resolution photos and graphics available that can be used for publication, and (3) link the pressroom to the company home page.

Media Interviews

Not all outreach to traditional media requires the preparation of news releases or other materials. Indeed, a great deal of media coverage is generated by reporters calling an organization's spokesperson or working through the public relations department to arrange an interview with an executive or expert.

The ability of a spokesperson to answer a journalist's questions in a concise manner or give a major speech to an audience requires thought and preparation. Andrew D. Gilman, president of CommCore in New York City, emphasizes the need for preparation. He says, "I would no more think of putting a client on a witness stand or through a deposition without thorough and adequate presentation than I would ask a client to be interviewed by a skillful and well-prepared journalist without a similar thorough and adequate preparation."

Preparing for an Interview

In all interviews, the person being questioned should say something that will inform or entertain the audience. The public relations practitioner should prepare the interviewee to meet this need. An adroit interviewer attempts to develop a theme in the conversation—to draw out comments that make a discernible point or illuminate the character of the person being interviewed. The latter can help the interviewer—and his or her own cause as well—by being ready to volunteer specific information, personal data, or opinions about the cause under discussion as soon as the conversational opportunity arises.

In setting up an interview, the public relations person should obtain from the interviewer an understanding of the interview's purpose. Armed with this information, the practitioner can assemble facts and data for the client to use in the discussion. The practitioner also can aid the client by providing tips about the interviewer's style.

Some journalists ask "cream puff" questions, whereas others bore in, trying to force the interviewee into unplanned admissions or embarrassment. Thus, it is especially important to be well acquainted with the interviewer's style, whether the interviewer is someone from a local newspaper, a TV reporter, or a *Wall Street Journal* columnist. Short, direct answers delivered without hesitation help a person project an image of strength and credibility. These types of answers also provide better quotes or broadcast soundbites, which the media value.

The Print Interview

An interview with a newspaper reporter may last about an hour and take place perhaps at lunch or over coffee in an informal setting. The result of this person-to-person talk may be a published story of perhaps 400 to 600 words. The interviewer weaves bits from the conversation together in direct and indirect quotation form, works in background material, and perhaps injects personal observations about the interviewee. The latter has no control over what is published, beyond the self-control he or she exercises in answering the reporter's questions. Neither the person being interviewed nor a public relations representative should ask to approve an interview story before it is published. Such requests are rebuffed automatically as a form of censorship.

Magazine interviews usually explore the subject in greater depth than those in newspapers, because the writer may have more space available. Most magazine interviews have the same format as those in newspapers. Others appear in question-and-answer form. These require prolonged, taped questioning of the interviewee by one or more writers and editors. During in-depth interviews, the interviewee should answer the questions, but refrain from going off on tangents.

Radio and television interviews will be covered in the next chapter.

News Conferences

A more formal approach to a media interview is the *news conference*, which is often referred to as a *press conference*. A news conference makes possible quick, widespread dissemination of a person's comments and opinions to a number of reporters at the same time. It avoids the time-consuming task of presenting the information to the news outlets individually and ensures that the intensely competitive newspapers and electronic media hear the news simultaneously. Increasingly, bloggers that cover the particular industry are also invited to attend a news conference.

Most news conferences are positive in intent and project the host's plans or point of view. A corporation may hold a news conference to unveil a new product whose manufacture will create many new jobs, or a civic leader may do so to reveal the goals and plans for a countywide charity fund drive she will head. Such news conferences should be carefully planned and scheduled well in advance under the most favorable circumstances.

Public relations specialists also must deal frequently with unanticipated, controversial situations, such as a business firm, an association, or a politician becoming embroiled in a difficulty that is at best embarrassing, and possibly incriminating. Press and public demand an explanation. A bare-bones printed statement will not be enough to satisfy the clamor and may draw greater press scrutiny of the stonewalling organization.

A well-prepared spokesperson may be able to achieve a measure of understanding and sympathy by issuing a carefully composed statement when the news conference opens.

No matter how trying the circumstances, the person holding the news conference should create an atmosphere of cooperation and project a sincere intent to be helpful. The worst thing he or she can do is to appear resentful of the questioning. In addition, the person never should succumb to a display of bad temper. A good strategy is to admit that the situation is bad and stress that the organization is doing everything in its power to correct it. The approach is described by Professor Timothy Coombs at Wayne State University as the "mortification" strategy, which was discussed in Chapter 10.

Most news conferences are planned in advance, but they can also be somewhat spontaneous. Such a situation might involve the recipient of a Nobel Prize meeting reporters right after the award is announced, or an Olympic athlete who has just won a gold medal and is breathlessly describing his feelings. Celebrities, in particular, give a lot of impromptu news conferences to announce everything from a divorce to a new multimillion-dollar contract. The other type is the regularly scheduled conference held by a public official at stated times, even when there is nothing special to announce. Usually this is called a *briefing*—the daily State Department briefing, for example.

Planning and Conducting a News Conference

First comes the question "Should we hold a news conference or not?" Frequently the answer should be "No!" The essential element of a news conference is news. If reporters and camera crews are summoned to a conference and receive information of minor news value to their readers or listeners, they go away disgusted. Their valuable time has been wasted—and it is valuable. In other words, public relations professionals should realistically assess whether the information can just as effectively be distributed through a news release or media kit.

What hour is best? This depends on the local media situation. If the city has only an afternoon newspaper, 9:30 or 10 A.M. is good, because this gives a reporter time to write a story before the midday deadline. If the city's newspaper publishes in the morning, 2 P.M. is a suitable hour. Early afternoon is also good for local television stations because they then have time to prepare a story for the 6 P.M. newscast.

Bulldog Reporter, a West Coast public relations newsletter, suggests the following checklist for public relations staff organizing a news conference:

- Select a convenient location, one that is fairly easy for news representatives to reach with minimal travel time.
- Set the date and time. A time between midmorning and midafternoon is good. Friday afternoons are deadly, as are days before holidays. See Figure 14.6 for a media advisory about a news conference.
- Distribute a media advisory about the upcoming news conference when appropriate. This depends on the importance of the event.
- Write a statement for the spokesperson to give at the conference and make sure that he or she understands and rehearses it. In addition, rehearse the entire conference.
- Try to anticipate questions so that the spokesperson can readily answer difficult queries. Problem/solution rehearsals prepare the spokesperson.
- Prepare a media kit. This should include a brief fact sheet with names and titles of participants, a basic news release, and basic support materials.
- Prepare visual materials as necessary. These may include slides, photos, posters, or even a short video.
- Make advance arrangements for the room. Be sure that there are enough chairs and leave a center aisle for photographers. If a lectern is used, make certain that it is large enough to accommodate multiple microphones.
- Arrive 30 to 60 minutes early to double-check arrangements. Test the microphones, arrange name tags for invited guests, and distribute literature.

A practitioner should take particular care to arrange the room in such a way that photographers and TV crews do not obstruct reporters. Some find it good policy for the speaker to remain after the news conference ends and make brief on-camera statements for the broadcast media or even a blogger. A final problem in managing a news conference is knowing when to end it. The public relations representative serving as backstage watchdog should avoid cutting off the questioning prematurely. A moment will come, however, when the reporters run out of fresh questions. This is the time to step forward and say something like, "I'm sorry, but I know some of you have deadlines to make. So we have time for just two more questions."

Online News Conferences

The previous section focused on news conferences in a specific location, but many of the guidelines also apply to online news conferences. Many news conferences today are interactive webcasts so that journalists and bloggers around the world can participate.

time to play
Spring Showcase

April 27, 2010 04:02 AM Pacific Daylight Time

Time to Play Spring Showcase Highlights the Best in Play from Hot New Movie Items to Outdoor Toys

Visit the Altman Building, NYC on Tuesday, April 27th

More Than 20 Leading Toy Manufacturers and Entertainment Companies Showcase Hot Toys for Spring & Summer '10; Executives On Site for Interview

Press Conference at 10 AM Announcing the Coolest Toys for Spring and Summer Fun

--(BUSINESS WIRE)--Media Advisory:

WHAT: With spring in full bloom, are you looking for fun and playful story ideas? Look no further! The Time to Play Spring Showcase is truly a one stop shop for a comprehensive first look at what people will be buzzing about this season.

Join Jim Silver, editor in chief of TimetoPlaymag.com and Chris Byrne, content director, aka The Toy Guy® as they talk about the industry, what's hot for the season and unveil some of the coolest children's products for the spring & summer season. More than 20 leading toy and family entertainment companies will showcase the best new toys hitting store shelves, blockbuster movie 'must haves' and toys to make the most of outdoor playtime! Plus, interview opportunities are available with Jim, Chris and executives from participating companies.

Exhibitors include Mattel, Hasbro, JAKKS Pacific, Spin Master, LEGO, Playmobil, Nickelodeon, Disney Consumer Products and more!

TimetoPlayMag.com provides information, entertainment, and services on what's fun for children and their families.

WHEN: Tuesday, April 27th 10:00 AM - 2:30 PM
Press check in begins at 9:00 AM
Press conference 10 AM - 10:30 AM

WHERE: Altman Building
135 West 18th Street, between 6th & 7th Avenues, New York City

PHOTO/ INTERVIEW OPPORTUNITIES

- **Movie & TV toys** that bring the adventure of the big screen home for fans of all ages

- **Hottest toys for cool summertime fun** – products that help make the most of the warm weather: water and dart blasters, sports toys, swing sets, beach and bubble toys, poolside accessories and rideables

- **Best new toys hitting store shelves** – tech toys, board games and everything in between

- **More than 20 leading toy manufacturers & entertainment companies with executives onsite for interviews**

- **Interview opportunities** with Jim Silver, editor in chief of TimetoPlaymag.com and Chris Byrne, content director, aka The Toy Guy®

Contacts

For more information or to RSVP, please contact:
Litzky Public Relations
Josslynne Welch/Marni Bahniuk, 201-222-9118
jwelch@litzkypr.com/mbahniuk@litzkypr.com

Figure 14.6   Time to Play News Conference Advisory

News conferences are often announced in media advisories. Media advisories usually provide the basic who, what, where, why information so that media organizations can decide whether to attend the event. In this case, the organization also provides a list of photo and interview opportunities that will be available.

Attendance is often better because journalists can view and even ask questions while sitting at their desks. In fact, if a news conference is for reporters across the country who are covering a particular industry, a webcast with company officials speaking to reporters via the Internet is not only more cost efficient but also more effective. Webcasts, including their use as news conferences, were discussed in Chapter 13. A media advisory for a webcast news conference is shown in Figure 14.7.

ECOLAB

April 12, 2010 01:30 PM Pacific Daylight Time ⬚

Ecolab Schedules Webcast and Conference Call on April 27th

ST. PAUL, Minn.--(BUSINESS WIRE)--Ecolab will host a live webcast of its first quarter investor conference call. A press release containing first quarter results and earnings guidance is expected to be issued before the market opens on April 27, 2010.

Details for the webcast are as follows:

TIME: 1:00 p.m. Eastern Time
DATE: Tuesday, April 27, 2010
DURATION: One hour
LOCATION: http://www.ecolab.com/investor
ARCHIVE: A replay of the webcast and supplementary materials will be available on Ecolab's web site.

To access the webcast, go to the Investor Information portion of the Company's Web site at http://www.ecolab.com/investor and click on the webcast icon. Listening to the webcast requires Internet access and the Windows Media, RealPlayer or other compatible streaming media player.

With sales of $6 billion and more than 26,000 associates, Ecolab Inc. (NYSE: ECL) is the global leader in cleaning, sanitizing, food safety and infection prevention products and services. Ecolab delivers comprehensive programs and services to the foodservice, food and beverage processing, healthcare and hospitality markets in more than 160 countries. More news and information is available at www.ecolab.com.

(ECL-C)

Contacts

Ecolab Inc.
Michael J. Monahan, 651-293-2809

Figure 14.7   Ecolab Webcast Advisory

News conferences are frequently conducted online so that reporters in locations around the world can easily attend without even getting up from their desks. This advisory by Ecolab gives the basic information about the webcast, but also lets reporters know that a replay and other materials will be available on the organization's website if they can't attend the actual webcast.

Media Tours and Press Parties

The purpose of the typical news conference is to transmit information and opinion from the organization to the news media in a businesslike, time-efficient manner. Often, however, an organization wishes to brief the media or get to know journalists and editors on a more personal basis. There are two approaches for doing this. One is the media tour and the other is the dinner or cocktail party. Both require intense attention to every possible detail and an ability to juggle multiple logistics.

Media Tours

There are three kinds of media tours. The most common is a trip, often disparagingly called a "junket," during which editors and reporters are invited to inspect a company's manufacturing facilities in several cities, ride an inaugural flight of a new air route, or watch previews of the television network programs for the fall season in Hollywood or New York. The host usually picks up the tab for transporting, feeding, and housing the reporters. Many publications, however, insist on paying transportation and housing to avoid any potential conflict of interest. In either case, the public relations staff should give reporters the option of being paid guests of the organization or paying for their own transportation and housing.

A variation of the media tour is the *familiarization trip*. "Fam trips," as they are called, are offered to travel writers and editors by the tourism industry (see Chapter 18). Convention and visitor bureaus, as well as major resorts, pay all expenses in the hope that the writers will report favorably on their experiences. Travel articles in magazines and newspapers usually result from a reporter's "fam trip."

In the third kind of media tour, which is widely used in high-technology industries, the organization's executives travel to key cities to talk with selected editors; for example, top Apple Computer executives toured the East Coast to talk with key magazine editors and demonstrate the capabilities of the new Apple iPad. Depending on editors' preferences, the executives may visit a publication and give a background briefing to key editors, or a hotel conference room may be set up so that the traveling executives may talk with editors from several publications at the same time.

Press Parties

This gathering may be a luncheon, a dinner, or a cocktail party. Whatever form the party takes, standard practice is for the host to rise at the end of the socializing period and make the "pitch." This may be the launch of a new product, a brief policy statement followed by a question-and-answer period, or merely a soft-sell thank-you to the guests for coming and giving the host an opportunity to know them better. Guests usually are given press packets of information, either when they arrive or as they leave. Parties giving the press a preview of an art exhibit, a new headquarters building, and so forth are widely used.

The advantages to the host of a press party can be substantial under the proper circumstances. During conversation over food or drink, officials of the host organization become acquainted with the media people who write, edit, broadcast, or blog about them. Although the benefit from the host's point of view is difficult to measure immediately, the party opens the channels of communication.

Also, if the host has an important policy position to present, the assumption—not necessarily correct—is that editors and reporters will be more receptive after a social hour. However, the host who expects food and drink to buy favorable press coverage may receive an unpleasant surprise. Conscientious reporters and editors will not be swayed by a free drink and a plate of prime rib followed by baked Alaska. In their view, they have already given something to the host by setting aside a part of their day for the party. They accept invitations to press parties because they wish to develop potential news contacts within the host's organization and to learn more about its officials.

Gifts in the form of a pen, note pad, or company paperweight are often given to reporters attending a press party, but anything costing more than a token amount should be avoided. Some large newspapers will not even permit their staffs to accept token gifts, as discussed in Chapter 3.

Summary

The News Release

- The news release is the most commonly used public relations tactic.

- News releases are sent to journalists and editors for possible use in news columns, and they are the source for a large percentage of articles that are published.

- News releases must be accurate, informative, and written in journalistic style.

- Online news releases are similar to traditional news releases, but the format is condensed and single-spacing is used. Most widely distributed news releases are now sent by e-mail or posted on organizational websites.

■ Multimedia news releases harness the capabilities of the Internet and social media by embedding photos, video, links, social tags, etc., into the basic news release.

Publicity Photos

■ Publicity photos often accompany news releases to make a story more appealing.

■ Photos must be high resolution and well composed.

■ A photo can be made more interesting by manipulating the camera angle and lighting and by showing scale and action.

■ Color photos are now commonly used in most publications.

Media Kits

■ A media kit, or press kit, was traditionally a folder containing news releases, photos, fact sheets, and features about a new product, event, or other newsworthy projects undertaken by an organization.

■ Electronic press kits (EPKs) are now commonly used and are produced on CD, e-mailed, or placed on organizational websites.

Mat Releases

■ A mat release is a form of news release that primarily has a feature angle instead of hard news. Mat releases provide consumer information and tips in an objective manner, with only a brief reference to the client that is distributing the information via a distribution firm such as Family Features.

■ These canned features appear in the food, travel, automotive, and business sections of a newspaper.

Media Alerts and Fact Sheets

■ Advisories, or alerts, let journalists know about an upcoming event such as a news conference or photo or interview opportunities.

■ Fact sheets give the five Ws and H of an event in outline form. Fact sheets also can be used to provide background on an executive, a product, or an organization.

The Art of Pitching a Story

■ Public relations personnel "pitch" journalists and editors with story ideas about their employer or client.

■ Such pitches can be telephone calls, e-mails, or even text messages and Tweets.

■ A good pitch is based on research and a creative idea that will appeal to the journalist or editor.

Distributing Media Materials

■ Electronic news services such as Business Wire provide an efficient way to distribute news releases around the world.

■ Online newsrooms are often part of an organization's website. They allow the media and the public to access news releases, photos, videos, and other public relations materials.

Media Interviews

■ Journalists often seek interviews with sources, and the role of the public relations person is to facilitate their requests.

■ Public relations personnel often do media training to ensure that sources give competent media interviews.

News Conferences

■ Such events should be held rarely and only when there is major news or intense media interest.

■ Public relations personnel are usually in charge of logistics and arrangements for news conferences.

■ Online news conferences are popular because journalists in different locations can easily attend.

Media Tours and Press Parties

■ Company executives often go on a media tour to visit editors in various locations and discuss a new product, such as the iPad.

■ Press parties are primarily social events that allow an organization's executives to meet journalists and develop working relationships.

Case Activity   Promoting the Opening of a New Library

A new university library will open next month. The $100 million building is an eight-story wonder of glass and steel beams designed by the famous architectural firm BK Skinner and Associates. The library has over 125 commissioned works of art and 2,500 Internet plug-ins for students and their laptops. In addition, the library has several computer labs for students and meeting rooms for university and community organizations. And, in a special coup, author J. K. Rowling of *Harry Potter* fame will be the guest of honor at the official opening.

Write an online news release about the new library and its planned grand opening. Second, write an e-mail pitch letter to the local media encouraging them to do feature stories about the new library in advance of the opening. Third, write a media alert letting the media know that J. K. Rowling will be available for interviews on a particular day. Include appropriate quotations and information that you deem necessary.

Questions   for Review and Discussion

1. What is the basic purpose of a news release?
2. What are the basic components of an online news release?
3. What are the characteristics of a multimedia news release?
4. What is SEO and why is it important?
5. Why is it a good idea to include a photograph with a news release? What are the six aspects of a good publicity photo?
6. What is a mat release? How is it different from a regular news release?
7. What's the difference between a media advisory and a fact sheet?

8. What's a media kit? What does a media kit typically contain?
9. Before pitching a story to a journalist or editor, why is it a good idea to first do some basic research on the individual or the publication?
10. What are the capabilities of an electronic news service?
11. What are the characteristics of an online newsroom?
12. How should you prepare for a media interview?
13. What are the mechanics of organizing a news conference?
14. What's the difference between a media tour and a press party?

Media Resources

Brown, D. (2010, April 28). Where next for the news release? Retrieved from PRBreakfastClub website: www.prbreakfastclub.com

Horwitz-Bennett, B. (2010, March 22). Ten ways you can keep the media coming back for more. Retrieved from www.ragan.com

Kent, C. (2009, September). Eight pitches that caught reporters' attention. *RaganReport*, pp. 24–25.

McQuade, G. S. (2010, January). Experts discuss electronic press kit protocol. *O'Dwyer's PR Report*, 64.

Mengel, A. (2010, March 15). The social media release is not a PR panacea. Retrieved from www.ragan.com

Miller, L. (2009, November 3). Poll: Don't trash press releases yet. Retrieved from www.ragan.com

Miller, L. (2010, January). Four techniques for spicing up corporate photos. *RaganReport*, 30–31.

The quick guide to writing your first online press release. (2010) Retrieved from PRWeb website: www.prweb.com

Skogrand, B., & Peterson, C. (2009, March). If they can find it, they will come: Optimizing your online newsroom. *Public Relations Tactics*, 18.

Strong, F. (2010, March 10). PR pros should write for search engines. Retrieved from www.ragan.com

Wilcox, D. L. (2009). *Public relations writing & media techniques* (6th ed.). Boston, MA: Allyn & Bacon.

Woodall, I. (2009, June 19). From old media to social media: Survey reveals the essential elements for today's online newsroom. *PR Tactics and the Strategist Online*. Retrieved from www.prsa.org/supportfiles/news

Young, S. (2010, May 4). Ten ways to pitching your story and getting publicity. Retrieved from www.ragan.com

Radio and Television

After reading this chapter, you will be able to:

Write radio news releases and video news releases

Prepare public service announcements (PSAs) for broadcast

Understand the components of radio media tours and satellite media tours

Know the procedure for booking a guest on a talk show

Understand the strategy of product placement on television shows

The Reach of Radio and Television

Radio and television are important channels of communications for public relations specialists because they reach the vast majority of the American public on a daily basis. Radio reaches almost 80 percent of the American population, second only to television, which reaches 95 percent of the population on a daily basis.

> Radio's power comes from its accessibility. People can listen to radio in almost any location—at home, the car, or work—and it remains a free medium for listeners.
>
> *David Beasley, marketing manager at News Generation, a public relations firm specializing in radio*

Nielsen Media Research also reports that, at the end of 2009, the average American was spending about 11 hours a week listening to broadcast radio and about 37 hours a week watching television. In contrast, the average American was spending about 8.5 hours a week on the Web/Internet, excluding the use of e-mail.

Both radio and television continue to thrive in the Internet Age for three reasons. First, radio and television content has expanded to other digital platforms. More than 40 million people, for example, listen to the radio weekly via the Internet, satellite radio, or iPod/MP3 players. Television programs are also widely downloaded to computers and smartphones. Second, broadcast media generate larger audiences for a particular program or event than any other single media platform. The 2010 Super Bowl, for example, attracted 116 million viewers. Other television programs, such as *Dancing With the Stars*, generate a typical weekly audience of more than 20 million.

The third reason is that radio and television are what the *Economist* describes as "an inherently lazy form of entertainment." Listening to either medium is a passive form of activity and doesn't require much work on the part of the individual. Radio is readily available in the home, in the car, and even at work by turning a switch. Radio also has the ability to reach niche audiences, whether they are housewives, baby boomers, or Hispanics. See also the Insights box on page XXX about Hispanic broadcast media. Both media also easily accommodate multitasking; a person can text, Tweet, and do a number of other tasks while listening to a radio or watching TV.

Tapping broadcast media for public relations purposes, however, requires a special perspective. Practitioners must constantly think about producing messages in audio and visual terms. This chapter discusses the various tactics used by public relations personnel to distribute information via radio and television, and to secure opportunities for their clients and employers to appear on a variety of broadcast shows.

Radio

The following sections will discuss (1) audio news releases, (2) radio public service announcements, and (3) radio media tours. A section toward the end of the chapter will discuss general guidelines for pitching broadcast outlets and arranging guest appearances on both radio and television talk shows.

Audio News Releases

Radio news releases in the industry are called *audio news releases*, or ANRs. They differ in three ways from online news releases, which were discussed in the last chapter. The most important difference is that a radio news release is written for the ear. The

on the job

A MULTICULTURAL WORLD

Reaching Out to the Hispanic Audience

The numbers tell the story. Hispanics are the largest and fastest-growing minority in the country and, by 2050, will constitute almost 30 percent of the U.S. population. This gives public relations professionals a special impetus to include this audience when executing a campaign that includes radio and television.

The Hispanic audience is important for several reasons. First, Latino consumers spend more than $685 billion annually on goods and services. A second reason is the average household size of 3.4 persons; this makes the Latino audience attractive to retailers of such goods as clothes, telephone services, and groceries.

Radio and television are particularly good communication channels for the Hispanic audience. First, in terms of Hispanic media, there are now about 600 Spanish-language radio stations and 75 Hispanic television stations in the United States. In addition, Univision is now the fifth largest network in the country.

Second, research studies show that the Hispanic audience outpaces the general population in terms of listeners and viewers. Hispanics, for example, average 24 hours a week listening to the radio, and one out of every three radio stations in the top

10 media markets is Hispanic. In terms of television, Hispanics daily view an average of one hour more than non-Hispanic whites. Seventy percent watch both English and Spanish programs.

This means that the full range of radio and television tactics, such as news releases, PSAs, media tours, and video news releases (VNRs), should be prepared with the Hispanic audience in mind. However, more is involved than simply translating an English version of the same material into Spanish. As a monograph from Medialink says, "A direct translation from English to Spanish, in many cases, simply does not make sense from a grammatical and syntax perspective." Instead, a public relations professional should practically start from scratch and have translations done by someone completely fluent in Spanish.

Radio and television media tours, called RMTs and SMTs, have their own special requirements. It is important to have a Hispanic spokesperson who speaks Spanish as his or her native language.

Although Spanish is the common denominator, it's also important to have spokespersons who appeal

to different age groups. A good example is television PSAs prepared by Strauss Radio Strategies on behalf of the Hispanic Heritage Awards Foundation (HHAF). Celebrity spokespersons included Gloria Estefan, Carlos Ponce, Jon Secada, and Shalim, as well as television personalities Judy Reyes from NBC's *Scrubs* and sports announcer Andres Cantor.

Another tip from Strauss Radio Strategies is to remember that many Hispanic radio and television stations operate on a shoestring budget and don't have the latest technologies. So, instead of satellite transmission, it's often necessary to distribute VNRs and PSAs by CD and an e-mailed MP3 file. In terms of pitching radio and television stations, a public relations person fluent in both English and Spanish is highly recommended.

> Make sure that PSAs are scripted, reviewed, and voiced by fluent native Spanish speakers.
>
> *Raul Martinez,*
> *Strauss Radio Strategies*

emphasis is on strong, short sentences that average about 10 words and can be easily understood by a listener.

A second difference is that an ANR is more concise and to the point. Instead of a news release that may run several hundred words, a standard one-minute ANR is about

125 words. The timing is vital, because broadcasters must fit their message into a rigid time frame that is measured down to the second.

The third difference is writing style. An online news release is more formal and uses standard English grammar and punctuation. Sentences often contain dependent and independent clauses. In a radio release, a more conversational style is used. In such a style, partial or incomplete sentences are OK. The following are some guidelines from the Broadcast News Network on how to write a radio news release:

- Time is money in radio. Stories should be no longer than 60 seconds. Stories without actualities (soundbites) should be 30 seconds or less.
- The only way to time your story is to read it out loud, slowly.
- A long or overly commercial story is death. Rather than editing it, a busy radio newsperson will discard it.
- Convey your message with the smallest possible number of words and facts.
- A radio news release is not an advertisement; it is not a sales promotion piece. A radio news release is journalism—spoken.
- Announcers punctuate with their stories; not all sentences need verbs or subjects.
- Releases should be conversational. Use simple words and avoid legal-speak.
- After writing a radio news release, try to shorten every sentence.
- Never start a story with a name or a vital piece of information. While listeners are trying to figure out the person speaking and the subject matter, they don't pay attention to the specific information.

Format A radio news release can be sent to stations for announcers to read, but the most effective approach is to provide a radio station with a recording of someone with a good radio voice reading the entire announcement. The person doing the reading may not be identified by name. This, in the trade, is called an *actuality*.

A second approach is to have an announcer and also include what is called a *soundbite* from a satisfied customer or a company spokesperson. This approach is better than a straight announcement because the message comes from a "real person" rather than from a nameless announcer. This type of announcement is also more acceptable to radio stations, because the station's staff can elect to use the whole recorded announcement or take the role of announcer and use just the soundbite.

An example of an effective ANR was the one produced for the American Psychological Association (APA). The APA, using the firm News Generation, got soundbites from a number of researchers presenting papers on topical issues at its national convention. One soundbite, for example, was about the differences in how men and women hear and smell. A number of radio stations used the ANR, reaching a potential audience of 20 million.

The following is a 60-second ANR that includes a soundbite from a spokesperson. It was produced by Medialink for its client, Cigna Health Systems, and distributed to radio stations via satellite.

Worried at Work

New Survey Shows American Workers Are Stressed Out But Can Take Simple Steps to Ease Workplace Tension

SUGGESTED ANCHOR LEAD: If you're feeling stressed out at work, you're not alone. A new survey shows economic uncertainty, dwindling retirement savings, and ongoing terrorist concerns have American workers increasingly stressed out. But as Roberta Facinelli explains, employees and employers alike can do things to counteract all this tension.

SCRIPT: If you're like most American workers, you're facing increased stress on and off the job. In fact, according to a new nationwide study conducted by employee assistance experts at CIGNA Behavioral Health, almost half of employees surveyed have been tempted to quit their jobs over the past year, have quit, or are planning to soon, given the series of pressures they're facing. But according to CIGNA's Dr. Jodi Aronson Prohofsky, there are things you can do to ease workplace tension.

CUT (Aronson Prohofsky): Simple changes in your lifestyle can help reduce stress. Exercising more often, volunteering, making time to read or engaging in a favorite hobby are all easy steps we can take. Many of us also take time out for reflection and meditation to deal with daily pressures.

SCRIPT: Employees often find workplace support programs a good place to start, so check with your employer. Many provide programs such as counseling services, flexible work schedules as well as nutrition and health programs—all of which can help reenergize stressed out workers to achieve a better work–life balance. I'm Roberta Facinelli.

SUGGESTED ANCHOR TAG: If you're interested in learning more about workplace stress reduction tips, visit www.cignabehavioral.com

The Cigna script is an example of an ANR that gives information and tips to the listener in a conversational way. It contains helpful information about how to reduce stress and is not overly commercial. Cigna is mentioned in the context of the story, but primarily as a source of information. A station newsperson, no doubt, would find the subject current and newsworthy for the station's audience.

Production and Delivery   Every ANR starts with a carefully written and accurately timed script. The next step is to record the words. When recording, it is imperative to control the quality of the sound. A few large organizations have complete recording studios, and some hire radio station employees as consultants; but most organizations use a professional recording and distribution service such as Strauss Radio Strategies.

These services have state-of-the-art equipment and skilled personnel who can take a script, edit it, record it at the proper sound levels, and package it for distribution to broadcast outlets via telephone, CDs, MP3 format, Web servers, and even through such networks as ABC and CNN radio.

Radio stations, like newspapers, have preferences about how they want to receive news releases. One survey by DWJ Television found that almost 75 percent of the radio news directors prefer to receive actualities by phone. This is particularly true for late-breaking news events in the station's service area. When a forest fire threatened vineyards in California's Napa Valley, a large winery contacted local stations and offered an ANR with a soundbite from the winery's president telling everyone that the grape harvest would not be affected. About 50 stations were called, and 40 accepted the ANR for broadcast use.

Use of ANRs   Producing ANRs is somewhat of a bargain compared with producing materials for television. Ford Motor Company, for example, spent less than $5,000 for national distribution of a news release on battery recycling as part of Earth Day activities. More than 600 radio stations picked up the ANR, and about 5 million people were reached.

Despite their cost-effectiveness, ANRs should not be sent to every station. Stations have particular demographics. A release about the benefits of vitamin supplements for senior citizens isn't of much interest to a station specializing in hip-hop. Various media databases such as Cision and Burrelles help practitioners select the right stations for their ANRs.

The use of ANRs is increasingly popular with radio stations. Thom Moon, director of operations at Duncan's American Radio Quarterly, told *PRWeek* that he thinks the major reason for this is the consolidation of ownership in radio broadcasting, which has resulted in cost-cutting and fewer news personnel.

Jack Trammell, president of VNR-1 Communications, echoed this thought. He told *pr reporter*, "They're telling us they're being forced to do more with less. As long as radio releases are well produced and stories don't appear to be blatant commercials, newsrooms are inclined to use them." Trammell also said news editors look for regional interest stories, health information, and financial news. They also like technology stories, children's issues, politics, seasonal stories, and local interest issues.

Public Relations Tactics gives some additional tips from Trammell:

- **Timeliness.** Stories should be timed to correspond with annual seasons, governmental rulings, new laws, social trends, and so on.

- **Localization.** Newsrooms emphasize local news. A national release should be relevant to a local audience. Reporters are always looking for the "local angle."

- **Humanization.** Stories should show how real people are involved or affected. Impressive statistics mean nothing to audiences without a human angle.

- **Visual appeal.** Successful stories provide vibrant, compelling soundbites that subtly promote, but also illustrate and explain.

Radio PSAs

In PSAs, speak to the common man. . . . Make it as simple as possible.

Christiana Arbesu,
VP of production, MultiVu

Public relations personnel working for nonprofit organizations often prepare *public service announcements* (PSAs) for radio stations.

A PSA is defined by the FCC as an unpaid announcement that promotes the programs of government or voluntary agencies or that serves the public interest. In general, as part of their responsibility to serve the public interest, radio and TV stations provide airtime to charitable and civic organizations to make the public aware of and educate them about such topics as heart disease, obesity, safe driving, and AIDS.

Format and Production   Radio PSAs are written in uppercase and double-spaced. Their length can be 60, 30, 20, 15, or 10 seconds. And, unlike radio news releases, the standard practice is to submit multiple PSAs on the same subject in various lengths. To prepare PSAs in various lengths, the writer should use the following guidelines setting margins for a 60-space line:

  2 lines = 10 seconds (about 25 words)

  5 lines = 20 seconds (about 45 words)

  8 lines = 30 seconds (about 65 words)

  16 lines = 60 seconds (about 125 words)

The idea is to give the station flexibility in using a PSA of a particular length to fill a specific time slot. DWJ Television explains: "Some stations air PSAs in a way that

on the job
INSIGHTS

Radio PSAs Should Have Varying Lengths

The following is a basic PSA, produced by the American Red Cross, that shows how the same topic can be treated in various lengths:

20 seconds

Ever give a gift that didn't go over real big? One that ended up in the closet the second you left the room? There is a gift that's guaranteed to be well received. Because it will save someone's life. The gift is blood, and it's desperately needed. Please give blood. There's a life to be saved right now. Call the American Red Cross at 1-800-GIVE LIFE.

60 seconds

We want you to give a gift to somebody, but it's not a gift you buy. We want you to give a gift, but not necessarily to someone you know. Some of you will be happy to do it. Some of you may be hesitant. But the person who receives your gift will consider it so precious, they'll carry it with them the rest of their life. The gift is blood and, every day in America, thousands of people desperately need it. Every day, we wonder if there will be enough for them. Some days, we barely make it. To those of you who give blood regularly, the American Red Cross and the many people whose lives you've saved would like to thank you. Those of you who haven't given recently, please help us again. There's a life to be saved right now. To find out how convenient it is to give blood, call the American Red Cross today at 1-800-GIVE-LIFE. That's 1-800-GIVE-LIFE.

relates length to time of play, for example, placing one length in their early news shows and another in the late news shows. Supplying both lengths allows a campaign to be heard by those who only listen to one of these shows." See the Insights box above for an example of two lengths used in a radio PSA.

Adding Sound The basic audio news release or radio PSA is a person reading a script. That's OK, but adding sound and other voices can make a radio PSA more interesting. Many PSAs use background music to add a dramatic touch or create a particular mood. Sound effects also work. A PSA for the National Heart Lung and Blood Institute, for example, used the sound of a stock car engine as an analogy to the idea that good air flow in a person's lungs is just as important as good air flow to an engine. Another common approach is to have the voices of several people in the PSA. Here is a 60-second radio PSA about the disease MRSA, which was highlighted in Chapter 8 on page 204.

Different kids using "mom-isms"
    Kid 1: Eat your fruits and veggies.
    Kid 2: Brush your teeth.
    Kid 3: Put on a coat; it's cold outside.
    Kid 4: Did you finish your homework?
    Kid 5: Wash your hands before you eat.

Announcer: So, mom, have you heard about MRSA? Methicillin-resistant *Staphylococcus aureus* is a type of staph bacteria that is resistant to certain antibiotics and may cause skin and other infections. The good news is, the earlier it's caught and treated, the better the outcome. So, if anyone in your family develops a bump that looks red, swollen, full of pus—or just plain infected—cover it with a bandage and contact a healthcare professional—especially if there's also a fever.

For more information, call 1-800-CDC-INFO or visit cdc.gov/MRSA, that's cdc.gov/MRSA.

A message from the U.S. Department of Health and Human Services' Centers for Disease Control and Prevention.

Delivery   PSAs can be distributed in four ways: (1) mailing a script to the station's public service director, (2) sending a CD with announcements of varying lengths, (3) providing an 800 number, or (4) providing downloads from a sponsoring organization's Web server. The Advertising Council (www.adcouncil.org), for example, provides radio and television PSAs on its website for a number of national nonprofit campaigns. The Centers for Disease Control (www.cdc.gov) also provides PSAs for broadcast media on a variety of health subjects. An example of PSAs provided in CD format is below.

Use of Radio PSAs   Almost any topic or issue can be the subject of a PSA. Stations, however, seem to be more receptive to particular topics. A survey of radio station public affairs directors by West Glen Communications, a producer of PSAs, found that local community issues and events are most likely to receive airtime, followed by children's issues. About 70 percent of the Advertising Council's PSA campaigns, for example, now address issues that affect children, from asthma and obesity to underage drinking.

Radio Media Tours

Another public relations tactic is the *radio media tour* (RMT). Essentially, a spokesperson from a central location conducts a series of around-the-country, one-on-one interviews with several radio stations. A public relations representative prebooks telephone interviews with DJs, news directors, or talk show hosts around the country, and the personalities simply give interviews over the phone that can be broadcast live or recorded for later use.

A major selling point of the RMT is its relatively low cost and the convenience of conducting numerous short interviews from one central location. Laurence Moskowitz, president of Medialink, told *PRWeek*, "It is such an easy, flexible medium. We can interview a star in bed at his hotel and broadcast it to the country. Radio is delicious."

Sample Radio PSA in CD Format

A popular method for distributing radio PSAs is by CD. This one, produced by the American Veterinary Medical Association, uses graphics to give the CD more visibility on the desk of a public affairs director at a radio station. The subjects of the PSAs are noted, and the varying lengths are given.

Is your cat healthy?

What pet owners should know about subtle signs of illness in cats.

1. :60 Radio PSA
2. :30 Radio PSA
3. :10 Radio PSA

American Veterinary Medical Association
1931 N. Meacham Road • Schaumburg, Illinois 60173
Phone (847) 925-8070 • www.avma.org

A major multinational pharmaceutical concern, Schering-Plough, used an RMT to point out that most smokers in the United States fail to recognize the warning signs of chronic bronchitis. (Of course, the company makes a drug for such a condition.) The RMT was picked up by 88 stations, with a total audience of more than 2.8 million. The RMT was part of a campaign that also used a *satellite media tour* (SMT) for television stations. SMTs are discussed in the next section.

However, public relations practitioners setting up an RMT need to do their homework. As Richard Strauss, president of Strauss Radio Strategies, told *PRWeek*, "It's not enough just to know the show exists. Listen to the show, understand the format, read the host's bio, and know past guests to gain some kind of familiarity." Another guideline is to tie the RMT to an event, premiere, holiday, or current news that links to the listening audience. "For example, seat-belt safety campaigns are most effective around Thanksgiving and the Fourth of July, when Americans take to the roads in record numbers," says Curtis Gill of News Generation, a firm that arranges RMTs for clients.

Timing is also a consideration. Most interviews are on morning talk shows between the hours of 8 A.M. and noon. This means that the spokesperson, either an expert or a known celebrity, must be prepared to give early morning interviews to cover all the time zones. Other experts also give the tip that an organization should select a spokesperson with some endurance—he or she might be giving one interview after another for three or four hours.

Television

Television is a powerful and influential medium because it taps both sight and sound. It's also pervasive in American society and occupies more of the average American's time than any other medium, including the Internet. Consequently, public relations specialists work very hard to harness this medium in most public relations campaigns.

There are several approaches for getting an organization's news and viewpoints on television. They are:

■ Send a standard news release. If the news director thinks the topic is newsworthy, the item may become a brief, 10-second mention by the news announcer. A news release may also prompt the assignment editor to think about a visual treatment and assign the topic to a reporter and a camera crew to conduct an on-camera interview or get additional video.

■ Send a media alert or advisory informing the assignment editor about a particular event or occasion that would lend itself to video coverage. Media alerts, which were discussed in Chapter 14, can be sent via e-mail, fax, or even regular mail.

■ Make a pitch by phone or e-mail to the assignment editor to have the station do a particular story. The art of making a pitch to a television news editor is to emphasize the visual aspects of the story.

■ Produce a *video news release* (VNR) package that, like an ANR, is formatted for immediate use, with a minimum of effort by station personnel. The alternative, increasingly used, is to offer B-roll material, which will be explained shortly.

■ Conduct a satellite media tour (SMT) in which a spokesperson can be interviewed by multiple stations at separate times.

- Arrange for your spokesperson to appear on a television talk or magazine show.
- Do product placement in television entertainment shows.

Several of these approaches will be explored in the rest of the chapter.

Video News Releases

Large organizations seeking enhanced recognition for their names, products, services, and causes are the primary clients for VNRs. The production of VNRs can be more easily justified if there is potential for national distribution and multiple pickups by television stations and cable systems. Increasingly, costs are also justified because a VNR package can be reformatted for an organization's website, be part of a multimedia news release, and be posted on an organization's YouTube channel.

> Today's VNRs are much more than just broadcast placement tools. They are being targeted to a variety of audiences through Web syndication, strategic placements in broadcast, cable, and site-based media in retail outlets and hospitals.
>
> *Tim Bahr, managing director of MultiVu, a broadcast production firm*

A typical 90-second VNR, says one producer, costs a minimum of $20,000 to $50,000 for production and distribution. Costs vary, however, depending on the number of location shots, the number of special effects, the use of celebrities, and the number of staff required to produce a high-quality tape that meets broadcast standards.

Because of the cost, a public relations department or firm must carefully analyze the news potential of the information and consider whether the topic lends itself to a fast-paced, action-oriented visual presentation. A VNR should not be produced if it contains only talking heads, charts, and graphs. Another aspect to consider is whether the topic will still be current by the time the video is produced. On average, it takes four to six weeks to script, produce, and distribute a high-quality VNR. In a crisis situation or for a fast-breaking news event, however, a VNR can be produced in a matter of hours or days.

Format   The traditional VNR package is like a media kit prepared for print publications, which was discussed in the last chapter. It has various components that provide the television journalist with everything he or she needs to produce a television news story. According to MultiVu, a production firm, this includes the following:

- Ninety-second news report with voiceover narration on an audio channel separate from that containing soundbites and natural sound.
- A B-roll. This is the video only, without narration, giving a television station maximum flexibility to add its own narration or use just a portion of the video as part of a news segment.
- Clear identification of the video source.
- Script, spokespeople information, media contacts, extra soundbites, and story background information provided electronically.

Conceptualizing and writing a VNR script is somewhat complicated because the writer has to visualize the scene, much like a playwright or screenwriter. In fact, a script for a VNR usually includes two columns. The left column lists the visual components and the right column outlines the audio elements, such as the anchor lead-in, narration, and a list of any soundbites. See a sample VNR script in Figure 15.1.

Medialink

Figure 15.1
Sample VNR Script

The script of a video news release requires thinking about the visuals at the same time that you write copy and plan for interview excerpts. This two-column format, showing visual and audio components, illustrates how a script is written.

VISUAL	AUDIO
FADE IN:	
Suggested Anchor Lead-in:	Despite the economy and world events, things are going "GRAPE" in California's wine country. The "CRUSH," officially underway in the heart of wine country, is the most exciting time of year. Grapes generate (help generate) billions of dollars in travel, tourism, jobs and sales. Especially in the Napa Valley where wine makers consistently create some of the world's finest wine. The buzz this year? A later than usual harvest may produce even higher quality wines.
	As Mother nature places the finishing touches on this year's grape harvest, wine lovers are out in force, pursuing their passion in restaurants, hotels and wine tasting rooms. If the bottom line is good taste, Elizabeth Anderson uncorks some vintage secrets.
	NAT SOT (:04 approx)
	NARRATION
	Coming to a glass near you...
Pour Nouveau-Beringer	The grapes of California's crush.
Crush, picking-harvest	92% of America's wine is produced in California...some of the world's best in Napa Valley.
Wine, grapes	Beringer's Nouveau, the first wine of the 2002 vintage, will beat all California wines to market. Of the Golden
Napa beauty shot	State's 847 wineries, this landmark is the oldest in Napa Valley...bottling award-winning magic for 125
Wine picking, crush-harvest.	years.
Nouveau, Beringer beauty shots, famous	**NAT SOT Beringer Winemaker**
Exteriors, wine is poured.	"The grapes are ready...just the right sugar content."
See Beringer name of famous real estate	
Historical video (from tv cmxl)	
B-roll to complement what he says	
Continuously show various vineyards – St. Clements, Stags Leap	

VISUAL	AUDIO
	NAT SOT :03 (harvest-crush-machinery)
	NARRATION
Crush activity. Grapes splash into camera	The crush proves good things come in small packages: grapes are the state's 3rd leading crop.providing 145-thousand jobs and a $33 billion dollar bottom line.
Agricultural activity	
Regional shots, tourists, perhaps purchasing wine.	
Wining, dining. Tourism, tourists in wine room	NAT SOT (cheers!)

Production   Although public relations writers can handle the job of writing a rough draft of a VNR script, the final scripting and production of a VNR is another matter. The entire process is highly technical, requiring trained professionals and sophisticated equipment.

Consequently, public relations departments and firms usually outsource production to a firm specializing in scripting and producing VNR packages. Public relations personnel, however, usually serve as liaison and give the producer an outline of what the VNR is supposed to accomplish. The public relations person also will work with the producer to line up location shots, props, and the individuals who will be featured. Medialink, a major producer and distributor of VNRs, gives some tips about the production of VNRs that best meet the needs of television news directors:

- Give television news directors maximum flexibility in editing the tape using their own anchors or announcers.

- Produce the VNR with news footage in mind. Keep soundbites short and to the point. Avoid commercial-like shots with sophisticated effects.

- Never superimpose your own written information on the actual videotape. Television news departments usually generate their own written notes in their own typeface and style.

- Never use a stand-up reporter. Stations do not want a reporter who is not on their own staff appearing in their newscast.

- Provide television stations with a local angle. This can be done by sending supplemental facts and figures that reflect the local situation. This can be added to the VNR when it is edited for broadcast.

- Good graphics, including animation, are a plus. Stations are attracted to artwork that shows things in a clear, concise manner.

The New Trend: B-Roll Packaging

It has already been mentioned that a VNR package should always include two or three minutes of B-roll, which contain additional soundbites and video that television news staffs can use for repackaging the story. In fact, a Nielsen Media Research survey of 130 television news directors found that 70 percent wanted a VNR with B-roll attached. Today, even more television news directors want B-roll packages instead of fully scripted VNRs.

One reason is that VNRs have come under fire in recent years because television stations often used them without attribution. Watchdog groups complained to the Federal Communications Commission (FCC) that stations using VNR content without telling the viewers about the source were presenting "fake news." The Center for Media and Democracy, for example, conducted a six-month probe and found that 46 stations in 22 states aired unsourced video material supplied by VNR production firms on behalf of clients.

The controversy over television's use of VNRs also put the spotlight on the public relations industry. The issue was whether public relations firms and the VNR producers were adequately labeling VNR packages so that they identified the sponsor or client. There was also criticism that "reporters" appearing in a VNR just said, "This is Nancy Williams, reporting from New York" and didn't add the line, "on behalf of X Company." As a consequence, the National Association of Broadcast Communicators (NABC) issued new standards for disclosure and transparency, which were discussed in Chapter 3.

Given the criticism, however, video production firms have increasingly moved to just producing B-roll packages on behalf of clients. Such packages provide plenty of video files and soundbites, but are not formally scripted into a complete story. This allows television news staffs to easily pick and choose material to produce their own stories.

One example of a B-roll package was done by the Hoffman Agency, a public relations firm, on how a new surveillance product produced by Sony and A4S Security could withstand extreme conditions and provide video coverage even after the detonation of a bomb in a bus or a building. The B-roll showed a bus being blown up with 10 pounds of explosives and the surveillance device recording the interior of the bus during the explosion. Such dramatic video, accompanied by soundbites from company executives and government officials, was a hit with local and network television news directors.

Bader TV News, a production company based in New York, also produced a B-roll package on behalf of Shell about a college competition to create vehicles that would get exceptional gasoline mileage. Components of the "Shell Oil Eco-Marathon 2010" campaign are shown in the PR Casebook on page 396. VNRs and B-roll packages are also distributed to television stations via satellite.

Television PSAs

Television stations, like radio stations, use PSAs on behalf of governmental agencies, community organizations, and charitable groups. In fact, a survey by News Broadcast Network found that the typical television station runs an average of 137 PSAs per week as part of its commitment to public service.

Many of the guidelines for radio PSAs, which were discussed previously, apply to television PSAs. They must be short, to the point, and professionally produced. Television is different, however, in that both audio and visual elements must be present. Even a simple PSA consisting of the announcer reading text must be accompanied by a photo or artwork that is shown on the screen at the same time. A good example is the sample 30-second television PSA from Rotary International shown on page 399.

Another approach is to have a spokesperson, such as a celebrity, talk directly into the camera for 30 seconds. In the trade, such a PSA is known as a *talking head*. This means that the format is relatively simple, involving just one person speaking to the camera. Ogilvy Public Relations Worldwide, for example, produced PSAs for the Centers for Disease Control and Prevention to build awareness about preventative colorectal cancer screenings. The PSAs featured celebrities such as Katie Couric and Morgan Freeman, both with personal ties to the cancer.

A more complex approach is to involve action and a number of scenes to give the PSA more movement and visual appeal. Good examples are PSAs produced by UNICEF United States Fund, which are downloadable from its website (www.unicefusa.org). Some of the sample downloadable PSAs available are shown on page 399.

Satellite Media Tours

The television equivalent of the radio media tour is the *satellite media tour* (SMT). Essentially, an SMT is a series of prebooked, one-on-one interviews from a fixed location (usually a television studio) via satellite with a series of television journalists or talk show hosts. Interviews via satellite are regularly seen on a number of network news shows, including *CNN News* and PBS's *The News Hour with Jim Lehrer*.

PRCasebook

B-Roll Drives Shell's Eco-Mileage Competition

Video production firms are increasingly producing B-roll packages instead of VNRs for clients because television stations want to format their own coverage. The following materials were sent to television stations via the Internet, and news directors could choose which of the several formats was most compatible with their technical needs. According to Domenic Travano of Bader TV, "The reason behind different formats (QTime, HD, SD and Windows Media are because of all the different set-ups broadcasters use. Unfortunately, there is no set standard in video equipment, so we try to make as many formats available to broadcasters as we can (those three being the most common)." In addition to video, it's also standard to include a script in Word document form so television news directors can determine the nature of the story.

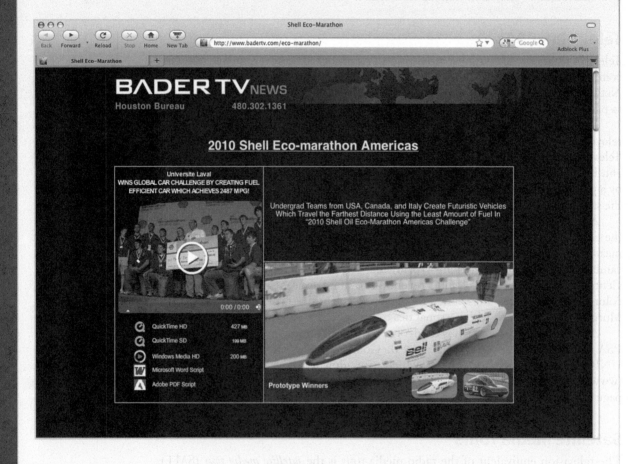

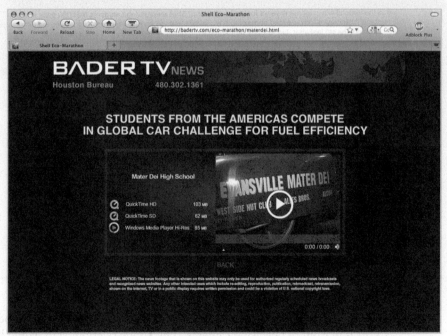

(continued)

BADER TV NEWS   Automotive Technology News
Media Information

Undergrads Go The Eco Distance!

LAVAL UNIVERSITY WINS SHELL MILEAGE CHALLENGE
FUEL EFFICIENT ENTRY ACHIEVES 2487 MPG!

**Undergrad Teams from USA, Canada and Italy Create Futuristic Vehicles which Travel the
Farthest Distance Using the Least Amount of Fuel in
"Shell Oil Eco-Marathon 2010" Challenge**

This B-Roll package is free to use without restrictions or obligations for regularly scheduled news, business, lifestyle,
sports and automotive TV news broadcasts and its corresponding websites only, covering the finals of the
2010 Shell Eco-marathon Americas: Here is the story overview:

Sunday, March 28, 2010, Houston, Texas: With a vehicle that achieved an amazing 2487 miles per gallon,
students from Laval University, Quebec, won the 2010 Shell Eco-marathon Americas. The competition,
hosted by the Shell Oil Company, challenges undergrad and high school teams, comprised of the brightest
engineering students to design a vehicle which travels the farthest distance utilizing the least amount of fuel.

SOT Full: Rodolfo Martinez / Monrovia High School, Los Angeles, CA

Nearly 50 teams from across North America and as far away as Italy faced-off over the weekend at
Houston's Discovery Green urban park. It's the first time the competition has been staged on city streets in
Shell's hometown and the first time that members of the public were invited to view the event, which was
held at the George R. Brown Convention Center.

SOT Full: Steven Zamora / University of Houston

SOT Full: Ted Pesyna / Purdue University (Pronounced: pes-ee-nah)

SOT Full: Nick Llanos / Loyola Marymount University, Los Angeles, California (Driver)

It was the second win in as many years for the Laval team. Shell awarded the students a $5000 prize in the
"Prototype" category, which is aimed at maximum technical creativity and minimal restrictions. The school
won the same award last year, but its entry performed even better, achieving 2757.1 miles per gallon.

SOT Full: Emilie Michaud / Laval University (Driver)

SOT Full: Philippe Bouchard / Laval University

Second and third prizes in the "Prototype" category went to Mater Dei High School, Evansville, Indiana,
which achieved 1892.3 miles per gallon and Rose-Hulman Institute of Technology, Terre Haute, Indiana,
whose entry reached 1803.3 miles per gallon. A solar powered vehicle from Politechnico di Milano, Italy
also took part in the event on an exhibition basis.

SOT Full: Evan Vibbert / Mater Dei High School (Prototype)

SOT Full: Barbara Arrowsling / Rose-Hulman Institute of Technology, Terre Haute, Indiana

SOT Full: Kevin Thine / Cicero North-Syracuse High School, Syracuse, NY

    The SMT concept started several decades ago when companies began to put their
CEOs in front of television cameras. The public relations staff would line up reporters
in advance to interview the spokesperson via satellite feed during allocated time frames
of one to five minutes. This way, journalists could personally interview a CEO in New
York even if they were based in San Francisco or Chicago. For busy CEOs, the SMT
was a time-efficient way to give interviews.

_vo_ Does peace really have a chance within our lifetime? At Rotary, we believe it does. We've created programs at universities around the world dedicated solely to teaching peace to a new generation. There is a new symbol for peace. Rotary. Humanity in motion. Symbols :30

Sample Television PSA

Rotary International distributes a variety of television PSAs on CD format to television stations and cable operators. This is the storyboard for one PSA.

Sample Downloadable PSA

Organization's websites often have PSAs that they encourage media and the public to download for viewing or embed on another website or blog. These images are from _Achieving Zero_ by UNICEF United States Fund (www.unicefusa.com).

Today, the SMT is a staple of the public relations and television industries. In fact, a survey by West Glen Communications found that nearly 85 percent of the nation's television stations participate in satellite tours.

The easiest way to do an SMT is to simply make the spokesperson available for an interview at a designated time. Celebrities are always popular, but an organization also can use articulate industry experts. In general, the spokesperson sits in a chair or at a desk in front of a television camera. Viewers usually see the local news anchor asking questions and the spokesperson on a large screen, via satellite, answering them in much the same way that anchors talk to reporters at the scene of an event.

Another popular approach to SMTs is to get out of the television studio and do them on location. When the National Pork Producers Council wanted to promote outdoor winter grilling, its public relations staff hired a team from Broadcast News Network to fire up an outdoor grill in Aspen, Colorado, and put a celebrity chef in a parka to give interviews, via satellite, while he cooked several pork recipes. E & J Gallo Winery was also creative about using a location to promote its products to the blue-collar crowd. The SMT site was a tailgate party at Giants Stadium in San Francisco, where instead of hot dogs and beer, the menu was shrimp and wine. Habitat for Humanity, on the other hand, used one of its home building sites for an SMT. The Insights box on page 401 gives some guidelines for planning an SMT.

A somewhat innovative approach involves what are called co-op SMTs. D S Simon Productions, for example, allows organizations to be represented on an SMT with a common theme or topic. One Simon co-op opportunity has the theme of Holiday Video Games, and an expert spokesperson does SMTs that mention the products of several companies. The Simon company also offers Internet video tours. Video interviews and demonstrations from a trade show, for example, are offered to bloggers and other websites.

News Feeds   A variation on the SMT is a news feed that provides video and soundbites of an event to television stations across the country via satellite or through webcasts. The news feed may be live from the event as it is taking place (real time) or it could be video shot at the event, edited, and then made available as a package.

In either case, the sponsoring organization hires a production firm to record the event. Major fashion shows, which take place in New York or Europe, often arrange for video feeds to media outlets around the world. Major auctions also send video feeds to media outlets and even gatherings of interested buyers.

DWJ Television, for example, was hired by Christie's to cover the auction of 56 outfits worn by women at Academy Award ceremonies. Stations could air the entire auction or simply make a video clip for use in later newscasts. In the case of a Pokémon's party in New York City, a news feed was arranged so that stations and Pokémon fans across the country could also participate. News feeds also are regularly used when the president gives a news conference or a company makes a major announcement at a news conference or trade show.

Guest Appearances

Radio and television stations increasingly operate on round-the-clock schedules, which require vast amounts of programming to fill the time available.

Thus far, this chapter has concentrated on how to prepare and generate timely material for newscasts and public service announcements. This section focuses on how

on the job

INSIGHTS

Guidelines for a Satellite Media Tour

Television stations get hundreds of opportunities to participate in satellite media tours (SMT), and anecdotal evidence indicates that four out of five pitched SMTs don't get aired. You can increase the odds if you follow these "do's" and "don'ts" compiled by *PRWeek*:

Do

- Include a relevant angle for the stations in every market you pitch.
- Use an interesting, visually appealing background or set. It often makes the difference between your SMT getting on the air and not getting on the air.
- Get stations involved by sending items that will help them perform and promote the interview.

- Respect producers' wishes when they tell you they will get back to you. Incessant follow-up will only annoy those whom you are trying to convince.
- Localize your SMT. If local audiences aren't going to be interested, neither will the producers airing the story be interested.
- Be clear in your pitch. Provide producers with the who, what, when, and why right away.
- Use credible, knowledgeable spokespersons who project confidence and are personable.

Don't

- Let the SMT become a commercial. If producers think

there is the possibility of too many product mentions, they won't book it.

- Be dishonest with producers about the content of your SMT.
- Pitch your SMT to more than one producer at a station.
- Be conservative with the amount of talent. A boring medical SMT will pack more punch if you include a patient along with the doctor.
- Surprise the producer. Newscasts are planned to the minute, and unexpected events (spokesperson cancels) will not be appreciated.

to get spokespersons on talk and magazine shows. In such situations, the public relations person's contact is no longer the news department, but the directors and producers of various programs. The most valuable communication tools in reaching these people are the telephone and the persuasive pitch, which will be discussed shortly.

Before contacting directors and producers, however, it is necessary for the public relations staff to do their homework. They must be totally familiar with a show's format and content, as well as the type of audience that it reaches. Media databases, such as Cision, are available that give key information about specific programs, such as the names and addresses of producers, the program format, audience demographics, and the purpose of the show.

A second approach, and one that is highly recommended, is to actually watch the program and study the format. In the case of a talk or interview show, what is the style of the moderator or host? What kinds of topics are discussed? How important is the personality or prominence of the guest? How long is the show or its segments? Does the show lend itself to product demonstrations or other visual aids? The answers to such questions will help determine whether the show is appropriate for the chosen spokesperson and how to tailor a pitch letter to achieve maximum results.

The possibilities for public relations people to have their clients interviewed on the air are immense. The current popularity of talk shows, on both local stations and syndicated satellite networks, provides many opportunities for on-air appearances in which the guest expresses opinions and answers call-in questions. A successful radio or television show guest appearance has three requirements:

1. **Preparation.** Guests should know what key message should be emphasized.

2. **Concise speech.** Guests should answer questions and make statements precisely and briefly. They shouldn't hold forth in excessive detail or drag in extraneous material. Responses should be kept to 30 seconds or less, because seconds count on the air: The interviewer must conduct the program under severe time restrictions.

3. **Relaxation.** "Mike fright" is a common ailment for which no automatic cure exists. It will diminish, however, if the guest concentrates on talking to the interviewer in a casual, person-to-person manner and forgets the audience as much as possible. Guests should speak up firmly; the control room can cut down their volume if necessary.

A public relations advisor can help the guest on all of these points. Answers to anticipated questions may be worked out and polished during a mock interview in which the practitioner plays the role of broadcaster. A tape recording or videotape of a practice session will help the prospective guest to correct weaknesses.

All too often, the hosts on talk shows know little about their guests for the day's broadcast. The public relations advisor can compensate for this difficulty by, in advance, sending the host a fact sheet summarizing the important information and listing questions the broadcaster might wish to ask. On network shows such as David Letterman's, nationally syndicated talk shows such as Oprah Winfrey's, and local programs on metropolitan stations, support staffs do the preliminary work with guests. Interviewers on hundreds of smaller local television and radio stations, however, lack such staffs. They may go on the air almost "cold" unless provided with volunteered information.

Talk Shows

Radio and television talk shows have been a staple of broadcasting for many years. KABC in Los Angeles started the trend in 1960, when it became the first radio station in the country to convert to an all-news-and-talk format. Today, more than 1,110 radio stations have adopted this format. Stations that play music also may include talk shows as part of their programming. In fact, it is estimated that there are now more than 4,000 radio talk shows in the United States.

The same growth applies to television. Phil Donahue began his show in 1967. Today, there are more than 20 nationally syndicated talk shows and a countless number of locally produced talk shows. For the past decade, the number-one syndicated daytime talk show has been *The Oprah Winfrey Show*, which attracts about 8 million viewers on a daily basis. On the network level, three shows are the Holy Grail for publicists: NBC's *Today*, ABC's *Good Morning America*, and CBS's *Early Show*. Collectively, these three shows draw about 14 million viewers between 7 and 9 A.M. every weekday. Other popular venues, particularly for entertainers promoting their most recent film or show, are *The Tonight Show* with Jay Leno and the *Late Show* with David Letterman.

The advantage of talk shows is the opportunity to have viewers see and hear the organization's spokesperson without the filter of journalists and editors interpreting and deciding what is newsworthy. Another advantage is the ability to be on the program longer than the traditional 30-second soundbite in a news program. Gresham Strigel, a senior producer, shared his thoughts with *Bulldog Reporter*, a media placement newsletter, about the ideal guest from the media's perspective:

- Guests should be personable and approachable when producers conduct preinterviews on the phone. They should also be forthright but not aggressive. "If you're wishy-washy, non-committed, or stilted, you're not going much further."

- Guests should have strong opinions. "We don't call certain people back because they have been trained not to say anything. The stronger your position is, and the higher up it is, the more media attention you're going to get. Nobody likes guests who play it safe."

- Guests should be passionate about the subject. "We don't want people who are robotic—who just spit out facts. If you convey passion about what you're talking about, you jump off the screen."

- Guests should be able to debate without getting personal or mean-spirited. "Smile....Audiences like to see someone who is comfortable on-screen—someone who is happy to be there."

- Guests should have engaging, outgoing personalities. "Talking heads and ivory-tower types don't do well on television. They're better suited for print, where their personality—or lack of it—can't turn audiences off."

> We expect our spokespersons to be able to put the products in a newsworthy context and answer unexpected questions.
>
> *Michael Friedman,*
> *EVP of DWJ Television*

Magazine Shows

The term *magazine* refers to a television program format that is based on a variety of video segments in much the same way that print magazines have a variety of articles. These shows may have a guest related to the feature that's being shown, but the main focus is on a video story that may run from 3 to 10 minutes. At the network level, CBS's *60 Minutes* is an example of a magazine program.

Many human-interest magazine shows are produced at the local level. A sampling of magazine shows in one large city featured such subjects as a one-pound baby who survived, a treatment for anorexia nervosa, a couple who started a successful cookie company, remedies for back pain, tips on dog training, a black-belt karate expert, blue-collar job stress, and the work habits of a successful author.

Most, if not all, of these features came about as the result of someone making a pitch to the show's producers. Such pitches, which are further discussed below, must convince a show's producer that not only does the proposed guest have an interesting story, but there are also opportunities for video illustration of the story. The objective of the segments, at least from the perspective of the people featured, is exposure and the generation of new business. The tips on dog training, for example, featured a local breeder who also operated a dog obedience school. The karate expert ran a martial arts academy, and even the story of the one-pound baby was placed by a local hospital touting its infant-care specialty.

Pitching a Guest Appearance

The rules for pitching a radio or television talk show are the same as for pitching a print publication, which was discussed in the last chapter. The public relations staff has

> What I love is a catchy subject line for your e-mail pitch. That's the key. It can't be some long sentence with a lot of details.
>
> *Dina Bair, reporter on WGN, Chicago*

to do their homework, be creative, and be succinct. An e-mail has to have a good subject line, and a telephone call has to tell the story in 30 seconds or less.

When thinking about booking a spokesperson on a local or syndicated talk show, here's a checklist of questions to consider:

- Is the topic newsworthy? Does it have a new angle on something already in the news?
- Is the topic timely? Is it tied to some lifestyle or cultural trend?
- Is the information useful to viewers? How-to and consumer tips are popular.
- Does the spokesperson have viewer appeal? A celebrity may be acceptable, but there must be a natural tie-in with the organization and the topic to be discussed.
- Can the spokesperson stay on track and give succinct, concise statements? The spokesperson must stay focused and make sure that the key messages are mentioned.
- Can the spokesperson refrain from getting too commercial? Talk show hosts don't want guests who sound like an advertisement.

It is particularly important that the public relations specialist be familiar with the program, its style, and its content. A staff member for *60 Minutes* told media database company Cision, "Follow the show and keep track of what certain producers like to cover. The next step is preparing a formal letter to the producer; ... it is not recommended to call before you have sent a letter."

The contact for a talk show may be the executive producer or assistant producer of the show. If it is a network or nationally syndicated show, the contact person may have the title of *talent coordinator* or *talent executive*. Whatever the title, these people are known in the broadcasting industry as *bookers* because they are responsible for booking a constant supply of timely guests for the show. To this end, about 4,000 radio/TV producers also read the *Radio/TV Interview Report*, a twice-monthly online magazine published by Bradley Communications Corp., to find guests that are listed by public relations firms and other organizations.

One common approach to placing a guest is to call the booker, briefly outline the qualifications of the proposed speaker, and state why this person would be a timely guest. Publicists also can send an e-mail telling the booker the story angle, why it's relevant to the show's audience, and why the proposed speaker is qualified to talk on the subject. Each show, however, has different preferences on how to be contacted. The production team of the *Daily Show with Jon Stewart*, for example, prefers to receive pitches by regular mail. The producers of *60 Minutes*, on the other hand, prefer a faxed letter; *The Early Show* on CBS prefers e-mail.

In many cases, the booker will ask for video clips of the spokesperson on previous TV shows or newspaper clips relating to press interviews. It's important to be honest about the experience and personality of the spokesperson, so that the booker isn't disappointed and the public relations professional retains his or her credibility for another day.

In recent years, there has been controversy over guests who are invited because they are celebrities and have large audience appeal but who, once they get on the show, endorse various products or are paid advocates of special interests. See the Ethics box on page 405. In general, talk shows book guests three to four weeks in advance. Unless a topic or a person is extremely timely or controversial, it is rare for a person to be booked on one or two day's notice. Public relations strategists must keep this in mind as part of overall campaign planning.

Product Placements

Television's dramas and comedy shows, as well as the film industry, are good vehicles for promoting a company's products and services. It is not a coincidence that the hero of a detective series drives a Ford Fusion or that the heroine is seen boarding a United Airlines flight.

Such product placements, sometimes called *plugs*, are often negotiated by product publicists and talent agencies. This is really nothing new. *IPRA Frontline* reports, "In the early 1900s, Henry Ford had an affinity for Hollywood and perhaps it is no coincidence that his Model T's were the predominant vehicle appearing in the first motion pictures of the era."

Product placements, however, came of age with the movie *E.T.* in the early 1980s. The story goes that M&M Candies made a classic marketing mistake by not allowing

on the job
ETHICS

Should TV Guests Reveal Their Sponsors?

Actress Lauren Bacall, appearing on NBC's *Today*, talked about a dear friend who had gone blind from an eye disease and urged the audience to see their doctors to be tested for it. She also mentioned a drug, Visudyne, that was a new treatment for the disease.

Meanwhile, over at ABC's *Good Morning America*, actress Kathleen Turner was telling Diane Sawyer about her battle with rheumatoid arthritis and mentioned that a drug, Enbrel, helped ease the pain. A month later, Olympic gold medal skater Peggy Fleming appeared on the show to talk about cholesterol and heart disease. Near the beginning of the interview, Fleming said, "My doctor has put me on Lipitor and my cholesterol has dropped considerably."

What the viewing audience didn't know was that each of these celebrities was being paid a hefty fee by a drug company to mention its product in prime time. Spokespersons being paid to advocate a particular cause have also come under criticism. A report in *The Nation*, for example, said that numerous lobbyists and public relations experts have appeared on CNN, *Fox News*, MSNBC, and CNBC to promote the financial and political interests of an unidentified client. Fairness and Accuracy in Media (FAIR) believes broadcasters have an obligation to their audience to ensure that guests and their clients or employers are properly identified.

This raises a dilemma for public relations personnel, who often book guests on various radio and television talk shows. Should you tell the show's producer up front that a celebrity is under contract as an endorser of a particular product? If you do, it may mean that your spokesperson won't be booked, because programs such as NBC's *Today* tend to shy away from what is called "stealth marketing."

What are your responsibilities? What is the responsibility of the talk show hosts? Should the public know that Peggy Fleming is appearing as an endorser of a product or that a political pundit is also on the payroll of a defense contractor or a health care insurance company?

the film to use M&M's as the prominently displayed trail of candy that the young hero uses to lure his big-eyed friend home. Instead, Hershey's Reese's Pieces jumped at the chance, and the rest is history. Sales of Reese's Pieces skyrocketed, and even today, more than 20 years after the film's debut, the candy and *E.T.* remain forever linked in popular culture and in the minds of a whole generation of *E.T.* fans.

Since E.T. went home, product placements have proliferated in television shows and movies. Reality shows such as *Survivor*, *The Apprentice*, and *American Idol* have recently been at the forefront of integrating products into television and have even changed the landscape of product placements by charging hefty fees for manufacturers to have their products featured.

The *Wall Street Journal* explained how the popular *American Idol* engages in product placement:

> The series launched in summer 2002 with a few sponsors, namely Coca-Cola Co., which paid to have a big Coke cup sitting in front of the three judges in every episode. . . . In the current season, Fox abandoned any pretense at subtlety. The Coke cups are still there. . . , but now Coca-Cola's famous logo appears prominently onscreen for part of each show; fizzy bubbles fill a screen behind contestants as they describe what song they will sing each week. . . . And each episode is loaded with other hard sells for a truckload of other merchandise, ranging from Cingular phones and text-messaging services to Kenny Rogers' new CD.

In other series, such as *The Sopranos*, the product placement is more subtle but still blatant in terms of brand name-dropping. Carmela drives a new Porsche Cayenne and Tony has a Cingular wireless phone. Clothing manufacturers and other retailers are particularly active in product placements because studies show that today's youth get most of their fashion ideas from watching television shows. This is why Buffy the Vampire Slayer wore jeans from The Gap.

Automakers are particularly active in product placements on television and the movies. GM cars, for about $3 million, got a starring role in *Transformers*, and the second installment of *Transporter* had an Audi A8 as a central prop. Perhaps the most successful product placement in recent years was Pontiac's appearance on *The Oprah Winfrey Show* at the beginning of a new season. Everyone in the studio audience—all 267 people—received a free Pontiac G6, and Oprah told her national audience that Pontiac is a great car. It cost General Motors almost $8 million, but the automaker reached an estimated 8 to 9 million viewers and reaped a flood of media publicity for its news model throughout the United States and the world. KFC also used Oprah's show for product placement and goodwill, but in that case, the event was almost too successful. See the Insights box on page 407.

Another opportunity for product exposure on television is game shows. *The Price Is Right*, for example, uses a variety of products as prizes for its contestants. In one episode, for example, the prize was a tent, a camp table and chairs, and lanterns. It was great product placement that cost Coleman less than $200.

Public relations specialists should always be alert to opportunities for publicity on television programs and upcoming movies. If a company's service or product lends itself to a particular program, the normal procedure is to contact the show's producers directly or through an agent who specializes in matching company products with the show's needs.

In some cases, it's a matter of mutual benefit. A television series needs a resort location, for example, and a resort makes an offer to house and feed the cast in exchange for being featured on the program. At other times, it's a matter of whether Pepsi or

on the job

INSIGHTS

KFC Gets Grilled on *Oprah*

It was a great product publicity idea. KFC President David Eaton appeared on the highly coveted *Oprah Winfrey Show* to tell the world two things: (1) KFC now offers grilled chicken, and (2) consumers could download a coupon from *Oprah.com* to get a free meal that included two pieces of grilled chicken, two sides, and a biscuit.

What KFC didn't anticipate, however, was the power of Oprah to motivate millions of consumers to download the coupon in a 36-hour period. KFC couldn't meet the demand and the promotion came to an abrupt halt, as a tidal wave of consumers flooded stores demanding their free meal. Negative media coverage followed, and it was beginning to look like a major blow to KFC's reputation.

KFC, however, took the initiative and apologized to its fans. It also added a free Pepsi to the rain checks that were issued to consumers. Media coverage improved, and Eaton even had a second appearance on *Oprah*, which is a rare occurrence. And as *PRWeek* noted, "Is there anyone that doesn't now know the Colonel offers grilled chicken in addition to its more crunchy—er, fried—varieties?"

Coke is used in the scene, and there's often a negotiated fee. A 20-second product placement in *Desperate Housewives*, at the height of its popularity, went for $400,000—about the same cost as a 30-second commercial shown during the commercial breaks. Such fees place product placement more in the category of advertising and marketing than in the category of public relations.

Issues Placement

A logical extension of product placements is convincing popular television programs to write an issue or cause into their plotlines. Writers for issue-oriented shows such as *The West Wing*, *ER*, and *Law & Order* are constantly bombarded with requests from a variety of nonprofit and special interest groups.

The National Campaign to Prevent Teen Pregnancy, for example, works very hard to get the issue of teen pregnancy placed into television programming. The WB's *Seventh Heaven* included an episode in which the Camden family supported Sandy as she went into labor. *The George Lopez Show* on ABC discussed teen pregnancy when George and Angie's teenage daughter, Carmen, planned to get pregnant to keep her boyfriend. Many social and health organizations also lobby the producers of daytime soap operas to write scripts in which the major characters deal with cancer, diabetes, drug abuse, alcoholism, and an assortment of other problems.

The idea is to educate the public about a social issue or a health problem in an entertaining way. Someone once said, "It's like hiding the aspirin in the ice cream." Even the federal government works with popular television programs to write scripts that deal with the dangers and prevention of drug abuse. All of this has not escaped the notice of the drug companies; they seek opportunities for getting their products mentioned in plotlines, too.

The flip side of asking scriptwriters to include material is asking them to give a more balanced portrayal of an issue. The health care industry, for example, is concerned about balance in such programs as *ER*. The popular program deals with a variety of health issues and, in many cases, health maintenance organizations (HMOs) are portrayed in an unfavorable light. Even the American Bar Association gets upset about the portrayal of lawyers in some series. Consequently, these organizations often meet with the program's scriptwriters to educate them about the facts so that the program is more balanced.

Ultimately, however, the programs are designed as entertainment. Scriptwriters, like newspaper editors, make their own evaluations and judgments.

DJs and Media-Sponsored Events

Another form of product placement is agreements with radio stations to promote a product or event as part of their programming. The most common example is a concert promoter giving DJs 10 tickets to a "hot" concert, which are then awarded as prizes to listeners who answer a question or call within 30 seconds.

A nonprofit group sponsoring a fund-raising festival also may make arrangements for a radio station (or television station) to cosponsor an event as part of the station's own promotional activities. This means that the station will actively promote the festival on the air through PSAs and DJ chatter between songs. The arrangement also may call for a popular DJ to broadcast live from the festival and give away T-shirts with the station's logo on them. This, too, is good promotion for the festival and the radio station, because it attracts people to the event.

The station's director of promotions or marketing often is in charge of deciding what civic events to sponsor with other groups. The station will usually agree to a certain number of promotional spots in exchange for being listed in the organization's news releases, programs, print advertising, and event banners as a sponsor of the event.

Stations will not necessarily promote or cosponsor every event. They must be convinced that their involvement will benefit the station in terms of greater public exposure, increased audience, and improved market position. Events and promotions are discussed in the next chapter.

Summary

The Reach of Radio and TV

- In today's society, radio and television reach the vast majority of people on a daily basis.

- The average American spends about 37 hours a week watching television, which is more than the time spent with any other medium, including the Internet.

Radio

- Radio releases, unlike those for print media, must be written for the ear and should be no longer than 60 seconds.

- A popular format is the audio news release (ANR), which includes an announcer and a quote (soundbite) from a spokesperson.

- Public service announcements (PSAs) are distributed by nonprofit organizations that wish to inform and educate the public about health issues or upcoming civic events.

- PSAs should be written in various lengths to give maximum flexibility for broadcast use.

- A radio media tour (RMT) involves a spokesperson being interviewed from a central location by journalists across the country. Each journalist is able to conduct a one-on-one interview for several minutes.

Television

- The video news release (VNR) is produced in a format that television stations can easily use or edit based on their needs.
- VNRs are relatively expensive to produce, but they have great potential for reaching large audiences through TV stations, websites, or even YouTube channels.
- B-rolls, the compilation of video clips and soundbites, are increasingly preferred by television news departments.
- Television PSAs must have audio and visual elements.
- Satellite media tours (SMTs) allow television newscasters to interview a spokesperson on a one-to-one basis.
- With a news feed, an organization arranges for coverage of a particular event, and television stations across the country can watch it in "real time" or receive an edited version of it for later use.

Guest Appearances

- Public relations personnel often book spokespersons on radio and television talk shows. The guest must have a good personality, be knowledgeable, and give short, concise answers.
- Booking a guest on a talk or magazine show requires a creative pitch to get a producer's attention.

Product Placements

- Companies are increasingly making deals with producers to get their products featured on television shows or movies. Nonprofit organizations also lobby to have scripts mention key health messages and deal with various social issues.
- Radio and television stations often cosponsor a civic event with an organization, which leads to increased visibility for the station and the civic organization.

Case Activity   Getting Broadcast Time for Peanut Butter

Jif has been making peanut butter for 50 years, but this basic product isn't exactly newsworthy. Jif, however, has an idea about generating media attention by publicizing a creative peanut butter sandwich contest for children. The idea is that cooking is linked to fostering creativity among children, so the contest also encourages parents to invite their kids into the kitchen to spend some quality time together. The child chef with the winning peanut butter sandwich will receive a $25,000 college scholarship; runners-up will receive smaller scholarships.

Your public relations firm is retained to come up with some ideas for broadcast publicity and story placement. One goal is to get on a national network show such as the *Today* show. Other tactics include (1) producing a B-roll package for distribution to television stations, (2) doing a satellite media tour (SMT), and (3) getting some product placement of Jif on some television entertainment shows. Write a memo outlining your pitch to the *Today* show. In addition, give your detailed ideas about producing a B-roll and an SMT, and getting a jar of Jif on a popular TV program.

Questions   For Review and Discussion

1. Why should public relations personnel consider radio and television as major tools in reaching the public?
2. Radio news releases must be tightly written. What's the general guideline for the number of lines and words in a 30-second news release? What other guidelines should be kept in mind when writing a radio news release?
3. How does an audio news release (ANR) differ from a standard news release?
4. Review the audio news release on pages 386–387 from Cigna Health Care Systems. What aspects of this release illustrate good guidelines for writing an effective release?
5. What is a public service announcement (PSA)?
6. What is the advantage of a radio media tour (RMT) or a satellite media tour (SMT) to the organization and journalists? Are there any disadvantages?
7. What are some guidelines for a successful SMT?

8. List four ways that an organization can get its news and viewpoints on local television.
9. What are the format and characteristics of a video news release (VNR)?
10. What is a B-roll? Why are they increasingly used?
11. What's a news feed, and how is it used in public relations?

12. What makes an ideal radio or television talk show guest/spokesperson?
13. Companies increasingly are working with television programs to get their products featured as part of the programs. What do you think of this trend?
14. How can a public relations person work with radio and television stations on joint promotions?

Media Resources

Beasley, D. (2008, November). New technology connects to radio's loyal listeners. *O'Dwyer's PR Report,* 12.

Kent, C. (2009, November). How to pitch radio. *RaganReport,* 25–26.

Piazza, J. (2010, April 25). The top ten most egregious product placements in film. Retrieved from www.popeater.com

Center for Media Research. (2009, November 9). Radio dominant audio device. Retrieved from news@media post.com

Stanley, A. (2009, June 7). Commercials you can't zap: Product placement is everywhere. *New York Times,* p. MT1–2.

Sweetland, B. (2009, December). How to pitch a busy TV reporter. *RaganReport,* 20–21.

Wilcox, D. L. (2009). Writing for radio and television. [Chapter 9 of] *Public relations writing & media techniques.* Boston, MA: Allyn & Bacon.

Wolfson, S. (2009, January). How to prepare your CEO for a TV interview. *RaganReport,* 25.

Meetings and Events

chapter

After reading this chapter, you will be able to:

Know the logistics of organizing a meeting

Plan a banquet, reception, or cocktail party

Organize an open house, exhibit, or plant tour

Understand the multiple aspects of organizing a convention

Recognize the basic elements of a trade show

Creatively think about promotional events that will attract attention

A World Filled with Events

Meetings and events are vital public relations tools. Their greatest value is that they let the audience participate, face-to-face, in real time. In this era of digital communication and information overload, there is still a basic human need to gather, socialize, and be part of a group activity.

Individuals attending a meeting or event use all five of their senses—hearing, sight, touch, smell, taste—so they become more emotionally involved in the process. Marketing and public relations professionals, for example, often use events to foster more brand awareness and loyalty. Procter & Gamble's Charmin toilet tissue event in New York's Times Square, highlighted in the PR Casebook on page 413, illustrates the point. Sharon Bates, an expert on experiential marketing, told *Corporate Events* magazine, "The Charmin event was a true testament of a successful event, as it reflected the brand in a positive manner, was memorable, and allowed participants to interact with the brand on various levels."

> Events deliver face time between consumers and brands. They also introduce consumers to new products.
>
> *Yung Moon, associate publisher of* Self *magazine, as reported in* PRWeek

Meetings and events, of course, come in all shapes and sizes. A committee meeting of a civic club or an office staff meeting may include only four or five people. Corporate seminars may be for 50 to 250 people. At the other end of the scale is a trade show such as the Consumer Electronics Show (CES) in Las Vegas, which attracts 130,000 attendees over a three-day period. Annual membership conferences, such as that of the Public Relations Society of America (PRSA) or the International Association of Business Communicators (IABC), attract more than 2,000 attendees. The travel research firm PhoCusWright estimates that spending on U.S. corporate meetings is almost $80 billion annually.

Effective meetings and events, however, don't just happen. Detailed planning and logistics are essential to ensure that defined objectives are achieved, whether the public relations specialist is organizing a banquet, an open house, a national conference, or a trade show. Post-event evaluation is also needed to assess the success and effectiveness of the efforts. See the Insights box on page 414.

Group Meetings

Having meetings seems to be part of human nature. There are literally thousands of civic clubs, professional societies, trade associations, and hobby groups that have meetings that attract millions of people every year. In addition, many of these organizations sponsor workshops, seminars, and symposia on a regular basis.

Planning

The size and purpose of the meeting dictate the plan. Every plan must consider these questions: How many people will attend? Who will attend? When and where will the meeting be held? How long will it last? Who will speak? What topics will be covered? What facilities will be needed? Who will run it? What is its purpose? How do we get people to attend? A checklist for planning a club meeting is on page 415.

PRCasebook

When Going to the Restroom Is an Event

Toilet tissue isn't exactly an item that generates a lot of consumer interest or even brand loyalty. Procter & Gamble, however, organized a creative "event" that was literally a "royal flush" for its brand, Charmin. The idea was to install 20 luxury restrooms in New York's Times Square during the Christmas season for harried shoppers on the go who had to "go."

This was not just a bunch of fancy portable potties. As visitors entered a room with plush carpeting and framed portraits of the Charmin bears, hosts in attractive uniforms greeted them and directed them to a reception desk and a Flush-O-Meter chart that tracked visitors' hometowns. In addition to residential-style restrooms, a handful of special New York–themed stalls were created, including a Broadway stall decorated like a theater dressing room. Another stall had a Wall Street theme with an actual working stock ticker that scrolled Charmin messages.

The restrooms were only part of the experience. More than 20 TV monitors played an instructional Potty Dance video and there was even a dance floor to practice. Visitors could also get their pictures taken with a giant stuffed Charmin bear riding a toboggan. Other visitors could relax on white couches in a room with a working fireplace.

> I was dying to pee and headed for McDonalds and saw you here. Charmin, you are my hero.
>
> *A visitor to New York City*

In the space of November 20 through December 31, more than 400,000 families from all 50 states and more than 100 nations visited the luxury Charmin bathrooms. The average family visit was 22 minutes, which *Corporate Event* magazine called "an impressive amount of time for consumers to interact with any brand, but especially one whose product normally doesn't generate much thought." One visitor was so impressed that she wrote, "I took more pictures at the Charmin restrooms than my whole trip in New York." More than 400 visitors posted video clips of the restrooms on YouTube.

The event garnered extensive coverage in the traditional media. The "Disneyland of Bathrooms," as the *New York Times* dubbed it, generated about 200 million impressions(circulation and broadcast audience numbers). The restrooms and Charmin even got coverage on the major morning television programs such as *Good Morning America*, *Today*, and *Fox and Friends*.

Adam Lisook, a brand manager for Charmin, makes the case for the event, telling *Corporate Events*, "We will always do advertising, but this kind of event can directly interface with hundreds of thousands of consumers, and bring an element of understanding as to what it is they need."

on the job

INSIGHTS

Asking the Right Questions After an Event

Post-event analysis is important to determine the success of an event from the standpoint of what worked, and what lessons can be learned for planning the next event. The following diagnostic chart, compiled by Bruce Jeffries-Fox of measurement firm KD Paine and Partners, provides a good starting point.

EVENT COMPONENT	DIAGNOSTIC QUESTIONS
Publicity	Did the event receive substantial coverage among your target public?
	Was the coverage of your event accurate? Did the coverage contain your key messages?
	Was the coverage favorable?
	Was the coverage cited by survey respondents as a substantial source of awareness of your event?
The event experience	Did adequate numbers of people attend your event?
	Were your event's attendees aware of your sponsorship?
	Did attendees enjoy the event?
Influence on attitudes, perceptions, purchase intent, etc.	Did your event have a positive impact on these?
	Were there any unexpected negative impacts?
The event as a whole	Was your event cost effective?
	Did your event take up more resources than expected?
	Did your event have positive impacts that you hadn't anticipated?

Location   If the meeting is to be held on the premises of the organization, it's often necessary to reserve the room in advance with the person responsible for scheduling the room. Many firms have rooms that are made available to nonprofit groups or to employees who are hosting a meeting. A meeting in a hotel or restaurant usually requires making arrangements with the catering manager.

The meeting room must be the right size for the expected audience. If it is too large, the audience will feel that the meeting has failed to draw the expected attendance. If it is too small, the audience will be uncomfortable. Most hotels have a number of meeting rooms ranging in size from small to very large. Having selected a room, the public relations professional must make sure that the audience can find it. The name of the meeting and the name of the room should be registered on the hotel or restaurant's schedule of events for a particular day.

Seating   A variety of seating arrangements can be used, depending on the purpose of the meeting. A monthly club meeting, for example, often features a luncheon or dinner. In this case, attendees are usually seated at round tables of six or eight, where they first have a meal and then listen to a speaker.

on the job

INSIGHTS

How to Plan a Meeting

Every meeting requires its own specialized checklist, but here is a general "to do" list for a local dinner meeting of a service club or a professional association.

In Advance

- What is the purpose of the meeting? Business? Social? Continuing education? Combination?

- What date and time are best for maximum attendance?

- What size audience do you realistically expect?

- Select restaurant facility at least four to six weeks in advance.

- Confirm in writing the following: date, time, menu, cocktails, seating plan, number of guaranteed reservations, and projected costs.

- Enlist speaker four to six weeks in advance. If speaker is in high demand, make arrangements several months in advance. Discuss nature of talk, projected length, and whether audiovisual aids will be used that require special equipment.

- Publicize the meeting to the membership and other interested parties. This should be done a minimum of three weeks in advance. Provide complete information on speaker, date, time, location, meal costs, and reservation procedure.

- Organize a phone committee to call members 72 hours before the event if reservations are lagging. A reminder phone call is often helpful in gaining last-minute reservations.

On the Meeting Day

- Get a final count on reservations, and make an educated guess as to how many people might arrive at the door without a reservation.

- Check speaker's travel plans and last-minute questions or requirements.

- Give catering manager revised final count for meal service. In many instances, this might have to be done 24 to 72 hours in advance of the meeting day.

- Check room arrangements one to two hours in advance of the meeting. Have enough tables been set up? Are tables arranged correctly for the meeting? Does the microphone system work?

- Prepare a timetable for the evening's events. For example, cocktails may be scheduled from 6:15 to 7 P.M., with registration going on at the same time. Dinner from 7 to 8 P.M., followed by 10 minutes of announcements. At 8:10 P.M., the speaker will have 20 minutes to talk, followed by an additional 10 minutes for questions. Your organizational leaders,

as well as the serving staff, should be aware of this schedule.

- Set up a registration table just inside or outside the door. A typed list of reservations should be available, as well as name tags, meal tickets, and a cash box for making change. Personnel at the registration table should be briefed and in place at least 30 minutes before the announced time.

- Decide on a seating plan for the head table, organize place cards, and tell VIPs as they arrive where they will be sitting.

- Designate three or four members of the organization as a hospitality committee to meet and greet newcomers and guests.

After the Meeting

- Settle accounts with the restaurant, or indicate where an itemized bill should be mailed.

- Check the room to make sure no one forgot briefcases, handbags, eyeglasses, or other belongings.

- Send thank-you notes to the speaker and any committee members who helped plan or host the meeting.

- Prepare a summary of the speaker's comments for the organization's newsletter and, if appropriate, send a news release to local media.

Seminars, designed primarily for listening, usually have what is called "theater" seating, in which rows of seats are set up facing the speakers. Such meetings may be held in theaters or auditoriums.

A workshop or a small seminar, on the other hand, may use what is called "lunchroom" seating, which has long tables with chairs on one side so that attendees can take notes or set up laptop computers.

Occasionally, large meetings are broken into discussion groups. Typically, the audience starts in one large room, where a speaker gives information and states a problem. The audience then moves into another room, or set of rooms, where round tables seating 8 or 10 people are available. A discussion leader is designated for each table. After the problem has been discussed, the leaders gather the opinions and the audience returns to the first room, where reports from each group are given to the entire assembly.

Facilities A small meeting may not need much in the way of facilities, whereas a large and formal one may require a considerable amount of equipment and furnishings. Following are things that should be considered—and supplied if needed. The public relations person should check everything one or two hours before the meeting.

- **Meeting identification.** Is it posted on the bulletin board near the building entrance? Are directional signs needed?
- **Lighting.** Is it adequate? Can it be controlled? Where are the controls? Who will handle them?
- **Charts.** Are they readable? Is the easel adequate? Who will handle the charts?
- **Screen or monitors.** Are they large enough for the size of the audience?
- **Microphones, projectors, and video equipment.** Are they hooked up and working? Who should be contacted at the facility if there are technical difficulties?
- **Seating and tables.** Are there enough seats for the audience expected? Are they arranged properly for a clear view of the stage or podium?
- **Wiring.** For all electrical equipment, can wires be kicked loose or trip someone?
- **Speaker's podium.** Is it positioned properly? What about a reading light?
- **Water and glasses.** For speakers? For audience?
- **Audience and speaker aids.** Are there programs or agendas? Will there be notepaper, pencils, and handout materials?
- **Name tags.** For speakers? For all attendees?

Invitations For clubs, an announcement in the newsletter, a flyer, or an e-mail should be adequate. For external groups—people who are not required to attend but whose presence is desired—invitations via the mail or e-mail are necessary. They should go out early enough for people to fit the meeting into their schedules—three to six weeks is a common lead time.

The invitation should tell the time, day, date, place (including the name of the room), purpose, highlights of the program (including names of speakers), and a way for the person to RSVP. This may be a telephone number, an e-mail address, a reply card to mail back to the event's organizers, or even the Web address of an online registration service that handles everything from making the reservation to processing the credit card information to pay for the event. Using an online reservation service is discussed further in the section on conferences and conventions. A map showing the location and parking facilities is advisable if the facility is not widely known.

Registration

If everyone knows everyone else, registration and identification can be highly informal, but if the group is large, it is customary to have a registration desk or table at the entrance of the room. Here the names of arrivals are checked against lists of individuals who said they would attend. If there is no invitation list and the presence or absence of any of the people who were invited is not important (as at a regular meeting of a club or association), the arrivals generally sign in on a plain sheet of paper, and no one checks the membership roster.

Greeting   A representative of the sponsoring organization should be at the entrance of the room. If the number attending is not large, a personal welcome is in order. This isn't possible when hundreds of people are expected, but the chairperson should greet the audience in his or her opening remarks.

Name Tags   Name tags are a good idea at almost any meeting. The public relations person should use label-making software to prepare name tags for everyone with advance reservations. Names should be printed in bold, large block letters so that they can be read easily from a distance of four feet. If the person's affiliation is used, this can appear in smaller bold letters.

For people showing up without advance registration, felt-tip pens can be available to create on-the-spot name tags. However, a nice touch is to designate one person at the registration desk to make these tags so that they look neat and consistent. Another approach is to use a laptop and print out name tags. Most tags are self-adhesive. Plastic badges with clamps or a chain are popular for large meetings such as conventions.

Program

At any meeting, the word "program" has two meanings. It is what goes on at the meeting, and it is also the printed listing of what goes on.

The meeting must have a purpose. To serve that purpose, it is necessary to have a chairperson who controls and directs the meeting, introduces the speakers, and keeps discussions from wandering. It is also necessary to have speakers who will inform, persuade, or motivate the listeners.

The printed program that is handed out to the audience in a workshop or seminar tells them what is going to happen, when, and where. It lists all the speakers, the time they will speak, coffee breaks, lunch breaks, and any other facts attendees should know about the meeting. Because speakers may have last-minute changes in their plans, the programs should not be printed until the last possible moment.

Speakers   Speakers should be selected early—several months in advance, if possible. They should be chosen because of their expertise, their crowd-drawing capacity, and their speaking ability. It is a good idea to listen to any prospective speaker before tendering an invitation, or at least to discuss the intention with someone who has heard the person speak before. Many prominent people are simply not effective speakers.

When a speaker has agreed to give a talk, it is essential to make sure that the speaker has all the information he or she needs to prepare remarks and get to the meeting. A thorough briefing will do much to ensure that the speaker will deliver a relevant talk and meet the expectations of the meeting's organizers. The Insights box below gives a checklist of what invited speakers need to know about the meeting.

Meals Club meetings and workshops often occur at a mealtime. In fact, many meetings include breakfast, lunch, or dinner.

Early morning breakfast meetings have the advantage of attracting people who cannot take the time during the day to attend such functions. A full breakfast, served buffet style, is a popular choice because it allows everyone to select what he or she normally eats for breakfast. People attending a half-day or full-day workshop often partake of a self-serve continental breakfast—rolls, juice, and coffee—during the registration period just prior to the start of the meeting.

Luncheons are either sit-down affairs with a fixed menu or a buffet. A 30- to 45-minute cocktail period may precede a luncheon, usually during registration as guests arrive. A good schedule for a typical luncheon is registration at 11:30, luncheon at

on the job
INSIGHTS

A Checklist for Invited Speakers

The organizers of any meeting or conference should ensure that invited speakers have all the background and information necessary to do an effective job with no logistical glitches. Barbara Nichols, owner of a hospitality management firm in New York City, gave this comprehensive checklist to *Meeting News* regarding what invited speakers need to know about your meeting:

- Information about the meeting sponsor and attendees
- Meeting purpose and objectives

- Presentation location, including meeting room, date, and hour
- Topic and length of presentation
- Anticipated size of the audience
- Session format, including length of time allowed for audience questions
- Names of those sharing the platform, if any, and their topics
- Name of person who will make the introductions
- Speaker fee or honorarium

- Travel and housing arrangements
- Meeting room setup and staging information
- Audiovisual equipment needed
- Dress code (business attire, resort wear, black tie)
- Handout material requested
- Signed release for organization to tape or videotape the remarks
- Arrangements for spouse, if invited

12 noon, and adjournment at 1:30. In rare instances, the adjournment can be as late as 2 P.M., but it should never be later than that.

Dinner meetings are handled in much the same way as luncheons. A typical schedule is registration and cocktails at 6 P.M., dinner at 7 P.M., speaker at 8 P.M., and adjournment between 8:30 and 9 P.M. A speaker should limit his or her remarks to 20 or 30 minutes; after that, attendees get restless.

The public relations person will need to have an accurate count of people who will attend a meal function. The hotel or restaurant facility will need a count at least 24 hours in advance to prepare the food and set up table service. The standard practice is for the organization to guarantee a certain number of meals, plus or minus 10 percent. If fewer than what is guaranteed show up, the organization still pays for the meals.

Banquets

Banquets, by definition, are fairly large and formal functions held to honor an individual, raise money for a charitable organization, or celebrate an event such as an organization's anniversary. Because they are in the category of a "special" event, they require a well-designed invitation package that is mailed to prospective guests. A sample invitation is shown below.

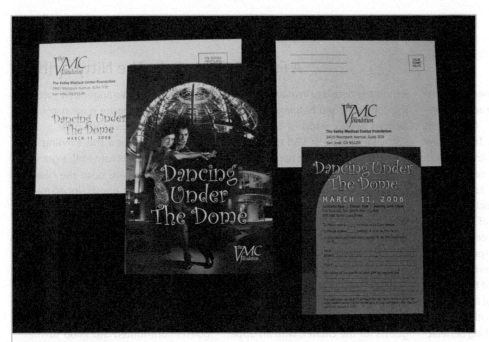

Sample Invitation

Attractive, well-designed invitations are necessary for banquets and other "special" occasions. Reply cards must be attached, often with a self-addressed envelope, so that attendees can register their names, meal preferences, and credit card information. This invitation was prepared by PRX Public Relations on behalf of Valley Medical Center of San Jose (CA) for its annual fund-raising dinner dance.

A banquet may have 100 or 1,000 people in attendance, and staging a successful one takes a great deal of planning. The budget, in particular, needs close attention. A banquet coordinator has to consider such factors as (1) food, (2) room rental, (3) bartenders, (4) decorations and table centerpieces, (5) audiovisual requirements, (6) speaker fees, (7) entertainment, (8) photographers, (9) invitations, (10) tickets, and (11) marketing and promotion. Major fund-raising galas have additional logistics in terms of generating attendance and donations. A behind-the-scenes look at a fund-raising event is highlighted in the Insights box below.

All these components, of course, must be factored into establishing the per-ticket cost of the event. The attendees are paying $75 to $100 not just for the traditional rubber chicken dinner but for the total cost of staging the event. If the purpose is to raise money for a worthy charitable organization or political candidate, tickets might go for $100 to $250. The actual price, of course, depends on how fancy the banquet is and how much the organization is paying for the speaker. See the Insights box on page 421 for a checklist on how to prepare a budget for a special event.

on the job
INSIGHTS

A Fund-Raising Gala: The Nitty-Gritty

The New York Women's Foundation hosted its first autumn benefit in midtown Manhattan, according to *New York Times* writer Laura Lipton. The organizers considered time, place, menu, centerpieces, entertainment, guest list, seating arrangement, and so much more. "To produce the few hours of gaiety, five chairwomen and a brigade of behind-the-scenes workers had spent months vetting every detail, from the hors d'oeuvres to the guests of honor. Such considerations are crucial for a gala to succeed amid scores of other parties, all for organizations seeking benefactors for their good works," Lipton wrote.

The chairwomen set a budget of $175,000 and a theme of "Stepping Out and Stepping Up." They hired CMI Event Planning and Fundraising to handle the details of invitations, catering contracts, and helping the chairwomen keep on top of the details. Cathy McNamara of CMI told Lipton, "We're the professional nags."

One of the chairwomen described how she spent Labor Day writing personal notes in 70 to 100 invitations. "'The New York Women's Foundation is extremely important to me. Please help support these extraordinary women,'" she said she wrote. "Then I might put, 'Say hi to your husband' or 'Hope you're well.'"

The foundation guaranteed 300 guests for the caterer, with an upper end of 350. As the event drew nearer, the chairwomen met to test and select appetizers (the mini hamburgers), select floral arrangements (coppery bowls were selected, but woven green reeds in one arrangement were rejected), and choose napkin colors (olive green was given the nod).

Lipton described the evening of the benefit: "At Gotham Hall, a grand, lofty space that was once the headquarters of a bank, guests sipped martinis and applauded the speeches. A mambo performance by a dozen school-age dancers momentarily transfixed the room." While the competition among benefits is strong and the economy in which this event found itself was weak, the organizers counted it as a success when 280 guests contributed $675,000 to the foundation through the event.

Source: L. Lipton. (2008, October 3). Benefit season: What goes on behind a scene." *New York Times*.

on the job

INSIGHTS

Making a Budget for a Banquet

All events have two sides of the ledger: costs and revenues. It is important to prepare a detailed budget so that you know exactly how much an event will cost. This will enable you to also figure out how much you will need to charge so that you at least break even. Here are some items that you need to consider:

Facilities

Rental of meeting or reception rooms.

Set up of podiums, microphones, audiovisual equipment

Food Service

Number of meals to be served

Cost per person

Gratuities

Refreshments for breaks

Bartenders for cocktail hours

Wine, liquor, soft drinks

Decorations

Table decorations

Direction signs

Design and Printing

Invitations

Programs

Tickets

Name tags

Promotional flyers

Postage

Postage for invitations

Mailing house charges

Recognition Items

Awards, plaques, trophies

Engraving

Framing

Calligraphy

Miscellaneous

VIP travel and expenses

Speaker fees

Security

Transportation

Buses

Vans

Parking

Entertainment

Fees

Publicity

Advertising

News releases

Banners

Postage

Office Expenses

Phones

Supplies

Complimentary tickets

Staff travel and expenses

Data processing

A well-known personality as a banquet speaker usually helps ticket sales, but it can also be a major expense in the budget. Karen Kendig, president of the Speaker's Network, told *PR Tactics* that the going rate is $3,000 to $10,000 for "bread and butter," business-type talks, $15,000 and up for entertainment celebrities, and $50,000 to $60,000 for well-known politicians. A number of firms, such as the Washington Speaker's Bureau and the Harry Walker Agency, represent celebrity speakers.

Such fees cannot be fully absorbed into the cost of an individual ticket, so in addition to sending out individual invitations, there usually is a committee that personally asks corporations and other businesses to underwrite the event and buy a table for employees, clients, or friends. A corporate table of eight, for example, may go for $25,000 or more, depending on the prestige and purpose of the event. Many local organizations, to minimize speaker cost and maximize fund-raising for a good cause, avoid outside speakers and use a prominent local person, such as the CEO of a major company, to give an address. At other times, the event is primarily a dinner dance and no speaker is necessary.

Working with Catering Managers

When organizing a banquet, the public relations staff usually contacts the catering or banquet manager of the restaurant or hotel at least three or four months before the event. He or she will discuss menus, room facilities, availability of space, and a host of other items to determine exactly what the banquet needs.

Hotels and restaurants have special menus for banquets, which are often subject to some negotiation. If the banquet will be held during the week, for example, the restaurant or hotel might be willing to give more favorable rates because weeknights aren't ordinarily booked. However, if the organization insists on having a banquet on a Friday or Saturday night—which is the most popular time—it can expect to pay full rates.

A banquet usually has a fixed menu, but a vegetarian dish should be available to those who request it. In general, a popular choice for a meat entree is chicken or fish. Pork may be objectionable on religious grounds, and many people refrain from red meats such as beef. Offering two entrees requires the extra work of providing coded tickets for the waiters, and the hotel or restaurant may charge more for the meal. The public relations specialist should get the catering manager's advice before ordering multiple entrees.

When figuring food costs, many amateur planners forget about tax and gratuity, which can add 25 percent or more to any final bill. That $25 chicken dinner on the menu is really $30.75 if tax and gratuity add up to 23 percent. In addition, there are corkage fees if the planner provides the liquor or wine. In many establishments, corkage fees are set rather high to discourage people from bringing their own refreshment. At one banquet, for example, the organizers thought it was a great coup to have the wine donated, only to find out that the hotel charged a corkage fee of $20 per bottle.

Logistics and Timing

Organizing a banquet requires considerable logistics, timing, and teamwork. First, it's necessary to establish a timeline for the entire process—from contacting catering managers to sending out invitations and lining up a speaker. Second, a detailed timeline for the several days or day of the event is also needed to ensure that everything is in place. A third timeline is needed for the event itself so that it begins and ends at a reasonable time. A good example of a banquet timeline is shown in Figure 16.1.

In addition, the public relations planner needs to work out the logistics to ensure that registration lines are kept to a minimum and everyone is assigned to a table. Table numbers must be highly visible. If the group is particularly large (1,000 or more), it's a good idea to provide a large seating chart so that people can locate where their seats are. Another, more personalized approach is to have staff inside the hall directing people to their seats.

**CONSERVATION AWARDS BANQUET
JW MARRIOTT HOTEL
WASHINGTON, DC
WEDNESDAY, MAY 13**

Crew Agenda

3:30 – 5:00 p.m.	Program agenda review–participants and staff only. Live run-through of C. Ghylin's remarks. (Grand Ballroom)
5:00 – 6:00	Private pre-reception for honorees, judges, staff. Honoree photo session including E. Zern and J. Sullivan. (Suite 1231)
6:30 – 7:15	Greetings and reception, open bar. Photo opportunities available. (Grand Ballroom Foyer)
7:15 – 7:30	Close bar, enter Grand Ballroom.
7:30 – 7:35	C. Ghylin: Welcome and opening remarks.
7:30 – 8:20	Dinner served.
8:20 – 8:25	C. Ghylin: Introduces special guests at head table, introduces E. Zern.
8:25 – 8:30	E. Zern: Welcome, honoree toast, introduces judges, completes remarks.
8:30 – 8:35	C. Ghylin: Introduces J. Sullivan.
8:35 – 8:45	J. Sullivan: Remarks.
8:45 – 8:50	C. Ghylin: Introduces slide presentation.
8:50 – 9:25	Slide presentation. (C. Ghylin remains at podium) (a) Introduces/explains honoree category; (b) Comments on professionals. Introduces/explains honoree category. (c) Comments on citizens. Introduces/explains organizations' honoree category.
9:25 – 9:40	C. Ghylin: Comments on organizations. Invites J. Sullivan and E. Zern for plaque presentation. Plaque presentation.
9:40 – 9:45	C. Ghylin: Final remarks.
9:45 p.m	America the Beautiful.

**Figure 16.1
Event Timeline**

The compilation of a timeline, and going over it with the master of ceremonies, helps keep the event on schedule.

Receptions and Cocktail Parties

A short cocktail hour, as mentioned previously, can precede the start of a club's luncheon or dinner. It can also be part of a reception. Its purpose is to have people socialize; it also is a cost-effective way to celebrate an organization's or an individual's achievement, to introduce a new chief executive to the employees and the community, or simply to allow college alumni to get together.

In any event, the focus should be on interaction, not speeches. If there is a ceremony or speech, it should last a maximum of 5 to 10 minutes.

A reception lasts up to two hours, and the typical layout is a large room where most people stand instead of sit. This facilitates social interaction and allows people to move freely around the room. Such gatherings, like any other event, require advance planning and logistics.

Don't make a lengthy presentation part of an event. You'll lose the attendees' attention.

Erica Iacono, reporter for PRWeek

It is important, for example, that food be served in the form of appetizers, sandwiches, cheese trays, nuts, and chips. People get hungry, and food helps offset some effects of drinking. The bar is the centerpiece of any reception, but there should be plenty of nonalcoholic beverages available, too. Urns of coffee, punch, and tea should be readily available in other locations around the room.

Such precautions will limit the organizer's liability if someone does get drunk and is involved in an accident on the way home. Liability can also be limited if there is a *no-host bar*, which means that guests buy their own drinks.

Most receptions, however, have a *hosted bar*, meaning that drinks are free. This is particularly true when a corporation is hosting the cocktail party or reception for journalists, customers, or community leaders. In every case, it is important that bartenders be trained to spot individuals who appear to be under the influence of alcohol and to politely suggest a nonalcoholic alternative.

Organizations also try to control the level of drinking by offering only beer or wine instead of hard liquor. Still others issue one or two free drink tickets to arriving guests, with the understanding that they will need to pay for additional drinks.

A reception, like a meal function, requires the planner to talk with the catering manager to order the finger food and decide how many bartenders are needed. As a rule of thumb, there should be one bartender per 75 people. For large events, bars are situated in several locations around the room to disperse the crowd and shorten lines.

It is also important to find out how the facility will bill for beverages consumed. If the arrangement is by the bottle, bartenders have a tendency to be very generous in pouring drinks because more empty bottles mean higher profits for the caterer.

Starting a cocktail party is easy—just open the bar at the announced time. Closing a party is not so easy. The invitation should give a definite time for the reception to end, but the planner should not assume that people will be ready to leave at the stated ending time. Toward the end of the cocktail party, particularly if the crowd is in a celebratory mood, a vocal announcement may be needed. The smoothest tactic is to say, "The bar will close in 10 minutes." This gives guests a chance to get one more drink. It's also important to ensure that the bartender closes the bar at the designated ending time of the cocktail party.

Open Houses and Plant Tours

Open houses and plant tours are conducted primarily to develop favorable public opinion about an organization. Generally they are planned to show the facilities where the organization does its work and, in plant tours, how the work is done. A factory might have a plant tour to show how it turns raw materials into finished products. A hospital open house could show its emergency facilities, diagnostic equipment, operating rooms, and patient rooms.

Open houses are customarily one-day affairs. Attendance is usually by invitation, but in other instances, the event is announced in the general media, and anyone who chooses to attend may do so. This is particularly relevant when there is an open house to view a traveling exhibit of some kind. See page 425 for a sample flyer announcing an open house for an exhibit.

Many plants offer daily tours on a regular schedule while the plant is in operation. These tours are most common among producers of consumer goods such as beer, wine, food products, clothing, and small appliances. These daily tours are geared to handle only a few people at any one time, whereas open houses generally have a large number of guests, and normal operations are thus not feasible during the tour.

Since the purpose of an open house or a plant tour is to create favorable opinion about the organization, the tour must be carefully planned, thoroughly explained, and smoothly conducted. The visitors must understand what they are seeing. This requires careful routing, control to prevent congestion, signs, and guides. All employees should understand the purpose of the event and be thoroughly coached in their duties.

The following are the major factors to consider in planning an open house:

- **Day and hour.** The time must be convenient for both the organization and the guests.
- **Guests.** These may be families of employees, customers, representatives of the community, suppliers and competitors, reporters, or others whose goodwill is desirable.
- **Publicity and invitations.** These materials should be distributed at least a month before the event.
- **Vehicles.** Parking must be available, and there should be a map on the invitation showing how to get there and where to park.
- **Reception.** A representative of the organization should meet and greet all arriving guests. If guests are important people, they should meet the top officials of the organization.

Sample Flyer

This flyer was distributed to various community groups to promote the grand opening of a new exhibit. It gives the basic five Ws and also entices the public with what kinds of photographs will be displayed.

- **Focal Point of Activity.** An area should be designated for exhibits, product demonstrations, or even entertainment acts for children and adults.
- **Restrooms.** If a large crowd is expected, portable toilets should be arranged to supplement the regular facilities.
- **Safety.** Hazards should be conspicuously marked and well lighted. Dangerous equipment should be barricaded.
- **Routing.** Routes should be well marked and logical (in a factory, the route should go from raw materials through production steps to the finished product). A map should be given to each visitor if the route is long or complicated.
- **Guides.** Tours should be led by trained guides who have a thorough knowledge of the organization and can explain in detail what visitors are seeing on the tour.
- **Explanation.** Signs, charts, and diagrams may be necessary at any point to supplement the words of the guides. The guides must be coached to say exactly what the public should be told. Many experts can't explain what they do, so a prepared explanation is necessary.

- **Housekeeping and attire.** The premises should be as clean as possible. Attire should be clean and appropriate. A punch press operator doesn't wear a necktie, but his overalls need not be greasy.
- **Emergencies.** Accidents or illness may occur. All employees should know what to do and how to request appropriate medical assistance.

Conventions

A convention is a series of meetings, usually spread over two or more days. Its purpose is to gather and exchange information, meet other people with similar interests, discuss and act on common problems, and enjoy recreation and social interchange.

Most conventions are held by national membership groups and trade associations. Because the membership is widespread, a convention is nearly always "out of town" for many attendees, so convention arrangements must give consideration to this.

Planning

It is necessary to begin planning far in advance of the actual event. Planning for even the smallest convention should start months before the scheduled date; for large national conventions, it may begin several years ahead and require hundreds or thousands of hours of work. The main components in planning a convention are (1) timing, (2) location, (3) facilities, (4) exhibits, (5) program, (6) recreation, (7) attendance, and (8) administration.

Timing   Timing of the convention must be convenient for the people who are expected to attend. Avoid peak work periods. Summer vacation is appropriate for educators, and after harvest is suitable for farmers. Preholiday periods are bad for retailers, and mid-winter is probably a poor time in the northern states but may be very good in the South. Here, as in every other area dealing with the public, it is imperative to know the audience and to plan for their convenience.

Location   As real estate agents say, location, location, location is very important. A national convention can be anywhere in the country, but one in Fairbanks, Alaska, is unlikely to be successful; yet one in Honolulu or New Orleans could be a great success because the glamour of the location would outweigh the cost and time of travel. Many organizations rotate their conventions from one part of the state, region, or country to another to equalize travel burdens.

Another factor in choosing a location is availability of accommodations. There must be enough rooms to house the attendees and enough meeting rooms of the right size. Timing enters into this, because many such accommodations are booked months or even years in advance. Large cities usually have large convention facilities and numerous hotels, but early reservations are necessary for such popular cities as San Francisco, New York, New Orleans, San Diego, and Las Vegas. The premier location for large conventions and trade shows is Las Vegas, which has a total of 140,000 hotel rooms. Once a tentative location has been selected, the planner must find out if the convention can be handled at the time chosen. Early action on this can forestall later changes. The planner must be sure to get a definite price on guest rooms as well as meeting rooms.

Small conventions are often held in resorts, but accessibility is a factor. If the visitors have to change airlines several times or if the location is hard to reach by automobile, the locale's glamour may fail to compensate for the inconvenience.

Facilities For every meeting of the convention, it is necessary to have a room of the right size and the equipment needed for whatever is to go on in that room. The convention might start with a general meeting in a large ballroom, where seating is theater fashion and the equipment consists of a public address system and a speaker's platform with large video monitors. After opening remarks, the convention might break into smaller groups that meet in different rooms set up for different speakers.

One speaker may require a computer projector; another may need a whiteboard or an easel for charts; still another may need a VCR and monitor. In one room the seating may be around conference tables; another may have theater seating. To get everything right, the planner must know in advance exactly what the speaker needs, who is going to participate, and when.

Exhibits The makers and sellers of supplies that are used by people attending conventions frequently want to show their wares. This means that the convention manager must provide space suitable for that purpose. Most large convention centers have facilities that can accommodate anything from books to bulldozers. There is a charge for the use of these rooms, and the exhibitors pay for the space they use.

The exhibit hall may be in the hotel where the convention is being held or in a separate building. For example, McCormick Place is an enormous building on the Chicago lakefront. It is an easy taxi trip from the Loop, where conventions are usually based

The Registration Area for a Book Expo

Conventions attract millions of attendees every year who belong to professional groups, trade groups, nonprofits, and a host of hobby-activity organizations.

and where the visitors sleep. Eating facilities, ranging from hot dog stands to elaborate dining rooms, can be found in almost any such building. Exhibits will be covered in more detail when trade shows are discussed.

Program

A convention program usually has a basic theme. Aside from transacting the necessary organizational business, most of the speeches and other sessions will be devoted to various aspects of the theme. Themes can range from the specific "New Developments in AIDS Research" to the more general "Quality Management and Productivity." Some groups use an even broader theme such as "Connections" or "At the Crossroads."

With a theme chosen, the developer of the program looks for prominent speakers who have something significant to say on a particular topic. In addition, there may be a need for discussions, workshops, and other sessions focusing on particular aspects of the general theme.

The printed program for the convention is the schedule, which tells exactly when every session will be, what room it will be in, and who will speak on what subject. Large conventions often schedule different sessions at the same time. Attendees then choose which session they prefer.

Ideally, the program schedule should be small enough to fit in a pocket or a handbag. Large programs may look impressive, but they are cumbersome to hold on to and easy to misplace. One compromise is to give attendees a large program, which contains paid advertising, at registration but to also include a tear-out "crib" sheet that summarizes the time and location of the major presentations. If the convention is on multiple floors of a hotel or convention center, it's also a good idea to provide a floor plan so that attendees can easily find the various meeting rooms. Printing of the program should be delayed until the last possible moment because last-minute changes and speaker defaults are common.

Recreation and Entertainment   This is a feature of practically all conventions and may range from informal get-togethers to formal dances. Cocktail parties, golf tournaments, sightseeing tours, and free time are among the possibilities. Sometimes recreational events are planned to coincide with regular program sessions, for spouses and delegates who would rather relax than listen to a speaker. Evening receptions and dinners at interesting venues such as an art gallery or museum are often planned for both attendees and their significant others.

Attendance   Getting people to attend a convention requires two things: (1) an appealing program and (2) a concerted effort to persuade members to attend. Announcements and invitations should go out several months in advance, to allow attendees to make their individual arrangements. A second and even a third mailing often are sent in the weeks preceding the convention. Reply cards should be provided, accompanied by hotel reservation forms. Many corporations and organizations now use specialty firms such as *cvent* that prepare digital invitations and provide event management tools. See the Insights box on page 429 about using Web-based invitation services.

Administration   Managing a convention is a strenuous job. The organization staff is likely to see very little of the program and few delegates. Among the things that must

on the job
INSIGHTS

Making Reservations on the Web

The digital age has made event planning more precise. A number of companies now offer event planners the ability to send Invitations via the Internet and to also track the response rate.

E-mail invitations are used for any number of organizational meetings and corporate events, including college students having a party to celebrate their 21st birthday. E-mail invitations, according to *cvent* (www.cvent.com), a firm offering such services, should have eye-catching graphics, an effective subject line, and relevant content such as the five Ws and H.

Most individuals just concern themselves with generating a list of Yes, No, and Maybe answers, but clubs and professional or trade groups also bundle the e-mail invitation with software that enables attendees to pay registration fees online. According to

cvent, event planners can achieve up to three times the standard response rate by integrating e-mail, direct mail, and phone calling campaigns.

Meeting planners like the capabilities of software programs and online systems that allow them to manage an entire event. StarCite and *cvent*, for example, offer a variety of meeting management services—from gathering hotel bids to sending electronic invitations and tracking registrations online. Software can even compile data on the reasons individuals aren't coming to the event—which may help in planning future meetings. Once someone registers, the site also allows him or her to book hotel, airline, and car reservations at the same time.

Electronic tracking is also helpful for figuring out exactly how many hotel rooms are needed; bad estimates, cancellations, and no-shows can add up to substantial hotel

cancellation fees. Other management tools allow groups to track the flow of registrations. If registrations are lagging, it's a signal to send another round of e-mails and direct mail to bolster attendance. You can even track attendance at various sessions. If breakfast sessions, for example, aren't well attended, it might be wise to plan fewer early morning meetings next year.

Although e-mail invitations are economical and efficient, they are most appropriate for business-related meetings and events. It's still considered tacky to send an e-mail invitation to your wedding or to a major fundraising dinner for a community cause. In this instance, mailed invitations and replies are the norm. If you send out a mailed invitation, you can still provide an e-mail address or phone number for people to respond if they don't want to fill out the reply card.

be done are arranging for buses to convey delegates from the airport to the convention (if it is in a remote location) and to take delegates on tours. Meeting speakers and getting them to the right place at the right time is another task.

People arriving at the convention headquarters must be met, registered, and provided with all the essentials (name tags, programs, and any other needed materials). Special arrangements should be made for the media. A small convention may interest only a few people from trade publications, but larger conventions may draw attention from the major media. In this case, a newsroom should be set up with telephones, fax machines, tables, and other needed equipment. Newsrooms are further discussed in the next section, on trade shows.

Trade Shows

Trade shows are the ultimate marketing event. According to *Tradeshow Week* magazine, about 6,000 trade shows are held annually in the United States. They range in size from more than 100,000 attendees to those in very specialized industries, which attract only several thousand people. It is estimated that about 65 million people attend trade shows on an annual basis.

The Consumer Electronics Show (CES), sponsored by the Consumer Electronics Association, illustrates the power and influence of a trade show. The show, open only to industry professionals, attracts 130,000 attendees to the Las Vegas Convention Center every January. Almost 3,000 companies show their new consumer products, taking up about 3 million square feet of exhibit space. Some news gadgets introduced at the CES in 2010 included an 82-inch home theater with 3-D technology, a touch-screen tablet PC, a waterproof case for those who want to use their Kindle in the bathtub, and backpacks and briefcases with solar chargers for today's digital road warriors.

Exhibit Booths

Although food and entertainment costs are high, the major expense at a trade show is the exhibit booth. At national trade shows, it is not unusual for a basic booth to start at $50,000, including design, construction, transportation, and space rental fees. Larger, more elaborate booths can easily cost between $500,000 and $1 million.

Any booth or exhibit should be designed for maximum visibility. Experts say booths have about 10 seconds to attract a visitor as he or she walks down an aisle of booths. Consequently, companies try to outdazzle each other in booth designs. Here is how Karen Chan of Dow Jones International News described one booth at the Telecoms trade show in Geneva:

> Hewlett-Packard Co.'s stand features a huge, upside-down glass pyramid with ever ascending pink neon lights rising from its tip. The 3-floor stand took 30 men three months to build and contains 56 tons of steel, 20 tons of glass, 7 truckloads of lumber, 1,000 meters of neon, and 5 miles of cable. Let's not forget the 5,000 bolts holding it all together.

Not every company has the resources of HP, but here are some points to keep in mind for planning an exhibit booth:

- Select the appropriate trade shows that have the best potential for developing contacts and generating future sales.
- Start planning and developing the exhibit 6 to 12 months in advance. Exhibit designers and builders need time to develop a booth.
- Make the display or booth visually attractive. Use bright colors, large signs, and working models of products.
- Think about putting action in the display. Have a video or slide presentation running all the time.
- Use involvement techniques. Have a contest or raffle in which visitors can win a prize. An exhibitor at one show even offered free foot massages.
- Give people an opportunity to operate equipment or do something.

Trade Shows Attract Millions of People Annually

They provide an opportunity to see new products from a number of companies, generate sales leads, and attract media coverage. Various companies displayed new gadgets such as 3-D television sets at the 2010 Consumer Electronics Show (CES) in Las Vegas. The show attracted 130,000 industry professionals. Almost 3,000 companies filled about 3 million square feet of exhibit space.

- Have knowledgeable, personable representatives on duty to answer questions and collect visitor business cards for follow-up.
- Offer useful souvenirs. A key chain, a shopping bag, a luggage tag, or even a copy of a popular newspaper or magazine will attract traffic.
- Promote your exhibit in advance. Send announcements to potential customers and media kits to selected journalists four to six weeks before the trade show.

Most organizations feel that the large investment in a booth at a trade show is worthwhile for two reasons. First, a trade show facilitates one-on-one communication with potential customers and helps generate sales leads. It also attracts many journalists, so it is easier and more efficient to provide press materials, arrange one-on-one interviews, and demonstrate what makes the product worth a story. Second, a booth allows an exhibitor to demonstrate how its products differ from the competition's. This is more effective than just sending prospects a color brochure. It also is more cost effective than making individual sales calls.

Hospitality Suites

Hospitality suites are an adjunct to the exhibit booth. Organizations use them to entertain key prospects, give more in-depth presentations, and talk about business deals.

The idea is that serious customers will stay in a hospitality suite long enough to hear an entire presentation, whereas they are likely to stop at an exhibit hall booth for only a few minutes. Although goodwill can be gained from free concerts and cocktail parties, the primary purpose of a hospitality suite is to generate leads that ultimately result in product sales.

Pressrooms and Media Relations

Trade shows such as CES and MacWorld attract hundreds of journalists. About a thousand reporters, for example, descend on MacWorld every year. Consequently, every trade show has a pressroom where the various exhibitors distribute media kits (usually in digital form) and other information to journalists. Pressrooms typically have phone, fax, and Internet facilities for reporters to file stories with their employers.

> For people to pay attention at a trade show, you need real news.
>
> *David Rich, SVP of the George P. Johnson marketing company, as reported in* PRWeek

An important task of public relations staff is to personally contact reporters several weeks before a trade show to offer product briefings and one-on-one interviews with key executives. The competition is intense, so the staff members have to be creative in pitching ideas and showing why their client's products or services merit the journalist's time when multiple other companies are also pitching them. If the planner can arrange as many pre-show interviews and briefings as possible, the public relations firm will be more effective and successful.

A survey by Access Communications, for example, found that more than 90 percent of journalists assigned to a trade show want to hear about the company and product news before the show even starts. Michael Young, SVP of Access, told *PRWeek*, "Journalists have limited bandwidth at the show. They can only do so much, so they want to know what the news is before getting there." In other words, the media relations work starts before the show; it continues throughout the show, and then the public relations specialist has to do follow-up with reporters to provide additional information.

Sarah Skerik, director of trade show markets for *PR Newswire*, provides some additional tips for working with the media during a trade show:

- Plan major product announcements to coincide with the show.
- Include the name of the trade show in your news releases so that journalists searching databases can log on using the show as a keyword.
- Include your booth number in all releases and announcements.
- Make it easy for journalists to track down key spokespeople and experts connected with your product by including cell phone, pager, and e-mail addresses in your materials.
- Have your spokespeople trained to make brief presentations and equip them with answers to the most likely asked questions.
- Consider a looped videotape to run in the booth with copies available to the media.
- Provide photos that show the product in use, in production, or in development.
- Provide online corporate logos, product photos, executive profiles, media kits, and PowerPoint presentations to those journalists who cannot attend or who prefer to lighten their suitcase by having everything in digital format.
- Keep hard copies of news releases, fact sheets, and brochures at the booth and in the pressroom.

Promotional Events

Promotional events are planned primarily to promote a product, increase organizational visibility, make friends, and raise money for a charitable cause. There is also the category of corporate event sponsorship, which is highlighted in the Insights box on page 434.

The one essential skill for organizing promotional events is creativity. There are multiple "ho hum" events that compete for media attention and even attendance in every city, so it behooves the public relations professional to come up with something "different" that creates buzz and interest. A good example is the annual Belgrade Beer Festival, which was created to increase tourism and visibility for Serbia. See the Multicultural World box on page 435.

Other somewhat creative events include Hasbro's 60th anniversary celebration of Candy Land, in which the company turned San Francisco's famed Lombard Street into a large version of the board game. There was extensive media coverage of an aerial photo showing the street decked out in multiple colors, and Yahoo! reported that it was the most e-mailed photo of the week on its site. Intel, on the other hand, used the Central Park Zoo in New York to launch its Classmate PC and show off its ability to incorporate applications regarding robotics and scientific measurement tools. The event was made available to the media via B-roll video and high-resolution photos.

Grand openings of stores or hotels, for example, can be pretty dull and generate a collective yawn from almost every journalist in town, let alone all the chamber of commerce types that attend such functions. So how do public relations professionals come up with something new and different instead of the same old thing? First, they throw out the old idea of having a ribbon cutting. Second, they start thinking about a theme or idea that fits the situation and is out of the ordinary. A good example is the PR Casebook on page 413 about Procter & Gamble's "event" in New York's Times Square, which literally scored a "royal flush."

The reopening of the Morgan Hotel in San Antonio is another good example. The hotel featured a new restaurant, Oro (meaning gold in Spanish), so the theme for the opening night reception was gold—gold flowers, gold curtains, and even bikini-clad women who were coated with gold paint and served as living mannequins. A new hotel in Beijing, using a different approach, hired professional climbers to scale the 25-story building, which attracted extensive media coverage and large crowds.

> Events bring you face-to-face with your customer and can often serve as qualifying tools in reaching decision makers. Most often, the individuals that attend events are there by choice.
>
> *Jennifer Collins, Event Planning Group, as quoted in* PRWeek

Using Celebrities to Attract Attendance

A public relations person can also increase attendance at a promotional event by using a television or film personality. The creative part is figuring out what "personality" fits the particular product or situation. A national conference on aging for policy-makers, government officials, and health care experts attracted attendees because former senator and astronaut John Glenn was a major speaker. Unilver, on the other hand, wanted to reach an Hispanic audience through a series of events promoting its Suave and Caress brands, so the company tapped famous stylists Leonardo Rocco and Fernando Navarro to give hair and beauty advice to women attending the events.

on the job

INSIGHTS

Corporate Sponsorships: Another Kind of Event

Many corporations, in order to cut through the media clutter and establish brand identity, sponsor any number of events that, in turn, are covered by the media. In North America alone, about $10 billion is spent by corporations to sponsor various events. According to the *Economist*, about two-thirds of this total is sponsorship fees for sporting events.

The Olympics is the World Series of corporate sponsorships. Companies such as Coca-Cola, General Electric,

Visa, and Samsung are among the top 12 official sponsors of the Olympics. In fact, Coca-Cola has been an official sponsor since 1928 and marked its 80th anniversary of sponsorship at the Beijing Olympics in 2008. These top sponsors, in the three years leading up to the Olympics, provided almost $1 billion in financial support, goods, and services. In addition, another $800 million was raised by the Beijing organizing committee from a number of other corporations operating in China.

If your employer or client is thinking about sponsoring an event, here are some guidelines you should apply:

■ Can the company afford to fulfill the obligation? The sponsorship fee is just the starting point. Count on doubling it to have an adequate marketing and public relations campaign to publicize the event and your particular event.

■ Is the event or organization compatible with the company's values and mission statement?

■ Does the event reach the organization's primary audiences?

■ Are the event organizers experienced and professional?

■ Will the field representatives be able to use the event as a platform for increasing sales?

■ Does the event give the organization a chance to develop new contracts and business opportunities?

■ Can you make a multiple-year sponsorship contract that will reinforce brand identity on a regular, consistent basis?

■ Is there an opportunity to get employees involved and raise their morale?

■ Is the event compatible with the personality of the organization or its products?

■ Can you do trade-offs of products and in-kind services to help defray the costs?

> It is recommended that for each dollar spent in sponsorship, the sponsor spend twice that much to leverage the sponsorship, and that is true no matter how large or small the project.
>
> *Rodger Roeser, writing in KD Paine's* Measurement Standard *online newsletter*

Hiring a celebrity or "personality," as they are called in the trade, is not exactly the most creative solution to every situation, but it's a time-honored way to increase the odds that the media will cover the event, because "prominence" is considered a basic news value.

A personality, however, can be a major budget item. Stars such as Oprah Winfrey and Jennifer Lopez, typically charge $100,000 for an appearance, as do Sarah Palin and

on the job

A MULTICULTURAL WORLD

A Beer Fest Puts Belgrade on the Map

Europeans usually head for the countryside during the summer months, and the citizens of Belgrade, Serbia, are no exception. All this changed in August 2003, however, when billboards and flyers around the city announced a four-day beer festival to be held beneath the imposing Kalemegdan fortress at the confluence of the Sava and Danube rivers.

Thousands of people showed up for good beer and music, and the annual fest was launched much to the elation of Serbians, who haven't had much to celebrate since the Balkan wars of the 1990s. The Belgrade Cultural Network (BCN), a non-governmental organization, worked closely with business and government agencies to promote the beer fest, with the objective of putting the city on the map as a tourist destination.

The beer fest has grown in size and prominence every year. In 2005, the four-day event attracted 250,000 people. By 2009, attendance had exceeded all expectations, with more than 650,000 visitors making it the most popular annual event in Central Europe. In that four-day period, 47 musical groups performed and over 1 million liters of beer were consumed. Almost 50 beer brands (domestic and foreign) took part in the festival, and more than 600 articles were published about the event.

The motto of the 2009 fest was "Biram da recikliram" ("I Choose to

Recycle"), and fans turned in almost 75,000 beer cans for recycling. According to the organizers, "Through this campaign, we have raised the people's awareness, having the festival which promoted the very important subjects of recycling and environmental protection." Funds from the recycling effort were used to locate recycling containers in Belgrade schools.

Public relations and marketing for the beer fest is now a year-round effort, but activity is highest in the three months leading up to the August event. One major vehicle is the website, www.BelgradeBeerfest.com, which was visited by 200,000 people in the three months prior to the 2009 fest. Posters, flyers, billboards, website

postings, and story placement in the region's mass media are used, but outreach is also made to have influential travel writers visit the fest and write about it. Another tactic is contacting the publishers of travel guides to include the beer fest in their listings and recommendations. The beer fest is even on *Wikipedia* now, giving an entire history of the event and the musical groups that have performed through the years.

Dejan Grastic, general manager of BCN, was optimistic about the 2010 event: "Diligence and hard work can successfully transform Serbia's image. We expect a significant turnout of tourists from the entire Europe and we will do our best to make this year's festival the best so far."

Al Gore. At the $50,000 level, a planner can book basketball player Charles Barkley, actor Angela Bassett, or tennis star Anna Kournikova. If the budget isn't big enough for that, the planner has to make do with what the business calls the "up and coming" or the "down and going." A star of a popular television program can be booked for $10,000 and a soap opera star gets about $5,000 to $10,000 for an appearance. Supermodel Naomi Campbell is a bit more expensive; she charges about $15,000 to show up. Such fees are the primary reason events using celebrities are usually underwritten by corporations.

If the event is for a charity that the celebrity supports as a personal cause, on occasion he or she will reduce or waive an appearance fee. The planner should note, however, that the organization is often expected to pay for the celebrity's transportation (first-class, of course), the hotel suite, and room service. In addition, an organization pays the cost of assistants, hair stylists, valets, and other personnel accompanying them. Such arrangements can greatly increase the costs, even if the celebrity is "free."

One source for finding celebrities for promotional events is Celebrity Source (www.celebritysource.com). It matches requests with the 4,500 names in its database and handles all the details of negotiating fees, expenses, and transportation logistics for the organization. The value of a firm such as Celebrity Source or Celebrity Access (www.celebrityaccess.com) is that they have regular contact with celebrities' business agents and publicists. An organization trying to figure out whom to contact for a particular celebrity, let alone how to contact that person, may have less success.

Celebrity Source, on its website, gives some tips on what the firm needs to know in order to select the right celebrity for the event. The following is a good checklist if an organization is thinking about using a celebrity:

- What exactly do you want the celebrity to do?
- Who do you want to appeal to by having a celebrity? Is it the public, the media, or the sponsors?
- What do you want to accomplish by having a celebrity participate? Sell tickets or add glamour?
- What are the demographics of your audience or attendees?
- What is your budget?
- What is the maximum that you're willing to spend for the right celebrity?
- Are you prepared to pay for first-class expenses for the celebrity and at least one staff person?
- Do you have access to any perks or gifts that will help motivate the celebrity to say "yes"?

> Security at public events is a significant aspect that should get as much attention as lighting, sound, or signage.
>
> *Matt Glass, managing partner at Eventage, as reported in* PRWeek

Planning and Logistics

Events that attract large crowds require the same planning as an open house. The public relations specialist should be concerned about traffic flow, adequate restroom facilities, signage, and security. Professionally trained security personnel should also be arranged to handle crowd control, protect celebrities or government officials from being hassled, and make sure no disruptions occur to mar the event.

Liability insurance is a necessity, too. Any public event sponsored by an organization should be insured, just in case there is an accident and a subsequent lawsuit charging negligence. If the organization doesn't already have a blanket liability policy, the planner should get one for the event.

Charitable organizations also need liability insurance if they are running an event to raise money. This is particularly relevant if the organization is sponsoring an event that requires physical exertion, such as a 10-K run, a bicycle race, or even a hot-air balloon race.

Participants should sign a release form that protects the organization if someone suffers a heart attack or another kind of accident. One organization, which was sponsoring a 5-K "fun run," had the participants sign a statement that read in part: "I know that a road race is a potentially hazardous activity.... I assume all risk associated with running in this event, including, but not limited to, falls, contact with other participants, the effects of the weather, including high heat/or humidity, traffic and the conditions of the road."

Promotional events that use public streets and parks also need permits from various city departments. If the organization is sponsoring a run, the public relations person needs to get a permit from the police or public safety department to block off streets and also hire off-duty police to handle traffic control. Permits for the Avon Walk for Breast Cancer, for example, are arranged months in advance because there are many requests for "runs" and many cities have imposed a limit on how many will be permitted each year.

A food event such as a chili cook-off or a German fest requires permits from the public health department and, if liquor will be served, a permit from the state alcohol board. If the event is held inside a building, a permit is often required from the fire inspector.

The public relations planner must also deal with the logistics of arranging cleanup, providing basic services such as water and medical aid, registering craft and food vendors, and posting signs. Promotion of an event can often be accomplished by having a radio or TV station or local newspaper cosponsor the event, which was discussed in the last chapter.

Summary

A World Filled with Events

- Events and meetings are important tools of public relations because they reach people on a one-to-one basis, and attendees are more involved because events involve the five senses.

- Events and meetings don't just happen. They must be planned with attention to every detail. Nothing should be left to chance.

Group Meetings

- Club meetings and workshops require attention to such factors as time, location, seating, facilities, invitations, name tags, menu, speakers, registration, and costs.

Banquets

- Banquets are more formal affairs that require extensive advance planning.

- In addition to the factors necessary for a group meeting, decorations, entertainment, audiovisual facilities, speaker fees, and seating charts must be considered.

Receptions and Cocktail Parties

- Cocktail parties and receptions require precautions about the amount of alcohol consumed and the availability of food and nonalcoholic drinks. Possible liability is an important consideration, too.

Open Houses and Plant Tours

■ Open houses and plant tours require meticulous planning and routing, careful handling of visitors, and thorough training of all personnel who will be in contact with the visitors.

Conventions

■ Conventions require the skills of professional managers who can juggle multiple events and meetings over a period of several days.

■ A convention may include large meetings, cocktail parties, receptions, tours, and banquets.

Trade Shows

■ Trade shows are the ultimate marketing events and attract millions of attendees annually. Exhibit booths may cost from $50,000 to $1 million.

Promotional Events

■ A celebrity at a promotional event will attract crowds and media attention, but appearance fees can be costly.

■ A promotional event may be a "grand opening" of a facility, an event to announce a new product, or a 10-K run sponsored by a charitable organization. It is important to consider such factors as city permits, security, and liability insurance.

Case Activity   Plan a Banquet

The School of Business at your university has scheduled its annual awards banquet, which will be held in six months. It usually attracts about 500 alumni and members of the local business community. Traditionally, a speaker with a national reputation is asked to give the major address at the banquet.

In addition, outstanding students will be recognized. Prepare a detailed outline of what must be done to plan the banquet, including a timeline or calendar of what must be done by specific dates.

Questions   for Review and Discussion

1. Why are meetings and events a vital public relations tool even in the digital age of texting and social media?
2. Name at least four factors that must be considered in planning a meeting for a group.
3. What information should be provided to an invited speaker for an event?
4. In general, how long should a speaker talk at a luncheon or a dinner meeting?
5. Discuss the variety of items that must be budgeted in planning a banquet.
6. What is the recommended length of time for a reception or cocktail party?
7. What questions should you ask a catering manager when planning an event?

8. What logistics must be considered when planning an open house or a plant tour?
9. What are the components of planning a convention?
10. A booth at a trade show requires some thought. What would you do to attract visitors?
11. What are the pros and cons of using a celebrity as part of a promotional event?
12. Why is it important to consider security and liability issues for a promotional event?
13. What kinds of questions should be asked after an event to determine its success?

Media Resources

Fritz, J. (2009, March 17). Growth slows for charity walks and runs, but still worth billions. Retrieved from Joanne's nonprofits blog: http://nonprofit.about.com

Iacono, E. (2007, September 28). Events can be key to a dazzling debut. *PRWeek*, 18.

Janes, E. R. (2007, Fall). Charmin scores a royal flush. *Corporate Event*, 54–57.

Jeffries-Fox, B. (2005). A guide to measuring event sponsorships. Retrieved from Institute for Public Relations website: www.instituteforpr.org

Kent, C. (2008, March 14). How to make the most of your time at a trade show. Retrieved from www.ragan.com

Kent, C. (2009, April). Trade shows: Go or stay home in 2009? *RaganReport*, 23–24.

Kilkenny, S. (2006). *The complete guide to successful event planning*. Ocala, FL: Atlantic Publishing.

McPherson, S. (2010, January). A 12-month guide: How to enhance your company's trade show performance. *Public Relations Tactics*, 114.

Packing them in: Millions of people visit Las Vegas each year to display their wares at meetings and conventions [Advertising supplement]. (2009, December 28). *Time*.

Parker, G., & Hoffman, R. (2006). *Meeting excellence: 33 tools to lead meetings that get results*. San Francisco, CA: Jossey-Bass.

Roeser, R. (2009, June). How to make the most of your sponsorships. KD Paine's Measurement Standard website: www.themeasurementstandard.com

Trottman, M. (2008, March 31). In search of the cheaper meeting: Planning corporate gatherings is getting a lot easier—and a lot less expensive. *New York Times*, pp. R1, R6.

Ward, D. (2007, December 10). Taking full advantage of trade shows. *PRWeek*, 18.

Corporations

After reading this chapter, you will be able to:

Describe the role of public relations in corporations

Explain how media relations contributes to the success of corporations

Understand the crucial roles of the customer, the investor, and the employee in the corporate communication program

Describe the main supportive functions of public relations for corporate marketing efforts

Explain the environmental relations process

Define corporate philanthropy and the part public relations plays in corporate giving

Today's Modern Corporation

Today, giant corporations have operations and customers around the world. International conglomerates control subsidiary companies that often produce a grab bag of seemingly unrelated products under the same corporate banner. These companies deal with a number of governments at many levels. Their operations affect the environment, control the employment of thousands, and impact the financial and social well-being of millions.

Although such corporations make up a tiny proportion of all companies, corporations are often associated with powerful conglomerates. The large size of these corporations, however, also brings remoteness. A corporation has a "face" because its products, logo, and brand are readily visible in advertising and billboards from Azerbaijan to Zimbabwe and all the nations in between. However, the average consumer really can't comprehend organizations such as Wal-Mart, with $405 billion in worldwide sales, or Exxon/Mobil, with $442 billion in global sales. These figures boggle the mind, and they represent more than the combined gross national product (GNP) of many nations.

Ordinary citizens become distrustful of the power, influence, and credibility of such giant corporations, often transferring their mistrust to business in general. When U.S. gasoline prices rise rapidly, for example, suspicion spreads that "Big Oil" has conspired to gouge the public, a distrust that the oil companies never fully allay. Major corporate financial scandals in recent years and the misdeeds of corporate executives also take their toll on the public's trust. See the PR Casebook on page 442 about BP's struggles to earn credibility regarding its response to its enormous oil spill in the Gulf of Mexico.

On the other hand, former Shell Oil President John Hofmeister reflects on the inevitability of risk when humans take on huge enterprises on behalf of all of us:

> There are risks associated with hydrocarbon extraction in the same way there are risks in every industrial pursuit, whether aircraft, marine or food processing. In the case of hydrocarbons, when things go wrong, they go spectacularly wrong. But not having a sound energy policy is what has pushed us into ever-deeper waters.

Hofmeister makes the point that the American thirst for fossil fuels consumes 10,000 gallons of oil per second.

> People all over this country feel an incredible frustration that they are seeing their neighbors lose their jobs and the government is helping companies like A.I.G. and Goldman Sachs and then the next thing they are reporting huge profits and huge compensation. I think people are incredulous that this system is working this way.
>
> Senator Sherrod Brown, D, Ohio

Microsoft Worldwide

Large corporations need to balance their responsibilities to their stockholders with the worldwide public perceptions.

PRCasebook

BP's Gulf Oil Spill Causes a Gusher of PR Problems

BP caused a major environmental disaster when one of its oil rigs caught fire in April 2010 and an unplugged well started gushing oil into the Gulf of Mexico. In such a situation, the CEO of a company becomes the major spokesperson and often sets the tone of the response to public concerns.

Tony Hayward, chief executive of BP, immediately found himself under intense scrutiny by the media as he tried to explain what had happened and what BP was doing about what was soon to become the largest oil spill in history. Hayward, a geologist by training, wasn't very adept at being in the limelight and made a series of statements that reduced his credibility and eroded public trust in BP's initial efforts to contain the spill.

His first gaffe was blaming TransOcean, the company that had leased the oil rig to BP—which is the denial defense, as outlined in Chapter 10. This came across in the media as BP not being willing to take responsibility for the oil spill. His second mistake was to boast that BP had everything under control and was well prepared for the disaster, which proved false several weeks later, after various attempts to seal the well failed. Hayward also tried another defense, minimizing the problem. At a news conference, he said, "The Gulf of Mexico is a very big ocean. The amount of volume of oil and dispersant we are putting into it is tiny in relation to the total water volume."

Two weeks later, as the oil continued to spread throughout the Gulf and surrounding coastal areas, Hayward told *Fox News*, "There is no one who wants this thing over more than I do. You know, I'd like my life back." That statement was particularly ridiculed by government officials and Gulf Coast citizens because it was perceived as insensitivity to the fact that 11 men had lost their lives in the oil rig fire that had started the disaster in the first place. The *New York Daily News* editorialized that Hayward was rapidly becoming "the most hated and clueless man in America." Even President Obama gave a speech saying Hayward would have been fired if he was working for him.

> **If the international oil company is to survive the disaster, it will need to get its communications right, as well as plugging the leak and cleaning up the spill.**
>
> Financial Times

Part of Hayward's problem, some pundits believe, was cultural. BP is a British company and Hayward was taking a typically British approach to communication, which is somewhat unemotional and understated. Because Americans, in contrast, are much more expressive in their feelings, Hayward came across as not really understanding the gravity of the situation. He also had the British tendency to make a joke or smile to defuse tension, which didn't play well in the televised news conferences about the mushrooming environmental disaster.

Meanwhile, BP initiated other public relations efforts. It hired Brunswick public relations, another British firm, to disseminate daily information about what was being done to contain the spill. The company also spent about $50 million on full-page newspaper ads to assure the public that it was committed to stopping the oil leak and would do whatever necessary to clean up the mess. In another move, BP used search phrases such as "oil spill" and "oil spill claims" on Google and Yahoo! to ensure that the first link on both search engines would be a sponsored ad that led to BP's "Gulf of Mexico response." Such a move was endorsed by Kent Jarrell, an SVP of Apco Worldwide, who told the *Chicago Tribune*, "In any crisis situation, one of the first things you do is look at what's happening on Google—it's a pretty cut and dried tactical move."

But the *Financial Times* duly notes, "Even the most sensitive communications strategy is likely to have been swamped by the wave of bad news from the spill." It's also an axiom that all the public relations in the world won't save BP from public condemnation if the company fails to restore the Gulf to its previous condition and make compensation to thousands of citizens affected by the oil spill. Just ask Exxon about the Valdez oil spill of 1989 in Prince Edward Sound, Alaska.

The vast enterprise required to meet such a thirst is set up for failure and recrimination at some point. Environmental impacts, safety errors, and injustices in the workforce are never going to disappear. The sheer scale of human activity required to deliver energy to keep Americans comfortably ensconced in their preferred lifestyle, not to speak of providing food and goods to 300 million Americans, is fraught with environmental and fiscal hazards.

Public relations professionals representing government, consumers, and corporations wrangle about what is an acceptable level of risk and catastrophe in cases such as the BP oil blowout in the Gulf. Hofmeister and other corporate leaders affirm that corporations can never let up in their efforts to manage what they do in the best interests of all the publics they serve. But media and ordinary citizens should also bring some perspective about the scale and complexity of what corporations do to deliver what consumers demand worldwide.

This is seldom the case; fewer than 3 in 10 Americans (27 percent) feel that most large U.S. corporations are trustworthy, according to a recent Roper survey. And a Gallup poll reveals that business leaders and stockbrokers have joined used-car dealers in the category of "least trusted" individuals in American society. Gallup polls also indicate that 82 percent of the public believe that the top executives of larger corporations receive outrageous salaries in the millions of dollars and, at the same time, improperly use corporate funds to adopt lavish lifestyles.

Public perceptions of greed and corporate misdeeds are reinforced by stories in the media. For example, hundreds of stories were written about Bernard Madoff's pyramid scheme, which ruined powerful investors in his funds as well as many worthy charities that invested heavily with him. His indictment, subsequent plea bargain, and imprisonment for vast and ruthless investment fraud increased the public's sense of alienation from and cynicism about the world of business. Such sentiments are natural, but unfair to the majority of companies and businesspeople who work in moderate-sized or even small businesses to make an honest living for themselves and their investors.

Corporate public relations practitioners face a delicate balance between arguing for realism and making lame excuses on behalf of their companies. Realistically, huge enterprises that make and do things will also make huge mistakes—spills, worker injuries, and the evils of fraud and price abuse. Society rightfully requires corporate communicators and media to expose illegal and incompetent dealings, but with some consideration of how hard corporations of all sorts strive to provide the best value they can, not only for profit but also from a need to have a worthy purpose in life.

The Role of Public Relations

The extensive negative publicity about corporations and business in general over the past several years has made it imperative that companies make a special effort to regain public credibility and trust. Thus, the concept of *corporate social responsibility* (CSR) is now high on the priority list of executives and their public relations staffs, who

> There are risks associated with hydrocarbon extraction in the same way there are risks in every industrial pursuit, whether aircraft, marine or food processing. In the case of hydrocarbons, when things go wrong, they go spectacularly wrong. But not having a sound energy policy is what has pushed us into ever-deeper waters.
>
> *John Hofmeister, Director,*
> *Citizens for Affordable Energy*

are charged with improving the reputation and citizenship of their employers. The Reputation Institute supports this goal with research indicating that 40 percent of a company's reputation derives from perceived corporate citizenship and sound governance.

Indeed, the public relations professional regularly takes steps to outline a plan of action for rebuilding public trust in business. "These are people who deal with trust issues all the time," says James Murphy, global managing director of communication for Accenture. "Therefore, we're in a good position to address them." American businesses and their leaders need to act in three main areas:

1. adopt ethical principles,
2. pursue transparency and disclosure, and
3. make trust a fundamental precept of corporate governance.

See the Insights box on page 445 for survey evidence of how important transparency is to building a solid corporate reputation.

The importance of public relations in CSR is explained by Jack Bergen, senior vice president of marketing and communication for Siemens Corporation. He told *PRWeek*:

> We are the eyes and ears of an organization. The best way to be socially responsible is to have your eyes and ears trained on all the stakeholders, to know what they want and need from the company. These are classic public affairs issues and the idea that they should be handled by anyone else would show a lack of understanding.

A number of strategies and tactics can be used to implement CSR, which involves corporate performance as well as effective communication. One of the more important roles of the public relations executive is counseling the CEO.

The public relations executive serves as a link between the chief executive and the realities of public opinion in the marketplace and the organization, according to Mark Schumann, global communication practice leader with Tower Perrin. He told an international IABC conference that CEOs are often "disconnected" and surrounded by other executives who simply agree with whatever the CEO says. Schumann told *PRWeek*, "...everyone sucks up and lies to them." Schumann believes corporate public relations professionals should be the "...playwright and director, but we also need to be the toughest critics" to ensure that the CEO comes across as concerned and involved with employees and customers. As critics, public relations professionals often hold a mirror up for the top leadership to see an unwelcome but valuable view of themselves and their performance.

Corporations seek a better reputation for a variety of reasons. First, responsible business practices ward off increased government regulation. Demonstrating what can happen when companies fail to police themselves, the U.S. Congress passed new laws regarding accounting practices and disclosure as a result of major financial scandals during the first decade of the century. Second, there is the matter of employee morale; companies with good policies and a good reputation tend to have less employee turnover. A good corporate reputation also favorably affects the bottom line. For example, a survey of executives by the Center for Corporate Citizenship

> Communication is good training for the vision, strategic thinking, and leadership that executive decision-makers are called upon to provide. I have come to think of myself as a generalist, with a strong focus in communications.
>
> *Bill Novelli, CEO, AARP*

on the job
INSIGHTS

Transparency: The Key to Corporate Reputation

Transparent and honest practices are the most important factor in determining a corporation's reputation, according to the 2010 Edelman Trust Barometer. In fact, it was the first time in 10 years that transparency ranked slightly higher than high-quality products or services.

Richard Edelman, CEO of Edelman public relations, said, "We're seeing a vastly different set of factors driving reputation than we did 10 years ago. Trust is now an essential line of business to be developed and delivered."

The Trust Barometer is an annual survey conducted by Edelman public relations, which has 3,200 employees in 51 offices worldwide. Almost 5,000 college-educated adults in 22 nations were surveyed to assess public trust in various institutions such as corporations, governments, and NGOs.

Figure 17.1 gives the percentage of respondents who ranked the importance of various factors in determining a corporation's reputation.

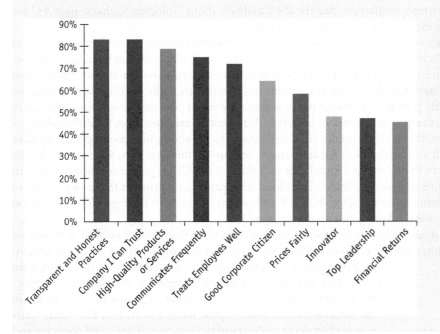

Figure 17.1 Factors in Corporate Reputation

Source: Edelman, *2010 Edelman Trust Barometer* report, www.edelman.com

and the Hitachi Foundation found that 82 percent of the respondents believe that good corporate citizenship contributes to meeting the organization's financial objectives. In addition, 53 percent say corporate citizenship is important to their customers.

Being a good corporate citizen is an admirable goal, but corporations also face a number of pressures and counterpressures when making decisions and forming policies. General Electric, one of the world's largest corporations, with a market value of about

$340 billion, once outlined four key factors that have to be considered at all times when making a decision:

- **Political.** How do government regulations and other pressures affect the decision?
- **Technological.** Do we have the engineering knowledge to accomplish the goal?
- **Social.** What is our responsibility to society?
- **Economic.** Will we make a profit?

The following sections discuss various facets of today's modern corporation and the activities that require the expertise and counsel of public relations professionals.

Media Relations

The media are a major source of public information and perceptions about the business world and individual companies. In recent years, the news about corporate behavior hasn't been all that favorable.

Major financial scandals and other negative coverage can cause a corporation's reputation to plummet. Wal-Mart, once ranked number one in corporate reputation, saw its position drop to seventh in the space of six months after coverage regarding the hiring of illegal immigrants and the filing of a class-action suit that claimed it discriminated against female employees. See the PR Casebook about Goldman Sachs on page 447 for another example of a rapid drop in reputation.

This volatility leads corporate executives to be defensive about how journalists cover their business, because they feel that too much emphasis has been given to corporate misdeeds and exaggeration of impacts on the environment and workforce even when companies devote effort to minimizing emissions, spills, and accidents. From the corporate perspective, you make mistakes only when you are doing things; the more you do, the greater the risk of criticism. Many corporate executives have several ongoing complaints about media coverage: inaccuracy, incomplete coverage, inadequate research and preparation for interviews, and an antibusiness bias. One survey by the American Press Institute found that one-third of the CEOs polled are dissatisfied with the business news they find in their local newspapers, a sentiment that is not exclusive to the business sector. (See the PR Casebook in Chapter 19 on page 497 for more on BP, President Obama, and media pressure.)

Business editors and reporters respond that often they cannot publish or broadcast thorough, evenhanded stories about business because many company executives, uncooperative and wary, erect barriers against them. Writers complain about their inability to obtain direct access to decision-making executives, which forces them to rely on news releases that don't contain the information they need. Journalists assert, too, that some business leaders don't understand the concept of balanced coverage and assume that any story involving unfavorable news about their company is intentionally biased.

Journalists also say it's a major mistake for corporate executives to slash public relations and communication budgets during times of financial scandal and economic downturn. A survey of journalists conducted by Middleberg Euro RSCG, a public relations firm, and the Columbia University Graduate School of Journalism, found that journalists also believe corporations should focus on delivering more

> You [executives] should communicate factually, frequently, and consistently. Use this time wisely, say the journalists, to position yourself.
>
> *Don Middleberg,*
> *public relations executive*

PRCasebook

Goldman Sachs
Smart, Greedy, Dangerous?

Goldman Sachs, the renowned global investment banking and securities firm, received billions of U.S. taxpayers' dollars from the Troubled Assets Relief Program (TARP) in 2008. It paid the government back quickly and taxpayers made a tidy profit in the transaction. So why did Goldman Sachs still have a public relations problem?

Maybe because when much of the U.S. economy was still suffering from a recession in 2009, Goldman Sachs had a record-setting year in terms of profits, and the average pay for its 30,000 employees was $595,000, according to the *New York Times*. Lloyd Blankfein, Goldman Sachs CEO, told *The Times of London* that he was aware that "people are pissed off, mad, and bent out of shape" about the banking mess. He added, "I know I could slit my wrists and people would cheer."

In January 2010, *Vanity Fair* summarized its investigative piece on Goldman Sachs with this sentence: "One of the biggest disconnects on Wall Street today is between the way Goldman Sachs sees itself (they're the smartest) and the way everyone else sees Goldman (they're the smartest, greediest, and most dangerous)." For example, Goldman Sachs put together investment packages, sold them, and then sold short, essentially betting against clients. This was justified during congressional testimony as "making markets," but it's doubtful that those who were sold bonds would find comfort in the seller profiting from failure of the item.

Goldman Sachs responded to public critiques in a variety of ways. In October 2009, the firm announced it would donate $200 million to its charitable foundation, nearly doubling the philanthropic organization's size. It also announced a $500 million program, dubbed "10,000 Small Businesses," which was intended to "unlock the growth and job-creation potential of 10,000 small businesses...through greater access to business education, mentors and networks, and financial capital."

Further, the company made plans to expand its existing program that requires executives and top managers to give a percentage of their earnings to charity. Public relations executive David Langness told *PRWeek*:

We understand that [Goldman Sachs] has been through a very tough year with negative press. The bottom line is, they had to do something. In this environment where

> The bottom line is, they had to do something. In this environment where there's such declining trust in major corporations, CSR [corporate social responsibility] campaigns have risen to the top of the list as far as importance level. It used to be CSR campaigns were unusual, now they're common practice. They're a part of the PR toolbox.
>
> *David Langness, public relations executive*

there's such declining trust in major corporations, CSR [corporate social responsibility] campaigns have risen to the top of the list as far as importance level. It used to be CSR campaigns were unusual, now they're common practice. They're a part of the PR toolbox.

The investment corporation also announced changes in compensation for its top 30 executives and used its website as a forum to respond to many of the critiques in the media. In February of 2010, *BusinessWeek* reported, "Goldman Sachs, the most profitable securities firm in Wall Street history, this year cut the percentage of revenue earmarked for pay to the lowest in a decade as a public company. The New York-based firm aimed to allay anger about banks whose profits and pay rebounded within a year of taking government bailouts while the U.S. jobless rate was about 10 percent."

Although the Dow Jones Media Lab noted that most media mentions of Goldman Sachs in October 2009 were negative, by mid-November more positive coverage was on the rise. Martin Murtland of Dow Jones told *PRWeek*, "The data indicates that on a percentage basis, positive coverage of Goldman has increased by four percentage

(Continued)

points, moving the needle from 14 percent to 18 percent positive coverage. This is a significant achievement; however this example is also evidence that an organization's reputation cannot be rebuilt over night."

Were Blankfein's acknowledgments of public outrage just pithy soundbites, or were his statements strategic?

Which public relations tactics do you see at work in the Goldman Sachs story?

Which strategies could financial institutions employ to engender more public trust in the aftermath of the government bank bailout?

fact-driven messages. Don Middleberg, director of the survey, told *PRWeek*, "You [executives] should communicate factually, frequently, and consistently. Use this time wisely, say the journalists, to position yourself."

Public relations practitioners serving businesses stand in the middle. They must interpret their companies and clients to the media, while showing their chief executive and other high officials how open, friendly media relations can serve their interests. One major interest that executives have is corporate reputation, and this is often tarnished or enhanced by the type of media coverage that an organization receives.

Savvy public relations professionals understand that business reporters often don't have adequate business preparation. For this reason, they spend a great deal of time and energy providing background to brief reporters on the business operations of their clients and employers. It's one way of ensuring that coverage will be more accurate and thorough.

One study by Hill & Knowlton, for example, found that Canadian CEOs believe that print and broadcast media criticism is the biggest threat to their companies' reputations, even ahead of such things as disasters and allegations by the government about employee or product safety. At the same time, executives know that communicating through the media is probably the most effective way for an organization to get its message across and to achieve its business goals.

Customer Relations

Customer service, in many respects, is the front line of public relations. A single incident, or a series of incidents, can severely damage a company's reputation and erode public trust in its products and services. Customer satisfaction is important because of word of mouth. A person who has a bad experience, surveys indicate, shares his or her story with an average of 17 people, whereas a person with a good experience will tell an average of 11 people.

The rapid growth of the Internet and blogs, however, has considerably changed the math. Today, a dissatisfied customer is capable of informing thousands, or even millions, of people in just one posting. According to the *New York Times*, corporations have become less accommodative of malcontents repeatedly posting comments to the Internet. Instead, companies are filing defamation suits against such individuals. Free speech advocates, on the other hand, call such lawsuits a SLAPP (Strategic Lawsuit Against Public Participation).

One somewhat embarrassing example is what happened to Comcast. A customer videotaped a Comcast repairman sound asleep on the couch in his home and posted it on www.Snakesonablog.com. The clip was then picked up by a technology blog and then was also shown on an MSNBC program. In no time, about 200,000 people saw the video, and Comcast was embarrassed enough to immediately send a team of technicians to the customer's home to fix the problem. The video, however, reached an even greater audience with a story about the video in the *New York Times*, which noted that the repairman had fallen asleep while trying to get through to the cable company's repair office on the phone.

Further illustrating the problem, *Pittsburgh Post-Gazette* reporter Teresa Lindeman wrote:

> . . . companies that consider ignoring tales of dissatisfied customers might want to take a look at a study released yesterday by the Wharton School of the University of Pennsylvania. Researchers there found that more than 50 percent of Americans said they wouldn't go to a store if a friend had a bad shopping experience there. Even worse, when someone has a problem, it gets embellished with every retelling, and pretty soon that store has a really, really big problem.

Product recalls, in particular, test the patience of consumers and bring into question the credibility of the entire company as far as its ability to provide safe and quality products. Toy maker Mattel had to recall more than 20 million toys because figures of famous icons such as Barbie, Elmo, and Dora the Explorer were tainted with lead paint used by Chinese subcontractors. Mattel vacillated initially, but soon took responsibility for quality control. Over time, this move reassured consumers, enabling Mattel to begin rebuilding its reputation. For more insight on how to handle a product recall, see the PR Casebook about Toyota in Chapter 10 on page 266.

Traditionally, customer service has been separate from the communication or public relations function in a company. Bob Seltzer, a leader in Ruder Finn's marketing practice, told *PRWeek*, "I defy anyone to explain the wisdom of this. How a company talks to its customers is among, if not the, most critical communication it has." Rande Swann, director of public relations for the Regional Airport Authority of Louisville, Kentucky, agrees, saying, "Our reputation is probably based more on how we serve our customers than any other single thing. If we don't have a reputation for great service, we don't have travelers."

> How a company talks to its customers is among, if not the, most critical communication it has.
>
> *Bob Seltzer, marketing expert at Ruder Finn*

Increasingly, however, corporations are realizing that customer relations serves as a telltale public relations barometer. Many public relations departments now regularly monitor customer feedback in a variety of ways to determine what policies and communication strategies need to be revised. One common method is to monitor customer queries to the organization's website. Indeed, most companies have a "contacting us" link on their websites. Another method is the content analysis of phone calls to the customer service center.

This sharing of information is valuable from the standpoint of getting public relations professionals involved in active listening so that they can strategize on what steps a company should take to ensure a good reputation among customers. As Andy Hopson, CEO of Burson-Marsteller's northeast region, told *PRWeek*, "Ignoring complaints can ultimately damage a company's reputation."

> Ignoring complaints can ultimately damage a company's reputation.
>
> *Andy Hopson, Burson-Marsteller executive*

Managing Conflict

The astute public relations practitioner must keep a watchful eye on the mood of the public while building diverse markets. Controversy over immigration policy, for example, affects multiple publics.

Public relations professionals also pay attention to consumer surveys. One such mechanism is the American Customer Satisfaction Index, which is the definitive benchmark of how buyers feel about what business is selling to them. The index, which has been tracking customer satisfaction for 200 companies in 40 industries for over a decade, has found that a company offering the lowest prices may not necessarily get the highest satisfaction rating.

Reaching Diverse Markets

The United States is becoming more diverse every year, which is now being recognized by corporate marketing and communication departments. As racial and ethnic minorities continue to increase in number and become more affluent, they will constitute a larger share of the consumer marketplace. See also Chapter 11 about diverse audiences.

According to Gina Amaro, director of multicultural and international markets for PR Newswire, "Companies that focus solely on one audience when creating products are missing an enormous opportunity. Furthermore, companies that do not incorporate a multicultural marketing and PR campaign to communicate these products and services to their many niche audiences will miss even larger opportunities."

As with many initiatives in public relations, there are two sides to most arguments. Efforts to accommodate Spanish speakers are met with criticism from some quarters. In the aftermath of the controversial Arizona illegal immigration enforcement law, those who feel illegal immigration is out of control have gained confidence from the popular support for the law in nationwide polls. They freely criticize bilingual efforts in education and marketing as pandering to the tidal wave of illegal immigration. Others in the Hispanic community have their own objections, claiming that special marketing programs, offers, and appeals are often merely token gestures. Clearly, public relations is strategic conflict management much of the time, and the astute professional keeps a vigilant eye on seemingly innocent, positive communication programs that may stir controversy.

Consumer Activism

A dissatisfied customer can often be mollified by prompt and courteous attention to his or her complaint or even by an offer from the company to replace the item or provide some discount coupons toward future purchases. A more serious and complex threat to corporate reputation, which can also affect sales, is consumer activists who demand changes in corporate policies.

Tyson Foods, a major American producer of meat and poultry products, was accused of inhumane treatment of animals by various animal rights groups, such as the People for the Ethical Treatment of Animals (PETA). The corporate response was to establish an office of animal well-being to assure retailers and consumers that it takes humane animal handling seriously.

Ed Nicholson, Tyson's director of media and community relations, told *PRWeek*, "The people from PETA are not going to be satisfied unless we go out of business, but there are consumers less radical than PETA who are still concerned about animal-handling practices." The new wellness office, headed by a veterinarian, will oversee audits of animal-handling practices and make them available to customers on request.

KFC also has been targeted by PETA and other animal rights groups, whose efforts have received extensive media publicity. The charges of inhumane animal treatment and how chickens are slaughtered can and do affect consumer buying decisions, especially when activists are outside a franchise wearing T-shirts that say, "KFC Tortures Animals." In such a situation, the public relations staff has the difficult job of defending the company against what it believes are unfounded allegations and to simultaneously assure the public that KFC's policies do provide for the humane slaughter of its chickens. The public relations professional also represents the external communication climate to management in a way that calls for redoubled efforts to do what is right.

Consequently, when it came to light that a KFC subcontractor was mistreating chickens, the company immediately called the abuse by workers appalling and told the subcontractor to clean up its act—or lose its contract. In this instance, because of the company's quick response, the media were able to include KFC's response in the story about the abuses, which were documented on videotape.

Coca-Cola also has reputation problems. Some activist groups charged the giant bottler with contributing to childhood obesity by selling its products in schools. Karl Bjorhus, director of health and nutrition communication for the bottler, told *PRWeek*, "We have been listening and trying to understand what people's concerns are."

As a result, the company partnered with the American Beverage Association and the Alliance for a Healthier Generation to voluntarily shift to lower-calorie and healthier beverages in school vending machines. In a company news release, Don Knauss, president of Coca-Cola North America, said:

> By combining our product offerings with the nutrition and physical education programs we support, such as Live It!, Triple Play and Copa Coca-Cola, we can help put schools at the forefront of the efforts to create a healthier generation. . . .

Another activist group had other concerns. One campaign, Stop Killer Coke, claimed that Coca-Cola was using paramilitary thugs in Colombia to intimidate workers and prevent unionization. The company said the charges were "false and outrageous," but that didn't stop the campaign's organizers from spreading the word to colleges, high schools, and unions. As a result, at least six colleges booted Coke beverages off their campuses, and several food co-ops decided to stop selling Coke products. In such a situation, even false allegations can affect the sales of a product. See the PR Casebook about the schools' soft-drink policy change on page 561 in Chapter 21.

In today's climate of media attention focused on health-related topics such as obesity, every food product company is suspect. McDonald's was the subject of a movie

> The people from PETA are not going to be satisfied unless we go out of business, but there are consumers less radical than PETA who are still concerned about animal-handling practices.
>
> *Ed Nicholson, Tyson Foods spokesperson*

We're responding aggressively because the film is a gross misrepresentation of what McDonald's is about. The scam in the movie is that he has given the impression that he only ate three basic meals a day, but the reality is that he stuffed himself with 5,000 to 7,000 calories, which is two or three times the recommended amount.

Walt Riker, VP of McDonald's

documentary, *Super Size Me*, in which the producer decided to eat three meals a day at McDonald's for several months. The movie, of course, details how all the "junk food" made him overweight and prone to major health problems.

In this case, McDonald's reaction was aggressive, reflecting a stance on the advocacy end of the continuum of strategic conflict management presented in Chapter 10. Walt Riker, vice president of corporate communication at McDonald's, told *PRWeek*,

We're responding aggressively because the film is a gross misrepresentation of what McDonald's is about. The scam in the movie is that he has given the impression that he only ate three basic meals a day, but the reality is that he stuffed himself with 5,000 to 7,000 calories, which is two or three times the recommended amount.

According to *PRWeek*, "McDonald's has been engaging the media in interviews and the company has made its global nutritionist, Cathy Kapica, available." Kapica appeared on CNN and CNBC, and gave a number of newspaper interviews about the film producer's "extreme behavior." The company also distributed a VNR and an ANR giving its views on smart choices in diet and exercise. It also sent briefing materials to its 2,700 franchises so they could talk to local media in an informed way.

Ford Motor Company also faced reputation and trust problems with consumers after Bluewater, an environmental group, took out full-page ads in various newspapers to accuse the automaker of continuing to make "America's worst gas guzzlers." The ads went on to say, "Don't Buy Bill Ford's Environmental Promises. Don't Buy His Cars." However, such public discourse and outright conflict can lead to positive change. Ford is now viewed as a leading maker of fuel-efficient and hybrid vehicles. See the Insights box on page 462 for more on Ford's use of social media to make this turnaround possible.

At the strategic level, a company weighs the potential impact of the charges or allegations on potential customer reaction and possible effect on sales before deciding on a course of action. This threat appraisal concept was discussed in Chapter 10. Activist consumer groups are a major challenge to the public relations staff of an organization. Do you accommodate? Do you stonewall? Do you change policy? Issues management is fully presented in Chapter 10, but here are some general guidelines from Douglas Quenqua on how to be proactive, which appeared in *PRWeek*:

Do

- Work with groups who are more interested in solutions than getting publicity.
- Offer transparency. Activists who feel you're not open aren't likely to keep dealing with you.
- Turn their suggestions into action. Activists want results.

Don't

- Get emotional when dealing with advocacy groups.
- Agree to work with anyone making threats.
- Expect immediate results. Working with adversaries takes patience—establishing trust takes time.

Consumer Boycotts

The *boycott*—a refusal to buy the products or services of an offending company—has a long history and is a widely used publicity tool of the consumer movement.

PETA, for example, announced that consumers should boycott Safeway until it improved conditions for farm animals. The key aspect of theater for this protest was Safeway's annual stockholders' meeting at which activists would unfurl a banner saying, "Safeway means animal cruelty." It had, as *PRWeek* says, "all the makings of a PR person's worst nightmare."

Safeway, however, headed off a boycott by negotiating. Just days before the annual meeting, the company's public affairs staff began working with PETA and quickly announced new standards for monitoring the conditions at its meat suppliers. Instead of a protest, PETA supporters showed up at the annual meeting with a large "Thank You" sign for entering stockholders. In addition, PETA ended its 20-state boycott of the chain. The director of public affairs for Safeway said the boycott didn't have any effect on sales, but PETA took a different tack. Its director told *PRWeek*, "It's just a truism that you don't want your corporation targeted by activists. My hunch is the timing of the call [from Safeway public affairs] was not purely coincidental."

The success of consumer boycotts is mixed. Various activist groups have boycotted Procter & Gamble for years, but without much effect, because the company makes so many products under separate brand names that consumers can't keep track of everything P&G makes. A single product name can sometimes be more vulnerable to a boycott than a large company that markets its goods and services under multiple brand names. When the iPhone was introduced in Canada, Rogers Communications had the only network on which the technology would work. Rogers offered its monthly data plans ranging from $60 to $115—much more than the $30 plans offered in the United States by AT&T. Canadian consumers threatened a boycott of Rogers Communications; 56,000 people signed an online petition against the company at *ruinediphone.com*. Ultimately, Rogers Communications responded by offering a $30 monthly data package for a limited time, and the boycott was averted.

Activists point out that a boycott doesn't have to be 100 percent effective in order for it to change corporate policies. Even a 5 percent drop in sales will often cause corporations to rethink their policies and modes of operation. Nike got serious about sweatshop conditions abroad only after activist groups caused its stock and sales to drop. Nike was losing market share, so it decided to formulate new policies for its subcontractors abroad and become active in a global alliance of manufacturers to monitor working conditions in overseas factories.

Employee Relations

Employees have been called an organization's "ambassadors." Consequently, the public relations department, often working with the human resources department, concentrates on communicating with employees just as vigorously as it concentrates on delivering the corporate story to the outside world. A workplace that respects its management, has pride in its products, and believes it is being treated fairly is a key factor in corporate success. See the Insights box on page 454 about using internal communication to define a company's shared identity.

Surveys indicate, however, that the success of communication efforts varies widely among organizations. According to a survey of 1,000 U.S. workers by Towers Perrin, 20 percent believe their organization does not tell them the truth. About half

on the job

INSIGHTS

A Brave New Brand

To create a unified corporate brand identity, Shire Pharmaceutical's corporate communications team started by asking all employees what makes the company so special. This process of fundamental, tried-and-true research that also goes by the name "listening" was the basis for Shire discovering what it is.

Many long-time employees saw Shire as intrinsically and historically brave, prompting a wonderful narrative around which the communication department could build a new corporate culture. The team then devised a multifaceted Brave initiative that ultimately became the cornerstone for new values and performance evaluations at Shire.

The award-winning internal communication campaign engaged all 3,700 Shire employees, with 100 percent buy-in from the 110 vice presidents, who would then become ambassadors for the new narrative to define the company. Elements used to engage the vice presidents included films of patients' stories and executives' own brave stories. Top managers were invited to the "brave room." Stories were shared in a podcast series and videos on Shire's intranet. The company used its global employee magazine to drive messaging, and a brave tour then allowed employees an opportunity to tell their own stories on video. All staffers also received a "Book of Brave," which included images and captions leading the reader into the Shire world. Some of the images were turned into large-scale wall art and integrated into office spaces.

A survey showed 98 percent of VPs agreed or strongly agreed with campaign messaging, and 96 percent felt the messages captured the spirit of Shire. The video and podcast pages became top 10 pages in the company intranet's history, each getting 3,500+ hits in the first two months. More than 100 staffers told stories during the "brave tour." The program also inspired a CEO blog, a more relaxed dress code, and a less hierarchical allocation of space in offices.

This campaign showcases the value of listening to employees and then being creative to build a genuine narrative about the company that helps to define the corporate culture.

Source: PRWeek 2010 Awards.

of the respondents say their company generally tells employees the truth, and about the same percentage believe that their employers try too hard to "spin" the truth. Another finding: Almost half believe they get more reliable information from their direct supervisors than from senior executives.

The extensive media coverage of corporate scandals also has taken its toll in terms of employee perceptions. A Fleishman-Hillard survey of workers, for example, found that 80 percent believe that greed is driving corporate scandals. The majority also agree that corporations care more about stock value than customers' needs. On the plus side, however, more than 70 percent of the respondents think the information they receive from their employer is "adequate" to "very comprehensive."

The value of credible and trustworthy communication cannot be overestimated. Mark Schumann of Towers Perrin told *Public Relations Tactics,* "Regardless of the topic, an organization will find it difficult to motivate, engage, and retain their most talented employees if their messages are not believed." Don Etling of Fleishman-Hillard told *PRWeek*, "We look at internal communication as something that affects performance, whether you have two or 200 employees. Companies that do a good job of explaining their values, not just to their partners, investors, and clients, but also to their employees, seem to enjoy better results....Companies really need to look at this as a performance issue."

A good example of successful corporate policies that build employee loyalty is the annual survey by *Working Mother* magazine that compiles a list of the 100 best companies for working mothers. A comparison of these 100 best companies with other organizations shows the following:

> Companies that do a good job of explaining their values, not just to their partners, investors, and clients, but also to their employees, seem to enjoy better results. . . . Companies really need to look at this as a performance issue.
>
> *Don Etling, Fleishman-Hillard*

- 100 percent of the 100 best companies offer flextime, versus 55 percent of companies nationwide.
- 99 percent of the 100 best offer an employee assistance program, versus 67 percent nationwide.
- 98 percent of the 100 best offer elder-care resource and referral services, versus 20 percent nationwide.
- 96 percent of the 100 best offer child-care resource and referral services, versus 18 percent nationwide.
- 94 percent of the 100 best offer compressed workweeks, versus 31 percent nationwide.
- 93 percent of the 100 best offer job-sharing, versus 22 percent nationwide.

Many employee issues must be addressed by a company, and public relations professionals often are involved in counseling not only what policies should be created but also how they should be implemented and communicated. One such issue is health and medical benefits. Company information about benefits should be written in plain English instead of legalese so that employees thoroughly understand what is covered. If there is a change in a health plan, the company must spend time and effort, often through small-group meetings, to explain the changes and why they are necessary.

Another issue is sexual harassment. This worries both employees and management for both legal and ethical reasons. The U.S. Supreme Court ruled in *Monitor Savings Bank v. Vinson* (1986) that a company may be held liable in sexual harassment suits even if management is unaware of the problem and has a general policy condemning any form of verbal or nonverbal behavior that causes employees to feel "uncomfortable" or consider the workplace a "hostile environment."

Organizations, to protect themselves from liability and the unfavorable publicity of a lawsuit, not only must have a policy, they must also clearly communicate the policy to employees and conduct workshops to ensure that everyone thoroughly understands what might be considered sexual harassment. See the discussion on page 319 in Chapter 12 about a company's legal rights to monitor employee e-mails.

Layoffs and Outsourcing

Layoffs present a major public relations challenge to an organization, especially in the current recession, in which layoffs are a common event. Julie Hood, an editor of *PRWeek*, says it best: "The way in which a company handles job reductions can have a significant

> The way in which a company handles job reductions can have a significant impact on its reputation, its share price, and its ongoing ability to recruit and maintain good staff. And that presents a major challenge for communication departments.
>
> *Julie Hood, editor of* PRWeek

impact on its reputation, its share price, and its ongoing ability to recruit and maintain good staff. And that presents a major challenge for communication departments."

Although human resource (HR) departments are most often involved in layoffs, it's also a situation in which the expertise of the public relations department is harnessed to ensure employee understanding and support. One cardinal rule is that a layoff is never announced to the media before employees are first informed. Another cardinal rule is that employees should be informed in person by their immediate supervisor; the traditional "pink slip" or an e-mail message is unacceptable. Employees who are being retained should also be called in by their immediate supervisor to let them know their status.

The rumor mill works overtime when there is uncertainty among employees about their job security, so it's also important for the company to publicly announce the layoffs and the impact as quickly as possible. Companies should be very forthright and upfront about layoffs; this is not the time to issue vague statements and "maybes" that just fuel the rumor mill.

Companies that are interested in their reputation and employee trust also make every effort to cushion the layoff by implementing various programs. Merrill Lynch, for example, laid off 6,000 employees by giving them the option of "voluntary separation" in exchange for one year's pay and a percentage of their annual bonus. Other companies offer outplacement services, the use of office space, and other programs. Such programs do much to retain employee goodwill even as workers are being laid off. And in recent years, employee communicators have paid more attention to sadness and depression among the survivors of layoffs who feel guilty about their good fortune.

A contentious issue, and one that has become an emotional and political football in recent years, is the matter of outsourcing white-collar jobs. This practice is commonly called *offshoring*. Today many American companies are employing lower-paid professionals in India and other Asian nations to handle everything from customer service to software engineering and accounting. The trend toward increased use of offshoring presents major internal communication challenges for public relations departments. See the Ethics box on page 457 for evidence of the financial benefits of ethical behavior.

Investor Relations

Another major component of keeping a company's health and wealth is communicating with shareholders and prospective investors. *Investor relations* (IR) is at the center of that process.

The goal of investor relations is to combine the disciplines of communication and finance to accurately portray a company's prospects from an investment standpoint. Some key audiences are financial analysts, individual and institutional investors, shareholders, prospective shareholders, and the financial media. Increasingly, employees are an important public, too, because they have stock options and 401 retirement plans.

Individuals who specialize in investor or financial relations, according to salary surveys, are the highest-paid professionals in the public relations field. One reason for this is that they must be very knowledgeable about finance and a myriad of

on the job

ETHICS

Ethical Behavior Pays Dividends

The World's Most Ethical Companies designation recognizes companies that truly go beyond making statements about doing business "ethically" to translating those words into action. WME honorees demonstrate real and sustained ethical leadership within their industries, putting into real business practice the credo of the Ethisphere Institute: "Good. Smart. Business. Profit."

The credo and the findings of the Ethisphere offer the sort of support

that public relations practitioners can use to represent the ethical concerns of media and ordinary folks who live outside the management bubble of major corporations. When a public relations person calls for ethical response to layoffs or environmental trade-offs or product recall on behalf of the many reporters and grassroots groups assailing the company, being able to argue that ethical behavior pays off at the bottom line is powerful backing.

Investing in ethics is beneficial for any company, even in a recession. Figure 17.2 compares the "WME Index" of all publicly traded 2010 World's Most Ethical Company honorees against two stock market indices since 2005. The ethical companies depicted in orange consistently outperformed the market every year.

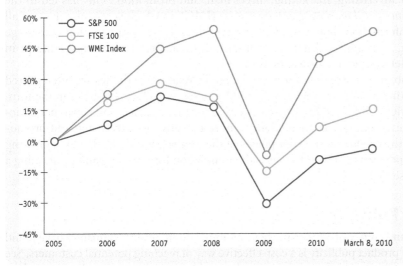

Figure 17.2   It Can Pay to Be Ethical

Source: Ethisphere Institute, 2010 report, www.ethisphere.com

regulations set down by the SEC on initial public offerings (IPOs) of corporate stock, mergers, accounting requirements, the contents of quarterly financial reports, and public disclosure of information. A company going public for the first time, for example, is required by the SEC to observe a "quiet period" in which company executives do not talk about the offering to analysts or the financial press so that they don't "hype" the stock.

Google's initial public offering (IPO) of its stock on the New York Stock Exchange had to be delayed because CEO and founder Marc Benioff had made some comments about the stock offering in a major magazine interview during the SEC's mandated "quiet period." The foul-up gave Google a rocky start in terms of positioning its stock and building a good impression among Wall Street analysts. See Chapter 12 for more information about the SEC.

Investor relations staff must be very comfortable with numbers, as they primarily communicate with institutional investors, individual investors, stockbrokers, and financial analysts. They are also sources of information for the financial press such as the *Wall Street Journal*, *Barron's*, *Bloomburg.com*, and the *Financial Times*. In their jobs, they make many presentations, conduct field trips for analysts and portfolio managers, analyze stockholder demographics, oversee corporate annual reports, and prepare materials for potential investors.

Marketing Communication

Many companies use the tools and tactics of public relations to support the marketing and sales objectives of their business. This is called *marketing communication* or *marketing public relations*.

Thomas L. Harris, author of *A Marketer's Guide to Public Relations*, defines marketing public relations (MPR) as "The process of planning, executing, and evaluating programs that encourage purchase and consumer satisfaction through credible communication of information and impressions that identify companies and their products with the needs, wants, concerns, and interests of consumers."

In many cases, marketing public relations is coordinated with a company's messages in advertising, marketing, direct mail, and promotion. This has led to the concept of *integrated marketing communication* (IMC), in which companies manage all sources of information about a product or service in order to ensure maximum message penetration. This approach was first discussed in Chapter 1 as a major concept in today's modern public relations practice.

In an integrated program, for example, public relations activities are often geared toward obtaining early awareness and credibility for a product. Publicity in the form of news stories builds credibility, excitement in the marketplace, and consumer anticipation. These messages make audiences more receptive to advertising and promotions about the product in the later phases of the campaign. Indeed, there is a growing body of support that public relations is the foundation for branding and positioning a product or service.

Product Publicity

As the cost and clutter of advertising have mounted dramatically, companies have found that creative product publicity is a cost-effective way of reaching potential customers. See page 405 in Chapter 15 for more on product publicity and branding. Even mundane household products, if presented properly, can be newsworthy and catch media attention.

Food & Wine magazine, along with America Online, announced to the world the survey results that the supermarket checkout line is the most popular choice of where to meet a mate. It also found that whipped cream is the sexiest food, but that chocolate mousse is better than sex. Product publicity can be generated in other ways. Old Bay Seasoning sponsors shrimp eating contests; Briggs & Stratton, which makes small engines for lawnmowers, compiles an annual top 10 list of beautiful lawns; Hershey Foods set a Guinness record by producing the world's largest Kiss—a chocolate candy that weighed several tons.

Product Placement

Product placement refers to the appearance of a product as part of a movie or television program, thereby helping to promote the brand. The Mercedes-Benz that the characters in the movie drive to the airport, the United Airlines flight that takes them to a destination, the Hilton where they stay, and the Grey Goose vodka martinis they drink in the bar are all examples of product placement.

Increasingly, product placements are the result of fees paid to film studios and television producers. Sometimes, there is a benefit to both parties. For example, when The Gap volunteers to provide the entire wardrobe for a television show, such a deal reduces the cost of production for the producer and at the same time gives the clothing firm high visibility. See Chapter 18 for more on entertainment and sports public relations.

According to Stuart Elliott and Julie Bosman, writing in the *New York Times*, opportunities to promote products inside television shows

> come in the form of what is called branded entertainment or product integration. They include mentioning brands in lines of dialogue, placing products in scenes so they are visible to viewers, and giving advertisers roles in plots of shows, whether it is a desperate housewife showing off a Buick and a shopping mall or a would be apprentice trying to sell a new flavor of Crest toothpaste.... The goal of branded entertainment is to expose ads to viewers in ways that are more difficult to zip through or zap the traditional commercials. Devices like digital video recorders and iPods are making it easier than ever to avoid or ignore conventional sales pitches.

Cause-Related Marketing

Companies in highly competitive fields, where there is little differentiation among products or services, often strive to stand out and enhance their reputation for CSR (corporate social responsibility) by engaging in *cause-related marketing*. In essence, this means that a profit-making company collaborates with a nonprofit organization to advance the latter's cause and, at the same time, increase the former's sales. A good example is Yoplait yogurt, which tells customers that 10 cents will be donated to support breast cancer research for each pink Yoplait lid customers send in.

> Never do it for publicity. Do it for building your business, your brand equity, and your stakeholder relations.
>
> *Cone/Roper research firm*

Companies supporting worthy causes have good customer support. One study, by Cone/Roper, found that 79 percent of Americans feel companies have a responsibility to support causes as part of their corporate citizenship. More important, 81 percent said they are likely to switch brands, when price and quality are equal, to support the brand that supports a cause.

American Express was not the first company to engage in cause-related marketing, but its success in raising money in 1984 to restore the aging Statue of Liberty and Ellis Island set a new benchmark for effectiveness. The company spent $6 million publicizing its program, in which one penny of every dollar spent on its credit cards would be donated to restoration efforts. American Express ended up raising $1.7 million for the cause. It also saw the use of its cards jump 28 percent, and applications for new cards increase 17 percent. In addition, the marketing campaign proved to be an excellent branding strategy that promoted an association in the public's mind between American Express and an American icon.

Selecting a charity or a cause to support involves strategic thinking. A chain of pet care stores, for example, would be better served by sponsoring projects with the

Humane Society of America than by contributing a percentage of its sales to the American Cancer Society. By the same token, a company such as Bristol-Myers Squibb that makes drugs to treat cancer would find a relationship with the American Cancer Society a good fit. Here are some tips for conducting cause-related marketing:

- Look for a cause related to your products or services or that exemplifies a product's quality.
- Consider causes that appeal to your primary customers.
- Choose a charity that doesn't already have multiple sponsors.
- Choose a local organization if the purpose is to build brand awareness for local franchises.
- Don't use cause-related efforts as a tactic to salvage your image after a major scandal; it usually backfires.
- Understand that association with a cause or nonprofit is a long-term commitment.
- Realize that additional budget must be spent to create public awareness and build brand recognition with the cause.

Corporate Sponsorships

A form of cause-related marketing is corporate sponsorship of various activities and events such as concerts, art exhibits, races, and scientific expeditions.

According to IEG, Inc. (www.sponsorship.com), companies annually spend about $10 billion sponsoring activities ranging from NASCAR races, the Kentucky Derby, the Academy Awards, PGA golf tournaments, and even the concert tour of Kelly Clarkson. Many of these events, unlike causes, are money-making operations in their own right, but a large part of the underwriting often comes from sponsorships provided by other corporations. Sports sponsorships are further discussed in Chapter 18.

Sponsored events offer four benefits:

1. They enhance the reputation and image of the sponsoring company through association.
2. They give product brands high visibility among key purchasing publics.
3. They provide a focal point for marketing efforts and sales campaigns.
4. They generate publicity and media coverage.

Sponsorships can be more cost effective than advertising. Visa International, for example, spends about $200,000 annually sponsoring the USA-Visa Decathlon Team, or about the price of a 30-second prime-time television commercial. Speedo, the swimwear manufacturer, sponsors the U.S. Olympic swim team, getting its name before millions of television viewers. At the Beijing Games, nearly 90 percent of the Olympic swimmers wore Speedo gear, which meant brand dominance in terms of sales.

Local stadiums and concert halls almost everywhere now have corporate names. Bank of America agreed to pay $7 million per year to put its name on the Carolina Panthers home stadium in Charlotte, North Carolina, until 2024. Federal Express is paying $7.6 million each year through 2025 for naming rights to FedEx Field, home of the Washington Redskins. In Philadelphia, Lincoln financial group, not exactly a household name, snapped up naming rights for the new stadium for the Eagles pro-football team. The company's reasoning: its name will become recognized as a major brand by those attending Eagles games and the 10 million fans who watch NFL games at home on television. By the same logic, the online-only University of Phoenix enrolls over 100,000 students at 200 locations, but has no traditional main campus. It does, however, have the University of Phoenix stadium, home of the NFL's Arizona Cardinals.

On occasion, a company will sponsor an event for the primary purpose of enhancing its reputation among opinion leaders and influential decision makers. Atofina Chemicals, for example, usually sponsored events and advanced science education. Nevertheless, it agreed to sponsor an exhibit of ballet-themed works by Dégas at the Philadelphia Art Museum to highlight the company's history as a Paris-based corporation. One objective of this sponsorship was to increase employee pride. The company's 1,200 employees in Philadelphia and their families were invited to an exclusive showing at the museum, where the exhibit was open to the public. In addition, the company used the exhibiting museum as its centerpiece for entertaining customers and their significant others. It also organized events for and donations of products to the Philadelphia High School for the Creative and Performing Arts.

Viral Marketing

Long before the rise of the Internet, professional communicators recognized the value of favorable recommendations and "buzz" about a product or service. For public relations programs, the primary objective has always been to enhance or maintain the reputation of the company or celebrity. Today, thanks to technology, "word of mouth" can be used to generate greater traffic to a website, where both marketing and public relations objectives can be met. The primary purpose of viral marketing is to stimulate impulse purchases or downloads, but increasingly, pass-it-on techniques on the Web are also intended to help public relations professionals meet goals for reputation management and message dissemination. Generating excitement about the release of a musician's latest CD and touting the opening of a movie are two common ways viral marketing is employed in the entertainment business. See the Insights box on page 462 about Ford's social media efforts.

Viral marketing has adopted a new terminology and some special techniques that take advantage of new technology to stimulate the natural inclination of people to tell others about a good deal, a good service, or a good group. One classic example of viral marketing is Burger King's subservient chicken website (www.subservientchicken.com), which was launched in 2004. The site features a human in a chicken suit who responds to whatever command the Web viewer types in. If a viewer tells the chicken to dance, it dances. If a viewer instructs it to jump, it jumps.

The connection to Burger King is twofold: (1) It plays on the restaurant's long-time slogan "Have it your way" and (2) it promotes the hamburger giant's chicken sandwich offerings. "The intent here is to speak specifically to young adults in their 20s and 30s," Burger King spokesperson Blake Lewis told the *Wall Street Journal*. "These are people that are very Internet savvy. They are very active. They may not mirror a lot of the traditional TV, newspaper, or radio consumption patterns that older adults have come to adopt." When the site was launched, only 20 people, friends of employees in the agency that created the campaign, were told about the website. From those 20 people, use of the site exploded exponentially, to the point that the site garnered 46 million hits in its first week of operation. The popularity of the subservient chicken spawned an Xbox game in 2006 and a Halloween costume in 2007. The chicken is still taking orders and spreading virally through a "Tell a Friend" feature on the company's website.

on the job

INSIGHTS

Building a More Social Ford

In 2009, car companies took a major hit in sales and reputation. Ford, the only domestic automaker to reject a government bailout, had an interesting story to tell and turned to social media to reach its audience, car buyers of any age or location.

Assembling a team of outside agencies, Ford sought to forge new relationships, improve the brand perception, and develop breakthrough social media programs. Ford and Ogilvy interacted with bloggers and online influencers using Twitter, YouTube, and other social media elements. It allowed drivers to experience multiple-day test drives, filming their experiences with flip cams.

Ford used social media to follow the Ford Fusion Hybrid 1000 Mile Challenge, demonstrating the car's fuel efficiency, and hosted tweet ups with Ford executives and events for blogging groups such as BlogHer. The campaign was wide reaching, engaging with more than 300 bloggers and gaining nearly 70,000 online views of Ford-branded multimedia content.

This change in communication strategy was met positively with a *PRWeek* 2010 Award for Social Media. One judge of the *PRWeek* awards called the effort a "game changing effort that has become part of the fabric of the company."

During the campaign, Ford saw its image evolve from "boring gas guzzlers" to "innovative" and "forward

thinking." Additionally, Ford research found that, prior to the campaign, an average of 29 percent of bloggers would've considered purchasing a Ford. Post-campaign, that number jumped to 89 percent. As a matter of fact, social media promotion of the

Ford Fiesta, a sprightly new fuel-efficient model targeted to younger drivers, actually received significant numbers of online preorders of the vehicle, sight unseen—not counting the thousands of virtual sightings by virtual customers.

Some viral marketing firms devise ways to stimulate the natural spread of recommendations through financial incentives called cohort communication. Going beyond the relatively organic spread of information via tactics such as Burger King's "Tell a Friend" feature, viral marketing specialists use more calculated tactics such as careful dissemination of favorable reviews. Software systems track referrals to a website or recommendations sent to friends, with senders chalking up cash or merchandise credits. Recommending a CD to friends might earn the recommender credit or free downloads of music tracks, for example.

Detractors worry that viral marketing is too easily recognizable as commercial manipulation, except among hard-core enthusiasts. Others say that it is deceptive and unethical to facilitate or reward what should be a natural process of trusted friends exchanging tips and links about great deals or great websites. When the music industry, for example, recruits fans to log on to chat rooms and fan websites to hype a band's new album, some liken the process to the questionable practice of "payola" in the radio industry, in which disc jockeys are paid to play certain tracks.

Viral marketing companies argue that the technique will work only when the idea, the movement, or the product earns genuine support from the marketplace. Public relations professionals need to make careful and ethical decisions to decide how best to use the Web to spread messages. The fairly staid Microsoft marketing people created a suggestive online video with hopes for a viral spread of buzz about the company's new Kin mobile phone. A young man in a soft focus video puts a camera under his shirt, snaps a shot of his chest, and sends the photo to a young woman. The video certainly caught the attention of critics, who felt it verged on the promotion of sexting, a worrisome activity among some teens sharing a little too much of themselves.

To explore viral marketing and to consider how to adapt techniques to your own public relations activities on campus, visit the websites for the following viral marketing companies:

Caffeine Online Marketing Solutions	www.getcaffeinated.com
Mindcomet	www.mindcomet.com
Oddcast	www.oddcast.com

Environmental Relations

Another aspect of corporate responsibility that is gaining momentum is corporate concern for the environment and sustainable resources. The end of the 20th century witnessed major clashes between corporations and activist nongovernmental organizations (NGOs) about a host of environmental and human rights issues. See page 534 in Chapter 20 for more on NGOs. The current trend, however, favors cooperation and partnerships among these former adversaries. Many companies, such as Shell, now issue annual corporate responsibility reports and work with environmental groups to clean up the environment, preserve wilderness areas, and restore exploited natural resources. See the Multicultural World box on page 464 for the worldwide greening of business.

Take American Apparel, a clothing company founded by Dov Charney, which has long been known for its activism. Both the company and Charney have been plagued

A MULTICULTURAL WORLD

Green Keeps Global Corporations in the Black

Here are an all-too-common head and subhead for a newspaper story:

"Green moves help keep corporations in the black

Eco-friendly ideas not just a PR stunt

CINCINNATI (AP)"

When a reporter combines the words "PR" and "stunt," conscientious public relations professionals wince. When laudable, constructive, actual behavior of a corporation is reflected in a special event, promotion, news release, or groundbreaking/ribbon cutting, it is not a stunt, it's just good "PR" in support of good behavior.

In recent years, going green has become good business when it's based on good behavior. Sales of green products such as organic foods and natural personal care items have jumped 15 percent since 2006, according to research from Minitel International. Public relations staffs are staying very busy telling the green story about their companies.

Hanes says it can put you in eco-friendly underwear, Frito-Lay offers some chips from a bag you can toss in the compost pile, and Target stores invite you to use their recycling bins.

Some of this may be image buffing for a pale green performance, but

environmentalists say that corporations, the major drivers of American consumer culture, are starting to make real strides. "It's a far cry from where we were," says Elizabeth Sturkin, manager of corporate partnerships for the Environmental Defense Fund.

The green revolution goes beyond just product offerings. The companies themselves are cutting lighting and heating costs, using less packaging, streamlining transportation to save gas, recycling more instead of throwing away.

According to the editor of Greener World Media, ". . . Most big companies have been taking significant steps. The fact is they're doing it for all the right business reasons."

"The behemoth that might drive even more serious improvements is retailer Wal-Mart stores Inc.," according to the AP. Wal-Mart is urging suppliers to reduce 20 million metric tons of greenhouse gas emissions by the end of 2015, on top of its own moves to build more energy-efficient stores, use more alternative fuels in its trucks, and reduce packaging. Wal-Mart says it is not only earth friendly, but remains wallet friendly, passing along the savings from energy efficiency to its customers.

Fellow behemoth Procter & Gamble has begun a major sustainability drive within its organization. The company

focuses on finding new uses for manufacturing byproducts that would normally go into incinerators and landfills. "So now, Clairol hair color ingredients help make tires shine, Duracell batteries help make bricks, and materials from Pampers diapers and Always maxi pads absorb industrial leaks and spills."

One area where product makers still need to improve, activists say, is in telling consumers in detail about ingredients so they can make their own decisions. Another problem is touting the product as green when it may have only one natural or organic ingredient that really qualifies. In other words, there is still too much greenwashing out there—the covering up of questionable environmental records with glitz and product marketing. Public relations professionals can play a key role in shaping corporate policies so that boomerang effects are avoided when customers see through the greenwash. Providing warnings against backlash makes the public relations professional a key management leader in ensuring that companies avoid phony green initiatives. Ironically, one of those most interested in avoiding "PR stunts" is the public relations person.

by negative press surrounding sexual harassment lawsuits filed against the company. In addition, American Apparel's public image has been forged through controversial, edgy advertising campaigns that some critics believe to be in questionable taste. Offsetting the sometimes negative press that has dogged the company, however, is the positive publicity generated by its exemplary social and environmental policies.

In 2009, *Apparel* magazine named American Apparel as one of the first Sustainability All-Star Award winners. Among the environmentally friendly steps taken by the company is the development of a product line made entirely from the scraps of material that are byproducts of manufacturing. These scraps are made into headbands and belts rather than sent to the landfill. The scraps are also made into underwear. This program recycles approximately 30,000 pounds of cotton per week.

According to American Apparel spokesperson Ryan Holiday, "We weren't thinking: 'How do we save the environment?' We were thinking: 'How can we do something fashionable with all these scraps? It's not an act of charity, because the belts make money." American Apparel offers a Sustainable Edition of its clothing as well. The sustainable line is made of 100 percent organic and certified pesticide-free cotton. And the company does not stop there: it generates 20 to 30 percent of its energy from solar panels, and it recycles cardboard boxes and cell phones. Timers and motion sensors save electricity in unused rooms. Employees are encouraged to use company bicycles to peddle back and forth to work. They are also supplied with bus passes to limit their driving.

Other large corporations around the world are forging alliances with various NGOs to preserve the environment, promote human rights, and provide social/medical services. The following are some examples of long-term CSR programs:

- The Royal Dutch/Shell Group wants to abolish child labor. Shell companies in 112 nations have procedures in place to prevent the use of child labor.

- Unilever, the food and consumer products company, is helping to restore a dying river estuary in the Philippines. The campaign is one of several programs in the company's global Water Sustainability Initiative.

- Volvo Corporation is working with the UN High Commissioner for Human Rights on a project addressing discrimination in the workplace.

- LM Ericsson, a Swedish telecommunication company, has a program to provide and maintain mobile communication equipment and expertise for humanitarian relief operations.

- Merck, the pharmaceutical giant, is a partner with the Bill and Melinda Gates Foundation on a five-year AIDS project in Botswana and is selling its drugs at cost in developing nations.

Corporate Philanthropy

Another manifestation of CSR is *corporate philanthropy*, the donation of funds, products, and services to various causes. Donations range from providing uniforms and equipment to a local Little League baseball team to a multimillion-dollar donation to a university for upgrading its programs in science and engineering. In many cases, the organization's public relations department handles corporate charitable giving as part of its responsibilities.

American corporations gave $15.4 billion in 2008 to a variety of causes. Although there is a common perception that corporate philanthropy provides the lion's share of donations, the actual percentage is very small. Of the total $308 billion given in 2008, only 5 percent was from corporations. The largest amount of money given, 75 percent, was given by individuals. See Chapter 21, on nonprofits, for more information on charitable contributions.

Corporations, of course, have long used philanthropy to demonstrate community goodwill and to polish their reputations as good citizens. There's also evidence that corporate giving is good for business and retaining customers, with 76 percent of Americans claiming to take corporate citizenship into consideration when purchasing products. At the same time, 76 percent believe that companies participate in philanthropic activities to get favorable publicity, and only 24 percent believe corporations are truly committed to the causes they support.

Getting good publicity, no doubt, is a factor in philanthropy, but companies should not view this as the ultimate objective of being charitable. The survey organization Cone/Roper says companies should be very careful about bragging about their good deeds, because the public will be skeptical about the motivation. Instead, companies should concentrate on the people they help, and the programs they showcase should be more than "window dressing." The research firm further states, "Never do it for publicity. Do it for building your business, your brand equity, and your stakeholder relations."

It also should be noted that companies don't donate to just anything and everything. A series of small grants to a wide variety of causes doesn't really help any particular charity, and it dilutes the impact of the contributions. Home Banc Mortgage Corporation, for example, used to give $300,000 annually in small grants to a variety of causes, but it eventually realized that the available funds could have more impact (and visibility) if it heavily funded just one or two causes. Consequently, the company now gives most of its charitable funds to Habitat for Humanity, a nonprofit that builds homes for low-income families.

In Home Banc's case, funding Habitat for Humanity is a strategic decision to funnel contributions into a cause directly related to home ownership, which is the business of the mortgage company. HP also is strategic in deciding where to place its charitable contributions. It contributes considerable money to a scholarship program and summer jobs for minority and female engineering and computer science majors. In another major initiative, HP gives its computers, medical equipment, and test equipment to institutions of higher learning. The company's giving philosophy is clearly stated: "HP giving to colleges and universities meets university needs for products while attracting higher skilled workers to the industries we support."

Strategic philanthropy is defined by Paul Davis Jones and Cary Raymond of IDPR Group as "the long-term socially responsible contribution of dollars, volunteers, products, and expertise to a cause aligned with the strategic business goals of an organization." Such giving, they say, can reap a number of benefits for the corporation, including:

- Strengthened reputation and brand recognition
- Increased media opportunities
- Improved community and government relations
- Facilitation of employee recruitment and retention
- Enhanced marketing

- Access to research and development
- Increased corporate profitability

Corporate philanthropy, despite its potential benefits, does have its limitations. A large grant by a corporation, for example, cannot offset a major financial scandal or the negative publicity of a class-action suit for discrimination of female employees. Philanthropy, as Philip Morris found out, also can't erase public concern about the promotion and marketing of tobacco products. Wal-Mart, faced with community opposition to "big-box" stores, probably won't change its opponents' minds by giving several million dollars to local schools.

Another downside to corporate philanthropy can arise when special interest groups object to the cause that's being funded. Pro-life groups, for example, often target companies that give grants to Planned Parenthood and ask their supporters to boycott the company's products. Bank of America was caught in a controversy when it decided to stop funding the Boy Scouts of America because of the group's refusal to admit gays. Although gay activists were pleased by the decision, a storm of protest arose from bank customers who supported the Boy Scouts. Many canceled their accounts and encouraged others to do the same.

According to Paul Holmes in a *PRWeek* column, there's even a Washington, D.C., group called the Capital Research Center that seeks to "end the liberal bias in corporate philanthropy." The group objects to company donations to "antibusiness" charities such as the National Wildlife Federation.

All this leaves corporations somewhat in a quandary about what charities are "safe" and which ones might raise controversy and protests at annual stockholder meetings. There's also the consideration of what special groups are most influential or have the ability to cause headaches for the corporation through boycotts, pickets, and demonstrations. In bottom-line terms, the corporation also thinks about what decision would be best to keep its overall customer base. For example, pro-life groups had originally forced Dayton-Hudson Corporation, a department store chain, to cancel its contributions to Planned Parenthood, but the company reversed its decision after hundreds of irate customers sent in cut-up credit cards.

Despite the possible downsides and controversies, corporate philanthropy is a good tool for enhancing reputation, building relationships with key audiences, and increasing employee and customer loyalty. It also serves the public interest in many ways.

Summary

Today's Modern Corporation

- Giant corporations have operations and customers around the globe.

- The public is often distrustful of these large entities because of their perceived wealth and power.

- Corporate financial scandals in recent years have further eroded public trust.

- Corporations must make special efforts to win back their credibility and the public's trust, and to tell the story of what corporations contribute to quality of life.

- The concept of corporate social responsibility (CSR) is high on the list of public relations priorities.

- Public relations plays a role in corporate transparency and ethical principles of conduct to improve corporate governance.

Media Relations

- The public's perception of business comes primarily from the mass media.

- Corporations must build a rapport with business editors and reporters by being accessible, open, and honest about company operations and policies.

Customer Relations

- Customer service, in many ways, is the front line of public relations.

- Customer satisfaction is important for building loyalty and telling others about the product or the reputation of the company.

- Public relations professionals solicit customer feedback as often as possible and act to satisfy customers' needs for communication and service.

- The U.S. population is becoming more diverse.

- Companies are now establishing communication programs, as well as marketing strategies, to serve this growing diverse audience.

- Special interest groups exert pressure on corporations to be socially responsible.

- Companies cannot avoid activist groups; they must engage in dialogue with them to work out differences.

- Consumer boycotts also require public relations expertise to deal effectively with a group's demands.

Employee Relations

- Employees are the "ambassadors" of a company and are the primary source of information about the company.

- Employee morale is important, and a good communication program does much to maintain high productivity and employee retention.

- The cardinal rule of corporate communications is to first talk to employees in person before announcing a layoff to the public.

- Many companies ease the impact of a layoff by providing a severance package.

- Offshoring is a rising concern of American workers, and companies must be sensitive to possible criticism.

Investor Relations

- Public relations professionals who work in investor relations must be knowledgeable about communication and finance.

- This highest-paying field in public relations requires extensive knowledge of government regulations.

Marketing Communication

- Companies often take an integrated approach to campaigns, with public relations, marketing, and advertising staffs working together to complement each other's expertise.

- Product publicity and product placement are part of marketing communication.

- Cause-related marketing involves partnerships with nonprofit organizations to promote a particular cause.

- Another aspect of marketing communication is corporate sponsorships.

Environmental Relations

- A new trend line is for corporations and activist organizations to have a dialogue and engage in collaborative efforts to change situations that damage the environment or violate human rights.

Corporate Philanthropy

- Companies give about $15 billion a year to worthy causes.

- Corporations select a charity that is complementary to their business and customer profile.

- Corporate philanthropy is part of an organization's commitment to be socially responsible.

Case Activity   PR in Maquiladora Zone Factories

You've just begun work with a global corporation that operates a number of factories in maquiladora zones along the U.S. border with Mexico. The manufacturer's home offices are located in Chicago, but because of your Spanish-language major and your two internships with Latin American companies, you've been hired to do public relations in the Mexico City office that handles plant communication for the four plants along the Texas border and the two

plants along the California border. How will you prepare for this assignment? What do you need to know about the company, its operations, and its relationship with key stakeholders in Mexico and the United States? Who are the key stakeholders? Make a "to do" list for yourself to help you effectively prepare for your new job and hit the ground running when you relocate to Mexico.

Questions   For Review and Discussion

1. What is the concept of corporate social responsibility (CSR), and why is it important to today's corporations? What is the role of public relations professionals in this concept?

2. Corporate executives indicate that they are wary of the media. What reasons do they give? Do you think their concerns are valid? Journalists also are critical of business executives. What are their complaints?

3. Why is it important for corporate executives to have a good relationship with the mass media?

4. Why is it important for companies to consider diversity in their marketing and public relations strategies?

5. If an activist group has called for the boycott of a particular company's products, would you be inclined to stop buying the company's products? Why or why not?

6. Why is employee relations so important to a company's image and reputation?

7. How should a company tell its employees about a layoff?

8. Give some examples of product publicity and product placement.

9. What is cause-related marketing? Give some examples.

10. Give four reasons why corporate sponsorship of concerts, festivals, and even the Olympics is considered a good marketing and public relations strategy.

11. Corporate philanthropy is now strategic. Do you think this makes corporate philanthropy too self-serving? Why or why not?

Media Resources

Bowen, S. (2010, Winter). An examination of applied ethics and stakeholder management on top corporate websites. *Public Relations Journal, 4*(1). Retrieved from www.prsa.org

Davis, A. (2010, March 5). How communications can re-engage employees. *The Public Relations Strategist.* Retrieved from www.prsa.org

Duhé, S. C. (2009). Good management, sound finances, and social responsibility: Two decades of U.S. corporate insider perspectives on reputation and the bottom line. *Public Relations Review, 35*(1), 77–78.

Fathi, S. (2009, September). When good companies give bad tweets. *O'Dwyer's PR Report,* 29.

Gable, T. (2009, June 12). Image as part of corporate strategy: Building reputation and results for any business. *The Public Relations Strategist.* Retrieved from www.prsa.org

Grupp, R. W. (2010, April 12). Trends in trust—a call to action. Retrieved from Institute for Public Relations website: www.instituteforpr.org

Heath, R. L., & Ni, L. (2010, April 8). Corporate social responsibility: Different fabrics. Retrieved from Institute for Public Relations' Essential Knowledge Project website: www.instituteforpr.org

Jacques, A. (2009, October 24). Domino's delivers during crisis: The company's step-by-step response after a vulgar video goes viral. *The Public Relations Strategist.* Retrieved from www.prsa.org

Keath, J. (2010, June). 21 unique location examples from Foursquare, Gowalla, Whrrl, and MyTown. Retrieved from www.socialfresh.com

Kelly, K. S., Laskin, A. V., & Rosenstein, G. A. (2010). Investor relations: Two-way symmetrical practice. *Journal of Public Relations Research, 22*(2), 182–208.

Kim, S.-Y., & Reber, B. H. (2008). Public relations' place in corporate social responsibility: Practitioners define their role. *Public Relations Review, 34*(4), 337–342.

Mackey, S. (2010). The original bailout of U.S. corporations: The public relations bailout. *Public Relations Review, 36*(1), pp. 1–6.

Quenqua, D. (2010, June 1). Public ire demands account for excessive CEO payments. Retrieved from www.prweekus.com

Schock, N. (2010, January 6). Communicate your environmental achievements in the new year. *Public Relations Tactics.* Retrieved from www.prsa.org

Williams, S. (2009, February 9). How PR can help solve the executive compensation riddle. Retrieved from Institute for Public Relations website: www.instituteforpr.org

18

Entertainment, Sports, and Tourism

Tiger Woods used a press conference to apologize to his fans and business partners for his unacceptable behaviors.

After reading this chapter, you will be able to:

Understand the role of public relations in the entertainment industry and the opportunities for employment

Describe the nature of celebrity culture and how publicists and media create celebrities

Use techniques to promote a play, concert, or other entertainment event

Outline the tactics used by public relations staff to promote a sports team

Describe the work of public relations personnel in the tourism industry

A Major Part of the American Economy

Many public relations specialists work for corporations, which was discussed in the last chapter, but a large number are also attracted to the more glamorous fields of entertainment, sports, and tourism. Indeed, these industries are a major part of the American economy and compete in the marketplace for the disposable income of virtually all Americans.

The scale of the entertainment and recreation industries is reflected in some general statistics:

- Attendance at movies in 2009 generated about $10 billion in revenues for the film industry.
- The Academy Awards, started during the 1929 depression as a way to promote movie attendance, continues to draw a TV audience of 30 million every year.
- The Super Bowl, originally designed to extend the football season and generate more revenue, had a TV audience of 116 million in 2010.
- Fans, even in the 2009 recession, plunked down $4.4 billion to attend concerts in North America.
- Sales of albums, despite iTunes and other digital downloads, generated almost $400 million in 2009.
- In the 2008 racing season, 400 companies put up more than $1.5 billion to sponsor races, cars, and drivers. NASCAR alone had revenues of $3 billion that year.
- Corporate sponsors of the Beijing Olympics paid almost $1 billion in sponsorship fees. Broadcasters paid $1.7 billion to televise the games.
- The hotel industry in the United States is a $135 billion business.
- Cruise lines are a $40 billion industry and generate more than 350,000 jobs.
- Fifty-eight million overseas visitors came to the United States in 2008.

Corporations and other organizations offering a wide array of activities and venues expend considerable amounts of money on advertising, marketing, and public relations to attract customers. This chapter gives an overview of entertainment, sports, and tourism and the vital role that public relations specialists play in these industries' success. It also discusses how public relations tactics are used to promote a variety of recreational activities and some of the challenges that public relations personnel must overcome in their work.

Celebrities, however, are a major component of the entertainment and sports industries, so this chapter begins with an exploration of today's celebrity culture and how publicists, with the help of the media, are instrumental in creating and promoting celebrities.

The Cult of Celebrity

According to historian Daniel Boorstin, a celebrity can be defined as a person well known in one of a wide variety of fields such as science, politics, or entertainment. In other words, anyone well known such as Barack Obama or the Pope can be considered a celebrity. Being a celebrity today, however, doesn't necessarily mean that it's based on some sort of outstanding achievement or accomplishment.

Cleveland Amory made that distinction more than a half-century ago as editor of the book *Celebrity Register*. He said that celebrity covers a multitude of sins and "It doesn't mean, for example, accomplishment in the sense of true or lasting worth—rather it often means simply accomplishment in the sense of popular, or highly publicized, temporary success."

The entertainment industry, in particular, is fueled by the constant publicizing and glorification of personalities. Individuals such as movie stars, pop music divas, television personalities, and talk show hosts generate a great deal of publicity in the media and on the Web, but today's celebrity status is often only temporary, as there are continually new celebrities who try to take the place of established celebrities in the public's esteem and interest.

> The advent of celebrity culture now drives the entertainment news cycle.
>
> *Rachel McCallister and Mark Pogachefsky, writing in* Public Relations Tactics

Stephen Cave, reviewing a number of books about fame and celebrity in the *Financial Times*, makes several observations. First, he says, "Fame is a product of certain industries—most notably the mass entertainment business—not a gold star given by the good fairy to the deserving." He goes on, "Fame is not what it used to be. Once it was granted to those who did something useful like discover gravity or win a world war. Now it is heaped on anyone who is runner-up in a television talent show, subsequently strips for a lads' magazine, then writes their life story age 25 while on day-release from rehab."

Cave says Paris Hilton is probably the poster child of today's celebrity culture. He observes:

> Although she is one of the most Googled people on earth, nobody can quite remember why we're interested in her. Guinness World Records lists her as the most overrated celebrity, but it's not even clear what she's overrated at. If you believe the pundits, she is the embodiment of our vacuous age, the bare-breasted figurehead at the prow of a booze-cruise party boat adrift without a moral compass.

Such criticism of today's celebrity culture is not particularly new. Francis Bacon wrote 400 years ago that "fame is like a river that beareth up things light and swollen, and drowns things weighty and solid." But what makes today's celebrity culture different, says Cave, is modern communications. He writes, "The fame trade has radically changed. The rise of instant communications, digital media, and mass literacy has all fueled the market for stars. Dedicated TV channels, websites, and magazines such as Heat and People have exponentially increased the speed and volume of celebrity gossip—and the number of celebrities."

An example of the media's fixation on celebrity was the coverage of the death of pop star Michael Jackson in mid-2009. In the 24 hours after his death, the Pew Research Center for Excellence in Journalism found that 60 percent of the total news coverage was devoted to his death, his life story, and his legacy. The coverage eclipsed all other major news stories such as health care reform, major political violence in Iran, the greenhouse gas bill, and even the saga of another instant celebrity, Governor Mark Sanford of South Carolina, who admitted that he was not really on a hiking trip but in Argentina having an affair.

The media's explanation for the wall-to-wall coverage of Jackson's death was that the public was highly interested in the story. Indeed, one survey indicated that almost 60 percent of Americans said they followed the story "very closely" or "fairly closely." At the same time, in a somewhat contradictory manner, 66 percent also said that the media gave too much coverage.

The three-hour memorial service for Jackson at Staples Center in Los Angeles, however, seemed to confirm the media's assessment that there was tremendous public interest in the story. The *New York Times* dubbed it "one of the most watched farewells in history" because the service attracted a television audience of 31 million and almost 8 million online viewers. Later that day, 20 million watched the prime-time specials offered by the major TV networks.

The massive coverage of Jackson's death and memorial service caused some to ruminate about fame and celebrity in America. Congressman Peter T. King (R-New York) was quoted in a YouTube video as saying, ". . . giving this much coverage to him, day in and day out, what does it say about us as a country?" And a newspaper columnist thought it was ironic that no one remembers that astronaut Gene Cernan was the last person to walk on the moon, whereas another "moon-walker" is a household name.

The death of a celebrity, particularly under unusual circumstances, generates massive media coverage, but so does the birth of a child to the "right" celebrity couple. Angelina Jolie and Brad Pitt, for example, received $14 million from *People* magazine for an exclusive interview and photos of their newborn twins in 2008. It was the best-selling issue of *People* in seven years. Earlier, the magazine had scored another exclusive and a spike in sales by paying Jennifer Lopez $6 million for exclusive photos of her twins.

The Public's Fascination with Celebrities

Psychologists offer varied explanations of why the public becomes impressed—"fascinated" might be the more accurate word—by highly publicized individuals. In pretelevision days, the publicity departments of the motion picture studios promoted their male and female stars as glamorous figures that lived in a special world of privilege and wealth. The studios catered to the universal need for fairy tales, which often have a rags-to-riches theme. Dreaming of achieving such glory for themselves, young people with and without talent go to Hollywood to try to crash through the magical gates, almost always in vain.

Many ordinary people leading routine lives also yearn for heroes. Professional and big-time college sports provide personalities for hero worship. Publicists emphasize the performances of certain players, and television sports announcers often build up the stars' roles out of proportion to their actual achievements; this emphasis creates hero figures for youthful sports enthusiasts to emulate. Syndicated gossip columnist Liz Smith once tried to explain the American cult of personality by saying, "Maybe it's because we all want someone to look up to or spit on, and we don't have royalty."

In addition to admiration for individual performers, members of the public develop a vicarious sense of belonging that creates support for athletic teams. Sports publicists exploit this feeling in numerous ways. A winning baseball team becomes "our" team in conversations among patrons of a bar. To signify their loyalty, children and adults alike wear baseball caps bearing the insignia of their favorite Major League teams. It isn't surprising that alumni of a university gnaw their fingernails while watching their school basketball team in a tight game, but the same intensity of support is found among fans who have no direct tie to the school.

> The hero is distinguished by his achievement; the celebrity by his image or trademark. The hero created himself; the celebrity is created by media. The hero is a big man; the celebrity is a big name.
>
> *Daniel Boorstin, author of* The Image: A Guide to Pseudo-Events in America, *1961*

Still another factor behind the public's fascination is the desire for entertainment. Reading fan magazines or listening to TMZ report on the personal lives and troubles of celebrities gives fans a look behind the curtain of celebrity. Such intimate details provide fuel for discussion among friends or even something to Tweet about. Even lining up in front of a box office hours before it opens to get a ticket to a championship game or a popular concert brings variety and a little excitement to the daily routine of life.

A public relations practitioner assigned to build up the public image of an individual should analyze the ways in which these psychological factors can be applied. Because the client's cooperation is vital in promotional work, a wise publicist explains this background and tells the client why various actions are planned.

The Work of a Publicist

A public relations practitioner working in the entertainment industry is usually called a *publicist* because his or her primary responsibility is getting publicity in the media for his or her organizations and individual clients. In the early days of public relations, which were discussed in Chapter 2, many of these individuals were called *press agents*.

In fact, the term *press agent* is still used on Broadway, and the union representing them is called the Association of Theatrical Press Agents and Managers. Ralph Blumenthal, a reporter for the *New York Times*, explains the basic process in the early days: "Broadway producers hired press agents to type out news releases about their shows and hand-carry them to the press so the press would write stories about the shows and people would buy the papers, read the stories and go to the shows, and the producers would be happy and the press agents would keep their job."

Press agents also dreamed up creative stunts to get publicity. David Merrick's *Look Back in Anger* wasn't doing too well at the box office so his press agent hired a woman in the audience to storm the stage and slap the leading actor. Another press agent, Jim Moran, was famous for his media-grabbing stunts. He publicized the book *The Egg and I* by sitting on an ostrich egg for 19 days until it hatched. On another occasion, he led a bull through a china shop to help the flagging career of an actor.

Hollywood publicists were also creative at generating publicity. Fox Studios insured Betty Grable's legs for $1 million in 1943. Mark Borkowski, owner of an entertainment public relations firm in Los Angeles, recounts a number of publicist exploits in his book *The Fame Factory: How Hollywood's Fixers, Fakers, and Star Makers Created the Celebrity Industry*. He says the role of publicists was maintaining Hollywood's fairy-tale image, despite the stars' real lives, which were fueled by sex and drugs.

According to Borkowski, publicists had as much trouble keeping their charges out of the news as in it. Fabricated biographies were the norm. Actor Micky Rooney later confessed that he had been "collecting blondes, brunettes, and redheads" when the studio claimed he was "collecting stamps, coins, and matchboxes." According to Stephen Cave's review of Borkowski's book, "The best paid publicists spent their time arranging back-street abortions, covering up affairs, and making suicide attempts look like gardening accidents."

Today's publicists tend to avoid the antics of Hollywood's "golden era." In fact, Howard Bragman writes in his book *Where's My 15 Minutes* that "A good PR person monitors the relationship between perception and reality and keeps things in check." However, while today's entertainment publicists still work to put a positive "spin" on the foibles of their celebrity clients, their tactics are more sophisticated in the age of the Internet. Borkowski, for example, says modern communications has "...killed off the ability to lie so freely." In other words, the intense scrutiny of traditional media, blogs, and entertainment websites makes it difficult to cover up damaging information.

Mel Gibson, for example, was picked up for drunken driving and allegedly made anti-Semitic comments to arresting officers, which was extensively reported within hours. His tirades and alleged physical abuse of his former wife in 2010 caused another round of negative publicity. And Lindsay Lohan's problems with alcohol and rehab are practically daily news items. But reputational damage can be minimized if celebrities listen to seasoned public relations counselors. Rubenstein Communications, for example, advised David Letterman when reports started to circulate that he was being blackmailed by another CBS staffer for having sex with members of his female staff. Letterman rapidly acknowledged the affairs and apologized on the air to his staff, fans, and wife for his transgressions. Tiger Woods took a different approach, with more distastrous results, which is highlighted in the PR Casebook on page 476.

Angelina Jolie was also able to overcome a potential public relations crisis when she became romantically involved with Brad Pitt. The fear was that the tabloid press would portray her as a predator who stole Pitt from his wife, Jennifer Aniston. According to the *New York Times*, Jolie's charitable work helped change the story. She and Pitt went to Pakistan, where she visited Afghan refugees, and then went on to Kashmir to bring attention to earthquake victims. According to Michael Levine, a celebrity publicist, "Presto, they come out looking like serious people who have transformed a silly press obsession into a sincere attempt to help the needy."

Crisis communications on behalf of superstars is one aspect of entertainment public relations, but rank-and-file entertainment publicists in New York and Los Angeles spend most of their working days doing more routine activities. Many work for film studios to generate publicity and buzz for new films. Paramount, for example, relied almost exclusively on publicists to generate fan interest on blogs and in traditional media for its horror film *Paranormal Activity*. And Univeral Pictures bolstered coverage for its *Couples Retreat* by taking newspaper and TV reporters on a lavish junket to Bora Bora, where the film was being shot. When 20th Century Fox released the DVD for *Ice Age: Dawn of the Dinosaurs*, publicists invited reporters to witness the construction of a 48-foot-tall ice sculpture resembling the star of the movie, Scrat the squirrel.

Loads of give-aways to the media are also standard in the TV and movie business. Walt Disney, for example, shipped jars filled with 90 toy soldiers to promote *Toy Story 3*. For the film *The Princess and the Frog*, which was set in New Orleans, the studio sent reporters one-pound boxes of beignet mix.

Brooks Barnes, writing in the *New York Times*, notes that "social networks like Facebook and Twitter have also changed the publicity game in Hollywood." She continues, "The PR apparatus has largely assumed the responsibility of monitoring, shaping, and creating attention on that part of the Web. Movie characters now have Twitter profiles and Facebook pages, for instance. Guess who updates the accounts?"

Teams of digital publicists also pay great attention to the hundreds of bloggers that cover the entertainment industry. Publicists issue bulletins on practically every detail of a movie being made, but they are also responsible for monitoring bloggers to find

PRCasebook

Tiger Tees Off His Fans and Sponsors

Sports, entertainment, and celebrity are intertwined. Never was that more obvious than when the world's most marketable sports personality, Tiger Woods, fell from grace as a result of an odd, 2:25 A.M. auto accident on Thanksgiving weekend of 2009.

Following the accident, in which Woods' wife, Elin Nodegren, was reported to have used a golf club to break a window in his Cadillac Escalade to rescue an unconscious Woods, rumors quickly circulated. Investigators said alcohol was not involved. Instead, a marital dispute was posited as the possible cause of the accident. Woods initially refused to talk with Florida Highway Patrol investigators, which fueled even more speculation and rumor about what had actually happened. In fact, in the 36 hours after the accident, more than 3,000 news stories were published worldwide in print and electronic form.

Such extensive media coverage reminded Sam Tanenhaus, writing in the *New York Times*, of historian Daniel Boorstin's statement about the power of the media to shape perceptions. Boorstin wrote in 1961, "The very agency which first makes the celebrity in the long run inevitably destroys him. He will be destroyed, as he was made, by publicity. The newspapers make him, and they unmake him."

Three days after the "Escalade escapade," as the *Christian Science Monitor* dubbed it, Woods dropped out of a tournament that benefited his Tiger Woods Foundation—and news reports of his infidelity began to surface. By early 2010, the number of "alleged paramours" had reached 14, and *Vanity Fair* predicted that it was "a figure bound to multiply." A *USA Today*/Gallup poll showed that what in 2005 had been Woods' 87 percent approval had now dropped to 33 percent following the accident and allegations of infidelity. According to the Davie-Brown Index, which tracks America's esteem for celebrities, Woods fell from No. 9 to No. 2,411 in a matter of days. Tiger's once-golden reputation was in a tailspin.

Woods' initial public relations strategy was to lie low. On his website he wrote, "This situation is my fault, and it's obviously embarrassing to my family and me. . . . This is a private matter and I want to keep it that way."

However, the statements on his website failed to quell the public's and the media's fascination with the story, and Woods remained reclusive as several corporate sponsors, such as Accenture, Gillette, and AT&T, dropped him like a hot potato. Other sponsors such as Nike adopted a wait-and-see attitude. Woods, who had earned $100 million annually in endorsements before the accident, saw his endorsement deals dwindle in a matter of weeks.

Experts in crisis communications faulted Tiger's team of advisors, mostly lawyers, for stonewalling the media and not taking control of the situation within the first 24 hours. In fact, Kevin McCauley, writing in *O'Dwyer's PR Report*, said, "The Tiger Woods sex scandal will go down in PR history as a classic example of a crisis made worse by poor communications." The recommended strategy in such situations is to immediately admit transgressions, sincerely apologize, promise to do better, and then move on.

It wasn't until February 2010, however, that Woods finally appeared in public and gave a 15-minute statement that was broadcast via video feed around the world. It was billed as a "news conference," but the only people in the room were his friends and supporters. Reporters were allowed to watch the video but couldn't ask any questions. This caused more media criticism of Woods, but communications consultant Howard Rubenstein told the *Wall Street Journal*, "It was a good but tiny baby step toward an image rehabilitation job."

In March, the embattled golfer hired Ari Fleischer, former press secretary to President Bush, and now owner of a sports communications firm. Fleischer, who also advised disgraced slugger Mark McGwire to admit use of steroids, helped Woods plan his return to golf in April by having an actual news conference at the beginning of the Master's Tournament in Augusta.

This time, Woods answered questions from the media and got better marks for being candid, sincere, and open about his problems. Tripp Frohlichstein, owner of a firm specializing in media and presentation coaching, wrote on *Ragan.com*, "This is something he should have done a long time ago. He could have saved himself a lot of hassle and probably a lot of money by keeping the sponsors who bailed if he had gotten this out of the way."

Woods, as a brand, probably will never regain the public adulation and endorsements that he had once commanded as the leading celebrity in sports, but experts expect that memories of the scandal will fade—especially if he continues to win golf tournaments.

mycommunicationlab

out which ones are influential and what they are saying. The reality of the Internet age is that one negative blog post can start an online brushfire that must be immediately addressed.

In sum, publicists and their work are an integral part of the entertainment industry. They are valued for their ability to grab attention through screenings, panel discussions, film festivals, and parties and for their ability to use current issues or controversies to get publicity—which is much cheaper than paid advertising. At Fox Searchlight Pictures, for example, a third of the company's executive roster is assigned to publicity or promotions.

> Executives have publicists. Stars have publicists. The tiniest movies will arrive in April at the Tribeca Film Festival with publicity teams, often three or four of them. Sometimes, it seems, even the publicists have publicists.
>
> *Michael Cieply, reporter for the* New York Times

In addition to the movie studios and television networks, publicists also work in public relations firms. A typical Los Angeles–area public relations firm specializing in personalities and entertainment has two staffs: one staff of "planters," who distribute stories about individual clients and the projects in which they are engaged, and another staff of "bookers," who place clients on talk shows and in other public appearances. Some publicity stories are for general release; others are prepared especially as an "exclusive" for a syndicated Hollywood columnist, a major newspaper, or an influential blogger.

Entertainment firms may also specialize in arranging product placement in movies and television programs. Usually the movie or television producers trade visible placement of a product in the show in exchange for free use of the item in the film. The movie *Up in the Air* is an example. It's no accident that George Clooney, the star, stays at Hilton Hotels throughout the film. Hilton offered free lodging to the film crew, provided the sets, and even promoted the movie on its key cards and its in-room television channel. In the movie *Soccer Mom*, Chrysler arranged for its Dodge Caravan to play a leading role. This kind of product placement, called "branded entertainment," was thoroughly discussed in Chapter 15.

Conducting a Personality Campaign

A campaign to generate public awareness of an aspiring star or other individual should be planned just as meticulously as any other public relations project. Practitioners conducting such campaigns follow a standard step-by-step process.

Interview the Client

The client should answer a detailed personal questionnaire. The practitioner should be a dogged, probing interviewer, digging for interesting and possibly newsworthy facts about the person's life, activities, and beliefs. When talking about themselves, individuals frequently fail to realize that certain elements of their experiences have publicity value under the right circumstances.

Perhaps, for example, the client is a little-known actress who has won a role as a Midwestern farmer's young wife in a motion picture. During her get-acquainted talks with the publicist, she happens to mention in passing that while growing up in a small town, she belonged to the 4-H Club. Not only must practitioners draw out such details from their clients, they must also have the ingenuity to develop these facts as story angles. When the actress is placed as a guest on a television talk show, the publicist should prompt her in advance to recall incidents from her 4-H experience. Tossing two or three humorous anecdotes about mishaps with pigs and chickens into the interview give it vitality.

Prepare a Biography

The basic biography should be limited to four typed pages, perhaps fewer. News and feature angles should be placed near the top of the "bio," as it is termed, so an editor or producer can find them quickly. The biography, a portrait, photos, and even video clips should be assembled in a media kit.

Plan a Marketing Strategy

The practitioner should determine precisely what is to be marketed. Is the purpose only to increase public awareness of the individual, or is it to publicize the client's product, such as a new television series, motion picture, or book? Next, the practitioner should decide which audiences are the most important to reach. For instance, an interview with a romantic operatic tenor on a rock music radio station would not be wise. But an appearance by the singer on a public television station's talk show would be right on target. A politician trying to project herself as a representative of minority groups should be scheduled to speak before audiences in minority neighborhoods and placed on radio stations whose demographic reports show that they attract minority listeners.

Conduct the Campaign

In most cases, the best course is to schedule the client on multiple media simultaneously. Radio and television appearances create public awareness and often make newspaper feature stories easier to obtain. The process works in reverse as well. Using telephone calls and "pitch" letters to editors and program directors, the publicist should propose print and on-air interviews with the client. The publicist should also include news or feature angles for the interviewer to develop. Because magazine articles take longer to reach the printed stage, the publicist should begin efforts to obtain them as early as feasible.

An interview in an important magazine—a rising female movie star in *Cosmopolitan* or *People*, for example—can have major impact among women readers. Backstage maneuvering often takes place before such an interview appears. Agents for entertainers on their way up eagerly seek to obtain such an interview. When a personality is "hot" or at the top of the ladder, however, magazine editors compete for the privilege of publishing the interview. The star's agent plays them off against each other, perhaps offering exclusivity but demanding such rewards as a cover picture of the star, the right to choose the interviewer (friendly, of course), and even approval of the article. Editors of some magazines yield to publicists' demands. Other publications refuse to do so.

News Releases   News releases are an important publicity tool, but the practitioner should avoid too much puffery.

Photographs   Photographs of the client should be submitted to the print media as often as justifiable. Media kits usually include the standard head-and-shoulders portrait, often called a "mug shot." Photographs of the client doing something interesting or appearing in a newsworthy group may be published merely with a caption, without an accompanying story. The practitioner and the photographer should be inventive, putting the client into unusual situations. The justification for a submission may be weak if the picture is not colorful and/or timely.

Public Appearances   Another way to intensify awareness of individual clients is to arrange for them to appear frequently in public places. Commercial organizations at times invite celebrities of various types or pay them fees to dress up and attend dinner meetings, conventions, and even store openings.

Awards   A much-used device, and a successful one, is to have a client receive an award. The practitioner should be alert for news of awards to be given and nominate the client for appropriate ones. Follow-up communications, along with persuasive material, may convince the sponsor to present the award to the client. In some instances, a practitioner proposes the idea of an award to an organization, which then conveniently declares the practitioner's client the first recipient.

Websites and Social Media   A website for the personality is a necessity. In addition, it's now standard for a personality to have a Facebook page and a Twitter account. It's important to update these sites on a regular basis.

Promoting an Entertainment Event

Attracting attendance to an event—anything from a theatrical performance to a fund-raising fashion show or a street carnival—requires a well-planned publicity campaign.

Publicity to Stimulate Ticket Sales

The primary goal of any campaign for an entertainment event is to sell tickets. An advance publicity buildup informs listeners, readers, and viewers that an event will occur and stimulates their desire to attend. Rarely, except for community events publicized in smaller cities, do newspaper stories and broadcasts about an entertainment event include detailed information on ticket prices and availability. Those facts usually are deemed too commercial by editors, who feel they should instead be announced in paid advertising. However, some newspapers may include prices, times, and so on in tabular listings of scheduled entertainments. Performance dates usually are included in publicity stories.

Stories about a forthcoming theatrical event, motion picture, rock concert, book, or similar event should concentrate on the personalities, style, and popularity of the activity or product. Every time the product or show is mentioned, public awareness grows. Thus, astute practitioners search for fresh news angles to produce as many stories as possible.

An Example: Publicizing a Play

The methods for publicizing a new play are the same whether the work will be performed on Broadway by professionals or in the local municipal auditorium by an amateur community theater group.

Stories include an announcement that the play will be presented, followed by news releases reporting the casting of lead characters, the beginning of rehearsals, and the opening date. Feature stories, or "readers," discuss the play's theme and background, with quotations from the playwright and director included to emphasize important points. In interviews, the play's star can tell why he or she finds the role significant or amusing.

Lady Gaga

Entertainment is big business and employs many publicists. In 2009, fans shelled out $4.4 billion to attend concerts in North America.

Photographs of show scenes, taken with actors in costume during rehearsal, should be distributed to the media and posted on a website to give potential customers a preview. As a reminder, a brief "opening tonight" story may be distributed. If a newspaper lists theatrical events in tabular form, the practitioner should submit an entry about the show. In some instances, publicity also can be generated through the use of e-mail and the World Wide Web.

The "Drip-Drip-Drip" Technique

Motion picture studios, television production firms, and networks apply the principle of "drip-drip-drip" publicity when a show is being shot. In other words, there is a steady output of information about the production. A public relations specialist, called a unit man or woman, is assigned to a film during production and turns out a flow of stories for the general and trade press and plays host to media visitors to the set. The television networks mail out daily news bulletins about their shows to media television editors. The networks assemble the editors annually to preview new programs and interview their stars. The heaviest barrage of publicity is released shortly before the show opens.

A much-publicized device is to have a celebrity unveil his or her star in the cement of the Hollywood Walk of Fame, just before the celebrity's new film appears. Videotaped recordings of the event turn up on television stations across the country.

One danger of excessive promotion of an event, however, is that audience expectations may become too high, the result being that the performance proves to be a disappointment. A skilled practitioner stays away from the "hype" that can lead to a sense of anticlimax.

The Business of Sports

The obsession with sports is flourishing in the United States and around the world. One indication of this is that a large percentage of the searches on Google every day are done by people looking for sports information. Simon Kuper, writing in the *Financial Times*, even says, ". . . checking for sports news online is now probably the most common way of consuming sport ahead of watching or playing or talking about it." He also reports that the most researched athletes in the world are Cristiano Ronaldo, David Beckman, Tiger Woods, and Lance Armstrong.

> Sport has become a global business, as well as a recreation for billions.
>
> *Patrick Lane, writing in the* Economist

Sports are also the most watched events on television around the world. Indeed, the global television audience for the Beijing Olympics was about 3 billion people, who watched 11,000 athletes from almost 200 nations compete in 28 sports. The 2010 FIFA World Cup in South Africa attracted an even larger global TV audience, estimated to be between 3.5 and 4 billion people.

This first World Cup ever held in Africa attracted almost 500,000 visitors, who spent about $850 million, and created more than 400,000 jobs in the South African hotel, restaurant, and tourism industries. To pull it off, more than 250 governmental and professional organizations in advertising, marketing, and public relations (including the Public Relations Institute of Southern Africa) coordinated a national communications effort to promote the World Cup at the country, continental, and global levels.

Indeed, all sports are stimulated by intense marketing and public relations efforts. Programs at both professional and big-time college levels seek to arouse public interest in teams and players, sell tickets to games, and publicize the corporate sponsors who subsidize many events. The Insights box on page 482, for example, highlights Coca-Cola's involvement in the 2010 World Cup. Increasingly, too, sports publicists work with marketing specialists to promote the sale of booster souvenirs and clothing, a lucrative sideline for teams.

Sports publicists use a variety of public relations tactics. They prepare media kits, write bios on players, compile stacks of statistics, wine and dine sports reporters, maintain the press box, arrange media interviews, book player appearances on television and radio sports shows, handle crises when players run afoul of the law, maintain the team website, write a team blog, and provide constant updates for fans on Facebook and followers on Twitter. Most professional teams have Twitter accounts now, and they also encourage their players to generate fans and support by tweeting. A good example is the Phoenix Suns, which was highlighted on page 347 in Chapter 13.

Tweeting, however, has been a mixed blessing for teams. On one hand, as Dan Schawbel, a personal branding

> The NHL [National Hockey League] social networking website boasts nearly 50,000 members, who can post profiles, photos, and fan blog entries to the site. The portal also features more than 84,000 photos and 1,500 videos, all posted by fans.
>
> *Frank Washkuch, writing in* PRWeek

on the job
INSIGHTS

Coke Scores a Goal at the World Cup

Sponsorship of international sporting events is an opportunity for corporations to give high visibility to a brand, reinforce brand preference, and even increase product usage. That's why Coca-Cola partnered with the 2010 FIFA World Cup that was held in South Africa.

One of Coke's initiatives was organizing a tour of U.S. cities, where the star attraction was the display of the World Cup trophy before the start of the games. The event, in which the price of admission was an empty Coca-Cola can, featured a 3-D World Cup movie, ball juggling acts, and entertainment by internationally known pop singers such as David Bisbal. Visitors, of course, could also get a souvenir photo of themselves posing with the original World Cup trophy. During the day, Coke partnered with Adidas to host a series of clinics with professional soccer players as part of its worldwide "Live Positively" program of making contributions to communities around the world.

Other Coke initiatives connected to the World Cup included (1) an international soccer camp for teenagers from around the world held in Pretoria, South Africa, and (2) a soccer-themed global program, RAIN "Water for

Schools," to help provide safe drinking water for schoolchildren in Africa and around the world. To increase brand awareness, Coke also decorated its cans in World Cup themes that featured dynamic graphics, soccer imagery, and vibrant colors.

A number of other major corporations also partnered with the World Cup. Visa, which also sponsors the Olympics, produced a visitor's guide

for the games and South Africa, launched a "Go Fans" marketing campaign, and produced a free World Cup–branded video game that combined the world's most popular sport with a financial literacy curriculum for schools. It also produced a theatrical production, focusing on financial literacy education in an entertaining way, that toured South African communities.

expert, says, "Twitter is how athletes and celebrities win fans for life." The downside is that players often embarrass themselves and the team by posting ill-considered Tweets. For example, Kansas City Chiefs star Larry Johnson got a two-week suspension for posting homophobic slurs on his personal Twitter account. And San Diego Chargers football player Antonio Cromartie was fined $2,500 for tweeting about the awful food at training camp. Even team owners get into trouble. Dallas Mavericks owner Mark Cuban was fined $25,000 by the National Basketball Association for criticizing the referees after a game.

Community Relations

Another important duty of the public relations staff of a professional team is community relations. Players are rarely from the local community, and a good relationship with the community is necessary for ticket sales, so every team does charitable work.

A good example is how Jason Zillo, media relations director of the New York Yankees, organized a "Hope Week." The impetus for the week, in part, was that the team had been criticized over ticket prices in their new stadium and that there was local grumbling about the taking of park land to build the stadium. Zillo arranged for Yankees players to do such things as visit sick children in hospitals, make appearances at local schools, talk with a Little Leaguer who had cerebral palsy, and visit two developmentally challenged workers in a law firm's mailroom.

Other teams, such as the San Francisco 49ers, have a community foundation that raises money through team-sponsored golf tournaments and other events for the purpose of funding various community organizations that work with disadvantaged children.

> When we started this program, we agreed that you just don't reach out to a community. You must invite them to be a part of the family before saying, "Here's how you buy tickets."
>
> *Jason Pearl, VP of the San Francisco Giants*

Sports publicists, by definition, are cheerleaders. They constantly work to build fan and community enthusiasm for the team and make star players celebrities. For college publicists, this means creating enthusiasm among alumni and making the school seem glamorous and exciting in order to recruit high school students. At other times, college sports publicists organize massive promotional campaigns to promote a player for a national award such as the Heisman Trophy.

Sometimes, usually when the team is a winner, these efforts succeed spectacularly. When a team is an inept loser, however, the sports publicist's life turns grim. He or she must find ways to soothe the public's displeasure and, through methods such as having players conduct clinics at playgrounds and visit patients in hospitals, create a mood of hopefulness: "Wait 'til next year!"

Win or lose, the immense popularity of sports makes it extremely difficult to find an entry-level public relations position in the field. Major league teams have hundreds of applicants for internship positions, and even full-time employment has a reputation for low salaries. Yet if a student takes a broader view, there are opportunities in college sports, the minor leagues, and even corporate sports-sponsorship programs.

The Tourism Industry

Tourism is one of the world's largest industries. It employs almost 8 percent of the world's workers (220 million) and generates almost 10 percent of global income, or about $5.5 trillion. Tourism's contribution to the GNP in the United States is about 10 percent, but in countries such as Thailand, it rises to almost 15 percent of GNP.

With money in their pockets, people want to go places and see things. Stimulating that desire and then turning it into the purchase of tickets and reservations is the goal of the travel industry. Public relations has an essential role in the process, not only in attracting visitors to destinations but also in keeping them happy once they arrive.

Like entertainment and sports, travel draws from the public's recreation dollars. Often its promoters intertwine their projects with those of entertainment and sports entrepreneurs.

Phases of Travel Promotion

Traditionally, the practice of travel public relations has involved three steps:

1. Stimulating the public's desire to visit a place
2. Arranging for the travelers to reach it
3. Making certain that visitors are comfortable, well treated, and entertained when they get there

Stimulation is accomplished through travel articles in magazines and newspapers, alluring brochures distributed by travel agents and by direct mail, travel films and videos, and presentations on the Web. Solicitation of associations and companies to hold conventions in a given place encourages travel by groups.

Public relations specialists in travel also stage creative events to attract attention. Weber Shandwick drove traffic to its YouTube video campaign for the Bahamas by sending 200 swimtog-clad commuters to walk through New York's Grand Central Station. Bikini-clad models visited Times Square with a giant beach ball to promote the U.S. Virgin Islands. The Fontainebleau Hotel in Miami also used models to promote a fashion show for Victoria's Secret at events celebrating the reopening of the hotel. Qantas airline took the celebrity approach. To inaugurate new service to Los Angeles, the Australian airline held a news conference for its global goodwill ambassador, John Travolta, and his *Grease* co-star, Olivia Newton-John, who served as a special celebrity flight attendant. Probably the most successful staged event in terms of worldwide publicity was Queensland's "Best Job in the World" promotion, which is highlighted in the Insights box on page 485.

> Travel public relations has become increasingly strategic and marketing driven.
>
> *Lorra M. Brown, former executive with Ogilvy Public Relations and Weber Shandwick Worldwide*

National and state travel agencies distribute literature, sponsor travel fairs, and encourage group travel by showing destination films at meetings. Cities and states coordinate their convention and travel departments to encourage tourism. A widely used method of promoting travel is the familiarization trip, commonly called a "fam trip," in which travel writers and/or travel salespeople are invited to a resort, theme park, or other destination for an inspection visit. In the past, fam trips often were loosely structured mass media junkets. Today they are smaller and more focused. See the Insights box on page 486 about the junkets for travel writers.

Good treatment of travelers is a critical phase of travel promotion. If a couple spends a large sum on a trip, and then encounters poor accommodations, rude hotel clerks, misplaced luggage, and inferior sightseeing arrangements, they go home angry. And they will vehemently tell their friends how bad the trip was.

on the job

INSIGHTS

The Best Job in the World

How would you like to be the caretaker of an island in Australia's Great Barrier Reef for six months, get a salary of about $100,000, and live in a three-bedroom villa with a pool?

That was the deal offered by the Queensland Tourism Authority in its "Best Job in the World" public relations campaign, which attracted 34,000 applicants from almost 200 nations. The job required "Excellent communication skills, good written and verbal English skills, an adventurous attitude, willingness to try new things, a passion for the outdoors and good swimming skills, and enthusiasm for snorkeling and/or diving."

Applicants were asked to audition via video clips and, of course, many clips made their way onto YouTube and other video-sharing sites, as hopeful candidates presented themselves in all sorts of creative ways, from stripping to getting a tattoo. According to *Advertising Age*, all this was ". . . part of a massive viral explosion aided and abetted by an enormous amount of TV and print coverage."

Mainstream media and social network coverage continued as the judges selected 50 semifinalists and then narrowed the field to 15, who represented a similar number of nations. They were flown to Hamilton Island for a final round of interviews that included plenty of swimming, snorkeling, sailing, and gourmet dinners, all of which was recorded by more than a dozen camera crews from news organizations around the world.

The winner was 34-year-old Ben Southall from England, who impressed the judges with his "true passion for Queensland." As part of his caretaker job, Southall wrote a blog about his island experiences, kept a photo diary, did video updates, and conducted media interviews. This kept the "best job in the world" campaign an ongoing story over a number of months. Indeed, the Queensland Tourism Authority estimates that its campaign to publicize the wonders of the Great

Barrier Reef as a tourist destination was worth about $130 million in media coverage.

The campaign received the Grand Prix award in the public relations category at the International Advertising Festival in Cannes, France.

Even the best arrangements go awry at times. Planes are late, tour members miss the bus, and bad weather riles tempers. This is where the personal touch means so much. An attentive, cheerful tour director or hotel manager can soothe guests, and a "make-good" gesture such as a free drink or meal does wonders. Careful training of travel personnel is essential. Many travelers, especially in foreign countries, are uneasy in strange surroundings and depend more on other people than they would at home.

on the job
INSIGHTS

How Many "Freebies" to Accept?

Newspaper and magazine stories about travel destinations, which are essential in tourism promotion, can pose a problem for writers and public relations people. Who should pay for the writers' expenses in researching these stories?

Some large newspapers forbid their travel writers from accepting free or discounted hotel rooms, meals, and travel tickets. They believe that such subsidies may cause writers to slant their articles too favorably, perhaps subconsciously.

Many smaller publications and most freelance writers cannot afford to abide by such a rule, however, and following it would prevent them from preparing travel articles. Freelance travel writer Jeff Miller, in *Editor & Publisher* magazine, took the publishing industry to task for paying just $150 per newspaper story and $500 to

$1,000 per magazine story while banning writers from taking subsidized trips. Travel writers claim the hypocritical policy makes the publications look good but is regularly ignored by travel writers, who simply cannot make a living without subsidized trips. The writers contend that pride in their professional objectivity keeps them from being influenced by their hosts' "freebies." Some point to critical articles they have written on subsidized trips.

For the public relations director of a resort, cruise, or other travel attraction, the situation presents two problems: (1) How much hospitality can be given to the press before the "freebies" become a form of bribery? and (2) How does the director screen requests from self-described travel writers who request free housing or travel?

The Society of American Travel Writers (SATW) sets the following guideline:

Free or reduced-rate transportation and other travel expenses must be offered and accepted only with the mutual understanding that reportorial research is involved and any resultant story will be reported with the same standards of journalistic accuracy as that of comparable coverage and criticism in theater, business and finance, music, sports, and other news sections that provide the public with objective and helpful information.

What do you think of the SATW guidelines? What about the "no sponsored trips" policy at some newspapers and magazines?

Travel Business Booms on the Internet

Airline tickets, hotel accommodations, and travel packages can be readily shopped for and then booked on the Web. Consumers have found the convenience and the discounted Internet specials to be highly attractive, which has resulted in a major increase in online travel transactions. Websites such as *Travelocity.com* not only offer complete airline booking services but also provide e-mail notification of fare changes for itineraries selected by the online user. Airlines and hotels find that last-minute inventory of seats or rooms can be sold effectively online. Because of such online commerce, hotels, resorts, and cruise lines can afford to mount extensive websites and even post YouTube videos that provide outstanding information to consumers and journalists alike.

Guam, a U.S. territory, is following the lead of many tourism agencies by actively establishing a presence in social media and providing mobile-enabled information on smartphones. It already had a website, *VisitGuam.org*, but has now expanded to establish more blog sites and utilize search engine optimization (SEO) to get its message disseminated.

Appeals to Target Audiences

Travel promoters identify target audiences and then create special appeals and trips for them. Great Britain's skillfully designed publicity in the United States is a successful example. Its basic appeal is an invitation to visit the country's historic places and pageants. It also offers London theatrical tours, golf expeditions to famous courses in Scotland, genealogical research parties for those seeking family roots, and tours of the cathedrals. Special tours can be arranged for other purposes as well.

Packaging   Packaging is a key word in travel public relations. Cruises for family reunions or school groups, family skiing vacations, university alumni study groups, archaeological expeditions, and even trips to remote Tibet are just a few of the so-called niche travel packages that are offered. A package usually consists of a prepaid arrangement for transportation, housing, most meals, and entertainment, with a professional escort to handle the details. Supplementary side trips often are offered for extra fees.

Appeals to Seniors   The largest special travel audience of all is older citizens. Retired persons have time to travel, and many have ample money to do so. Hotels, motels, and airlines frequently offer discounts to attract them. As a means of keeping old-school loyalties alive, many colleges conduct alumni tours, heavily attended by senior citizens.

A large percentage of cruise passengers, especially on longer voyages, are retirees. Alert travel promoters design trips with them in mind, including such niceties as pairing compatible widows to share cabins and arranging trips ashore that require little walking. Shipboard entertainment and recreational activities with appeal to older persons—nostalgic music for dancing rather than current hits, for example—are important, too.

Coping with Threats and Crises

Tourism, however, is a somewhat volatile business even in the best of times. Public relations professionals must be prepared to cope with unexpected situations and even crises that can seriously impact

Royal Caribbean's *Oasis of the Seas*

There's always something new in the travel industry. Royal Caribbean, for example, launched the *Oasis of the Seas* in early 2010 and generated considerable media coverage because it was the world's largest cruise ship. Many stories focused on the sheer size of the ship (longer than four football fields) and the logistics of accommodating up to 6,300 passengers, to say nothing of the 2,100 crew members. One unusual recreational feature is shown in the photograph; it's a zipline above the ship's boardwalk and cabin balconies that gives passengers a bird's-eye view of the entire ship.

the operations of hotels, cruise lines, airlines, or even the entire tourism business of a city, state, or country.

The economic situation is one level of threat that calls for immediate response in terms of creative strategies to entice tourists. The worldwide recession in 2009, for example, hit the tourism industry very hard. The World Travel & Tourism Council (WTTC) estimated that the travel industry contracted 3.5 percent and shed 10 million jobs by early 2010.

The lingering effects of the recession still affect the tourism industry, but other threats can also have a devastating effect. A good example is how Mexican tourist officials had to deal with an outbreak of swine flu, which caused a significant drop in tourists within a few weeks. This situation is highlighted in the Multicultural World box on page 489.

Other events and environmental factors also threaten tourism. America's Gulf Coast, for example, had a major drop in tourism in 2010 when an oil rig caught fire and sank, leaving a well that spewed millions of barrels of oil into the Gulf Stream. Tourism officials in Alabama, Mississippi, and Florida had to redouble their promotional efforts to convince tourists that the regions still offer good value and reassure them that the damage to pristine beaches was being contained. See the PRCasebook in Chapter 17 on page 442.

The three states immediately launched an advertising and publicity effort to shore up their $20 billion tourism industry. BP, responsible for the oil spill, was also asked to pay for the advertising and publicity effort. In a letter to BP, Florida Governor Charlie Crist made the basic point: "Unfortunately, because of the constant images of millions of gallons spilling into the Gulf of Mexico, potential visitors are receiving negative and false information. We need your urgent assistance to correct the record. This action is critical to our economic survival." In the meantime, Mississippi's tourism agency posted a YouTube video featuring tourism director Mary Beth Wilkerson declaring, "The state is open for business."

In another situation, Alaska tourism officials had to ease travelers' concern over the eruption of Mount Redoubt. The eruption provided great video and photographs for the mass media, but didn't do much to persuade potential tourists to visit the state. The Alaska Travel Industry Association hired a public relations firm to reassure the public. The firm sent out news releases and advisories to the media stressing that the resulting ash cloud was not significantly affecting Anchorage airspace and that the fall of debris had been "limited to a few small, remote communities."

Civil and political unrest can also affect tourism in a big way. Athens, for example, had major riots and demonstrations when the Greek economy went into a tailspin and austerity measures were introduced. Images of demonstrators battling police in the streets of Athens caused many tourists to cancel trips to the country. Thailand was also racked with political unrest, and a two-month encampment by demonstrators in Bangkok closed major hotels and shopping malls. Arrivals in Bangkok's international airport declined by 33 percent and hotel occupancy dropped to less than 30 percent. To compound the problem, various governments issued advisories to citizens to defer all nonessential travel to Thailand.

In such a situation, it's a major challenge for public relations professionals to counter the headlines and images portrayed in the news media that imply the whole city or country is under siege, when in reality, the unrest is usually restricted to a small area. According to a *New York Times* story, "In fact, much of Bangkok is peaceful, as are virtually all parts of the provinces." That statement, however, was not in the headline but buried near the end of the story. In any case, tourism officials and

on the job

A MULTICULTURAL WORLD

Mexican Tourism Responds to H1N1 Virus

When the H1N1 virus hit Mexico in late April 2009, it wreaked havoc on Mexico's $13 billion tourist industry, directly affecting the 2 million Mexicans who work in that industry. Just two weeks into the crisis, Mexico's finance secretary estimated that the outbreak had cost the Mexican economy $2.2 billion.

Mexico City, the country's capital, was the epicenter of what ended up becoming a pandemic. City officials immediately shut down nightclubs, movie theaters, museums, restaurants, and other places where people normally gather. Hotel occupancy rates plummeted 85 percent.

Other Mexican tourist destinations were affected as well. Cruise ships were rerouted to bypass Cancun and other port cities. In the initial days of the outbreak, 64 port calls were canceled by cruise companies, resulting in the absence of nearly 134,000 tourists. In May, the number of visitors on cruise ships declined by 95 percent. A popular T-shirt sold to the few remaining tourists proclaimed, "I went to Mexico and all I got was the swine flu."

The Mexican Tourist Board, given the dire situation, decided to launch a major public relations effort to counter the perceived fears of potential tourists and convince them that the authorities had taken effective steps to contain the virus. Contracts totaling $1.7 million were given to two firms, APCO Worldwide and Qorvis Communications.

A number of tactics were implemented. First, focus groups and surveys probed public perceptions of Mexico so that a response could be tailored to immediate concerns. Second, a number of journalists for national publications were contacted and briefed to counter prior media coverage that had tended to exaggerate the actual situation. A third tactic was to have organizations such as the Centers for Disease Control and the Harvard School of Public Health issue statements congratulating the Mexican government for effectively countering the swine flu virus. In addition, various celebrity testimonials lauding Mexico's great beaches, food, and culture were organized.

There was also extensive Internet outreach. The website for the Mexican embassy in Washington, D.C., was revamped to answer queries about the situation in Mexico and whether it was safe to travel there. Several blogs were started to discuss Mexico's response to the outbreak, and various videos were syndicated via social media to give the country's perspective.

Mexico's hotel and restaurant industry also conducted a number of promotions, offering cut-rate prices for rooms, meals, drinks, and souvenirs. One owner of a small hotel in Tepoztian even started a Twitter account to update his guests and prospective guests about the H1N1 virus. A sign of normalcy came after several weeks of crisis; the hotel owner Tweeted, "prepared lunch for family w/odds and ends but turned out well—spicy shrimp & chicken stir fry with mangoes, jicama, celery and carrots."

Time, extensive advertising, and public relations helped Mexico's tourism recover, as cruise ships, winter "snow birds," conventioneers, and spring breakers slowly returned.

PEARSON
mycommunicationlab

their public relations staffs often have to redouble their efforts to entice tourists back to a country.

A state's legislation can also affect tourism. Arizona passed strict legislation regarding immigrants and undocumented workers and reaped considerable criticism from civil rights groups. As a result, some cities and national organizations announced a boycott of the state. In the first weeks of the passed legislation, almost 25 meetings and conventions were cancelled. In addition, Fenton Communications handled a public relations drive on behalf of *MoveOn.com* and *Presente.org*, a Hispanic group, to convince Major League Baseball to yank its 2011 All-Star Game from Phoenix. Public relations staff for the state and the hotel industry countered that any boycott hurts tourist-related jobs, which are often held by Hispanics.

On a different level, the luxurious ocean liner *Queen Elizabeth II* departed on a high-priced cruise before refurbishing was completed. Many passengers had unpleasant trips because some facilities were in disrepair, leading to one news report describing the ship as a floating construction project. Others had their reservations cancelled because their cabins had not been completed. After bad international publicity and a class-action suit filed by some passengers, the Cunard cruise line offered a settlement. It gave full refunds of cruise fares plus a travel credit for a future cruise. See the Ethics box on page 491 about an ethical dilemma for Royal Caribbean lines using Haiti as a port of call.

The tourism industry must also be prepared for crises and terrorism. The Caribbean island of Aruba, for example, is a popular destination of U.S. tourists, about 1 million annually, but its exotic image of clear water, beautiful beaches, and swaying palm trees was considerably shaken when Natalee Holloway, an 18-year-old from Alabama on a class graduation trip, disappeared from one of Aruba's resorts. The disappearance—and the strong implication of foul play—became a major story in the print and broadcast media. At one point, 60 foreign reporters were on the Dutch island covering the case. Howard Kutz, media critic for the *Washington Post*, said, "Cable TV is treating this as the crime of the century, or at least, the obsession of the moment." He told the *Christian Science Monitor* that Aruba had garnered more media coverage over Holloway than it had in the previous 20 years.

The Holloway story was a major crisis for the Aruba tourism industry, and other Caribbean islands were concerned that their tourism would also decline because of the negative coverage. The story continued to garner headlines as Holloway's mother gave extensive interviews and loudly complained about the lack of progress the Aruba police were making in finding her daughter. The Alabama legislature even got into the act and threatened a boycott of the island until the case was solved.

Aruba's public relations firm, Quinn & Co. in New York, originally retained to promote the island's beaches and resorts, had to immediately switch gears and do crisis management. One tactic was to centralize information about the police investigation and to give regular updates on progress in the case. The firm also worked with cruise lines, travel agents, and airlines to assure them that Aruba was safe and still an attractive destination. The government also issued a statement saying, "This comes as a shock to Aruba where crime against tourists is almost non-existent," noting the island's repeat visitor rate of 40 percent, the highest in the Caribbean. The disappearance of Holloway has never been solved, and the mystery still hangs over the island's image, although tourism has somewhat rebounded to former levels.

Terrorism is also a factor that requires immediate response. Public relations staff at Marriott headquarters in Maryland had their Saturday interrupted when a suicide bomber smashed his explosive-packed truck into the Islamabad, Pakistan, Marriott Hotel, killing 40 people and severely injuring hundreds more, before a gas leak eventually ignited and destroyed the whole hotel.

A five-part crisis team was immediately assembled. The *research and writing team* was responsible for being in touch with hotel staff in Pakistan and issuing the first statement within 15 minutes after gathering initial information. The *media team*

on the job

ETHICS

Cruise Ship Passengers Stumble Ashore in Haiti

Should a luxury liner continue to use a private beach in Haiti to entertain its passengers while, about 50 miles away, an estimated 275,000 Haitians are dead and several million have lost their homes in a devastating earthquake?

That was the ethical dilemma of Royal Caribbean Cruise Lines, which has been using the heavily guarded private resort of Labadee on the north coast for a number of years. One week after the earthquake that practically leveled the entire capital city of Port-au-Prince, the 4,370-berth *Independence of the Seas* used the resort, and passengers enjoyed swimming, parasailing, and rum cocktails delivered to their hammocks. And a second luxury liner was scheduled the following week.

The public image of tourists enjoying the "good life" while large numbers of Haitians didn't even have water or food caused many critics to complain

that Royal Caribbean Cruise Lines was being insensitive and putting profit before human suffering. Even some of the ship's passengers had misgivings. One passenger, for example, posted a note on the Cruise Critic Internet forum saying, "It was hard enough to sit and eat a picnic lunch at Labadee before the quake, knowing how many Haitians are starving; I can't imagine having to choke down a burger there now."

Whether to continue stopping in Haiti was also the subject of debate within the company, but the decision was eventually made that the cruise line would help more Haitians by continuing to include Labadee in its scheduled stops. The rationale was that the resort employed 230 Haitians and another 300 benefitted from their employment. In addition, the ships could be used to deliver food to the island. The company also pledged to donate all profits from the visit to help

the Haitian people. Any finally, Royal Caribbean also pledged $1 million to the relief effort, using part of the amount to help its 200 Haitian crew members.

Do you think Royal Caribbean Cruise Lines made the right decision to continue its visits to Labadee despite the devastating earthquake? What, if anything, should the cruise line do about public perceptions and media stories of rich tourists enjoying a private beach in Haiti while the native population was struggling to find adequate drinking water and food? Do you think Royal Caribbean Cruise Lines acted in an ethical manner? Why or why not?

PEARSON
my**communication**lab

---

received information from the research team and prepared news releases and statements for the media. The *internal communications team* got information to employees. The *community relations team* communicated with the Red Cross and other government agencies. The *logistics team* set up a "war room" to ensure that all communications technologies were readily available and also set up a Pakistan location. The first statement was posted on Bill Marriott's well-known blog expressing sadness at the loss of lives and the injuries to people. Marriott's senior vice president for Asia was dispatched to Islamabad to coordinate rescue efforts and communications while the staff at headquarters posted updates to the employee intranet and asked supervisors to cascade information down to other employees. The basics of crisis communications were discussed in Chapter 10.

Summary

A Major Part of the American Economy

- Entertainment, sports, and tourism are big business. Billions of dollars are spent every year on movies, concerts, sporting events, and travel.

- Because there are multiple options for people to spend their discretionary income, each industry spends a great deal of money on advertising, marketing, and public relations to compete with each other and entice customers.

The Cult of Personality

- Today's mass media focus on the publicizing and glorification of celebrities in the fields of sports and entertainment and even high-profile criminals and politicians.

- Celebrities are motivated by fame (or notoriety), self-glorification, the attempt at positive image creation, and the desire for monetary gain. The public is impressed because of wish fulfillment, hero worship, a vicarious sense of belonging, and a desire for entertainment.

- Public relations people are generally called *publicists* in the entertainment industry because their primary job is to generate publicity for a film, a concert, or an individual star.

- Entertainment publicists are often called upon to do "damage control" when a celebrity runs afoul of the law or makes an ill-considered statement.

Conducting a Personality Campaign

- A practitioner planning a campaign to generate public awareness of an individual must interview the client, prepare a biography, plan a marketing strategy, and conduct the campaign through news releases, photographs, and public appearances.

Promoting an Entertainment Event

- Publicity campaigns to promote events may include publicity to stimulate ticket sales.

- The "drip-drip-drip" technique involves a steady output of information as the event is being planned. The motion picture industry defines target audiences.

The Business of Sports

- Sports publicists promote both big-time college and professional teams.

- Some publicity focuses on building images of star players.

- A major aspect of sports is corporate sponsorships, which generate billions of dollars.

- Social media such as Facebook fan pages and personal Twitter accounts for athletes are now common.

The Tourism Industry

- The tourism industry in the United States generates almost 10 percent of the nation's GNP.

- Travel promotion involves encouraging the public's desire to visit a place, arranging for them to reach it, making sure they enjoy their trip, and protecting their safety.

- Campaigns may include a familiarization trip to increase travel agents' awareness. Retirees are a major audience for the tourism business.

- Tourism is a volatile business. There are threats such as economic recession, political unrest, and oil spills, but there are also crises such as a terrorist attack or an accident that kills or injures tourists.

Case Activity   Promoting the Azores

The Azores Islands are an autonomous region of Portugal, located 1,000 miles off its coast in the middle of the Atlantic Ocean. This makes the Azores the part of Europe that's closest to North America—only a four-hour flight from New York or Boston. This string of nine islands has diverse landscapes, historic sites, and an unspoiled feel. What they don't have are American tourists.

Azores Express Airlines, in partnership with a group of boutique hotels, wants to generate more business from American tourists, so it has contacted your public relations firm to help it generate more awareness of the Azores as a vacation spot for travelers looking for a fresh destination.

The client doesn't have money for an advertising campaign, so it wants to use public relations tactics to reach opinion leaders in travel and groups of experienced American travelers who have already seen Europe and are looking for a new destination. Some preliminary research also indicates a possible market in New England, which has a number of people of Azorean descent and a strong dose of Portuguese culture.

You have a $200,000 budget for a year-long program of public relations and marketing. The objective is to increase the number of American tourists who travel to the islands by 25 percent. What program would you recommend? *Note of caution:* Although the Azores are islands, they don't offer the traditional sand and surf of the more popular Caribbean islands. The president of Azores Express Airlines tells you point-blank, "Don't promote the place as a beach location."

Questions   for Review and Discussion

1. Give some figures or statistics verifying that the industries of entertainment, sports, and tourism are important segments of the American economy.
2. What constitutes a celebrity today in American society? What are the roles of publicists and the media in creating celebrities?
3. When pop star Michael Jackson died, the media devoted blanket coverage of his death and memorial service. Do you think the coverage was excessive? Why or why not?
4. Magazines such as *People* pay millions of dollars for exclusive photos of a celebrity couple's newborn children. Are such payments justified? Why or why not?
5. Give some reasons why the public is fascinated with the personal lives of celebrities or develops strong attachments to sports teams.
6. Describe the work of an entertainment publicist. Would being an entertainment publicist appeal to you as a career? Why or why not?
7. What is your assessment of the Tiger Woods sex scandal? Do you agree with him that this should have remained a private matter and not have been subjected to extensive media coverage? Why or why not?
8. What is "branded" entertainment? Can you give some examples?
9. What is the process for developing a publicity campaign for a personality?
10. How would you create publicity or "buzz" about a new play or musical performance?
11. If you worked in sports public relations for a team, what kind of duties would you have on a daily basis?
12. What are the three phases of promoting a tourism destination?
13. Tourism promotion requires creative thinking in terms of staging events that draw public and media attention. Can you give any examples from the text?
14. Tourism is described as a volatile business. What kinds of threats and crises do public relations personnel have to cope with when these crises occur?

Media Resources

Barnes, B. (2008, November 21). Story behind the cover story: Angelina Jolie and her image. *New York Times,* pp. 1, A20.

Barnes, B. (2009, November 22). Ad budget tight? Call the PR machine. *New York Times,* p. B7.

Borkowski, M. (2009). *The fame formula: How Hollywood's fixers, fakers and star makers created the celebrity industry.* London, England: Sidgwick & Jackson, Ltd.

Brown, L. M. (2009, June). Tracking the development of travel and tourism public relations. *Public Relations Tactics,* 11.

Cave, S. (2009, January 29). Fall of fame: Every age has its Paris Hiltons, but what does it take to achieve lasting recognition? [Life & Arts section]. *Financial Times,* 13.

Cieply, M. (2008, February 24). Your publicist should call my publicist. *New York Times.* Retrieved from www.nytimes.com

Gingerich, J. (2008, July). Experiences, trends, options make travel news, not places. *O'Dwyer's PR Report,* 1, 25.

Lane, P. (2008, August 2). Fun, games, and money: A special report on the sports business. *Economist,* 1–16.

McAdams, S. (2009, January). How Marriott communicators responded to the Islamabad bombing. *RaganReport,* 15–18.

McCallister, R., & Pogachefsky, M. (2009, January). Movie stars and cell phone screens: Evolution in entertainment public relations. *Public Relations Tactics,* 18.

McCauley, K. (2009, July). Mexico gears PR rebound from swine flu. *O'Dwyer's PR Report,* 17–18.

Tanenhaus, S. (2009, December 13). The 15-minute game: A few thoughts on modern celebrity [Week in Review]. *New York Times,* pp. 1–6.

Zuk, R. (2009, March). Tweeting up with THE_REAL_SHAQ: Phoenix Suns PR pros embrace Twitter. *Public Relations Tactics,* 12.

Politics and Government

19

chapter

After reading this chapter, you will be able to:

Describe the basic purposes and functions of public relations in government

Explain what public relations professionals do at the federal, state, and local levels

Define public affairs, government relations, and lobbying

Describe the roles public relations plays in election campaigns

Government Organizations

Federal, state, and local governments and agencies have a common bond in that all engage in the same types of public relations tasks in order to succeed and thrive. Government agencies and administrations share characteristics such as tax exemption and an intent to serve the public good. All operate within the framework of regulations regarding the external distribution of funds to individuals or entities. The public relations functions of government agencies consist primarily of disseminating information. Government agencies often promote the policies of the current administration and seek support from citizens. Such public relations efforts are typically associated with reelection campaigns. Although both major parties, when not in power, decry leadership characterized by election campaign tactics, in recent decades each party has practiced a political campaign style of leadership when in office. See the PR Casebook on page 497 on President Obama's response to the BP oil disaster in the Gulf for examples of campaign style leadership.

Government entities employ public relations specialists to promote their services, orchestrate fund-raising, spread news of their successes or crises, assist with smooth daily operations or crisis management, implement campaigns that address social issues, and help develop long-range plans and visions. This variety means that aspiring public relations professionals won't want to overlook opportunities for employment in government.

Corporations and other nonprofit organizations also have specialized functions with regards to government organizations that are generally tied to lobbying. This lobbying activity serves to counterbalance the actions of governmental bodies at the local, state, and federal levels that influence the business environment for corporations as well as nonprofit organizations. These functions typically involve gathering, analyzing, and disseminating information, in line with individual organization interest.

> For students and young professionals who have an interest in public affairs and public service, the city [Washington, D.C.] can provide an amazing opportunity for learning both.
>
> *Tom Martin, former VP of corporate communication at FedEx Corp.*

Basic Purposes of Government Public Relations

Ideally, the mission of government is public service; no one makes private profit directly from the operation of governments, and governments are noncommercial. In practice, a widespread perception exists that administrations fall far short of these ideals, but the shortcomings of some government officials and employees should not blind citizens to the tangible benefits of the democratic system. In order for federal, state, and local governments to function efficiently, each branch needs to communicate effectively with its constituents. From election campaigns to military recruitment to floating a bond issue, a common thread runs through governmental public relations: the circulation of information. This core function of all public relations is a particularly prominent aspect of government communication. Skilled public relations professionals are required at every level of our government to ensure that information is disseminated clearly, efficiently, and to the widest number of people. See the Insights box on page 499 for an example from the CDC of information dissemination—crucial scientific findings that debunk the myth that Ecstasy is a safe party drug.

PRCasebook

Obama Forced into Campaign Mode on BP Gulf Disaster

The President of the United States is so powerful that he usually can set the agenda for media coverage by making sure that everyone in the White House is "on message." But not so in the case of the BP Gulf oil spill.

Pressure from the media caused President Obama to turn up the intensity of his efforts to deal with the oil well blowout 5,000 feet below the surface of the Gulf of Mexico even though he is not a petroleum engineer or a Coast Guard officer. Media coverage questioned Obama's management of the world's worst environmental disaster, developing the following critical themes:

- Slow to respond in any serious and concerted manner after the blowout and spread of oil

- Unemotional tone when discussing the environmental disaster and the economic impact

- No direct talks with BP, not even by telephone, for seven weeks after the spill began

- Expressed that there was no real point in communicating with BP

- Stereotyping by Obama of the oil industry and business executives as always telling the public what it wants to hear

- Calling for a drilling moratorium in the Gulf, which would compound job loss and economic catastrophe

- Mandating a freeze by BP of all dividend payments to shareholders, which earned immediate backlash from British pundits and officials looking out for the interests of British pensioners counting on BP payments

Is it any wonder that a modern President would turn to political campaign tactics in place of governing from the Oval Office even though that is where the world's most powerful leader could probably be most effective in dealing with the disaster and the many other issues on the presidential plate? The criticism became so pitched that some media reports viewed BP's then-CEO, Tony Hayward, more favorably than the U.S. chief executive. Ironically, Hayward seemed to benefit from his frequent interaction with journalists and his regular willingness to speak to the media, even when his words were not always borne out by decisive actions. Even his saying off the cuff that he "wanted his life back," disrespecting the 11 lives lost during the oil rig explosion, seemed only to make him more human in the eyes of reporters. Overall, Hayward's responsiveness to press requests and his exposure on a regular basis worked to neutralize even this terrible gaffe.

In a news story with the headline "White House Message Machinery Spinning Faster Than Ever," Steven Thomma pointed to the White House bureaucracy's devotion to managing public imagery in an era when what Theodore Roosevelt called "the bully pulpit" no longer is enough. As critical media pressure mounted, the message machinery turned toward the environmental catastrophe with full force, portraying President Obama as on the job in managing, from the top down, the world's worst environmental disaster. Of course, the campaign elements were also intended to win back public favor and global respect for President Obama as a caring manager and a confident leader.

Campaign-style moves by Obama included:

- More frequent, more visible visits to the Gulf, with ample photo opportunities of the President talking with local residents and examining oil pollution

- One such visit was punctuated by Obama's pointed effort to become more emotional and

Tony Hayward

(Continued)

more responsive concerning the catastrophe by saying he needed to go on-scene so that he would know "whose ass to kick."

- The White House developed arguments for the moratorium on drilling in U.S. waters that initially seemed to be a no-brainer, until many Louisiana leaders expressed bitterness that this would only make matters worse in the region where fishing and tourism were already decimated.

- Obama acknowledged that the biggest economic driver in the region, the oil industry, would be crippled by a six-month stoppage and urged the review team to move expeditiously to prevent drilling rigs shifting to other parts of the world and likely never returning to the Gulf.

- First formal speech from the White House after his first overnight stay in the Gulf region, which included a visit to three impacted states

- Polished videography of Obama's visit to the Gulf by media professionals in the White House posted online

- Obama, who was criticized for not meeting with or even speaking by phone to the CEO of BP, scheduled a high-profile meeting with top BP executives in the White House.

- Diplomatic overtures from the White House led to a call by British Prime Minister David Cameron for cooler heads to prevail regarding a freeze of BP dividends.

- The BP Chairman apologized to the American people during the visit to the White House and voluntarily pledged to freeze dividends to provide $20 billion in reparation funds to the Gulf.

The outcome:

Media pressure played an important role not only in gearing up the message machine in the White House, but also in the formulation of a substantive response to the disaster. Oil abatement efforts across the sensitive Gulf ecosystem gained momentum and focus. But the most dramatic results pertained not so much to the intractable environmental or engineering challenges, but to the media's respect accorded to Obama. With that base restored, leadership of reparation and recovery efforts at last appeared to be a more manageable task.

Source: S. Thomma. (2010). White House message machinery spinning faster than ever. McClatchy Newspapers.

PEARSON
mycommunicationlab

The Federal Government

One of our more scholarly and inquisitive founding fathers succinctly stated the case for federal information services in a democratic system: "A nation of well-informed men who have been taught to know and prize the rights which God has given them cannot be enslaved. It is in the region of ignorance that tyranny begins," said Benjamin Franklin. Today, the U.S. government may well be both the world's premier collector of information and one of the world's greatest disseminators of information. Advertising is a key governmental activity. Federal agencies spend several hundred million dollars a year on public service advertising, primarily to promote military recruitment, government health services, and the U.S. Postal Service.

The White House

At the apex of government public relations efforts is the White House. The President receives more media attention than Congress and all the federal agencies combined. It is duly reported when the President visits a neighborhood school, tours a housing development, meets a head of state, plays basketball with staff, or even takes his wife to New York City on a date. The focus on the President in the

on the job
INSIGHTS

CDC Warns of Ecstasy Overdose "Clusters" at Raves

Two quotes from a *USA Today* article showcase the importance of spending tax dollars on government public relations:

First, the lead—"What seems like a carefree night of revelry at a 'rave' can quickly turn tragic when the club drug ecstasy is involved, finds a new report on one such event from the US Centers for Disease Control and Prevention."

The lead serves as an important safety advisory to youth, young adults, and their parents.

Second, paragraph 6—"The report appears in the June 11 issue of the US Centers For Disease Control and Prevention's (CDC), Morbidity and Mortality Weekly Report."

This unobtrusive paragraph acknowledges a highly cost effective, basic source of newsworthy health information. The hallowed weekly news roundup known among health reporters as the MMWR receives thousands of media visits and generates hundreds of important health stories every year. The humble MMWR is a fount of story ideas that alert citizens and begin investigations as well as reforms in the interests of the health and well-being of American citizens.

As a matter of fact, the 18 hospitalizations and one death reported in the MMWR—and in *USA Today*—at a 2010 New Year's Eve rave in Los Angeles might have been reduced or even eliminated if youth and young adults, along with their ever watchful parents, had been aware that the party drug is not safe, in spite of all the lore to the contrary. According to the MMWR, the reality has less to do with fun and more to do with seizures, the breakdown of muscle tissue, kidney failure requiring hemodialysis, and liver failure.

Bottom line: Government public relations professionals play a crucial role in communicating risk, health, and science information provided by disinterested and professional research groups to citizens every day.

coverage of the BP oil spill exemplifies this attention. Lax regulators in the Department of the Interior and congressional responsibility for legal guidelines of oil exploration have effectively gotten a free pass when compared with the pressure brought to bear on President Obama.

All Presidents have taken advantage of the intense media interest to implement public relations strategies to improve their popularity, generate support for programs, and explain embarrassing policy decisions. And each President has his own communication style, which arises naturally from his experience and personality, but is accentuated by speech writers and media coaches.

Ronald Reagan was considered by many to be a master communicator. A former actor, he was extremely effective on television and could make his remarks seem spontaneous even when he was reading a teleprompter. He understood the importance of using symbolism and giving simple, down-to-earth speeches with memorable, personal appeal. Reagan's approach was the effective use of carefully packaged soundbites and staged events.

George H. W. Bush (senior) was no Ronald Reagan as a public speaker, but he did project enthusiasm for his job and had a friendly, but formal, working relationship with the White House press corps. Bill Clinton, on the other hand, was more populist in his communication style. He was at home with information technology and made effective use of television talk shows. Clinton was most effective when he talked one on one with an interviewer or a member of the audience, which explains why historians already consider his most effective response to the Lewinsky and impeachment ordeal to be an extended *60 Minutes* interview with his wife at his side. Although the interview was at times excruciating, the fallibility and humanity of the President left a lasting impression.

President George W. Bush adopted Reagan's approach to stagecraft and symbolism. A team of television and video experts made sure that every Bush appearance was well choreographed for maximum visual effect. The Bush administration's concept of stagecraft manifested itself in tight control of information and limited media access. Bush, for example, gave substantially fewer press conferences, interviews, and other media events than either Bill Clinton or his father in their first two years in office.

Barack Obama has also proved to be a master of the media. His presidential campaign rallies frequently were compared to rock concerts. However, Obama has been criticized for emphasizing style and rhetorical flourish over gravity and substance. Others have worried alternately that his presentation, not unlike that of Vice President Joe Biden or Senator John Kerry (D-Massachusetts), sometimes tends to be a little too verbose and intellectual, even unemotional, as in the media criticism of his response to the Gulf oil environmental catastrophe. Nevertheless, Obama is a skilled orator with a riveting presence, in the tradition of John F. Kennedy, Ronald Reagan, and Dr. Martin Luther King.

One of the major accomplishments of President Obama early in his term has been to employ his warmth and charismatic oratory in foreign affairs, warming relations with nearly every foreign country and organization. The years from 2001 to 2009 had not been kind to the image of America abroad. A survey of 24 nations conducted in 2008 by the Pew Charitable Trusts indicated that 42 percent of French citizens had a favorable view of the United States. And that was the good news; only 31 percent of Germans, 22 percent of Egyptians, and 12 percent of Turks had a positive view of the United States. As a result, tourism declined sharply, foreign investment in the United States was threatened, and allies openly expressed hostility to American political decisions. *The Guardian*, a liberal newspaper in England, predicted "the end of the era of American Dominance."

But as Mark Twain famously said, "Reports of my death are greatly exaggerated." In one fell swoop, the election of Barack Obama in February 2008 heralded a new era of good feelings abroad about America and her prospects. Set to the sounds of Obama's rousing slogan "Yes, We Can," the election represented the public desire for changes, not only at home but overseas as well. "Most French people saw Obama's election as a breath of fresh air and a reaffirmation of American values," said Seth Goldschlager, an American public relations professional working in France. Germans held banners reading, "Obama for Chancellor" when he visited during the campaign.

Obama for Chancellor

Obama's popularity in other countries has helped to bolster worldwide public opinion of the United States.

For many non-Americans, Obama was the new face of America. Recognized as the personification of renewed optimism about international cooperation, Obama was awarded the Nobel Peace Prize in the fall of 2009. In some ways, the President's Nobel Peace Prize was earned in anticipation of what Obama could bring to building global cooperation and harmony based on his hopeful positions and oratory during the presidential campaign prior to his taking office or even making any official overtures on the international scene. And although the President's poll numbers declined significantly at home by late 2010, surveys abroad continued to suggest that he, and by extension the United States as a whole, remain popular abroad.

Lou Capozzi, PRSA fellow and senior counselor at Manning, Selvage & Lee, argued in a 2009 article in the *Public Relations Strategist* that public relations professionals can build on the good feelings abroad and play an important role in repairing connections between the United States and the rest of the world. He argued for a foundational approach—marshalling communication skills with cultural sensitivity, publicizing the good things that are being done by industry and organizations, and advocating for the United States. These are lofty outcomes worthy of the best in public relations practice.

Congress

The House of Representatives and the Senate are major disseminators of information. Members regularly produce a barrage of news releases, newsletters, recordings, brochures, taped radio interviews, e-mails, electronic newsletters, and videos (often uploaded to YouTube), all designed to inform voters back home about Congress as well as to keep the congressperson in the minds of voters. In fact, in a recent nine-month period, members of Congress spent about $3.5 million on electronic outreach.

Some question whether this venerable benefit, called a franking privilege, unduly hurts the challenger in a close campaign and helps incumbents hold their position in office. Critics are certainly correct that most of these materials are self-promotional and have little value. The late Senator John Heinz, a Republican from Pennsylvania, once distributed 15 million pieces of mail, financed by taxpayers, during one election year.

Each member of Congress also employs a press secretary, who is a public relations person fulfilling perhaps the most long-standing and basic function in the profession, managing media relations. Says Edward Downes, of Boston University:

> Capitol Hill's press secretaries play a significant role in the shaping of America's messages and consequent public policies. In their role as proxy for individual members, the press secretaries act as gatekeepers, determining what information to share with, and hold from, the media; thus, they have command over news shared with the citizenry.

Capitol Hill's press secretaries play a significant role in the shaping of America's messages and consequent public policies. In their role as proxy for individual members, the press secretaries act as gatekeepers, determining what information to share with, and hold from, the media; thus, they have command over news shared with the citizenry.

Edward Downes, Boston University

White House historians and media watchers describe President Obama's press secretary, Robert Gibbs, as one of the more authoritative and bold examples of a public relations person asserting a strategic role during daily press briefings. Congressional press secretaries are seldom given this sort of authority or visibility, serving more as the information disseminators envisioned by Benjamin Franklin.

Federal Agencies

Public affairs officers (PAOs) and public information specialists engage in tasks common to the public relations department of corporations. They answer press and public inquiries, write news releases, work on newsletters, prepare speeches for top officials, oversee the production of brochures, and plan special events. Senior-level public affairs specialists counsel top management about communication strategies and how the agency should respond to crisis situations. For major projects, departments will collaborate with public relations agencies to design and implement research-based, creative campaigns to achieve high-priority goals for an agency or a department. For details of such a campaign, which helped to stem the tide of panic spreading to regional and local banks during the recent financial decline and collapse, see the Insights box on page 503.

One of the largest public affairs operations in the federal government is conducted by the U.S. Department of Defense (DOD), the cabinet-level agency that oversees the armed forces. Its operations vary from the mundane to the exotic.

One of the longest-running public relations efforts has been the preparation and distribution of "hometown" releases by the military. The Fleet Hometown News Center, established during World War II, sends approximately 1 million news releases annually about the promotions and transfers of U.S. Navy, Marine Corps, and Coast Guard personnel to their hometown media.

on the job

INSIGHTS

Government Public Relations Allays Fear Itself

As the first decade of this new century came to a close, government public relations efforts were crucial to alleviating panic and preventing bank runs reminiscent of the infamous bank closures of the Depression in the 1930s. At that time, President Franklin D. Roosevelt led our country out of the Depression by restoring confidence. He emphasized that "We have nothing to fear but fear itself," in identifying failure of nerve as an essential problem in maintaining bank systems. The same approach was essentially the theme of an award-winning campaign created by the public relations firm Porter Novelli and the Federal Deposit Insurance Corporation, or FDIC, in the first decade of the new century.

After IndieMac Bank failed in July 2008 and the FDIC took over, customers withdrew more than $1.3 billion in 11 business days. The FDIC feared that rising panic might create a domino effect nationwide that would pose a serious threat to the beleaguered financial system. The FDIC thus sought Porter Novelli's aid. The team responded with a public service effort that provided guidance to broad audiences through public service announcements, spokespeople, and a website named *myfdicinsurance.gov*.

The public relations firm, in this textbook example, began with intensive research that helped define two broad categories of audiences:

1. The anxious public and
2. High-balance depositors.

The campaign used plain-talk messages for general audiences, as well as culturally appropriate versions for Hispanic, Asian, and African American segments. Renowned personal finance expert Suze Orman was featured in campaign materials, and a Univision media personality, Julie Stav, was able to relate the campaign to Spanish-speaking audiences.

One day after the launch of the campaign, the website got nearly 3.4 million hits, which earned media coverage topping 291 million impressions and multiple days of coverage on high-profile outlets like *The Oprah Winfrey Show* and *Good Morning America*.

Human suffering and tragedy were alleviated by stemming the panic that could have resulted in a collapse of regional banking, if not also national bank systems. The experience helped make the FDIC a stabilizing and steadying force the following year as Wall Street collapsed and national banking empires were shaken. Many ordinary Americans derived great reassurance from knowing that their savings in banks are guaranteed with the full faith and backing of the federal government.

Source: Public Sector Campaign of the Year, 2010; retrieved from www.prweekus.com

A particularly exotic assignment for a military public affairs officer is giving background briefings and escorting the journalists who cover battlefield military operations. When the military initiated the policy of "embedding" journalists within military units during the 2003 invasion and occupation of Iraq, it assigned a large number of PAOs as escorts. The policy of "embedded" journalists is continuing with U.S. forces in Afghanistan. Journalists sometimes complain about restrictions on their freedom. For example, there has been criticism of the military's recent decision to forbid embedded journalists from photographing troops killed in action in Afghanistan.

However, a national survey found that U.S. media outlets unreservedly use the embedded reports, especially those from their own organization or network. The degree of insight and detail made possible by being embedded with troops is valued. Public affairs officers in combat areas also noted that modern warfare without clearly defined battle lines and uniformed combatants imposes new constraints:

1. Soldiers' lives are at stake—so information must be managed carefully.
2. Reporters' lives are at stake—venturing out for independent reporting puts journalists in harm's way, from impromptu airstrikes or guerrilla explosive devices.

Public affairs officers in the military face a classic question: what constitutes public information versus propaganda? And to make such a question even more problematic, how does a military unit that is violently imposing its will on a region restrain itself when it comes to imposing its will on the media content of the occupied territory? According to a *Los Angeles Times* report, the Pentagon, a common name for the Department of Defense derived from the shape of the agency's headquarters, contracted with Washington, D.C.-based Lincoln Group to plant more than 1,000 "good-news" stories in several Iraqi Arab-language papers. The contract specified that Lincoln would inform the Iraqi people of American goals and the progress being made, in order to gain public support. At issue was how they accomplished the goal. Lincoln paid the editors at papers such as *Azzaman* and *al Sabah* between $40 and $2,000 to publish articles that were supposedly written by local journalists. In reality, however, many of the stories were prepared by Lincoln staffers, soldiers at "Camp Victory," and military public relations officers.

According to *New York Times* reporters Jeff Gerth and Scott Shane, the source of the articles and opinion pieces was concealed. Lt. Col. Steven A. Boylan defended the practice, arguing that such "pay for play" was necessary because Iraqi papers "normally don't have access to those kinds of stories." Michael Rubin, formerly of the Coalition Provisional Authority, stressed the need for "an even playing field," implying that because the insurgents use deceptive messages, Lincoln's tactics were justified. However, Gen. Peter Pace found the practice to "be detrimental to the proper growth of democracy" and then-President George W. Bush was reportedly "very troubled" by the disclosure. A Pentagon review found the program basically "appropriate," though it recommended adhering to guidelines about attribution of authorship. The contract with Lincoln continued, with some modifications. In September 2008, Lincoln was one of four firms awarded a $300 million contract for "information operations" in Iraq.

Journalists have widely denounced the practice of pay for play. "Ethically, it's indefensible," said Patrick Butler, vice president of the International Center of Journalists in Washington. Likewise, the Public Relations Society of America has issued a condemnation of the practice. Pamela Keaton, director of public affairs for the congressionally funded Institute for Peace, worries about the long-term effects of what she labels a propaganda campaign: "It will get to the point where the news media won't trust anybody, and the people won't trust what's being quoted in news articles."

The Pentagon also engages in recruitment drives. One tactic used to bolster recruitment goals was paying $36,000 to United Airlines to run a 13-minute video news release entitled "Today's Military" as part of the in-flight entertainment package. The campaign, which described exciting military jobs such as Air Force language instructor and animal care specialist based in Hawaii, was designed to appeal to parents or other adult role models who might recommend the military to their children or relatives.

Another major operation of the Pentagon is assisting Hollywood with the production of movies. More than 20 public information specialists are liaisons with the film and television industries. They review scripts and proposals, advise producers on military procedures, and decide how much assistance, if any, a film or TV show portraying the military should receive. Movies portraying the military in a positive light, such as *Transformers: Revenge of the Fallen* (2009), *Iron Man* (2008), *Pearl Harbor* (2001), or *Saving Private Ryan* (1998), are more likely to receive assistance from the military than movies with less flattering or ambiguous messages, such as *Stop Loss* (2008), *Redacted* (2007), *Jarhead* (2005), or *Broken Arrow* (1996).

Other federal agencies also conduct campaigns to inform citizens. In many cases, the agency selects a public relations firm through a bidding process. Ogilvy Public Relations Worldwide was awarded six government contracts in October 2009. Their clients included the Centers for Disease Control, the U.S. Department of Health and Human Services, and the Department of Veteran Affairs. The Reardon Group, a public relations firm based in Washington, D.C., received a $1.5 million contract from the Pentagon to assess the "perspective, style and tone" of journalists reporting on military subjects. The contract was canceled in August 2009 because of pressure from advocacy groups such as the First Amendment Center, which questioned "the line between government review of the press and censorship." Politicians often capitalize on their connections to get work from lobbying or public relations companies.

For a review of another information campaign that has received a great deal of attention and criticism, see the Insights box on page 506 about the promotion and outright advocacy for the No Child Left Behind program, first introduced and championed by President George W. Bush.

Information campaigns are fairly common in most federal agencies. At times, however, public affairs staffs can find themselves on the front lines of a crisis or a controversy that involves handling hundreds of press calls in a single day. The Department of Homeland Security, which became operational on January 26, 2003, was formed by merging 22 different agencies. As was to be expected in light of such a major reorganization, DHS experienced a variety of growing pains. One problem was cohesion; it took time to get public affairs staffs from so many agencies to operate as a unit. There were also problems in message formulation. Dennis Murphy, director of public affairs for border and transportation security, told *PRWeek*, "We want to get the word out quickly . . . but operations folks want to make sure we're not saying too much." Another example of a communication breakdown between government agencies and the public was the dissemination of information to the public about the Cash for Clunkers Program in 2009. Started on July 27, and ended abruptly on August 24, the program provided cash incentives for consumers to trade in their older vehicles for newer, more fuel-efficient ones. Early on, lack of clear information about how long the program would last, what cars qualified for trade in, and how dealers would be reimbursed with rebates created confusion. Nevertheless, subsequent economic analysis showed significant stimulation of the economy through new car sales in a besieged economic sector. The same was true in foreign markets, with Germany reporting strong stimulus from a similar cash for clunkers program.

on the job

INSIGHTS

Promoting No Child Left Behind

Does the government have the right to promote its programs using taxpayer money even when partisan issues are involved? Should government agencies acknowledge their role in public relations campaigns? Promotion of the No Child Left Behind (NCLB) Act during the Bush administration raised ethical questions that politicians and the public relations professionals working for them will have to deal with in the coming years.

Signed into law by President Bush in 2001, the NCLB Act requires every school to provide adequate educational opportunities for all its students. From the outset, the Bush administration used public relations strategies to gain support for the NCLB Act from communities and families. The Department of Education paid the public relations firm Ketchum $1 million to produce and distribute video news releases that promoted the programs and evaluate media coverage.

However, investigative journalists discovered that part of the contract with Ketchum included paying conservative commentator Armstrong Williams $240,000 to promote the NCLB

The Photo Op

A key element in any presidency is the carefully staged photo opportunity. Here, President Bush speaks about the No Child Left Behind legislation with appropriate signage behind him.

Act in television and radio appearances. Representative George Miller (D-California) was among the many who questioned what appeared to be an illegal promotion of the administration's initiative in order to gain political advantage.

Also at issue was the use of video news releases (VNRs), which are often run by TV stations without attribution,

a common broadcasting practice. Federal law specifically prohibits the government from using public funds to actively promote or support a partisan issue. The Government Accounting Office ruled that Ketchum had failed to openly acknowledge the government's role in the production of the NCLB VNRs and that, as such, the VNRs were covert propaganda.

Global travel, migration, and mass media have brought corners of the world closer together as neighbors and collaborators in communication efforts. Integrated global communication in health matters probably rivals the best work of multinational corporations when it comes to health challenges such as containing viral epidemics. Cooperation between Mexico and the United States serves as a fine example. Health officials announced the outbreak of the H1N1 virus, also known early on as swine flu, in Mexico on March 18, 2009. By late April, news of 80 deaths and about 3,600 confirmed cases had been disseminated to the American public. Swine flu was declared a public emergency and the World Health Organization (WHO) announced a pandemic alert level of 5, the second highest level. In the United States, the Centers for Disease Control (CDC) in Atlanta served as a clearing house for information about the progress of the disease.

Although the U.S. response in general, and the CDC's in particular, have been widely praised by health officials, politicians, and journalists, comparatively little credit has been given to Mexican health and public information officials. Their swift action and the sacrifices made by the Mexican people appear to have prevented an international pandemic. But the overnight response did not really happen overnight. Years, even decades, of crisis management planning were required.

In the mid-1980s, Mexico established a network of 11,000 disease-surveillance units. Mexico was among the first countries to implement the program, designed by the CDC. A similar template was employed successfully by the European CDC, based in Stockholm Sweden, in spite of the challenges of providing risk and crisis communication for a loose federation of independent countries.

Effective communication ensured that residents complied with the order. The streets of Mexico City, normally jammed with traffic, were all but empty. Messages were disseminated over a variety of channels. Public communications stressed, for example, that anyone exhibiting symptoms should see a physician for immediate treatment. Most importantly, health officials and government agencies, for the most part, followed the rules of effective public relations. They delivered messages that were factual, consistent, and repeated. Thus, panic did not ensue. Most importantly, closing the country probably averted a pandemic. It did, however, wreak havoc on the Mexican tourism industry and probably cost the country up to 0.5 percent of its annual GDP.

State Governments

Like the federal government, each of the 50 states disseminates information about its programs to various constituents. States also compete to develop campaigns to encourage tourism, to attract new residents, and to advance the interest of the state. State public information officers are often tasked with encouraging business and economic development. Often, the work is subcontracted to private public relations firms. Delaware, a small state with fewer than 800,000 people, awarded a public relations firm a $600,000 contract to create a campaign to attract business investment in the state. The public relations firm used the slogan "It's good being first," referring to Delaware's being the first colonial state to ratify the U.S. Constitution. The public relations firm admitted it was a difficult assignment. But the slogan seems to have been a success, as it allowed a number of tie-ins to promote tourism. For example, playing on the theme of "first," the state ran a promotion in 2009 that offered a free first night if visitors booked at least two nights of lodging at one of a number of participating hotels.

Publicizing quality of life issues has emerged as a highly competitive arena that draws on the resources of public relations professionals across many divisions or branches of state government. North Carolina, for example, saw a 2.2 percent decline in the aggregate crime rate from 2007 to 2008. Public affairs officers from the State Bureau of Investigation, the Attorney General, and the Department of Justice publicized the decline. A particular point of pride was that the city of Carey was named the fourth safest city in the United States, according to "City Crime Rankings 2008–2009: Crime in Metropolitan America."

Every state provides an array of public information services. In California, the most populous state, there are about 175 public information officers (PIOs) in about 70 state agencies. On a daily basis, PIOs provide routine information to the public and the press on the policies, programs, and activities of the many facets of the state's government.

State agencies also conduct a variety of public information and education campaigns, often with the assistance of public relations firms that have been selected via a bidding process. In a typical bidding process, a state agency will issue a request for proposal (RFP) and award a contract on the basis of presentations from competing firms.

One primary campaign area is health and safety. Most states, in recent years, have spent considerable money trying to convince people not to smoke. The funds, from the national tobacco settlement and state-imposed cigarette taxes, have provided somewhat of a windfall in available funds. California generates about $120 million annually from tobacco taxes, and about 10 percent of that is devoted to anti-smoking advertising and public relations. In a somewhat ironic twist, however, it is turning out that as smoking decreases, the amount of taxes collected also decreases, and there is thus less money for such campaigns. For health communicators this would be the ultimate in proverbial good problems to have: no more "customers" for smoking cessation programs.

One of the most concerted and visible communication functions of state government is health communication. For example, the California Department of Health Services (DHS) runs campaigns on a variety of health issues, such as childhood immunizations, breast cancer screening, and teen pregnancy prevention. The California Highway Patrol (CHP) also conducts safety campaigns. One recent campaign was an effort to increase seat belt use and decrease drunk driving accidents among African Americans because statistical data indicate that this audience is less likely to use seat belts and is more likely to die in an alcohol-rated crash than other demographic groups. Even though the implications drawn by some about behavioral patterns could be construed as judgmental, the health benefits of using these observations to develop strategies to reduce deaths are clear. Focusing on such disparities in health outcomes is a frequent, proven means of getting media attention, which can then be leveraged to change knowledge and behavior by reaching large audiences. The jury is still out among health communication researchers, however, whether emphasizing the divide in health outcomes motivates or discourages the target group.

States also promote tourism through advertising and public relations campaigns. Tourism and conventions are the second largest industry in Wisconsin, so its Department of Tourism concentrates on branding Wisconsin as a destination for cheese lovers (350 types of cheese are produced there) and beer drinkers ("Beer Capital of the U.S."). The Illinois Department of Commerce and Economic Opportunity recently awarded a $6.5 million contract to Edelman Worldwide to develop a tourism campaign. Tourism is also big business in Texas. About 500,000 people are employed in the Lone Star State's tourism industry, which generates about $57 billion in spending on an annual basis. In 2009, the state spent almost $2 million on public relations and advertising just in an effort to lure European travelers.

Local Governments

Cities employ information specialists to disseminate news and information from numerous municipal departments, which include the airport, transit district, redevelopment office, parks and recreation, convention and visitors bureau, police and fire, city council, and the mayor's office.

The information flow occurs in many ways, but the objectives are always to inform citizens about, and to help them take full advantage of, government services. The city council holds neighborhood meetings; the airport commission sets up an exhibit showing the growth needs of the airport; the recreation department promotes summer swimming lessons; and the city's human rights commission sponsors a festival promoting multiculturalism.

Cities also promote themselves to attract new business. *PRWeek* reported, "The competition for cities and wider regions to attract businesses is as intense as ever, experts say, with an estimated 12,000 economic development organizations vying for the roughly 500 annual corporate moves/expansions that involve 250 or more jobs each." Many cities pump millions of dollars into attracting new business through a variety of communication tools, including elaborate brochures, placement of favorable "success" stories in the nation's press, direct mail, telemarketing, trade fairs, special events, and meetings with business executives.

Detractors question whether expensive campaigns—combined with free land, tax incentives, and donated infrastructure from local government—ever get paid off through purported economic growth. Public relations professionals can better plan for this criticism of business recruitment if they understand the life cycle of an issue and the role of public relations and strategic conflict management, as presented in Chapter 10.

Cities often promote themselves in an effort to increase tourism. One example of this is the campaign by the Panama City (Florida) Convention and Visitors Bureau to position Panama City as a prime destination for college students during spring break. According to *PRWeek*, the bureau spent about $300,000 promoting the city through posters, news releases, brochures, advertising, and special events to let students know that they are welcome to visit.

Cities often promote tourism through cultural attractions and special events. Initiatives range from traditional tactics, such as issuing press releases, to more ambitious efforts at outreach, such as creating interactive media sites. For example, the city of Little Rock, in 2009, took an active role in promoting the exhibition "World of the Pharaohs: Treasures of Ancient Egypt Revealed" at the Arkansas Arts Center by issuing press releases and providing other news subsidies. The city of Boston operates a social media center (http://www.cityofboston.gov/news/socialmedia.asp) with links to Facebook, Twitter, YouTube, and LinkedIn sites.

Frequently cities compete for federal funds to undertake ambitious projects such as increasing nonmotorized commuting through health campaigns in conjunction with improved bikeways and sidewalks. The infusion of significant state or federal dollars enables local public information departments to engage in more systematic, campaign-based communication programs than can be done with local budgets alone. This movement has actually resulted in a friendly competition among cities vying to be the most bike friendly, touting the miles of trails and downtown bike-loan programs. See the Multicultural World box on page 510 for an example of a sophisticated campaign to increase applications from African American and Latino high school students for financial aid funds for higher education in Charlotte, NC; Long Beach, CA; and Philadelphia, PA.

on the job

A MULTICULTURAL WORLD

It Takes a Community

The U.S. Department of Education has not often been in the limelight in recent years for exemplary communication performance. But the judges at *PRWeek* recognized a combination of fine communication tactics and a worthwhile goal in the department's campaign to increase participation in higher education by minority populations in the United States.

The three-year program in three test markets—Philadelphia, PA; Charlotte, NC; and Long Beach, CA—was devised to increase submissions to the Free Application for Federal Student Aid (FAFSA) from African American and Latino high school students. Research in the three test markets encouraged Crosby Marketing to craft customized messages for target audiences based on zip code and graduation rates. With the widespread adoption of Global Information Systems, or GIS, a wide array of health and pro-social campaigns are able to develop highly targeted campaign efforts to address disparities in health outcomes, or in this

case, participation in the American dream through post–high school education. Focus groups revealed that both ethnic groups would listen to peers and mentors more than parents about college and FAFSA.

Although tactics were tailored to each market, they all were rooted in leveraging existing college access groups, as well as other community and local education stakeholders, to support increased awareness about FAFSA. These influentials enabled a two-step flow approach to increase the persuasive value of the campaign on undecided high school students. The team also provided media relations support as well as public service announcements in each market. Recruitment and training of volunteers for one-on-one support in learning about FAFSA and filling out the applications were critical.

This is a classic case of using mass media to "condition the market," much as one would do in integrated marketing communication efforts for the sale

of a consumer product, which is then finalized through personal "closing" by the community volunteers. Media impressions approached 3.5 million, providing increased awareness and predisposition to at least consider applying to college with support from financial aid sources.

Results were outstanding, as the rate of original FAFSA submissions exceeded previous years in both Charlotte and Philadelphia. The Latino effort in Long Beach surpassed its first-year goal for FAFSA completion by 24 percent.

To extend the reach of the pilot program, a 66-page evaluation report was created by Crosby, and a toolkit for establishing FAFSA outreach programs in other markets included how-to advice and templates for college access coordinators and other education stakeholders.

Source: Multicultural Marketing Campaign of the Year, 2010; retrieved from www.PRWeekus.com

Public Information and Public Affairs

Ever since the ancient Egyptians established the first unified state more than 5,000 years ago, governments have engaged in what is now known as public information and public affairs. It is not an exaggeration to say that human history is, to a large degree, rooted in the history of public relations.

There has always been a need for government communications, if for no other reason than to inform citizens of the services available and the manner in which they may be used. In a democracy, public information is crucial if citizens are to make intelligent judgments about policies and the activities of their elected representatives. Governments provide information in the hope that citizens will absorb the necessary background to participate fully in the formation of government policies. Public relations plays an important, but not an uncheckered, role in helping citizens make more informed choices at the ballot box, in the grocery store, at the doctor's office, behind the wheel of a car—basically, throughout all walks of life.

People, especially journalists, often criticize government public information activities as simply producing reams of useless news releases promoting individual legislators or justifying questionable policies. Such criticisms, coupled with snide news stories about the cost of maintaining government "public relations" experts, rankle dedicated public information officers (PIOs) at the various state and federal agencies who work very hard to keep the public informed with a daily diet of announcements and news stories. One PIO for a California agency said, "I'd like to see the press find out what's going on in state government without us."

Indeed, a major source of media hostility seems to stem from the fact that reporters are heavily dependent on news subsidies. One study found that almost 90 percent of one state government's news releases were used by daily and weekly newspapers. In fact, according to mass media scholars Peter Sandman, David Rubin, and David Sachsman, "If a newspaper were to quit relying on news releases, but continued covering the news it now covers, it would need at least two or three times more reporters."

Public information efforts can be justified in terms of cost savings. The U.S. Department of Agriculture's public affairs office, for example, receives thousands of inquiries a year. Two-thirds of the requests can be answered via a simple pamphlet, brochure, or link on its website, which solves problems for food producers, large and small, all provided under the umbrella of public information.

Preventive public relations also saves money. The taxpayers of California spend about $7 billion annually to deal with the costs associated with teenage pregnancy. Consequently, $5.7 million spent on a successful sex education campaign potentially could save the state welfare costs, as well as human costs such as personal despair and lost childhoods for young mothers.

One Associated Press reporter acknowledged in a story that government information does have value. He wrote:

> While some of the money and manpower goes for self-promotion, by far the greater amount is committed to an indispensable function of a democratic government—informing the people. What good would it serve for the Consumer Product Safety Commission to recall a faulty kerosene heater and not go to the expense of alerting the public to its action? An informed citizenry needs the government to distribute its economic statistics, announce its antitrust suits, tell about the health of the President, give crop forecasts.

I'd like to see the press find out what's going on in state government without us.

A public information officer for a California governmental agency

If a newspaper were to quit relying on news releases, but continued covering the news it now covers, it would need at least two or three times more reporters.

Peter Sandman, David Rubin, and David Sachsman, in Media: An Introductory Analysis of American Mass Communications

Government Relations by Corporations

Government relations, closely related to lobbying, is a specialized component of corporate communication. This activity is so important that many companies, particularly in highly regulated industries, have separate departments of government relations. The reason is simple: The actions of governmental bodies at the local, state, and federal levels have a major impact on how businesses operate. Government relations specialists, often called public affairs specialists, have a number of functions: They gather information, disseminate management's views, cooperate with government on projects of mutual benefit, and motivate employees to participate in the political process.

As the eyes and ears of a business or industry, practitioners in government relations positions spend considerable time gathering and processing information. They monitor the activities of many legislative bodies and regulatory agencies to keep track of issues coming up for debate and possible vote. This intelligence gathering enables a corporation or an industry to plan ahead and, if necessary, adjust policies or provide information that may influence the nature of government decision making.

Businesses monitor government in many ways. Probably the most active presence in Washington, D.C., and many state capitals is that of the trade associations that represent various industries. A Boston University survey found that 67 percent of the responding companies monitor government activity in Washington through their trade associations. The second monitoring effort cited on the list was frequent trips to Washington by senior public affairs officers and corporate executives; 58 percent of the respondents said they engage in this activity. Almost 45 percent of the responding firms reported that they have a company office in the nation's capital.

Government relations specialists also spend a great deal of time disseminating information about the company's position to a variety of key publics. Their tactics can include informal office visits to government officials or testimony at public hearings. In addition, public affairs people are often called on to give speeches or to write speeches for senior executives. They may write letters and op-ed articles, prepare position papers, produce newsletters, and place advocacy advertising.

Although legislators are the primary audience for government relations efforts, the Foundation for Public Affairs reports that 9 out of 10 companies also communicate with their own employees on public policy issues. Another 40 percent communicate with retirees, customers, and other publics such as taxpayers and government employees.

Lobbying

The term *lobbyist* may have originally been coined by President Ulysses S. Grant, who often sought refuge with a cigar and brandy in the Hotel Willard's lobby in Washington, D.C. He is said to have used the term to describe the people who sought favors from him when he was thus engaged.

Today, lobbying is more formal and more closely aligned with governmental relations or public affairs; in fact, the distinction between the two often blurs. This is because most campaigns to influence impending legislation have multiple levels. One level is informing and convincing the public about the correctness of an organization's viewpoint, which is the domain of the public affairs specialist. Lobbyist efforts, another level, are aimed at the defeat, passage, or amendment of legislation and regulatory agency policies.

Lobbyists work at the local, state, and federal levels of government. California has about 900 registered lobbyists, who represent more than 1,600 special interest groups. The interests represented in the state capital, Sacramento, include large corporations, business and trade groups, unions, environmental groups, local governments, nonprofit groups, school districts, and members of various professional groups.

The number and variety of special interests increase exponentially at the federal level. James A. Thurber, a professor of government at American University and a lobbying expert, estimates that Washington, D.C., now has about 260,000 lobbyists, including support staff. This number, says Thurber, doubled in the past decade. According to him, lobbying is now a $2 billion industry. See the Ethics box below about lobbying by the student loan industry, for an example of how lobbying can be called an "insider's game." Not only do lobbyists need to get inside the government to impact legislation, but because the issues are so specialized, oftentimes only an insider, a lobbyist, can sort them out.

on the job

ETHICS

Student Loan Industry Launches Lobbying Campaign

Public relations people face ethical dilemmas in the course of their work, often without the challenge being formally identified or anyone hitting a "moral pause button" while the pros and cons are deliberated.

Although we may think of ethical considerations as requiring a complicated set of deliberations that follow from religious or philosophical principles, we are just as likely to encounter ethical questions as the natural consequences of doing our jobs for an organization that we believe in.

For example, lobbying in Washington affects all legislation, including student loan programs. The Obama administration introduced legislation to bypass private lenders and make loans directly to college students, but the student loan industry mounted a lobbying campaign to defeat such legislation. Sallie Mae, the nation's biggest student lender, with $22 billion in student loans, spent $8 million on lobbying in 2009, and other private lenders spent millions of dollars more, according to the Center for Responsive Politics. In

addition, political action committees (PACs) for lenders and company employees made $2.1 million in political contributions during 2009 to various democratic and republican candidates.

Some of the industry's lobbying tactics were sit-down sessions with key legislators, town hall meetings, and petition drives to help mobilize opposition to the legislation. The strategy was to persuade legislators that the proposal would do more harm than good for the estimated 10 million students who get loans every year.

The student loan industry argued that direct federal loans to students would force it out of business and cause unemployment among its 35,000 workers around the country. Industry lobbyists also claimed that a "federal takeover" of the student loan business would deny students the opportunity to talk directly with a loan counselor and to choose from a selection of loan packages. The industry also said that it could do a better job than the government of ensuring that students pay back their loans.

All of these arguments are plausible and those making them undoubtedly felt doing so was perfectly ethical.

The Obama administration countered that the government would save about $80 billion over the next decade in fees paid to private lenders for handling federally backed student loans. These savings could then be used for early learning programs, community colleges, and the modernization of public school facilities.

Again, what could be morally wrong with making these points in the debate?

The outcome, due to the intense lobbying of the student loan industry, was compromise legislation that gives private companies a more active role in originating student loans than what had been proposed in the original legislation.

A conservative or even libertarian critic of large government would say that industry efforts stemmed at least part of the tide of inefficient large government, making the lobby effort a highly ethical undertaking. On the other hand, the Obama administration remained convinced that it'd had the best interests of students in mind when it took an ethical stand to propose elimination of private student loans.

So, who can claim the moral high ground in this case?

The simple answer to this riddle might be to applaud a compromise, but that may just be wishy-washy moral reasoning. Perhaps a better approach would be to take a close look at your own value system and to seek work in your career for organizations that mesh with your view of the world. Once you are on board with the mission and worldview of your employer, make your case in public debates as best you can in the

interests of all concerned. And do not hesitate to say that "the moral pause button" is needed to sort things out for yourself—and for your employer.

Lobbyists represent the interests of virtually the entire spectrum of U.S. business, educational, religious, local, national, and international pursuits. Lobbying is also conducted on behalf of foreign governments and interests. The American-Israel Public Affairs Committee (AIPAC), for example, is a major player in Washington because of its impressive resources. According to the *Economist*, "AIPAC has an annual budget of around $60 million, more than 275 employees, an endowment of over $130 million, and a new $80 million building on Capitol Hill."

The variety of lobbying groups at the federal level is apparent when we consider the debate and maneuvering about health care that continued even after the major reform bill had been passed. This sort of thing occurs because federal insiders know that the real impact of legislation is largely filled out in the detailed regulations and procedures developed to implement the will of Congress. Opposing the details of this new regulation are: (1) insurance companies, (2) HMO trade groups, (3) the U.S. Chamber of Commerce, (4) the National Federation of Independent Businesses, and (5) the American Association of Health Plans. Groups supporting patient rights include: (1) a broad coalition of consumer groups, (2) the American Medical Association, and (3) the Trial Lawyers of America. The drug and biotech industries, for example, spent about $110 million in the first nine months of 2009 to influence health care legislation; that translates to about $600,00 a day. According to *Time* magazine, "The drug industry's legion of registered lobbyists numbers 1,228, or about 3.3 lobbyists for every member of Congress."

Much of this activity enables influence by vested interests. However, lobbyists also bring to bear expertise and input from many contending perspectives, which help to forge the actual guidelines and procedures in ways that legislative aides cannot always accomplish. In spite of our concerns as citizens for the undue influence of those with much to gain, the system of making legislation a working reality in government offices now requires lobbyists' expertise and resources.

Ideally, competing lobbying efforts often cancel each other out. This leaves legislators and regulatory personnel with the chore of weighing the pros and cons of an issue before voting. Indeed, *Time* magazine notes that competition among lobbyists representing different sides of an issue "do[es] serve a useful purpose by showing busy legislators the virtues and pitfalls of complex legislation."

A perennial conflict that lobbyists weigh in on is the debate between saving jobs and improving the environment. A coalition of environmental groups constantly lobbies Congress for tougher legislation to clean up industrial pollution or protect endangered species. Simultaneously, local communities and unions may counter that the proposed legislation would result in the loss of jobs and economic chaos. The galvanizing effect of the world's largest single environmental disaster in the Gulf is only now beginning to shift the lines of that discourse for what will be at least the next half decade, with environmental concerns likely to have more credence than has been true for several decades.

Most groups claim to be lobbying in the "public interest." Is it in the "public interest," a lobbyist may ask, to throw thousands of people out of work or to legislate so many restrictions on the manufacture of a product that it becomes more expensive for the average consumer? Or, should the community risk possible long-term and irreversible damage to the environment? The answer, quite often, depends on whether one is a steelworker, a logger, a consumer, or a member of the World Wildlife Federation. Much of the debate takes place against the backdrop of minimal or no changes in the conservation lifestyle of most Americans. Without dramatic changes in consumption that will be largely shaped by government policy, combined with the crucial role of public relations and government communication, the debate about whether vice presidential candidate Sarah Palin's famous chant "Drill Baby Drill" was right or not will be moot. A shift in the will and determination of American citizens will ultimately be a communication accomplishment, followed by technical innovation, not the reverse.

Pitfalls of Lobbying

Although a case can be made for lobbying as a legitimate activity, deep public suspicion exists about former legislators and officials who capitalize on their connections and charge large fees for doing what is commonly described as "influence peddling." Indeed, the roster of registered lobbyists in Washington includes a virtual who's who of former legislators and government officials from both the Democratic and Republican Parties. According to the watchdog group Center for Public Integrity, more than 12 percent of current lobbyists are former executives and legislative branch employees. This includes more than 200 former members of Congress (175 from the House, 34 from the Senate), and 42 former agency heads.

The Ethics in Government Act forbids government officials from actively lobbying their former agencies for one year after leaving office. Critics say, however, that this law has had little or no impact. A good case study is the U.S. Department of Homeland Security. Tom Ridge was head of the agency when it was established in 2002; he has since left to become a lobbyist with a long list of clients from the security industry who seek contracts with Homeland Security, which has a budget of more than $40 billion to spend. Ridge is not alone. A *New York Times* article written during the Bush administration reported that at least 90 former officials at the Department of Homeland Security or the White House Homeland Security office, two-thirds of the most senior executives, have become lobbyists.

Unlike federal agency personnel, members of Congress can become lobbyists immediately after leaving office. Consider former Representative J. C. Watts (R-Oklahoma), who announced the formation of a group of lobbying and public affairs firms exactly one day after leaving office. High-ranking members of Watts' congressional staff moved with him to his new offices to begin their careers as lobbyists of their former colleagues.

Instances of people "cashing in" on connections give the press and the public the uneasy feeling that influence peddling is alive and well in the nation's capitol. This practice also gives credence to the cliché "It's not what you know, but who you know." The scandal involving lobbyist Jack Abramoff reveals how closely tied legislators are to lobbyists. Abramoff's financial mismanagement and willingness to dispense illegal perks to legislators earned him a lengthy prison sentence. Further, Republican House Majority Leader Tom Delay (R-Texas) had to resign his leadership post and Ohio Congressman Bob Ney pleaded guilty to two counts of conspiracy and making false statements in the Abramoff scandal. About half a dozen other legislators and dozens of congressional aides and other government officials remain under scrutiny.

Grassroots Lobbying

Politicians in both parties have regularly decried the influence of lobbyists, but reform has taken a half-century. At least 10 times since the first loophole-riddled lobbying regulations were passed in 1946, efforts to update the law failed to get past the legislative obstacles. In 1995, however, Congress did pass a measure designed to reform lobbying, and President Clinton signed it. Part of the impetus, no doubt, were the polls indicating that the public believed lobbyists had runaway influence in Washington.

One key provision was an expanded definition of who is considered to be a "lobbyist." The 1995 law defined a lobbyist as "someone hired to influence lawmakers, government officials or their aides, and who spends at least 20 percent of his or her time representing any client in a six-month period." Another key provision requires lobbyists to register with Congress and disclose their clients, the issue areas in which lobbying is being done, and roughly how much is being paid for it. Violators face civil fines of up to $50,000.

One area exempted from the lobby reform bill is financial disclosures for so-called grassroots lobbying, the fastest-growing phenomenon in the political persuasion business.

Grassroots lobbying is now an $800 million industry, according to *Campaigns and Elections*, a bimonthly magazine for "political professionals." What makes it so attractive to various groups is that there are virtually no rules or regulations. The tools of this sort of lobbying are advocacy advertising, toll-free phone lines, bulk faxing, websites, and computerized direct mail aimed at generating phone calls and letters from the public to Congress, the White House, and governmental regulatory agencies.

Grassroots lobbying also involves coalition building. The basic idea is to get individuals and groups with no financial interest in the issue to speak on the sponsor's behalf. The premise is that letters and phone calls from private citizens are more influential than arguments from vested interests. Such "grassroots" campaigns make public interest groups wonder if they really shouldn't be called "Astroturf" campaigns, since the "grass" is often artificial. Michael Pertschuk, codirector of the Advocacy Institute in Washington, D.C., told *O'Dwyer's PR Services Report*, "Astroturf groups are usually founded with corporate seed money that is funneled through PR firms."

Election Campaigns

Public affairs activities and lobbying, either in the halls of Congress or at the grassroots level, are year-round activities. During election years, either congressional or presidential, an army of fund-raisers, political strategists, speech writers, and communication consultants mobilize to help candidates win elections.

The high cost of running for office in the United States has made fund-raising virtually a full-time, year-round job for every incumbent and aspirant to office. In fact, American-style campaigning is the most expensive in the world.

Candidates retain professionals to organize fund-raising activities. A standard activity in Washington, D.C., and other major cities across the country is the luncheon, reception, or dinner on behalf of a candidate. The *Wall Street Journal*, for example, reported that 14 such events were held on a single day in October, raising $650,000 for congressional incumbents. Individual donors and lobbyists for various organizations regularly attend these events. Although a chicken dinner or a cheese platter with crackers and champagne is not exactly worth $2,000 a person in literal terms, the event shows support of the candidate and allows donors to have contact with him or her. No business is actually discussed, but the occasion gives both individuals and lobbyists for special interests an opportunity to show the "flag" and perhaps indirectly influence legislation or open the door for personnel appointments at a later date after the election, if the candidate wins.

Some consultants specialize in direct mail and telemarketing. They are assisted by firms that specialize in computer databases and mailing lists. Aristotle Publishers, for example, claims to have records on 128 million registered voters. A candidate can obtain a tailored list of prospects using any number of demographic variables, including party affiliation, voting record, contribution record, age, geographic location, and opinions on various issues.

Other firms handle mass mailings on behalf of candidates. Kiplinger Computer and Mailing Services, for example, is capable of running envelopes at 10,000 per hour and printing personalized letters at 120 pages per minute.

The latest tool for fund-raising and reaching supporters is the Internet, with one key use in political campaigns being research. The *Wall Street Journal*, for example, reported that a Kerry support organization in Concord, New Hampshire, was able to track down Democratic women voters, aged 18 to 30, who were interested in abortion rights; within seconds, the computer was able to generate the names of 812 such women and also provide a street map marking their addresses. Members of Planned Parenthood and other Kerry supporters followed up with door-to-door visits on behalf of the presidential candidate.

The Internet was used for campaign fund-raising and building grassroots support during the 2000 presidential election. However, its effectiveness was not realized until the 2004 election, when former Vermont Governor Howard Dean used the Internet to build a grassroots network, motivate potential voters, and—perhaps most importantly—raise funds. Dean also used social networks such as *Meetup.com* to interact with constituents. Dean's campaign initially had fewer financial resources than campaigns of his competitors, but by making efficient use of the Internet, he soon leveled the playing field by raising a large amount of money thanks to thousands of small donations.

Candidates during the 2008 campaign wisely followed Dean's strategy of using the Internet. Although some have argued that no one candidate exploited its full potential, Barack Obama achieved notable success by leveraging technology to build core support among college students, young professionals, and independents. Effective use of social media was one crucial factor that allowed the relatively unknown candidate to outmaneuver more experienced and better-financed contenders to secure the Democratic Party nomination and eventually defeat Republican candidate John McCain.

Like Dean, Barack Obama raised an enormous sum of money online by soliciting small donations. In March 2008, for example, he raised $40 million, 90 percent of which came from donations of $100 or less. Advisors helped him craft a strategy to interact

The Obama campaign has come closest to achieving the Holy Grail of politics on the Internet—converting online enthusiasm to offline action.

Andrew Rasiej, a leading analyst of online politics

with supporters online by encouraging them to submit content via sites such as Facebook, YouTube, and Twitter. YouTube videos by ObamaGirl were particularly memorable examples of his online grassroots support. Obama interacted with wired voters by posting regularly on his Facebook page and sending a constant stream of Tweets, which recapped each campaign stop and shared news of upcoming rallies and events. By contrast, candidate John McCain made what was perhaps the fatal error among younger voters by admitting that he knew almost nothing about computers or the Internet. See the Insights box below for more on the rising importance of social media in political campaigns.

Of course, there is a downside to relying on the Internet and social media. Candidates surrender some measure of control over

on the job

INSIGHTS

Social Media and the 2008 Election

The Internet and social media sites such as Facebook, MySpace, and *Meetup.org* took a more prominent role during the 2008 presidential election than ever before. Barack Obama, John McCain, and Hillary Clinton all employed social media to raise funds and mobilize support. However, while all major candidates used social media somewhat effectively in 2007 and 2008, no one consistently integrated social media into his or her campaign strategy. "Many [candidate] sites are poorly structured, are built without regard to best practices or search strategy, and don't seem to be part of a cohesive unit," asserts J. Barbush of independent public relations agency RPA. Also, social media initiatives have usually been geared toward younger demographics, limiting their appeal to 20- and 30-somethings. Given this fact, it may not be the case that candidates have not fully

exploited the potential of new media, as much as it is the case that the number of voters capable of, or interested in, receiving messages via social media has not reached a critical mass.

Despite these issues, there were some encouraging developments. Obama was particularly effective in raising millions of dollars by soliciting small donations on sites such as Facebook. Libertarian fringe candidate Ron Paul (R-Texas) raised $4M in a single day. And *McCainblogett.com*, a blog operated by John McCain's daughter, Meghan, was well conceived, according to Barbush. He notes that it helped to "reframe perceptions and infuse humanity into the otherwise confusing area of campaign-based rhetoric." Barbush even adds this, about reading the blog: "I was relating to McCain as a father."

It is likely that there will be a gradual evolution in campaign strategies, as

candidates and political parties become more sophisticated in their use of new media and move toward realizing the full potential of social media.

1. If you were in charge of the new media initiatives for a political candidate, what are some of the strategies and tactics that you might use to gain an advantage over competitors?

2. What social media–focused public relations activities would be appropriate for government organizations to use at the federal, state and local levels?

3. What are the potential risks of using social media in corporate government relations or lobbying, and how can they be avoided?

PEARSON
mycommunicationlab

the message and discussion. Any gaffes are instantly amplified through re-tweets and message boards. Constant vigilance is needed to rebut gossip and misinformation. And the opposition can create rogue websites that spoof or mimic that of the candidate. Despite these caveats, the Internet and social media have proven to be effective as both public relations tactics and strategy. Kate Kenski, of the National Annenberg Election Survey, notes, "Considering that over half of young adults are using the Internet for obtaining political information, the Internet will continue to capture a larger share of where people get their political information with each passing election cycle." Candidates in the future will ignore it at their peril.

Candidates in election campaigns also employ groups of consultants and other technicians such as position paper writers, speech writers, graphic artists, computer experts, webmasters, media strategists, advertising experts, radio and television producers, public affairs experts, pollsters, and public relations specialists. A highly visible and critical job is done by advance people, who spend many hours organizing events, arranging every detail, and making sure there's a cheering crowd, with signs, when the candidate arrives. On a single day, for example, a presidential candidate may give five to seven talks at rallies in multiple states. As is the case with most of the public relations activities and events described in this chapter, a cadre of individuals often works behind the scenes to orchestrate these events and initiatives. To ensure that the candidate's speech is received under the best possible circumstances, public relations professionals mobilize the audience and the media, manage potential risks, avert or handle crises that arise, and provide assessment of the results with polls and reports after each speech.

Summary

Government Organizations

- Governments have always engaged in campaigns to educate, inform, motivate, and even persuade the public.

- In the United States, Congress forbids federal agencies from "persuading" the public, so the emphasis is on "public information" efforts.

The Federal, State, and Local Governments

- The U.S. federal government is the largest disseminator of information in the world.

- The apex of all government information and public relations efforts is the White House; the President's every move and action are chronicled by the mass media. Presidents throughout history have used this media attention to lead the nation, convince the public to support administration policies, and get reelected.

- All agencies of the federal government employ public affairs officers and public information specialists. Members of Congress also engage in extensive information efforts to reach their constituents.

- Various states employ public information officers to tell the public about the activities and policies of various

agencies. In addition, state agencies conduct a number of campaigns to inform the public about health and safety issues and to promote the state as a tourist destination.

- All major cities employ public information specialists to tell citizens about city services and promote economic development.

Public Information and Public Affairs

- A major component of corporate communication is public affairs, which primarily deals with governmental relations at the local, state, national, and even international levels.

- Public affairs specialists build relationships with civil servants and elected officials and also monitor governmental actions that may affect the employer or client.

- Trade groups, representing various professions and industries and primarily based in state capitals or Washington, D.C., have public affairs specialists who engage in governmental relations.

- A public affairs specialist primarily provides information about an organization's viewpoint to the public and government entities. A lobbyist has the more specialized function of directly working for the defeat, passage, or amendment of legislation and regulatory agency policies.

■ In recent years, there has been public concern about "influence peddling" in terms of former legislators and other officials becoming lobbyists and "cashing in" on their knowledge and connections. To curb abuse, several laws have been passed to regulate lobbyists.

Government Relations by Corporations

■ Although closely related to lobbying, government relations involves the broader functions of gathering information, disseminating management's views, and cooperating with government on projects of mutual benefit as well as motivating employees to take part in the political process.

■ One of the most active forms of corporate government relations is the work of trade associations in Washington, D.C., and state capitals on behalf of industries.

Lobbying

■ Lobbyists represent the interests of virtually the entire spectrum of U.S. business, educational, religious, local, national, and international pursuits.

■ Lobbying is a formal process closely aligned with corporate and organizational governmental relations.

■ Lobbyist efforts are aimed at the defeat, passage, or amendment of legislation and regulatory agency policies in the interests of the corporation or advocacy organization.

Election Campaigns

■ An army of specialists, including public relations experts, are retained by major candidates to organize and raise money for election campaigns.

■ In recent years, the Internet has played an important role in raising money, generating high visibility for candidates, and increasing the number of registered voters.

Case Activity   How Do You Communicate Proactively?

Disaster response in Louisiana has improved vastly since Hurricanes Katrina and Rita devastated the coast and flooded New Orleans. Katrina and Rita had horrific impacts, in both a physical and an emotional sense. And as they attacked the state, it became immediately clear that they represented communication disasters as well, by revealing a lack of comprehensive risk management.

One of the dilemmas faced by local, state, and federal governments when a hurricane looms is how, and when, to warn residents of the danger. If government officials issue warnings too often or too early or raise the alarm in cases where a major hurricane does not end up hitting land, there is a risk that residents will become desensitized and learn to disregard the warnings. On the other hand, officials face criticism and loss of public trust if they fail to warn citizens in a timely manner.

Consider a scenario in which another Category V storm looms off the coast of New Orleans. National Oceanic and Atmospheric Administration (NOAA) meteorologists predict that there is a 65 percent chance that the storm will hit the city in four days. There is also a chance that it will miss the city entirely. If you were a public affairs specialist for the mayor of New Orleans, what steps would you take immediately to inform the public? What channels of communication would you use? How would you structure your message? What steps would you recommend taking regarding communication with the public if the wrong decisions are made and the situation becomes a catastrophe? Working with a small group, quickly brainstorm a communication plan.

Questions   for Review and Discussion

1. What are the basic purposes and functions of government relations?

2. What is the difference between someone working in corporate public affairs (government relations) and a lobbyist?

3. Many lobbyists are former legislators and government officials. Do you think they exercise undue influence on the shaping of legislation? Why or why not?

4. Fund-raisers play a crucial role in elections. Would you like to be a political fund-raiser? Why or why not?

5. Why do government agencies engage in "public information" efforts instead of "public relations" activities? Are there any laws involved? If so, what are they?

6. Federal agencies engage in any number of public information campaigns. What is your opinion of this? Are these campaigns just a waste of taxpayer dollars, or are they legitimate and necessary?

7. What are some examples of public relations campaigns run by state or local governments?

8. How does public relations at the local level differ from public relations efforts at the state and federal levels? What channels are typically used by federal and local officials to disseminate messages to the public?

9. How do grassroots groups use technologies to disseminate their messages? What are the benefits and risks of using social media to promote an agenda within a political arena?

Media Resources

Appelbaum, B., & Lichtblau, E. (2010, May 9). Banks lobbying against derivatives trading ban. *New York Times*. Retrieved from www.nytimes.com

Berg, K. T. (2009). Finding connections between lobbying, public relations and advocacy. *Public Relations Journal, 3*(3).

Connolly-Ahern, C., Grantham, S., & Cabrera-Baukus, M. (2010). The effects of attribution of VNRs and risk on news viewers' assessments of credibility. *Journal of Public Relations Research, 22*(1), 49–64.

Flights, girls and cash buy Japan whaling votes. (2010, June 13). *The Sunday Times*. Retrieved from www.timesonline.co.uk

Gelders, D., & Ihlen, Ø. (2010). Government communication about potential policies: Public relations, propaganda or both? *Public Relations Review, 36*(1), 59–62.

Gordon, R. (2010, February 1). The Goog, Microsoft, Facebook and K street. *PRWeek*. Retrieved from www.prweekus.com

Lee, K. (2009). How the Hong Kong government lost the public trust in SARS: Insights for government communication in a health crisis. *Public Relations Review, 35*(1), 74–76.

McLean, K. (2010, April 1). Election advocacy still driven more by political climate than Supreme Court ruling. *PRWeek*. Retrieved from www.prweekus.com

Murphree, V., Reber, B. H., & Blevens, F. (2009). Superhero, instructor, optimist: FEMA and the frames of disaster in Hurricanes Katrina and Rita. *Journal of Public Relations Research, 21*(3), 273–294.

Pinkham, D. (2009, December 1). White House efforts to curb special interests is a blow to government access. *PRWeek*. Retrieved from www.prweekus.com

Titus, W. (2009, September 11). Public affairs and government issues management [Podcast]. Retrieved from podcast.prsa.org

Wiseman, P. (2010, June 11). Auto dealers could see new financial regulations. *USA Today*. Retrieved from www.usatoday.com

20
Global Public Relations

After reading this chapter, you will be able to:

Appreciate the practice of public relations in other nations

Know the various cultural values that shape a nation's communication patterns

Recognize the impact of the global economy and the role that public relations plays in that economy

Recognize ways that foreign governments and corporations attempt to influence U.S. legislation and policies

Appreciate the major role that NGOs now play in shaping public opinion

Understand the job opportunities available in global public relations

What Is Global Public Relations?

Global public relations, also called international public relations, is the planned and organized efforts of a company, institution, or government to establish and build relationships with the publics of other nations. These publics are the various groups of people who are affected by, or who can affect, the operations of a particular firm, institution, or government. Increasingly in today's global economy, almost all public relations activity has international aspects.

International public relations can also be viewed from the standpoint of its practice in individual countries. Although public relations is commonly regarded as a concept developed in the United States at the beginning of the 20th century, some of its elements, such as countering unfavorable public attitudes through publicity and annual reports, were practiced by railroad companies in Germany as far back as the mid-19th century, to cite only one example.

Even so, it is largely U.S. public relations techniques that have been adopted throughout the world, even in authoritarian nations. Today, although in some languages there is no term comparable to *public relations*, the practice has spread to most countries, especially those with industrial bases and large urban populations. This is primarily the result of worldwide technological, social, economic, and political changes and the growing understanding that public relations is an essential component of advertising, marketing, and public diplomacy.

Development in Other Nations

Public relations as an occupation and a career has achieved its highest development in the industrialized nations of the world—the United States, Canada, the European Union (EU), and parts of Asia. It develops more rapidly in nations that have (1) multiparty political systems, (2) a relatively free press, (3) considerable private ownership of business and industry, (4) large-scale urbanization, and (5) relatively high per capita income levels, which also impact literacy and educational opportunities.

China's rapid industrialization and movement toward a free-market economy, in particular, has led to explosive growth in its public relations industry. Public relations revenues for the past several years have experienced double-digit gains, and China is now the second largest national economy in the world.

The United States and European nations began exporting their public relations expertise to the People's Republic of China in the mid-1980s. Hill & Knowlton, active in Asia for more than 30 years, began a Beijing operation in a hotel room with three U.S. professionals and a locally hired employee. Today, every global public relations firm has a Beijing or Shanghai office to represent U.S. and European companies in the Chinese market.

Working in China has its challenges. One is the nature of the press, which is state-owned or highly controlled. Although the media are getting more sophisticated, Chinese journalists are still poorly trained and underpaid. As Cindy Payne, director of Asia Pacific Connections, says, "Journalists in China are arguably the worst paid, so to offset the reality of public transportation woes, you are expected to provide a travel allowance."

Global public relations firms and advertising agencies are now buying stakes or affiliating with successful Chinese firms. Porter Novelli, for example, is affiliated with Blue Focus, one of the largest Chinese-owned firms in the country. Gyroscope, a consultancy, estimates that there are about 2,000 public relations firms in China, but most of them are one- or two-person operations primarily dealing with publicity, media

The future of China lies in exporting Chinese brands to the world. That means increasing the value of the "Chinese product" and the "Chinese brand." PR has a vital role in building and maintaining brand value—and a nation which cannot master PR is at an enormous disadvantage.

Public relations executive in Gyroscope's report in The Public Relations Landscape in China

relations, and staging events. Gyroscope notes, "The vast majority of PR spending is on low-value, low-worth publicity, inexpertly planned and delivered, with a small number of clients and agencies focusing on high-value, high-worth strategic consultancy."

Fueling the development of public relations in China have been several major international events. The Beijing Olympics in 2008 placed China on the world stage, and the Shanghai Expo of 2010 affirmed China's influence on the global economy. The six-month Expo attracted an estimated 70 million visitors, and 193 countries erected pavilions and other exhibits. Saudi Arabia, for example, spent $164 million on its pavilion. In addition, thousands of companies from around the world organized other events and exhibits, hoping to make lucrative deals and find new customers.

Other nations and regions, to varying degrees, also have developed larger and more sophisticated public relations industries within the past decade. Here are some thumbnail sketches from around the globe:

Africa   South Africa is a relatively mature market, with a long tradition of public relations education, professional development for practitioners, and large corporations with international outreach. In 2010 South Africa became the first African nation to host the World Cup, which required an extensive international public relations and marketing strategy. Nigeria, the most populous nation in Africa, has made strides in developing its public relations industry, and so has Ghana. Kenya has a relatively well-developed public relations industry because of tourism, but most nations in Africa are still somewhat undeveloped in terms of public relations as an occupation.

Australia, Singapore, and Hong Kong   These are relatively mature public relations markets, offering a variety of services ranging from financial relations to media relations and special event promotion. More attention is given to overall strategic planning and integrating communications for overall corporate objectives. A major growth area in Singapore is in the hospitality and service industries, as the island nation adds new resorts and casinos.

The Shanghai Expo of 2010

Public relations expansion in China is fueled by international events that attract worldwide attention.

Brazil   This country is the largest in South America in terms of population (186 million) and economic power. There are about 1,000 public relations firms, primarily in the São Paulo area. To date, few global public relations firms have established a presence, but this is rapidly changing because the nation's booming economy has made it a major player in the world economy. Brazil will also host the 2016 Olympics, which will generate more development of its public relations industry. Brazil has become a mature business market, and its CEOs are increasingly recognizing the importance of image, reputation, and social responsibility. In addition, the public relations industry in Argentina and Chile also are well developed.

India The Indian market, with more than 1 billion people, is a major market for products, services, and public relations expertise. There are at least 1,000 large and small public relations firms serving the subcontinent, but training and educating qualified practitioners continues to be a major problem. The Public Relations Society of India has increased professionalism among practitioners, but much of the work involves getting visibility in the media. The country's population of more than 1 billion makes it an attractive location for foreign investment and international public relations firms. In addition, Indian firms are now expanding to the global market, and the level of public relations is getting more sophisticated.

Japan Business and industry are still at the stage of perceiving public relations as primarily media relations. Public relations firms and corporate communications departments work very closely with the 400-plus reporters' clubs that filter and process all information for more than 150 news-gathering organizations. Major advertising agencies tend to dominate the public relations field, and there has been little development regarding strategic positioning or how to do crisis communications. Toyota's somewhat inept handling of a product recall in 2010 is an example.

Mexico Traditionally, small public relations firms in Mexico dominated the market and provided primarily product publicity. With the North American Free Trade Agreement, international firms have established operations with more sophisticated approaches to strategic communications.

Middle East The Middle East comprises 22 nations and more than 300 million people. In general, the public relations industry is relatively immature and unstructured, and lacks trained personnel. There is government-censored media and fear of transparent communications. Dubai, which is in the United Arab Emirates, in recent years has positioned itself as a major business center and has attracted many international companies. Consequently, it's expected that public relations services will continue to expand in Dubai as the world's economy recovers from a major recession.

Nordic Countries Public relations is highly developed in these countries, and the *Paul Holmes World Report* quotes one executive as saying, "The PR Industry in the Nordic region is quite developed and on a more strategic and analytic level than in other countries." Norway, Denmark, Sweden, and Finland also have a culture of corporate social responsibility,

INOUE

Public relations is now an international enterprise and every country has its own industry. This ad is for a Japanese public relations firm.

environmental sustainability, labor rights, and gender equality high on the political agenda, so public relations counselors often facilitate programs in these areas.

Russian Federation and the Former Soviet Republics   The rise of a market economy and private enterprise has spurred the development of public relations activity, but continuing problems in the Russian economy have stunted its development. The press and journalists are still very dependent on supplemental income, and news coverage can be "bought" with cash or through political connections. A key issue is the training of public relations professionals; college curriculums are still very weak. Gyroscope, a consultancy, predicts that public relations will continue to develop from its roots in political campaigning to become more corporate and consumer oriented. Ukraine, once part of the Soviet Union, now has a developed public relations industry but suffers some of the same problems as Russia in continuing to develop it.

Thailand   The nation has a great deal of foreign investment and is becoming established as an assembly center for automobiles. It's the primary hub in Southeast Asia for international tourism, and a number of public relations firms and corporations have well-qualified staffs to handle media relations, product publicity, and special event promotion. However, Thailand lacks a cohesive national public relations organization to promote professional development.

International Corporate Public Relations

This section explores the new age of global marketing and addresses the differences in language, laws, and cultural mores that must be overcome when companies conduct business in foreign countries. We also discuss how U.S. public relations firms represent foreign interests in this country as well as U.S. corporations in other parts of the world.

The New Age of Global Marketing

For decades, hundreds of corporations based in the United States have been engaged in international business operations, including marketing, advertising, and public relations. All these activities exploded to unprecedented proportions during the 1990s, largely because of new communications technologies, development of 24-hour financial markets almost worldwide, the lowering of trade barriers, the growth of sophisticated foreign competition in traditionally "American" markets, and shrinking cultural differences, all of which bring the "global village" ever closer to reality.

In the case of Coca-Cola, probably the best-known brand name in the world, international sales account for 70 percent of the company's revenues. In addition, large U.S.-based public relations firms such as Burson-Marsteller and Edelman are now generating between 30 and 40 percent of their fees serving foreign clients.

Today, almost one-third of all U.S. corporate profits are generated through international business. At the same time, overseas investors are moving into American industries. It is not uncommon for 15 to 20 percent of a U.S. company's stock to be held abroad. The United Kingdom, for example, has a direct foreign investment in the United States exceeding $122 billion, followed by Japan and the Netherlands, with nearly half that sum each, according to the U.S. Department of Commerce.

Fueling the new age of global public relations and marketing is the pervasive presence of the Internet. It allows every corporation to have instant contact with any and all of its operations around the world, but the downside is that any problem or crisis in one plant or country is instantly known throughout the world. In addition, satellite television, fax, fiber optics, cellular telephone systems, and technologies such as integrated services digital network (ISDN) enable a blizzard of information via voice, data, graphics, and video. For example, Hill & Knowlton has its own satellite transmission facilities, and General Electric has an international telecommunications network, enabling employees to communicate worldwide using voice, video, and computer data simply by dialing seven digits on a telephone. Using three satellite systems, Cable News Network (CNN) is viewed by more than 200 million people in more than 140 countries. England's BBC World Service also reaches an impressive number of nations, including the 40-plus member nations of the British Commonwealth. A number of newspapers and magazines are also reaching millions with international editions. The *Wall Street Journal* and the *Financial Times* have daily editions in the United States, Europe, and Asia. Other publications, such as the *Economist*, have worldwide distribution.

Much of the jousting for new business takes place on Western European terrain, where the European Union (EU) is a formidable competitor with U.S. firms in the global market. Although hampered by recession in recent years, public relations expenditures have increased significantly. Many European companies extensively use advertising, marketing, and public relations strategies to lure business from nations around the world. A good example is Finnair, which is featured in the Insights box below.

on the job
INSIGHTS

Finnair Looks at the Future of Flying

Will we be flying faster than sound in 2093? Will planes look like flying saucers? And what about space? Will we have business and leisure flights there?

Those were the questions that Finnair, the national carrier of Finland, posed to help celebrate its 85th anniversary and project the image of a forward-looking company with a strong focus on sustainability. A secondary objective was to promote optimism among consumers and employees about the future of travel and aviation.

The major communications vehicle for the campaign was the publication of a book titled *Departure 2093: Five Visions of the Future of Flying*, which featured the forecasts of five experts representing various aspects of the aviation field. The date 2093 was chosen because it tied into the next 85 years of Finnair. The primary target audience was frequent travelers between Europe and Asia. The key public relations messages were to raise awareness of (1) Finnair's long history and (2) its operation of one of the world's most modern fleets of planes.

The airline launched the book in Helsinki with a news conference and also organized speaking engagements in a number of Finnair's Asian destinations such as Delhi, Beijing, and Seoul. At a news conference in Delhi, for example, about 50 journalists attended. Other communication tactics included a *departure2093* website, a tabloid newspaper distributed at various airports around Europe, and videos uploaded on YouTube that illustrated some of the visions portrayed in the book.

The book and the various media events generated about 100 print articles in Europe and Asia. In addition, there were 115 blog posts about *Departure 2093*.

Saudi Aramco World Magazine

International corporations often publish high-quality magazines for distribution to opinion leaders in various nations to increase visibility and enhance their reputation and brand. This quarterly magazine of Saudi Aramco is designed to increase cross-cultural understanding of the Middle East and the Muslim world, where the company has extensive oil operations.

Although the EU promoted the phrase "a single Europe," corporations and public relations firms still face the complex task of communicating effectively to 400 million people in 25 countries speaking multiple languages. Differences in language, laws, and cultural mores among countries are a continuing challenge to culturally sensitive public relations practice. There also is a need for both managers and employees to act locally and think in global terms. Already, Burson-Marsteller, with offices in many countries, is spending more than $1 million a year on training tapes and traveling teams of trainers to foster a uniform approach to client projects.

Language and Cultural Differences

Companies operating in other nations are confronted with essentially the same public relations challenges as those operating in the United States. Their objectives are to compete successfully and to manage conflict effectively, but the task is more complex on an international and intercultural level. Google, for example, had to make cultural adjustments in Japan, which is highlighted in the Multicultural World box on page 529.

Public relations practitioners need to recognize cultural differences, adapt to local customs, and understand the finer points of verbal and nonverbal communication in individual nations. Experts in intercultural communication point out that many cultures, particularly non-Western ones, are "high-context" communication societies. In other words, the meaning of the spoken word is often implicit and based on environmental context and personal relationships rather than on explicit, categorical statements. The communication styles of Asian and Arab nations, for example, are high context.

In contrast, European and American communication styles are considered low context. Great emphasis is placed on exact words, and receivers are expected to derive meaning primarily from the written or verbal statements, not from nonverbal behavior cues. Legal documents produced in the West are the ultimate in explicit wording.

Geert Hofstede, a company psychologist for global giant IBM, studied national/cultural differences among employees around the world back in the 1970s and came up with five basic cultural dimensions. Today, students still rely on his typology to understand various national cultures. Professors David Guth and Charles Marsh of

on the job

A MULTICULTURAL WORLD

Google in Japan: One Size Does Not Fit All

Global companies continue to learn that their products, marketing, and public relations must be "localized" for individual nations. Even Google, the world's leading search engine, found that it had to make some adaptations in the Japanese market.

Google had been in Japan since 2001, but the web giant was a distant second in market share (34 percent) compared to Yahoo! Japan, which handled almost 60 percent of all search queries. One problem was that Yahoo! Japan was the first Web-based search engine in the country. A second problem was that Yahoo! had 35 percent local ownership, so users perceived it as a Japanese company that had mostly Japanese employees. As Nobuyuki Hayashi, a technology analyst, told the *New York Times*, "Google's still a foreigner who's learned to speak some Japanese."

Google wanted to increase market share, but it first had to confront some cultural differences. One was the spare design of Google's opening page. Japanese prefer pages with a lot of graphics and links, so Google added links to YouTube, Gmail, and other services. Google also had to change its "street views" to capture views 15 inches lower because the Japanese complained that the service could peek into people's homes and invade their privacy. Google also found that its map service,

A New Partnership

Google executive Omid Kordestani (C) shakes hands with Japanese communication giant NTT DoCoMo executives Takeshi Natsuno (L) and Kiyoyuki Tsujimura (R).

which usually directs people to the center of town in the United States, was inappropriate because the Japanese heavily rely on mass transit and want maps that direct them to bus and train stations. Google also developed a spelling service to help non-native English speakers with their queries.

Although Google's YouTube was already the most popular video site in Japan, the company refined its features by adding text captions, linked with automatic translation into 50 languages, to many videos on the site. In another innovation, Japanese consumers can buy songs featured in YouTube videos and download them on their cell phones for use as ring tones.

To announce all these "localized" innovations, Google launched an extensive advertising and public relations campaign. One attention-getting publicity stunt involved inviting people on the street in Tokyo to float in the air with the aid of 2,500 multicolored balloons.

the University of Kansas summarize Hofstede's cultural dimensions in their book *Adventures in Public Relations: Case Studies and Critical Thinking*:

1. *Power distance* measures how tolerant a society is about unequally distributed decision-making power. Countries with a high acceptance of power distance include Mexico and France. Countries with a low acceptance include Austria and the United States.

2. *Individualism*, as contrasted with collectivism, pits loyalty to one's self against loyalty to a larger group. Countries in Asia and Latin America gravitate toward collectivism, while the United States, Canada, and most European countries gravitate toward individualism.

3. *Masculinity/femininity* contrasts competitiveness (traditionally masculine) with compassion and nurturing (traditionally feminine). Masculine nations include Australia, Germany, and Japan. Feminine nations include Sweden and Spain.

4. *Uncertainty avoidance* measures how well a society tolerates ambiguity. Nations that have difficulty tolerating uncertainty include Japan, Belgium, and Greece. Nations that tolerate ambiguity include Great Britain, the United States, and Sweden.

5. *Long-term versus short-term orientation* measures a society's willingness to consider the traditions of the past and carry them into the future. China and other East Asian nations tend to have long-term orientations in terms of a process or plan evolving over a number of years. The United States, in contrast, has a short-term orientation. Americans, for example, get impatient if recovery from a recession takes more than one or two years.

Public relations professionals and American executives must keep Hofstede's dimensions in mind as a general guide, but they must also be sensitive to the cultural differences that present themselves on a daily basis. Some examples:

■ In China, tables at a banquet are never numbered. The Chinese think such table assignments appear to rank guests and that certain numbers are unlucky. Thus it's better to direct a guest to the "primrose" or the "hollyhock" table.

■ Americans are fond of using first names, but it's not proper business etiquette to do so in Europe and Asia unless you have been given permission.

■ Americans should avoid using expressions such as "full-court press" or even "awesome" or "cool" since many foreigners will have no idea what you are talking about.

■ In the UK, the word "scheme" refers to a business proposition and holds no connotation of deceit as it does in the United States.

■ Early morning breakfast meetings are not conducted in Latin America; by the same token, a dinner meeting may not start until 9 or 10 P.M.

■ In Thailand and other Asian cultures, it's inappropriate to criticize an employee in front of others because the employee will "lose face." Also, it's a crime in Thailand to make disrespectful remarks about the royal family, particularly the king.

■ In Latin America, greetings often include physical contact such as hugging the other person or grabbing him or her by the arm. Men and women commonly greet each other with a kiss on the cheek in Argentina and Chile.

■ News releases in Malaysia should be distributed in the four official languages to avoid alienating any segment of the press.

on the job

INSIGHTS

Giving the "Ugly American" a Makeover

Business for Diplomatic Action Inc., a nonprofit organization, works with U.S. companies to improve the reputation of the United States around the world. To that end, it has compiled guidelines on how business travelers (as well as tourists) should behave abroad. Here are some tips from its brochure "World Citizens Guide":

Read a map. Familiarize yourself with the local geography to avoid making insulting mistakes. Knowledge of current events and public issues is a real plus.

Dress up. In some countries, casual dress is a sign of disrespect.

Talk small. Talking about wealth, power, or status—corporate or personal—can create resentment. Bragging about America's greatness is a real turnoff.

No slang. Even casual profanity is unacceptable.

Slow down. Americans talk fast, eat fast, move fast, live fast. Many other cultures do not.

Listen as much as you talk. Ask people you're visiting about themselves and their way of life.

Speak lower and slower. A loud voice is often perceived as bragging.

Exercise religious restraint. In many countries, religion is not a subject for discussion.

Exercise political restraint. Steer clear . . . if someone is attacking U.S. politicians or policies. Agree to disagree.

Learn some words. Learning some simple phrases in the host country's language is most appreciated.

- Gift giving is common in Asian cultures. Executives, meeting for the first time, will exchange gifts as a way of building a social relationship.
- In Muslim nations, particularly the Middle East, men should not stand near, touch, or stare at any woman.

Other suggestions for American travelers abroad are given in the Insights box above. Americans and others not only must learn the customs of the country in which they are working, but they also should rely on native professionals to guide them. Media materials and advertising must be translated, and the best approach for doing so is to employ native speakers who have extensive experience in translating ad copy and public relations materials. On some occasions, despite the best intentions, a company stumbles. See the Ethics box on page 532.

Foreign Corporations in the United States

Corporations and industries in other countries frequently employ public relations and lobbying firms to advance their products, services, and political interests in the United States. In fact, the Center for Public Integrity (CPI) reported that in a six-year period, 700 companies with headquarters in about 100 nations spent more than $520 million lobbying the U.S. government. The Center's analysis continued, "Over that time, those companies employed 550 lobbying firms and teams of 3,800 lobbyists, more than 100 of whom were former members of Congress."

Uproar in India: A $23,000 Pen Honoring Gandhi

Montblanc, the Swiss pen maker, wanted to raise its profile in India. One initiative was to produce a gold-and-silver fountain pen to commemorate Mahatma Gandhi, a man widely revered for leading the independence movement and for his austere, simple life.

The limited-edition Mahatma Gandhi pen, engraved with Gandhi's image and featuring a saffron-colored garnet on the clip, was unveiled in Delhi just before the national holiday honoring Gandhi's birthday. In a news release, Montblanc said the pen, priced at $23,000, "... embodied Gandhi's timeless philosophy of non-violence and respect for all living creatures."

Indian companies, however, generally don't use the image of Gandhi for commercial purposes because of his sainted status, so the unveiling of the pen was severely criticized. The head of the Gandhi Ashram in Sabarmati expressed dismay in a *Financial Times* article, saying, "I cannot imagine why anybody has done this. We cannot recognize this." Suhel Seth, a brand expert said, "Look at the illogical marketing. Montblanc is an elite product. Gandhi stood for everything that was non-elitist. When you tinker around with that symbol of credibility, respect, and honor, you risk a backlash that no brand needs or deserves."

Not everyone, however, was critical. Montblanc, for example, had received the blessing of Gandhi's great-grandson, who received $146,000 from the pen maker to build a shelter for rescued child laborers. He told the *Financial Times*, "I know there is a contradiction between the man and the product they are commemorating him with, but you can't expect a company like Montblanc to come out with a cheap thing."

What do you think? Was it ethical for Montblanc to use the image of Gandhi for commercial purposes? Do you think the Swiss company considered the cultural sensitivity of the Indian public? Does Montblanc's donating money for a shelter justify its decision to produce an expensive pen honoring Gandhi?

Not surprisingly, international trade was by far the most common issue foreign companies reported lobbying on, followed by defense and taxation.

The Center for Public Integrity

Companies from the United Kingdom (UK) top the list, having spent more than $180 million during the six-year period. This included BP (British Petroleum) and the pharmaceutical giant GlaxoSmithKline, which has extensive operations in the United States. BP, on the other hand, lobbies on matters relating to environmental standards and oil and gas issues. Companies from Germany were second on the list, spending about $70 million on lobbying. Swiss corporations were third, with about the same expenditures, and Japanese companies were fourth, spending about $60 million during that six-year period.

On a global level, there is intense lobbying to influence negotiations on a global climate change treaty. The fossil fuel industries and other heavy carbon emitters are using public relations strategies and lobbying to slow any progress on the control of greenhouse emissions. According to a report by the International Consortium of Investigative Journalists, "Employing thousands of lobbyists, millions in political contributions, and widespread fear tactics, entrenched interests worldwide are thwarting the steps that scientists say are needed to stave off a looming environmental calamity."

The Center for Public Integrity, which partnered with the journalists on its report, says lobbying can be seen most clearly in developed nations because they have disclosure regulations. In the United States, for example, CPI says, "There are now about 3,000 climate lobbyists—five lobbyists for every member of Congress—a 400 percent jump from six years earlier."

Carl Levin, vice president and senior consultant of Burson-Marsteller, Washington, D.C., lists five major reasons foreign corporations retain public relations counsel in the United States:

1. To hold off protectionist moves that threaten their companies or industries
2. To defeat legislation affecting the sale of their products
3. To provide ongoing information on political, legal, and commercial developments in the United States that could affect their business interests
4. To support expansion of their markets in the United States
5. To deal with a crisis situation that threatens the financial health or reputation of their organization

U.S. Corporations in Other Nations

Many U.S. corporations are global in scope, with employees, products, manufacturing plants, and distribution centers around the world. The largest U.S. giants in terms of 2009 sales, according to *Fortune* magazine, are (1) Exxon/Mobil, $442 billion; (2) Wal-Mart, $405 billion; (3) Chevron, $263 billion; (4) Conoco Phillips, $230 billion; and General Electric, $183 billion. Such revenues, which dwarf the total GNPs of most nations, mean that these companies affect the lives of millions and leave a massive environmental footprint on the entire planet.

These top five giant corporations, as well as hundreds of other U.S. companies, engage in extensive public relations and lobbying activities in other nations for virtually the same reasons that foreign countries lobby in the United States. The total amount expended on public relations and lobbying abroad is not known because U.S. companies don't have to report such expenditures to the U.S. government.

Public relations professionals who work for these giants as well as a host of other American companies are heavily involved in global activities, because their work involves the companies' employees and operations in many nations. The corporate headquarters usually decides what key messages will be communicated worldwide, but relies on public relations staffs and local public relations firms in each country to ensure that the messages are properly translated and implemented. Many of these corporations also retain global public relations firms such as Burson-Marsteller and Hill & Knowlton to provide services from offices in major cities around the world. The global efforts of public relations firms were discussed in Chapter 4.

At the start of the 21st century and in the aftermath of the 9/11 terrorist attacks in 2001, American companies have faced a number of challenges abroad: competing with other large corporations headquartered in other nations; dealing with sustainable development; being boycotted by nations that disagree with American foreign policy; and striving to act as good corporate citizens at the local and national levels.

Every organization is going to have to deal with new rules and expectations for communication as the world becomes more competitive and as organizations interact with new markets.

Ray Kotcher, CEO of Ketchum, at the International Public Relations Association (IPRA) World Congress in Beijing

David Drobis, a former senior partner and chair of Ketchum, outlined some of these challenges in a speech before the International Communications Consultancy Organization (ICCO). Drobis declared that one major challenge is to better communicate to the world's people the economic advantages of globalization. The *Economist*, for example, has also called globalization a massive communications failure because the public and private sectors have done such a poor job of communicating globalization's benefits, being transparent about their activities, and building important alliances.

Drobis believes that public relations professionals are best suited to explain the benefits of globalization. These benefits must be communicated to three key groups: (1) company management; (2) nongovernmental organizations, known as NGOs; and (3) international institutions such as the United Nations.

Corporations   The first group is the companies themselves, which must realize that international capitalism has a bad connotation in many parts of the world. Companies, according to Drobis, have done little to correct this view despite the efforts of a few highly responsible companies who have outstanding programs. He asserts, "Companies must take into consideration a broad group of stakeholders as they pursue their business goals globally. And by doing so, there are tangible and intangible business benefits. In this way, good corporate citizenship is not a cost of doing business, but rather a driver of business success. What's good for the soul is also good for business."

Drobis adds, "Companies that pursue initiatives—be they related to the environment, labor standards, or human rights—are rewarded with improved business success in a number of areas, including shareholder value, revenue, operational efficiencies, higher employee morale and productivity, and corporate reputation."

NGOs   The second group that must be informed of the benefits of globalization is nongovernmental organizations (NGOs). Although many NGOs are outright hostile to all private enterprise, American companies must realize that NGOs can become an important seal of approval and branding. Indeed, major mainstream NGOs such as the World Wildlife Federation and Greenpeace are working with corporations on sustainable development programs. The *Financial Times* notes, "A new type of relationship is emerging between companies and NGOs, where NGOs act as certification bodies, verifying and, in many cases, permitting the use of their logos, showing that products and services are being produced in socially responsible and environmentally friendly ways."

The next five to ten years will be challenging for companies that operate on a world stage with the rise of technologically enabled activism.

Public Affairs Council President Doug Pinkham in PRWeek

Indeed, hundreds of nongovernmental organizations expend considerable energy to get international support for their programs and causes. Organizations such as Greenpeace, Amnesty International, Doctors Without Borders, Oxfam, and even a number of groups opposed to globalization have been effective in getting their messages out via the World Wide Web, e-mail, and demonstrations. They have been successful not only in setting the agenda for discussion issues, but also in influencing legislation at the national and international levels. A good example is Oceana's efforts to preserve the world's fisheries, which is highlighted in the PR Casebook on page 535.

PRCasebook

NGO Campaign Goes After Fishing Subsidies

Nongovernmental organizations, commonly known as NGOs, have become very influential in terms of shaping public opinion on global issues because the public widely perceives NGOs as being highly sincere and credible. For example, Oceana, an international conservation group, influenced the World Trade Organization (WTO) and national governments regarding the threat of overfishing.

Oceana worked on a three-year campaign to generate support from and action by the WTO to reduce nations' subsidies to their fishing fleets. The campaign, "Cut the Bait," used an extensive communications program to convince the WTO that reducing or eliminating subsidies would be the greatest contribution to preserving the world's oceans. A series of steps were involved in the campaign.

Step One Oceana commissioned scientists at the University of British Columbia to assess the extent of fishing subsidies. The study found that governments were spending a combined total of $20 billion annually in subsidies to the fishing industry, an amount equal to 25 percent of the world's fish catch.

Step Two Extensive interviews were undertaken with WTO officials, country diplomats, and other trade experts to gain technical and political insights. In addition, Oceana did a political analysis of the U.S. Congress on environmental issues. It also reviewed existing public opinion research and did a content analysis of how the media were covering the issue to date.

Step Three A communications strategy that included media relations, advertising, events, and stakeholder advocacy was established to increase visibility on the issue and create pressure on WTO representatives. Science-based messages were used, and Oceana also created a life-size mascot, called "Finley the Fish," to establish a highly visible logo that would appeal to the public. Other collateral materials produced were magnets and a snow globe containing Finley surrounded by floating boats with fish hooks and money "confetti."

Step Four More than 500 meetings were conducted with WTO delegations. More than 175 briefings were conducted with U.S. trade and congressional offices. Technical briefings were conducted in Geneva, headquarters of the WTO, by scientists and experts. In addition, scientists were mobilized for advocacy. A letter signed by 125 scientists from 27 nations was sent to the WTO director general. Other activities included sponsoring billboards in Geneva saying, "Stop Fishing Subsidies" and enlisting television and movie celebrities to make public statements. Oceana also partnered with 11 other environmental groups, who publicly provided support.

The outcome was gratifying to Oceana. As a result of its "Cut the Bait" campaign, the WTO produced a first-draft agreement on fishing subsidies that included most of Oceana's recommendations. The agreement, as of 2009, had not been ratified but the draft agreement still remains the basis for negotiations. Nine nations, including the United States, have also strongly endorsed Oceana's recommendations, and even the U.S. Congress passed a resolution supporting the reduction of fishing subsidies.

In terms of media coverage, Oceana generated more than 1,000 media placements—including in influential publications such as the *Financial Times*, the *New York Times*, and the *Wall Street Journal*—in 37 nations. The campaign and the resulting media coverage also positioned Oceana as the leading spokesperson on fishing subsidies and related WTO negotiations. In 2009, the International Public Relations Association (IPRA) awarded Oceana a Golden World Award for an outstanding campaign by an NGO.

One study by StrategyOne, the research arm of Edelman Worldwide, showed that media coverage of such organizations more than doubled over a four-year period, and NGOs were perceived by the public to be more credible than the news media or corporations when it came to issues such as labor, health, and the environment. Thought leaders, for example, indicate that they trust NGOs more than government or corporations because they consider the NGOs' motivation to be based on "morals" rather than "profit." Public Affairs Council President Doug Pinkham has said the StrategyOne report should be taken as a "wake-up call" by large corporations that have failed to embrace greater social responsibility and transparency.

International Institutions   The third group is international institutions such as the World Trade Organization (WTO), the World Bank, the International Monetary Fund (IMF), and even the United Nations. Drobis says these organizations are unfairly criticized as being undemocratic, but fairly criticized for being nontransparent. An article in *Foreign Affairs* puts it this way: "To outsiders, even within the same government, these institutions can look like closed and secretive clubs. Increased transparency is essential. International organizations can provide more access to their deliberations, even after the fact."

Drobis, in giving advice to American companies doing business abroad, concludes by saying that the era of "relationship building" is over. Instead, he says, the 21st century is an era of "confidence building" in the international arena so that various publics not only trust corporations to do the right thing, but also believe globalization is a benefit to hundreds of millions of poor people around the globe.

Public Relations by Governments

The governments of virtually every country have multiple departments involved in communicating with political leaders and citizens in other nations. Much effort and billions of dollars are spent on the tourism industry to attract visitors, whose expenditures aid local economies. Even larger sums are devoted to lobbying efforts to obtain favorable legislation for a country's products; for example, Costa Rica conducted a public relations and lobbying campaign to convince the U.S. Congress to reduce tariffs on the import of its sugar.

Conflict and war between nations also lead to extensive public relations efforts by both sides to influence world public opinion that their actions are justified. Both Russia and Georgia, for example, hired American public relations firms to help each country convince the world that the other side was the aggressor in 2008 when a war broke out over the somewhat disputed territory of South Ossetia. Russia claimed it was responding to an unprovoked attack on the Russian population of Ossetia (officially part of Georgia), but the Georgians claimed that giant Russia was bullying the small former Soviet Republic. "This is part of warfare these days that you get your story out," Kleine Brockhoof, a German journalist, told *PRWeek*. The Israeli-Palestinian conflict is also a war of words and dueling videos. See the Insights box on page 537.

Countries engage in persuasive communication campaigns for a number of reasons. Burson-Marsteller's Carl Levin says their goals when dealing with the United States are to:

- Advance political objectives
- Assess probable U.S. reaction to a projected action by the country

on the job

INSIGHTS

The War of Words: Israel Takes the Offensive

In times of war and conflict, each side hauls out the heavy artillery of public relations to sway world public opinion that its cause is just. The Israeli-Palestinian conflict is a continuing war of words with no resolution in sight.

Israel, however, has stepped up its public relations efforts in recent years to counter criticism of its actions and policies regarding the Gaza Strip and its continuing battle with Hamas, which it considers a "terrorist" group. Indeed, a 2010 poll of citizens in 28 nations conducted by the BBC (see the Insights box on page 542) indicated that only 19 percent of the respondents viewed Israel in a favorable light. A survey in 2009 had found that even U.S. support of Israel was slipping, with 44 percent of Americans supporting Israel and another 41 percent being against it.

The catalyst for increased public relations was Israel's military opera-

tion in Gaza at the end of 2008, when world opinion was sharply critical of what it perceived as excessive use of force that caused the death of many Palestinian civilians. Israel countered by communicating to the American mainstream media that it was "under attack" and had the right to defend itself against terrorism. It also devoted resources to social media efforts, including broadcasting a two-hour news conference via Twitter, establishing blogs, and posting updates on MySpace, Facebook, and YouTube pages.

The government also blocked foreign reporters' access to the Gaza Strip but did make platoons of official spokespersons available to reporters. A website was also established featuring selected videos that, according to the *Economist*, documented the "humane action and operational success" of Israeli forces. Another

public relations tactic was to enlist thousands of volunteers around the world and give them "talking points" so that they could "nudge editors, journalists, and commentators to see news from Israel's perspective."

In June 2010, Israel had another public relations war on its hands when commandos stopped a flotilla of boats carrying aid to the Palestinians from landing on the Gaza coast, which was blockaded by Israel. Nine activists were killed on one ship, and each side released a blizzard of videos to blame the other side for aggression. The Israeli military was particularly active, posting nearly 20 videos on its YouTube channel. James F. Hodge, editor of *Foreign Affairs*, told the *New York Times*, "On matters like this, public opinion is awfully important in terms of determining which image is really going to last."

- Advance the country's commercial interests—for example, sales in the United States, increased U.S. private investment, and tourism
- Assist in communications in English
- Help win understanding of and support for specific issues that undermine the country's standing in the United States and the world community
- Modify laws and regulations inhibiting the country's activities in the United States

Under the Foreign Agents Registration Act (FARA) of 1938, all legal, political, fund-raising, public relations, and lobbying consultants hired by foreign governments to work in the United States must register with the Department of Justice. They are also required to file reports with the attorney general listing all activities

on the job

INSIGHTS

U.S. Firms Represent a Variety of Nations

The following is a representative sample of contracts signed by U.S. public relations firms to work on behalf of foreign governments, as reported in *O'Dwyer's Newsletter*.

Edelman Worldwide: $160,000 to help Switzerland emphasize its "close economic, political, and cultural relationship with the U.S."

BKSH & Associates: $240,000 to work with Albania on public policy issues and to improve its relationship with the U.S. government, Congress, and other American political dignitaries.

Samuels International: $675,000 to facilitate Angola's public image, improve U.S.-Angolan military-to-military relations, and foster sister-city relationships.

Ketchum: $2.9 million to promote Russia's leadership and national policies. The contract calls for outreach to major American media, arranging for "top-tier global media leaders" to have high-level discussions with President Dmitri Medvedev, and promoting the speeches of Russia's top leadership at various world economic forums.

Brunswick: $900,000 to work with Dubai on "anticipating potential issue areas, messaging, positioning, media training and events."

Cassidy & Associates: $700,000 to help Pakistan "promote the evolution of U.S. policy in favor of Pakistan's specific goals."

APCO Worldwide: $420,000 to promote Malaysia as a moderate Islamic state and to improve its ties with the United States, its largest trading partner.

on behalf of a foreign principal, compensation received, and expenses incurred. See the Insights box above for a list of U.S. public relations firms representing various nations.

Normally hired by an embassy after openly bidding for the account, the firm first gathers detailed information about the client country, including past media coverage. Attitudes toward the country are ascertained both informally and through surveys.

The action program decided on will likely include the establishment of an information bureau to provide facts and published statements of favorable opinion about the country. In many cases, a nation may also use paid issue advertising in publications such as the *New York Times*, the *Washington Post*, the *Wall Street Journal*, and the *Financial Times* that reach a high percentage of opinion leaders and elected officials. The Republic of Kazakhstan, for example, placed full-page ads in major American newspapers after its national elections to reinforce public perceptions that it is a democracy. The ad's headline was "Today, Kazakhstan has another asset besides oil, gas and minerals. Democracy."

Appointments also are secured with key media people and other influentials, including educators, business executives, and leaders of various public policy groups. In many cases, the primary audiences are key members of congressional committees, heads of various governmental agencies, and even the White House staff. These people are often invited to visit the client country on expense-paid trips, although some news media people decline on ethical grounds.

Gradually, through expert and persistent methods of persuasion (including lobbying), public opinion may be changed, favorable trade legislation may be passed, foreign aid may be increased, or an influx of American tourists may go to the country.

Some of the toughest problems confronting public relations firms who work for foreign governments include:

- Deciding whether to represent a country, such as Myanmar (Burma) or Zimbabwe, whose human rights violations may reflect adversely on the agency itself
- Persuading the governments of such nations to alter some of their practices so that the favorable public image sought will reflect reality
- Convincing the officials of a client country in which the government totally controls the flow of news internally that the American press is independent from government control and stressing that the officials should thus never expect coverage that is 100 percent favorable
- Deciding whether to represent a nation such as Ecuador, whose president, Rafael Correa, is an ally of Venezuela's Hugo Chavez and a bitter critic of U.S. Latin American policies

Why do some U.S. firms choose to work for other governments, perhaps even those that are unpopular? Says Burson-Marsteller's Carl Levin: "I do not think it is overreaching to state that in helping friendly foreign clients we also advance our national interests. And we help in ways that our government cannot."

A case in point is China, which has ramped up its public relations and lobbying efforts in recent years to counter criticisms (and fears) in the United States about its growing economic and military power. It hired the Patton Boggs firm to lobby on a wide range of issues before Congress, including trade tariffs, intellectual property, currency exchange rates, and Taiwan.

In addition to using American public relations firms, the Chinese government has embarked on a massive global effort to enhance its image and reputation. The Beijing Olympics and the Shanghai Expo, for example, did much to generate positive media coverage around the world and alter popular misconceptions of China.

China is also expanding its influence worldwide by creating TV networks, starting English-language newspapers, leasing radio stations on all continents, and broadcasting TV news to a worldwide audience in six languages. The UK's *Guardian Weekly* notes, "Beijing's response is typically massive and ambitious: a $6.6 billion global strategy to create media giants that will challenge agenda-setting western giants such as News Corp, the BBC, and CNN." On another level, China has greatly expanded its outreach to educational institutions around the world. See the Insights box on page 540.

American Public Diplomacy

The American government is the major disseminator of information around the world. This is called *public diplomacy*, because it is an open communication process primarily intended to present

> In the modern age, whichever nation's communication methods are most advanced, whichever nation's communications capacity is strongest . . . has the most power to influence the world.
>
> *President Hu Jintao of China*

on the job
INSIGHTS

China's Educational Outreach to the World

Countries use a variety of "public diplomacy" initiatives to enhance their national reputation and influence opinion leaders in other nations. One such initiative is an extensive program by China to establish Confucius Institutes at universities around the world.

Hanban, an agency affiliated with China's Ministry of Education, was started in 2004 for the purpose of "... enhancing the world's understanding of Chinese language and culture, deepening the friendship between China and the rest of the world, and promoting global cultural diversity." By 2009, Hanban had established and funded almost 350 Confucius Institutes in more than 80 nations and regions around the world.

A sampling of American universities with Institutes includes the University of Tulsa, the University of Florida, Northwestern University, Stanford University, Texas A&M University, and the University of Minnesota. Confucius Institutes on such campuses provide instruction on Chinese culture and language by providing teachers, partnering with various university academic departments, and donating instructional resources.

The number and distribution of teaching resources to schools is impressive. According to a recent annual report by Hanban, (1) 1.3 million volumes of teaching materials were donated to more than a thousand institutions in 100 nations, (2) 2,000

teachers and volunteers were sent to 109 nations to teach Chinese, (3) 16,512 secondary school teachers from 47 nations received language training, and (4) *Everyday Chinese* is published in 38 languages.

Hanban also has an extensive international exchange program. More than 800 primary and secondary school principals, for example, visited China in a recent year. In addition, 800 foreign high school students visited China and participated in "Chinese Bridge" summer camps. University students also receive funding to visit China and learn about Chinese culture and language. In January 2010, for example, more than 400 American

college students from universities such as SUNY, Cornell, Yale, and San Jose State University spent three weeks at Chinese universities. The government also has an extensive scholarship program for foreign students to study at Chinese universities.

According to the Chinese government, "The vigorous development of Confucius Institutes reflect[s] the common wish of all peoples in the world to learn from one another, strengthen communication and cooperation, and enhance friendship and understanding, as well as the inner demands of China to open-up and reform, face the world, and achieve win-win cooperation."

American society in all its complexity so that citizens and governments of other nations can understand the context of U.S. actions and policies. Another function is to promote American concepts of democracy, free trade, and open communication around the world.

The United States Information Agency (USIA), created in 1953 by President Dwight Eisenhower, was the primary agency involved in shaping America's image abroad. USIA, in many ways, was the direct descendant of George Creel's Committee on Public Information (CPI) during World War I and Elmer Davis's Office of War Information during World War II. See Chapter 2.

After World War II, the new threat was the outbreak of the Cold War between the United States and the Soviet Union and the Communist bloc nations in Eastern Europe. The Cold War was a war of words on both sides to win the "hearts and minds" of governments and their citizens around the world.

Some early USIA activities included (1) the stationing of public affairs officers (PAOs) at every American embassy to work with local media, (2) publication of American books and magazines, (3) distribution of American films and TV programs, (4) sponsorship of tours by American dance and musical groups, (5) art shows, (6) student and faculty exchange programs such as the Fulbright Program, and (7) sponsorship of lecture tours by American authors and intellectuals. The USIA was abolished in 1999 after the end of the Cold War and the implosion of the Soviet Union, but many of these activities continue today under the auspices of the U.S. Department of State, which has an undersecretary of state for public affairs and diplomacy.

The 9/11 attacks on the United States created a new impetus to "sell" America and the U.S. decision to invade Afghanistan and Iraq. The cry was to "win the hearts and minds" of the world's people and to gain public, as well as international, support for U.S. actions. Diplomatic efforts have had mixed results, and American foreign policy is still not popular in many of the world's capitals. The international reputation of the United States, however, started to improve in 2009. See the Insights box on page 542.

One major vehicle of communication is the Voice of America (VOA), which was created in 1942. It traditionally broadcast news, sports, and entertainment around the world via shortwave, but VOA has also established AM and FM radio transmitters throughout the world. In addition, the agency supplies many radio and television stations throughout the world with various news, music, and talk programs free of charge. The VOA also offers audio streaming on the World Wide Web. The worldwide audience for VOA is difficult to judge, given all the distribution methods, but estimates are that it has several hundred million listeners.

> U.S. sponsored radio and TV broadcasts remain critical weapons in the struggle for freedom around the world.
>
> *James K. Glassman, chair of the Broadcasting Board of Governors*

More recently, Congress has set up radio and television services focusing on Iraq and the Middle East. Radio Sawa injects news tidbits written from an American perspective into a heavy rotation of American and Middle Eastern pop music. A similar radio service aimed at Iranian youth is Radio Farda. On the television side, the U.S. government started Al Hurra. According to the *New York Times*, Al Hurra is "a slickly produced Arab-language news and entertainment network that [is] beamed by satellite from a Washington suburb to the Middle East." It is the American government's answer to Al Jazeera, the popular pan-Arab television service.

on the job

INSIGHTS

Reputation of U.S. Begins to Improve

Nations, like organizations, worry about their reputation, and the United States is no exception. The good news, however, is that the United States is viewed more favorably today by other nations than it was in 2008.

A 2010 poll by BBC *World News* and GlobeScan/PIPA of adults in 28 nations found that, on average, 46 percent of foreign citizens view the United States favorably and say the country has a mostly positive influence in the world. According to GlobeScan Chairman Doug Miller, "People around the world today view the United States more positively than at any time since the second Iraq war. . . . the U.S. is clearly on the rise again."

This compares with a 2008 Pew Center poll of 24 nations, which found that only 42 percent of the French, 33 percent of Spaniards, and 31 percent of Germans viewed the United States favorably. In Pakistan, the percentage dropped to 19 percent, while only 12 percent of the Turks had a positive impression. The BBC poll found that this hasn't changed. The only two countries to have majorities with negative views of the United States remain Turkey

(70 percent) and Pakistan (52 percent).

In the BBC poll, the countries that are viewed more favorably than the United States, with its 46 percent rating, are Germany (59 percent), Japan (53 percent), the United Kingdom (52 percent), Canada (51 percent), and France (49 percent). In contrast, Iran is the least favorably viewed nation (15 percent), followed by Pakistan (16 percent), North Korea (17 percent), and Israel (19 percent).

A change of administrations in Washington is given the most credit for the improvement of America's reputation. Steven Kull, director of PIPA, said, "After a year, it appears that the 'Obama effect' is real. Its influence on people's views worldwide, though, is to soften the negative aspects of the United States' image, while the positive aspects are not yet coming into strong focus."

In other words, Obama is viewed very favorably abroad as a charismatic personality, but citizens in other nations also base their perceptions of the United States on its actions and policies. John Paluszek, senior counsel of Ketchum and president of the Global Alliance of national public rela-

tions associations, puts it more bluntly. He wrote in *PRWeek*, "It's the policy, stupid."

He continues, "It is policy—and related action—that matters most in successful PR. Recent opinion polls tell us that it's current American foreign policy, not traditional American values, that is unacceptable to many people in the Middle East." Indeed, an Advisory Group on Diplomacy for the Arab and Muslim World appointed by Congress concluded, ". . . much of the resentment toward America stems from our policies" and ". . . in this time of peril, public diplomacy is absurdly and dangerously underfunded."

Funding for public diplomacy has increased under the Obama administration, but changing American policies is a much more difficult political process. Judith McHale, chief of U.S. public diplomacy efforts, told an audience in Europe that President Obama and Secretary of State Clinton recognize public diplomacy as a key cog in restoring U.S. leadership around the world: "They recognize public diplomacy as an essential ingredient of 21st century stagecraft."

VOA, and services such as Radio Sawa, are not directed at U.S. citizens. Under the United States Information and Educational Exchange Act of 1948, Congress prohibited the government from directing its public diplomacy efforts toward Americans, because of fears that the government would propagandize its own citizens.

Opportunities in International Work

The 1990s, according to many experts, represented a new golden age of global marketing and public relations. The opening of the European market, coupled with economic and social reforms in the former Soviet Union, hastened the reality of a global economy.

These developments led Jerry Dalton, past president of the PRSA, to say, "I think more and more American firms are going to become part of those overseas markets, and I expect a lot of Americans in public relations will be living overseas." Indeed, Dalton believes that the fastest-growing career field for practitioners is international public relations. He adds, "Students who can communicate well and are fluent in a foreign language may be able to write their own ticket." But the coming of the "global village," as Marshall McLuhan once termed it, still means that there will be a multiplicity of languages, customs, and values that public relations professionals will have to understand.

Gavin Anderson, chairman of Gavin Anderson & Company, a pioneer in international public relations, penned the following observations some years ago—but the message is still relevant today:

> Practitioners of either global or international public relations are cultural interpreters. They must understand the business and general culture of both their clients (and employers) and the country or countries in which they hope to do business. Whether as an outside or in-house consultant, the first task is to tell a U.S. company going abroad (or a foreign party coming to the United States) how to get things done. How does the market work? What are the business habits? What is the infrastructure? The consultant also needs to understand how things work in the host country, to recognize what will need translation and adaptation. . . .
>
> The field needs practitioners with an interest in and knowledge of foreign cultures on top of top-notch public relations skills. They need a good sense of working environments, and while they may not have answers for every country, they should know what questions to ask and where to get the information needed. They need to know where the potential dangers are, so as to not replenish the business bloopers book.

The decision to seek a career in global public relations should ideally be made during the early academic years, so that a student can take multiple courses in international relations, global marketing techniques, the basics of strategic public relations planning, foreign languages, social and economic geography, and cross-cultural communication. Graduate study is an asset. As a desirable starting point, students should study abroad for a semester or serve an internship with a company or organization based in, or with operations in, another nation. Students may want to apply for the Fulbright Program, which funds travel and study abroad. Rotary International offers a student foreign study scholarship as well.

Different people in different parts of the world need and expect different things. Understanding and responding to the demands and expectations of the populations emerging from changing demographics and immigration patterns is vital. PR professionals must guide an informed and sensitive response to those needs and expectations.

Deanna Pelfrey and Juan-Carlos Molleda, writing in The Strategist

Further, American students should not assume that they have an "inside" track on working for an American-based global corporation. Increasingly, global corporations are looking at a worldwide pool of young talent—some of whom are excellent candidates because they know several languages and are accustomed to intercultural communications. Hewlett-Packard is one example of an organization that casts a global net; it prefers to hire European- or American-trained Russians for its corporate communications efforts in Moscow and the Russian Federation.

Taking the U.S. Foreign Service Officers examination is the first requirement for international government careers. However, foreign service work with the innumerable federal agencies often requires a substantial period of government, mass media, or public relations service in the United States before foreign assignments are made.

Summary

What Is Global Public Relations?

- Public relations work today involves dealing with employees, customers, vendors, communities, and government officials in multiple nations.

- Public relations is a well-developed industry in many nations around the world. China, in particular, has a rapidly expanding public relations industry that is getting more sophisticated every year.

International Corporate Public Relations

- In the new age of global marketing, public relations firms represent foreign interests in the United States as well as the interests of American corporations around the world.

- The practitioner must deal with issues of language and cultural differences, including subtle differences in customs and etiquette and even ethical dilemmas such as paying for news coverage.

- A great deal of public relations work for companies and governments involves lobbying a nation's elected officials or government agencies for favorable trade agreements.

- Nations also use global public relations to enhance their global image and gain influence in various regional and international groups.

- NGOs are now major players in setting the agenda for discussion of global issues and influencing the policies of corporations and governments.

- NGOs are widely believed to be more credible by the news media and the public on such issues as labor, health, and the environment, partly because they are perceived as lacking the self-interest ascribed to governments and corporations.

- There is increasing evidence that giant corporations are adopting a more accommodative stance and cooperating with activist NGOs to form more socially responsible policies.

Public Relations by Governments

- Most governments seek to influence the foreign policies of other countries as well as the opinions and actions of their publics. These communications can range from promoting tourism to influencing trade policies and promoting foreign investment.

- U.S. public relations firms work for foreign governments, helping them advance their political objectives and commercial interests, counseling them on probable U.S. reactions to their proposed actions, and assisting in communications in English.

  - War and conflict between nations usually results in a barrage of public relations activity on both sides to justify their actions. The Russia-Georgia conflict, as well as the Israel-Palestine impasse, are examples.

- The U.S. government refers to its international information efforts as *public diplomacy*, which involves activities to enhance understanding of American culture and promote U.S. foreign policy objectives. The Voice of America (VOA) radio broadcasts are part of this program.

Opportunities in International Work

- As global marketing and communications have expanded in recent years, so too have opportunities for international public relations work.

- Fluency in a foreign language is a valued skill but not a prerequisite; also important is a background in international relations, global marketing techniques, social and economic geography, and cross-cultural communication.

Case Activity   Promoting Tourism for Turkey

Turkey has a problem. Prior to 9/11, the country was on track to become the fastest-growing destination for Americans. That projection was derailed by the terrorist attacks and the subsequent invasions of Afghanistan and Iraq, which caused many Americans to think twice about visiting a Muslim nation—even one like Turkey, which has a secular government and a strong European orientation.

Indeed, Turkey remains a virtual treasure-house of art, culture, and cuisine that would appeal to seasoned travelers looking for a new experience and destination. To this end, the Turkish Culture and Tourism Office has retained your public relations firm to conduct a media relations program in the American press (and to some extent the European media) to increase awareness of Turkey as a desirable tourist destination.

Research and interviews with Turkish tourism authorities indicate that gearing campaigns to separate audience segments would be more fruitful than a general campaign. Travelers interested in food and wine, for example, might be reached by articles about the cuisine of Turkey. Music lovers might be interested in the new jazz sounds of Turkish musicians, and even shoppers looking for vintage jewelry and exotic products such as carpets in the famous bazaars of Istanbul would be a good specialized public. Then, of course, there are the history buffs, who would be interested in visiting the sites of ancient civilizations.

Now that you know the possible interests of several target audiences, develop a public relations plan that will use appropriate media and events to reach these various audiences. Your plan should outline possible feature stories for print and broadcast media, as well as the venues for special events.

Questions   For Review and Discussion

1. What is global public relations? What are some of the reasons for its growth in recent decades?
2. The field of public relations develops best in a nation that has some special characteristics. What are some of those characteristics?
3. How does public relations contribute to the global operations of large companies?
4. What objectives do foreign nations seek to accomplish by hiring U.S. public relations firms to represent them in America?
5. The successful practice of international public relations requires knowledge of a nation's history and political sensitivities. It also requires knowledge of proper manners and cultural sensitivity. What advice is given for business executives who travel abroad?
6. Dave Drobis of Ketchum identifies three key audiences to whom public relations personnel need to promote the benefits of globalization. What are they?
7. What is an *NGO*? Why have NGOs gained influence in terms of influencing corporations and even governments regarding such issues as global warming?
8. The Israeli-Palestinian conflict has been going on for years. In your opinion, which side is winning the "war of words" in terms of worldwide public opinion?
9. What is China doing to enhance its international reputation and promote itself as a leading nation in the global economy?
10. What kinds of "public diplomacy" efforts does the United States undertake to promote its way of life and foreign policy objectives?
11. If you decided to have a career in global public relations, would you choose a global corporation, an international NGO, or the U.S foreign service? Explain your rationale.

Media Resources

Cambie, S., & Ooi, Y.-M. (2009). *International communication strategy: Developments in cross-cultural communications, PR, and social media.* London, England: Kogan, Page Publishers.

Cull, N. J. (2008). *The Cold War and the United States Information Agency.* London, England: Cambridge Press.

Global views of United States improve while other countries decline. (2010). Retrieved from www.worldpublicopinion.org

Khalaf, R. (2010, June 2). Pr campaign cannot turn off spotlight now on Gaza. *Financial Times,* 2.

Maltby, E. (2010, January 19). Expanding abroad? Avoid cultural gaffes. *Wall Street Journal,* p. B5.

Molleda, J.-C. (2009). Global public relations. Retrieved from Institute for Public Relations, Essential Knowledge Project website: www.instituteforpr.org

Netzley, M (2008, December). Peering through the walls: Special report: Asia/Pacific. *Communication World,* 31–40.

Peijuan, C., Ting, L. P., & Pang, A. (2009). Managing a nation's image during crisis: A study of the Chinese government's image repair efforts in the "Made in China" controversy. *Public Relations Review, 35*(3), 213–218.

Seitel, F. (2009, July). Dealing with the foreign press. *O'Dwyer's PR Report,* 34.

Tang, L., & Li, H. (2009). Corporate social responsibility communication of Chinese and global firms in China. *Public Relations Review, 35*(3), 199–212.

Ylisela, J. (2009, May). Six secrets of global communication. *RaganReport,* 30–31.

Nonprofit, Health, and Education

The Nonprofit Sector

Nonprofit organizations, which are often referred to as *charities*, encompass a broad area of public relations work. In the United States, there are almost 2 million such groups, according to GuideStar, an organization that compiles information on nonprofits.

More than 6.5 million people work in the nonprofit sector. The range of nonprofit institutions is astounding, from membership organizations, advocacy groups, and social service organizations, to educational organizations, hospitals and health agencies, small-city historical societies, and global foundations that disperse million-dollar grants.

The main purpose of nonprofit organizations is to serve the public interest. By definition, nonprofit organizations do not distribute monies to shareholders or owners. This is not to say that nonprofit organizations cannot generate income or hold assets, but there are a number of restrictions regulating how their income may be generated and how these funds may be used to support the organization's stated objectives. From the public relations perspective, nonprofit organizations are often represented as fostering goodwill, and as beacons of social responsibility.

Nonprofits are tax exempt. The federal government grants them this status because they enhance the well-being of their members, in the case of trade associations, or enhance the human condition in some way, in the case of environmental groups or medical research organizations. Many nonprofit organizations could not survive if they were taxed. Because they do not have shareholders or sell goods and services to customers, they face the never-ending task of asking for donations to pay expenses, finance projects, and recruit volunteers.

Competition, Conflict, and Cooperation

For many nonprofit organizations, partnerships are mutually beneficial. The United Way is a good case in point—many business and nonprofit organizations ranging from the National Football League to the Advertising Council, as well as numerous local organizations, partner with the United Way. This maximizes donations that are distributed to hundreds of associated charities. However, the frustrating reality is that nonprofits, instead of partnering, often compete with each other for members, funds, and other resources. For example, universities or colleges within the same state compete for funding from their respective state governments, even as they enter into collaborative partnerships with each other to obtain federal funding. Hospitals compete for "customers," but must work together to resolve shared concerns and issues.

Competition among nonprofit agencies for donations is intense. For many nonprofit groups, fund-raising of necessity is their most time-consuming activity. Without generous contributions from companies and individuals, nonprofit organizations could not exist. The scope of philanthropy in the United States and the amount of money needed to keep voluntary service agencies operating are staggering.

Nonprofit organizations have a willingness to cooperate but must also compete for limited or scarce resources. Sometimes nonprofit groups enter into partnerships based on common interests, such as the United Way, but generally, in advocating their individual interests, they are no different from business organizations that must struggle for market share.

Activist groups who espouse certain causes, in contrast, can come into conflict with other organizations whose values are different. Such conflicts can be high profile. In recent years, a number of religious organizations have come into conflict with groups that advocate for secular values.

For example, the American Civil Liberties Union (ACLU), a nonprofit organization founded in 1920 "to defend and preserve the individual rights and liberties guaranteed to every person in this country by the Constitution and laws of the United States," often comes into conflict with the American Center for Law and Justice, a conservative group founded by Pat Robertson to preserve "religious liberty, the sanctity of human life, and the two-parent, marriage-bound family." Although both organizations state their commitment to preserving "liberty," their respective views of what constitutes "liberty" are often diametrically opposed. This wrangle in the marketplace of ideas was introduced in Chapter 10 to emphasize the value in a free society that arises from allowing contending voices, many of them nonprofit organizations, to express themselves.

On an international level, there can also be competition and conflict. Many international organizations and government agencies, for example, supply aid funds to Africa, but some wonder if such aid is effective. See the Multicultural World box below.

on the job

A MULTICULTURAL WORLD

Dead Aid: Are Public Relations Fund-Raising Efforts Going to Waste?

Who is not moved by heart-rending depictions of children suffering from malaria or waterborne disease, whether within our own borders or in far-flung locales? Most of us are familiar with high-profile celebrities contributing time and talent to raise funds that address tragic conditions. Showcased by artists such as Bono or the popular judges from the talent show *American Idol*, we see squalor, disease, and violence-torn regions crying out for our help.

But what if all that goodwill from governments, corporate partners, and generous individuals—evoked by effective message strategies, much of them executed through the skills of

Dambisi Moyo

Bono

"This reader was left wanting a lot more Moyo, and a lot less Bono." Niall Ferguson, from the foreword to *Dead Aid*.

public relations people working behind the scenes—is actually doing more fundamental harm to emerging economies than good?

Dambisi Moyo, a native of Zambia with advanced economics degrees

from Harvard and Oxford, argues in her controversial book *Dead Aid: Why Aid Is Not Working and How There Is a Better Way for Africa* that "the majority of sub-Saharan countries flounder in a seemingly never-ending cycle of

(continued)

corruption, disease, poverty, and aid dependency," despite the fact that these countries have received more than $300 billion in development assistance since 1970. The book argues that despite the widespread Western belief that the rich should help the poor and that the form of this help should be aid, the reality may be that aid has helped make the poor poorer and growth slower.

Dr. Moyo focuses on concessional loans and grants, which are large transfers of nonemergency funds that actually spur aid dependency, corruption, market distortions, and greater poverty. A former World Bank strategic economist, Moyo argues that aid programs need to be reinvented to ensure that enormous single payments do not go to corrupt organizations and individuals, who manage to funnel off much of the largesse. For example, Zaire's president may have stolen as much as $5 billion, equal to the entire external debt of his country.

Moyo, a former economist for Goldman Sachs, now notorious for its reckless role in the 2009 banking collapse, is certainly not without her detractors, charitable organizations and aid recipients alike.

But setting aside the need for some final verdict on celebrity fundraising events and governmental aid programs, perhaps Moyo offers public relations professionals the chance to alter strategies and tactics in light of provocative points made in her book:

From 1970 to 1998, when aid flows to Africa were at their peak, the poverty rate in Africa actually rose from 11 percent to a staggering 66 percent.

Celebrity fund-raising events are feel-good celebrations of world generosity that condemn recipient countries to grimly negative stereotypes such as incompetent, feckless, and uncaring.

Moyo estimates that at least $10 billion, nearly half of Africa's 2003 foreign aid receipts, leaves the continent every year.

As a conservative economist, Moyo sees merit in the Chinese practice of not giving aid, but setting up businesses that provide employment and raise living standards in spite of daily wages at Chinese factories that are shockingly low.

For Africa ever to gain true prosperity, it must wean itself from aid and shift to a culture of enterprise and self-sufficiency.

Questions for our profession:

One of the points of pride for the public relations profession is the impact of our skills on fundraising for worthy causes. But could we do more to have a positive effect on long-term outcomes for developing economies by showing not only the desperate needs but also the determination and the progress of some in struggling communities?

Dr. Moyo's personal journey through life has taken her from Zambia to Harvard and Oxford and Wall Street—then back home again. Does Moyo's experience bring a multicultural perspective that informs her critique of aid and charitable giving? Or is she promoting

principles of self-reliance from Wall Street to peoples who just need to survive another day?

Do you think that the Chinese business approach to create jobs in developing regions offers a more lasting "hand up" instead of a "handout"? Or is it opportunism?

Do critiques and exposés of the failings of charitable aid only exacerbate despair, heightening compassion fatigue about evidently intractable conditions in many parts of the world? In other words, does criticism give prospective donors such as you and me an excuse—it's not good for the recipients?

How can celebrity public relations professionals, who play a central role in showcasing human suffering and raising funds to alleviate it, shift strategies to ensure that generosity has maximal impact on the needy, not on fat-cat administrators and politicians?

Do such critiques of charitable giving actually enable us to become better and more effective in providing "precision aid" to those most in need?

> The notion that aid can alleviate systemic poverty, and has done so, is a myth.
>
> *Dambisi Moyo, in* Dead Aid: Why Aid Is Not Working and How There Is a Better Way for Africa

Membership Organizations

Membership organizations are composed of people who share common business or social interests. Their purpose is mutual help and self-improvement. Membership organizations often use the strength of their common bond to promote the professionalism of their members, endorse legislation, and support socially valuable causes. Their main function is to advocate for the well-being of their members.

Professional Associations

Members of a profession or skilled craft organize for mutual benefit. Examples include the Royal Institute of British Architects or the Federal Law Enforcement Agency. Others serve highly specialized or niche groups, such as the National Association of Professional Organizers or the seemingly anachronistic Society of Gilders. Some professional organizations, such as the American Medical Association, also function as some of the largest advocacy and lobbying groups. In many ways, their goals resemble those of labor unions in that they seek improved earning power, better working conditions, and public appreciation of their roles in society.

Professional associations place their major emphasis on setting standards for professional performance, establishing codes of ethics, determining requirements for admission to a field, and encouraging members to upgrade their skills through continuing education. In some cases, they have quasi-legal power to license and censure members. In most cases, however, professional groups rely on peer pressure and persuasion to police their membership.

In general, professional associations are national in scope. Larger organizations often have district, state, or local chapters. Many scientific and scholarly associations, however, are international, and have chapters in many nations. The Public Relations Society of America (PRSA) and the International Association of Business Communicators (IABC) are examples of professional associations.

Public relations specialists for professional organizations use the same techniques as their colleagues in other branches of the field. And like their counterparts in trade groups and labor unions, many professional associations maintain offices near the seat of government in Washington, D.C., and in the various state capitals, employing lobbyists to make their voices heard.

Trade Groups

The membership of a trade association usually consists of manufacturers, wholesalers, retailers, or distributors in the same field. Corporate entities, not individuals, are the members. A few examples of trade associations include the American Beverage Association, the Property Casualty Insurers Association, and the National Association of Home Builders. There are about 6,000 trade and professional associations in the United States.

Because federal laws and regulations often can affect the fortunes of an entire industry, about one-third of these groups are based in the Washington, D.C., area. There, association staffs can monitor congressional activity, lobby for or against legislation, communicate late-breaking developments to the membership, and interact with government officials on a regular basis.

Although individual members of trade associations may be direct rivals competing for market share, it is often to their advantage to work together to promote an entire industry, generate public support, and share information. By representing an entire industry, an association often is a more effective news source than individual companies can be. When a news situation develops involving a particular field, reporters frequently turn to the spokesperson of its association for comment. To promote their industry, many trade organizations compile statistics, establish online newsrooms, provide speakers to schools, sponsor trade shows, and even maintain a YouTube channel.

Labor Unions

Like trade associations, labor unions represent the interests of an entire industry. However, labor unions advocate on behalf of employees, whereas trade associations typically represent the interests of management. As with other membership organizations, labor unions lobby for better working conditions, higher wages, increased safety regulations, better benefits, and education for their members.

Since their apex in the late 1970s, labor unions have suffered serious membership losses and, as a consequence, political clout. Union membership declined from 20.1 percent of workers in 1983 to 12.4 percent in 2008, according to the Department of Labor's Bureau of Statistics. However, the number of union members rose by about 400,000 between 2007 and 2008, perhaps a reflection of worker concern about job security during the economic recession. Workers in education, government, and libraries tend to have the highest union representation. Government workers are five times more likely to belong to a union than are their private sector counterparts.

Media portrayals often suggest that unions are corrupt, inflexible, and lacking in concern for anyone except their members. Nevertheless, labor unions have been largely responsible for many positive things that Americans today take for granted: the end of child labor, the 40-hour workweek, laws against discrimination in hiring and firing, and the minimum wage. Unions are still very much a part of the American scene, representing teachers, players in the National Basketball Association, UPS employees, and other familiar groups.

Unions rely on public relations tools to assert their strength and influence. Unions seek to build their memberships, protect members' job security, and improve their public images. Unions also employ public relations when communicating with their internal audiences in various companies or organizations because unions must keep their memberships informed about what they receive in return for their dues, which includes recreational and social programs and representation in communication and negotiations with company management.

Labor unions are often in conflict with management, which is dominant in terms of both financial strength and political clout. In every national political campaign, unions spend millions of dollars to support candidates they regard as friendly to their cause. Some of this money goes directly to the candidates, but significant amounts are devoted to "issue ads" that do not explicitly endorse an individual. This practice—which despite rhetoric to the contrary, represents a fraction of the money spent on issue ads supporting pro-business interests—enables support of candidates beyond individual campaign spending limits.

Chambers of Commerce

A chamber is an association of business professionals who work to improve their city's commercial climate and to publicize its attractions. Above all, chambers of commerce serve as boosters of local business growth. State chambers of commerce and, nationally, the U.S. Chamber of Commerce help guide local chambers and speak for business interests before state and federal government.

According to the Center for Public Integrity, the U.S. Chamber of Commerce spent almost $530 million on lobbying activities between 1998 and 2009. Its closest competitor, the American Medical Association, spent less than half that amount. In 2008–2009, both groups concentrated on lobbying efforts to shape the Democratic health care bill. The U.S. Chamber of Commerce also lobbies against legislation regarding global warming, but this has caused some companies to drop their membership. See the Ethics box below about Apple dropping its membership.

on the job

ETHICS

Apple Decides to Walk the Talk on Climate Change

On October 5, 2009, Apple Corporation resigned from the U.S. Chamber of Commerce, the country's largest industry advocacy group, citing a difference of opinion over proposed climate change legislation.

The letter sent to Chamber President Thomas Donahue by Apple's vice president of worldwide government affairs, Catherine A. Novelli, indicated that "we strongly object to the Chamber's recent comments opposing the EPA's efforts to limit greenhouse gases" and that the "Chamber's position differs so sharply from Apple['s]." Other companies had previously resigned: Exelon, PNM Resources, and Pacific Gas & Electric. However, Apple was, according to *BusinessWeek*, "the first highly visible consumer brand" to split with the Chamber on the issue.

The Chamber has long opposed, through lobbying, many of the provisions of the Clean Air Act and

initiatives to reduce carbon emissions through cap-and-trade. Apple, on the other hand, has gradually emerged as a leading "green" company. Indeed, Apple has recently emphasized its efforts to reduce the carbon footprint associated with its products, to be true to its position and avoid charges of merely "greenwashing"—covering up policies that make Apple's carbon footprint larger, instead of smaller.

At issue are two worldviews. According to polls, public opinion in the United States is split just about evenly on the issue of climate change. One view, represented by the Chamber and, presumably, most of its 3 million members, is that global warming has been exaggerated and that curbing it will hurt American competitiveness—and, worse. impoverish people worldwide. The other position, adopted by Apple, suggests that the evidence for climate change is overwhelming and that steps to reduce emissions are necessary.

According to *Newsweek*, Apple has recognized that arguing against climate change or carbon limits may be "bad for business." More importantly, doing so would pose a moral compromise and a hypocritical approach to take an accommodative stance toward the green movement while supporting one of that movement's main adversaries, the Chamber.

What are some of the ways that the Chamber can respond to Apple's resignation?

When Apple took the moral high ground, did the Chamber's equally principled position suffer or can both coexist without winners and losers?

What are the benefits and risks of the Chamber's position?

What strategies and tactics would you, as a PR professional, recommend to reopen the dialogue?

Local chambers of commerce play the role of community booster: Chambers spotlight the unique characteristics of their cities and sing their praises to anyone who will listen. Chambers often coin a slogan for a city, such as "Furniture Capital of Indiana" (Berne) or "Business at its Best since 1926" (Belfast, Maine).

Often, a chamber of commerce serves as the public relations arm of city government. The chamber staff generally produces the brochures and maps sent to individuals who seek information about visiting the city or who consider moving to the area. Chambers also conduct polls and compile statistics about the economic health of the city, including data on major industries, employment rates, availability of schools and hospitals, housing costs, and so on. Attracting conventions and new businesses to the city also is an important aspect of chamber work.

Advocacy Groups

Affecting communities to varying degrees are a number of pressing issues, from social matters such as poverty, abortion, and racism to threats such as epidemic diseases and environmental degradation. Organizations that fight for social causes can have significant impacts, both positive and negative. For example, the environment is prominent on the public agenda, primarily because of vigorous campaigns by environmental organizations. By advocating for recycling, eliminating toxic waste sites, purifying the air and water, and preserving natural resources, such organizations strongly influence our collective consciousness.

Advocacy groups include activist organizations such as Greenpeace and People for the Ethical Treatment of Animals (PETA) and social issue organizations such as the National Rifle Association (NRA) and the American Family Association (AFA). They advocate to promote their own causes, but may be perceived as lobbying for the good of the whole society. Their causes are often in conflict with one another. For example, the AFA frequently expresses views that conflict with those of the Gay and Lesbian Alliance Against Defamation (GLAAD).

The principal ways in which advocacy groups work to achieve their goals are lobbying, litigation, mass demonstrations, boycotts, reconciliation, and public education. Some of these organizations work relatively quietly through lobbying or reconciliation. Others are stridently confrontational and use more hard-core tactics such as litigation or mass demonstrations.

Activist Groups

Greenpeace, an organization that operates in 41 countries including the United States, is perhaps the best known of the confrontational groups. With 2.8 million members, Greenpeace is second in size, among environmental groups, to the much-less-flamboyant National Wildlife Foundation. Recently, contributions to Greenpeace have declined; so has the group's political influence. However, their movement is still vital.

Television viewers are familiar with the daredevil efforts of Greenpeace members in small boats to stop nuclear warships and whaling vessels. Right to Life, a highly visible abortion opponent, spent almost $500,000 on lobbying efforts in 2009. This was down slightly from 2004, the year that George W. Bush won his second election.

On the other hand, pro-choice groups such as Planned Parenthood spent a record $1.75 million in 2008 during the run-up to the presidential race. Christian denominations sometimes adopt an activist role. The Southern Baptist Convention mounted a boycott of Disney Corporation and all of its subsidiaries in protest of sex and violence in Disney entertainment productions. The boycott was mounted in response to "gay days" at Disney's theme parks.

Other groups, such as the American Family Association, press advertisers to drop sponsorship of television shows that the groups consider contrary to family values. They have been particularly active countering what they identify as "affirmation of homosexual behavior." An ongoing boycott of Pepsi-Cola started when the AFA asked Pepsi to "remain neutral in the culture war." As of November 2009, almost 400,000 supporters had signed an online petition. AFA maintains a Facebook page entitled "Boycott Pepsi," which has about 36,000 followers.

Public Relations Tactics

This section describes the principal ways in which advocacy groups work to achieve their goals.

Lobbying   Much of this is done at state and local government levels. In just one example, approximately 150 organizations have campaigned for laws to forbid smoking in public places and to restrict the sale of tobacco around the country.

Litigation   Organizations file suits seeking court rulings favorable to their projects or attempting to block unfavorable projects. The Sierra Club did so in a multiyear action that resulted in a landmark decision by the U.S. Fish and Wildlife Service declaring the northern spotted owl an endangered species.

Odds of a child becoming a top fashion designer: 1 in 7,000

Odds of a child being diagnosed with autism: 1 in 110

Some signs to look for:
No big smiles or other joyful expressions by 6 months. | No babbling by 12 months. | No words by 16 months.

To learn more of the signs of autism, visit autismspeaks.org

AUTISM SPEAKS
It's time to listen.

Autism Speaks

The Advertising Council (www.adcouncil.org) often partners with major nonprofits and governmental health agencies to conduct a major information campaign to raise public awareness about a disease or health condition. The Ad Council prepares radio and television PSAs, print ads, and billboard messages. This print ad was part of a national campaign to inform the public about autism.

Mass Demonstrations   Designed to demonstrate public support for a cause and in some cases to harass the operators of projects to which a group objects, mass demonstrations require elaborate public relations machinations. Organizers must obtain permits, inform the media, and arrange transportation, housing, programs, and crowd control. A small but vocal rally can also generate media coverage.

Boycotts   Some boycotts achieve easily identifiable results. Others stay in effect for years with little evident success. One success story occurred when the Rainforest Action

Network boycotted Burger King because the company had been buying Central American beef raised in cleared rain forests; the fast-food chain subsequently agreed to stop such purchases.

Reconciliation   Some environmental organizations have achieved good results by cooperating with corporations to solve pollution problems. The Environmental Defense Fund joined a task force with McDonald's to deal with the fast-food chain's solid waste problem, which eventually led to the company's decision to phase out its polystyrene packaging and take a leading role in reducing the waste entering landfills.

Fund-Raising   Raising money to conduct programs is an ongoing and costly problem for nonprofit organizations. With so many groups in the field, competition for donations is intense. Some professional fund-raisers believe that as a whole, nonprofit groups depend too much on direct mail and should place more emphasis on face-to-face contacts. Ironically, while some environmental groups advocate preservation of forests, they also create mountains of wastepaper by sending out millions of solicitation letters to raise funds for their organization. See the section on fund-raising at the end of the chapter.

Social Service Organizations

Social service organizations include social service, philanthropic, cultural, and religious groups serving the public in various ways. Because communication is essential for their success, these organizations require active and creative public relations programs.

Organizations frequently have dual roles, both service and advocacy, and serve the needs of individuals, families, and society in many ways. Among prominent national organizations of this type are Goodwill Industries, the American Red Cross, the Boy Scouts and Girl Scouts of America, and the YMCA.

Their advocacy is rooted in a sense of social purpose and the betterment of society as a whole. Local chapters carry out national programs. Service clubs such as Rotary and Kiwanis raise significant amounts of money for local, national, and global charitable projects.

Foundations

Hundreds of tax-free foundations in the United States constitute about 9 percent of total charitable giving. These are started when money to establish a foundation is provided by a wealthy individual or family, a group of contributors, an organization, or a corporation. The foundation's capital is then invested, and earnings from the investments are distributed as grants to qualified applicants. The Bill and Melinda Gates Foundation, for example, made grants of $5.3 billion in 2008 on projects for education and global health.

The Gates Foundation was already the largest in the world, but in June 2006 became what one writer described as a "behemoth" when Warren Buffett, the world's second richest man, gave $30 billion—85 percent of his fortune—to the Gates Foundation. With a stroke of the pen, the Gates Foundation doubled in size to more than $60 billion, completely eclipsing

> Seeing a problem resolved is extraordinarily gratifying.
>
> *Evelyn Lauder, founder of the Breast Cancer Research Foundation, which has raised more than $250 million since its creation in 1993*

all other foundations in terms of wealth. The Ford Foundation, the second largest foundation in the world, has only about $11 billion in assets. The third largest is the Robert Woods Johnson Foundation, with about $9 billion, followed by the Lilly Endowment, with $8 billion.

In addition to these large, highly visible national foundations, which make grants to a variety of causes, are smaller organizations such as the Susan G. Komen Breast Cancer Foundation and the Avon Foundation, which are also well known. Many smaller foundations, some of them extremely important in their specialized fields, distribute critical funds for research, education, public performances, displays, and similar purposes. Most of these organizations not only dispense money but also engage in numerous fund-raising activities to raise money for foundation efforts.

Corporations often set up their own foundations for handling philanthropic activities. Often the majority of their grants are awarded not in cash but involve the companies' products. The IBM Foundation, as well as HP and Apple, often make grants of computers and other high-tech equipment to educational institutions. When it became a public corporation, Google also set up a foundation (www.google.org) for the purpose of awarding grants in several issue areas, including global poverty, health, energy, and the environment.

Cultural Groups

Generating interest and participation in the cultural aspects of life often is the responsibility of nonprofit organizations in America. So, too, in many instances, is the operation of libraries; musical organizations, such as symphony orchestras; and museums of art, history, and natural sciences. Such institutions frequently receive at least part of their income from government sources; in fact, many are operated by the government.

But even government-operated cultural organizations such as the Smithsonian Institution depend on private support to raise supplementary funds. Cuts to government programs that subsidize the arts at the state and federal levels have increased the urgent need for private support for cultural institutions. For example, federal funding for the National Endowment for the Arts in 2010 was only $167.5 million.

Cultural organizations have a great need for public relations professionals. The constant efforts to publicize exhibitions, performances, and events, as well as support ongoing fund-raising, present many opportunities. Most cultural institutions have in-house divisions of public relations and marketing, but others, such as the Getty Museum or the New York Philharmonic, employ outside agencies.

Religious Groups

The mission of organized religion, as perceived by many faiths today, includes much more than holding weekly worship services and underwriting parochial schools. Churches also distribute charity, conduct personal guidance programs, provide leadership on moral and ethical issues in their communities, and operate social centers where diverse groups gather.

Public Relations Tactics

A number of public relations strategies and tactics are used to advance the goals of social service organizations.

Publicity   The news media provide well-organized channels for stimulating public interest in nonprofit organizations and are receptive to newsworthy material from these groups. Newspapers usually publish stories and announcements about meetings, training sessions, and similar routine activities. Television and radio stations broadcast important news items about organizations and are receptive to feature stories and guest appearances by organization representatives. Public relations practitioners should look for unusual or appealing personal stories, such as a retired teacher helping Asian refugee children to learn English.

Creation of Events   Events make news and attract crowds and are another way to increase public awareness. Such activities might include an open house in a new hospital wing or a concert by members of the local symphony orchestra for an audience of blind children. Novel stunts sometimes draw more attention to a cause than their intrinsic value would seem to justify. For example, a bed race around a shopping center parking lot by teams of university students who are conducting a campus fund drive for the March of Dimes is bound to attract curious spectators as well as local television and newspaper coverage.

Use of Services   Closely tied to increasing overall public awareness are efforts to encourage individuals and families to use an organization's services. Free medical examinations, free clothing and food for the needy, family counseling, nursing services for shut-ins, cultural programs at museums and libraries, offers of scholarships, and many other services provided by nonprofit organizations cannot do anyone any good unless potential users know about them. Written and spoken material designed to attract these publics should emphasize ease of participation and privacy of services. An example of this approach is the American Cancer Society's widely publicized campaign to encourage people to be screened for colon cancer.

Creation of Educational Materials   Public relations representatives of nonprofit organizations spend a substantial proportion of their time preparing written and website materials to educate the public. The quickest way to introduce people to an organization is to hand them a brochure or refer them to a website. Organizations also strive to design logos, or symbols, to help make their materials memorable to the public.

Newsletters   Another basic piece of printed material is a news bulletin, usually monthly or quarterly, mailed to members, the news media, and a carefully composed list of other interested parties. In addition to the publication and distribution of brochures explaining an organization's objectives, periodic newsletters distributed to opinion leaders are a quiet but effective way to tell an organization's story. And more and more organizations are using online newsletters through their listserv or social networking sites. See the newsletter for Guide Dogs for the Blind on page 559.

Health Organizations

There are two types of organizations in the health sector. The first type is hospitals, some of which are nonprofit and some of which are for-profit. Because hospitals sell a product (improved health), parallels exist between their public relations objectives and those of other corporations.

Hospitals

Hospitals focus on diverse audiences, both external and internal; involve themselves in public affairs and legislation because they operate under a maze of government regulations; and stress consumer relations, which involves keeping patients and their families satisfied as well as seeking new clients. Hospitals produce publications and publicity for these external and internal audiences. They also develop networks of volunteers who assist hospital staff in working with patients and their families.

Hospital public relations programs have four basic audiences: patients, medical and administrative staffs, news media, and the community as a whole. The four audiences overlap, but each demands a special approach and focus. Careful scrutiny can identify significant subaudiences within these four—for example, the elderly; pregnant women; victims of heart disease, cancer, and stroke who need support groups after hospitalization; potential financial donors to the hospital; and community opinion leaders, whose goodwill helps to build the institution's reputation. Each group can be cultivated by public relations techniques.

The public relations staff of a hospital has two primary roles: (1) to strengthen and maintain the public's perception of the institution as a place where medical skill, compassion, and efficiency are paramount, and (2) to help market the hospital's array of services such as surgery and cancer treatment. Many hospitals have sought to redefine themselves as community health centers. Basically, hospitals, like hotels, must have high room-occupancy rates to succeed financially. They augment this fundamental source of income by creating and marketing supplementary services such as cosmetic surgery, an area that offers opportunities and challenges for public relations people.

Guide Dog News

Nonprofits use newsletters in print and online format to keep donors informed about their activities. Regular communication with donors and prospective supporters helps generate support in the competitive world of fund-raising. This 8-page quarterly newsletter is published by Guide Dogs for the Blind, San Rafael, California.

Health Agencies

The second type of organization is private and government health agencies, which serve the public interest by providing health care, funding for health initiatives, and oversight. The most familiar health agencies are those administered at the federal and state levels, such as Medicare, Medicaid, and the Children's Health Insurance Program (CHIP). Nonprofit health agencies range from national organizations such as the American Heart Association, the American Cancer Society, and the National Multiple Sclerosis Society, to smaller groups such as the Conservation, Food & Health Foundation in Boston.

The Department of Health and Human Services (HHS) is the federal government's leading health agency. Its budget ($800 billion in 2010) amounts to nearly one-quarter of all federal spending. HHS provides more than 300 programs, including emergency preparedness, Head Start for preschoolers, maternity and infant programs, disease prevention and immunizations, and insurance programs such as Medicaid and Medicare. Divisions include major initiatives such as the Food and Drug Administration, the Centers for Disease Control and Prevention (CDC), and the National Institutes of Health (NIH). The NIH is the largest branch, with an annual budget of $31.2 billion in 2010 and more than 17,000 employees. Established in 1887, the NIH annually supports about 35,000 research and other grant projects.

On occasion, health public relations professionals must be prepared to handle crisis situations. For example, the CDC's Director of Media Relations, Dr. Glen Nowak, faces a 24/7 workweek when major health events unfold, such as the 2009 H1N1 flu epidemic. Nowak puts it this way:

> Communications is quickly at the forefront when there's an emergency or potentially great threat to people's health and well being. Many people, including the news media, want information as fast as possible, and throughout the emergency. As such, communications and media staff need to be prepared to put in many hours, perhaps for weeks or months.

Both governmental and nonprofit health agencies offer numerous job opportunities for public relations professionals. Those who specialize in health communication can have an impact on all Americans who are concerned about personal health risks as well as threats to financial security from burdensome medical costs. Essentially, health communicators strive to convey health information, prevention measures, and emergency response information as a means of reducing health risks.

Health Campaigns

Health campaigns to prevent and respond to diseases, and to promote health and quality of life, began applying social marketing practices in the late 1980s. A number of public relations strategies and techniques have been implemented for these initiatives, mainly by federal and state governments and private health agencies.

Campaigns to promote breast cancer awareness, the importance of diet and exercise, and the importance of screenings for colon cancer are examples of recent health promotion efforts sponsored by government and nonprofit health organizations. The American College of Emergency Physicians (ACEP), for instance, sponsors a Risky Drinking Campaign, an alcohol awareness program; Failure Is Not an Option, a project to alert the public to the symptoms of heart failure; and the Partnership for Anthrax Vaccine Education, which provides the latest information about vaccination initiatives. In addition to having altruistic motives, the ACEP sponsors these campaigns as a public relations tool to build goodwill and a positive public image.

A recent health campaign launched by the food industry arose from a serious health scare involving

> Communications is quickly at the forefront when there's an emergency or potentially great threat to people's health and well being. Many people, including the news media, want information as fast as possible, and throughout the emergency.
>
> *Dr. Glen Nowak, director of media relations at the Centers for Disease Control and Prevention*

PRCasebook

Schools Find Common Ground with Beverage Industry on Soft-Drink Sales to Students

In May of 2010, the American Beverage Association announced that it had decided on full cooperation with schools to remove sweetened soft drinks from school vending machines, reflecting a dramatic conflict management shift to accommodation by the industry.

Many contingent factors that influence public relations efforts, such as government regulation, activist groups' claims, and public perception, were at play. Interested parties competed through public relations efforts to win the hearts and minds of society and to reach a satisfactory or at least partially beneficial resolution for a wide array of participants.

Concern over the obesity rate of American children has pitted concerned parents, health officials, and some school districts against fast-food and soft-drink companies. According to the Centers for Disease Control and Prevention, nearly 1 out of 3 children is now obese. Health professionals generally cite a high-fat diet associated with increased soft-drink and fast-food consumption as a leading cause of childhood obesity.

The food industry's main strategy has been to reject the causal link between sugar and high-fat food and obesity, claiming that a sedentary lifestyle is the culprit. Groups with credible-sounding names such as the American Council of Fitness and Nutrition (ACFN), the Nutrition Advisory Council (NAC), and the Center for Consumer Freedom (CCF) have expressed their opposition to proposed bans. Because these groups are actually funded by the food industry, however, observers have labeled such grassroots organizations "Astroturf."

But the tide is turning. Many school districts have banned vending machine sales during school hours. For example, the Los Angeles County Unified School district voted to gradually eliminate the sale of soda and other sugary drinks. New York City approved a plan in October 2009 to promote healthy alternatives, with limited calories, carbonation, and sodium, to junk food in their vending machines.

One of those rejoicing was the milk industry, which had suffered diminished consumption as soft drink and sweetened juice sales rose, illustrating one final time that public relations professionals represent many divergent interests, each with a voice in the debate at the center of a free society.

---

bacterial contamination of precut vegetables. Television news producers often aired "buyer beware" segments on the dangers of precut salad ingredients, citing lists of common, harmless bacteria normally found on the vegetables and suggesting that their presence could mean that dangerous bacteria might appear. Health groups and activists have also pressured the beverage industry to offer more healthy beverages in school vending machines. See the PR Casebook above.

Indicative of the growing sophistication of health care public relations is the targeting of women for consumer information; 60 percent of doctor visits and 59 percent of prescription drug purchases are made by women, according to Kym White, managing director of Ogilvy Public Relations Worldwide's Health & Medical Practice. Audience targeting also was the thrust of a study entitled *Femstat 3 Report: American Women and Self-Care.* The study found that 50 percent of women get information mainly from their primary care doctors, 24 percent from magazines and newspapers, 7 percent from television and radio, and 5 percent from self-help books. Much of the health information that women receive is from public relations sources targeting this population.

Health information and advice on the Internet has grown exponentially over the past several years. The National Cancer Institute has a single database with over 650 articles on cancer risk. According to *O'Dwyer's PR Services Report*, 55 percent of the adult population has online access, and 86 percent of them use the Internet to find health-related information. Some experts estimate that nearly 25 percent of all Web searching is health related. Public relations companies now produce video and audio programming on the web for their health care clients, providing doctors, medical reporters, investors, and patients with medical and pharmaceutical information. Social media also are increasingly used to reach niche audiences. See the Insights box below about how health agencies are using texting to reach teenagers.

on the job
INSIGHTS

Need Info about Sex?: Text a Question

"If u have sex underwater, do u need a condom?" That is one of the hundreds of questions about sex that teenagers texted to the nonprofit Adolescent Pregnancy Prevention Campaign of North Carolina, which runs a Birds and Bees Text Line staffed by qualified adults.

State health educators were deeply concerned because North Carolina was ranked ninth in the nation in terms of teenage pregnancy rates, so they decided to dispense sex education via teenagers' favorite device—their cell phones. Questions are answered within 24 hours, and as journalist Jan Hoffman of the *New York Times* reports, "The Birds and Bees Text Line offers one-on-one exchanges that are private, personal, and anonymous. And they can be conducted free of parental scrutiny."

Other health agencies around the nation are also tapping into teenagers'

favorite technologies to fight disease and unwanted pregnancies. Some have used websites, such as Columbia University's *Go Ask Alice* and Atlantic Health's *TeenHealthFX.com*, that allow teenagers to post questions online. According to Hoffman, "Other programs in Washington, D.C., Chicago, Toronto, and San Francisco allow young people to text a number, select from a menu of frequently asked questions ('What 2 do if the condom broke') and receive automated replies, with addresses of free clinics." California also started HookUp 365247, a statewide text messaging service. The texter can type a zip code and get a local clinic referral as well as weekly health tips.

Professor Sheana Bull of the University of Colorado School of Public Health makes the key

point about using social media networking strategies, telling the *New York Times*, "The technology can be used to connect young people to trusted, competent adults who have competent information." The North Carolina program, for example, also has a blog, pages on MySpace and Facebook, and a Twitter account.

Educational Organizations

Educational institutions include programs that provide child care, instruction for primary and secondary students, colleges, universities, trade schools, and schools for special needs students. These organizations are often licensed or regulated by state and federal agencies, as in the case of primary and secondary schools, or by private accreditation bodies such as the Southern Association of Colleges and Schools.

Most educational institutions have nonprofit status insofar as they do not have shareholders who receive proceeds or profits from their operation and they are formed specifically for charitable, scientific, or educational purposes. Educational institutions take on a staggering array of organizational structures and functions. A public information officer for a local school district must constantly deal with parents, the school board, and other community and governmental organizations. A university director of public relations or even marketing communications, on the other hand, has less interaction with parents but must deal with ongoing student recruitment, campus controversies, and alumni relations. See the Insights box below for a job posting in university relations.

on the job
INSIGHTS

A Job in University Relations

Many public relations professionals find rewarding jobs in a university setting. A good example of a job description for a director of communications is the one posted by Empire State College, part of the State University of New York (SUNY) system. The following was posted on *prnewsonline.com*:

Job Description

The director's primary responsibility is the development, implementation, and management of an integrated communications plan that will raise the profile of the college across the state of New York, nationally, and internationally. The communications plan, which must include

key performance indicators, will be reviewed annually to ensure alignment with the college's strategic plan and attainment of measures of success. Empire State College was founded in 1971 as a comprehensive, public college within the State University of New York.

The director, which reports to the vice president for communications and government relations, is expected to:

Establish strategic media relations through active engagement with broadcast, print, and online outlet reporters and managers to broaden recognition and understanding of the college and its unique mission.

Work closely with various college constituencies, especially members of the writing, design, marketing, publication, and special events staffs to create documents and events that will support efforts to increase recognition of the college.

Engage with college deans regarding public relations in their geographic regions or areas of expertise.

Create and advise on internal communications and manage the college's electronic newsletter.

Prepare faculty and ress. interactions with *(continued)*

Assist in the preparation of briefing papers and advocacy pieces on public higher education policy.

Ensure consistency of messaging and accuracy of information.

Serve as official spokesperson for the college, as necessary.

Engage in extensive travel, be available for occasional weekend and evening hours.

Minimum Qualifications

Three to five years experience.

Bachelor's degree, preferably in public relations, journalism, marketing, or related field.

Extensive experience in developing and managing integrated communication activities.

Technological competence, computer mastery, and ease in communicating Web 2.0 and social media technologies.

Excellent oral and written communications and presentation skills, mastery of Associated Press writing style, expertise in editing.

Ability to work under tight and changing deadlines and manage multiple tasks simultaneously.

Experience in using a variety of media to advance policy changes in higher education.

Preferred Qualifications

Master's degree, preferably in public relations, journalism, marketing, or a related field.

Experience in higher education communications, marketing, and/or public relations.

Experience in creating video, webcast, and podcast content.

Experience working with national and international media outlets.

Experience in managing press communications in crisis situations.

Familiarity with Empire State College and the State University of New York (SUNY).

Colleges and Universities

Higher education is big business in the United States. California, the most populous state, with 38 million residents, spends $20 billion annually on four-year public colleges and universities. Another $6 billion is spent on two-year community colleges.

It's also a business that has millions of customers—students. In the United States, almost 17.5 million students are enrolled at more than 4,000 college and universities. Almost every one of these institutions has personnel working in such activities as public relations, marketing communication, and fund-raising.

In large universities, the top communication officer supervises the office of development, which includes a division for alumni relations and also an office of public relations; these functions are often combined in smaller institutions. Development and alumni personnel seek to enhance the prestige and financial support of the institution. Among other activities, they conduct meetings and seminars, publish newsletters and magazines, and arrange tours. Their primary responsibilities are to build alumni loyalty and generate funding from private sources.

The public relations director, generally aided by one or more chief assistants, supervises the information news service, publications, and special events. Depending on the size of the institution, perhaps a dozen or more employees will carry out these functions, including writing, photography, graphic design, broadcasting, and computer networking. See the organization chart for Stanford University's Office of Public Affairs in Figure 21.1.

The most visible aspect of a university public relations program is its news bureau. An active bureau produces hundreds of news releases, photographs, and special columns and articles for the print media in addition to other activities. It prepares programs of

Figure 21.1 Public Relations in a University

This is the organization chart for the office of public affairs at Stanford University. The vice president of public affairs reports directly to the president of the university.

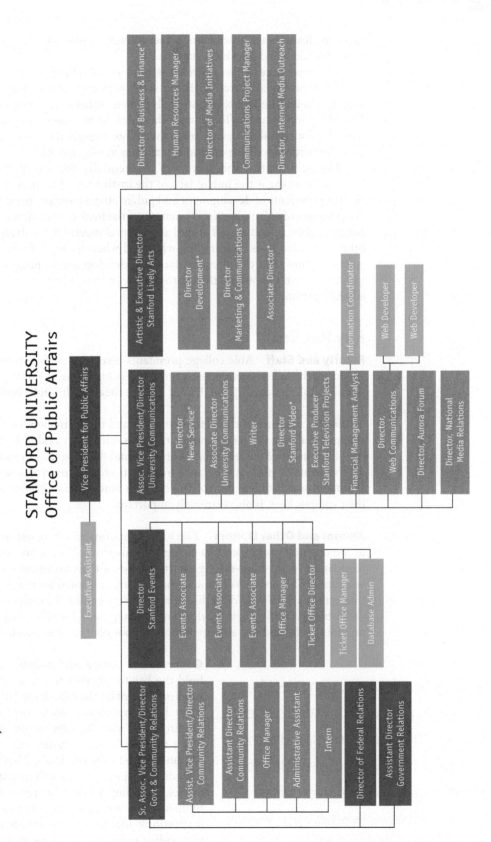

STANFORD UNIVERSITY
Office of Public Affairs

news and features about students' achievements, faculty activities, and campus person-alities for radio and television stations.

The news bureau also provides assistance and information for reporters, editors, and broadcasters affiliated with the state, regional, and national media. The staff responds to hundreds of telephone calls from members of the news media and the public seeking information. To enhance this interchange, many progressive news bureaus have developed online news portals that allow engagement and serve to tell the campus story without relying on traditional mass media outlets.

The president of the university is essentially the top public relations officer because he or she is the public face of the institution. The president relies, however, on vice presidents of development and public affairs to implement a consistent, coherent program of enhancing the reputation of the institution among a variety of publics. Ideally, public relations staff attend all top-level meetings involving the president and other administrators to learn the whys and wherefores of decisions made and lend counsel. Only then can they satisfactorily develop action programs and respond to questions from the publics those programs concern. They are indeed the voice of the administration.

Key Publics

Faculty and Staff   Able college presidents involve their faculty and staff in decision making to the fullest extent possible, given the complexities of running a major institution. Good morale, a necessity, is achieved in large measure through communication.

Students   Because of their large numbers and the many families that they represent, students make up the largest public relations arm—for good or bad—that a university has. The quality of the teaching they receive and their overall experience are the greatest determinants of student allegiance to an institution. However, a sound administrative attitude toward students, involving them as much as possible in decisions that affect their campus lives, is also extremely important.

Alumni and Other Donors   The loyalty and financial support of alumni are crucial to the ongoing operations of a college or university. Alumni are considered the major foundation of any fund-raising effort because of their immediate association with the institution. Donors who are not alumni also are cultivated for major gifts based on their interest in particular fields or disciplines. Colleges and universities raise money for such projects as recruiting new faculty, buying equipment, building student residence halls, providing scholarships, and upgrading campus computer networks.

When I say I'm a lobbyist, some people look at me as if I need a shower. It's a new business with the universities, and some people think it's a dirty business. But nothing's dirtier than not having resources.

Robert Dickens, coordinator of government relations for the University of Nevada at Reno

Government   State and federal governments often hold the key to whether universities receive sufficient monies to maintain their facilities, faculty, and programs. Most large institutions have someone who regularly monitors the state legislature on appropriations and issues ranging from laboratory experiments on animals to standardized tests and taxes. That person's work also includes competing with other state institutions for money, defending proposed increases in higher education budgets and arguing against cuts, establishing an institution's identity in the minds of legislators, and responding to lawmakers' requests for information.

The Community A college or university must maintain a good relationship with the members of the community in which it is situated. The greatest supporters that an institution may have are the people within its immediate geographic area.

Prospective Students Suffering from declining revenues, increased operation costs, and a dwindling pool of prospective students occasioned by lower birthrates and competition from online degree programs, many colleges have turned to highly competitive recruiting methods.

They commonly use extensive direct mail as a recruiting tool and attract students by offering free tuition scholarships and so on. Some, in the "hard-sell" classification, use extensive advertising in print and broadcast media and on the Web. Other colleges and universities have replaced their catalogs and brochures with slick, four-color materials that use bright graphics and catchy headlines to lure students. Most, if not all, now use the Web or other emerging social media such as Facebook or Twitter. In addition to exciting graphics, interactive features such as podcasts, blogs, links to Facebook sites, and Twitter feeds capitalize on prospective students' interest in technology and social media.

Fund-raising has increased dramatically at most public and private universities in recent years as costs have risen and allocations from state legislatures and federal agencies have dramatically declined. Total nongovernmental financial support for education was $40.9 billion in 2008, according to Giving USA, a unit of the Giving Institute, which publishes an annual tally of charitable contributions. This amount represents 13 percent of the total charitable giving in the United States, which was $307 billion in 2008. In addition to annual operating fund campaigns, universities are increasingly conducting long-range capital campaigns for large amounts of money. Fund-raising is the topic of the next section.

Fund-Raising and Development

Finding ways to pay the bills is a critical problem for virtually all nonprofit organizations that advocate social or environmental causes, offer social services, provide health care, and even provide education from kindergarten to college. Many also receive government funding, but the amount usually covers only part of the operating costs. Consequently, an important component of any nonprofit is fund-raising, which is often called *development* or *advancement*.

Although the largest, most publicized donations are made by corporations and foundations, individual contribution totals far exceed combined corporate and foundation giving. In fact, individual contributions amount to about 76 percent of annual U.S. philanthropic donations, or about $223 billion.

Depending on their needs, nonprofit organizations may try to catch minnows— hundreds of small contributions—or angle for the huge marlin, a large corporate gift. Some national organizations raise massive sums. In 2008, for example, the American Red Cross raised about $3.2 billion, followed by Food for the Poor ($1.5 billion), Feed the Children ($1.2 billion), World Vision ($1.1 billion), and the Brother's Brother Foundation ($1.1 billion). Charities often receive a flood of donations following catastrophes, such as Hurricane Katrina or the massive earthquake in Haiti.

Public relations professionals participate directly in fund-raising by organizing and conducting solicitation programs or by serving as consultants to specialized development departments in their organizations. However, organizations may instead employ professional firms to conduct their fund-raising campaigns on a fee basis. In those instances, the organizations' public relations professionals usually serve a liaison function.

Motivations for Giving

An understanding of what motivates individuals and companies to give money or volunteer their time is important to anyone involved in fund-raising. An intrinsic desire to share a portion of one's resources, however small, with others—an inherent generosity possessed in some degree by almost everyone—is a primary factor of this motivation.

The Independent Sector commissioned the Gallup Organization to do a survey on volunteerism and giving. The survey found that 53 percent of those responding cited "assisting those who are less fortunate" as their personal motive for volunteering and giving. The second most frequently cited reason was gaining a feeling of personal satisfaction; religion was third. Only 6 percent cited tax considerations as a major reason for giving.

Another motivation, quite simply, is ego satisfaction. The donor who makes a large contribution gets a building named for his or her family, and individuals get their names published in a list of contributors. Peer pressure—overt or subtle—is another factor. Saying "no" to a direct request from a friend, neighbor, or coworker is difficult, and the cliché about "keeping up with the Joneses" applies here as well.

Despite the downturn in the economy, a Gallup poll also found that the number of people who donated to charitable causes declined only slightly and volunteerism actually rose between 2008 and 2009. (See the Insights box on page 570 for details on giving.)

Fund-raising involves risks as well as benefits. If an organization is to maintain public credibility, adherence to high ethical standards when soliciting contributions and close control of fund-raising costs are essential to ensure that expenses constitute a reasonable percentage of the funds collected. Numerous groups have had their reputations severely damaged by disclosures that only a small portion of the money they raised was actually applied to the causes they advocate, with the rest consumed by solicitation expenses and administrative overhead.

Fund-Raising Methods

There are a number of methods that nonprofits use to raise money for their services and programs.

Corporate and Foundation Donations   Public relations professionals generally implement different types of campaigns for fund-raising efforts, depending on whether they are targeting corporations or individuals. Organizations seeking donations from major corporations normally do so through the local corporate offices or sales outlets. Some corporations give local offices a free hand in making donations to local groups up to a certain amount. Even when the decisions are made at corporate headquarters, local recommendations are important. Requests from foundations generally should be made to the main office, which typically provides application forms.

Increasingly, corporations undertake programs that match employee donations. Most commonly, matching is done on a dollar-for-dollar basis: If an employee gives $1 to a philanthropic cause, the employer does the same. Some corporations match at a two-to-one rate, or even higher. Corporations make contributions to charities in less direct ways, too, some of which are quite self-serving.

When applying for a charitable donation, applicants are best served if they submit a "case for support" letter that covers the following elements: background of the organization, current status of the organization's services, need for the organization's services, sources of current funding, administration of the organization, community support, current needs of the organization, and the benefits to the community of the donation.

Structured Capital Campaigns The effort to raise major amounts of money for a new wing of a hospital, an engineering building on a university campus, or even the reconstruction and renovation of San Francisco's famed cable car system is often called a *capital campaign*.

In a capital campaign, emphasis is placed on substantial gifts from corporations and individuals. One key concept of a capital campaign is that 90 percent of the total amount raised will come from only 10 percent of the contributors. For example, in a $10 million campaign to add a wing to an art museum, it is not unusual for the lead gift to be $1 or $2 million.

Capital campaigns require considerable expertise, and for this reason, many organizations retain professional fund-raising counsel. A number of U.S. firms offer these services; the most reputable ones belong to the Giving Institute, formerly known as the American Association of Fundraising Counsel.

Donors often are recognized by the size of their gifts, and terms such as *patron* or *founder* are designated. Major donors may be given the opportunity to have rooms or public areas in the new building named after them. When they are soliciting gifts, hospitals may even prepare "memorial" brochures that show floor plans and the cost of endowing certain facilities.

Direct Mail Although direct mail can be an expensive form of solicitation because of the costs of developing or renting mailing lists, preparing the printed materials, and mailing the solicitations, direct mail is increasingly competitive. An organization can reduce costs by conducting an effective local, limited direct mail campaign on its own, if it develops an up-to-date mailing list of "good" names known to be potential donors. Regional and national organizations, and some large local ones, either employ direct mail specialists or rent carefully chosen mailing lists from list brokers.

Attractive, informative mailing pieces that motivate recipients to donate are keys to successful solicitation. The classic direct mail format consists of a mailing envelope, letter, brochure, and response device, often with a postage-paid return envelope.

Recently, however, the *Chronicle of Philanthropy* has reported a sharp decline in direct mail contributions to several large national organizations, such as Disabled American Veterans and Easter Seals. The widespread adoption of online media may be exacerbating the prevailing view that direct mail is an "uninvited guest" in the home. The publication asserts, "Americans have become increasingly fed up with direct-mail appeals from charities."

Event Sponsorship The range of events a philanthropic organization can sponsor to raise funds is limited only by the imagination of its members. Participation contests are a popular method, as are events such as walkathons, which appeal to the American desire to exercise more. Nationally, the March of Dimes holds an annual 32-kilometer WalkAmerica in 1,100 cities on the same day.

Staging parties, charity balls, concerts, exhibitions, and similar events in which tickets are sold is another widely used fund-raising approach. Often, however, big parties create more publicity than profit, with 25 to 50 percent of the money raised going to expenses. Other methods include sponsorship of a motion picture premiere, a theater night, or a sporting event. Barbecues flourish as money-raisers in western U.S. cities. Seeking to attract donors from the under-30 age group, some organizations use the fun approach by raffling off pop culture items, as when one group raffled Madonna's sequined brassiere (for $2,500) and a T-shirt by artist Felix Gonzalez-Torres with the message "Nobody Owns Me" (for $50).

Television Solicitations A television station sometimes sets aside a block of airtime for a telethon sponsored by a philanthropic organization. Best known of the national telethons are the ones conducted by the Public Broadcasting System, often involving broadcasts of classic rock concerts. Another high-profile event was the celebrity telethon to aid victims of Hurricane Katrina.

Telephone Solicitations Solicitation of donations by telephone is a relatively inexpensive way to seek funds but is of uncertain effectiveness. Many people resent

on the job

INSIGHTS

Contributions Decline for First Time in Nearly a Quarter Century

Charitable giving is a well-established American institution. More than $300 billion was given in 2007 as well as in 2008, and there was a 2 percent drop between them. According to Giving USA Foundation, donations to charitable organizations totaled $314.07 billion in 2007 and $307.65 billion in 2008. With the country going through serious economic downturns, 2008 experienced a decline, the first decline since 1987. Del Martin, chair of the Giving USA Foundation, said,

We definitely did see belt-tightening. This drop in giving meant that nonprofits have had to do more with less over the past year, but it could have been a lot worse...

individuals, corporations and foundations still provided more than $307 billion to causes they support, despite the economic conditions.

According to the research conducted by the Center for Philanthropy at Indiana University, the major sources of U.S. donations were rounded as shown in Figure 21.2.

Figure 21.2 2008 charitable giving. Total: $307.65 billion

Source: Giving Foundation USA 2009

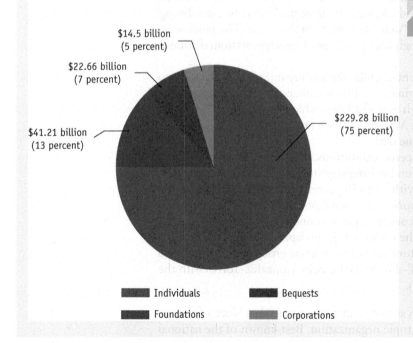

$14.5 billion
(5 percent)

$22.66 billion
(7 percent)

$41.21 billion
(13 percent)

$229.28 billion
(75 percent)

■ Individuals ■ Bequests
■ Foundations ■ Corporations

We definitely did see belt-tightening. This drop in giving meant that nonprofits have had to do more with less over the past year, but it could have been a lot worse... individuals, corporations and foundations still provided more than $307 billion to causes they support, despite the economic conditions.

Del Martin, chair of the Giving
USA Foundation

Except for religion, public-society benefit, and international affairs, there was a slight decline in donations received. Religious organizations, with an increase of 5 percent from the previous year, received 35 percent of the total in 2008. It was the second year that giving to religion exceeded $100 billion. Public-society benefit received 8 percent of total giving and the increase was 5 percent. The growth for international affairs organizations was 0.6 percent. For other types of recipients, decreases were from 5 percent (education; environment and animals) to 19 percent (foundations). Figure 21.3 shows a breakdown of the various categories by distribution of $307.65 billion.

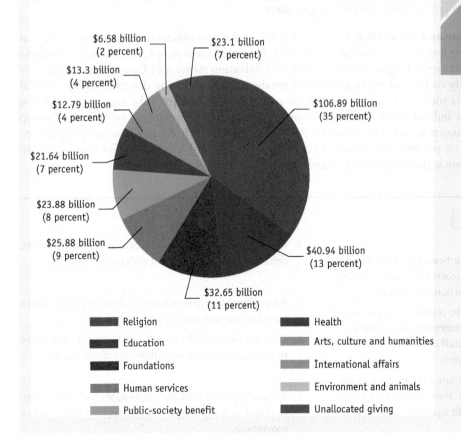

$6.58 billion
(2 percent)

$13.3 billion
(4 percent)

$12.79 billion
(4 percent)

$21.64 billion
(7 percent)

$23.88 billion
(8 percent)

$25.88 billion
(9 percent)

$32.65 billion
(11 percent)

$23.1 billion
(7 percent)

$106.89 billion
(35 percent)

$40.94 billion
(13 percent)

Religion

Education

Foundations

Human services

Public-society benefit

Health

Arts, culture and humanities

International affairs

Environment and animals

Unallocated giving

Figure 21.3 Types of recipients of contributions, 2008. Total: $307.65 billion

Source: Giving Foundation USA 2009

receiving telephone solicitations, particularly if the recipient of the call is unfamiliar with the cause. In addition, the national do-not-call registry prevents fund-raisers from randomly calling people, although legitimate charities are exempt from the regulation. Converting verbal telephone promises into confirmed written pledges also is problematic. And the widespread switch from landline phones to cell phones adds to the complexity of using telephone solicitations, particularly for "cold calling" those with no loyalty to or affinity for an organization.

Increasingly, calling is driven by automatic dialers known as "robocalls." A number of political candidates and political action committees made effective use of so-called robocalls during the 2008 presidential election. Automated calls cost the candidate or organization between five and eight cents. Despite messages being targeted to potential voters likely to support the candidate's message, many people have expressed objections to the impersonal nature of robocalls.

Endorsements and Tie-Ins   Rather than depending entirely on contributions, some nonprofit organizations go into business on their own or make tie-ins with commercial firms from which they earn a profit. Use of this approach is growing, but entails risks that must be carefully assessed. Three types of commercial money-raising are the most common: (1) licensing use of an organization's name to endorse a product and receiving payment for each item sold, such as the American Heart Association's commission for its endorsement of Healthy Choice frozen dinners; (2) sharing profits with a corporation from sales of a special product, such as Newman's Own salad dressing; and (3) operating a business that generates revenue for the organization, such as the Metropolitan Museum of Art's gift shop.

Online and Social Media   Using the Internet is cost efficient, compared with the cost of sending thousands of pieces of mail. However, most people remain wary of online solicitations. Organizations such as the Salvation Army and Greenpeace, which are highly visible and trusted, have had greater success soliciting donations online. Social media such as blogs, Twitter, Facebook, LinkedIn, and YouTube are vital tactics that allow individuals to interactively engage causes that they support or oppose. A group of women in India, for example, developed the Pink Chaddi (underwear) campaign to oppose paternalistic views. They regularly blog and maintain a Facebook page to chronicle their fight for women's rights.

Summary

The Nonprofit Sector

- Nonprofit organizations have been given tax-exempt status because their primary goal is to enhance the well-being of their members or the human condition.

- Fund-raising is a major public relations task of these groups, in which they create communication campaigns and programs, and require a staff (including volunteers) to handle their fund-raising work.

- For many nonprofit organizations, partnerships among members are necessary for their common interest. Competition among nonprofit agencies for their share of donations is intense.

- Many nonprofit groups advocate differing positions, resulting in ongoing conflict with one another.

Membership Organizations

- A membership organization is made up of people with a common interest, either business or social.

- Such groups include professional associations, trade groups, labor unions, and chambers of commerce.

Advocacy Groups

- Advocacy groups work for social causes such as the environment, civil rights, gun ownership, or the pro-choice movement.

■ Their efforts include lobbying, litigation, mass demonstrations, boycotts, reconciliation, and public education.

Social Service Organizations

■ Service groups and philanthropic, cultural, and religious organizations all fall into the category of social service organizations.

■ Their public relations goals include developing public awareness, getting individuals to use their services, creating educational materials, recruiting volunteers, and fund-raising.

Health Organizations

■ Hospitals and health agencies are the two major organizations serving the public's health needs.

■ Public relations professionals help communicate information about medical advances, the availability of health services, and potential health risks.

Educational Organizations

■ Public relations at colleges and universities involves both development, or fund-raising, and enhancing the prestige of the institution.

■ The office of development and public relations may conduct meetings, publish newsletters, and arrange tours.

■ The audiences for communication include alumni, students, prospective students, faculty and staff, government, and the general public.

Fund-Raising and Development

■ Fund-raising is a critical issue for nonprofit organizations. Depending on their mission and strategy, nonprofits seek donations from large corporations or foundations or small contributions from individuals.

■ Recruiting volunteer labor is often crucial to making up for lack of operating funds and involving the community in reaching the nonprofit's goals.

Case Activity   Creating a Social Media Strategy

Nonprofits are constantly exploring ways to expand their social media strategy to increase community visibility and raise money for their various projects.

The president of Goodwill Industries in your city asks you to develop a social media strategy for the nonprofit. The organization already has a website, but it doesn't seem to generate many visitors. She has also heard about blogs, Facebook, texting, YouTube, Twitter, and mobile phone "apps," but like many executives in the over-50 age group, she readily admits that she doesn't know how all these "things" work.

She outlines some of Goodwill's activities and projects. Goodwill, for example, operates two stores in the city where donated vintage clothing and other goods are sold. In addition, the nonprofit has an annual fashion show that highlights many of the quality clothing items that can be found in the stores. The purpose of both activities, of course, is to raise money for operations and to drive traffic to the stores. There is also an annual community fund-raising banquet that features a known personality or celebrity. Of course, Goodwill also promotes its sites where the public can drop off donated items.

Given Goodwill's activities outlined above, what social media strategies would you recommend? Be specific about how each would be used to promote Goodwill and its various activities. The president would also appreciate suggestions on how to make the website "more interesting and exciting."

Questions   For Review and Discussion

1. What are the differences and similarities among trade associations, labor unions, professional associations, and chambers of commerce?
2. Identify public relations strategies and tactics that advocacy groups use to further their causes.
3. Name and describe some types of social service agencies.
4. What motivates people to serve as volunteer workers?
5. What are major roles of public relations professionals in health organizations?

6. What are some components of successful health campaigns?
7. How can social media be used to promote various health campaigns?
8. With what primary public does a sound university public relations program begin? List other major publics that must be addressed in such a program.
9. Describe commonly used types of fund-raising.
10. What is a capital campaign?

Media Resources

Elliott, S. (2009, November 12). For causes, it's a tougher sell. *New York Times*, pp. 1F, 16.

Goldberg, M. (2010, May 8). Is foreign aid a bad thing? *The American Prospect*. Retrieved from www.prospect.org

Hoffman, J. (2009, May 3). When the cellphone teaches sex education: Health officials use teenagers' favorite technologies to fight disease and unwanted pregnancies. [Sunday Styles section]. *New York Times*, pp. 1, 8.

Lariscy, R., Avery, E., & Sohn, Y. (2010, April). Health journalists and three levels of public information: Issue and agenda disparities. *Journal of Public Relations Research, 22* (2), pp. 113–135.

Lavrusik, V. (2009, July 23). Ten ways universities are engaging alumni using social media. Retrieved from www.mashable.com

Miller, L. (2009, November). Lupus Foundation builds a network, pulls in donations through Facebook. *RaganReport*, 5–16.

Moyo, D. (2009). *Dead aid: Why aid is not working and how there is a better way for Africa*. New York, NY: Farrar, Straus, Giroux.

Pogrebin, R. (2009, November 12). The chain store: Patron of the arts. *New York Times*, p. 6.

Public sector unions: Welcome to the real world. (2009, December 12). *Economist*, 31.

Simon, S. (2009, August 17). Hard-hit schools try public relations push. *Wall Street Journal*. Retrieved from www.online.wsj.com/article

Sisco, H., Collins, E., & Zoch, L. (2010, March). Through the looking glass: A decade of Red Cross crisis response and situational crisis communication theory. *Public Relations Review, 36*(1), 21–27.

PEARSON
mycommunicationlab

The Pearson Public Relations Podcast. "Careers in PR: Nonprofit."

Directory of Useful Web Sites

Public relations requires research and facts. Here's a sampling of sites on the Internet where you can find information.

General Information

www.highbeam.com: Provides full-text articles from multiple sources, including newspapers, newswires, magazines, etc.

www.pollingreport.com: Compilation of findings from surveys regarding trends in public opinion.

thomas.loc.gov: Site of the Library of Congress and the starting point for legislative and congressional information.

www.infoplease.com: Online almanacs on various topics from business to history and sports.

www.biography.com: Backgrounds on current and historical figures.

www.acronymfinder.com: Definitions of acronyms, abbreviations, and initialisms.

www.howstuffworks.com: Descriptions, diagrams, and photos that show how devices work.

www.statistics.com: Statistics from government agencies and other sources on a range of subjects.

www.ipl.org: The Internet Public Library, a University of Michigan site that gives links to all kinds of sources, from dictionaries to writing guides to newspapers.

resourceshelf.freepint.com: A favorite among reference librarians.

www.salary.com: Salaries in all fields, including public relations.

www.norc.org/GSS+website: General Social Survey, which examines social trends in the United States.

Public Relations

www.about.com: Provides multiple guide sites. Public relations site offers articles, directories, forums, etc.

http://prcentral.wordpress.com: General information about public relations.

www.businesswire.com, www.prnewswire.com, www.prweb.com: News releases by company and industry.

tweepml.org/Starter-Pack-for-PR-Students/: Useful Twitter feeds for PR students to follow.

www.prmuseum.com: The (online) Museum of Public Relations houses information on early pioneers in the field.

www.workinginpr.com: Public relations jobs and salaries by classification and geographical area.

Organizations

www.awpagesociety.com: Arthur W. Page Society.

www.pagecenter.comm.psu.edu: Arthur W. Page Center at Pennsylvania State University.

www.cgpr.uncc.edu: Center for Global Public Relations, University of North Carolina at Charlotte.

www.prfirms.org: Council of Public Relations Firms.

www.globalalliancepr.org: Global Alliance for Public Relations and Communication Management.

www.instituteforpr.com: Institute for Public Relations (IPR).

www.iabc.com: International Association of Business Communicators (IABC).

www.ifea.com: International Festivals and Events Association (IFEA).

www.ipra.org: International Public Relations Association (IPRA).

www.niri.org: National Investor Relations Institute (NIRI).

www.plankcenter.ua.edu: Plank Center for Leadership in Public Relations at the University of Alabama.

www.pac.org: Public Affairs Council.

www.prsa.org: Public Relations Society of America (PRSA).

www.prssa.org: Public Relations Student Society of America (PRSSA).

www.annenberg.usc.edu/sprc: Strategic Public Relations Center at the University of Southern California Annenberg School for Communication.

Trade Publications

www.adage.com: *Advertising Age*.

www.briefings.com: *Communication Briefings*.

www.iabc.com/cw: *Communication World* (requires IABC membership).

www.odwyerpr.com: *O'Dwyer's PR/Marketing News*; can also sign up for weekly e-mail newsletter.

http://www.prnewsonline.com/: *PRNews* (requires subscription).

http://www.ragan.com: Articles and general information about public relations.

http://www.prsa.org/Intelligence//: PRSA publications (*Tactics, Strategist*), blogs, and podcasts.

www.prweekus.com: *PRWeek*; also features blogs, including *The Cycle* (news), *Insider* (industry), and *Editor's Blog*.

Bibliography of Selected Books, Directories, and Periodicals

General Books

Bobbitt, R., & Sullivan, R. (2005). *Developing the public relations campaign: A team-based approach.* Boston, MA: Allyn and Bacon.

Botan, C., & Hazelton, V. (2006). *Public relations theory II.* Mahwah, NJ: Lawrence Erlbaum Associates.

Broom, G. M., Cutlip, S., & Center, A. (2009). *Effective public relations* (10th ed.). Upper Saddle River, NJ: Prentice Hall.

Cameron, G. T., Wilcox, D. L., Reber, B. H., & Shin, J.-H. (2008). *Public relations today: Managing competition and conflict.* Boston, MA: Allyn & Bacon.

Coombs, W. T., & Holladay, S. (2007). *It's not just PR: Public relations in society.* Malden, MA: Wiley-Blackwell.

Coombs, W. T., & Holladay, S. (2010). *PR strategy and application: Managing influence.* Malden, MA: Wiley-Blackwell.

Grunig, J. E. (Ed.). (1992). *Excellence in public relations and communication management.* Hillsdale, NJ: Lawrence Erlbaum.

Grunig, L. A., Grunig, J. E., & Dozier, D. M. (2002). *Excellent public relations and effective organizations.* Mahwah, NJ: Lawrence Erlbaum.

Guth, D. W., & Marsh, C. (2008). *Public relations: A values-driven approach* (4th ed.). Boston, MA: Allyn and Bacon.

Hansen-Horn, T., & Neff, B. D. (2008). *Public relations: From theory to practice.* Boston, MA: Allyn & Bacon.

Heath, R. L. (Ed.). (2004). *Encyclopedia of public relations.* Thousand Oaks, CA: Sage Publications.

Heath, R. L. (Ed.). (2010). *The SAGE handbook of public relations.* Thousand Oaks, CA: Sage Publications.

Heath, R. L., & Coombs, W. T. (2006). *Today's public relations: An introduction.* Thousand Oaks, CA: Sage Publications.

Ihlen, Ø., van Ruler, B., & Fredriksson, M. (2009). *Public relations and social theory: Key figures and concepts.* New York, NY: Routledge.

Lattimore, D., Baskin, O., Heiman, S. T., Toth, E., & VanLeuven, J. K. (2008). *Public relations: The profession and the practice* (3rd ed.). New York, NY: McGraw-Hill.

L'Etang, J., & Pieczka, M. (2006). *Public relations: Critical debates and contemporary practices.* Mahwah, NJ: Lawrence Erlbaum Associates.

Newsom, D., Turk, J. V., & Kruckeberg, D. (2007). *This is PR: The realities of public relations* (9th ed.). Belmont, CA: Thomson/Wadsworth.

Seitel, F. P. (2011). *The practice of public relations* (11th ed.). Upper Saddle River, NJ: Prentice Hall.

Shankman, P. (2007). *Can we do that?! Outrageous PR stunts that work?!* New York, NY: John Wiley & Sons.

Smith, R. D. (2009). *Strategic planning for public relations* (3rd ed.). Mahwah, NJ: Lawrence Erlbaum.

Tench, R., & Yeomans, L. (2009). *Exploring public relations* (2nd ed.). Prentice Hall.

Toth, E. L. (Ed.). (2006). *The future of excellence in public relations and communication management: Challenges for the next generation.* Routledge.

Toth, E. L., & Heath, R. L. (Eds.). (2009). *Rhetorical and critical approaches to public relations* (2nd ed.). Hillsdale, NJ: Lawrence Erlbaum.

Wilcox, D. L., & Cameron, G. T. (2011). *Public relations: Strategies and tactics* (10th ed.). Boston, MA: Allyn and Bacon.

Wilcox, D. L., Cameron, G. T., Reber, B. H., & Shin, J.-H. (2012). *Think: Public relations.* Boston, MA: Allyn & Bacon.

Wilson, L. J., & Ogden, J. (2008). *Strategic program planning for effective public relations campaigns* (5th ed.). IA: Kendall-Hunt, 2008.

Special Interest Books

Business/Management

Austin, E. W., & Pinkleton, B. E. (2006). *Strategic public relations management* (2nd ed.). Mahwah, NJ: Lawrence Erlbaum.

Belasen, A. T. (2007). *The theory and practice of corporate communication: A competing values perspective.* Thousands Oaks, CA: Sage Publications.

Berger, B. K., & Reber, B. H. (2006). *Gaining influence in public relations: The role of resistance in practice.* Mahwah, NJ: Lawrence Erlbaum Associates.

Caywood, C. (Ed.). (1997). *The handbook of strategic public relations and integrated communications.* New York, NY: McGraw-Hill.

Cornelissen, J. P. (2008). *Corporate communication: A guide to theory and practice* (2nd ed.). SAGE Publications.

Goodman, M. B., & Hirsch, P. B. (2010). *Corporate communication: Strategic adaptation for global practice.* New York, NY: Peter Lang.

Ledingham, J. A., & Bruning, S. D. (2001). *Public relations as relationship management.* Mahwah, NJ: Lawrence Erlbaum.

McKee, K. B., & Lamb, L. F. (2009). *Applied public relations: Cases in stakeholder management* (2nd ed.). New York, NY: Routledge.

Careers

Cassio, J., & Rush, A. (2009). *Green careers: Choosing work for a sustainable future.* New Society Publishers.

Gregory, M. (2008). *The career chronicles: An insider's guide to what jobs are really like.* Novato, CA: New World Library.

Mogel, L. (2002). *Making it in public relations: An insider's guide to career opportunities* (2nd ed.). Mahwah, NJ: Lawrence Erlbaum.

Ross, B. I., & Johnson, K. F. (Eds.). (2009). *Where shall I go to study advertising and public relations?* [Pamphlet]. Lubbock, TX: Advertising Education Publications. Retrieved from http://communication.utexas.edu/WSIG/

Case Studies

Courtright, J. L., & Smudde, P. M. (2007). *Power and public relations.* Cresskill, NJ: Hampton Press.

Guth, D. W., & Marsh, C. (2005). *Adventures in public relations: Case studies and critical thinking.* Boston, MA: Allyn & Bacon.

Hagley, T. (2005). *Writing winning proposals—Cases.* Boston, MA: Allyn & Bacon.

Hendrix, J. A., & Hayes, D. C. (2009). *Public relations cases* (8th ed.). Belmont, CA: Thomson/Wadsworth.

Lamb, L. F., & McKee, K. B. (2009). *Applied public relations: Cases in stakeholder management* (2nd ed.). Mahwah, NJ: Lawrence Erlbaum.

May, S. (2006). *Case studies in organizational communication: Ethical perspectives and practices.* Thousand Oaks, CA: Sage Publications.

Sheehan, M., & Xavier, R. (2009). *Public relations campaigns.* New York, NY: Oxford University Press.

Swann, P. (2010). *Cases in public relations management.* New York, NY: Routledge.

Communication/Persuasion

Bryant, J., & Oliver, M. B. (2008). *Media effects: Advances in theory and research* (3rd ed.). Hillsdale, NJ: Lawrence Erlbaum.

Jowett, G. S., & O'Donnell, V. (2005). *Propaganda and persuasion* (4th ed.). Thousand Oaks, CA: Sage Publications.

Larson, C. U. (2006). *Persuasion: Reception and responsibility* (11th ed.). Belmont, CA: Thomson/Wadsworth.

Moloney, K. (2006). *Rethinking public relations: PR propaganda and democracy* (2nd ed.). London, England: Routledge.

Perloff, R. M. (2010). *The dynamics of persuasion: Communication and attitudes in the 21st century* (4th ed.). Routledge.

Samovar, L., Porter, R., & McDaniel, E. R. (2009). *Intercultural communication: A reader* (12th ed.). Belmont, CA: Wadsworth.

Simons, H. W., & Jones, J. (2011). *Persuasion in society* (2nd ed.). Routledge.

Stacks, D. W., & Salwen, M. B. (2009). *An integrated approach to communication theory and research* (2nd ed.). New York, NY: Routledge.

Crisis Communications

Coombs, W. T. (2007). *Ongoing crisis communication: Planning, managing, and responding* (2nd ed.). Thousand Oaks, CA: Sage Publications.

Fearn-Banks, K. (2010). *Crisis communications: A casebook approach* (4th ed.). Mahwah, NJ: Lawrence Erlbaum.

Harmon, J. F. (2009). *Feeding frenzy: Crisis management in the spotlight.* New York, NY: Eloquent Books.

Hearit, K. M. (2005). *Crisis management by apology: Corporate response to allegations of wrongdoing.* Routledge.

Heath, R. L., & O'Hair, H. D. (2009). *Handbook of risk and crisis communication.* New York, NY: Routledge.

Millar, D. P., & Heath, R. L. (Eds.). (2004). *Responding to crisis: A rhetorical approach to crisis communications.* Mahwah, NJ: Lawrence Erlbaum.

Ulmer, R. R., Sellnow, T. L., & Seeger, M. W. (2007). *Effective crisis communication: Moving from crisis to opportunity.* Thousand Oaks, CA: SAGE Publications.

Zaremba, A. J. (2010). *Crisis communication: Theory and practice.* Armonk, NY: M.E. Sharpe.

Cultural Diversity/Gender

Alexander, A., & Hanson, J. (Eds.). (2010). *Taking sides: Clashing views on controversial issues in mass media and society* (11th ed.). New York, NY: McGraw-Hill.

Brief, A. P. (2008). *Diversity at work.* New York, NY: Cambridge University Press.

Creedon, P. J., & Cramer, J. (2007). *Women in mass communication.* Thousand Oaks, CA: SAGE Publications.

Grunig, L. A., Toth, E. L., & Hon, L. C. (2001). *Women in public relations: How gender influences practice.* New York, NY: Guilford Publications.

Education

Bagin, D., Gallagher, D., & Moore, E. H. (2007). *The school and community relations* (9th ed.). Boston, MA: Allyn and Bacon.

Kowalski, T. J. (2007). *Public relations in schools* (4th ed.). Upper Saddle River, NJ: Prentice Hall.

Employee Relations

D'Aprix, R. (2008). *The credible company: Communicating with today's skeptical workforce.* San Francisco, CA: Jossey-Bass.

Harris, T. E., & Nelson, M. D. (2008). *Applied organizational communication: Theory and practice in a global environment* (3rd ed.). New York, NY: Lawrence Erlbaum Associates.

Holtz, S. (2003). *Corporate conversations: A guide to crafting effective and appropriate internal communications.* AMACOM/American Management Association.

Jablin, F. M., & Putnam, L. (Eds.). (2004). *The new handbook of organizational communication: Advances in theory, research, and methods.* Thousand Oaks, CA: Sage Publications.

Modaff, D. P., DeWine, S., & Butler, J. A. (2008). *Organizational communication: Foundations, challenges, and misunderstandings* (2nd ed.). Boston, MA: Pearson/Allyn and Bacon.

Ethics

Bivins, T. (2009). *Mixed media: Moral distinctions in advertising, public relations, and journalism* (2nd ed.). New York, NY: Routledge.

Fitzpatrick, K. R., & Bronstein, C. (2006). *Ethics in public relations: Responsible advocacy.* Thousand Oaks, CA: Sage Publications.

May, S., Cheney, G., & Roper, J. (2007). *The debate over corporate social responsibility.* New York, NY: Oxford University Press.

McElreath, M. P. (1997). *Managing systematic and ethical public relations.* Dubuque, IA: Brown and Benchmark.

Stauber, J., & Rampton, S. (2000). *Toxic sludge is good for you: Damn lies and the public relations industry* [Critical analysis]. Monroe, ME: Common Courage Press.

Wilkins, L., & Christians, C. G. (2009). *The handbook of mass media ethics.* New York, NY: Routledge.

Financial/Investor Relations

Bragg, S. M. (2010). *Running an effective investor relations department: A comprehensive guide.* Hoboken, NJ: John Wiley & Sons.

Guimard, A. (2008). *Investor relations: Principles and international best practices of financial communications.* Palgrave Macmillan.

Fund-Raising/Development

Ciconte, B. K., & Jacob, J. G. (2004). *Fund raising basics: A complete guide* (2nd ed.). Gaithersburg, MD: Aspen Publications.

Rosso, H. (2003). *Achieving excellence in fund-raising* (2nd ed.). San Francisco, CA: Jossey-Bass.

Weinstein, S. (2009). *The complete guide to fund-raising management* (3rd ed.). New York, NY: John Wiley & Sons.

Government/Public Affairs

Feld, L., & Wilcox, N. (2008). *Netroots rising: How a citizen army of bloggers and online activists is changing American politics.* Westport, CT: Praeger.

Fitzwater, M. (2000). *Call the briefing: A memoir ten years in the White House with Presidents Reagan and Bush.* Xlibris Corporation.

Klein, W. (2008). *All the presidents' spokesmen: Spinning the news—White House press secretaries from Franklin D. Roosevelt to George W. Bush.* Westport, CT: Praeger.

Lee, M. (2007). *Government public relations: A reader.* CRC Press.

Lerbinger, O. (2005). *Corporate public affairs: Interacting with interest groups, media, and government.* Routledge.

McMillen, W. (2010). *From campus to capitol: The role of government relations in higher education.* Baltimore, MD: The Johns Hopkins University Press.

Walsh, K. T. (2002). *Feeding the beast: The White House versus the press.* Xlibris Corporation.

Warnick, B. (2007). *Rhetoric online: Persuasion and politics on the World Wide Web.* New York, NY: Peter Lang, 2007.

History

Cutlip, S. M. (1994). *The unseen power: Public relations: A history.* Hillsdale, NJ: Lawrence Erlbaum.

Cutlip, S. M. (1995). *Public relations history: From the seventeenth to the twentieth century.* Hillsdale, NJ: Lawrence Erlbaum.

Ewen, S. (1998). *PR! A social history of spin.* New York, NY: Basic Books.

Griese, N. (2001). *Arthur W. Page: Publisher, public relations pioneer, patriot.* Atlanta, GA: Anvil Publishers.

Lee, M. (2005). *The first presidential communications agency: FDR's Office of Government Reports.* Albany: State University of New York Press.

Miller, K. S. (1999). *The voice of business: Hill & Knowlton and post-war public relations.* Chapel Hill: University of North Carolina Press.

Tye, L. (2002). *The father of spin: Edward L. Bernays and the birth of public relations.* Holt Paperbacks.

International

Cambie, S., & Ooi, Y.-M. (2009). *International communications strategy: Developments in cross-cultural communications, PR, and social media.* Philadelphia, PA: Kogan Page.

Curtin, P. A., & Gaither, T. K. (2007). *International public relations: Negotiating culture, identity, and power.* Thousand Oaks, CA: Sage Publications.

Freitag, A. R., & Quesinberry Stokes, A. (2009). *Global public relations: Spanning borders, spanning cultures.* New York, NY: Routledge.

Grunig, L. A., & Grunig, J. E. (2002). *Excellent public relations and effective organizations: A study of communication management in three countries.* Mahwah, NJ: Lawrence Erlbaum.

Jandt, F. E. (2010). *An introduction to intercultural communication* (6th ed.). Thousand Oaks, CA: Sage Publications.

Moss, D., Powell, M., & DeSanto, B. (2010). *Public relations cases: International perspectives* (2nd ed.). New York, NY: Routledge.

Newsom, D. (2007). *Bridging the gaps in global communication.* Malden, MA: Blackwell Publishing.

Parkinson, M., & Ekachai, D. G. (2006). *International and intercultural public relations: A campaign case approach.* Boston, MA: Allyn & Bacon.

Rudd, J. E. (2007). *Communicating in global business negotiations: A geocentric approach.* Thousand Oaks, CA: Sage Publications.

Samovar, L. A., Porter, R. E., & McDaniel, E. R. (2008). *Intercultural communication: A reader* (12th ed.). Belmont, CA: Thomson/Wadsworth.

Schmidt, W. V., Conaway, R. N., Easton, S. S., & Wardrope, W. J. (2007). *Communicating globally: Intercultural communication and international business.* Thousand Oaks, CA: Sage Publications.

Sriramesh, K., & Vercic, D. (2009). *The global public relations handbook: Theory, research, and practice* (2nd ed.). Mahwah, NJ: Lawrence Erlbaum Associates.

Tilson, D. J., & Alozie, E. C. (2004). *Toward the common good: Perspectives in international public relations.* Boston, MA: Pearson Education.

Internet/Social Media

Breakenridge, D. (2008). *PR 2.0: New media, new tools, new audiences.* Upper Saddle River, NJ: FT Press.

Brown, R. (2009). *Public relations and the social web: Using social media and web 2.0 in communications.* Philadelphia, PA: Kogan Page.

Duhe, S. C. (2007). *New media and public relations.* New York, NY: Peter Lang.

Kelleher, T. (2006). *Public relations online: Lasting concepts for changing media.* Thousand Oaks, CA: Sage Publications.

Safko, L., & Brake, D. K. (2009). *The social media bible: Tactics, tools, and strategies for business success.* Hoboken, NJ: John Wiley & Sons.

Scott, D. M. (2010). *The new rules of marketing and PR: How to use social media, blogs, news releases, online video, and viral marketing to reach buyers directly* (2nd ed.). New York, NY: John Wiley & Sons.

Shih, C. (2009). *The Facebook era: Tapping online social networks to build better products, reach new audiences, and sell more stuff.* Boston, MA: Pearson Education.

Solis, B., & Breakenridge, D. (2009). *Putting the public back in public relations.* Boston, MA: FT Press/Pearson Education.

Vorvoreanu, M. (2008). *Web site public relations: How corporations build and maintain relationships online.* Amherst, NY: Cambria Press.

The Yahoo! style guide: The ultimate sourcebook for writing, editing, and creating content for the digital world. (2010). Retrieved from Amazon.com

Issues Management

Heath, R. L., & Palenchar, M. J. (2009). *Strategic issues management: Organizations and public policy challenges* (2nd ed.). Thousand Oaks, CA: Sage Publications.

Mitroff, I. I., & Anagnos, G. (2001). *Managing crises before they happen.* New York, NY: AMACOM.

Law

Gower, K. K. (2007). *Legal and ethical considerations for public relations* (2nd ed.). Prospect Heights, IL: Waveland Press.

Haggerty, J. F. (2009). *In the court of public opinion: Winning strategies for litigation communications* (2nd ed.). Chicago, IL: American Bar Association.

Kerr, R. L. (2008). *The corporate free speech movement: Cognitive feudalism and the endangered marketplace of ideas.* New York, NY: LFB Scholarly Publishing.

Middleton, K., & Lee, W. E. (2011). *Law of public communication* (8th ed.). Boston, MA: Allyn and Bacon.

Moore, R. L., Collins, E., & May, C. (2010). *Advertising and public relations law* (2nd ed.). New York, NY: Routledge.

Parkinson, M., & Parkinson, M. L. (2007). *Public relations law.* Routledge.

Pember, D. R., & Calvert, C. (2010). *Mass media law* (17th ed.). New York, NY: McGraw-Hill.

Marketing

Blakeman, R. (2007). *Integrated marketing communication: Creative strategy from idea to implementation.* Lanham, MD: Rowman & Littlefield Publishers.

Dilenschneider, R. L. (2010). *The AMA handbook of public relations.* New York, NY: AMACOM.

Gillis, T. (2006). *The IABC handbook of organizational communication: A guide to internal communication, public relations, marketing and leadership.* New York, NY: John Wiley & Sons.

Morse, D. R. (2009). *Multicultural intelligence: Eight make-or-break rules for marketing to race, ethnicity, and sexual orientation.* Ithaca, NY: Paramount Market Publishing, Inc.

Weiner, M. (2006). *Unleashing the power of PR: A contrarian's guide to marketing and communication.* San Francisco, CA: Jossey-Bass.

Media/Press Relations

Favorito, J. (2007). *Sports publicity: A practical approach.* Burlington, MA: Butterworth-Heinemann.

Gower, K. K. (2007). *Public relations and the press: A troubled embrace.* Evanston, IL: Northwestern University Press.

Hart, H. (2007). *Successful spokespersons are made, not born* (Expanded ed.). Bloomington, IN: AuthorHouse.

Howard, C. M., & Mathews, W. K. (2006). *On deadline: Managing media relations* (4th ed.). Prospect Heights, IL: Waveland Press.

Mindich, D. T. Z. (2005). *Tuned out: Why Americans under 40 don't follow the news.* New York, NY: Oxford University Press.

Wallack, L., Woodruff, K., Dorfman, L. E., & Diaz, I. (1999). *News for a change: An advocate's guide to working with the media.* Thousand Oaks, CA: Sage Publications.

Nonprofit Groups/Health Agencies

Andreasen, A. R. (2005). *Social marketing in the 21st century.* Thousand Oaks, CA: Sage Publications.

Bonk, K., Tynes, E., Griggs, H., & Sparks, P. (2008). *Strategic communications for nonprofits: A step-by-step guide to working with the media.* San Francisco, CA: John Wiley & Sons.

Brinckerhoff, P. C. (2010). *Mission-based marketing: Positioning your not-for-profit in an increasingly competitive world* (3rd ed.). Hoboken, NJ: John Wiley & Sons.

Feinglass, A. (2005). *The public relations handbook for nonprofits: A comprehensive and practical guide.* New York, NY: John Wiley & Sons.

Publicity

Borkowski, M. (2008). *The fame formula: How Hollywood's fixers, fakers, and star makers created the celebrity industry.* London, England: Pan MacMillan, Ltd.

Levine, M. (2008). *Guerrilla P.R. 2.0: Wage an effective publicity campaign without going broke.* New York, NY: HarperCollins.

Also see entries in Special Events and Writing in Public Relations sections.

Reputation

Alsop, R. J. (2006). *The 18 immutable laws of corporate reputation: Creating, protecting, and repairing your most valuable asset.* London, England: Kogan Page Ltd.

Aula, P., & Mantere, S. (2008). *Strategic reputation management.* New York, NY: Routledge.

Brogan, C., & Smith, J. (2009). *Trust agents: Using the web to build influence, improve reputation, and earn trust.* Hoboken, NJ: John Wiley & Sons.

Doorley, J., & Garcia, H. F. (2010). *Reputation management: The key to successful public relations and corporate communication* (2nd ed.). New York, NY: Routledge.

Fertik, M. (2010). *Wild west 2.0: How to protect and restore your reputation on the untamed social frontier.* AMACOM.

Firestein, P. (2009). *Crisis of character: Building corporate reputation in the age of skepticism.* New York, NY: Sterling Publishing Co., Inc.

Gaines-Ross, L. (2008). *Corporate reputation: 12 steps to safeguarding and recovering reputation.* New York, NY: John Wiley & Sons.

Research Methods

Daymon, C. (2010). *Qualitative research methods in public relations and marketing communications* (2nd ed.). New York, NY: Routledge.

Demers, D. P. (2005). *Dictionary of mass communication and media research: A guide for students, scholars and professionals.* Spokane, WA: Marquette Books.

Frey, L. R., Botan, C. H., & Kreps, G. L. (2005). *Investigating communication: An introduction to research methods* (3rd ed.). Boston, MA: Allyn and Bacon.

Friesen, B. K. (2010). *Designing and conducting your first interview project.* San Francisco, CA: Jossey-Bass.

McQuarrie, E. F. (2006). *The market research toolbox: A concise guide for beginners* (2nd ed.). Thousand Oaks, CA: Sage Publications.

Priest, S. H. (2009). *Doing media research: An introduction* (2nd ed.). Thousand Oaks, CA: Sage Publications.

Stacks, D. W. (2010). *Primer of public relations research* (2nd ed.). New York, NY: The Guilford Press.

Warren, C. A. B., & Xavia Karner, T. (2009). *Discovering qualitative methods: Field research, interviews, and analysis* (2nd ed.). New York, NY: Oxford University Press.

Special Events

Allen, J. (2007). *The executive's guide to corporate events and business entertaining: How to choose and use corporate functions to increase brand awareness, develop new business, nurture customer loyalty and drive growth.* New York, NY: John Wiley & Sons.

Allen, J. (2009). *Event planning: The ultimate guide to successful meetings, corporate events, fundraising galas, conferences, conventions, incentives and other special events* (2nd ed.). New York, NY: John Wiley & Sons.

Bowdin, G. (2010). *Events management* (3rd ed.). Oxford, England: Butterworth-Heinemann.

McGillivray, D., Foley, M., & McPherson, G. (2011). *Event policy: From theory to strategy.* New York, NY: Routledge.

Wendroff, A. L. (2003). *Special events: Proven strategies for nonprofit fundraising* (2nd ed.). New York, NY: John Wiley & Sons.

Speeches/Presentations

Beebe, S. A., & Beebe, S. (2008). *Public speaking: An audience-centered approach* (7th ed.). Boston, MA: Allyn and Bacon.

DiSanza, J. R., & Legge, N. J. (2008). *Business and professional communication: Plans, processes, and performance* (4th ed.). Boston, MA: Allyn and Bacon.

Engleberg, I., & Daly, J. A. (2008). *Presentations in everyday life: Strategies for effective speaking* (3rd ed.). Boston, MA: Allyn and Bacon.

Fujishin, R. (2008). *The natural speaker* (6th ed.). Boston, MA: Allyn and Bacon.

Writing in Public Relations

Aronson, M., Spetner, D., & Ames, C. (2007). *The public relations writer's handbook: The digital age* (2nd ed.). New York, NY: John Wiley & Sons.

Bivins, T. H. (2007). *Public relations writing: The essentials of style and format* (6th ed.). Boston, MA: McGraw-Hill.

Diggs-Brown, B. (2006). *The PR style guide: Formats for public relations practice.* Belmont, CA: Thomson/Wadsworth.

Marsh, C., Guth, D., & Short, B. P. (2008). *Strategic writing: Multimedia writing for public relations, advertising and more* (2nd ed.). Boston, MA: Allyn and Bacon.

Morton, L. P. (2006). *Strategic publications: Designing for target publics.* Best Books Plus.

Newsom, D., & Haynes, J. (2010). *Public relations writing: Form and style* (9th ed.). Belmont, CA: Thomson/Wadsworth.

Smith, R. D. (2007). *Becoming a public relations writer: A writing process workbook for the profession.* New York, NY: Routledge.

Whitaker, W. R., Ramsey, J. E., & Smith, R. D. (2008). *Media writing: Print, broadcast, and public relations* (3rd ed.). New York, NY: Routledge.

Wilcox, D. L. (2009). *Public relations writing and media techniques* (6th ed.). Boston, MA: Allyn and Bacon.

Zappala, J. M., & Carden, A. R. (2009). *Public relations writing worktext: A practical guide for the profession* (3rd ed.). New York, NY: Routledge.

Directories

Directories are valuable tools for public relations personnel who need to communicate with a variety of specialized audiences. The following is a selected list of the leading national and international directories.

Media Directories

The All-In-One Media Directory. Gebbie Press, Box 1000, New Paltz, NY 12561.

Bacon's Media Directories: Newspaper/Magazines, Radio/TV/Cable, Media Calendar, Business Media, International Media Directory, New York Publicity Outlets, Metro California Outlets, Computer & High-Tech Media, and Medical & Health Media. Bacon Information, Inc., 332 S. Michigan Avenue, Chicago, IL 60604.

Broadcasting Cable Yearbook. Broadcasting & Cable Magazine, PO Box 7820, Torrance, CA 90504.

Bulldog Reporter's National PR Pitch Book; PR Agency and Services Directory. Infocom Group, 5900 Hollis Street, Suite R2, Emeryville, CA 94608-2008.

Burrelle's Media Directories: Newspapers and Related Media, Magazines and Newsletters, Radio, Television, and Cable. Burrelle's Media Directory, 75 E. Northfield Rd., Livingston, NJ 07039.

Cable & TV Station Coverage Atlas. Warren Communications, 2115 Ward Court NW, Washington, D.C. 20037.

The College Media Directory. Oxbridge Communications, 150 Fifth Avenue, Suite 302, New York, NY 10011.

Directory of Small Press/Magazine Editors and Publishers. Dustbooks, PO Box 100, Paradise, CA 95967.

Directory of Women's Media. Women's Institute for Freedom of the Press, 1940 Calvert Street NW, Washington, D.C. 20009.

Gale Directory of Publications and Broadcast Media. Gale Group, PO Box 9187, Farmington Hills, MI 48333.

Hudson's Washington News Media Contacts Directory. Hudson Associates, PO Box 311, Rhinebeck, NY 12572.

Literary Marketplace. R. R. Bowker Company, 245 W. 17th St., New York, NY 10011.

National Directory of Community Newspapers. American Newspaper Representatives, 1700 W. Beaver Road, Suite 340, Troy, MI 48084.

National Directory of Magazines. Oxbridge Communications, 150

Fifth Avenue, Suite 302, New York, NY 10011.

News Media Directory. Bowker/Proquest, 630 Central Avenue, New Providence, NJ 07974.

The Society of American Travel Writers' Directory. Society of American Travel Writers, 7044 South 13th Street, Oak Creek, WI 53154.

Standard Rate and Data Services: Business Publications, Community Publications, Newspapers, and Spot Radio. SRDS, 3004 Glenview Rd., Wilmette, IL 60091.

International Media Directories

The Asia Pacific Media Directory. Haymarket Media, 60 Wyndham Street, Central, Hong Kong.

Benn's Media. Benn's Business Information Services, Riverbank House, Angelhare, Tonbridge, Kent, England TN9 1SE.

Dun's Europe. Dun & Bradstreet Information Services, 3 Sylvan Way, Persipanny, NJ 07054.

Encyclopedia of International Media and Communications. Academic Press, Elsevier, 30 Corporate Drive, #400, Burlington, MA 01803.

Hollis PR Annual and Hollis Europe. Harlequin House, 7 High Street, Teddington, England TW11 8EL.

Urlich's Global Serials Directory. Serial Solutions, 501 North 34th Street, Suite 400, Seattle, WA 98103.

Willings Press Guide. Cision House, 16-22 Baltic Street West, London, England EC1Y 0UL.

World Radio/TV Handbook. WRTH Publications, 8 King Edward Street, Oxford, England, OX1 4HL.

Other Selected Directories

Adweek Directory. The Nielsen Company, 770 Broadway, New York, NY 10003.

Asian Americans: A Statistical Sourcebook. Information Publications, 2995 Woodside Road, Woodside, CA 94062.

Awards, Honors, and Prizes. Gale Research, PO Box 9187, Farmington Hills, MI 48333.

Business Organizations, Agencies, and Publications Directory. Gale

Research, PO Box 9187, Farmington Hills, MI 48333.

The Celebrity Source. The Celebrity Source, 8033 Sunset Boulevard, Suite 1108, Los Angeles, CA 90046.

Congressional Yellow Book; Federal Yellow Book. Leadership Directories, 1301 Pennsylvania Avenue NW, Suite 925, Washington, D.C. 20004.

CorpTech® Directory of Technology Companies. CorpTech, 12 Alfred Street, Suite 200, Woburn, MA 01801-9998.

Encyclopedia of Associations: International Organizations. Gale Research, PO Box 9187, Farmington Hills, MI 48333.

GreenBook Directory of Marketing Research and Focus Group Companies. New York American Marketing Association, 116 E. 27th Street, 6th floor, New York, NY 10016.

Hispanic Americans: A Statistical Sourcebook. Information Publications, 2995 Woodside Road, Woodside, CA 94062.

Hispanic Americans Information Directory. Gale Group, 27500 Drake Road, Farmington Hills, MI 48331-335.

IEG Sponsorship Sourcebook. IEG Inc., 640 N. LaSalle #600, Chicago, IL 60610.

National Directory of Corporate Public Affairs. Columbia Books, 8120 Woodmont Avenue, #110, Bethesda, MD 20814.

O'Dwyer's Directory of Corporate Communications; Directory of PR Executives; Directory of PR Firms. O'Dwyer's, 271 Madison Avenue, New York, NY 10016.

Oxbridge Directory of Newsletters. Oxbridge Communications, 150 Fifth Avenue, Suite 302, New York, NY 10011.

Professional Freelance Writer's Directory. National Writer's Association, 1450 South Havana Street, Suite 424, Aurora, CO 80012.

Research Services Directory. Greyhouse Publishing, 185 Millerton Road, Millerton, NY, 12546.

The Source Book of Multicultural Experts. Multicultural Marketing Resources, 332 Bleeker Street, Suite G41, New York, NY 10014.

Yearbook of Experts, Authorities, and Spokespersons. Broadcast Interview Source, 2233 Wisconsin Avenue NW, Suite 301, Washington, D.C. 20007.

Periodicals

CASE Currents. Council for Advancement and Support of Education, 11 Dupont Circle, Washington, D.C. 20036. Monthly.

Communication Briefings. Briefings Publishing Group, 2807 N. Parham Road, Suite 200, Richmond VA, 23294. Monthly.

Communication World. International Association of Business Communicators (IABC), One Hallidie Plaza, Suite 600, San Francisco, CA 94102. Bimonthly.

Investor Relations Update. National Investor Relations Institute (NIRI), 8045 Leesburg Pike, Suite 600, Vienna, VA 22182. Monthly.

Jack O'Dwyer's PR Newsletter. O'Dwyer's, 271 Madison Avenue, New York, NY 10016. Weekly.

Journal of Public Relations Research. Routledge, 7625 Empire Drive, Florence, KY 41042-2919. Quarterly.

O'Dwyer's PR Services Report. O'Dwyer's, 271 Madison Avenue, New York, NY 10016. Monthly.

PRWeek. Haymarket Media, 220 Fifth Avenue, New York, NY 10001. Weekly.

Public Relations Review. Elsevier, 3251 Riverport Lane, Maryland Heights, MO 63043. Quarterly.

Public Relations Strategist. Public Relations Society of America (PRSA), 33 Maiden Lane, New York, NY 10038-5150. Quarterly.

Public Relations Tactics. Public Relations Society of America (PRSA), 33 Maiden Lane, New York, NY 10038-5150. Monthly.

Index

Credits

Chapter 14

p. 353: Kyodo/Newscom; p. 359: Stuart Baker, Inoue Public Relations; p. 361: Frank Strong, Vocus Communications; p. 362: Jung Yeon-Je/AFP/Getty Images/Newscom; p. 365: Melissa Kruth, Shedd Aquarium; p. 367: Brian Agnes, Family Features; p. 371: © Kathy deWitt/Alamy; p. 374: Gary Rainville, HP.

Chapter 15

p. 383: POA/ARB/Newscom; p. 390: Sharon Curtis Granskog, American Veterinary Medical Association; pp. 396–398: Domenic Travano, Bader TV; p. 399: (top) Courtesy of Rotary; (bottom) Photos by UNICEF.

Chapter 16

p. 411: Milos Aleksic/Belgrade Cultural Network; p. 413: Reuters/Mike Segar; p. 419: Elizabeth Handler, PRX public relations, and Valley Medical Center; p. 425: Courtesy of the Martin Luther King, Jr. Library, San Jose, California; p. 427: Robyn Beck/AFP/Getty Images/Newscom; p. 431: Robyn Beck/AFP/Getty Images/Newscom; p. 435: Milos Aleksic/Belgrade Cultural Network.

Chapter 17

p. 440: © Richard Levine/Alamy; p. 441: © Lou Linwei/Alamy; p. 442: Steven Johnson/MCT/Newscom; p. 450: AP Photo/Ross D. Franklin, File; p. 462: Rob Crandall/Newscom.

Chapter 18

p. 470: Lori Moffett/UPI/Newscom; p. 480: STR/EPN/Newscom; p. 482: Adolphus Opara/Twenty Ten/Africa Media Online/The Image Works; p. 485: Torsten Blackwood/AFP/Getty Images/Newscom; p. 487: Scott Keeler/St. Petersburg Times/PSG/Newscom.

Chapter 19

p. 495: Win McNamee/POOL-CNP-PHOTOlink.n/Newscom; p. 497: Zhang Jun/Xinhua/Photoshot/Newscom; p. 499: ©Newscom; p. 501: A3397 Gero Breloer/Newscom; p. 506: Jason Reed/Reuters/Landov19; p. 514: Jeff Greenberg/Alamy.

Chapter 20

p. 522: Alexander Joe/AFP/Getty Images/Newscom; p. 524: © Stan Rohrer/Alamy; p. 525: IPA Frontline; p. 528: Courtesy of Saudi Aramco; p. 529: Yoshikazu Tsuno/AFP/Getty Images/Newscom; p. 535: Oceana; p. 540: Dennis Wilcox.

Chapter 21

p. 547: STR/AFP/Getty Images/Newscom; p. 549: (left) © Geraint Lewis/Alamy; (right) © Marina Spironetti/Alamy; p. 555: Advertising Council; p. 559: Joanne Ritter, Guide Dogs for the Blind.

Text Credits

Chapter 1

p. 25, Insights Box: Source: Public Relations Student Society of America (PRSSA), New York.

Chapter 4

p. 97, Fig. 4.1: (c) 2009 IBM Corporation. Courtesy of Jon Iwata, SVP of communications, IBM Corporation.; p. 98, Fig. 4.2: Courtesy of David Kroll, VP of global communications for AMD.; p. 101, Fig. 4.3: Source: Corporate Communication International, 2009 Corporate Communication Practices and Trends Survey, www.corporatecomm.org.

Chapter 7

p. 165, Table 7.1: Source: Kirk Hallahan (in press). Public relations media. In R. L. Heath (Ed.), *Handbook of public relations* (pp. 623–641). Los Angeles: Sage. Table p. 626. *The SAGE handbook of public relations* by Heath, Robert L., Copyright 2011 by SAGE Publications Inc. Books. Reproduced with permission of SAGE Publications Inc. Books in the format Textbook via Copyright Clearance Center.

Chapter 8

p. 193, Fig. 8.1: Source: Ketchum, New York, published in *Public Relations Quarterly*.; p. 201, Fig. 8.3: Charts courtesy of Frank Strong, Vocus.

Chapter 10

p. 263, Insights Box: Wilcox, et al., *Think Public Relations*, "Classic Crisis Management Campaigns" p. 57, © 2011 by Pearson Education, Inc. Reproduced by permission of Pearson Education, Inc.

Chapter 14

p. 357, Fig. 14.1: Courtesy of ABI Research. Bhavya Khanna and Jake Saunders, Analysts.; p. 359, Fig. 14.2: Courtesy of Inoue Public Relations, Tokyo, Japan.; p. 361, Fig. 14.3: Courtesy of Frank Strong, Vocus.; p. 373, Fig. 14.5: Courtesy of Business Wire,; p. 378, Fig. 14.6: Courtesy of Litzky Public Relations.; p. 379, Fig. 14.7: Source: Ecolab Inc. Copyright Business Wire 2010. Used with permission.

Public Relations
CASEBOOKS IN PUBLIC RELATIONS
Strategies and Tactics Tenth Edition